Bootwise

D1334516

6/51

/03

9.00

Class No. 796.334   Ac

football

the beautiful game

796.334

This is a **FLAME TREE** Book
Second edition published in 2003
First edition published in 2002

04 05 03

3 5 7 9 10 8 6 4 2

FLAME TREE PUBLISHING
Crabtree Hall, Crabtree Lane,
Fulham, London SW6 6TY
United Kingdom

Visit our website: www.flametreepublishing.com

Flame Tree is part of The Foundry Creative Media Company Limited

Copyright © The Foundry 2003

ISBN 1-904041-77-9

All rights reserved. No part of this publication may be reproduced, stored in a retrieval system, or
transmitted in any form or by any means, electronic, mechanical, photocopying, recording or otherwise,
without the prior permission of the publisher.

A copy of the CIP data for this book is available from the British Library

Printed and bound in Spain by Bookprint, S.L., Barcelona

Thanks to everyone involved with this project:
Ray Barnett, Frances Bodiam, Michelle Clare, Jeff Fletcher, Chris Herbert, Mariano Kälfors,
Scott Morgan, Sonya Newland, Melinda Revesz, Julia Rolf, Colin Rudderham, Graham Stride,
Nick Wells, Richard Whiting at Allsport and Polly Willis

football

the beautiful game

Nick Holt & Guy Lloyd

Foreword: Sir Bobby Robson

FLAME TREE
PUBLISHING

CONTENTS

INTRODUCTION

Football is unique amongst sports in the degree of passion it arouses in non-combatants. Not for the football fan the pure voyeurism of watching two people belt the living daylights out of each other in a ring, nor the tortuous but cerebral intrigue of a fluctuating test match. Football is about intensity, the thrill of a moment, the excitement of a game revolving around a single piece of action. The fans live every moment, feel every moment, kick every ball.

We've done our share of suffering watching Chelsea under-perform and Bolton get relegated (but not this time, at least for another year!). We've also done our fair share of running around screaming as Chelsea win the FA Cup or Bolton win at Highbury. We've tried to write this book from a fan's perspective, and capture some of the agony and the ecstasy, the hysteria and the humour.

This is not a list of stats; Rothmans and others cover that. Nor is it an in-depth history of the game; that involves too much stuff that no one really cares about – and too much work! This book tries to identify key people and events and themes that have changed or enlivened the game for better or worse. From Hidegkuti to Hairstyles, Nou Camp to Nicknames, we've given a page – no more - to the best and worst of the Beautiful Game. If we think a player was talented but a bit of a lightweight, we've said so; if we think a side was dirty or arrogant, we've said so. We've said so not just because we think we're right, but because football fans want an opinion and an argument.

KEY

Throughout the book you will note that each player or manager has a legend rating. These are based on the following criteria:

Players:

Achievement: how much the player achieved in football – very little sympathy is accorded players who eschew 'the big move' in this mark.
Skill: pure talent.
Teamwork: ability to turn a game with a moment of skill or leadership.
Passion: overall contribution to a side, heart.
Personality: charisma, personal style.

Managers:

Achievement: as above.
Tactical Awareness: ability to read the way a game is going or will go and to act accordingly.
Motivation: gung-ho up-and-at 'em style or man-management – whatever it takes to get the best out of your best.
Transfer Dealing and Team Selection: the ability to distinguish a Cantona from a Marco Boogers.
Personality: as above.

Like the Dream Teams, these are based on opinion, rather than any tangible measurement, and are meant to invite discussion and disagreement. If you think we've rippled Row F rather than the back of the net with our selections, please e-mail us with your abuse (not too ripe!), or your own selections. You could even e-mail us if you agree – but where's the fun in that?

Nick Holt and *Guy Lloyd*

FOREWORD

The outstanding success of the 2002 Word Cup Finals in Japan and South Korea demonstrated once again the global popularity of our wonderful game of football.

The remarkable skills of the players – especially the dazzling Brazilians, of course; the amazingly high levels of fitness and stamina, plus the hard-nosed tactical battles fought out by the coaches, made fascinating viewing for all those watching the World Cup matches.

Football continues to evolve, and the balance of power may be shifting. It is predicted that an African country will win the World Cup in the near future – and we had better not rule out the possibility of an Asian team from probably becoming World Champions.

Football in the early years of the twenty-first century remains the highest-profile sport on the planet and its future looks very bright indeed. All those lucky enough to earn a living from football – including players, managers and those involved in the media – owe a huge debt to the past giants of the sport.

The players and managers make today's headlines, but it is the supporters of the game of football that form the bedrock of the sport. It is their passion, their enthusiasm and, ultimately, their money that helps keep the game alive.

Thousands of books on football have been published over the years. Some have been notorious and self-seeking, others well-crafted works of literature. And many excellent reference books, containing all kinds of information and statistics, have been produced.

Football: The Beautiful Game by Nick Holt and Guy Lloyd is a worthy addition to the list. It has been written and compiled by genuine football fans and is aimed at genuine football fans. The book is not a just a list of statistics, nor an in-depth history of the game, but one that tries to identify key people, events and themes that have changed or enlivened the game for better or worse.

It pays tribute to the past and present heroes of the game. *Football: The Beautiful Game* takes an honest, thoughtful and affectionate view of our marvellous sport and will be a good read for all football fans, young and old.

Sir Bobby Robson

Sir Bobby Robson
Summer 2002

Adams, Tony

Arsenal, England

IN HIS EARLY YEARS Adams was frequently subjected to cries of 'donkey' from the terraces, as he appeared to be a traditional English centre-half – physically dominant but maladroit with the ball at his feet. The fact that he is now treated with universal respect wherever he plays is testimony to the commitment and hard work he has shown in eliminating many of those early deficiencies from his game. The back line of David Seaman, Lee Dixon, Nigel Winterburn and Adams, with first Steve Bould and later Martin Keown, could reasonably lay claim to being the best-ever British club defence.

An outstanding reader of the game, he became a natural leader and an inspirational talisman for England and Arsenal, both of whom were notably weaker in his absence. Adams' fight against alcohol addiction became a symbol of his strength of character, and his readiness to address personal flaws earned him respect well beyond the football world. His brief stretch in prison gave him a glimpse of life that few of today's pampered professionals would comprehend.

VITAL STATISTICS

Place of Birth: Romford, England

Date of Birth: 10 October 1966

Died: n/a Caps: 66 (England) Goals (International): 5

Clubs: Arsenal

Appearances: Club (League): 504

Goals: Club (League): 32

Trophies: LT 1989, 1991, 1998, 2002; FAC 1993, 1998, 2002; LC 1987, 1993; CWC 1994

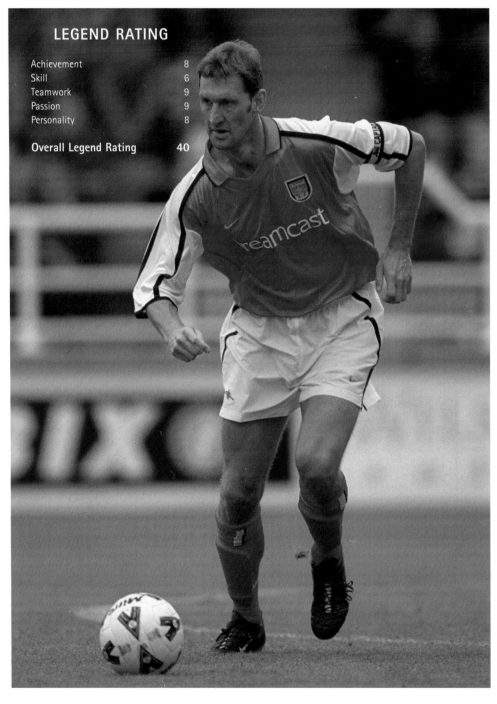

LEGEND RATING

Achievement	8
Skill	6
Teamwork	9
Passion	9
Personality	8
Overall Legend Rating	**40**

◁ Arsenal's miserly defence conceded only 18 goals as they waltzed away with the Championship in 1991.

◁ Adams took over two years to score his first league goal, finally bagging against Liverpool in 1986.

◁ His autobiography, *Addicted*, sold well beyond the normal audience of a one-club footballer.

◁ In Adams' 11 matches as England captain they were only beaten once.

◁ Adams' honesty and self-awareness has mistakenly led some journalists to paint him as a sage and philosopher, when he is clearly neither. He is a decent man who has learned to grow up.

Ademir Marques de Menezes

Vasco da Gama, Brazil

BRAZIL ENTERED the 1950 World Cup in state of high expectation. They were the hosts, and the previous year they had won the Copa América with some sensational performances. The stars of the show were their trio of sparkling forwards – Jair Rosa Pinto, Zizinho and Ademir. All slim, nippy and moustachioed, they moved the ball with amazing skill and speed.

Ademir had been playing as an outside left for Vasco da Gama and for his country, but when Brazil moved him inside alongside the other two maestros the results were spectacular. Shimmies, dummies, overhead kicks, half-volleys ... all the magic we associate with the 1958 and 1970 Brazil teams was there. Four goals of stunning quality in the final pool match against Sweden was probably Ademir's greatest moment. Only in the last match of the 1950 tournament, when Uruguay detailed their experienced captain, Varela, to mark him, did anyone work out how to cope with his tricks.

VITAL STATISTICS

Place of Birth: Recife, Brazil

Date of Birth: 8 November 1922

Died: 11 May 1996   Caps: 39 (Brazil)

Goals (International): 32

Clubs: FC Recife, Vasco da Gama, Fluminense

Trophies: BLT 1945, 1946, 1947, 1949, 1950, 1952

LEGEND RATING

Achievement	8
Skill	9
Teamwork	7
Passion	8
Personality	7
Overall Legend Rating	**39**

Ademir with the Brazilian World Cup squad in 1950 – our man is third from right on the bottom row.

- No TV footage exists to prove it, but Ademir was said to use a trick of trapping the ball in his heels and hopping over the goalkeeper, still moving at some speed.
- The famous English referee Arthur Ellis rated Ademir's overhead kick against Sweden as the best goal he'd ever witnessed.

- By the time the 1954 World Cup came around, Ademir, Jair and Zizinho had all gone, and it was 1958 before the next crop of outrageous talent arrived.
- So many coaches pulled an extra defender back to counter Ademir that Brazil adopted a 4-2-4 system to help create space for him.

- In the 1949 Copa América, Brazil, without Ademir, lost to Paraguay and were forced into a play-off. Our boy put it to rest as Brazil won said play-off 7-0, with Ademir hitting a hat-trick.

African Nations

THE AFRICAN NATIONS EMERGED as serious contenders at world level in the 1980s. The continent has since become a recruiting hotbed for the big European clubs. Although the players cannot be blamed for fleeing their homelands, their migration is undermining Africa's efforts to develop its game to its true potential.

This is a great side, full of massive talents. Radebe, so unlucky with injury, was a major force at Leeds as they built a challenging side in the 1990s. Taribo West, green hair notwithstanding, had some great moments at Milan, and Sammi Kuffour has been the corner-stone of Bayern Munich's recent re-emergence as a European force.

Oman Biyick scored some spectacular goals for Cameroon alongside the engaging Milla, and Okocha was a joy to watch in the World Cups of 1994 and 1998. Madjer masterminded Algeria's memorable defeat of West Germany in 1982, one of the World Cup's most enjoyable moments. And who could forget George Weah? The Liberian striker was the first African player to make a serious impact on the world stage, and at his peak with AC Milan was deservedly named World Player of the Year. His mantle as the daddy of African football has now passed to Arsenal's Nwankwo Kanu who, as part of a brilliant Ajax team, conquered Europe before his 21st birthday.

Manager: Roger Lemerre
3-3-1-3

Thomas Nkono (Cameroon)

Lucas Radebe (S. Africa) Taribo West (Nigeria) Sammi Kuffour (Ghana)

J-J Okocha (Nigeria) Oman Biyick (Cameroon) Mustafa Hadji (Morocco)

Rabah Madjer (Algeria)

Roger Milla (Cameroon) George Weah (Liberia) Nwankwo Kanu (Nigeria)

Subs: Peter Rufai (Nigeria) (G) Mark Fish (S. Africa) (D) Ahmed Ramzy (Egypt) (M) Abedi Pele (Ghana) (M) El Hadji Diouf (Senegal) (F)

Cameroon with the 2002 African Nations Cup.

◁🔊 World Cup 1982: Algeria beat West Germany and Chile, and were unlucky not to reach the second phase.

◁🔊 World Cup 1986: Morocco held England and Poland, beat Portugal and progressed to the second round where they lost due to a late goal from Lothar Matthaus.

◁🔊 World Cup 1990: Cameroon beat holders Argentina, Romania and Colombia before defensive errors saw them eliminated by England after being 2-1 up.

◁🔊 World Cups 1994 and 1998: Nigeria played well in the group stages but again failed to cope with experienced European opposition in the knockout rounds.

Ajax

AJAX HAD NO PEDIGREE before Rinus Michels took over as coach in the 1960s, but since then they have twice developed the best club side in Europe – only to see it broken up by the lure of the lira and, occasionally, the peseta.

The first team was all-Dutch, and contained the cultured defenders Krol and Suurbier, the flying Piet Keizer, the steel of Neeskens and style of Haan in midfield. Oh, and they also had some bloke called Johan Cruyff. That team swept all before them, winning three consecutive European Cups. Only Feyenoord, with Rinus Israel, Wim Van Hanegem and the Swede Owe Kindvall, could compete with them at home while, in Europe, their only serious threat came from the Bayern Munich team of Beckenbauer, Breitner and Müller.

The second side was a much more cosmopolitan affair. By the 1990s, Ajax, like other Dutch sides, were blending home talent with clever imports. Rijkaard and Van Basten had left to team up with Gullit at Milan, but more good youngsters emerged: Reiziger, Davids, Seedorf, Kluivert and the De Boers from Holland, plus Kanu, Litmanen and Finidi George from abroad. Captained by Danny Blind, they won back the European Cup in 1995.

Manager: Rinus Michels

3-4-1-2

Edwin Van Der Sar (90s)

Wim Suurbier (70s) Danny Blind (80s/90s) Rudi Krol (C) (70s)

Piet Keizer (70s) Frank Rijkaard (80s/90s) Johan Neeskens (70s)
Jari Litmanen (90s)

Johan Cruyff (70s)

Marco Van Basten (80s) Dennis Bergkamp (90s)

Subs: Heinz Stuy (G) (70s) Frank De Boer (D) (90s) Arie Haan (M) (70s)
Nwankwo Kanu (F) (90s) Patrick Kluivert (F) (90s)

◁▷ Keizer was an underrated member of the early Ajax side. More direct and aggressive than many of his team-mates, he was often the one to inject some urgency when their play became over-elaborate.

◁▷ Young Patrick Kluivert was one of the most exciting prospects in European football when he emerged in the mid-1990s. His failure to fulfil that potential must be attributed in part to some unsavoury incidents in his private life.

◁▷ Guus Hiddink and Louis Van Gaal are accomplished coaches, but Michels is the undisputed father of modern Dutch football – and the only manager to get the best out of the notoriously temperamental Cruyff.

Albert, Florian

AS THE GREAT HUNGARIAN TEAM of the 1950s was dissolving, the seeds of a new team were being sown. It took a few years, but by the 1966 World Cup Finals some of the young talent was ripening. The jewel among them was Florian Albert, a playmaker with leading club side, Ferencvaros. A gifted centre-forward, he was at the heart of the last Hungarian side to truly compete on the international stage.

In 1962, Albert put paid to English World Cup hopes with a stylish winning goal, and followed it with a hat-trick against Bulgaria. In the 1966 tournament they were drawn in a tough group with Brazil and Portugal. The key game was a 3-1 victory over Brazil and it was a minor classic. Hungary's second, decisive goal involved an eye-blinkingly rapid movement from Albert to Ferenc Bene to Janos Farkas, who crashed in a volley that bulged the net in mouth-watering fashion. In the quarter-finals a strong Soviet side had done their homework; they close-marked Albert and cut off his supply from midfield, a tactic that contributed hugely to their 2-1 victory. The next time the sides met in a Finals tournament was in Mexico 1986. Albert was long gone and the USSR won 6-0.

VITAL STATISTICS

Place of Birth:	Hungary
Date of Birth:	15 September 1941
Died: n/a	Caps: 75 (Hungary)
Goals (International): 27	
Clubs: Ferencvaros	
Trophies: OLT 1963, 1964, 1967, 1968	

LEGEND RATING

Achievement	6
Skill	9
Teamwork	7
Passion	9
Personality	7
Overall Legend Rating	**38**

◁ Albert and Hungary won the Olympic gold in 1964 and 1968.
◁ Ujpest Dozsa winger Ferenc Bene, was a great foil for Albert. Quick, and a tidy finisher, he scored all the goals in a 6-0 win over Morocco at the 1964 Olympics.

◁ Albert's Ferencvaros became the only Hungarian club to win a European trophy when they beat Juventus in the 1965 Fairs Cup Final.
◁ Albert was named European Footballer of the Year in 1967.

◁ Ferencvaros returned to the Fairs Cup Final three years later, but lost 1-0 to Leeds over two legs. Bene's Ujpest Dozsa trod the same path the following year, but were beaten by Newcastle.

Allchurch, Ivor

Swansea, Newcastle, Cardiff, Wales

IVOR ALLCHURCH WAS one of the great pioneers of Welsh football. In the 1950s, along with John and Mel Charles, he brought recognition for a sport that had failed to arouse the same passion in Wales as it had in England and Scotland. Allchurch, who emerged with local team Swansea, was a cultured inside-left with a perception and maturity that was rare for players of his era.

He was one of those footballers who always seemed to be in the right place at the right time, and this opportunism helped make him a permanent inclusion in the Welsh national team for 15 years. Despite his early promise at Swansea, Allchurch did not play in the

First Division until Newcastle gave him the chance at the age of 28. The experience was short-lived though, as the Magpies were relegated three years later and Allchurch returned to Wales with Cardiff. He ended his league career as he had begun it, back at Swansea, and later played non-league football until into his 50s. A warm welcome will always be waiting for him at the Vetch Field.

VITAL STATISTICS

Place of Birth: Swansea, Wales
Date of Birth: 16 October 1919
Died: 9 July 1997   Caps: 68 (Wales)
Goals (International): 23
Clubs: Swansea, Newcastle, Cardiff
Appearances: Club (All Matches): 692
Goals: Club (All Matches): 251
Trophies: None

LEGEND RATING

Achievement	6
Skill	8
Teamwork	8
Passion	8
Personality	6
Overall Legend Rating	**36**

◁ He was awarded the MBE for services to football.
◁ Brother Len was also a Welsh international. When both brothers appeared against Northern Ireland in 1955, Wales also fielded a second pair of brothers in Mel and John Charles.
◁ He scored seven hat-tricks for Swansea, and one against them (playing for Newcastle in 1965).
◁ In 1956/57, Allchurch set a Swansea club record by scoring in nine consecutive fixtures.
◁ Allchurch's 68 Welsh caps remained a record for 20 years, until broken by Joey Jones.

Allez ... Oops!

France 0 Senegal 1, 2002

FOOTBALL HISTORY is littered with examples of top sides sauntering against less fancied opposition and getting their just desserts. The opening game of the 2002 World Cup Finals found France taking their turn at being Goliath. The Davids were the French-speaking Senegalese, playing in their first Finals tournament. Senegal were determined and robust, more than equal to the physical challenge of Desailly, Vieira and Petit. The excellent Fadiga was a patient prompter from the left, and El Hadji Diouf gave the French defence a torrid first half. The defence were outstanding; led by the formidable Aliou Cisse of Montpellier they were disciplined and committed without being dirty.

France, by contrast, were far from committed. Sluggish to begin with, their response to conceding a goal was unworthy of World and European champions. They were pedestrian at the back, where Leboeuf looked complacent and second-rate, and uninspired in midfield where the injured Zidane was sorely missed. The dream forward combination of Henry and Trezeguet was disjointed and disappointing; both hit the woodwork but overall they looked lightweight.

A sensational start to the tournament: the other fancied teams raised a collective eyebrow. For France it was the beginning of the end: they finished last in their group in a miserable defence of their title.

SCORERS: Senegal: PB Diop (30)
EVENT: Group A, opening match, World Cup Finals, Seoul, 31 May 2002

FRANCE
(Man: Roger Lemerre)

1	Barthez	8	Petit
2	Thuram	9	Djorkaeff
3	Desailly		(Dugarry)
4	Leboeuf	10	Henry
5	Lizarazu	11	Trezeguet
6	Wiltord		
	(D. Cisse)		
7	Vieira		

SENEGAL
(Man: Bruno Metsu)

1	Sylva	8	PB Diop
2	Coly	9	Diao
3	Diatta	10	Fadiga
4	A. Cisse	11	Diouf
5	PM Diop		
6	Daf		
7	Mou		
	Ndiaye		

Papa Boupa Diop leaves Desailly, Petit and Barthez floundering to score Senegal's winner.

▸ The French starting line-up featured no players from the French league. The Senegalese, by contrast, put out an entire team from their league.

▸ El Hadji Diouf had been nominated African Footballer of the Year earlier in the season. He looked the part in this tournament, leading the line with aggression and skill.

▸ The goal was an embarrassment for the much-vaunted French defence. An aggressive run by Diouf left Leboeuf a spectator; Petit failed to deal with the cross and Diop was left with a tap-in.

▸ Senegal failed to make qualification for the 1994 tournament: officials at their association forgot to enter them!

Allison, Malcolm

Manchester City, Crystal Palace

THE TACKY 1970s IMAGE should not disguise the ability of Malcolm Allison, one of England's finest post-war coaches. Like Ron Atkinson and Graham Taylor, Allison only truly established himself in football after hanging up his boots. A contributor to the West Ham 'academy' of the late 1950s, he was a senior professional at Upton Park when an awestruck Bobby Moore came under his tutelage. But it was at Manchester, first working as a coach during Joe Mercer's reign at Maine Road, that he honed his managerial abilities. Mercer and Allison presided over the most successful spell in the club's history, winning promotion in 1966, and the First Division title two years later.

In 1972 the marriage went sour and Allison was handed control of the team. He was a disastrous manager, and his graceless comments about Mercer earned him no plaudits. City lost seven of their first 10 league games and Allison jumped ship to Palace before the axe fell. The Eagles were relegated the same season. After Third Division Palace's Cup run brought them to within one game of Wembley in 1976, City forgave him and he returned to Maine Road. This time he was worse, squandering millions on mediocre players. He was sacked in 1980 and has since remained in the footballing wilderness, a sad demise for a man who shaped England's most famous captain.

VITAL STATISTICS

Place of Birth: Dartford, England
Date of Birth: 5 September 1927
Died: n/a   Caps: 0
Goals (International): 0
Clubs: As player: West Ham. As manager: Plymouth, Manchester City, Crystal Palace, Middlesbrough, Bristol Rovers
Trophies: LT 1968; FAC 1969; LC 1970 (all as assistant manager at Manchester City)

LEGEND RATING

Achievement	5
Skill	9
Teamwork	7
Passion	5
Personality	9
Overall Legend Rating	**35**

◄៕ 1968. Allison gave a famous half-time team-talk in City's final league game at Newcastle. With the score at 2-2 and a win needed, he remained completely silent, believing that the players knew the task ahead. They duly obliged.

◄៕ 'I've served more time than Ronnie Biggs did for the Great Train Robbery.' Allison reflecting ruefully on his lifetime touchline ban.
◄៕ 1978/79. Broke British transfer record, paying £1.4 m for Steve Daley. Other signings include £750,000 for Preston's Michael

Robinson, a player with a handful of league games, plus £250,000 for untried Palace teenager Steve MacKenzie.
◄៕ After City and Palace, Allison went to Farense in Portugal before returning to England to take over non-league Fisher Athletic.

Anderson, Viv

Nottingham Forest, England

VIV ANDERSON DID NOT SINGLE-HANDEDLY banish racism from the game of football, but he did advance the cause of enlightenment by becoming the first black player to win a full England cap. No tokenism here: Anderson was a cultured, overlapping full-back with genuine pace and an ease on the ball not normally associated with English defenders. His best club football came early in his career at Nottingham Forest where, under Brian Clough's tutelage, he became an integral member of their First Division and European Cup winning teams. His reputation was enhanced further at Arsenal, but faded after a later move to Manchester United where injuries hampered his

spell in the mid-1980s. Thus far, his coaching career has been a disappointment. Promoted from player to the backroom staff at Middlesbrough, he was Bryan Robson's assistant during their topsy-turvy Riverside reign that ended with them both being shown the door in 2001. Yet, while he still has much to prove in the management game, Anderson's legacy as a pioneer of black footballers is not something that can ever be taken away from him. Through his skill, courage and dignity he helped turn the volume down on the bigots. And for that alone, he deserves considerable respect.

VITAL STATISTICS

Place of Birth: Nottingham, England

Date of Birth: 29 August 1956

Died: n/a Caps: 30 (England) Goals (International): 2

Clubs: Nottingham Forest, Arsenal, Manchester United, Sheffield Wednesday, Barnsley

Appearances: Club (All matches): 574

Goals: Club (All matches): 31

Trophies: LT 1978; LC 1978, 1979, 1987; EC 1980

LEGEND RATING

Achievement	8
Skill	6
Teamwork	8
Passion	7
Personality	7
Overall Legend Rating	**36**

◄╏▸ Played his first cap against Czechoslovakia in 1979. Anderson was sent a bullet in the post before the game; the accompanying note claimed the next one was for him if he played.

◄╏▸ Anderson was Alex Ferguson's first signing at Man United.

◄╏▸ He should have won far more than 30 caps (right-back plodder Phil Neal reached 50).

◄╏▸ Anderson remained a professional for 23 years, almost unheard of for a modern outfield player.

◄╏▸ Anderson was awarded an MBE in 2000.

Archie's Passion

GOING INTO THIS MATCH, Scotland's hopes of glory at the 1978 World Cup Finals were already in tatters. With only one point from their first two games they were virtually out of the competition – a fate they could only avoid by beating the mighty Holland by three clear goals. Unbelievably, they came close to pulling it off.

The Scots gave everything. They hit the bar, had a goal disallowed and found themselves a goal down for their troubles, when Rensenbrink converted a penalty. Dalglish volleyed a deserved equaliser just before half-time, and Gemmill scored from the spot after Souness was brought down. Then came the goal that set

Scottish hearts beating like the clappers. Gemmill, picking the ball up wide on the right, swerved past two defenders, nutmegged a third and coolly chipped the advancing Jongbloed. As he turned away Gemmill's face was a glorious and unforgettable fusion of elation, determination and passion. A midget player with a giant's heart had scored one of the greatest goals in the history of the game. Sadly for Gemmill, Dalglish and the rest, Scotland could not force a fourth, and had their hopes finally, and emphatically, extinguished by Johnny Rep's 30-yard howitzer three minutes later.

SCORERS:	Holland: Rensenbrink (pen), Rep	
	Scotland: Dalglish, Gemmill 2 (1 pen)	
EVENT:	World Cup group match, Mendoza, 11 June 1978	

HOLLAND (Man: Ernst Happel)		SCOTLAND (Man: Ally MacLeod)	
1 Jongbloed	7 van der Kerkhof, R	1 Rough	8 Hartford
2 Suurbier	8 Rep	2 Kennedy	9 Jordan
3 Krol	9 Rensenbrink	3 Donachie	10 Souness
4 Jansen	10 Neeskens	4 Rioch	11 Dalglish
5 Rijsbergen	11 van der Kerkhof, W	5 Forsyth	
6 Poortvliet		6 Buchan	
		7 Gemmill	

◁» No less a judge than the great Dutch coach Rinus Michels had tipped Scotland as dark horses to win the tournament.

◁» Scottish winger Willie Johnston was sent home after the first match for taking a banned substance.

◁» Martin Buchan was chosen as full-back against Peru, where he struggled against Munante, one of the world's fastest wingers.

◁» Ally MacLeod stayed on as manager for one more game before resigning, blaming everyone else for a disastrous tournament.

◁» Complacent and off-key in the first two games, Scotland had been beaten by Peru and drawn with Iran, Ally McLeod having omitted Graeme Souness for both these games.

Ardiles, Osvaldo ('Ossie')

Argentina, Tottenham Hotspur

ARDILES WAS UNKNOWN IN EUROPE before the 1978 World Cup, where he was the fulcrum of the Argentina side that won the tournament, so when he and Ricky Villa were persuaded to come to England immediately after, it was, rightly, regarded as a stunning coup for Spurs. Ardiles returned to the World Cup stage in 1982, but Argentina found it harder work playing in Europe and lost their crown.

With the exception of his 1981 Cup Final performance Villa was only a partial success at Spurs. Ardiles, on the other hand, was a revelation. His push-and-go style was easy to adapt to English football, and he formed a hugely effective partnership with the more flamboyant Glenn Hoddle. A better defence would surely have seen Spurs win more than an FA Cup and UEFA Cup in the early 1980s.

As a manager, Ardiles proved surprisingly inept for such an intelligent player. After a reasonably successful spell at Swindon Town, he suffered disastrous tenures at Newcastle and back at Spurs where, despite bringing in expensive signings such as Jurgen Klinsmann, Gica Popescu and Ilie Dumitrescu, he could not mould the team into an effective unit.

VITAL STATISTICS

Place of Birth: Cordoba, Argentina

Date of Birth: 3 August 1952

Died: n/a   Caps: 53   Goals (International): 8

Clubs: Intstituto de Cordoba, Huracan, Tottenham Hotspur, Paris Saint Germain, Blackburn Rovers, Queen's Park Rangers

Appearances: Club (for Tottenham): 315

Goals: Club (for Tottenham): 25

Trophies: WorC 1978; FAC 1981, UEFAC 1984

LEGEND RATING

Achievement	8
Skill	8
Teamwork	9
Passion	8
Personality	7
Overall Legend Rating	**40**

- His only success as a manager, promotion with Swindon, was annulled due to financial irregularities under the previous incumbent, Lou Macari.
- Ardiles and Maradona only briefly overlapped for Argentina, when Ossie was past his energetic best. They would have been some combination in their mutual pomp.
- Ardiles' most embarrassing moment was a brief cameo in Spurs' 1981 FA Cup song. The memory of that squeaky little voice trilling out 'Tottingham' still sends shivers down the spine of music lovers everywhere.
- Ardiles owned a Yorkshire Terrier called Gazza.

Argentina

THIS DEFENCE IS FORMIDABLE. In front of arguably the finest South American goalkeeper ever sits a brutal back four. Ruggeri gets in ahead of Sensini and Olguin, while the cultured Ayala would make an interesting contrast with the 6 ft 3 in destroyer Rattin. Marzolini was a world-class attacking full-back and behind him sits one of the great sweepers, the uncompromising Daniel Passarella.

With Ardiles to do the donkey work, Maradona, Di Stefano and the silky pre-war inside forward, Omar Sivori, would be free to run at defences and link up with the lone forward (who needs more than one striker with those three in midfield?). Incredibly, there is no room even on the bench for some serious talent like Ortega, Onega, Veron or Valdano.

Selecting the lone forward was tough; Kempes just gets the nod over Batistuta, as his goals won a World Cup in 1978. No space either for the foppish Caniggia, Artime or Kempes' powerful partner, Luque.

Manager: Cesar Luis Menotti

1-4-4-1

Ubaldo Fillol (80s)

Daniel Passarella (c) (70s/80s)

Oscar Ruggeri (70s/80s)   Antonio Rattin (60s)
Reuben Ayala (90s)   Silvio Marzolini (60s)

Ossie Ardiles (70s/80s)   Diego Maradona (80s/90s)
Alfredo Di Stefano (50s/60s)   Omar Sivori (60s)

Mario Kempes (70s/80s)

Subs: Nery Pumpido (G) (80s) Roberto Ferreiro (D) (30s)
Jorge Burruchaga (M) (80s) Guillermo Stabile (F) (30s) Gabriel Batistuta (F) (90s)

◂◗ Guillermo Stabile was Argentina's finest pre-war player, a centre-forward in the team that reached the final of the 1930 World Cup.
◂◗ Silvio Marzolini and Roberto Ferreiro were members of the infamous 'Animals'. Ferreiro was a thug, but an effective defender, while Marzolini was a fine player and one of the less obnoxious members of that side.
◂◗ Ruggeri was a fine and consistent defender in the 1990s, while Burruchaga, though not the most naturally gifted player, developed into a capable lieutenant for Maradona.
◂◗ Both goalkeepers are highly capable – Brazil would look enviously at a bench containing Pumpido.

Armfield, Jimmy

AS HONEST, ONE-CLUB MEN GO, there was none finer than the pipe-smoking Jimmy Armfield. Arguably England's best-ever full-back, Armfield approached fixtures at Bloomfield Road or the Maracana with the same dedicated, professional attitude. The England international spent 20 seasons with Blackpool, starting as a fresh-faced team-mate of Stanley Matthews and ending it alongside the long-haired mavericks of the 1970s. Signed originally as an amateur, his sporting attitude brought him a reputation as a fine tackler but never a dirty one, while his speed and enthusiasm to link with the attack made him the English pioneer of the modern wing-back

position. His peak was the 1962 World Cup, where journalists voted him the tournament's best right-back. But, amazingly, he was dropped to accommodate George Cohen before the next Finals tournament and never regained his place. Thus, with Jimmy Greaves, he became one of the best England players of his generation not to collect a 1966 World Cup winner's medal (to add to his woes that year, he was also beaten to the PFA Player of the Year award by Bobby Charlton). Loyal even now, Armfield still lives in Blackpool where, like his original mentor Matthews, he continues to be held in high esteem by the locals.

VITAL STATISTICS

Place of Birth:	Manchester, England
Date of Birth:	21 September 1935
Died: n/a	Caps: 43 (England)
Goals (International): 0	
Clubs: Blackpool	
Appearances: Club (League): 568	
Goals: Club (League): 0	
Trophies: None	

LEGEND RATING

Achievement	5
Skill	8
Teamwork	8
Passion	7
Personality	7
Overall Legend Rating	35

- A natural sportsman, Armfield excelled as a schoolboy at cricket, swimming and athletics.
- Armfield holds the Blackpool record for league appearances (568) and is the club's most capped player (43).
- In 1959 he made his England debut at the Maracana in front of 120,000 fanatical Brazilians.
- In 1963 Armfield shocked Blackpool by requesting a transfer, although he played at Bloomfield Road for a further eight years.
- Now a summariser for BBC radio, Armfield was awarded the OBE in 2000.

Atkinson, Ron

West Bromwich Albion, Manchester United

QUITE HOW RON ATKINSON EMERGED as a flamboyant, big-time manager and media pundit is something of a surprise, given his nondescript playing career kicking round the lower divisions at places like Barrow and Oxford United. It speaks volumes for his self-confidence that he was able to manage players whose ability far exceeded his own and, despite never having won a league title, convince those around him that he was a success.

His best team, the late-1970s West Bromwich Albion of Bryan Robson, Cyrille Regis and Laurie Cunningham, gave him the opportunity to fry bigger fish at Old Trafford. A record of two third

places, three fourths and two FA Cups would have been more than good enough for most, but at United it cost him his job and heralded the arrival of Alex Ferguson. Perhaps it was signing Remi Moses for a ridiculous sum that the United board found unacceptable.

For four seasons United fans considered the Atkinson era a relatively golden one but, following their recent run of success, his tenure is now regarded as a failure. An Indian summer at Villa threatened an elusive title, but by this time his tanned presence was better known on television, where his unique jargon still entertains and irritates audiences in equal measure.

VITAL STATISTICS

Place of Birth: Liverpool, England
Date of Birth: 19 March 1939
Died:n/a Caps: 0
Goals (International): 0
Clubs: As player: Aston Villa, Oxford United. As manager: Kettering Town, Cambridge United, West Bromwich Albion, Manchester United, Atlético Madrid, Sheffield Wednesday, Aston Villa, Coventry City
Trophies: FAC 1983, 1985; FLT 1991, 1994

LEGEND RATING

Achievement	6
Tactical Awareness	6
Motivation	8
Transfer Dealing and Team Selection	8
Personality	9
Overall Legend Rating	**37**

◄ᴵᴵ Atkinson took Cambridge United from Fourth to Second Division in successive seasons.

◄ᴵᴵ 1988. Sacked from his only foreign job at Atlético Madrid after just 88 days by notorious president, Jesus Gil.

◄ᴵᴵ 1991. Vilified by Sheffield Wednesday fans after leaving for Villa, Atkinson was to return to Hillsborough six years later.

◄ᴵᴵ 1986. 'The sacking of Ron Atkinson is the best thing that could happen to Manchester United,' said former United boss, Tommy

Docherty on hearing the news. Despite comparisons, there was no love lost.

Azteca Stadium

Mexico City

THE NATIONAL STADIUM OF MEXICO, situated 2,240 m above sea level, has a reputation for sapping the strength of even the fittest players with its rarefied atmosphere. With its all-round roof, alarmingly steep stands and six-figure capacity, an Azteca packed to its three-tiered rafters leaves one breathless in more ways than one.

For England fans, the Azteca will always be remembered as the scene of Diego Maradona's infamous 'Hand of God' goal for Argentina against England in the 1986 Finals. Rising to meet Steve Hodge's back pass, the midfielder punched the ball past the stranded Peter Shilton and peeled away in delight. The officials failed to spot the incident and moments later Maradona danced his way past a string of English defenders to score the greatest-ever World Cup goal.

If Maradona was the star performer at the Azteca in 1986, Pele undoubtedly stole the show in 1970, proving that the best performers invariably raise their games on the greatest stages.

The Azteca could provide no greater inspiration. With the relative decline of the Maracana and the reduced capacity of the Bernabeu, there is no finer stadium in the world today.

VITAL STATISTICS

Location:	Mexico City, Mexico
Local Club:	América (other Mexican clubs use it for important matches)
Date Built:	1966
Current Capacity:	110,000
Max. Capacity:	114,590

Although known universally as the Azteca, its name was formally changed in 1997 to the Estadio Guillermo Canedo in memory of the late FIFA vice-president.

The Azteca is the only stadium to host two World Cup Finals, 1970 and 1986. In both tournaments, 19 games were played there, also a Finals record.

The Azteca staged the 1968 Olympic Games football final.

The stadium witnessed the finest ever national team performance, as Brazil outclassed Italy 4–1 to win the 1970 World Cup Final and keep the Jules Rimet trophy.

In 1999, at the end of a tour of Mexico, the Pope addressed 110,000 adoring followers at the Azteca.

Baggies' Best

MODERN BAGGIES' FANS will not remember their team's greatest years. Nor, come to that, would their fathers. One of the founder members of the league, two of West Brom's five FA Cup victories came in the nineteenth century, and their only league title was in 1920. Jesse Pennington, an upstanding and gentlemanly centre-half, was their leading name in those sepia-toned days.

Another competent side was built in the 1950s. They won the FA Cup in 1954, with much-capped Welsh right-back Stuart Williams, a young Bobby Robson, midfield worker Ray Barlow and the exciting centre-forward Ronnie Allen in their line up.

The rest of this dream team is made up of stars from the 1960s and 1970s; Albion maintained a respectable berth in the top flight for most of those years, including a third and a fourth place under Ron Atkinson. Their star turn was Bryan Robson, but left-winger Willie Johnston was an outstanding maverick and a real crowd favourite too. Latterly West Brom have struggled to hold on to their better players, and despite regular appearances in the top six in Division One, look ill-equipped to compete in the modern Premier League.

Manager: Ron Atkinson
4-4-2

John Osborne (60s/70s)

Don Howe (50s/60s) John Wile (C) (60s/70s)
Jesse Pennington (1890s/00s) Derek Statham (70s)

Ray Barlow (40s/50s) Bobby Robson (60s)
Bryan Robson (80s) Willie Johnston (70s)

Tony Brown (60s) Ronnie Allen (50s/60s)

Subs: Jim Cumbes (G) (60s/70s) Brendan Batson (D) (70s)
Asa Hartford (M) (70s) Cyrille Regis (F) (80s) Jeff Astle (F) (60s)

Baggies' legend Jeff Astle celebrates after scoring the winner in the 1968 Cup Final versus Everton.

◁ Ron Atkinson's departure spelt the end of the competitive years for Albion. Bryan Robson decamped to join him at Old Trafford, as did his midfield cohort, Remi Moses.
◁ Derek Statham was desperately unlucky. Three caps for England,

compared with 86 for Kenny Sansom should have been raised at Prime Minister's Question Time, as it clearly constitutes a national disgrace.
◁ Alongside Cyrille is the late Jeff Astle. Astle was a good centre-

forward who fell on hard times — why else would he have agreed to sing karaoke on Baddiel and Skinner's *Fantasy Football* show?
◁ Tony Brown remains the club's record goalscorer in all competitions. He relegated Cyrille Regis to the bench.

Baggio, Roberto

ONE OF ITALY'S most fêted-strikers of the last 20 years, the more talented Baggio brother played all his club football during the golden years of Serie A. A move outside Italy was never considered, not least because no one outside Serie A could afford the transfer fee. An outstanding schoolboy talent, he made his 1983 debut for Vicenza aged 15 and was snapped up by Fiorentina after only two years. His £8 m transfer in 1990 to Juventus sparked street riots, but it was five years before his goals finally won Serie A for the Turin giants.

A star of the *Azzuri*, his goals saw Italy through to the final of the 1994 World Cup, but the match proved to be his nadir. The memory of Baggio's final penalty sailing harmlessly over the bar to hand Brazil the trophy probably haunts him still, and started a decline that saw his previously unthinkable omission from the Euro 96 squad. A contentious choice for France 98, his chance to lay the World Cup ghost was unsuccessful as Italy again lost on penalties to the eventual winners.

VITAL STATISTICS

Place of Birth: Caldogno, Italy

Date of Birth: 18 February 1967

Died: n/a Caps: 55 (Italy) Goals (International): 27

Clubs: Fiorentina, Juventus, AC Milan, Bologna, Inter Milan, Brescia

Appearances: Club (League): 464

Goals: Club (League): 203

Trophies: EUFAC 1993; SA 1995, 1996

LEGEND RATING

Achievement	8
Skill	9
Teamwork	7
Passion	8
Personality	8
Overall Legend Rating	**40**

Baggio despairs after missing the final penalty in the 1994 World Cup Final.

◄ Baggio once refused to take a penalty for Juventus against Fiorentina out of loyalty to his former club – and was promptly substituted by an unsentimental coach.

◄ World and European Footballer of the Year in 1993.

◄ Baggio scored a sensational goal against Czechoslovakia in the 1990 World Cup, sauntering in from the left touchline, drifting past a couple of defenders and scoring in the corner. He produced a carbon copy against Bulgaria in the 1994 semis.

◄ Baggio is a style icon in Italy, his snappy dress-sense and trendy ponytail earning him film-star status with the media.

◄ Baggio has proved remarkably durable; his form in 2001 put him in the reckoning for a place in Italy's 2002 World Cup squad.

Balkan Select

Yugoslavia, Croatia, Slovenia: The Dream Team

WHEN YOU CONSIDER THE BITTERNESS and ferocity of the fighting in the Balkan Wars of the 1990s, it's a wonder the old Yugoslavia got 11 players to walk out on to the same field together. That fierce pride has often spilled over on to the football pitch; Yugoslavia and Croatia have been involved in some tempestuous games over the years.

The talent in this side is immense. Secularac, Dzajic, Stojkovic, Pancev and Savicevic all possessed extravagant skills, but they rarely managed to excel as a collective unit. The closest old Yugoslavia came was in the early 1960s when they reached the final of the inaugural European Championship. Two years later much the same team reached the semi-finals of the World Cup, losing to a less talented but more determined Czechoslovakia.

Some observers claim that a team uniting the talents of Yugoslavia, Croatia and Slovenia would have won a trophy in the 1990s, but that is to ignore a long history of failure to make their ability count. The Balkan sides are simply too easy to provoke into indiscretion, making them vulnerable to more experienced nations.

Manager: Bora Milutinovic
4-3-1-2

Vladimir Beara (50s)

Ivan Horvat (50s) Igor Stimac (C) (90s) Vladislav Bogicevic (70s) Robert Jarni (90s)

Zlatko Cajkowski (50s) Dragoslav Secularac (50s/60s) Dragan Dzajic (60s/70s)

Dragan Stojkovic (80s/90s)

Dejan Savicevic (90s) Davor Suker (90s)

Subs: Enver Maric (G) (70s) Vladimir Markovic (D) (60s) Zlatko Zahovic (M) (90s) Drazen Jerkovic (F) (60s) Darko Pancev (F) (90s)

◁▮ Of the older players, Beara was an athletic goalkeeper, Horvat a monolith of a defender, and Cajkovic an energetic ball-winner.

◁▮ Secularac was the early 1960s team playmaker. It also contained the excellent centre-half Markovic and quality striker Jerkovic.

◁▮ Zlatko Zahovic, the only Slovenian here, had an outstanding Euro 2000 and played a key role in securing Slovenia's qualification for Japan/Korea 2002, putting in fine performances against Romania in a play-off.

◁▮ Davor Suker was top scorer at the 1998 World Cup where Croatia, with a team containing Slaven Bilic, Robert Prosinecki, Aljosa Asanovic, Stimac and Jarni, made the semi-finals.

Ball, Alan

Everton, Southampton, England

THERE ARE FEW PLAYERS who reach their peak at 21, but as the youngest member of England's World Cup winning side, Alan Ball had the world at his feet. A teenage talent at Blackpool, his six-figure transfer to Everton the same year, the first of that size between English clubs, correctly identified Ball as one of English football's major talents. His Everton years saw Ball in his domestic pomp. With Howard Kendall and Colin Harvey he formed the 'Holy Trinity' that was the Everton midfield and saw them continue the north-west's dominance of the league title. Ball's adherence to the fiery redhead stereotype provided any team with its engine room,

but often brought him to the attention of referees and earned him the rare distinction of becoming one of only a handful of players to be sent off while playing for England.

After a lean period at Arsenal, during which his fall-out with Don Revie put paid to his international career, his renaissance at Southampton was typical of other ageing ex-England stars. However, he could not repeat his on-field success in management, where his record thus far reads promotions two, relegations five.

VITAL STATISTICS

Place of Birth: Farnworth, Lancashire, England
Date of Birth: 12 May 1945
Died: n/a Caps: 72 (England) Goals (International): 8
Clubs: Blackpool, Everton, Arsenal, Southampton, Bristol Rovers
Appearances: Club (League): 743
Goals: Club (League): 170
Trophies: WorC 1966; LT 1970

LEGEND RATING

Achievement	9
Skill	7
Teamwork	8
Passion	9
Personality	7
Overall Legend Rating	**40**

◅ Despite being a World Cup winner, his 1970 league title is Ball's only domestic trophy.

◅ He was the first player to make 100 league appearances for four different clubs (Blackpool, Everton, Arsenal and Southampton).

◅ He scored one of the quickest-ever First Division goals, in 12 seconds for Arsenal v Man Utd.

◅ His £220 k move to Arsenal made Ball England's most expensive player for a second time.

◅ Ball on Revie's England selections: 'Some of the players are donkeys. Give them a lump of sugar and they run all day and play bingo all night.'

Banged Up

SADLY, FOOTBALL'S RECORD is as long as your arm. It is not simply that the game is prey to match-fixing, betting scandals and brown envelopes. Some of its participants are just plain criminal.

Top of the crime league is Arsenal. Five players in as many years were banned from driving in the early 1980s, while Tony Adams went one better in 1990, earning a four-month sentence after wrapping his car around a telegraph pole while driving under the influence. Mind you, his efforts were nothing compared to former Gunner Peter Storey. His rap sheet included headbutting a lollipop man, forgery and living off immoral earnings. Small wonder that one of his later

trial judges sentenced him with the words 'you already know what prisons are like, Mr Storey'.

The most tragic case is probably that of George Best. The flawed Belfast genius drank and drove once too often but failed to show in court. Eventually tracked to his Chelsea flat, he escaped and later resisted arrest, a small squad of officers being occupied in the process. The magistrate failed to see the funny side and gave him three months. The bigger they are....

> 'For a man who commanded the respect of thousands of people, to find yourself here, believe me, it is heartbreaking.'
>
> Peter Storey's trial judge

1996: Colombian keeper Rene Higuita shows off his scorpion kick at Wembley.

◁)) Colombian keeper Rene Higuita is known to English audiences for his spectacular 'scorpion-kick' at Wembley in 1996. Less publicised was his absence from the 1994 World Cup Finals, when he was in jail as a result of kidnapping charges.

◁)) Duncan Ferguson's nickname of 'Duncan Disorderly' came after convictions for violence ended in a three-month jail term. Ferguson had assaulted Raith Rovers' fullback John McStay, a rare example of an on-field incident standing up in court.

◁)) Wrexham's Mickey Thomas was convicted of forgery in 1992. The incriminating evidence included his passing of dodgy banknotes to the club's YTS players.

Bankrupt

MOST CLUBS have been run habitually on a shoestring. Lower Division clubs have relied on nurturing and selling young talent and have proved valuable nurseries for the big clubs. After the Bosman ruling, and the ability of players to move without a fee once their contracts expired, TV money appeared to be the saviour.

With SKY's billions controlling the Premiership, ITV Digital's £315m, three-year deal gave them exclusive rights to transmit Nationwide games live. All the clubs got a piece, and work proceeded on ground and contract improvements. Barely halfway through the deal, ITV Digital was rocking. The figure of 1.2 m subscribers was way below target and had barely dented SKY's superiority. This need not have been a problem, parent companies Granada and Carlton had pockets deep enough to weather the storm. Their escape tunnel, however, had already been dug by the traditional incompetence of Football League chairmen, who had neglected to enforce their liability in the initial contract.

Early in 2002, ITV Digital offered to pay only £50 m from an outstanding total of £178 m. The clubs threatened legal action but it was only a gesture. With the money already spent, most are staring into a financial abyss. It remains to be seen which will disappear.

'ITV Digital Monkey Kills Imps'.

A Lincoln City protest banner captured the mood of many Nationwide clubs following the collapse of the pay-TV company.

◄¹⁾ ITV Digital lavished millions on an advertising campaign featuring comedian Johnny Vegas and an engaging monkey puppet. The latter could have done a better job as the company's accountant.

◄¹⁾ Clubs most seriously affected with administration following ITV Digital's collapse include Bury, York City and Chesterfield. Clubs recently relegated from the Premier League have found the drop in turnover almost too much to bear. Derby, Bradford City and Watford remain saddled with huge debts.

◄¹⁾ Even in the Premier League, Leeds United's attempts to keep up with the Champions League Joneses have resulted in a £100 m debt, a clearout of many top players and three managers in season 2002/03 alone.

Banks, Gordon

England

ENGLAND'S POST-WAR TRADITION is richer in goalkeepers than in any other position. The pick of a distinguished crop is a man once sacked from Romarsh Welfare in the Yorkshire League after conceding 15 goals in two games. Fortunately for England, Gordon Banks put this disappointment behind him to become his country's automatic choice for nine years, making his debut in Alf Ramsey's second game in charge. It was Ramsey who gave him all his 73 caps, but his worth to England's cause was perhaps most tellingly illustrated by a game he missed. Stricken by a stomach bug the night before the 1970 World Cup quarter-final against West Germany in

Mexico, Banks was forced to watch helplessly as his replacement, Peter Bonetti, conceded three goals as England let slip a 2-0 lead. Despite his ability Banks's club career was largely unsuccessful (Leicester and Stoke provided top-division football but little else). Indeed, Leicester practically gave him away to Stoke (£50,000), although they did have an ace up their sleeve in the form of a teenager called Peter Shilton to take over his mantle. The end of his career made headline news for the wrong reasons, the loss of the sight in his right eye following a car crash making his fitness and athleticism irrelevant.

VITAL STATISTICS

Place of Birth: Sheffield, England
Date of Birth: 20 December 1937
Died: n/a Caps: 73 (England) Goals (International): 0
Clubs: Chesterfield, Leicester City, Stoke City, Fort Lauderdale Strikers
Appearances: Club (Football League): 510
Goals: Club (Football League): 0
Trophies: WorC 1966; LC 1964, 1972

LEGEND RATING

Achievement	8
Skill	10
Teamwork	8
Passion	9
Personality	7
Overall Legend Rating	**42**

- He lost two FA Cup finals (1961 and 1963) with Leicester in three seasons.
- With Banks between the posts, England lost only nine of 73 games.
- He pulled off what is regarded as the world's greatest-ever save, diving to push a header from Pelé over the bar at the 1970 World Cup Finals in Mexico.
- During his spell with the Fort Lauderdale Strikers in the USA Banks was voted NASL's most valuable keeper. He could only see out of one eye at the time.
- In 1972 he became the first goalkeeper since Bert Trautmann (1956) to win the Footballer of the Year award.

Barcelona

THIS IS PROBABLY not the most talented line-up of Barcelona players, but that would include mainly foreign imports who took the pesetas for a year or two then scarpered for a fat signing-on fee elsewhere. The three overseas stars here stayed long enough to show they wore the red and blue with pride. Koeman was the foundation for the European Cup winning side, Schuster the playmaker throughout the 1980s, and Rivaldo the driving force behind the team in the last five years.

The rest are all Spanish stars, mostly Catalan, and all long-serving players. The defence, in front of the much-capped Zubizarreta, is tough and solid, with sufficient pace and aggression to allow Koeman the freedom to launch attacks with his trademark raking passes. The midfield, too, has strong runners and tacklers supporting the strikingly blond Schuster, and the explosive power of Rivaldo. In attack we have gone for the loyal Rexach, the current coach, alongside 1950s legend Kubala – both mobile and intelligent. Johan Cruyff will coach this team, which is why he doesn't feature in the starting line-up.

Manager: Johan Cruyff

4-4-2

Andoni Zubizarreta (C) (80s/90s)

Albert Ferrer (90s) Gustau Biosca (50s) Ronald Koeman (80s/90s) Migueli (70s/80s)

Bernd Schuster (80s) Jose Bakero (90s) Juan Manuel Asensi (70s) Rivaldo (90s)

Carlos Rexach (60s/70s) Ladislao Kubala (50s)

Subs: Antoni Ramallets (G) (40s/50s) Francisco Gallego (D) (60s/70s) Josep Maria Fuste (M) (60s) Paulino Alcantara (F) (10s/20s) Josep Samitier (F) (20s/30s)

◄♪ The players left out would make a team in their own right: not featured are Sandor Kocsis, Evaristo, Cesar, Mariano Martin, Ronaldo, Gary Lineker, Hristo Stoichkov, Diego Maradona, Patrick Kluivert, Javier Saviola and, of course, Steve Archibald.

◄♪ Kubala was Hungarian born. He came to Barca as an outcast and was only able to play after agreeing to adopt Spanish nationality. A goalscoring, inside-forward, many Barca people regard him as the club's best-ever player.

◄♪ Migueli's 649 appearances for Barcelona remains a club record, with Rexach not far behind.

◄♪ Pre-war icon Samitier later became president of the club, bringing stars like Kubala, Kocsis and Evaristo to Barcelona.

Baresi, Franco

IN A TEAM OF AC MILAN STARS, none shone brighter than the central defensive wall that was Franco Baresi. A one-club man in an era when most stars shopped around for greater riches, Milan's favourite son was nearly a schoolboy signing for rivals Inter, but big brother Giuseppe was favoured instead. Originally an attacking midfielder, his switch to the back in 1977 began a career for club and country as one of the world's finest and most uncompromising defenders.

His prolonged absence in 1980 with a blood disorder ensured Milan's worst season for years and eventual relegation following a betting scandal, but the ever-loyal Baresi matured still further; four

of his six Serie A titles came after he was 30. A third European Cup eluded him – he was suspended for Milan's 1994 triumph – but his biggest disappointment was bowing out of three World Cup tournaments as a loser on penalties, the most gut-wrenching being Italy's defeat to Brazil in the 1994 final. In 1997, the year of his retirement, he was voted Milan's most legendary player. The no. 6 banners that still fly at the San Siro ensure that Baresi's legacy will endure forever.

VITAL STATISTICS

Place of Birth: Travagliato, Italy

Date of Birth: 8 May 1960

Died: n/a Caps: 81 (Italy) Goals (International): 1

Clubs: AC Milan

Appearances: Club (League): 470

Goals: Club (League): 12

Trophies: SA 1979, 1988, 1992, 1993, 1994, 1996; EC 1989, 1990, 1994; WCC 1989, 1990

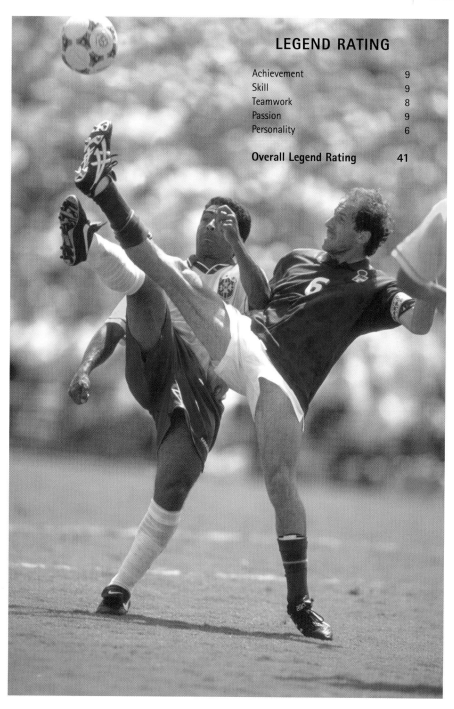

LEGEND RATING

Achievement	9
Skill	9
Teamwork	8
Passion	9
Personality	6
Overall Legend Rating	**41**

◀ Baresi's testimonial drew over 50,000 adoring Milanese to the San Siro.

◀ Baresi has never won the World Cup (although named in the victorious 1982 squad, he was not selected).

◀ Baresi played the first game of the World Cup Finals in 1994, was injured and only re-appeared for the final, having had a knee operation in the meantime! He still played a huge game.

◀ In the 1990 World Cup, Baresi marshalled a defence that didn't concede a goal until the sixth game of the tournament.

◀ Baresi scored the first penalty in the shoot-out against Argentina in 1990, but missed in the same circumstances against Brazil in 1994.

Bastin, Cliff

WHILE STILL A TEENAGER Cliff Bastin won a league title, the FA Cup and his first England cap. He carried on achieving great things, and who knows what he might have accomplished had the war not arrived while he was still only 27.

Herbert Chapman went to watch a player called Tommy Barnett at Watford, but ended up buying the opposition winger. Thus Bastin arrived at Highbury where his left-sided partnership with Alex James proved the creative core in the most successful club side of the 1930s. Most wingers at that time simply tried to go round their marker, but Bastin gave Arsenal an extra option by frequently cutting in and shooting, hence his remarkable goal tally for a winger.

When centre-forward Ted Drake joined Arsenal Bastin scored fewer goals, but his constant 'assists' for the barnstorming Drake helped Arsenal maintain their march towards three consecutive titles. Bastin was still with Arsenal after the war, but his increasing deafness and the legacy of earlier cartilage trouble meant he was a spent force, and he retired at the end of that first season.

VITAL STATISTICS

Place of Birth: Exeter, England
Date of Birth: 14 March 1912
Died: 4 December 1991
Caps: 21 (England)
Goals (International): 12 Clubs: Exeter City, Arsenal
Appearances: Club (for Arsenal): 395
Goals: Club (for Arsenal): 178
Trophies: LT 1931, 1933, 1934, 1935, 1938; FAC 1930, 1936

LEGEND RATING

Achievement	8
Skill	9
Teamwork	8
Passion	7
Personality	7
Overall Legend Rating	**39**

- Bastin was one of seven Arsenal players in the England team for the 1934 'Battle of Highbury' against Italy.
- His 33 goals in 1933 remains a record for a winger.
- Rome radio claimed Bastin was a POW during the war; actually he was an air-raid warden, unable to enter active service due to encroaching deafness.
- Bastin remained Arsenal's top scorer until Ian Wright eclipsed his record in 1997.
- Bastin joined other Arsenal stars as a pallbearer at Herbert Chapman's funeral.

Batistuta, Gabriel Omar

Fiorentina, Argentina

AS A TEENAGER Gabriel Omar Batistuta seemed destined to be a basketball star, but a switch to football at the age of 17 saw a remarkable turnaround. Not the quickest, but hard-working, powerful and sharp, the striker with the rock-star looks made an instant impact. 'Batigol' won the Copa Libertadores (Argentinean championship) at 19, and was top scorer as Argentina won the Copa América for the first time in 32 years in 1991. The inevitable move to Italy followed, but to Fiorentina, the Viola, not one of the Serie A giants. Despite his goals Fiorentina were relegated, but Batigol stayed, and they came back up. In 1999 the Viola pushed hard for the title, but a crucial injury to Batistuta cost them dearly. Finally in 2000 he left for Roma, and promptly inspired them to a Serie A title triumph, a victory his ability and commitment fully merited.

Batistuta played with distinction in two World Cup tournaments in his time at Fiorentina, proving he lacked no appetite for the big games. The 2002 finals proved to be Batistuta's swansong, as age and creaky legs caught up with him.

VITAL STATISTICS

Place of Birth: Reconquista, Santa Fe, Argentina

Date of Birth: 2 January 1969

Died: n/a **Caps:** 75 (Argentina) **Goals (International):** 55

Clubs: Newell's Old Boys, River Plate, Boca Juniors, Fiorentina, AS Roma

Appearances: Club (All Matches): 411

Goals: Club (All Matches): 220

Trophies: SA 2001

LEGEND RATING

Achievement	7
Skill	9
Teamwork	7
Passion	8
Personality	7
Overall Legend Rating	**38**

- Roma's Serie A title ended an 18-year drought for the club. Batistuta scored over 20 Serie A goals for the fifth time.
- Keegan on Batistuta: 'Batistuta is very good at pulling off defenders.' Whoops.

- Bati scored two hat-tricks in successive World Cups, against Greece in 1994 and Jamaica in 1998 (the one against Jamaica was the only one of the tournament).
- Batistuta is believed to have more websites dedicated to him

than any other player – all entirely down to his footballing talent, of course!
- The £22 m Roma paid for Batistuta was the second highest transfer fee at the time.

Baxter, Jim

A MIDFIELD, BALL-PLAYING GENERAL whose medal tally never matched those of a Billy McNeill or an Ally McCoist, but whose skill, personality and lifestyle filled endless column inches on the front and back pages of Scotland's press.

The architect of Rangers' dominance in the early 1960s, Baxter's talent elevated him to the status of team-mate to the likes of Alfredo Di Stefano, Ferenc Puskas and Eusebio in a Wembley appearance for the Rest of the World against England in 1963. Four years later it was the same venue and opponents who provided Baxter with a moment that epitomised his talent and sense of occasion when, during Scotland's famous defeat of the World Champions, he sat on the ball inviting the English players to dispossess him. While the tanner-ball Scottish stereotype suited Baxter, he also lived up to his nation's drinking traditions and a decline following a transfer to Sunderland in 1965 ensured he was never again to win a major trophy. His death at 61 in April 2001 jogged memories of a greater glory and prompted Rangers fans to line the streets in their thousands to mourn his passing.

VITAL STATISTICS

Place of Birth: Hill O'Beath, Fife, Scotland
Date of Birth: 29 September 1939
Died: 14 April 2001
Caps: 34 (Scotland)   **Goals (International):** 3
Clubs: Rangers, Sunderland, Raith Rovers, Nottingham Forest
Appearances: Club (for Rangers): 254
Goals: Club (for Rangers): 24
Trophies: SLT 1961, 1963, 1964; SFAC 1962, 1963, 1964

LEGEND RATING

Achievement	6
Skill	9
Teamwork	7
Passion	8
Personality	8
Overall Legend Rating	**38**

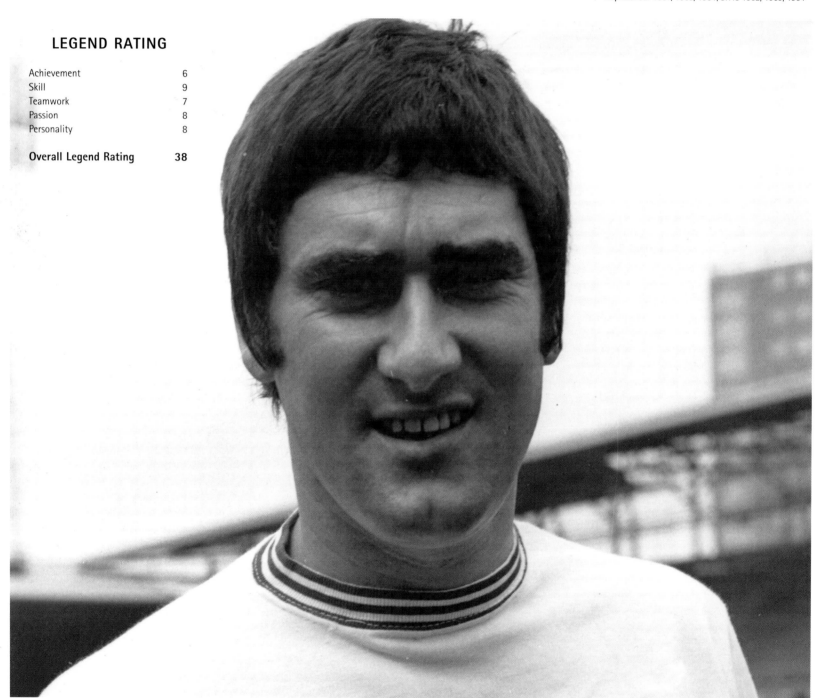

◁ Baxter's best-ever Rangers performance was probably the 1963 Cup Final replay against Celtic. He was imperious in a 3–0 victory.

◁ Scotland's failure to qualify for the 1966 World Cup Finals was put down largely to the absence of Baxter, who missed crucial qualifiers against Poland and Italy.

◁ Baxter never played in the finals of a major international tournament, so remains largely unknown outside Britain.

◁ After four unsuccessful years away, Baxter returned to Rangers for a last hurrah in 1969, but was not the force of old.

◁ Scotland's 1967 victory at Wembley condemned England to their first defeat since winning the World Cup a year earlier.

Bayern Munich

BAYERN'S TRUE HISTORY started in 1969 when they won their second league title. The first, in 1932, was in a weak league, and the club spent most of the following 30 years in the Second Division.

That all changed when the huge hands of Maier and the genius of Beckenbauer were allied to the finishing of Müller. With the uncompromising Schwarzenbeck at the back, Breitner surging up and down the left, and Hoeness quietly piecing it all together, this was a class act, and they won three consecutive European Cups to prove it.

Bayern have never quite hit those heights again, but they have remained at the top of German football, and have always been a threat in Europe (although it wasn't until 2001 that they won the European Cup again). A good percentage of Germany's best players have started with Bayern, often, like Matthaus and Klinsmann, returning for a second spell after doing the tourist bit in Italy, Spain or England. Bayern's unpopularity with other European clubs is based on their reputation for arrogance; this team would do nothing to alleviate that.

Manager: Franz Beckenbauer

1-4-3-2

Sepp Maier (60s/70s)

Franz Beckenbauer (C) (60s/70s)

Markus Babbel (90s) Georg Schwarzenbeck (70s) Samuel Kuffour (90s)
Paul Breitner (70s)

Uli Hoeness (70s) Lothar Matthaus (80s/90s) Stefan Effenberg (90s)

Gerd Muller (70s) Karl-Heinz Rummenigge (80s)

Subs: Jean-Marie Pfaff (G) (80s) Andreas Brehme (D) (80s) Klaus Augenthaler
(D) (80s) Mehmet Scholl (M) (90s) Jurgen Klinsmann (F) (90s)

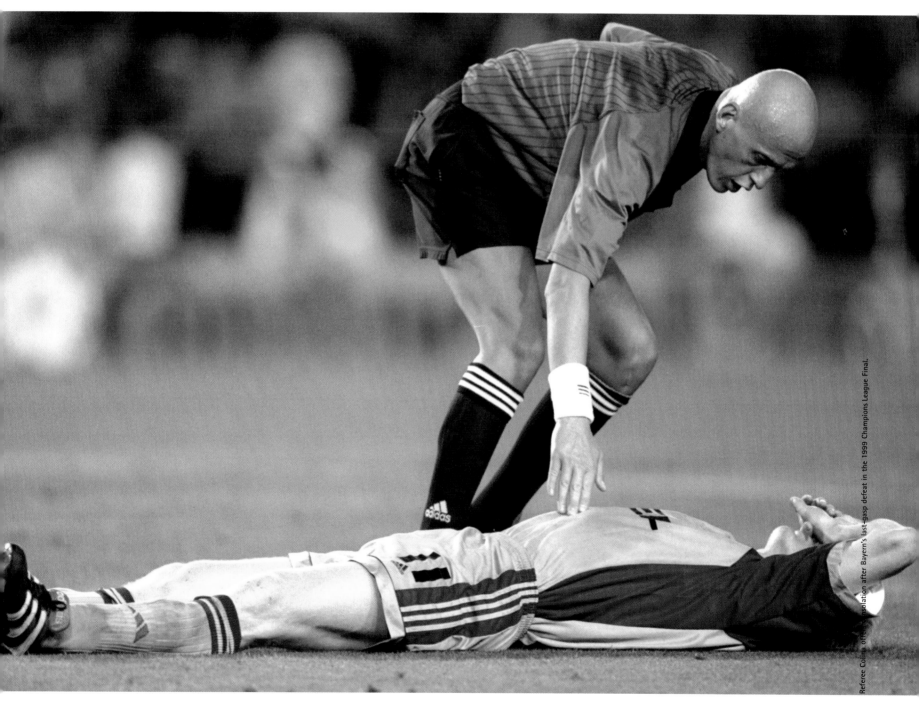

Referee Collina offers consolation after Bayern's last-gasp defeat in the 1999 Champions League Final.

◁) Markus Babbel, an aggressive and attack-minded defender, was enjoying an excellent spell at Liverpool when he was diagnosed with Guillain Barre syndrome. He missed most of the 2001/02 season because of the illness.

◁) Samuel Kuffour, the Ghanaian international, has become an integral part of the modern Bayern side; it was a surprise when he was not elected African Footballer of the Year in 2001.
◁) Apart from Kuffour, Belgian goalkeeper Pfaff is the only other

non-German in the side. The successor to Maier, he was one of the earlier successful imports into the Bundesliga.
◁) Uli Hoeness was an undemonstrative player, but his link play allowed the bigger egos to flourish.

Beckenbauer, Franz

Bayern Munich, Germany

'THE KAISER', as Franz Beckenbauer became known (such were the imperious nature of his displays for club and country), was one of the finest players in the history of the game. An outstanding captain and tactician, it was no surprise that he went on to win everything, including the World Cup as player and manager.

Beginning his international career as a deep-lying midfielder, Beckenbauer revolutionised the notion of the attacking sweeper, bursting out of defence to set up attacks, often even finishing them himself. He had every attribute a footballer requires: control, passing, strength and uncanny vision. Only Ruud Gullit has since shown a

comparable range of skills, but he lacked Beckenbauer's iron will. Retiring from international football in 1977, Beckenbauer teamed up with Pelé at New York Cosmos in the North American Soccer League, before returning to claim one last domestic honour with SV Hamburg.

Once retired he was appointed national coach almost immediately, and injected the same discipline and indomitable steel into the German side in the 1980s that it was famed for under his captaincy 10 years earlier. More success followed, and Beckenbauer, as President of Bayern Munich, remains at the forefront of German and European football to this day.

VITAL STATISTICS

Place of Birth: Munich, Germany
Date of Birth: 11 September 1945
Died: n/a Caps: 104 (West Germany) Goals (International): 15
Clubs: Bayern Munich, Hamburg, New York Cosmos
Appearances: Club (All Matches): 720
Goals: Club (All Matches): 94
Trophies: WorC 1974 (1990), Euro C 1972; BLG 1969, 1973, 1974, 1975, (1994); EC 1974, 1975; CWC 1967

Beckenbauer covets the World Cup with the West German team in 1974.

LEGEND RATING

Achievement 10
Skill 9
Teamwork 9
Passion 9
Personality 8

Overall Legend Rating 45

- Many commentators believe Beckenbauer's best performance came in the 3-2 win over England at the 1970 World Cup in Mexico. He inspired the Germans to a 3-2 win after they fell two goals behind.
- Only Mario Zagalo has equalled Beckenbauer's feat of World Cup medals as player and manager; Zagalo was not captain of Brazil.
- Beckenbauer was twice named European Footballer of the Year, in 1972 and 1976.
- He was picked for Germany after only 27 appearances for Bayern.
- Beckenbauer was detailed to man-mark Bobby Charlton in the 1966 World Cup final, and later admitted he was not ready for the challenge.

Beckham, David

WHEN DAVID BECKHAM curled a last-minute free kick over the Greek wall to win England a place at the 2002 World Cup Finals, it completed a comeback more remarkable than merely the context of England's qualifying campaign. It completed a transformation in the public's perception of the England captain.

Three years previously Beckham had been a national figure of hate, reviled after his petulant kick and red card during the game against Argentina had (at least in the eyes of the tabloids) contributed to England's defeat in the second round at France 98. If he had taken the easy option and moved abroad he may not have become what he is: the single-most influential player for his country. His passing and crossing are of the highest order, and his shooting from set pieces is almost Brazilian in its power and accuracy.

That he has matured beyond adolescent cockiness is more surprising, not least because his looks, style and pop-star wife have made 'Becks' the most hounded footballer since George Best. A United fan since his North London boyhood, Beckham had shown no desire to seek fresh challenges abroad, until his controversial ommission from the starting line-up in the 2002/3 Champions league quarter-final against Real Madrid fueled speculations of a move.

VITAL STATISTICS

Place of Birth: Leytonstone, England

Date of Birth: 2 May 1975

Died: n/a Caps: 59 (England) Goals (International): 11

Clubs: Manchester United

Appearances: Club (All Matches): 386

Goals: Club (All Matches): 86

Trophies: LT 1996, 1997, 1999, 2000, 2001, 2003; FAC 1996, 1999; EC 1999

Beckham lets rip after his last-minute free kick earns England's passage to the 2002 World Cup Finals.

LEGEND RATING

Achievement	9
Skill	8
Teamwork	10
Passion	8
Personality	6
Overall Legend Rating	41

- Beckham announced himself to English football with an outrageous 50-m goal at Wimbledon.
- France 98. National hero after scoring 25-m free kick against Colombia. Argentina and Diego Simeone were only days away...
- 1999. Married Spice Girl Victoria Beckham. 'Posh and Becks' become Britain's most photographed couple.
- 2001. Rumours of row with Alex Ferguson as Beckham was dropped for crucial game at Leeds. Beckham was also left out for seven games over the holiday period; no player is too big for United.
- December 2001. Voted BBC Sports Personality of the Year, and runner-up as World Footballer of the Year for a second time.

Bellamy, Craig

ASK ANY DEFENDER what they dislike most and they are sure to say it is a nippy forward running towards them at pace. They must loathe the sight of Craig Bellamy.

He was always lightning fast. Nationwide defences were one thing, coping with Europe's finest in the Premier League proved to be a test that Bellamy looked like flunking in the early months. His first touch and footballing brain have come on so rapidly in the last two seasons that this is no longer an issue.

Bought by Coventry from Norwich as a replacement for Robbie Keane, he filled his boots uncannily accurately. Following the Sky Blues' relegation in 2001, he was always going to be too hot a property to keep. Bobby Robson and a £6 m cheque proved an irresistible combination for player and club.

Bellamy has slotted in perfectly at St James's Park, owing a large debt to the guile of Shearer, who has proved his perfect attacking partner and mentor. His achilles heel is his temperament, eleven bookings in his first season made him a marked man for referees and wily defenders. At 24 years old, he is growing too old for youthful exuberance. What bodes well for Newcastle and ill for defenders is that his best days should still be ahead of him.

VITAL STATISTICS

Place of Birth: Cardiff, Wales
Date of Birth: 13 July 1979
Died: n/a Caps: 20 (Wales) Goals (International): 6
Clubs: Norwich City, Coventry City, Newcastle United
Appearances: Club: 196
Goals: Club: 64
Trophies: None

Bellamy (No. 10) is congratulated by mentor Shearer.

LEGEND RATING

Achievement	5
Skill	8
Passion & Commitment	8
Inspiration	7
Personality	6
Overall Legend Rating	34

◁ Red-carded twice for violent conduct in the 2002/03 Champions League campaign. The first is awarded retrospectively on video evidence. The second sees him depart in tears after only seven minutes following a moment of madness against Internazionale.

◁ Wales' emergence under Mark Hughes is due in no small part to the attacking options provided by Bellamy.
◁ Another flash of temper has seen Bellamy formally cautioned for assault after an incident in Newcastle's city centre.

◁ 2001/02 season ruined by knee injury, although the recovery has not slowed him down.
◁ First Welsh cap – 1998 as substitute v Jamaica.

Bergkamp, Dennis

Arsenal, Holland

DENNIS BERGKAMP BROKE INTO the Ajax team towards the end of the Gullit, Rijkaard, Van Basten era. Bergkamp gradually made his presence felt, and earned a high-profile move to Inter to replace Jurgen Klinsmann. Not suited to playing as a lone striker, the move did not work out and Inter offloaded him to Arsenal. Initially it seemed as if his spell at Highbury would be equally unfruitful, but the arrival of Arsène Wenger changed all that. Almost immediately Bergkamp was rejuvenated and, in tandem with Nicolas Anelka, inspired the Gunners to a League and Cup double in 1998.

After scoring the two goals at Wembley that effectively eliminated England in the qualifiers, Bergkamp had an outstanding 1994 World Cup in a transitional side. A better side flopped in Euro 96, getting hammered by England, but surprised many by the quality of their play at France 98. Bergkamp showed his divine poise and touch in scoring the goal of the tournament against Argentina. Since then Bergkamp's best has only been seen in glimpses, and he found himself exiled to the fringes of the Arsenal first team until a resurgence of form saw him help the Gunners win another double in 2002.

VITAL STATISTICS

Place of Birth: Amsterdam, Holland

Date of Birth: 18 May 1969

Died: n/a Caps: 79 (Holland) Goals (International): 36

Clubs: Ajax, Inter Milan, Arsenal

Appearances: Club (League): 472

Goals: Club (League): 189

Trophies: LT 1998, 2002; FAC 1998, 2002, 2003; DLT 1993; EUFAC 1992, 1994

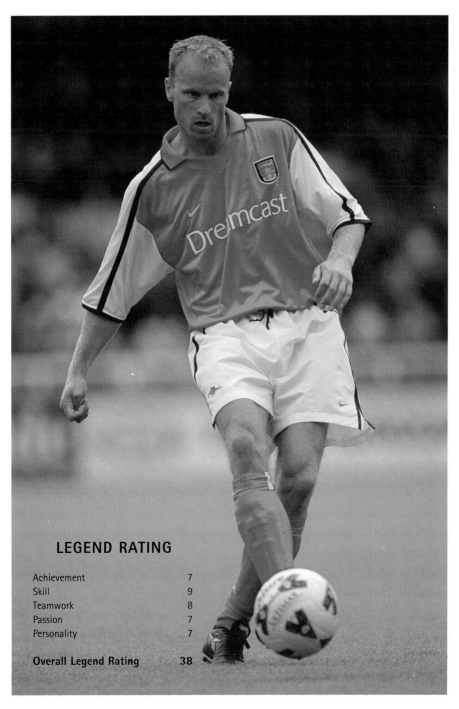

LEGEND RATING

Achievement	7
Skill	9
Teamwork	8
Passion	7
Personality	7
Overall Legend Rating	**38**

◄)) In August 1997 Bergkamp occupied the top three positions in the *Match Of The Day* goal-of-the-month competition. The winning goal, a cheeky control-and-finish against Leicester, also won the goal-of-the-season award.

◄)) Many Ajax coaches thought Bergkamp wasn't strong enough for pro football, but Johan Cruyff was quick to select him for the first team.

◄)) Bergkamp's fear of flying, which he thought he had conquered, was rekindled by a bomb alert as the Dutch team travelled to the 1994 World Cup in the USA. He has not flown since.

◄)) Bergkamp was named after Denis Law. His parents mistakenly spelt his first name with two 'n's instead of one.

Berlusconi's Dream

IN DEBT AND UNSUCCESSFUL, Milan were going nowhere until Silvio Berlusconi's millions (or billions, if we're talking lire!) provided coach Arrigo Sacchi with the funds to strip other European clubs of their prize assets. The ploy had served Milan well in the late 1950s, and was to do so again. The Dutch triumvirate of Gullit, Rijkaard and Van Basten was assembled in front of possibly the greatest club defence of all time; Tassotti and Maldini at full-back and, inside them, the peerless Baresi and Costacurta. In 1989, after a wait of 20 years, they brought home the European Cup, and won it again the following year.

Four years later, this time under Fabio Capello, the European Cup was again brought back to the San Siro, erasing the frustrations of a defeat against Marseille in 1993. The full-backs and the tousle-haired Donadoni were still there, and Marcel Desailly bestrode the midfield. There was a Balkan influence up front, with the Croatian Boban deployed alongside the enigmatic Yugoslav, Savicevic. That was the last great European year for Milan; Savicevic departed and was shortly followed by Desailly, while Baresi was to retire before the decade was out. Their replacements have so far proved to be unworthy successors.

Managers: Arrigo Sacchi and Fabio Capello

Key Players

Paolo Maldini (D) Franco Baresi (D) Alessandro Costacurta (D)
Frank Rijkaard (M) Ruud Gullit (M/F) Marcel Desailly (M)
Roberto Donadoni (M) Daniele Massaro (F)
Marco Van Basten (F) Dejan Savicevic (F)

Trophies

SA 1988, 1992, 1993, 1994 EC 1989, 1990, 1994

Van Basten and Gullit with the European Cup. Nice vest, Ruud!

◁ In the 1989 European Cup final the Dutch trio destroyed Steaua Bucharest 4-0, Van Basten and Gullit grabbing a brace each.

◁ Rijkaard's glory came the following year, as he scored the only goal in the 1-0 win over Benfica.

◁ In 1994 Savicevic was the tormentor-in-chief. Barcelona were confident of victory going into the game, but they were pulled apart by the Yugoslav genius as Milan again won 4-0.

◁ Following a corruption enquiry into their owner, Bernard Tapie,

Marseille were stripped of their 1993 European Cup title. Uefa decided not to award Milan the trophy by default.

◁ Franco Baresi missed Barcelona's crushing. It would have been fitting to have one of the club's great servants in their finest hour.

Bernabeu Stadium

Madrid, Spain

THE CHAMARTIN STADIUM WAS HOME to Real Madrid for their first 23 years. In 1944, ambitious club president Santiago Bernabeu saw work begin on his dream to construct an arena which would propel Real to the top of football's élite. Three years later the boast became reality.

The Bernabeu is a mighty work. It boasts twin towers, similar to those at Wembley, and its steep terraces make it one of the most intimidating football theatres in the world. The Bernabeu played host to the all-conquering Real side of the 1950s, and became a virtual fortress for the home team between 1957–65, as Real played a remarkable 114 matches in succession without defeat. Eight replica European Cups make the trophy room unique, a scale of victory unthinkable without the atmosphere and revenue generated by the Bernabeu.

The stadium was improved still further when Spain hosted the 1982 World Cup Finals. A new roof was added, increasing the crescendo still further. Naturally, the Bernabeu played host to the final itself, Italy beating West Germany 3-1.

VITAL STATISTICS

(Named after long-time Real Madrid president Santiago Bernabeau)

Location:	Madrid, Spain
Local Club:	Real Madrid
Date Built:	1947
Current Capacity:	105,000
Max. Capacity:	125,000

◁ The first game at the Bernabeu on 14 December 1947 saw Real Madrid beat the Portuguese team Os Belenenses 3-1.

◁ A record crowd of 124,000 watched Real beat Fiorentina 2-0 in the 1957 European Cup final.

◁ The capacity was drastically reduced in the 1990s following UEFA's insistence on all-seater stadiums.

◁ The Bernabeu has hosted three European Cup finals; 1957, 1969 and Nottingham Forest's 1-0 victory over Hamburg SV in 1980.

◁ A new stadium has been proposed on a site 5 km away. It has met with stiff opposition from traditionalists, despite the intention to return capacity to 120,000-plus.

Best Football Team in the World

...Ever

THIS WAS REALLY EASY TO PICK. So few players elevate themselves to the level of these 16 players that the process of elimination is almost automatic. The criteria? Great technical ability, appetite for battle, sustained excellence over a number of years, and an ability to inspire others, either by example or leadership.

None of these players were perfect (although Pelé came close at times) and none are pre-war (football was a cruder game back then and the competition was less fierce), but all satisfy the criteria in abundance. Six of them played in the 1950s, four more started in the 1960s, two in the 1970s, and the last four in the 1980s.

There are nine Europeans and five South Americans (no country has more than two players), and there are no out-and-out full-backs; the restrictive nature of the position makes it unattractive for the very best players. If 4-4-2 were required, Baresi would slot in alongside Moore, and Garrincha or Best would drop to the bench. Only Paolo Maldini is still in active service, and his career is coming to an end. Other current players were considered, but the likes of Luis Figo, Thierry Henry and David Beckham still have plenty to prove before they can be bracketed in this exalted company.

Managers: Guy Lloyd and Nick Holt

3-4-1-2

Lev Yashin (USSR)

Franz Beckenbauer (C) (W. Ger) Bobby Moore (Eng) Paolo Maldini (Ita)

Garrincha (Bra) Pelé (Bra)
Michel Platini (Fra) George Best (N. Ire)

Alfredo Di Stefano (Arg)

Johan Cruyff (Hol) Ferenc Puskas (Hun)

Subs: Gordon Banks (G) (Eng) Franco Baresi (D) (Ita) Diego Maradona (M) (Arg) Juan Schiaffino (F) (Uru) Gerd Muller (F) (W. Ger)

Lev Yashin (USSR)

Franz Beckenbauer (W. Ger)   (c)   Bobby Moore (Eng)   Paolo Maldini (Ita)

Garrincha (Bra)   Pelé (Bra)   Michel Platini (Fra)   George Best (N. Ire)

Alfredo Di Stefano (Arg)

Johan Cruyff (Hol)   Ferenc Puskas (Hun)

◁ No one got close to either of the goalkeeping slots; the next in line were Shilton, Schmeichel, Zoff and Jennings.
◁ Van Basten is another Dutchman unlucky to miss out, and Eusebio and Bobby Charlton wouldn't have looked out of place.

◁ Daniel Passarella had a case for inclusion, but was less sophisticated than the four defenders picked. Marcel Desailly falls just short of this status.
◁ Gullit is perhaps the most obvious omission from the midfield.

◁ Lothar Matthaus was a great player, but his biggest fan was Lothar Matthaus.
◁ Managing this collection of inflated egos would be impossible, so we thought we might as well appoint ourselves!

Best, George

'I THINK I'VE FOUND YOU A GENIUS,' claimed the Belfast scout in an excited telephone call to Matt Busby. He wasn't wrong. Signed as a professional on his 17th birthday, George Best thrilled the Old Trafford faithful like no player before or since. Had Best played for a stronger country than Northern Ireland he may now be spoken of with the same reverence as Pelé.

The cocktail of outrageous ball skills and smouldering good looks proved to be an explosive one; Best's transformation from Belfast innocent to international playboy seemed to capture the spirit of the 1960s. He was even dubbed 'El Beatle' by the Portuguese press after

a mesmerising display in Benfica's Stadium of Light. The free spirit that was Europe's most feared striker became society's hottest property, an advertiser's dream whose fame and fortune rocketed in a whirl of boutique openings and product endorsement. The inevitable falls from grace were frequent and glaring, and at 28 he was washed-up.

Despite an Indian summer at Fulham with fellow funster Rodney Marsh, and occasional spells in the NASL and elsewhere, the career of George Best has now been restricted to bar-room reminiscences for nearly 30 years.

VITAL STATISTICS

Place of Birth: Belfast, Northern Ireland
Date of Birth: 22 May 1946
Died: n/a **Caps:** 37 (Northern Ireland) **Goals (International):** 9
Clubs: Manchester United, Stockport County, Cork Celtic, Los Angeles Aztecs, Fulham, Hibernian, Fort Lauderdale Strikers, San Jose Earthquakes, Golden, Bournemouth
Appearances: Club (League: for Man Utd): 361
Goals: Club (League: for Man Utd): 137
Trophies: LT 1965, 1967; EC 1968 (all with Man Utd)

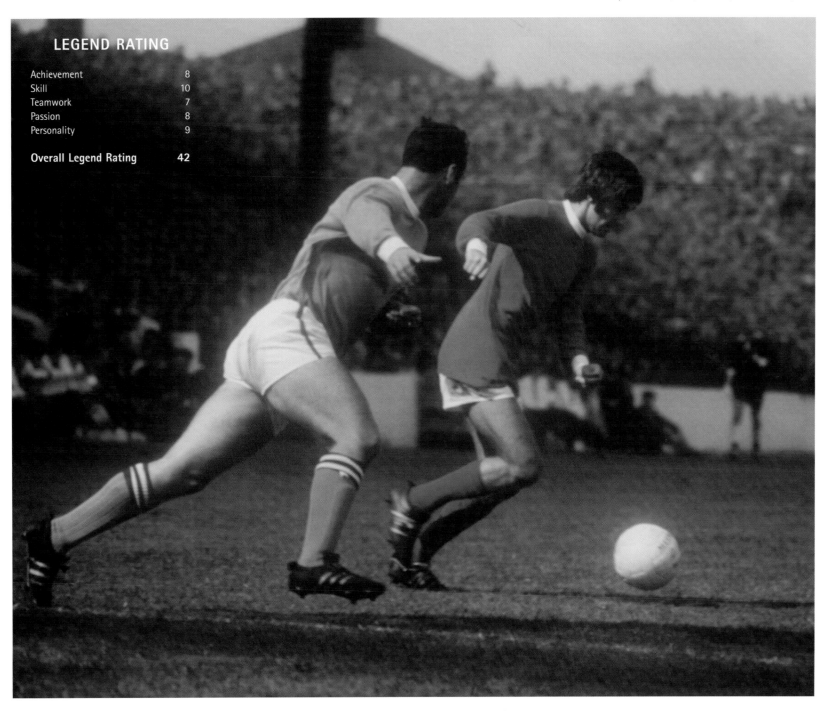

LEGEND RATING

Achievement	8
Skill	10
Teamwork	7
Passion	8
Personality	9
Overall Legend Rating	**42**

◄〗 Best was originally recommended to Leeds. Unimpressed, the scout left his trial match during the first half.

◄〗 1968. Best's *annus mirabilis*: Joint First Division top-scorer, European Cup winner, English and European Footballer of the Year.

◄〗 1970. Suspended for four weeks for bringing the game into disrepute. On his return, scored six in an 8–2 win at Northampton.

◄〗 1976. Scored after 71 seconds in his debut for Fulham. Also

became their first recipient of a red card.

◄〗 2001. Admitted to hospital following a long battle with alcoholism.

Bettega, Roberto

Juventus, Italy

'HE ALLIES TREMENDOUS ATHLETIC STRENGTH with impressive technical skills. He is particularly strong in the air and can kick the ball with either foot ... he will certainly be a force to be reckoned with'. Wise words indeed from the Varese coach on his 19-year-old scoring prodigy. The following year, Roberto Bettega was at Juventus to begin a liaison that would end 13 seasons later with a guaranteed place in the lofty pantheon of the Turin club's hall of fame.

He announced himself early with a back-heeled goal in the San Siro against Milan, but it wasn't until the arrival of Giovanni Trapattoni as coach that he moved to his trademark centre-forward position. Bettega enhanced his folk-hero status further by battling back from tuberculosis when medical opinion had written off his career at 21. From then on he dominated Juve's forward line, winning seven league titles in 11 years, and was an automatic choice as Italy's number nine. He was to bow out disappointingly in the 1983 European Cup final, but for Juventus fans nothing could spoil the legend.

VITAL STATISTICS

Place of Birth: Torino, Italy

Date of Birth: 27 December1950

Died: n/a Caps: 42 (Italy) Goals (International): 19

Clubs: Varese, Juventus

Appearances: Club (League: for Juventus): 326

Goals: Club (League: for Juventus): 126

Trophies: EUFAC 1977; SA 1972, 1973, 1975, 1977, 1978, 1981, 1982

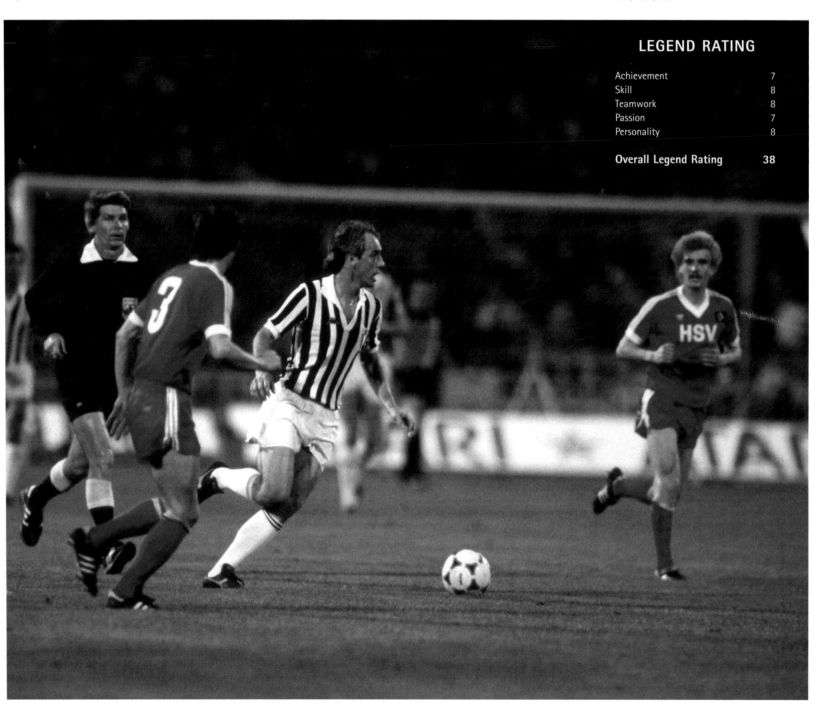

LEGEND RATING

Achievement	7
Skill	8
Teamwork	8
Passion	7
Personality	8
Overall Legend Rating	**38**

◀ᴵᴵᴵ He was known throughout his career as 'Bobby-gol' by the Juventus faithful.

◀ᴵᴵᴵ Best international goal: A stunning header in Rome sinks England in a 1976 World Cup qualifier.

◀ᴵᴵᴵ He missed Italy's 1982 World Cup Finals triumph after knee-ligament damage in 1981 ruled him out for nearly a year.

◀ᴵᴵᴵ Despite seven league titles, he never won the European Cup. His last game was as a losing finalist against Hamburg.

◀ᴵᴵᴵ He returned to Juventus after retirement as vice-president.

Bianconeri

AT THE BEGINNING of the 1980s Juventus were a deeply unfulfilled club. Their great rivals from Milan had both won the European Cup in the 1960s and 1970s, but despite a stream of Serie A titles, Juve were perennial failures in their quest for ultimate European glory (they had lost their only final appearance against Ajax in 1973). The defence was rock solid, a formidable barrier that contained experienced keeper Dino Zoff, Scirea at sweeper and the fabled hard-man Gentile in the middle. Coach Trapattoni had tried a number of permutations of overseas stars ahead of them, but it was the combination of Platini and the Polish star Boniek that would

prove the key. They came close in 1983, but came up against a stubborn Hamburg in the final. The following year was another dress rehearsal, a victory in the European Cup Winners' Cup over Porto. Sadly, when Juve finally landed their Holy Grail, their victory, against Liverpool in the 1985 final, was tainted with sadness. The deaths of 39 of their fans following the collapse of a wall in the Heysel stadium before kick-off reduced the match to a meaningless and hollow affair. The Cup was lifted, the crowd applauded but there was no joy in the celebrations.

Manager: Giovanni Trapattoni

Key Players

Dino Zoff (G) Claudio Gentile (D) Antonio Cabrini (D)
Gaetano Scirea (D) Marco Tardelli (M) Zbigniew Boniek (M)
Michel Platini (M/F) Paolo Rossi (F) Roberto Bettega (F)

Trophies

SA 1981, 1982, 1984, 1986 EC 1985 CWC 1984 WCC 1985 ESC 1984

Zbigniew Boniek, 'Il Bello di Notte', celebrates another goal.

- Zoff, Gentile, Cabrini, Scirea, Tardelli and Rossi all started the 1982 World Cup final. Zoff captained the side, Tardelli and Rossi both scored.
- Juve squeezed past Manchester United in the semi-finals of the 1984 European Cup Winners' Cup, a 2–1 home win seeing them home on aggregate by the odd goal.
- In 1983, on their way to the European Cup final, they disposed of English opposition, beating Aston Villa home and away.
- Platini settled the 1985 final with a penalty that shouldn't have been given. The great Frenchman contributed seven goals to Juve's campaign that year.

Bingham, Billy

THERE WAS A TIME in the not-too-distant past when Northern Ireland was not simply cannon fodder for the rest of the world. Lest we forget, the nation now lumped in the same bracket as Cyprus reached the 1958 World Cup quarter-finals, distinguished themselves in Spain in 1982 and qualified again for the Mexico Finals four years later. The one connection? Mr Billy Bingham.

As a small, nippy, right-winger, Bingham played in all five games during the 1958 campaign, but it was as manager that he made the greater impact. The blend was the key; from the vast experience of Pat Jennings to the 17-year-old exuberance of Norman Whiteside, Bingham built a well-balanced team. Unfancied before the 1982 World Cup Finals, Northern Ireland beat hosts Spain to win their group, and were later only undone by a Michel Platini-inspired France.

At the Mexico Finals four years later there was again no disgrace in losing to Spain and Brazil. Indeed, Bingham had earned international respect as a coach simply by qualifying again. Bingham's international record was in stark contrast to his record as a club manager; he achieved little as boss of a string of lowly club sides. But to the people of Ulster he will always be fondly remembered.

VITAL STATISTICS

Place of Birth: Belfast, Northern Ireland

Date of Birth: 5 August 1931

Died: n/a   Caps: 56 (Northern Ireland)

Goals (International): 10

Clubs: As Player: Glentoran, Sunderland, Luton Town, Everton, Port Vale; As Manager: Southport, Plymouth Argyle, Linfield, Everton, Mansfield

Trophies: None

LEGEND RATING

Achievement	5
Tactical Awareness	7
Motivation	9
Transfer Dealing and Team Selection	7
Personality	8
Overall Legend Rating	**36**

◁ᴺ He shared a record number of N. Ireland caps with Danny Blanchflower (56).

◁ᴺ 1959. Won FA Cup runners-up medal with Luton Town.

◁ᴺ 1963. League Championship winner with Everton.

◁ᴺ 1983. Coached Northern Ireland to a shock 1–0 win over West Germany in Hamburg.

◁ᴺ 1981. Awarded MBE for services to football.

Blanchflower, Robert Dennis (Danny) Tottenham Hotspur, Northern Ireland

DANNY BLANCHFLOWER is best remembered as the playmaker in the 1961 Spurs double-winning side. However, he was by then in the twilight of his career, having emerged in Irish football just after the war.

Not exceptionally quick or powerful, Blanchflower's game was all about passing. Blessed with exceptional vision, his ability to find team-mates with the ball was uncanny. His understanding of the game was deep and intuitive, and he used that knowledge to great effect on the pitch. 'Football is not really about winning ... it's about doing things in style,' he once wrote. Any modern footballer uttering those words would be sold the next day!

After retiring, Blanchflower had a few forays into management. He managed the Northern Ireland national team in a tough spell prior to the golden years of Billy Bingham, and was in charge at Stamford Bridge as Chelsea suffered relegation in 1979. Thereafter he concentrated on his career as a journalist, where his erudite thinking about the game served him better.

VITAL STATISTICS

Place of Birth: Belfast, Northern Ireland
Date of Birth: 10 February 1926
Died: 9 December 1993 **Caps:** 56 (Northern Ireland)
Goals (International): 2 **Clubs:** Glentoran, Swindon Town, Barnsley, Aston Villa, Tottenham
Appearances: Club (All Matches): 735
Goals: Club (All Matches): 40
Trophies: LT 1961; FAC 1961, 1962; CWC 1963

LEGEND RATING

Achievement	8
Skill	9
Teamwork	7
Passion	8
Personality	8
Overall Legend Rating	**40**

◀ He famously refused to take part in the programme *This Is Your Life* when Eamonn Andrews surprised him.

◀ Danny's younger brother, Jackie, played for Manchester United and was injured in the Munich air crash, never to play again.

◀ Blanchflower was captain of the Northern Ireland team that reached the quarter-finals of the 1958 World Cup.

◀ He was also captain when Northern Ireland beat England at Wembley for the first time in 1957.

◀ He was Player of the Year in 1958 and 1961.

Blohkin, Oleg

THE SOVIET UNION used to guard its assets with extreme jealousy, so football viewers to the west of the Iron Curtain only tended to see their stars when they came out of their shell in European competition. When Dynamo Kiev beat Ferencvaros in the 1975 European Cup Winners' Cup final they revealed some marvellous talent, not least their flying winger Oleg Blokhin, scorer of their third goal. Fast and with a penchant for cutting inside and heading for goal, Blokhin went on to terrorise the best club defence in Europe the following year, scoring a hat-trick in the 3-0 victory over Bayern Munich in the European Super Cup. Eleven years later Blokhin played

in another European Cup Winners' Cup final, this time as the old warhorse in the sublimely talented side coached by Valeri Lobanowski. He contributed a goal to a mesmerising performance in what was a fitting swansong at the top level. In Igor Belanov, another striker who enjoyed attacking from wide positions, Dynamo had a ready-made successor for Blokhin, and they have continued to cover for his absence impressively, nurturing several talented front men including Andrei Shevchenko and Sergei Rebrov.

VITAL STATISTICS

Place of Birth: Kiev, Russia

Date of Birth: 5 November 1952

Died: n/a Caps: 101 (USSR) Goals (International): 39

Clubs: Dynamo Kiev, Vorwarts Styer

Appearances: Club (League): 432

Goals: Club (League): 211

Trophies: LT 1971, 1974, 1975, 1977, 1980, 1981, 1985, 1986; CWC 1975, 1986

LEGEND RATING

Achievement	8
Skill	8
Teamwork	8
Passion	7
Personality	6
Overall Legend Rating	**37**

◁ Blohkin's cup exploits earned him the European Footballer of the Year award in 1975. His club-mate and compatriot Igor Belanov won the same honour in 1986.

◁ Kiev almost got to the final of the 1977 European Cup but,

after eliminating holders Bayern Munich, they lost 2-1 on aggregate to Borussia Monchengladbach in the semi-final.

◁ Blokhin became the first Soviet player to win 100 caps. Let's hope no one catches his final target of 101, because if they do

it means the tanks have rolled again.

◁ At the end of his career Blokhin was allowed to leave the Soviet Union and earn a pension in Austrian football. He later became manager of Olympiakos in Greece.

Blonde Bombshells

The Nordic Dream Team

SWEDEN AND DENMARK DOMINATE this strong selection, as befits the two Nordic countries with the greatest pedigree at international level. Eriksson is the most successful coach from any of those nations, so gets the manager's job. Sweden have been a competitive side since the war, reaching the final of the 1958 World Cup on home soil with a team including the adaptable Liedholm, the energetic Gren and the great goalscorer Gunnar Nordahl.

Denmark's remarkable win at Euro 92 put them on the footballing map, and the skills of the Laudrup brothers managed to keep them there throughout the 1990s. Ironically, their best team was one that

won nothing; at Mexico 86 a dynamic, attacking team containing Michael Laudrup, Preben Elkjaer, Soren Lerby and Jesper and Morten Olsen thrilled a global audience of millions but came away empty-handed after defeat to Spain in the second round.

Norway flirted with major tournaments in the 1990s but Egil Olsen's dour tactics always stifled their better players. Bratseth, a world-class defender, represents them here. Finland are an improving side, with Jari Litmanen an inspiration for future generations. And in qualification for Euro 2000 Iceland gave a superb account of themselves in a group containing France, Russia and Ukraine.

Manager: Sven-Goran Eriksson (Swe)
1-3-3-1-2

Peter Schmeichel (Den) (90s)

Morten Olsen (C) (Den) (80s)

Nils Liedholm (Swe) (50s) Bjorn Nordqvist (Swe) (60s/70s)
Rune Bratseth (Nor) (80s/90s)

Gunnar Gren (Swe) (50s) Jan Molby (Den) (80s)
Jari Litmanen (Fin) (90s) Michael Laudrup (Den) (90s)

Allan Simonsen (Den) (70s/80s) Gunnar Nordahl (Swe) (50s/60s)

Subs: Tomas Ravelli (Swe) (G) (80s/90s) Patrik Andersson (Swe) (D) (90s)
Kurt Hamrin (Swe) (M/F) Eidur Gudjohnsen (Ice) (F) (00s)
Brian Laudrup (Den) (F) (90s)

◁◁▷ Sweden have had several top-class international strikers. In the 1970s Ralf Edstrom was a towering player, Thomas Brolin was their playmaker in the 1990s, and their recent duo of Kennet Andersson and Henrik Larsson were both high-calibre finishers.

◁◁▷ Denmark, too, have had notable strikers. Preben Elkjaer and Fleming Povlsen were both excellent players, especially Elkjaer, whose stamina and industry made him a fine foil for the young Michael Laudrup.

◁◁▷ Iceland, and the future, are represented by Chelsea's Eidur Gudjohnsen, whose father also played for his country.

◁◁▷ With the precocious Mikael Forsell in their ranks, Finland gave England two tough matches in the 2002 World Cup qualifiers.

Bloomer, Steve

WITH HIS SLIGHT BUILD and sallow appearance, Steve Bloomer was an unlikely athlete. A dressing-room nickname of 'paleface' hardly suggested a man brimming with rude health but, during a remarkable career of 21 seasons, he became English football's first great goalscoring hero, and its undoubted star during the pre-First World War era.

His 352 league goals (a record that only Dixie Dean has beaten) were achieved courtesy of rare, two-footed skills that made him one of the game's most entertaining dribblers. His influence was exemplified by the 1903 FA Cup. Bloomer's goals had guided Derby to the final but, for the big day itself, he was absent with injury. Without him Derby succumbed 6-0 to Bury in what remains the heaviest final defeat of all time.

Two years later he made up one half of British football's then-biggest transfer, as Middlesbrough swooped for Bloomer and Sunderland's Alf Common in the first-ever four-figure deal. The gamble paid off. Boro, seemingly destined for relegation, hauled themselves clear in the final weeks of the season. For Bloomer, carrying inferior team-mates became the story of his career.

VITAL STATISTICS

Place of Birth: Cradley Heath, England
Date of Birth: 20 January 1874
Died: 16 April 1938
Caps: 23 (England) Goals (International): 28
Clubs: Derby County, Middlesbrough
Appearances: Club (League): 598
Goals: Club (League): 353
Trophies: None

Bloomer (front row, seated second from left) poses with the England team.

LEGEND RATING

Achievement	5
Skill	8
Teamwork	8
Passion	9
Personality	6
Overall Legend Rating	36

- He was England's seventh-highest scorer with 28 goals, despite winning only 23 caps.
- Bloomer never won a trophy, twice finishing on the losing side in the FA Cup final.
- 1914. Coaching in Berlin, Bloomer's career was only ended when he was interned at the onset of the First World War.
- Bloomer had a typically direct approach to the game: 'The purpose of play is the scoring of goals.'
- He was the leading league scorer five times in eight seasons.

Blue Heaven

The 1955 team may have won Chelsea's only title, but its sum was always greater than its individual parts. Hence captain and inspiration Roy Bentley is its only representative in this Dream Team, the remaining players being provided by teams of the 1970s and the late 1990s.

The agile Bonetti was a better goalkeeper than England fans will ever credit. The rest of the defence is dominated by the recent sides, with the exception of left-back where McCreadie shades the more talented but unpredictable Le Saux. With Gullit and the fabulous Marcel Desailly at the back, there's no shortage of ability on the ball.

Dennis Wise adds a bit of attitude to the midfield alongside the gifted yet underachieving Hudson. Gus Poyet provides all-day running and a decent goal quota. The puck-like skills of Gianfranco Zola are used in their best position, just behind the front two (the only downside to this being that ball artists Nevin and Cooke have to settle for a place on the bench).

In attack Osgood, a truly complete centre-forward who should have played more internationals for England, is a fine spearhead alongside the industrious Bentley. Hughie Gallacher, perhaps better known as a Newcastle player, makes a potent substitute.

Manager: Glenn Hoddle

4-3-1-2

Peter Bonetti (60s/70s)

Albert Ferrer (90s)   Marcel Desailly (90s)

Ruud Gullit (90s)   Eddie McCreadie (70s)

Dennis Wise (90s)   Alan Hudson (70s)   Gus Poyet (90s)

Gianfranco Zola (90s)

Roy Bentley (50s)   Peter Osgood (60s/70s)

Subs: Eddie Niedzewiecki (G) (80s) Graeme Le Saux (D) (90s) Pat Nevin (W) (80s) Charlie Cooke (W) (60s/70s) Hughie Gallacher (F) (30s)

Ron Harris (left) and Peter Osgood (right) brandish the FA Cup after Chelsea's victory in 1970.

◁ Gullit is included in defence, despite being better known as an attacking midfielder.

◁ No place for Jimmy Greaves. Despite 124 goals in 157 games, his name is synonymous with Spurs.

◁ Bonetti is one of Chelsea's shorter keepers, dwarfed by 'Fatty' Foulke and Ed de Goey.

◁ Osgood and Le Saux both had two spells at the club. Osgood is included for his first, Le Saux for his second.

◁ This is a cosmopolitan squad, with players from eight different countries, (Niedzewiecki played for Wales). Unlike current Chelsea squads, it includes eight England internationals.

Boniek, Zbigniew

AFTER EMERGING as a potential star with his local team, Zbigniew Boniek was picked up by Widzew Lodz, one of the top Polish sides. As his international reputation grew, so did the interest in him from scouts operating on behalf of the top clubs in Spain and Italy. He joined Juventus in 1982, forming an awesome midfield with Michel Platini and Marco Tardelli in one of the great European club sides.

Boniek was the perfect compliment to elegant playmaker Platini. Quick, skilful and industrious, he pulled defenders all over the pitch creating space and goals for both the Frenchman and striker Paolo Rossi.

At international level he appeared in three World Cups for Poland. On his first appearance, in 1978, he was still a raw novice, but by 1982 a strong Polish side was erected around his talents, and who knows what might have happened had he not been suspended for the semi-final against Italy? His last World Cup Finals appearance at Mexico 86 is probably best forgotten. Slow and ineffective playing as a sweeper, he was humiliated as a waning Polish team crashed 4-0 to Brazil in the second round.

VITAL STATISTICS

Place of Birth: Bydgoszcz, Poland
Date of Birth: 3 March 1956
Died: n/a   Caps: 80 (Poland)
Goals (International): 24
Clubs: Zawisza Bydgoszcz, Widzew Lodz, Juventus, Roma
Trophies: EC 1985; CWC 1984; SA 1984

LEGEND RATING

Achievement	8
Skill	8
Teamwork	7
Passion	9
Personality	7
Overall Legend Rating	**39**

◁ᴵᴵᴵ He was christened *Bello di Notte* ('Beauty of the Night') by Juventus president Gianni Agnelli for his stunning performances in night matches.

◁ᴵᴵᴵ He now works as a commentator on Polish TV.

◁ᴵᴵᴵ Boniek scored a great hat-trick in a second phase match against Belgium in the 1982 World Cup.

◁ᴵᴵᴵ He scored the winner in the 1984 European Cup Winners' Cup final against Porto.

◁ᴵᴵᴵ The £1.1 m Juventus paid for Boniek was a record for a Polish player.

Boot Room, The

IT SEEMS A LITTLE HARSH to lump this lot together and count them as one team, but to separate them would be to undervalue their core strength, namely the great continuity that ran through the club for nearly 30 years. Liverpool's legendary ability to hand over from one manager to the next, and to replace one great player with another was the platform on which their success was built.

Shankly stood down for Paisley and, briefly, Fagan. Lawrenson slotted in effortlessly for Thompson, Keegan became Dalglish – every few years the face of the team would morph like Dr Who and a new line-up would emerge, just as powerful as the last. The circuit seemed to have been broken with the installation of Dalglish as the team's first player-manager, but the mercurial Scot understood the Liverpool ethos, and brought more success, including the club's first League and Cup double in 1986.

Liverpool won games on reputation alone – lesser teams quailed at the prospect of playing them, and Anfield became a fortress. They lost only nine home league games in the 1970s, compared with 33 in the less successful 1990s.

Managers: Bill Shankly, Bob Paisley, Joe Fagan, Kenny Dalglish

Key Players
Ray Clemence (G) Emlyn Hughes (D) Phil Thompson (D)
Phil Neal (D) Alan Hansen (D) Mark Lawrenson (D)
Graeme Souness (M) Jimmy Case (M) Ray Kennedy (M)
Ronnie Whelan (M) John Barnes (W) Kevin Keegan (F)
Kenny Dalglish (F) Peter Beardsley (F) Ian Rush (F)

Trophies
LT 1973, 1976, 1977, 1979, 1980, 1982, 1983, 1984, 1986, 1988, 1990;
FAC 1986; LC 1981–84; UEFAC 1973, 1976; EC 1977, 1978, 1981, 1984

◁ Phil Neal, the right-back, amassed eight championship medals, a record held jointly with Hansen. Add 50 caps and you have a remarkable tally for a player of modest abilities.

◁ Ray Kennedy, a double winner with Arsenal in 1971, missed the chance to become the first player to achieve that feat with a second club when Liverpool were beaten by Manchester United in the 1977 FA Cup final.

◁ Ronnie Whelan was an underrated player – athletic and strong, he could run all day and was a wonderful foil for the less mobile talents of Souness and Jan Molby.

◁ Liverpool never replaced the solidity of Ray Clemence in goal; current keeper Jerzy Dudek looks the best they have had since.

Boro

IF THE MAXIM that money can't buy you success provokes hollow laughter from most football clubs nowadays, they are words that still ring true with fans of Middlesbrough. Despite becoming the first club to pay a £1,000 transfer fee in 1905 (for Alf Common), and spending lavishly on Juninho and Boksic in recent years, Boro's trophy cabinet remains empty.

Having been relegated in 1997, chairman Steve Gibson's faith in manager Bryan Robson was tested again three seasons later, when only the intervention of Terry Venables as coach saved them from the same fate. Middlesbrough's recent soft centre belies a tradition for

uncompromising players, never better illustrated than Jack Charlton's Second Division champions of 1974. Maddren, Boam, Craggs and centre-forward John Hickton steamrollered all before them that year, playing a brand of football that frightened their opponents half to death. But this triumph proved to be another false dawn; by 1986 Boro had nosedived into Division Three, and subsequently had their ground locked by administrators eager to put the brake on the club's spiralling debts. Today, the impressive Riverside Stadium and Premiership revenue mean those days are a distant memory – but that first major trophy remains elusive.

Manager: Jack Charlton

4-4-2

Jim Platt (70s)

John Craggs (70s) Tony Mowbray (80s) Willie Maddren (70s)
George Hardwick (30s/40s)

Eric McMordie (60s/70s) Graeme Souness (70s/80s) Wilf Mannion (50s)
Juninho (90s)

Brian Clough (50s/60s) George Camsell (20s/30s)

Subs: Stephen Pears (G) (80s/90s) Stuart Boam (D) (70s)
Paul Ince (M) (90s) Heine Otto (M) (80s) Alen Boksic (F) (00s)

▶ Record goal scorer George Camsell's total of 325 includes 59 in a single season, the best ever in Division Two.

▶ Boro's most famous striker was Brian Clough, their last player to score five in a match.

▶ Dutchman Heine Otto was a terrace favourite at Ayresome Park. Committed and skilful, he held the side together as they flirted with disaster in the 1980s.

▶ In 1974 Boro won Division Two by 15 points. If the 'three points

for a win' system had been in operation, the margin would have been a staggering 23.

▶ Full-back George Hardwick captained England in the 1930s. He survived an inauspicious start, scoring an own goal on his debut.

Bosman, Jean-Marc

FC Liege, Belgium

IN 1988, an unremarkable Belgian midfielder entered into a dispute with his club over what appeared to be nothing more than a contractual technicality. Seven years later, the outcome of this legal spat was to change football forever. Jean-Marc Bosman was signed by RFC Liege on a two-year contract in 1988. On its expiry, a prospective new deal would have reduced his wages by 60 per cent. A potential solution was offered in the form of French club Dunkerque, but their transfer valuation of Bosman was less than half the £250,000 that Liege were demanding. He remained stuck in Belgium. Undeterred, Bosman started a legal process that inched its way to the European Court of Justice. His argument was that by retaining his registration, and demanding a transfer fee even after his contract had expired, Liege were in breach of European Union law, which was supposed to safeguard the free movement of workers between member states. In December 1995, the court agreed and ruled in Bosman's favour. The ruling has made players more powerful than ever before, with many of them, like England stars Steve McManaman and Sol Campbell, choosing to see out their contracts in order to negotiate lucrative moves away from clubs where they had been nurtured, developed and idolised.

VITAL STATISTICS

Place of Birth: Belgium
Date of Birth: 30 October 1964
Died: n/a   Caps: 0
Goals (International): 0
Clubs: Ajax, FC Liege
Appearances: Club (League): 73
Goals: Club (League): 3
Trophies: None

LEGEND RATING

Achievement	4
Skill	6
Passion & Commitment	7
Passion	8
Personality	9
Overall Legend Rating	**34**

◄⁰⁾ The same ruling also quashed a UEFA regulation limiting the number of foreign players that could appear in European competition for a single club.

◄⁰⁾ The beneficiaries? Top players, as clubs began to offer improved wages to attract out-of-contract stars.

◄⁰⁾ The losers? Small clubs, who had relied on the transfer income from their rising talent. Bigger teams could now wait for their contracts to expire and pick them up for nothing.

◄⁰⁾ Bosman did not earn the same headlines. He appeared for Ajax in the 1988 European Cup Winner's Cup final, which they lost 1–0 to Mechelen.

Brady, Liam

Arsenal, Juventus, Republic of Ireland

LIAM BRADY'S SKILL on the ball was a joy to behold – great touch, excellent dribbling skills and a sublime left foot. Little wonder then, that Arsenal fans quickly took him to their hearts. 'Chippy', as he became known, inspired the Gunners to their dramatic 3-2 FA Cup final win over Manchester United in 1979, creating the winning goal for Alan Sunderland in the dying moments.

A year later he was instrumental in Arsenal's run to the final of the European Cup Winners' Cup but, on the night, it was Brady's missed penalty in the shoot-out that handed the Cup to Valencia.

Possibly operating on the philosophy of 'if you can't beat 'em join 'em', Brady later moved to the continent where he became a huge success, winning two Serie A titles with Juventus, where he played alongside greats like Roberto Bettega and Zbigniew Boniek in what many Juve fans still regard as their finest-ever team. Oddly though, Brady never played in a championship-winning side for Arsenal. In England Brady is perhaps best remembered for a goal he scored during a 5-0 thrashing of Spurs, an outrageous left-footed shot that curled into the top corner of the net.

VITAL STATISTICS

Place of Birth: Dublin, Ireland
Date of Birth: 13 February 1956
Died: n/a **Caps:** 72 (Republic of Ireland)
Goals (International): 9
Clubs: Arsenal, Juventus, Inter Milan, Ascoli, West Ham
Appearances: Club (for Arsenal): 306
Goals: Club (for Arsenal): 59
Trophies: FAC 1979; SA 1981, 1982

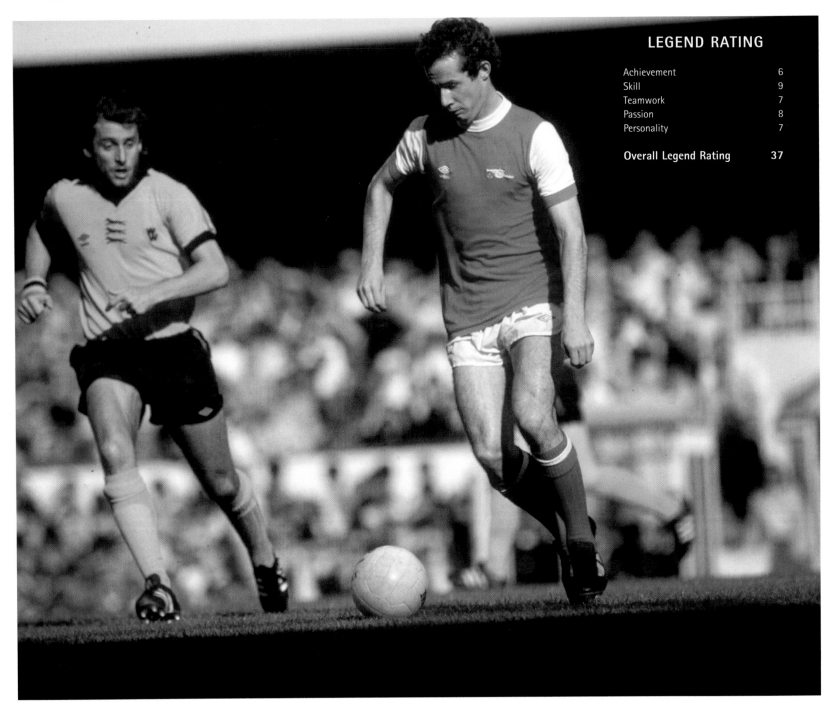

LEGEND RATING

Achievement	6
Skill	9
Teamwork	7
Passion	8
Personality	7
Overall Legend Rating	**37**

- Brady was voted PFA Player Of The Year in 1979.
- He scored the penalty that sealed Juve's second successive title in 1982.
- Both Brady's brothers played professional football in Ireland.
- Brady had an unhappy two years as manager of Celtic, citing internal politics as his reason for leaving.
- He won surprisingly little in England, just his 1979 FA Cup medal.

Breitner, Paul

GERMANY HAVE RARELY been short of a decent left-back. Andreas Brehme was justifiably acclaimed as the best player in the world in his position during the 1980s and early 1990s, but Paul Breitner had a range of skills that eclipsed even those of the former Inter star. Quick, strong and with a keen eye for the goal, Breitner was the complete full-back, a player so comfortable on the ball that in the latter stages of his career he developed into an equally impressive midfield player.

Breitner was picked for West Germany at 20 in 1971, and was a key member of the team that won the 1972 European Championship and the 1974 World Cup. After a dispute with the management he was absent from the international scene for a number of years, but returned to play in the 1982 World Cup as a midfield general, some say at the behest of Karl-Heinz Rummenigge. Breitner's club career saw him win a plethora of league titles with Bayern Munich and Real Madrid, and he also appeared in the first of Bayern's three consecutive European Cup wins in the mid-1970s.

VITAL STATISTICS

Place of Birth: Freilassung, Germany

Date of Birth: 5 September 1951

Died: n/a **Caps:** 48 (West Germany)

Goals (International): 10

Clubs: Bayern Munich, Real Madrid, Eintracht Braunschweig

Trophies: WorC 1974; EuroC 1972; EC 1974; PLA 1975, 1976; BLG 1972,1973,1974,1980,1981

LEGEND RATING

Achievement 10

Skill 8

Teamwork 8

Passion 7

Personality 8

Overall Legend Rating 41

- ◄)) Breitner scored in two World Cup Finals, a penalty in 1974, and West Germany's consolation in the 1982 final.
- ◄)) Breitner also scored in a World Cup final, putting away the penalty that beat Argentina at Italia 90.

- ◄)) Before the 1974 final, Breitner had already scored twice in the tournament against Chile and Yugoslavia.
- ◄)) Breitner was known for his left-wing political views; not a common trait in a professional footballer!

- ◄)) Breitner was known as 'Der Afro' on account of his disco-frizz hairdo.

Bremner, Billy

THE FIRST GREAT LEEDS SIDE may have been created by Don Revie, but Billy Bremner was its midfield heartbeat. An assessment of him could just as easily describe the team itself – tough-tackling, measured in the pass and with a combative spirit that was by turns inspirational and illegal.

Bremner was indispensable even in a team packed with pedigree, a fact emphasised by a glance at the Elland Road record books. Incredibly, Bremner led Leeds to six of the seven major trophy successes in their entire history (the championship win of 1992 being the only triumph in which he did not participate).

Often in trouble with referees, the sight of Bremner throwing his shirt to the ground after becoming, with Kevin Keegan, the first British player to be dismissed at Wembley, led to parliamentary calls for him to be permanently suspended.

It was similar at an international level. In 1974 he captained a Scotland squad that emerged from the World Cup Finals as the only unbeaten team, but was shortly banned for life following incidents in a Danish nightclub after a game. His departure from Elland Road to Hull City in 1976 signalled the break-up of the great Leeds team, a schism which took the Yorkshire club 16 years to recover from.

VITAL STATISTICS

Place of Birth: Stirling, Scotland
Date of Birth: 9 December 1942
Died: 7 December 1997 **Caps:** 54 (Scotland)
Goals (International): 3
Clubs: Leeds United, Hull City, Doncaster Rovers
Appearances: Club (League): 586 (for Leeds Utd)
Goals: Club (League): 90 (for Leeds Utd)
Trophies: LT 1969, 1974; FAC 1972; LC 1968; EUFAC 1968, 1971

LEGEND RATING

Achievement	8
Skill	7
Passion & Commitment	9
Passion	9
Personality	6
Overall Legend Rating	**39**

Wembley 1968: Bremner lifts Leeds' first major trophy, the League Cup.

◁» Bremner made his Leeds debut aged 17, as a winger.
◁» 1965. Scored Leeds' first-ever goal at Wembley but they lose 2-1 to Liverpool in the FA Cup final.
◁» 1970. Scored in British football's most epic club game, but Leeds went down to Celtic in a European Cup semi-final.
◁» 1985. Became Leeds' manager by popular demand. Failed to revive an average Second Division team and was sacked in 1988.
◁» 1997. His sudden death from a heart attack shocked and saddened the football world.

Brilliant Orange

PERHAPS NOT SURPRISINGLY, all these players are from the modern era. Holland were no great shakes until around 1960, when Rinus Michels began to bring through a generation of players at Ajax that would change the face of football for ever. His method of play became known as 'Total Football' and it spawned a team of creative, flexible players capable of performing wherever they happened to find themselves on the field.

All the defenders in this team are comfortable on the ball (although Koeman had a tendency to dwell on it), and all the midfield players could defend when necessary. Gullit and Rijkaard give the midfield strength and Rep, who is picked ahead of Van Hanegem, provides width. Their only genuine winger, Marc Overmars, has failed too often on the big occasion to warrant selection.

The forward line is wonderful. The movement of Cruyff and Bergkamp would have defences marking shadows, and the pure goalscoring genius of Van Basten means a decent percentage of the chances would be put away without fuss. In a Dream Team World Cup they would produce performances to drool over, probably surpassing even Brazil at their best. But they would inevitably lose in the final and all blame each other.

Manager: Rinus Michels

3-4-3

Hans Van Breukelen (80s)

Wim Suurbier (70s) Ronald Koeman (C) (80s/90s) Rudi Krol (70s)

Frank Rijkaard (80s) Ruud Gullit (80s)
Johann Neeskens (70s) Wim van Hanegem (70s)

Johann Crujff (70s) Marco Van Basten (80s) Dennis Bergkamp (90s)

Subs: Edwin Van Der Saar (G) (90s) Frank De Boer (D) (90s)
Arie Haan (M) (70s) Johnny Rep (M) (70s) Ruud Van Nistelrooy (F) (00s)

◄)》 The side lacks a quality goalkeeper like Sepp Maier, Gordon Banks or Dino Zoff.

◄)》 Only four of the XVI are still playing, Holland not being the force they were: no De Boer, Kluivert, Cocu or Davids.

◄)》 Bergkamp's inclusion is, of course, dependent on the fixtures being held in western Europe. Van Nistelrooy will fill in for away fixtures that require air travel.

◄)》 Van Nistelrooy gets in without any great international pedigree simply because we couldn't leave him out after his breathtaking displays for Man United. If Holland screw up in the next World Cup qualifiers he may become one of the greatest players never to make the Finals.

Bring on Brazil

LET'S GIVE DUE CREDIT to Karl-Heinz Schnellinger. This semi-final was drifting towards a sterile 1-0 Italian victory when he emerged in the last minute to smash a volleyed equaliser, thus setting up the greatest extra-time ever. Germany then appeared to have completed their smash-and-grab raid when Müller took advantage of an underhit back pass but, uncharacteristically, the German defence went to sleep, and two goals in six minutes saw the first period of extra-time finish with Italy 3-2 ahead.

The plot had yet more twists. An apparently harmless header from Müller was left by substitute Rivera – who had anticipated a goal kick – and the ball crept inside the post. But within a minute, the villain had turned hero, calmly placing the ball past a floundering Sepp Maier for the game's fifth goal in a breathless 22 minutes. In the light of what had gone before, a goalless last nine minutes was unexpected. By the final whistle, players and spectators were completely drained.

SCORERS: Italy: Boninsegna, Burgnich, Riva, Rivera
W. Germany: Schnellinger, Müller (2)
EVENT: World Cup semi-final, Azteca stadium, Mexico City, 17 June 1970

ITALY (Man: Feruccio Valcareggi)		WEST GERMANY (Man: Helmut Schoen)	
1 Albertosi	8 Mazzola	1 Maier	8 Seeler
2 Burgnich	9 Boninsegna	2 Vogts	9 Muller
3 Facchetti	10 Di Sisti	3 Patzke	10 Overath
4 Bertini	11 Riva	4 Beckenbauer	11 Lohr
5 Rosato		5 Schnellinger	
6 Cera		6 Schulz	
7 Domenghini		7 Grabowski	

Rivera wraps himself around a post as Müller levels the scores at 3–3.

◀)) England should have been playing in this match, but had blown a 2-0 lead against Germany in the quarter-finals.

◀)) Goals may have flowed in this game, but Burgnich's effort was rare: in his 66 internationals, this was his second and last.

◀)) The high altitude of Mexico produced enervating conditions. Extra-time was always likely to lead to a higher incidence of errors and goals.

◀)) This is not a game Franz Beckenbauer will remember fondly.

Germany's sweeper finished with four in the debit column and a heavily strapped arm.

◀)) For Italy, victory proved bittersweet. Brazil were waiting to pick them off in the final.

Brooking, Trevor

West Ham United, England

ONE-FOOTED, could not tackle, could not head the ball, really slow. How on earth did Trevor Brooking make it as a professional footballer, let alone win 47 caps? Largely because the one foot he used was a cracker, and he had the brains to use it. He got someone else to do the tackling and heading, and didn't need to be quick because his passing, anticipation and timing were so good.

Like many other Hammers, he was intensely loyal to the club – he remains a director – and thus sacrificed the opportunity to win a cupboard full of medals. At international level he developed a fine understanding with Kevin Keegan, another intelligent footballer, and

was unlucky to play in an ordinary team that struggled to qualify for major tournaments. When England did reach the World Cup Finals, in 1982, Brooking was injured and played only 20 minutes. In his retirement he has become a popular TV and radio commentator, famously dubbed 'Mr Creosote' due to his habit of sitting on the fence.

VITAL STATISTICS

Place of Birth:	Barking, London, England
Date of Birth:	2 October 1948
Died: n/a	Caps: 47 (England)

Goals (International): 5

Clubs: West Ham United

Appearances: Club (League): 528

Goals: Club (League): 88

Trophies: FAC 1975, 1980

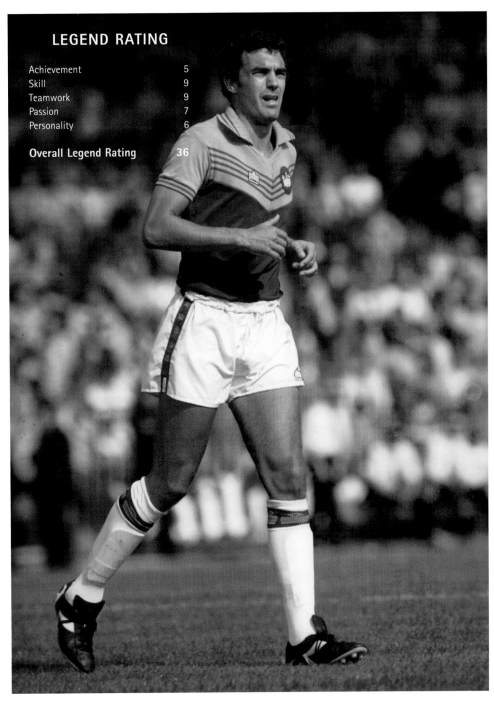

LEGEND RATING

Achievement	5
Skill	9
Teamwork	9
Passion	7
Personality	6
Overall Legend Rating	**36**

◖ Brooking scored the only goal of the 1980 FA Cup final – with his head, to his and everybody else's amazement.

◖ He scored twice in a World Cup qualifier in Budapest as England beat Hungary 3-1, probably his finest game for his country.

◖ He was appointed chairman of Sport England in 2000, a government advisory body.

◖ England's fortunes in the 1982 World Cup might have been different if Brooking and Kevin Keegan had been fit.

◖ Like his BBC colleagues Alan Hansen and Gary Lineker, he doesn't appear to have aged, apart from a few grey hairs. Is it the White City tea or the make-up?

Brothers' Farewell

Brazil 3 Denmark 2, 1998

BOTH TEAMS CAME into the match on good form. Brazil had thrashed Chile 4–1 in the second round of the tournament, and their most celebrated player, Ronaldo, had been in sparkling form. More surprisingly, Denmark, inspired by the gifted Laudrup brothers, had beaten the highly fancied Nigerians by the same score.

The brothers were awesome against Brazil, too. Brian Laudrup set up a simple goal after two minutes for Jorgensen, while Michael gave the Brazilian defence a torrid time all night, even when the favourites were enjoying the bulk of possession. Brazil's armoury was still formidable, though, and they quickly restored parity, Bebeto breaking away from his marker to score past Schmeichel. Then, before the first half came to a close, they took the lead through Rivaldo. In the second half a mistake by Roberto Carlos let in Brian Laudrup, and the Dane inflicted full punishment. Denmark then poured forward in search of a winning goal, but suddenly Dunga released Rivaldo, who finished with a trademark piledriver. Rieper was thrust into the attack and hit the bar as the Danes applied late pressure, but Brazil clung on. Both Laudrups retired from international football after this game, bringing a golden era of Danish football to an end.

SCORERS:	Brazil:	Bebeto 11 Rivaldo 27, 60
	Denmark:	Jorgensen 2 Brian Laudrup 50
EVENT:	World Cup quarter-final, Nantes, 3 July 1998	

BRAZIL
(Man: Mario Zagallo)

1 Taffarel
2 Cafu
3 Roberto Carlos
4 Junior Baiano
5 Aldair
6 Cesar
Sampaio
7 Leonardo
8 Dunga
9 Ronaldo
10 Bebeto
11 Rivaldo

DENMARK
(Man: Bo Johansson)

1 Schmeichel
2 Helveg
3 Heintze
4 Colding
5 Rieper
6 Hogh
7 Jorgensen
8 Nielsen
9 B.Laudrup
10 M. Laudrup
11 Moller

◄ Michael Laudrup threw his boots into the crowd at the end of the match – a clear statement of his intent. His younger brother followed him into retirement a few days later.

◄ Brazil's semi-final was another pulsating game, as Holland hung on, forcing a penalty shoot-out, but couldn't hold their nerve.

◄ The Danes, and the Dutch in the next round, exposed a weakness in the Brazilian defence that the French exploited in the final.

◄ After a disastrous Euro 2000, Denmark, coached by their former captain Morten Olsen (with Michael Laudrup assisting), have regrouped well, and qualified for the 2002 World Cup Finals with an unbeaten record.

Busby Babes

ANY MENTION OF THE Manchester United team that dominated English football in the late 1950s inevitably evokes images of the terrible Munich air crash. The death of eight of football's brightest young talents was a tragedy that touched the lives of football fans all over the world. But just as tragic is that the players who perished are now largely remembered as passengers on an ill-fated aircraft rather than for what they were: extraordinary and remarkable footballers who might easily have gone on to dominate Europe for a decade.

At the heart of the team was Duncan Edwards. Looking at photographs now, it seems impossible to believe that such an imposing presence was only 21 when he died. Mark Jones was a similarly towering presence at centre-half, while in goal Harry Gregg combined agility with rare courage (many press pictures of the time show him diving boldly at the feet of oncoming strikers).

Like all great United teams though, their strength lay in attack. Tommy Taylor was a fearless centre-forward in the best English tradition, and Dennis Viollet and Bobby Charlton both chipped in with more than their fair share of goals. This team was together for less than two seasons. Yet even in this short time they established themselves as a formidable and widely feared European force.

Manager: Matt Busby

Key Players
Harry Gregg (G) Duncan Edwards (D)
Tommy Taylor (F) Bobby Charlton (M/F) Bill Foulkes (D)
Dennis Viollet (M) Roger Byrne (D)

Trophies
LT 1956, 1957

The last line-up of the Busby Babes. 5 February, 1958, Belgrade.

◁᠉ Under Busby, United had already won the league in 1952, but that ageing side was dismantled to make way for the Babes.
◁᠉ United won the league in 1956 and 1957. They should have won the double in 1957, but lost to Aston Villa in the final.

◁᠉ United were the first British entrants to the European Cup in 1956/57, defying the wishes of the myopic Football League. They reached the semi-finals in their first two competitions.
◁᠉ The last league match played by the Busby Babes, five days

before Munich, was one of their most memorable games. Arsenal 4 United 5 brought the curtain down in typical style.
◁᠉ Of the Munich survivors, Bill Foulkes and Bobby Charlton were eventual European Cup winners in 1968.

Busby, Matt

IN 1945 MATT BUSBY became manager of Manchester United, a club whose 67 years had yielded just two league titles and a solitary FA Cup. The trophy cabinet had been bare for 34 years, Old Trafford was a bomb site and United were lodging at Maine Road. On his retirement in 1969, Matt Busby had added five Championships, two FA Cups and United had become England's first winners of the European Cup.

Although a remarkable haul, it would surely have been more but for the tragic Munich air crash in 1958 that robbed English football of one of its greatest-ever teams. It was indicative of his tenacity and strength of will that Busby not only cheated death himself in the disaster but that, within seven years, he had made United champions again, rebuilding his team around George Best, Denis Law and Bobby Charlton. The end of his tenure saw them relegated within five years.

A journey to Old Trafford today finishes with a walk down Sir Matt Busby Way to his statue. One senses a modest, hard-working Scotsman from humble, working-class origins would have been uneasy with such acclaim. However, for a club with legends to spare, it is fitting that the tribute is for him alone.

VITAL STATISTICS

Place of Birth:	Bellshill, Glasgow, Scotland
Date of Birth:	26 May 1909
Died:	20 January 1994
Caps: 1 (Scotland)	Goals (International): 0

Clubs: As Player: Manchester City, Liverpool;
As Manager: Manchester United

Trophies: FAC 1948, 1963; LT 1952, 1956, 1957, 1965, 1967; EC 1968

LEGEND RATING

Achievement	10
Tactical Awareness	9
Motivation	10
Transfer Dealing and Team Selection	9
Personality	8
Overall Legend Rating	**46**

▸ No mean player himself, Busby played for United's deadliest rivals Manchester City and Liverpool!

▸ He was born within a few miles of two other managerial legends, Jock Stein and Alex Ferguson.

▸ He was awarded a CBE in 1958 and knighted 10 years later.

▸ On winning the European Cup: 'When Bobby took the cup it cleansed me. It eased the pain of going into Europe. It was my justification.'

▸ He defied the Football League to enter United as England's first European Cup contestants in 1956. The rift took 26 years to heal, before Busby was elected Football League vice-president in 1982.

Butcher, Terry

IT IS RARE for an English player to make a move north of the border, and even more rare for one to do so at the height of his career, but in joining Rangers in the 1980s Terry Butcher bucked the trend. Fortunately Butcher was a player with enough resolve and spirit that the move saw him flourish, rather than fester as many had predicted.

A 6 ft 4 in giant, Butcher made his reputation as a central defensive totem during the latter days of Bobby Robson's reign at Ipswich. A natural leader, he was unfazed by international football at 21 and was a key player in an England spine of Peter Shilton, Bryan Robson and Gary Lineker. His iconic match came in 1989 during a World Cup qualifier in Sweden, a tedious 0–0 draw that was memorable only for Butcher who, after receiving an injury in an aerial challenge in the second-half, played the remainder of the match with blood oozing on to his white shirt from a head wound. His insistence on lasting the 90 minutes was typical. At Rangers, his partnership with Richard Gough was the rock on which their nine consecutive title wins were built. A broken leg in 1987 was followed by three more Scottish titles, before a brief, and largely unhappy, foray into management at Coventry. Of late he has steered a steady ship as boss at Motherwell.

VITAL STATISTICS

Place of Birth: Singapore
Date of Birth: 28 December 1958
Died: n/a Caps: 77 (England) Goals (International): 3
Clubs: As player: Ipswich Town, Glasgow Rangers, Coventry, Sunderland; As manager: Motherwell
Appearances: Club (League): 445
Goals: Club (League): 24
Trophies: EUFAC 1981; SLT 1987, 1989, 1990

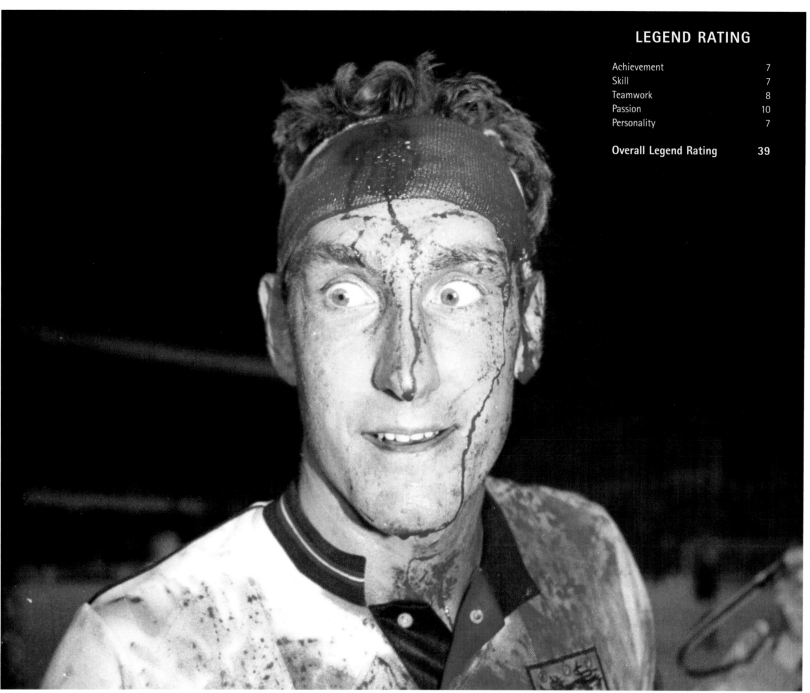

Sweden, 1989. Butcher donates blood for the England cause.

LEGEND RATING

Achievement	7
Skill	7
Teamwork	8
Passion	10
Personality	7
Overall Legend Rating	**39**

- 1987. Scored at Aberdeen in a 1–1 draw to clinch Rangers' first SPL title for 10 years
- 1987. One of three ordered off in an Old Firm clash, Butcher was later fined in a civil court for a breach of the peace.
- 1990. Untried in management, Butcher took charge as boss and player at Coventry.
- He is still heard on BBC Radio 5 Live as a summariser.
- Butcher is one of the few England players to play in three World Cups. He would have captained England in the final itself but for the penalty shoot-out loss to Germany in the semi-final at Italia 90.

Campbell, Sol

Tottenham, Arsenal, England

SOL CAMPBELL was destined for big things at an early age. A schoolboy prodigy, he was one of the early vindications of the FA School of Excellence before signing professional forms with Spurs in 1992.

He immediately started attracting the sort of praise normally reserved for continental central defenders. Not only could he take the knocks and command in the air, he possessed the first touch, distribution and prescience that brought comparisons with Bobby Moore.

Despite becoming a permanent fixture for England, it became clear that major domestic honours would elude Campbell at White Hart Lane. In the summer of 2001, as a free agent, he became the most talked-about transfer in years when he thought the unthinkable, broke Spurs' hearts and became a Gunner.

The inevitable yet depressing hate campaign followed, Campbell's dignified response was typical of a player who has always let his feet do the talking. The answer was the Double in his first season.

His blossoming partnership with Rio Ferdinand looks destined to be England's platform for several seasons to come. Even after a decade of Premiership football, Campbell remains a player at the top of his game.

VITAL STATISTICS

Place of Birth: London, England

Date of Birth: 18 September 1974

Died: n/a Caps: 54 (England) Goals (International): 1

Clubs: Tottenham Hotspur, Arsenal

Appearances: Club (League): 404

Goals: Club (League): 21

Trophies: LT 2002; FAC 2002; LC 1999

'What's up with you?', Sol Campbell asks of Brazil's Rivaldo during England's clash with Brazil on 21 June 2002.

LEGEND RATING

Achievement	7
Skill	9
Passion & Commitment	7
Inspiration	8
Personality	7
Overall Legend Rating	**38**

- December 1992 – scores on his first-team debut against Chelsea.
- Only 23 yellow cards in over 400 games are testament to Campbell's pace and clean tackling.
- At the 1998 World Cup Finals, Campbell has an 81st-minute 'winner' against Argentina disallowed for Shearer's earlier foul. Sadly the rest is history.
- Campbell's first international goal is England's opener at the 2002 World Cup Finals, as he powers home a header against Sweden.
- 2002 – Campbell is named in FIFA's Team of the World Cup Finals, surprisingly edging out the superior Ferdinand.

Cantona, Eric

WHETHER FOR HIS FOOTBALLING exploits or temperamental outbursts, few players have provoked headlines or incited debate like Eric Cantona. Not one to suffer fools gladly, he was too hot to handle for five French clubs.

An instant hit at Leeds, his arrival provided the Yorkshire club with the impetus to clinch the League title in 1992 but, while the fans idolised him, rumours of his clashes with manager Howard Wilkinson were rife. His shock £1.2 m transfer to Manchester United indicated Leeds' desire to be rid of him, but it turned out to be the most injudicious transfer sale of all time, as Cantona went on to inspire United to a period of domination unrivalled since Liverpool's run of success in the 1970s and 1980s.

It is a sad fact that Cantona will be remembered for one moment of madness when, at Crystal Palace in 1995, making his way off the pitch following yet another red card, Cantona launched a two-footed kung fu kick at a spectator who had racially abused him. A less gifted player may have been sacked, but Cantona survived and returned to lead United to more championship success. He retired at 31, and his recent incarnations as an actor and sports promoter have enhanced his reputation as the modern renaissance footballer.

VITAL STATISTICS

Place of Birth: Paris, France

Date of Birth: 24 May 1966

Died: n/a **Caps:** 45 (France) **Goals (International):** 19

Clubs: Martigues, Auxerre, Marseille, Bordeaux, Montpellier, Leeds United, Manchester United

Appearances: Club (for Man Utd): 142

Goals: Club (for Man Utd): 64

Trophies: LT 1992, 1993, 1994, 1996, 1997; FAC 1994, 1996

LEGEND RATING

Achievement	8
Skill	9
Teamwork	7
Passion	9
Personality	9
Overall Legend Rating	**42**

◁⁾ 1988. Banned from the French national side after describing manager Henri Michel as a 'sack of sh*t'.

◁⁾ PFA Player of the Year, 1994 and 1996. Footballer of the Year 1996.

◁⁾ 1994. Arrested and handcuffed by security guards after a row with officials at USA 94. Cantona was just there to watch.

◁⁾ He had five league titles in six English seasons 1992–97, missing out only in 1995.

◁⁾ He was voted Manchester United's most valuable player ever in 1999.

Capped and Cast-Off

An Ill-Treated England Team

THERE WILL ALWAYS be players who feel hard done by when international caps are handed out. But there can be good reasons why a player does not receive the international acclaim he feels he deserves. Sometimes players fail to reproduce their club form at international level (Steve McManaman), lack the touch to compete against the world's best (Les Ferdinand and Ian Wright), or simply don't fit into the framework of a team (Matt Le Tissier).

Most of this team do not fit into any of these categories. These players were omitted because their faces, for some reason, just didn't fit. In some cases a player was kept out of the side by another player who most people (except the manager) could see was inferior: Phil Neal kept out Dave Clement, and Kenny Sansom won 86 caps to Derek Statham's three. The woeful Peter Barnes was somehow selected ahead of Gordon Hill, and Alan Hudson had to sit on the sidelines while the likes of Colin Viljoen and Dave Thomas pulled on England jerseys. Clough and Shackleton were omitted for different reasons. Notoriously vocal and headstrong, both were rejected by an establishment that didn't like to be challenged.

Manager: Terry Venables

4-4-2

Shilton (125)

Dave Clement (5) Colin Todd (27)
Kevin Beattie (9) Derek Statham (3)

Alan Devonshire (8) Dennis Mortimer (0)
Alan Hudson (2) Jimmy Case (0)

Brian Clough (2) Len Shackleton (5)

Kevin Beattie, a nine-times capped player.

◁ Why Shilton? Because Ray Clemence and Chris Woods won 85 caps between them while Shilton was still playing. Clemence was a great keeper, but Shilton was better. Woods was not in the same league.

◁ Mortimer was the fetcher and carrier in the Aston Villa side that won the First Division title in 1981. He was an excellent team player and deserved England honours.

◁ Clough and Shackleton's exclusion was echoed in the 1970s,

when Revie's suspicion of flair players saw talents like Hudson, Bowles and Worthington miss out on international recognition.

◁ How did Sammy Lee win 14 caps and Jimmy Case none? Lee was a good player, but certainly no better than Case.

Capped and Clueless

All-Time Worst England Team

EVEN AT THEIR PEAK this lot would have struggled to win a pub league. Anyone with at least one partially functioning eye could see this, except, it seems, the England managers who selected them. You want detail? Okay, here we go: Beasant was error-prone and nervy.... Bardsley was nondescript.... Foster and Blockley were cumbersome and slow.... Ruddock was overweight and overrated.... Phelan looked a decent player at Norwich but became a laughing stock at Old Trafford ... while Geoff Thomas was a plodding journeyman elevated to the role of international playmaker (he and his Palace team-mate Andy Gray were selected on the basis of getting to the Cup final).

And who on earth was Nick Pickering? And Peter Ward? Brian Deane, meanwhile, has had his lack of international quality exposed by his subsequent failure to be retained by any club for more than a couple of seasons. This XI are by no means the only players who should never have been picked for England, but they remain the most startling examples.

Manager: Don Revie

4-4-2

Dave Beasant (2)

David Bardsley (2) Steve Foster (3)
Jeff Blockley (1) Neil Ruddock (1)

Michael Phelan (1) Geoff Thomas (9)
Andy Gray (1) Nick Pickering (1)

Peter Ward (1) Brian Deane (3)

Neil Ruddock, who made it into the England side one glorious time.

◁🕮 We've restricted ourselves to players from our own era. It's unfair to deride a player you've never seen.

◁🕮 Both Ward and Pickering made their appearances in tour friendlies against Australia.

◁🕮 Foster compounded his lack of ability by wearing that absurd headband. It didn't add anything to his game and looked ridiculous.

◁🕮 Ruddock had a nice left foot, but was too slow to cope with top-class forwards, and lacked the wit to make up for it with anticipation and experience.

69

Carter, Raich

Sunderland, Derby County, England

IF YOU ASKED YOUR GRANDDAD (who obviously thinks all modern players are cissies) whom he admired the most, he would probably say something like: 'Raich Carter, laddie, there was a player. He had everything: skill, vision, and he was a bit tasty in the tackle as well.' Granddad of course would be right. Horatio 'Raich' Carter was indeed a terrific player, and it remains a mystery how he was picked a measly 13 times for England (plus a few more unofficial wartime caps).

Carter's halcyon days were with his local team, Sunderland, whom he led with great distinction in the 1930s. Carter was hurt when Sunderland let him go after the war, and proved there was plenty left in the tank by leading Derby County to an FA Cup victory.

He was still playing as he approached 40, as player-manager of Hull City, and led the Tigers out of the Third Division. His managerial career continued at Leeds, where after taking a John Charles-inspired side out of Division Two, he failed to make an impact in the top flight.

VITAL STATISTICS

Place of Birth: Sunderland, England

Date of Birth: 21 December 1913

Died: 9 October 1994

Caps: 13 (England)   **Goals (International):** 7

Clubs: Sunderland, Derby County, Hull City

Appearances: Club (All Matches – for Sunderland): 276

Goals: Club (All Matches – for Sunderland): 127

Trophies: LT 1936; FAC 1937, 1946

LEGEND RATING

Achievement	6
Skill	8
Teamwork	8
Passion	7
Personality	7
Overall Legend Rating	**36**

- He was the only player to win FA Cup winners' medals either side of the Second World War.
- He scored the winning goal in 1937 Cup Final victory over Preston.

- Carter's first season at Hull saw the team begin the season with nine straight wins, end it with promotion, and fill in with a cup run ended by eventual winners Manchester United. Unsurprisingly, attendances at Boothferry Park doubled that year.

- He made his England debut against Scotland in 1934.
- He captained Sunderland to their last Championship in 1936, scoring 31 goals.

Catenaccio Kings

INTERNAZIONALE, or Inter Milan as they tend to be known in Britain, is a huge club which has never made the impact expected of them in European football. Except in the 1960s, that is. In the decade of flower power and the Beatles Inter, managed by Argentinian Helenio Herrera, were top dogs. Herrera was a fiery character and a flamboyant coach who had previously enjoyed spells with Barcelona and, briefly, the Spanish national team. At Inter he developed the formidable *catenaccio* system, the first formal tactical system to use a sweeper behind a back four. Wrongly interpreted by British observers as an entirely negative formation, it allowed the full-backs license to attack, and dispensed with the need for two wingers. Two successive European Cup wins in 1964 and 1965 were the fruits of Herrera's work, but defeat against Celtic in the 1967 final was the beginning of a decline in the club's fortunes. An ageing team reached the Final in 1972 but were no match for Ajax, particularly Johann Cruyff who destroyed them almost single-handedly.

Manager: Helenio Herrera

Key Players
Sarti (G) Tarcisio Burgnich (D) Giacinto Facchetti (D)
Guarneri (D) Jair (W) Sandro Mazzola (M)
Luis Suarez (M/F) Angelo Domenghini (M)

Trophies
SA 1963, 1965, 1966, 1971 EC 1964, 1965

1964: Internazionale carry off the European Cup, having beaten the mighty Real Madrid 3–1.

◁ Facchetti was one of the first beneficiaries of *Catenaccio*; tall for a full-back, quick and energetic, he was an early 'wing-back'. Facchetti was outstanding in Italy's 1970 World Cup campaign.
◁ Mazzola was a one-club man, and his rivalry with Milan's Gianni Rivera is legendary. He enjoys a status at Inter similar to that accorded Bobby Charlton at Manchester United.
◁ Inter haven't reached a European Cup Final since 1972, although they won three UEFA Cup trophies in the 1990s.
◁ Herrera's most significant signing was Luis Suarez from his old club, Barcelona. Suarez's combination with Mazzola gave Inter the ability to play keep-ball to a degree not previously seen in European club football.

Champions League

The Ultimate Test

THERE WAS A TIME when the European Cup was simple. If you won your domestic title, you qualified for a 32-team knockout competition, where each tie was a home and away two-legged affair. Then in 1992/93 the Champions League was born. As with most schemes approved by UEFA's bigwigs, it was a dog's dinner. In 1999, however, it became a canine banquet. The previous format of teams playing in a league system to qualify for the quarter-finals was complicated further by an expansion to 32 teams, with two group stages meaning 12 games now have to be played before the knockout stage of the last eight. Teams reaching the final must now play a total of 17 matches.

Of course, true competition has little to do with it. Rich European clubs, frustrated by their domestic authorities' refusal to sanction a breakaway super league, have simply dangled the sponsors cash in front of UEFA and created one anyway. The current revenue of £416 m is difficult to ignore. UEFA takes £112 m while the rest goes to the participating clubs. The problem is that saturation point has been reached. As TV audiences fall, the gravy train is about to hit the buffers.

> 'If we want to make more money we have to change the concept.'
>
> **UEFA's Gerhard Aigner explains the reasons for the further expansion of the Champions League in 1998**

Luis Figo in action for Real in their 2002 semi-final win against his former club Barcelona.

◁ Just qualifying for the Champions League in 2001/02 brought £1 m. Each match brings a further £1.25 m, irrespective of the result. Bayern Munich gathered £29.6 m for winning the competition in 2001.

◁ UEFA now insist that the front six rows of seats remain empty in many grounds to accommodate out-size advertising boards.

◁ Manchester United won the trophy in 1999 despite being runners-up in the Premier League the year before.

◁ Fortunately, some attractive football is still played. The best final was in 1994, when Milan cuffed Barcelona 4–0, probably the finest European club display since Real Madrid won 7–3 in 1960.

Channel, Mick

Southampton, England

MICK CHANNON'S WHEELING ARM as he turned away to celebrate another goal was one of the most memorable images of the 1970s. His pace and power, allied to good instincts, meant he had plenty of opportunities to practice that famous 'windmill' celebration. An unselfish player, equally adept at setting up chances for others as taking them himself, Channon was a product of the Southampton youth system. He first emerged at the club in the late 1960s, scoring on his debut as a 17-year-old in 1966. Though it took him time to break through fully, by 1969/70 he had established himself as Martin Chivers' natural successor and began a run that saw him finish as the club's top scorer every season until his departure to Manchester City in 1977. But it wasn't long before Channon returned to his beloved Saints; after just two years at Maine Road he came back to the Dell to enjoy a spell in what was Southampton's best-ever team that included no less than three former England captains (Peter Shilton, Mick Mills and Dave Watson).

VITAL STATISTICS

Place of Birth: Orcheston, Wiltshire, England
Date of Birth: 28 November 1948
Died: n/a   **Caps:** 46 (England)
Goals (International): 21
Clubs: Southampton, Manchester City, Norwich City
Appearances: Club (League: for Southampton): 510
Goals: Club (League: for Southampton): 185
Trophies: FAC 1976

1985: Channon's Wembley swansong v Sunderland in the 1985 League Cup Final.

LEGEND RATING

Achievement	5
Skill	7
Teamwork	8
Passion	8
Personality	7
Overall Legend Rating	**35**

- Channon remains Southampton's record goal-scorer, eclipsed not even by Matt Le Tissier.
- He briefly became a TV pundit on retirement, where his strong Wiltshire accent made him a target for good-natured teasing.
- He now has a highly successful career as a racehorse trainer.
- Channon has never played in the World Cup Finals.
- When asked once what made a good manager Channon replied, 'good players'.

Chanting

IN THE 1870s it would have appeared rather vulgar. One can't imagine the Old Carthusians goalkeeper standing resolute with flat cap and Victorian moustache to a backdrop of 'Who ate all the pies?' from the massed top hats of the Royal Engineers. Some contemporary chanting can claim a distinguished pedigree. 'The Pompey Chimes' were ringing out at Fratton Park for the title winning teams of over 50 years ago, while 'I'm Forever Blowing Bubbles' has been handed down through the generations at Upton Park (although opposition fans now tend to shout their own alternative over the cockney chorus).

Over the past 30 years, club choirs have broadened their repertoires considerably from the quaint 'Ee-aye-addio'. The greater televising of matches means that copyrights can be quickly violated – a player can be vocally ridiculed at Old Trafford one week and hear the identical chant at Stamford Bridge the next. One fact remains a certainty, though. Any player guilty of the merest physical deformity, tabloid headline or on-field mishap can be sure it will be pointed out. For anyone playing in front of more than two men and a dog, 'you can run but you can't hide' is the biggest truism of all.

> 'He's fat, he's round, he's never in the ground, Captain Bob.'
>
> Oxford fans to absent chairman Robert Maxwell

Gallic chic noticeably absent as French fans raise the roof.

◁ To opposition fans scarce in number: 'Is that all you take away?', 'You must have come in a taxi', or 'We'll see you both outside'.

◁ 'He's fat, he's round' also prefaced a memorable chant about Jan Molby, namely: 'He's fat, he's round, his car is in the pound.'

◁ To expensive opposition striker, preferably one who's just missed an open goal: 'What a waste of money', 'Hallo, hallo [insert previous club here] reject' (repeat to fade).

◁ Silliest chant: 'Boing! Boing! Baggies! Baggies!', accompanied by a vigorous pogo from West Bromwich Albion fans.

◁ References in this section to Elton John, Leslie Ash or Trevor Morley would be libelous. But you know what we're getting at, right?

Chapman, Herbert

MANY GREAT MANAGERS have built one great team at one club, but Herbert Chapman is among the élite who have done it twice. An unconventional manager, he surrounded himself with intelligent players who fed him ideas and tactics. He responded to a change in the offside law by introducing a 3-4-3 formation with a defensive centre-half, and he was the first manager to encourage his wingers, notably Cliff Bastin, to cut inside the full-back and go for goal.

His first great side was the Huddersfield Town team of the 1920s, built around the intelligent playmaker Clem Stephenson. He left Huddersfield for the challenge of managing Arsenal and turned them into the dominant side of the next decade. The Arsenal side featured many of the great players of that generation, often providing five, six or even seven players to the England team of that era. Under his stewardship Arsenal went on to win the title four times in five years, but tragically Chapman died of pneumonia in 1934, aged 55, and didn't enjoy the full fruits of his work. He was the game's first managerial genius.

VITAL STATISTICS

Place of Birth: Kiverton Park, England
Date of Birth: 19 January 1878
Died: 6 January 1934 **Caps:** 0
Goals (International): 0 **Clubs:** As Player: Kiverton Park, Ashton North End, Stalybridge Rovers, Rochdale, Grimsby Town, Sheppey United, Worksop, Northampton Town, Sheffield United, Notts County, Tottenham Hotspur; As Manager: Northampton Town, Leeds City, Huddersfield Town, Arsenal
Trophies: LT 1924, 1925, 1926, 1931, 1933; FA Cup 1922, 1930

LEGEND RATING

Achievement	10
Tactical Awareness	9
Motivation	9
Transfer Dealing and Team Selection	9
Personality	9
Overall Legend Rating	**46**

Chapman (left) was always ready to oblige the media.

◁ Chapman was a great innovator, and was an early advocate of floodlights, artificial pitches and numbered shirts.

◁ He was instrumental in the renaming of Gillespie Road tube station as 'Arsenal'.

◁ He was one of the first managers to offer a fee to lure big-name players away from other clubs. His purchase of David Jack from Bolton was the first £10,000 transfer.

◁ Most of the Arsenal team only heard of Chapman's death as they turned up to play a match. The pallbearers at the funeral were Cliff Bastin, Eddie Hapgood, Joe Hume, David Jack, Alex James and Jack Lambert.

Chapman's Champions

Arsenal, 1930s

WHEN HERBERT CHAPMAN took over as Arsenal manager in 1925 the team was a mid-table side who had won nothing. By the time war broke out they had won their first trophy, the FA Cup in 1930, and followed it with four league championships and another FA Cup in between. In 1932, one of their fallow years, they were runners-up in both competitions. Sadly Chapman was to die soon after, his life taken by a bout of pneumonia in 1934.

In the infamous England international against Italy that became known as 'The Battle of Highbury' Arsenal provided no less than seven players to the England team (Moss, Hapgood, Copping, Bastin,

Drake, Bowden and Male). Arsenal skipper Eddie Hapgood captained his country that day, and his successor in the role was the other Arsenal full-back, George Male.

The team's innovative tactics and willingness to spend money to bring in new, better players ensured they stayed at or near the top for the whole decade. Indeed, such was their residual strength that an ageing team continued to compete at the top of the table in the immediate post-war years. The only blot on their record in the decade was THE cup defeat by Third Division Walsall in 1933 – arguably the most seismic upset in FA Cup history.

Manager: Herbert Chapman

Key Players

Frank Moss (England, goalkeeper) Eddie Hapgood (England, full-back)
Alex James (Scotland, playmaker) Cliff Bastin (England, winger)
Joe Hulme (England, winger) David Jack (England, inside forward)
Jack Lambert (Scotland, centre forward) Ted Drake (England, Lambert's replacement) Wilf Copping (England, half-back, hard man)
Leslie Compton (England, half-back) George Male (England, full-back)

Trophies

LT 1931, 1933, 1934, 1935, 1938 FAC 1930, 1936

Arsenal players line up to pay their respects at the great man's funeral.

◄)) Male was a half-back converted to full-back by Chapman. Within a year he was in the England team. He remained with the club in various capacities until his retirement in 1975.

◄)) Lambert was a crunching, old-fashioned, centre-forward with a good goal scoring record. There were eyebrows raised when he was replaced with Drake, but the latter proved even more deadly.

◄)) Frank Moss was injured in a crucial league game against Everton in March, 1935. With no substitutes allowed he went out to the wing as a passenger leaving Hapgood to take over in goal. Arsenal won 2-0. Moss scored.

◄)) In the 'Battle of Highbury', Wilf Copping inspired his team to a 3-2 victory over the World Cup winners.

Charles, John

WHETHER OPERATING AT centre-half or centre-forward John Charles was the most complete footballer Wales has ever produced. Although a hero at Leeds and Cardiff, he became the first British player to settle successfully on the Continent, succeeding for five years in Italy where Jimmy Greaves and Denis Law were later to fail. So adored was he in Turin that Juventus fans dubbed him the 'Gentle Giant' due to his power and sportsmanship.

As an international, he was the key to Wales's most successful era, a period that culminated in their appearance in the 1958 World Cup quarter-final in Sweden. Sadly, Charles was absent through injury that day and the Welsh went down narrowly 1-0 to the eventual winners Brazil.

Lured back to Leeds by Don Revie, he failed to settle and returned to his adopted Italy with AS Roma before ending his career at Cardiff, adding thousands to the Ninian Park attendances. In a land where sporting heroes have traditionally played with an oval ball, Charles increased the stature of football in the Valleys like no player before or since.

VITAL STATISTICS

Place of Birth: Swansea, Wales

Date of Birth: 27 December 1931

Died: n/a Caps: 38 (Wales) Goals (International): 15

Clubs: Leeds United, Juventus, Roma, Cardiff City, Hereford United

Appearances: Club (League: for Juventus): 150

Goals: Club (League: for Juventus): 93

Trophies: SA 1958, 1960, 1961

LEGEND RATING

Achievement	7
Skill	9
Teamwork	8
Passion	9
Personality	7
Overall Legend Rating	**40**

◄❯ 1957. Charles moves from Leeds to Juventus for £70,000, more than double the British transfer record.

◄❯ He never won a trophy in Britain, but has three Italian titles and two cups to his name.

◄❯ The first rich British footballer, Charles' wages in Italy were £60 per week, more than four times the maximum permitted in Britain. A signing-on fee of £10,000 added to his fortune.

◄❯ He played with brother, Mel, in the same Welsh team as the Allchurch brothers, Len and Ivor. Two sets of brothers have never appeared together in any other international team.

◄❯ 1973. Years after retirement, Charles lined up for Europe, scoring a hat-trick against Great Britain in a friendly international.

Charlton, Bobby

Manchester United, England

HAVING SURVIVED THE Munich air crash, Bobby Charlton seized his chance to become one of England's most successful and admired players. He never commanded the huge transfer fees paid for Denis Law, nor could he boast the natural flair and ability of George Best, but in terms of achievement Charlton was by far the most successful of United's most famous forward line. His application was total. As a young player he would often train wearing just a slipper on his right foot – a ploy designed to make him practice shooting with his left until it could generate the same venomous power as his right.

For England, he became a national hero after helping them win the 1966 World Cup, but it was his substitution in the 1970 quarter-final against Germany that fans remember almost as vividly; brought off by Alf Ramsey with the score at 2-1 to England, Charlton's absence upset the balance of the team and they eventually capitulated 3-2. Charlton bowed out in 1973 – on the same day as his brother, Jack – when over 60,000 fans packed Old Trafford for his testimonial. Knighted in 1994, he remains a director at Old Trafford and ambassador for both United and the Football Association.

VITAL STATISTICS

Place of Birth: Ashington, Northumberland, England

Date of Birth: 11 October 1937

Died: n/a **Caps:** 106 (England) **Goals (International):** 49

Clubs: Manchester United, Preston North End

Appearances: Club (All Club Matches): 798

Goals: Club (League): 257

Trophies: WorC 1966; EC 1968; LT 1957, 1965, 1967; FAC 1963

LEGEND RATING

Achievement	10
Skill	8
Teamwork	9
Passion	8
Personality	7
Overall Legend Rating	**42**

- His league appearances (606) and goals (199) remain United club records.
- Best England goal? A 30-yard rasper versus Mexico in the 1966 World Cup Finals.
- 106 caps was an England record only Bobby Moore and Peter Shilton have overtaken, his 49 goals remain unequalled.
- 1966. English and European Footballer of the Year. He also received a special PFA merit award in 1974.
- He was one of only two Munich air crash survivors to play in the European Cup winning side 10 years later. Bill Foulkes was the other.

Charlton, Jack

Leeds, England, Republic of Ireland

AN ENGLAND WORLD-CUP WINNER he may have been, and the defensive rock of Don Revie's Leeds he undoubtedly was, but Jack Charlton's most celebrated achievements came more recently across the Irish sea. Foreign managers taking control of other countries' national teams no longer raises eyebrows, but Charlton's appointment to the Republic of Ireland post was a revolutionary step.

Using the no-frills approach that had served him well in English club management, Charlton rebuilt the Irish team. Eschewing continental niceties for a long-ball style that was effective rather than pretty, and recruiting players through long-lost Irish family connections, he affected a dramatic turnaround in their international fortunes. The Republic qualified for the European Championships and the World Cup in 1988 and 1990 respectively. The World Cup in Italy was his finest hour, especially the penalty shoot-out victory over Romania that set up a quarter-final with Italy, bringing the nation to a standstill. The Republic's 1-0 defeat to the Italians cemented his status as Ireland's second most popular icon after the Pope. USA 94 saw revenge against Italy, but Ireland's lack of imagination cost them. Imagination wasn't a word associated with him as a player either, but he stood tall against some of the best the game could throw at him.

VITAL STATISTICS

Place of Birth: Ashington, Northumberland, England

Date of Birth: 8 May 1935

Died: n/a

Caps: 35 (England)   Goals (International): 6

Clubs: As Player: Leeds United; As Manager: Middlesbrough, Sheffield Wednesday, Republic of Ireland national side.

Trophies: As Player: WC 1966; LT 1969; FAC 1972; LC 1968; None as manager

LEGEND RATING

Achievement	9
Skill	6
Teamwork	7
Passion	8
Personality	7
Overall Legend Rating	**37**
Achievement	6
Tactical Awareness	8
Motivation	9
Transfer Dealing and Team Selection	7
Personality	8
Overall Legend Rating	**38**

◁ Success arrived late for Charlton the player; not picked for England until nearly 30, he was a World Cup winner and Footballer of the Year (1967) in the two seasons that followed.

◁ 1965. Policeman intervened during a Fairs Cup tie to stop Charlton exacting revenge on a Valencia player. Charlton and two Spaniards were dismissed.

◁ 1973/74. His first season in management saw Middlesbrough win Division Two by 15 points.

◁ Charlton was criticised as Irish manager for seeking out players with distant Irish heritage, but the practice is now common.

◁ He is the only member of England's 1966 World Cup winning side who made a success of management.

Cheating

The Unacceptable Face

THE ORIGINAL CHEAT was also the biggest. One can only imagine what was going through William Webb Ellis's mind as he picked up the ball and sprinted for the goal-line. The referee's action was even more inexplicable. Instead of an automatic red, Ellis was slapped on the back and credited with inventing a new game. If only he'd gone to Our Lady of the Sacred Heart, rugby might never have got off the ground. In football, modern discussion is centred on the dive. While some xenophobic opinion incorrectly identifies diving as an exclusively foreign pastime, it is true that Jurgen Klinsmann raised the art to a new level. Still, at least he had the self-deprecating charm to diffuse the criticism that came his way, famously making an ironic plunge turfwards after scoring on his Spurs debut at Hillsborough. The Daddy of all cheats, though, is Maradona, who saved the 1986 World Cup quarter-final against England for his party piece. Although Diego lied, the camera didn't, and the image of his hand palming the ball past Peter Shilton still raises the ire of all England fans.

> 'It was scored partly by the hand of God and partly by the head of Maradona.'
>
> **Diego puts a personal spin on THAT goal, 1986**

The 'Hand of God' strikes. Maradona's hand reaches the ball marginally before Peter Shilton.

◁ Frank Skinner gag during Euro 92: 'I brushed past the television and Klinsmann fell over.'

◁ Drugs have played their part. Jaap Stam is one of the latest to fall foul of the authorities for use of banned substances.

◁ Referees are not untouchables. The Greek referee was widely believed to have cheated Leeds out of the 1973 European Cup Winners' Cup final. Even his countrymen in the Salonika crowd booed him at the final whistle.

◁ The complaint of players collapsing to the ground clutching non-existent head wounds provokes strong reactions. Leicester boss Dave Bassett accused Spurs' Mauricio Taricco of cheating after a league match in 2002; a bit rich from Robbie Savage's boss.

Chilavert, Jose Luis

THEY SAY GOALKEEPERS are a different breed, and there is no denying the position has boasted its fair share of larger-than-life characters. There's Yashin, Schmeichel and Higuita for starters. But even these men are bashful wallflowers compared to Jose Luis Chilavert. Paraguay's most famous player came from humble farming stock, but lost his humility at an early age. 'I'm the best goalkeeper in the world,' was a typical self-assessment. After quickly outgrowing Paraguayan domestic football he came to prominence in Argentina – and not just for his prowess between the sticks. 'El Chila' also insisted on taking free-kicks. Most keepers in opposition territory are generally regarded as little more than novelty acts, but Chilavert proved to be highly accomplished and deadly accurate; his 19 goals in the last five seasons probably make him the highest-scoring custodian in history. Chilavert's disciplinary record can be politely described as 'colourful'; the targets of his ire have included the president of the Paraguayan Olympic committee and a ballboy whom he berated for not doing his job with sufficient alacrity. Japan and Korea was a tournament too far: Chilavert was a parody of himself.

VITAL STATISTICS

Place of Birth: Luque, Paraguay

Date of Birth: 27 July 1965

Died: n/a Caps: 111 (Paraguay) Goals (International): 8

Clubs: Cerro Porteno, San Lorenzo, Velez, Sarsfield, RC Strasbourg

Appearances: Club (All Matches): 521

Goals: Club (All Matches): 24

Trophies: None

LEGEND RATING

Achievement	6
Skill	9
Teamwork	7
Passion	9
Personality	9
Overall Legend Rating	**40**

◄))) Chilavert's goalscoring exploits began in the last minute of an international against Colombia in 1989. With all his colleagues reluctant to take a penalty, Chilavert rushed up-field to smash the winner past Rene Higuita.

◄))) Chilavert is the only goalkeeper ever to win the South American Footballer of the Year award (1997).

◄))) His showmanship has brought volatile reactions from Argentine crowds. He was once narrowly missed by a knife, while a more accurately thrown firecracker left him with concussion.

◄))) He has stated his intention to run for the Paraguayan presidency on his retirement. Judging by the standard of his predecessors and his adored status in his native land, he is probably a good bet.

Christmas Trees and *Catenaccio*

IN THE EARLY PART of the last century, tactics did not invite the degree of discussion they do today. Teams played with two defenders, a centre-half, two half-backs – who were expected to do most of the running – two inside forwards to create and score, two wingers to supply, and a centre-forward. But in the 1930s innovative managers like Arsenal's Herbert Chapman and Italy's Vittorio Pozzo tweaked this system. In their teams the centre-half became a defender, and the inside forwards started to drop a little deeper. Wingers, too, were encouraged to add to their repertoire and tuck slightly further infield.

Throughout the 1950s Austria and Hungary introduced new attacking ideas and styles, and their intricate passing and use of a deep-lying centre forward initially confused many of their more conventionally structured opponents. Brazil's World Cup success started when they adopted a back four, with attacking full-backs and two forwards feeding off two wingers. The Italian club sides in the 1960s introduced the notion of the sweeper behind two centre-halves, and Franz Beckenbauer advanced that role. The Dutch threw away the book entirely in the 1970s, laying the foundations for the fluid, modern football we see today.

'I do want to play the long ball, and I do want to play the short ball. I think long and short balls are what football is all about.'

Bobby Robson

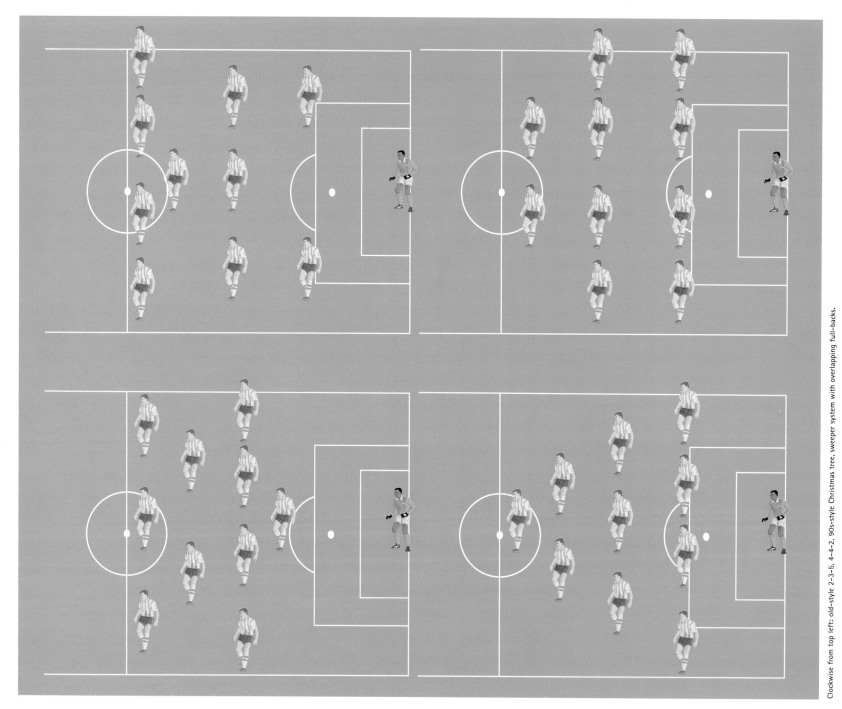

Clockwise from top left: old-style 2–3–5, 4–4–2, 90s-style Christmas tree, sweeper system with overlapping full-backs.

◁๗ 'Contrary to what some people might think I do not want to see the ball booted aimlessly up-field – but the truly great players hurt the opposition with one devastating pass.' Graham Taylor, defending the tactics of a team containing Geoff Thomas.

◁๗ The advent of substitutes and large squads has allowed managers more flexibility with tactics. 'I don't drop players, I make changes.' Bill Shankly.

◁๗ Once the players are out there it's beyond the manager's control:

'I went down to pass on some technical information to the team like the fact the game had started.' Ron Atkinson forsakes his seat in the stand as things don't go to plan.

Clough, Brian
Middlesborough, Derby County, Nottingham Forest, England

REMEMBERED BY MODERN SUPPORTERS as one of the great managers of his era, Clough was also a fine player. A phenomenal scoring record at Middlesbrough and then Sunderland was down to a sharp turn of speed and clinical finishing. Clough's playing career was cut short by a serious knee injury suffered on Boxing Day 1962, after which he concentrated on management, initially at Hartlepool, where he was joined by Peter Taylor, an old team-mate from his Middlesbrough days. The pair moved to Derby where Clough won his first league title in 1972. In October, 1973, Clough resigned from Derby and joined Brighton. In July, 1974, Clough was appointed by Leeds for his infamous 44 days. Elland Road just wasn't big enough for all those egos.

It was at Forest that Clough really hit the heights. Reunited with Taylor, he built a successful, well-organised side that continually managed to punch above its weight, winning two European Cups in 1979 and 1980. Clough finally left Forest towards the end of the 1992/93 season, with the club in some disarray, and amid accusations of excessive drinking. It was a sad end to a glorious and charismatic career.

VITAL STATISTICS

Place of Birth: Middlesbrough, England
Date of Birth: 21 March 1935
Died: n/a   Caps: 2 (England)   Goals (International): 0
Clubs: As Player: Middlesbrough, Sunderland;
As Manager: Hartlepool United, Derby County, Brighton & Hove Albion, Leeds United, Nottingham Forest
Trophies: LT 1972, 1975; 1978; EC 1979, 1980; LC 1978, 1979, 1989, 1990

LEGEND RATING

Achievement	6
Skill	9
Teamwork	7
Passion	8
Personality	7
Overall Legend Rating	**37**
Achievement	9
Tactical Awareness	9
Motivation	9
Transfer Dealing and Team Selection	8
Personality	10
Overall Legend Rating	**45**

◁ After resigning due to ill health, Peter Taylor returned to management at Derby, and promptly poached John Robertson, one of Forest's key players. He and Clough never spoke again before Taylor's death.

◁ Players at Derby threatened to strike when Clough left in 1973.
◁ Two caps was a risible return for such a fine striker.
◁ Forest were unbeaten for a record 42 league matches between November 1977 and December 1978.

◁ Forest only once finished outside the top 10 in the First Division during Clough's 18 years, prior to the relegation season.

Collins, Bobby

Celtic, Everton, Leeds, Scotland

FEW PLAYERS BECOME LEGENDS at more than one club. But invite fans of Celtic, Everton and Leeds to name their greatest characters, and Bobby Collins will feature prominently in all three lists. What he lacked in stature the 'Wee Barra' made up for in passion and skill. At 5 ft 4 in he was hardly an aerial target but, when it came to balance, control and pace, he had the edge over most of his opponents. For both his major clubs his haul of silverware was less impressive than the platform he helped build. Rangers were the Glasgow force in the 1950s, but Collins threw cash-strapped Celtic a financial lifeline when Everton offered £25,000 for him in 1958. After helping Everton

secure their future as a First Division club, Collins moved to Leeds in 1962, joining a team who were on the threshold of greatness. His transfer to Elland Road brought the club the Second Division title, just two years after he had almost single-handedly prevented them dropping into the Third Division. The great Revie side was built around him. He was always the architect, but seldom reaped the reward. Fortunately, the fans are still grateful.

VITAL STATISTICS

Place of Birth: Govanhill, Scotland
Date of Birth: 19 February 1931
Died: n/a Caps: 31 (Scotland) Goals (International): 10
Clubs: Celtic, Everton, Leeds, Bury, Greenock Morton, Oldham Athletic
Appearances: Club (for Leeds): 168
Goals: Club (for Leeds): 25
Trophies: SLT 1954, SFAC 1954

LEGEND RATING

Achievement	7
Skill	7
Teamwork	8
Passion	8
Personality	6
Overall Legend Rating	**36**

◁⫶ In 1965, Collins was the first Scot to become Footballer of the Year in England.

◁⫶ Curiously, despite a 14-year international career, Collins was not selected for six years between 1959–65.

◁⫶ Collins once scored a hat-trick of penalties, for Celtic against Aberdeen in 1953.

◁⫶ The rest of his playing, coaching and managerial days are best forgotten. He became a nomad, flitting between England,

Scotland, Ireland and Australia, but he had little success.

◁⫶ In 1968 Collins and John Charles were awarded a joint testimonial by Leeds. A fitting but belated reward for a player who had left Elland Road 11 years earlier.

Commentators

LOVE THEM OR LOATHE THEM, commentators are an integral part of the modern football-watcher's perception of the game. Initially, especially in Kenneth Wolstenholme's early broadcasts, commentary was simply a scientific narrative of the match, but as the art developed they became more intrusive, sharing opinions and statistical nuggets of information with their audience. John Motson became the master of the trivial aside, relishing every opportunity to embellish his reports with whimsical extras. ITV joined the fray, and Brian Moore's voice soon became as familiar as that of Motty and David Coleman.

New technology led to increased coverage, and an increase in the studio body count. Suddenly, presenters like Desmond Lynam were joined by teams of 'expert' summarisers, usually retired, or uninvolved current players. The two-commentator broadcast became ever-more popular, with a pundit sitting alongside a match commentator, sharing views and an occasional bit of banter.

All in all, football commentary and punditry has made a disappointing contribution to the game; intelligent and articulate people are shackled by fear of upsetting one faction or the other, or even a sponsor, and the result is too often bland and innocuous.

> 'Poland nil, England nil, though England are now looking better value for their nil.'
>
> Barry Davies, 1989

John Motson, poised to deliver another statistic.

⏴𝕝 The first radio broadcast was on 2 January 1927. The game? Arsenal versus Sheffield United.

⏴𝕝 The first TV broadcast was in 1936, and was followed a year later by the first live TV broadcast (1938 FA Cup final, Preston versus Huddersfield). The BBC tested their 'live' technology with a test broadcast of Arsenal versus Arsenal Reserves.

⏴𝕝 *Match of the Day* began in 1964, with Kenneth Wolstenholme as commentator.

⏴𝕝 Why ex-footballers or managers? Why not people trained professionally to talk, not play? That way we could avoid the cliché and banality offered by Messrs Brooking, Charlton, Pleat, Keegan, Francis and Atkinson.

Comptons, Denis and Leslie

THE COMPTONS are one of the most remarkable pairs of sporting brothers in history. Both represented England at soccer, and while Leslie never made the national team at cricket, he was a more than competent player for Middlesex for many years. His younger brother, Denis, was a lavishly talented cricketer, one of the greatest English batsmen of all time. It is unthinkable that this level of dual representation could be repeated in the modern sporting age.

Leslie Compton was good enough to play at centre-half in Herbert Chapman's legendary 1930s Arsenal team. Denis, a lively winger, arrived on the scene after Chapman's death, making his debut in 1936. Their careers were interrupted by the war, but both resumed where they had left off once Hitler had been defeated. Denis managed 12 caps for England, although he made fewer appearances than his brother for Arsenal due to his cricketing commitments (he spent long periods on tour overseas). Leslie's belated selection made him the oldest player, at 38, to win his first cap for England, a record that is likely to stand forever.

VITAL STATISTICS

Leslie/Denis Compton

Place of Birth: Woodford/Hendon, England

Date of Birth: 12 September 1912/23 May 1918

Died: 27 December 1984/23 April 1997

Caps: 2/12 (England) Goals (International): 0

Clubs: Arsenal

Trophies: LT 1948; FAC 1950

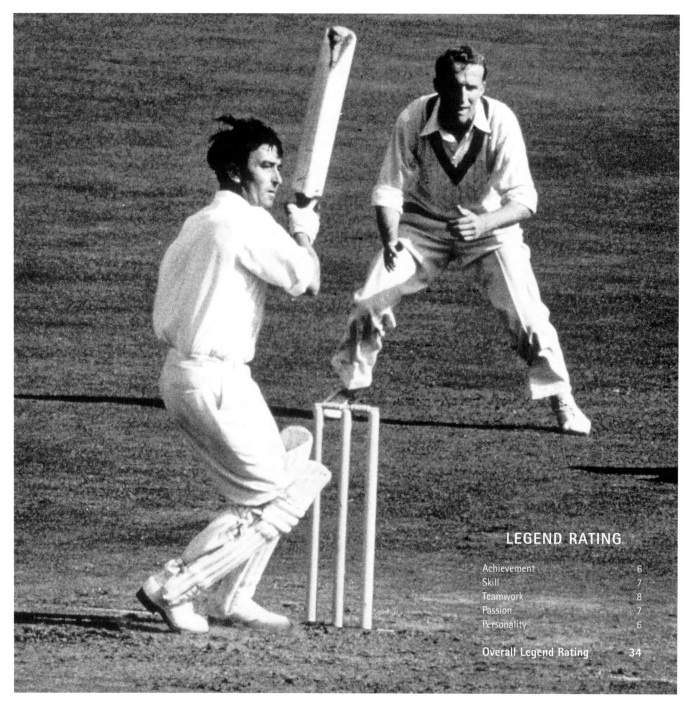

LEGEND RATING

Achievement	6
Skill	7
Teamwork	8
Passion	7
Personality	6
Overall Legend Rating	**34**

- Leslie scored an equaliser in the 1950 FA Cup semi-final against Chelsea – a header from Denis's corner.
- In the 1950 final, a concussed Denis was revived with a half-time brandy, then set up the second goal in a 2-0 win.

- Denis pioneered the modern vogue for product endorsement with a series of *Brylcreem* advertisements.
- Denis once caused outrage by airing controversial views on the emergence of black players in British football.

- Players continued to pursue parallel football and cricket careers into the 1970s (Phil Neale, Chris Balderstone and Ted Hemsley to name but three).

Corinthian Spirits

IN THE BEGINNING they were all amateurs. The game was born from the English public-school system when J.C. Thring published its prototype rules in 1862. A glance at the early winners of the FA Cup gives a strong indication of the amateurs' power; Oxford University, Old Etonians and Old Carthusians all battled it out in the early Finals. But by the mid-1880s, the balance of power had shifted, and more recognisable names began appearing on the honours board, notably the likes of Blackburn and Aston Villa.

A two-tier structure has co-existed ever since, with famous amateur sides continuing to fly the flag and provide a feeder system for the professional game. One of the best, Bishop Auckland, nurtured a certain Bob Paisley before he turned professional with Liverpool. In 1974, the term 'amateur' was officially abolished by the FA, who now class all participants in the game as 'players'. But for every park footballer, coach and manager who marvels at the wages of today's Premiership stars, the distinction remains clear enough.

'Ludere causa ludendi'.

Motto of original Scottish amateurs' Queen's Park. It translates as 'to play for the sake of playing'.

The Corinthian Casuals football team. FA Amateur Cup Final, March 20, 1956.

◁ᐧ The individual record for FA Cup winners' medals is still shared by three amateurs. The Hon. Alfred Kinnaird, Charles Wollaston and James Forrest all won five in the competition's first 20 years.

◁ᐧ The Corinthian Casuals' missionary tours helped bring the game to Brazil: one of its biggest clubs is named Corinthians.

◁ᐧ Corinthian Casuals struck a rare blow for amateurism in 1924, knocking First Division Blackburn out of the FA Cup.

◁ᐧ The original Scottish amateurs, Queen's Park, are the only remaining example of an amateur club playing in a wholly professional league.

◁ᐧ 1951. A record crowd of 100,000 attended the Amateur Cup Final at Wembley to see Pegasus beat Bishop Auckland 2-1.

Crawford's Cracker

Colchester United 3 Leeds United 2, 1971

'THE MOST FANTASTIC RESULT you'll ever see!' For once, this was a headline that avoided hyperbole. Although not non-leaguers, Fourth Division Colchester's feat was, in relative terms, more notable than any previous Cup giant-killing. This was Leeds. Don Revie's Leeds. The best team in the country, a line-up replete with seasoned internationals and a reputation for hard-man cynicism that made them the least likely of pushovers.

Colchester had one international up their sleeve. True, Ray Crawford's two England caps had been won nine years earlier and at 34 his star was hardly in the ascendant. But all this counted for nothing as Crawford's double swept Colchester to an incredible 3-0 lead just after half-time. Normal service was partly resumed as Hunter and Giles set up a frantic finish that saw Leeds keeper, Gary Sprake, reduced to a role as a distant onlooker. But his counterpart in the Colchester goal, Graham Smith, proved equal to the bombardment and the Essex club held out to produce a result that provoked open-mouthed astonishment across the country. Revie's Leeds had their share of big-match disappointments, but none was as humiliating as this.

SCORERS: Colchester: Crawford 2, Simmons
Leeds: Hunter, Giles
EVENT: FA Cup Fifth Round, Layer Road, Colchester, 13 February 1971

COLCHESTER UNITED (Man: Dick Graham)		LEEDS UNITED (Man: Don Revie)	
1 Smith G.	8 Simmons	1 Sprake	8 Clarke
2 Hall	9 Mahon	2 Reaney	9 Jones
3 Cram	10 Crawford	3 Cooper	10 Giles
4 Gilchrist	11 Gibbs	4 Bates	11 Madeley
5 Garvey		5 Charlton	
6 Kurila		6 Hunter	
7 Lewis		7 Lorimer	

Ray Crawford (left foreground) turns away after scoring one of his giantkilling goals.

◁╲╏ Colchester hero Ray Crawford has a league championship medal, won with Ipswich in 1962.

◁╲╏ Manager Dick Graham had promised a free fortnight's holiday for his players and their wives if they won. He paid up.

◁╲╏ A triumph for experience; six Colchester players were over 30.

◁╲╏ Colchester lost 5-0 at Everton in the sixth round.

Cruyff, Johann

JOHANN CRUYFF'S MOTHER worked as a cleaner at Ajax's ground in Amsterdam, and the club were persuaded to give the youngster trials. One suspects they didn't regret it. He was fortunate to develop under the legendary Ajax coach Rinus Michels, but not as fortunate as Ajax were to have such an extraordinary talent born on their doorstep.

Cruyff had the lot: pace and strength allied to nigh-perfect ball control, and a punishing finish with either foot. The Ajax and Dutch teams of the early 1970s took the passing and movement of the 1950s Hungarian side into a new era. But, as is often the case with men of genius, Cruyff had a flawed side to his personality. An

irritable and greedy nature saw him often at odds with authority and meant he was lost far too early to international football.

As a manager he was quixotic and opinionated too, and brought great success to Barcelona, landing them the coveted European Cup, but his tenure at the Nou Camp was plagued by clashes with key players, notably Hristo Stoichkov and the Brazilian striker, Romario.

Despite his arrogance and irritability, Cruyff will be remembered as a breathtaking footballer to rank with the best in the world. Living in his native Holland, he has retired from management after developing a heart problem due to his penchant for chain-smoking.

VITAL STATISTICS

Place of Birth: Amsterdam, Holland
Date of Birth: 25 April 1947
Died: n/a Caps: 48 (Holland) Goals (International): 33
Clubs: Ajax, Barcelona, Los Angeles Aztecs, Washington Diplomats, Levants, Feyenoord
Appearances: Club (All Matches): 704
Goals: Club (League): 392
Trophies: OLT 1966,1967, 1968, 1970, 1972, 1973, 1982, 1983, 1984, (1986, 1987); PLA 1974, (1991, 1992, 1993, 1994); EC 1971, 1972, (1992); CWC 1987, 1989

LEGEND RATING

Achievement	9
Skill	10
Teamwork	10
Passion	9
Personality	7
Overall Legend Rating	**45**
Achievement	9
Tactical Awareness	8
Motivation	6
Transfer Dealing and Team Selection	9
Personality	7
Overall Legend Rating	**39**

- Cruyff destroyed Inter in the 1972 European Cup final, scoring both goals in Ajax's 2–0 win.
- Legendary sports writer David Miller dubbed Cruyff 'Pythagoras in boots', such was the geometric precision of his passing.
- After a bust-up with Ajax at the end of his playing career, Cruyff responded by joining their arch-rivals Feyenoord as player-coach, promptly winning the double for the old enemy.
- He is one of only three players to have won the European Player of the Year award three times, in 1971, 1973 and 1974 (the others were Michel Platini and Marco van Basten).
- Cruyff's son Jordi was also a Dutch international, and had a spell at Manchester United.

Cubillas, Teofilo

Peru

'NENE' CUBILLAS IS Peru's most famous player, his two World Cup Finals' appearances, eight years apart, guaranteeing his status as national hero and international star. As an unknown 20-year-old in 1970, his attacking skills and combination with the experienced Hector Chumpitaz helped Peru reach the quarter-finals in Mexico and placed him in the international shop window. Curiously, it took three years before he left local club side Alianza for FC Basel, but an impressive spell in the Swiss league saw him transferred to FC Porto the following year. He was never to settle in Europe, however, and returned for a second spell with Alianza.

Back on home soil, Cubillas enhanced his reputation further by helping Peru fend off the twin giants of Brazil and Argentina to take the South American Championship in 1975, and three years later he was to score twice as Peru shocked Scotland in the 1978 World Cup Finals in Argentina. His performance that day was typical. Always one to raise his game on the big occasion, his two World Cup Finals' appearances brought him 10 goals, making him one of the highest scorers in the tournament's history.

VITAL STATISTICS

Place of Birth: Puente Piedra, near Lima, Peru

Date of Birth: 8 March 1949

Died: n/a   Caps: 117 (Peru)

Goals (International): 47

Clubs: Alianza, Basel, FC Porto, Fort Lauderdale Strikers

Goals: Club (for Alianza de Lima): 295

LEGEND RATING

Achievement	5
Skill	9
Teamwork	7
Passion	8
Personality	7
Overall Legend Rating	**36**

◁)) Cubillas finished his career in the NASL with Fort Lauderdale, where he enjoyed a striking partnership with George Best.

◁)) He was South American Footballer of the Year, 1972.

◁)) Cubillas inspired the Peru side that burst the Ally McLeod bubble in the 1978 World Cup Finals, scoring twice in seven minutes in a 3-1 victory.

◁)) Unlike Scotland, Cubillas was more than a match for Iran in that tournament, and helped himself to a hat-trick.

◁)) Cubillas' World Cup career came to a sadly undignified end in 1978. With Argentina requiring a heavy victory to progress, Peru capitulated 6-0 in abject fashion amidst whispers of bribery.

Cullis, Stan

Wolverhampton Wanderers, England

THE CLOSEST STAN CULLIS got to winning a major trophy as a player was the 1939 FA Cup final against Portsmouth. Wolves were the hot favourites that day – a status they partly owed to rumours that they had been fed on monkey glands (actually anti-flu injections) – but the bookies got it wrong as Pompey ran out comfortable 4-1 winners. Retiring soon after the war to take over from Major Frank Buckley as manager at Molineux, Cullis vowed that his team were not going to be bridesmaids for much longer. And he was as good as his word.

During his reign in the Black Country Wolves won the lot. Cullis' tactics were simple and direct, the Wimbledon of their day if you

like; the ball was played quickly and accurately up to forwards who were adept at holding it up and waiting for support, or getting to the line and crossing. His teams were also renowned for their fitness, discipline and unshakeable team spirit. Cullis had a reputation as a strict disciplinarian, an attitude fortified by his wartime experiences. It is unlikely that a manager of his intolerance would have been comfortable in the modern game.

VITAL STATISTICS

Place of Birth: Ellesmere Port, Cheshire, England

Date of Birth: 25 October 1916

Died: 27 February 2001

Caps: 12 (England)

Goals (International): 0

Clubs: As Player: Wolverhampton Wanders. As Manager: Wolverhampton Wanderers, Birmingham City

Trophies: LT 1954, 1958, 1959; FAC 1949, 1960

LEGEND RATING

Achievement	9
Tactical Awareness	9
Motivation	9
Transfer Dealing and Team Selection	8
Personality	7
Overall Legend Rating	**42**

◁ Under Cullis Wolves regularly attracted gates of over 40,000.

◁ 6, 2, 14, 16, 3, 1, 2, 3, 6, 1, 1, 2, 3, 18, 5, 16. Wolves' finishing positions in Division One under Cullis.

◁ In 1960 Wolves narrowly missed winning the double. They lost

to Spurs in the penultimate game, allowing Burnley to slip under the wire, but went on to beat Blackburn in the FA Cup final.

◁ Cullis was a redoubtable centre-half. It was his experience in that position that helped him persuade the 30-year-old Billy

Wright to drop back from his favourite half-back role to lengthen his career.

91

Dalglish, Kenny

Celtic, Liverpool, Scotland

KENNY DALGLISH EMERGED as a major force with Celtic in the early 1970s, in a side that dominated Scottish domestic football. It did not take him long to establish himself in the Scottish national team or to convince Liverpool to part with a massive £440,000 to take him to Anfield as a successor for the departing Kevin Keegan. Dalglish repaid their faith in him immediately forming a deadly combination with Ian Rush. It is hard to envisage a harder player to mark – subtle, strong and two-footed, he could turn defenders any which way he wanted.

When Liverpool needed a manager to keep up the boot-room succession, they surprised many by turning to Dalglish as player-manager in 1985. Again their faith was repaid. Dalglish became the first (and remains the only) player-manager to win the League and Cup double.

Dalglish later retired as Liverpool manager, blaming cumulative stress partially brought on by the Hillsborough disaster. A year later, though, he returned to football as manager of Blackburn Rovers, whom he led to the Premiership title in 1995. More recently spells at Newcastle and Celtic, where he took up a role as technical director, both ended in acrimony and failure. But who's to say he won't be back?

VITAL STATISTICS

Place of Birth: Glasgow, Scotland
Date of Birth: 4 March 1951
Died: n/a Caps: 102 (Scotland) Goals (International): 30
Clubs: Celtic, Liverpool
Appearances: Club (League): 559 Goals: Club (League): 230
Trophies: SLT 1972, 1973, 1974, 1977; SFAC 1972, 1974, 1975, 1977; EC 1978, 1981, 1984; LT 1979, 1980, 1982–4, (1986), (1988), (1990); LC 1981, 1982, 1983, 1984; FAC (1986), (1989)

LEGEND RATING

Achievement	9
Skill	8
Teamwork	9
Passion	9
Personality	7
Overall Legend Rating	**42**
Achievement	9
Tactical Awareness	8
Motivation	8
Transfer Dealing and Team Selection	7
Personality	6
Overall Legend Rating	**38**

◁ Dalglish scored Liverpool's only goal in the 1978 European Cup final against Bruges.

◁ He is the only player to score 100 goals for English and Scottish clubs.

◁ Dalglish is a superb golfer, and could have been good enough to play professionally.

◁ He was one of only three managers to win the English First Division with two different clubs.

◁ He was PFA and Football Writers' Player of the Year, 1983.

Danny's Boys

BY 1961 the general consensus among the football fraternity was that the League and Cup double was impossible. Aston Villa and Preston's achievements were distant memories that belonged to another century, while Cullis's Wolves and the Busby Babes had both faltered in recent years when the prize seemed within their grasp. The genesis of the team that finally cracked it was 10 years earlier, when Arthur Rowe's side won the title with a style its critics labelled 'push and run'. By the time Bill Nicholson took over in 1958, he realised that this style could be honed to greater effect. Rather than players remaining in static positions, Nicholson figured that if they

worked harder, passed the ball earlier and found space to receive it quickly, they would out-manoeuvre most opponents. It was a prototype of 'Total Football'.

The blend was irresistible, particularly in midfield where the silky passing of Blanchflower dovetailed perfectly with the powerhouse tackling of Mackay and the industry of John White. Maurice Norman was the rock at centre-half, while the free-scoring talents of Smith, Allen and Greaves ran riot through immobile defences. Their prime was the double season of 1961. They made it look easy.

Manager: Bill Nicholson

Key Players

Maurice Norman Danny Blanchflower (M) Dave Mackay (M)
John White (F) Cliff Jones (W) Bobby Smith (F) Jimmy Greaves (F)

Trophies

LT 1961 FAC 1961

Spurs won the League by eight points in 1961, setting records galore. They won their first 11 games, won 16 away matches and equalled Arsenal's 1931 points total of 66.

Jimmy Greaves arrived six months after the double was won, and

he was instrumental in maintaining Spurs' success. He helped Spurs retain the FA Cup the following year.

Nicholson knew early he was on to a good thing. His first game in charge finished Spurs 10 Everton 4.

Spurs were the first British team to win a European trophy, collecting the European Cup Winners' Cup in 1963.

Although Arthur Rowe's 1951 team was largely home grown, Nicholson's side was built with players from the transfer market.

Das Wunderteam

Either side of the war Austria had teams that were briefly rated as the world's best. In the early 1930s Jewish banker Hugo Meisl built 'Das Wunderteam', the finest Austrian side in history. They beat Scotland 5-0, Germany 6-0, Switzerland 8-1 and Hungary 8-2. In 1932 they lost 4-3 to England at Stamford Bridge in a fabulous game that gave English fans their first glimpse of the Austrians' elaborate passing movements. They went into the 1934 World Cup as the favourites, where they eliminated France and Hungary (after an ill-tempered clash), before meeting with hosts Italy on a muddy pitch in Milan. Sindelar, their pale but athletic playmaker, was

mauled by Luis Monti, and the Austrians were narrowly beaten 1-0. Another formidable side was built after the war but, as in 1934, the team was marginally past its best by the time the Finals came around in 1954. With Ocwirk pulling the strings, they hammered the Czechs thanks to a brilliant hat-trick from Probst, recovered from 3-0 down to beat Switzerland 7-5, but were then inexplicably trounced 6-1 by West Germany. The team had shot its bolt, and Austria's days as a major force were over.

**Managers: Hugo Meisl (pre-war)
Walter Mausch (post-war)**

Pre-War
Rudi Hiden (G) Pepi Smistik (M) Josef Bican (F)
Matthias Sindelar (F) Franz Binder (F).

Post-War:
Gerhard Hanappi (F/B) Ernst Happel (F/B)
Ernst Ocwirk (M) Robert and Alfred Korner (W)
Erich Probst (F)

Matthias Sindelar, the ill-fated Austrian play maker.

◁᎗ Matthias Sindelar looked more like a schoolteacher than a footballer, playing with a studiousness befitting his appearance. He was a Jew and didn't survive the German invasion.

◁᎗ Many others in the Austrian team were annexed to the German

squad for the 1938 World Cup, only a month after the Nazi invasion. 'Bimbo' Binder was one of them – he played 20 times for Austria and nine times for 'Greater Germany'.

◁᎗ Ernst Ocwirk was one of the finest attacking centre-halves in

the game, but by 1954 Austria's tactics were out of date, and the powerful German inside-forwards swamped their defence.

◁᎗ Hanappi and Happel were great defenders, and the versatile Hanappi often played at half-back and at inside-forward.

Day of the Dons

Aberdeen 2 Real Madrid 1, 1983

BASED ON the European pedigrees of these two clubs, this final looked like a mismatch. But this was no ordinary Scottish club side, and it was a Real side in a lean spell, struggling to make any real impact in European competition.

Alex Ferguson had forged Aberdeen into a durable and courageous team that boasted three international-class players in the shape of Gordon Strachan, Willie Miller and Alex McLeish. In winger Peter Weir, Fergie also had a talented maverick at his disposal. The rest were tough pros who would respond in a tight corner. In the quarter-final, after a grim draw in Munich, they were 2-1 down at home to

Bayern in the second leg with 15 minutes to go, but came back to stun the Germans with two goals in two minutes.

The final wasn't a classic. Aberdeen were the better side throughout, but as the match wore on it began to look as if they might be edged out. But then John Hewitt came on for Eric Black, scorer of the opening goal, and within minutes he was on hand to head home after a neat move between Mark McGhee and Weir.

SCORERS: Aberdeen: Black 4, Hewitt 112
          Real Madrid: Juanito (pen) 15
EVENT: European Cup Winners' Cup Final,
          11 May 1983, Gothenburg

ABERDEEN   REAL MADRID
(Man: Alex Ferguson)   (Man: Alfredo Di Stefano)

1 Leighton   7 Cooper   1 Agustin   7 Gallego
2 Rougvie   8 Black   2 Metgod   8 Stielike
3 McMaster   9 McGhee   3 Bonet   9 Juanito
4 Strachan   10 Simpson   4 Camacho   10 Santillana
5 Miller   11 Weir   5 Juan Jose   11 Isidro
6 McLeish   6 Angel

◁ Real's manager was none other than the legendary Alfredo Di Stefano. His coaching skills were not the equal of his playing ability, and he lasted just one season as boss.

◁ Aberdeen went on to beat European Cup winners Hamburg in the Super Cup, and reached the semi-finals of the European Cup Winners' Cup again a year later.

◁ In the following year's European Cup Winners' Cup, Mark McGhee scored a hat-trick in a 3-0 win over Ujpest Dozsa, overturning a 2-0 deficit from the first leg.

◁ Aberdeen won the double in 1984 and another title in 1985.

THE MOST effective striking partnerships are forged from a blend of complimentary skills. The holding abilities and experience of Shearer serve as a foil to the express pace of Bellamy's youth. The former's ability to adapt his game with age has produced the third fertile partnership of his career, his Blackburn and England alliances with Sutton and Sheringham respectively saw Shearer as the spearhead.

The intelligence of Sheringham's forward play has also borne fruit at club level. Eric Cantona and Andy Cole in particular benefited from their striking partner's ability to take out defenders by his own positioning or a shrewd through ball.

Sometimes it simply comes down to size. In the Seventies, the Liverpool target that was John Toshack created eyeholes through which a quicksilver Kevin Keegan would often thread.

With any duo, the sum is greater than either part. Mark Bright and Ian Wright were each other's equals at Crystal Palace but Bright was never the same player after they were separated. By contrast, Wright prospered at Arsenal.

One consistent feature is that despite the best utterances of managers and coaches, most striking partnerships succeed more by luck than judgement.

'He made my life easier because the opposition always put its best defender on him'.

Peter Beardsley pays tribute to England striking partner Gary Lineker

Shearer (left) and Sheringham on England duty.

Jack Rowley (175 goals) and Stan Pearson (149) were a post-War match for anything Manchester United have produced of late. They formed the first great partnership of the Busby era.

Best England partnership? Lineker and Beardsley. After forward lines that included the likes of Hateley and Mariner, their class made a pleasant and welcome change.

Tony Cottee and Frank McAvennie revitalised West Ham in the mid-Eighties, guiding them to a best-ever finish of third in 1986/87. Neither was as effective individually at other clubs.

Queen's Park Rangers fielded a twin-strike force of Flanagan and Allen in the Eighties. Mike and Clive were a far more entertaining act than their music hall namesakes.

Dean, William 'Dixie'

Everton, England

FOOTBALL'S MOST PROLIFIC pre-war goal machine was the original English centre-forward. Lawton, Lofthouse and Milburn may have carried on the tradition, but none of them scored goals like Dixie Dean. His British record of 379 is one that will stand forever. True, today's superior marking and packed defences would have prevented this avalanche, while Dean's bustling strength would have incurred the displeasure of modern referees, but none of this should overshadow the man's talent – at times he seemed to challenge Arsenal's dominance of the league title almost single-handedly, shooting Everton to a brace of league titles and an FA Cup in six seasons.

Dean was born, raised and remained in the north-west all his life, retiring in modest circumstances before a disgracefully overdue testimonial in 1964 drew 40,000 to Goodison Park. Fittingly Dean even took his last breath at his beloved Everton's ground, passing away at Goodison after watching a Merseyside derby in 1980.

VITAL STATISTICS

Place of Birth: Birkenhead, England
Date of Birth: 27 January 1907
Died: 1980 Caps: 16 (England) Goals (International): 18
Clubs: Tranmere, Everton, Notts County
Appearances: Club (League): 438
Goals: Club (League): 379
Trophies: LT 1928, 1932; FAC 1933

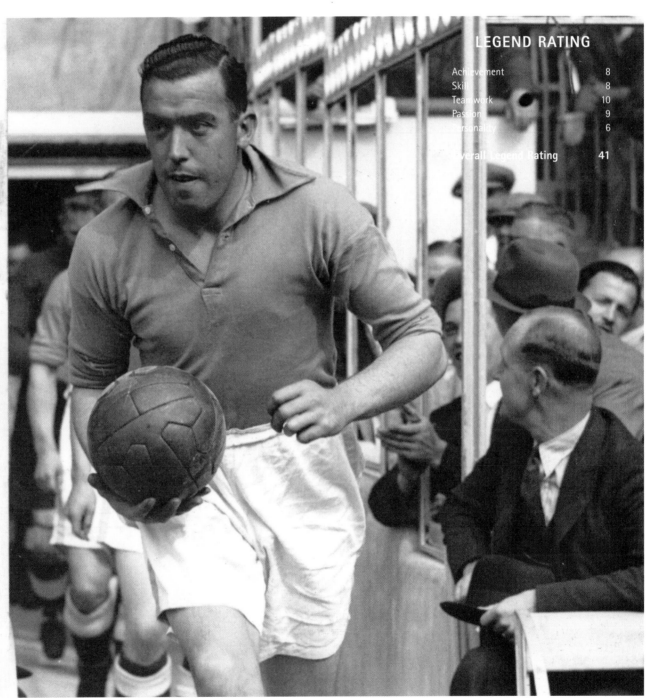

LEGEND RATING

Achievement 8
Skill 8
Teamwork 10
Passion 9
Personality 6

Overall Legend Rating 41

◄ 1928/29 season. Scored 60 goals in 39 games for Everton in the First Division, a record that still stands.
◄ Lived most of his life with a steel plate in his head, after fracturing his skull in a motorcycle crash as a youth.
◄ 1936. Overhauled Steve Bloomer's record of 352 league goals.
◄ Dean scored twice on his debut for England and hit hat-tricks in his second and fifth matches.
◄ He preferred his real name William to his life-long nickname Dixie.

Demons Exorcised

FOR ENGLAND, the opposition could not have been more formidable. This was Argentina, pre-tournament favourites, England's nemesis of 1986 and 1998. Early exchanges had the form-book pundits nodding sagely. Argentina were slick and confident: England had only another midfield casualty, Owen Hargreaves, to show for their efforts. Gradually the balance turned; as half-time approached the industry and passing of England's midfield, coupled with a growing assurance from the centre-backs, tipped the balance their way. They seemed out of luck when Owen's shot rebounded from a post, but the turning point was to come a minute before half time. Owen wriggled past Pochettino in the box and was clipped by his outstretched leg. Beckham put aside four years of resentment and delivered an emphatic penalty.

In the second half, Argentina were outplayed. England opened them up consistently for half-an-hour, strengthened by Sheringham's wit, and could have doubled their lead if Cavallero had not been equal to Scholes or Sheringham's thunderous volleys. In the final quarter, determined defence meant that only territory was surrendered. Seaman's smothering of Pochettino's header was the only heart-in-mouth moment. At the final whistle, the joy was unbridled: the weight had been lifted. It had been hard-earned and thoroughly deserved.

SCORERS: England: Beckham (pen.)
EVENT: Group F, second match, World Cup Finals, Sapporo, 7 June 2002

ARGENTINA
(Man: Marcelo Bielsa)

1	Cavallero
2	Pochettino
3	Samuel
4	Placente
5	Zanetti
6	Simeone
7	Veron
	(Aimar)
8	Sorin
9	Gonzalez
	(Lopez)
10	Ortega
11	Batistuta
	(Crespo)

ENGLAND
(Man: Sven Goran Eriksson)

1	Seaman
2	Mills
3	Ferdinand
4	Campbell
5	Cole
6	Beckham
7	Hargreaves
	(Sinclair)
8	Butt
9	Scholes
10	Owen
	(Bridge)
11	Heskey
	(Sheringham)

Beckham's face tells its own story of relief after scoring England's penalty.

◁))) This was Beckham's first penalty for England, despite his familiarity and record with dead balls outside the area. Although struck dead-centre, its pace beat Cavallero almost before he could react.

◁))) Beckham's penalty was a cathartic moment. Four years earlier his red card made him a scapegoat for England's exit at the hands of the same opponents. The Argentinian celebrations had rankled with the England captain.

◁))) This was Argentina's first defeat in two years and 18 matches, including Brazil twice in qualification: a measure of England's achievement.

Der Kaiser und Der Bomber

West Germany, 1970s

SO CONSISTENT have been their performances over the last 50 years, it seems almost ill-mannered to single out a particular German team for special praise. But, for their comprehensive domination of the early 1970s, the team of Beckenbauer, Breitner and Müller, stands out, even ahead of their all-conquering successors in the 1990s. After losing in an exciting semi-final against Italy in the 1970 World Cup, the Germans regrouped and emerged even stronger for the 1972 Euros. Inspired by Gunther Netzer, the brilliant, if unpredictable, midfielder, they won the tournament with ease, including an exemplary victory at Wembley to effectively eliminate England. Their

1974 World Cup winning side was typical West Germany. In defence they boasted an enviable array of talent including Bertie Vogts, a blond terrier of a full-back, the attacking marauder Paul Breitner, the redoubtable Karl-Heinz Schnellinger and, of course, Beckenbauer. Ahead of them stood a midfield of rare athleticism and energy, Grabowski's wing play providing an outlet for Wolfgang Overath's silky left foot, and ammunition for the urgent running of new star Rainer Bonhof. At the tip of their arrow was Gerd Müller, a striker with the priceless knack of producing a goal, even when the rest of his colleagues were struggling. This was no Dream Team. It was real.

Manager: Helmut Schoen

Key Players

Sepp Maier (G) Franz Beckenbauer (D/SW) Berti Vogts (D)
Paul Breitner (D) Wolfgang Overath (M) Uli Hoeness (M)
Rainer Bonhof (M) Gunter Netzer (M) Gerd Müller (F)

Trophies

EuroC 1972 1980 WorC 1974

West Germany line up before the 1974 WC Final. See if you can spot Paul Breitner's afro.

◁ West Germany, and later Germany, have been blessed with a succession of world-class forwards. Seeler was succeeded by Müller, and Rummenigge, Voller and Klinsmann followed.

◁ Jurgen Grabowski was a frustrating talent, brilliant one minute,

mediocre the next. His successor, Pierre Littbarski, though a potential match-winner, rarely rose to the big occasion.

◁ Uli Hoeness was the link player in the team, an unfussy player he rarely gave the ball away.

◁ West Germany won the 1974 World Cup the hard way, against a Dutch team regarded as one of the greats. The Germans hardly touched the ball for the first 20 minutes, but showed typical resilience to come back from a goal down to win 2–1.

Desailly, Marcel

AC Milan, Chelsea, France

THE FRENCH HAVE OFTEN mined foreign territories in search of new talent, with West Africa proving to be one of their richest seams. Among the gems to have been uncovered in their excavations is a tall, loose-limbed Ghanian by the name of Marcel Desailly. In France Desailly began his career with Nantes, later moving on to Bernard Tapie's Olympique Marseille where he became a mainstay of their French championship-winning teams of the early 1990s.

An imperious midfield general, his languid and nonchalant style has often brought accusations of arrogance, but he has proved to be a loyal and dependable professional, well-liked and respected by

colleagues wherever he's played. After Marseille's surprise win in the 1993 European Cup final, the vanquished Milan immediately signed him, and it was perhaps no coincidence that the trophy followed him to the San Siro the following season. By now Desailly was at the heart of the defence, from where he helped guide France to their triumphs at France 98 and Euro 2000. On his arrival at Chelsea in 1998, many thought him another fading foreign star in search of a final payday, but that was a criminal underestimation of both man and player. The bigger the opposition, the better he performs. 'The Rock' shows no sign of crumbling.

VITAL STATISTICS

Place of Birth: Accra, Ghana

Date of Birth: 7 September 1968

Died: n/a Caps: 104 (France) Goals (International): 3

Clubs: Nantes, Marseille, AC Milan, Chelsea

Appearances: Club (League): 491

Goals: Club (League): 17

Trophies: WorC 1998; Euro C 2000; EC 1993, 1994; SA 1994, 1996; FAC 2000

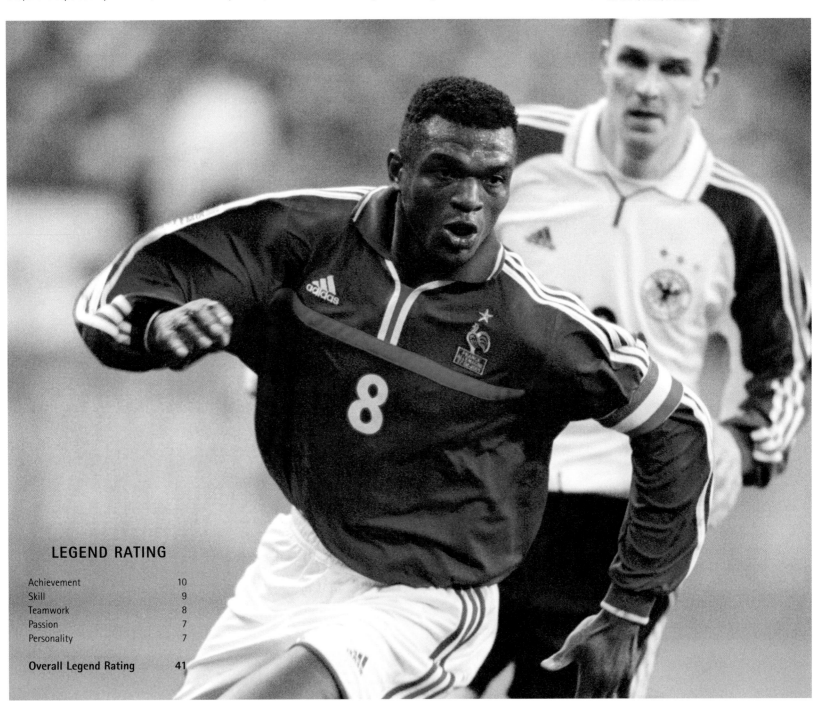

LEGEND RATING

Achievement	10
Skill	9
Teamwork	8
Passion	7
Personality	7
Overall Legend Rating	**41**

◀))) After financial scandal rocked Marseille and forced Tapie's hand, Desailly's transfer brought income that was desperately needed.

◀))) On his return to the San Siro with Chelsea, Desailly received a warmer reception than some members of the Milan team.

◀))) His goals are rare, but his canter through the Barcelona defence before applying the coup de grace in the 1994 European Cup final is an obvious highlight.

◀))) Playing with Angloma and Boli in a Marseille defence known as

the 'black guard', Desailly won over the crowd in France's most racist city.

◀))) His seven different major honours make Desailly's trophy cabinet one of the most complete, and varied, in Europe.

Di Canio, Paolo

Celtic, Sheffield Wednesday, West Ham United

LIKE FELLOW MAVERICK Eric Cantona, Paolo di Canio's talents have been more appreciated in Britain than in his home country. Volatility and indiscipline have led successive Italian managers to ignore him, and have resulted in a lengthy exile from his homeland following precocious beginnings at Milan. The case against was most vividly illustrated in 1998 when, reacting to being issued with a red card playing for Sheffield Wednesday against Arsenal, he pushed referee Paul Durkin to the ground. The shove inflicted only bruised pride, but left another manager resigned to parting with a wayward talent.

With passion and skill complementing his sublime touch and striker's instinct, Di Canio has been a folk hero at every club from the San Siro to Celtic Park, always resurrecting a career that has appeared irretrievably damaged. His hunger and commitment to the team are often obscured by his moments of indiscretion, but those that have watched him regularly will vouch for his skill and influence. Alex Ferguson's efforts to sign him for Manchester United in 2002 are an indication that, even at 34, he still had much to offer on football's biggest stages.

VITAL STATISTICS

Place of Birth: Rome, Italy
Date of Birth: 9 July 1968
Died: n/a Caps: 0 Goals (International): 0
Clubs: Terrana, Lazio, Juventus, Napoli, AC Milan, Celtic, Sheffield Wednesday, West Ham
Appearances: Club (League): 327
Goals: Club (League): 94
Trophies: None

LEGEND RATING

Achievement	4
Skill	9
Teamwork	8
Passion	10
Personality	9
Overall Legend Rating	**40**

- Di Canio even takes penalties in style; his trademark chips continue to embarrass keepers.
- 2000. Outrageous volley v Wimbledon wins BBC's goal of the season.
- 2001. Won Fair Play award after catching the ball to allow Everton's fallen keeper to receive treatment when he might have pulled the ball down and scored.
- He has never won a trophy in Britain.
- West Ham fans chant his name to the tune of an aria from Verdi's 'Rigoletto'.

Di Stefano, Alfredo

Real Madrid, Argentina, Colombia, Spain

ONE OF THE GREATEST-EVER strikers, Alfredo Di Stefano's name was initially made in South American football where, after leading a players' strike and starring in a breakaway league, he stood out as much for his militancy as his ability on the ball. Europe beckoned and it was as the captain and inspiration of the mighty Real Madrid team of the 1950s for which he is now best remembered.

His partnership with the brilliant Hungarian Ferenc Puskas was one of the great attacking combinations in the game's history and reached its high point in the last of Madrid's five consecutive European Cups from 1956–60. In a 7-3 demolition of Eintracht Frankfurt Di Stefano scored a hat-trick, while Puskas weighed in with the other four!

With the 'White Arrow' spearheading their attack, Real carried all before them in La Liga for nigh on a decade. After leaving Real in 1964, ending an 11-year love affair at the Bernabeu, he played one final season in Spain with Espanol but, at 38, he was unable to sustain the brilliance for which he was famed, sparkling only in flashes. Coaching spells in Spain and Argentina brought him a La Liga title with Valencia in 1970, but it is as a player of rare and inspirational skill that he left his most enduring imprint on the sport.

VITAL STATISTICS

Place of Birth: Barracas, Argentina
Date of Birth: 4 July 1926
Died: n/a **Caps:** 7 (Argentina); 2 (Colombia); 31 (Spain)
Goals (International): 7 (Argentina); 0 (Colombia); 23 (Spain)
Clubs: Los Cardales, River Plate, Huracan, Millonarios, Real Madrid, Espanyol
Appearances: Club (All matches for Real Madrid): 510
Goals: Club (All matches for Real Madrid): 418
Trophies: EC 1956, 1957, 1958, 1959, 1960; PLA 1954, 1955, 1957, 1958, 1959, 1961, 1963, 1964, (1971)

LEGEND RATING

Achievement	8
Skill	10
Teamwork	9
Passion	9
Personality	8
Overall Legend Rating	**44**

◁))) He is the only player to have played for three countries: Argentina, Colombia and Spain.

◁))) He was European Player of the Year 1957 and 1959.

◁))) Di Stefano's 49 European club goals remains a record.

◁))) Real beat Man United 5-3 on aggregate in a classic two-leg semi-final in the 1957 European Cup. But for the Munich disaster the two teams would have surely battled each other for Europe's top award for many years.

◁))) Di Stefano joins George Best as the only members of our World XI never to grace a World Cup Finals tournament – he pulled out of the 1962 finals after a row with Spanish coach Herrera.

Dirtiest Cup Final Ever

Chelsea 2 Leeds United 1, 1970

THIS INFAMOUS MATCH was a bloodbath. Chelsea were the fancydan southerners, flashy and inconsistent with a reputation for boozy late nights, while Leeds were the no-nonsense, cynical professionals whose pre-match evenings were spent playing dominoes. Both teams viewed each other with contempt. At Wembley, Eddie Gray had tormented Chelsea's right-back David Webb, and the tactic of switching Webb with Ron Harris for the replay had the desired effect within minutes. Gray became a limping passenger for the rest of the game. 'Chopper' had set the tone.

In a tit-for-tat response that would have brought approval from hardliners in the Middle East, Bonetti was taken out moments later, subsequently giving a commendable display on one leg. From then on, a pulsating and skilful Cup final was routinely punctuated by outbreaks of violence. Hutchinson and Charlton traded blows, while McCreadie's two-footed lunge at Bremner's neck introduced kung fu to a British audience several years before Bruce Lee.

Yet for all the 'southern softies' jibes, it was Chelsea who prevailed. A goal down at half-time, they hit back through a diving header from Osgood and scrambled a winner courtesy of Webb's right ear.

SCORERS: Chelsea: Osgood, Webb
         Leeds: Jones
EVENT: FA Cup Final Replay, Old Trafford,
         29 April, 1970

CHELSEA (Man: Dave Sexton)		LEEDS (Man: Don Revie)	
1 Bonetti	8 Cooke	1 Harvey	8 Clarke
2 Harris R	9 Osgood	2 Madeley	9 Jones
3 McCreadie	10 Hutchinson	3 Cooper	10 Giles
4 Hollins	11 Houseman	4 Bremner	11 Gray, E.
5 Dempsey		5 Charlton	
6 Webb		6 Hunter	
7 Baldwin		7 Lorimer	

Alan Clarke shoots for Leeds in the replay at Old Trafford.

◁║ When Chelsea finally went ahead in extra-time, it was the first time they had led in the tie. They had pegged Leeds back at Wembley with two equalisers.

◁║ Osgood's goal meant he had scored in every round.

◁║ This was the first FA Cup final settled outside Wembley since it became the venue in 1923.

◁║ Referee Jennings must have forgotten his pencil. Despite the violence not one player was cautioned.

◁║ David Harvey was the only change from the teams who contested the first match. Gary Sprake was left out after a trademark howler had gifted Chelsea their first equaliser.

FOOTBALL ATTRACTS MORE SPECTATORS than any other sport in the world. The downside to this is that when things go wrong they go wrong in a big way. Recent advances in stadium safety seem to have eradicated most of the problems, but it took a scandalously long time for the authorities to take action. In 1946, a wall collapsed under pressure from spectators eager to watch Bolton's FA Cup quarter-final against Stoke. Thirty-three people were crushed to death. After this the luck of the authorities held until 1971, when 66 people died at Ibrox. Rangers fans were filing down a staircase, believing their team to have been beaten in the New Year derby. A last-minute equaliser caused thousands to turn back and the crush barriers failed to take their weight.

Ibrox's legacy was the Safety of Sports Grounds Act, which, although a development, failed to address the problem of old wooden structures and fire risk. In 1985, this oversight resulted in the deaths of 56 fans from a fire started by one cigarette, dropped on to rubbish under a stand at Valley Park. Though most British grounds are safer now, the mixture of weak stadium, bad policing, hooliganism and panic can result in tragedy anywhere in the world. It is inevitable that, one day, this page will require updating.

> 'Football is not a matter of life and death – it's much more important than that!'
>
> In the context of Heysel and Hillsborough, Bill Shankly's words have a hollow ring

The dead and wounded are carried out of the first Ibrox disaster in 1902.

◄1ᵈ 1982. In a chilling echo of Ibrox, 340 people died at a European Cup match in Moscow after a late goal. Russian officials claimed the death toll was 61 in an attempt to disguise poor policing.

◄1ᵈ Locked gates and an exiting human tide have proved a fatal combination. 74 people were crushed at an Argentine game in 1968; 71 died for the same reason in Katmandu 20 years later.

◄1ᵈ In 1964 police fired shots as a crowd 'control' exercise in Lima. Over 300 people died in the resulting panic.

◄1ᵈ African crowd control has not kept pace with modern improvements. Three unnecessary uses of tear-gas have produced separate disasters in the last two years.

◄1ᵈ 26 people died at Ibrox in 1902 after a stand collapsed.

Docherty, Tommy

Chelsea, Manchester United, Scotland

FOR ALL HIS BREAST-BEATING and fondness for soundbites (he could have invented the term), Tommy Docherty built only two teams of note in a multi-club career. The first was at Chelsea, where a Second Division side still reeling from the loss of Jimmy Greaves became football's embodiment of the 'swinging sixties' and brought fame and recognition to the likes of Venables, Graham and Osgood.

A decade later, after first taking them down into the Second Division, he won promotion with Manchester United and built a swashbuckling attacking team whose stars, the likes of Coppell, Hill, Pearson, Macari and the brothers Greenhoff, replaced the heroes of the Busby era in the affections of the Old Trafford fans. But then, like always with Docherty, things turned sour. Within weeks of winning the FA Cup in 1977 he was found to have been having an affair with the club physio's wife, Mary Brown, and was sacked on the spot. He later tried his luck at a bewildering assortment of other clubs, but never hit the heights of his Old Trafford days again. Now he makes his money doing what he was always best at: rattling off one-liners and telling jokes on the lucrative after-dinner circuit.

VITAL STATISTICS

Place of Birth: Glasgow, Scotland
Date of Birth: 24 April 1929
Died: n/a Caps: 25 (Scotland) Goals (International): 1
Clubs: As Player: Celtic, Preston North End, Arsenal.
As Manager: Chelsea, Rotherham United, Queens Park Rangers, FC Porto, Hull City, Scotland national side, Manchester United, Derby County, Sydney Olympic, Preston North End, Wolverhampton Wanderers, Altrincham
Trophies: LC 1965; FAC 1977

LEGEND RATING

Achievement	4
Tactical Awareness	7
Motivation	6
Transfer Dealing and Team Selection	9
Personality	7
Overall Legend Rating	**33**

◄▮ Docherty only won two trophies as a manager, and never won the league.

◄▮ A mediocre Scotland manager, he left after a year to take the United job.

◄▮ Offered a TV acting role, to play a football manager (what else?).

◄▮ 'I've had more clubs than Jack Nicklaus,' Docherty on his ever-lengthening employment record.

◄▮ On being told his board were right behind him: 'I want them in front of me, that way I can see what they're doing'.

Doncaster Belles

THE DONCASTER BELLES have been a force in women's football in England since they were formed in 1969 by a group of women who sold 'Golden Goal' tickets for Doncaster Rovers. They won the Notts League a remarkable 11 times in 13 seasons between 1977 and 1989 and were without doubt the biggest women's club in the land during the 1980s and early 1990s. During a golden 12-year period they won the Women's FA Cup six times and were runners-up five times. In 1983 the entire Belles side represented England in Holland for the European Championships. The Belles lifted the first-ever national title in 1992, a feat they repeated in 1994, but in more recent seasons they have had to take a back seat to the likes of Arsenal and QPR. The Belles are one of the few women's clubs not to be directly affiliated to their male professional counterparts. They previously shared a humble ground with Brodsworth Welfare of the Northern Counties east league but recently moved to a new £1.8 m stadium with a 4,000 capacity and corporate entertaining facilities.

> 'We just don't like males and females playing together. I like feminine girls. Anyway it's not natural.'
>
> Ted Croker, FA Chief Executive (and Sexist), 1988

◁▷ Popular BBC TV series *Playing The Field* was inspired by author Pete Davies' book on the Doncaster side, *I Lost My Heart To The Belles*, that detailed events in the season after they won the double in 1994.

◁▷ Half the England midfield is made up of Belles – Burke, Exley and Hunt with Walker up front. Three ex-Belles are also regular members of the squad.

◁▷ Doncaster Belles are the last team in the 10-strong FA Women's Premier League to still have a woman at the helm. Manager Julie Chipchase is in her third season.

◁▷ Record Belles goalscorer Karen Walker carries the nickname of 'Wacker'. She has 61 England caps.

Don't Expect it to Happen Again   Liverpool 4 Newcastle United 3, 1996

IN 10 YEARS of the Premier League, there had never been a game quite like it. With the season approaching its climax, both teams were straining for the Champions League, while Newcastle were also slugging it out with Man United for the title.

Under the circumstances a cagey, low-scoring affair would have been understandable. Instead, both teams came at each other from the off, and after an extraordinary opening 15 minutes Newcastle were 2-1 to the good, having overturned Robbie Fowler's second-minute strike. A sense of normality returned for the following 30 minutes but half-time only served to recharge the batteries.

Fowler slid in an equaliser 10 minutes after the restart, only for Asprilla to restore Newcastle's lead within another two. A spectator for 68 minutes, Stan Collymore woke up sufficiently to turn in McAteer's cross to level the scores again. A draw seemed the fair result, but Ian Rush had other ideas. His appearance as an 82nd-minute substitute spurred Liverpool for one last effort and two minutes into injury time Anfield's greatest goalscorer turned provider, combining with John Barnes to set up an unmarked Collymore for the winner. Fairytale stuff.

SCORERS: Liverpool: Fowler (2), Collymore (2)
              Newcastle: Ferdinand, Ginola, Asprilla
EVENT: FA Premiership, Anfield, 3 April 1996

LIVERPOOL   **NEWCASTLE**
(Man: Roy Evans)   (Man: Kevin Keegan)

1 James   8 McManaman   1 Srnicek   8 Batty
2 Wright   9 Jones   2 Watson   9 Ginola
3 Scales   10 Fowler   3 Howey   10 Ferdinand
4 Ruddock   11 Collymore   4 Albert   11 Asprilla
5 McAteer   5 Beresford
6 Redknapp   6 Beardsley
7 Barnes   7 Lee

Michael Owen leaves Newcastle's Steve Watson floundering.

- 'If they score three, we'll score four.' Keegan's words earlier in the season characterised Newcastle's approach and so nearly proved prophetic.
- For Newcastle it was another away defeat in a stuttering run that cost them the title. They had been 12 points ahead at the turn of the year.
- Best moment of the match? Asprilla nutmegging Ruddock before scoring Newcastle's third.
- Radio Five Live's captain smugness, Alan Green, before the corresponding fixture the following season: 'Welcome to a packed Anfield. And do yourselves a favour folks: don't expect 4-3. That happens once every ten years.' You've guessed it....

Double, The

THE SIGHT OF an open-topped bus inching its way through an adoring throng is a familiar end-of-season ritual, but the spectacle of beaming players displaying both the League Championship and the FA Cup is relatively rare. Only seven clubs have achieved the double in over 100 seasons of competition (nine times in all). It seemed so easy when Preston won it in the league's first season, so when Aston Villa completed the same feat eight years later it barely raised an eyebrow. But for the next 64 years the double acquired the status of a holy grail as numerous teams stumbled near the summit. Chapman's Huddersfield and Arsenal, and the Busby Babes, all went close without igniting the proverbial cigar.

It was the push-and-run of Nicholson's Spurs that ended the drought, a feat repeated to general surprise by their North London neighbours a decade later. The fact that the double has been won relatively frequently in recent years is a symbol of the recent polarisation of power in the game. Indeed, following Man United's capture of the League, FA Cup and European Cup treble in 1999, the status of the domestic double has probably been undermined for good.

'We were the last Manchester club to finish as Champions ... and we'll be the next.'

Peter Swales, Manchester City chairman in 1992

Kenny Dalglish with the spoils in 1986.

◄» 1889. Preston North End remained unbeaten all season.
◄» 1897. Aston Villa's toughest obstacle was an FA Cup quarter-final epic with Preston lasting three games.
◄» 1994, 1996 and 1999. Manchester United raise the stakes with a 'double-double', followed by their *annus mirabilis* three years later.
◄» 1971. Arsenal climbed Everest the hard way, overhauling Leeds in the final game and coming from behind in the FA Cup Final.
◄» 1986. Liverpool's cake was iced by beating Everton in the first all-Merseyside Cup final.

Drake, Ted

WHEN HERBERT CHAPMAN decided he needed a replacement for his centre-forward Jack Lambert, he had only one target in mind: Ted Drake, the barnstorming Southampton striker. And so, for the princely sum of £6,500, Drake moved to Arsenal, becoming the latest piece in Chapman's ever-shifting jigsaw. The attacking line-up in the 1934/35 season read thus: Bastin, Jack, Drake, James and Hulme. Like Lambert, Drake was strong and fearless, often playing through injuries that would have ruled out lesser men. In 1935 Arsenal beat Aston Villa 7-1, a game in which Drake had nine attempts at goal. One was saved, one hit the bar and he scored with the other seven.

The vagaries of international selection in those days meant he played only five times for England; it is testimony to his striking instincts that he still managed to notch six goals. After the war Drake tried his hand at management, and enjoyed a nine-year spell at Chelsea, during which he led the club to its only league title, in 1955. A tall, handsome, athletic man, but without excessive vanity, Drake would have been a marketing manager's dream had he played today.

VITAL STATISTICS

Place of Birth: Southampton, England
Date of Birth: 16 August 1912
Died: 30 May 1995   Caps: 5 (England)
Goals (International): 6
Clubs: Southampton, Arsenal
Appearances: Club (All Matches for Arsenal): 184
Goals: Club (All Matches for Arsenal): 139
Trophies: LT 1935, 1938, (1955); FAC 1936

LEGEND RATING

Achievement	7
Skill	8
Teamwork	7
Passion	9
Personality	6
Overall Legend Rating	**37**

- Scored the only goal in the 1936 FA Cup Final.
- In 1963 Drake became a member of the first ever pools panel, convened in the 'big freeze' of that winter.
- Drake's tackle on Italy's Luisito Monti sparked off the 'Battle of Highbury', a bruising encounter between Italy and England in 1934. England won 3-2, Drake scored.
- He scored 42 league goals in his first season at Arsenal, including four in a match on four occasions.
- His seven goals against Aston Villa (see main text) were made even more remarkable by the fact that Drake played with a heavily-strapped knee.

Dream Dragons

HARDLY SCINTILLATING IS IT? Welsh football has had its moments, but they have tended to come in one-off matches rather than during sustained periods of excellence. Looking at this team it is not hard to see why. The squad of 16 contains no more than half a dozen genuinely world-class players.

Players have not been selected on the basis of appearances, otherwise the midfield might have comprised Peter Nicholas, Brian Flynn, Barry Horne and Mickey Thomas (assuming he's out of jail by now). At least the goalkeeper is top quality, and Kevin Ratcliffe was a hugely underrated defender. John Charles would start at the back,

but could also bolster the attack and the team does at least boast two decent wingers: Meredith from the early part of the century, and the whippet-like Cliff Jones, who was a member of Tottenham's 1961 double winning side.

We have picked Giggs in a floating role behind the strikers, hopefully allowing him to link up and run past them. Hughes was capable of giving anyone a hard game, even if he wasn't a prolific scorer, and Rush? He'll just stick the ball in the net like he always did.

Manager: Mike Smith

3-4-1-2

Neville Southall (80s/90s)

Kevin Ratcliffe (80s) Mike England (70s) John Charles (60s)

Billy Meredith (00s/10s) Fred Keenor (20s)
Ivor Allchurch (50s) Cliff Jones (C) (50s/60s)

Ryan Giggs (90s)

Mark Hughes (80s/90s) Ian Rush (80s)

Subs: Jack Kelsey (G) (50s) Len Allchurch (D) (50s)
Terry Yorath (M) (70s) Trevor Ford (F) (40s/50s) Ted Vizard (W) (20s)

John Charles, the greatest Welsh player of all, against Hungary in the 1958 World Cup.

◄ Fred Keenor was captain of the Welsh team that won the Home Internationals in the 1920s, and also skippered the Cardiff City side that won the 1927 FA Cup final.

◄ Mike Smith oversaw a Welsh team that achieved more than its

collective parts suggested it was capable of – which was more than many of his more illustrious successors managed.

◄ We went for a 3-4-3 formation to avoid picking Joey Jones.

◄ Hundreds of Jones's were considered for selection, as were Mark

Aizlewood, Glynn Hodges, Clayton Blackmore, Kenny Jackett and Eric Young. They didn't make it because they weren't very good.

◄ Wales might not have a team as strong as England's, but at least they have a national stadium. And a fine one at that.

Dreaming in Red

The Liverpool Dream Team

IT WAS SURPRISING, when we started to examine the Liverpool players of the last 35 years as individuals, how few of them stood out as genuine world-class performers. The likes of Tommy Smith, Brian Hall, Phil Neal, Sammy Lee and Jimmy Case were crucial parts of the Anfield jigsaw, but taken out of that context were relatively unremarkable players.

But an endless cycle of international players in recent years wasn't allowed to blur the fact that it was the more prosaic home-grown talents – the likes of full-backs Lawler and Hughes – that brought Liverpool their vast array of trophies over two decades.

Those two, with Lawrenson (narrowly over Ron Yeats) and Hansen – probably the best-ever pairing in English club football – and the redoubtable Clemence in goal make up a formidable back five.

In midfield we ignored the claims of St John, McDermott and Molby in favour of the skill and effort of Liddell, Souness and Callaghan. Keegan and Dalglish could interchange, and Rush would relish service of the quality this team could provide. If he didn't we could always call on Roger Hunt or Michael Owen to replace him.

Manager: Bill Shankly

4-4-2

Ray Clemence (70s/80s)

Chris Lawler (60s/70s) Mark Lawrenson (80s)
Alan Hansen (70s/80s) Emlyn Hughes (C) (70s)

Kevin Keegan (70s) Graeme Souness (80s)
Ian Callaghan (60s/70s) Billy Liddell (40s)

Kenny Dalglish (70s/80s) Ian Rush (80s)

Subs: Elisha Scott (G) (20s) Ron Yeats (D) (60s) Roger Hunt (F) (60s)
Steven Gerrard (M) (00s) Michael Owen (F) (90s/00s)

◄ The Kop, originally standing on a mound of ashes and cinders, was named after the Spion Kop, a hill successfully defended by the Boers in the Boer War.

◄ Club anthem 'You'll Never Walk Alone' came from a hit by

Merseybeat singer Gerry Marsden. The phrase is now carved into the wrought-iron gates at the ground.

◄ No Heighway, Toshack, Aldridge, Beardsley, Barnes, Fowler. Simply no room at the inn.

◄ Only Owen from the current crop – though in three or four years time Dudek and Hyppia may push for consideration.

◄ 'Mind you, I've been here during the bad times too – one year we came second.' Bob Paisley, Liverpool's most successful manager.

Dutch Revival

VAN GAAL TOOK OVER as head coach at Ajax in 1991 and, following the departures of Rijkaard, Van Basten, Bergkamp, Winter and Jonk, was immediately charged with the onerous task of finding suitable replacements. Three years later, with the returning Rijkaard in their team, they won the Dutch title and went on to reclaim their status as Europe's premier club side. Van Gaal was successfully able to blend emerging Dutch stars with well-chosen imports; Jari Litmanen, the imaginative Finnish playmaker, and two young Nigerians, Finidi George and the freakishly large-footed Nwankwo Kanu. They finally announced themselves in the 1995 Champions League, beating AC

Milan twice in the group stages and romping through to a tough semi-final against Bayern Munich. After a 0-0 draw in Munich, a similarly close second leg was expected. But, inspired by Litmanen, Ajax tore into Bayern, winning 5-2. A hard-fought match against AC Milan brought a third win against the Italians, and the return of the trophy Ajax had dominated in the early 1970s. Another fine campaign the following year ended in disappointment as they lost to Juventus on penalties in the final.

Manager: Louis Van Gaal

Key Players

Edwin Van Der Saar (G) Frank De Boer (D) Danny Blind (D)
Frank Rijkaard (D) Edgar Davids (M) Marc Overmars (W)
Jari Litmanen (F) Patrick Kluivert (F) Finidi George (F)
Ronald De Boer (W) Kanu (F)

Trophies

OLT 1994, 1995, 1996 EC 1995 UEFAC 1992
ESC 1995 WCC 1995

➤ During the 1995/96 European campaign, Van Gaal almost took his players off the pitch in Budapest in protest at the racial abuse being hurled at Ajax's black players. They settled for a 4-0 win.

➤ Van Gaal had a spell at Barcelona after Ajax; when Frank Rijkaard

resigned as Dutch coach after Euro 2000, Van Gaal took over.

➤ Ronald and Frank De Boer both moved to Barcelona from Ajax – the twins have since split up, Ronald moving on to Rangers.

➤ Since their European Cup win the team has broken up again; all

its best players have been sold (Van Der Saar, Overmars, Kanu, George and Litmanen all played in the Premiership).

➤ Ajax look to be on the rise again, claiming a domestic league and cup double in 2002.

Eastern Promise

THIS LINE-UP has class – in spades. Every one of the 16 players performed well at the highest level, but only rarely did their respective nations perform well as a team, the one notable exception being Czechoslovakia, who reached the 1962 World Cup final and won Euro 76. Poland reached two World Cup semi-finals, in 1974 and 1982, while Romania and Bulgaria both had to wait until the 1994 World Cup to make their first impact on a major tournament.

The defence is strong and would take no prisoners. Zmuda was a good organiser and Miodrag Belodedici a fearsome, hard-tackling opponent. In midfield the distribution and discipline of Deyna and

Masopust, allied to the pace of Boniek, would make a fine combination, but throw in the flair and trickery of Hagi as well and the prospect is mouth-watering. Lato adds pace up front and Stoichkov's left foot is one of the most lethal weapons of the last footballing decade.

Manager: Jacek Gmoch (Poland)

4-4-2

Borislav Mihailov (Bul) (80s/90s)

L. Nowak (Cze) (60s) W. Zmuda (Pol) (70s)
M. Belodedici (Rom) (90s) N. Lupescu (Rom) (70s)

Kazimierz Deyna (C) (Pol) (70s) Josef Masopust (Cze) (50s/60s)
Zbigniew Boniek (Pol) (90s) Gheorghe Hagi (Rom) (90s)

Grzegorz Lato (Pol) (70s) Hristo Stoichkov (Bul) (90s)

Subs: Viliam Schrojf (Cze) (G) (60s) Oldrich Nejedly (Cze) (M) (30s)
Iordan Letchkov (Bul) (M) (90s) Zdenek Nehoda (Cze) (M) (70s/80s)
Marius Lacatus (Rom) (W) (90s)

Poland's winning goal against Brazil in the 1974 World Cup.

Deyna and Lato both won over 100 caps for Poland. Deyna, the captain of Poland's best side, had a brief spell at Manchester City before moving to the USA where he died in a car crash.

Nehoda was the outstanding individual in the Czech team that won Euro 76, though Panenka wasn't far behind. Tomas Skuhravy, their excellent centre forward of the 1980s, was also close to inclusion.

The Romanians have traditionally underachieved. It was only when the gifted Hagi finally showed his true colours in a big event that they made an impact. The exciting Lacatus was another who too often exasperated manager and fans alike.

Edwards, Duncan

Manchester United, England

FROM THE MOMENT Duncan Edwards died in Munich, losing a desperate battle for life two weeks after seven team-mates had perished on the runway, his status as a footballing immortal was assured. Only 21 years of age when he died from his injuries, his achievements at the heart of the famous Busby Babes team were the pipe dreams of most players 15 years his senior. Wistful debates have continued for over 40 years as to what he might have achieved, but Sir Duncan Edwards with a World Cup winner's medal and a century of England caps is a realistic, some might say even conservative, projection.

Edwards was earmarked for stardom at an early age, excelling for England's under-14s and creating a queue for his signature that saw the wily Matt Busby at its head. He was equally at home at centre-half or half-back but his physique, strength and authority (unprecedented in a teenager) meant he could operate pretty much wherever Busby wanted him to. All deaths at Munich were individual tragedies of equal measure, but Edwards' loss was the biggest for English football.

VITAL STATISTICS

Place of Birth: Dudley, England
Date of Birth: 1 October 1936
Died: 21 February 1958
Caps: 18 (England)
Goals (International): 5   Clubs: Manchester United
Appearances: Club (League): 175
Goals: Club (League): 21
Trophies: LT 1956, 1957

LEGEND RATING

Achievement	7
Skill	8
Teamwork	9
Passion	9
Personality	7
Overall Legend Rating	**40**

◁)) 1953. Edwards made his professional debut for Manchester United aged only 16 years 185 days.

◁)) 1955. Became England's youngest debutant of the century at 18 years 183 days. Scotland are trounced 7-2.

◁)) He played for England at five different levels.

◁)) He won two league titles before his 21st birthday.

◁)) Had he lived, Edwards would now be a pensioner, having reached 65 in October 2001.

Eleven Lions in their Shirts

The England Dream Team

WE WERE TEMPTED by 3-5-2 due to lack of great full-backs, but that would not be England, so 4-4-2 it is. Unfortunately, this means we have had to omit one of the great centre-halves, the much-capped Billy Wright. Leaving out Moore was unthinkable, and the monolithic Duncan Edwards adds much-needed strength and attacking power. Eddie Hapgood switches to the right – he was the best of the pre-war, old-fashioned full-backs. Roger Byrne, who like Edwards had his life tragically cut short by the Munich air crash, gets in on the left ahead of Terry Cooper and Stuart Pearce. Finney wins our version of the ever-raging debate and gets in ahead of Sir

Stanley Matthews for his greater all-round contribution and for his goalscoring.

Beckham gives defences a different problem on the other side, and adds his set-piece flair. Meanwhile, Robson's tackling and stamina allow Charlton to push behind the front two. We went for the big man/quick man combination up front, with Lineker shading Greaves and Jackie Milburn for the quick-man role. Dean was a towering presence, creating as well as scoring goals with his aerial power. But then, to be fair, so would Drake, Lawton, Lofthouse or Tommy Taylor. Decisions, decisions....

Manager: Alf Ramsey

4-4-2

Gordon Banks (60s)

Eddie Hapgood (30s) Duncan Edwards (50s)
Bobby Moore (C) (60s) Roger Byrne (50s)

David Beckham (90s) Bobby Charlton (60s)
Bryan Robson (80s) Tom Finney (50s)

Gary Lineker (80s/90s) Dixie Dean (20s/30s)

Subs: Peter Shilton (G) (70s/80s) Billy Wright (D) (50s) Len Shackleton (M) (50s) Stanley Matthews (W) (40s/50s) Jimmy Greaves (F) (60s)

◀🔊 We would like to point out that we mean Billy Wright, as opposed to Mark Wright, or Ian Wright playing out of position.

◀🔊 The assumption that all players are operating at the peak of their career means only one of Bryan Robson's legs is currently broken.

◀🔊 Dean would need to be briefed on law changes as smacking the keeper into the net is simply not the done thing these days.

◀🔊 Alf Ramsey would only be given the job if he signed a contract agreeing to play wingers.

◀🔊 Lineker would take the penalties, as Le Tissier didn't make the 16, and Beckham would be spoilt for choice over who to pick out from free-kicks.

Emerald Eleven
The Republic of Ireland Dream Team

MANY PUNDITS have criticised Jack Charlton's Irish team for being negative and unimaginative, and point out that their achievements in the World Cup were, despite the hype, relatively modest. Fair enough, but they would do well to remember that until Charlton took over and started picking players with Irish grannies, the Republic had been swimming with the minnows. Suddenly a team emerged. Celtic goalkeeper Packy Bonner, Lawrenson, O'Leary, Brady and Stapleton were the core of the first side while Manchester United's long-serving full-back Dennis Irwin, Staunton, McGrath, Keane and Quinn took them into another decade and, some would

say, on to another level. In our team Johnny Carey is the sole representative of the old guard.

This side would do what Irish sides do best – scrap for everything and hope that their limited forwards (Stapleton was hard-working and intelligent, but not world class) made the most of the chances. Bonner became a top goalkeeper, and O'Leary and Lawrenson would be a genuine barrier, especially with McGrath in front of them. The midfield is superb, three world-class players with complimentary styles, and there are few better wingers in the game now than Duff.

Managers: Jack Charlton with Mick McCarthy
4-1-4-1

Packy Bonner (80s/90s)

Johnny Carey (50s) Mark Lawrenson (80s) David O'Leary (80s) Dennis Irwin (90s)

Paul McGrath (C) (80s/90s)

Damian Duff (00s) Johnny Giles (60s/70s) Roy Keane (90s) Liam Brady (70s/80s)

Frank Stapleton (70s)

Subs: Jim McDonagh (G) (70s) Steve Staunton (D) (90s)
Kevin Sheedy (M) (80s) Steve Heighway (M) (70s) Niall Quinn (F) (90s)

It does go in and Roy Houghton scores the goal that beats Italy in the 1994 World Cup.

⤺ The biggest challenge would be keeping Keane and Giles on the pitch – two great players, neither afraid of putting the boot in.

⤺ Charlton could bring out the best in players of limited ability, Mick McCarthy and Tony Cascarino being good examples.

⤺ The back-up midfield is top-quality, too. Sheedy was a talented player who achieved less than he should have and Heighway held down a place in a fantastic Liverpool team.

⤺ The redoubtable Mick McCarthy would be employed as a coach –

against expectations he has maintained the Republic's record of qualifying for tournaments from tough groups.

⤺ No place for John Aldridge – prolific at club level, consistently off target for his country.

England's Dreaming

THERE ARE MANY DIFFERENT opinions as to why England has unearthed such a rich seam of young footballing talent at the start of the twenty-first century. The FA will probably take the praise, but the main reason is certainly not the new academy system (it will be at least another decade before the fruits of that tree ripen). Perhaps the proliferation of the much-criticised foreign legion has forced the young English players to work that much harder to cement their place and prove themselves? Ashley Cole matured quickly as a Premiership player because he knew that any slip meant he would lose his place to Silvinho or Edu, and Steven Gerrard and Danny

Murphy had to compete for his place with internationals like Hamann, Berger and Smicer.

By 2006 many of the established players, like Beckham and Owen, may be struggling to maintain their motivation, and will be fighting off the challenge of another generation. The team that will appear in England colours will probably be a mixture of the names given here, plus a couple of as-yet unknown talents.

We may be a little premature; who knows, England might peak in at Euro 2004 – if they qualify! Below are some alternative potential line-ups.

Manager: Who knows? Alan Curbishley? Glynn Pardew? Perhaps Martin O'Neill?

4-4-2

(Ages as of 1 June 2006).

Chris Kirkland (25)

Gareth Johnson (22) Jonathan Woodgate (25) Rio Ferdinand (27) Ashley Cole (24)

Kieron Dyer (27) Steven Gerrard (26) Jermain Jenas (23) Gareth Barry (25)

Wayne Rooney (21) Alan Smith (25)

West Ham's Joe Cole, hopefully part of England's bright young future.

Other possible teams

◄⫶ Richard Wright (28), Paul Konchesky (25), John Terry (25), Joleon Lescott (23), Wayne Bridge (25), Joe Cole (24), Michael Carrick (25), Frank Lampard (27), James Milner (21), Malcolm Christie (26), Jermaine Defoe (23).

◄⫶ Paul Robinson (25), Danny Mills (29), Michael Dawson (22), Wes Brown (25), J. Lloyd Samuel (25), Kevin Nolan (23), Michael Tonge (23), Matt Jansen (28), Danny Murphy (29) Carlton Cole (22), Nick Chadwick (23).

Eriksson, Sven-Goran

IFK Gothenburg, Benfica, Lazio, England

UNASSUMING, softly spoken and seemingly dispassionate, Sven-Goran Eriksson has many qualities you would not expect to find in a football manager. He also possesses plenty of common sense, which appears to have stood him in good stead.

An unremarkable playing career was ended early by a knee injury; he then commenced a coaching career that has taken in a number of the biggest clubs in Europe and seen him collect an impressive list of national titles plus a smattering of European trophies.

Then the bombshell: for the first time in history, England appoint a foreigner as manager of the national team! Despite opposition from the sceptics – not all of them motivated by moronic nationalism – Eriksson quickly settled into his new role. Recognising the talent available to him Eriksson set about organising his players and, with improved tactics and discipline, virtually the same squad that lost at home to Germany in a World Cup qualifier under Kevin Keegan tore the Germans apart in the reverse fixture in Munich, winning 5-1 and sending a minor tremor through European football.

VITAL STATISTICS

Place of Birth: Torsby, Sweden
Date of Birth: 5 February 1948
Died: n/a   Caps: 0   Goals (International): 0
Clubs: As Player: KB Karlskoga; As Manager: Degerfors IF, IFK Göteborg, Benfica, AS Roma, Fiorentina AC, Sampdoria, Lazio, England national side
Trophies: SA 2000; SLT 1981; PLT 1983, 1984, 1991; UEFAC 1982; CWC 1999; ESC 1999

LEGEND RATING

Achievement	8
Tactical Awareness	9
Motivation	8
Transfer Dealing and Team Selection	8
Personality	7
Overall Legend Rating	**40**

◁ A five-year spell at Sampdoria was something of a mid-career hiccup for Eriksson, as he failed to galvanise the unfashionable side.

◁ Eriksson seems to have blunted the venom of the English tabloids by appearing to be unaware of their supposed influence and power. He simply pretends they aren't there.

◁ He cleverly installed Beckham as regular England captain and saw the player rise to spectacular new heights.

◁ Eriksson's appointment appears to have coincided with a decline in the influence of Howard Wilkinson on the England scene. Attaboy Sven!

Eusébio

MOZAMBIQUE-BORN Eusébio da Silva Ferreira was the first great African player and remains the continent's most famous footballing ambassador. His ability to run past players at pace, and hit fierce shots at speed, helped him maintain a goalscoring record so impressive that comparisons with Pelé are not inappropriate.

At Benfica, where he played most of his career, his goals tally was an unrivalled 316 from 294 games, and he appeared in four European Cup finals for the Lisbon club (sadly, wining only one).

English audiences warmed to Eusébio, having adopted him during the 1966 World Cup where, after North Korea had taken a 3-0 lead in the quarter-final, he hauled his side back into the game, scoring four as Portugal ran out 5-3 winners. The semi-final against England, where his duel with Nobby Stiles was the tournament's highlight, saw him in the role of gallant loser. His tears at the end of that Wembley clash were repeated at the same stadium two years later when Benfica lost out to Matt Busby's Man United in the European Cup final, a match in which the 'Black Panther' had a chance to give his team the lead in the dying moments but shot straight at United's Alex Stepney. Despite his disappointment Eusébio turned to shake hands with Stepney and applaud the save.

VITAL STATISTICS

Place of Birth: Lourenco-Marques (now Maputo), Mozambique
Date of Birth: 25 January 1942
Died: n/a **Caps:** 64 (Portugal) **Goals (International):** 41
Clubs: Sporting Club of Lourenco-Marques, Benfica, Monterrey, Boston Minutemen, Toronto, Metros-Croatia, Las Vegas Quicksilver
Appearances: Club (League: for Benfica): 294
Goals: Club (League: for Benfica): 316
Trophies: PLT 1961, 1963, 1964, 1965, 1967, 1968, 1969, 1971, 1972, 1973, 1974; EC 1962

LEGEND RATING

Achievement	8
Skill	10
Teamwork	8
Passion	9
Personality	7
Overall Legend Rating	**42**

◁ After a spell in the NASL, Eusébio retired after a serious knee injury, aged only 32.

◁ He was European Footballer of the Year in 1965.

◁ Benfica cheekily snatched the young Eusébio from rivals Sporting Lisbon; he had begun his career with Sporting's nursery club.

◁ He was top scorer in Europe twice (1968 and 1973), and also at the 1966 World Cup, with nine.

◁ A statue at Benfica's Estadio da Luz is a fitting tribute to a club and a nation's greatest footballer.

FA Cup

ON 16 OCTOBER 1871, 13 teams entered a knockout competition dreamt up by FA secretary Charles Alcock. It thrives today with the same name, the Football Association Challenge Cup.

Little did Alcock know what he had started. The first final was played in front of 2,000 spectators at the Kennington Oval. As the competition grew in stature, so did the venues, until the twin towers of the newly built Wembley became the permanent home for finalists in 1923. Even then, the Cup's popularity was underestimated; the first final was not all-ticket and over 200,000 turned up, leaving a white horse called Billy to shepherd spectators off the pitch.

The Graf Zeppelin's visit in 1930 ... Bert Trautmann massaging his broken neck in 1956 ... Jim Montgomery's miraculous save for Sunderland in 1973 ... the final has produced memories that have endured through generations, passed on from father to son. Once it was the dream of every minnow to reach the final. That has long passed but the Cup's value to the lesser lights should not be underestimated; one tie against a top division club can bring more revenue than they would usually amass in an entire season. Other competitions come and go, but the oldest and best will always be known, quite simply, as The Cup. And long may it continue.

'The Crazy Gang have beaten the Culture Club.'

John Motson describing Wimbledon's surprise victory over Liverpool in the 1988 final

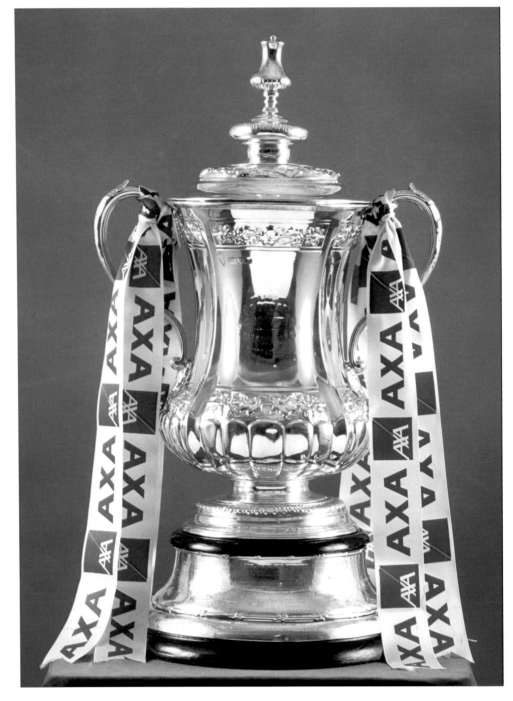

◁▷ Ten venues have staged the FA Cup final. In 1920 the final was scheduled for Stamford Bridge. Chelsea were knocked out in the semi by Aston Villa, saving the FA from the potentially embarrassing situation of having to rewrite their rule book (the final is supposed to be played on a neutral ground).

◁▷ The best final? It has got to be 1953 when, inspired by Stanley Matthews, Blackpool recovered from 3-1 down to win in the last minute.

◁▷ There have been four trophies. The first cost £20 to make but was stolen in 1895. The present design was created for the 1911 final by Italian silversmiths in Bradford, Messrs Fattorini and Sons. Appropriately, Bradford were its first winners.

Facchetti, Giacinto

ITALY HAS AN UNRIVALLED reputation for producing outstanding and uncompromising defenders, and Giacinto Facchetti is probably their finest piece of work. The rock of the Internazionale side that could claim to being the world's best in the 1970s, Facchetti had height, strength and deceptive pace. These qualities were used to pioneering effect by manager Helenio Herrera, who developed the defensive cattenaccio (doorbolt) system and gave it a counter-attacking option by using Facchetti as an attacking full-back. A defender overlapping his midfield and linking with attack was revolutionary, making Facchetti the inadvertent father of the modern wing-back.

Like so many Milanese defenders his loyalty to one club brought him a stack of domestic honours and, had he not had the misfortune to play in one of Italy's more modest international sides, his haul of medals would have been even higher. Facchetti's best chance of international reward was the 1970 World Cup final, but Italy's 4-1 drubbing put paid to his hopes. Yet it is important to point out that the result was a reflection of Brazil's dominance that day, and should not be used to diminish the memory of one of the finest full-backs ever to play the game.

VITAL STATISTICS

Place of Birth: Treviglio, Italy

Date of Birth: July 18, 1942

Died: n/a **Caps:** 94 (Italy)

Goals (International): 3

Clubs: Internazionale

Appearances: Club (League): 475

Goals: Club (League): 59

Trophies: SA 1963, 1965, 1966, 1971; EC 1964, 1965

LEGEND RATING

Achievement	9
Skill	8
Teamwork	8
Passion	7
Personality	7
Overall Legend Rating	**39**

◁ᴵᴵ His 94 caps was an Italian record, surpassed only by Zoff and Maldini.

◁ᴵᴵ He became Inter's ambassador to FIFA and UEFA after he retired.

◁ᴵᴵ Despite his reputation as a tough defender, Facchetti was sent off only once. Even this was mistaken identity, but video evidence to overturn dismissals was a long way off.

◁ᴵᴵ In the 1970s Facchetti converted from left-back to sweeper, where he played successfully for another six seasons.

◁ᴵᴵ Biggest club disappointment? The 1967 European Cup final. Facchetti pulled a hamstring with Inter leading 1-0, leaving Celtic to capitalise with two late goals.

Fanzines

IN 1986 BRITISH FOOTBALL had sunk as low as it could go; banned from Europe, attendances dwindling, the tragedies of Heysel and Bradford having left an indelible stain on the game. And yet football writing reflected none of this. As it had been for the previous 30 years, literature on the game was stuck in a rut of anodyne club programmes and childish annuals.

Enter *When Saturday Comes*. Here was a magazine that dared to treat football fans with a modicum of intelligence. It raised current football issues, was amusing, satirical and as likely to feature Leek Town as Liverpool. Originally a black-and-white pamphlet, *When*

Saturday Comes's glossy cover now rubs shoulders with the best of them at WH Smith.

The trend quickly caught on, and team fanzines sprang up all over the country. These independent publications produced a much-needed antidote to the official club line and are usually a better read. Many of their titles are a story in themselves, Lincoln's *Deranged Ferret* and Merthyr Tydfil's *Dial M for Merthyr* standing out from an entertaining crowd. Big business finally caught up in the 1990s with the launch of *FourFourTwo*, but the groundwork had been laid some 10 years earlier.

'More Dead Wood Than The Mary Rose.'
(Plymouth Argyle)

'Hyde! Hyde! What's The Score?'
(Preston, – they once beat Hyde United 26–0)

'It's Half Past Four And We're Two-Nil Down.'
(Dundee)

◄)) *WSC* was not the very first football fanzine, the excellent *Foul!* appeared in the early 1970s but failed to set the same trend.

◄)) Steve Tongue (*Foul!*) and Andy Lyons (*WSC*) are two fanzine pioneers who have crossed into mainstream football journalism.

◄)) Many of the early titles were not centred on the major clubs. Bradford's *City Gent*, Queen's Park's *The Web* and York City's *Terrace Talk* blazed a trail before the big boys.

◄)) The fanzine trend also spread to Europe. *The Stockholmian* reflects

the fortunes of AIK Stockholm, while *Der Ubersteiger* is the voice of St Pauli fans in Hamburg. There are many more.

◄)) Fanzine campaigns against racism and for the better treatment of supporters forced the hand of football's establishment.

THE CATEGORY WINNERS IN THE 'SILLIEST HAIR IN FOOTBALL' AWARDS ARE AS FOLLOWS:

CATEGORY	GOLD	SILVER	BRONZE
Mullet	Brian Kilcline	Kevin Keegan	Chris Waddle
Comb-Over	Ralph Coates	Sir Bobby Charlton	Uwe Seeler
Perm	Tommy Caton	Bob Latchford	Terry McDermott
Dreadlocks	Jason Lee	Henrik Larsson	Tony Daley
Pony-tail	Roberto Baggio	David Seaman	Darren Peacock
Beard	Trevor Hockey (aka Chewbacca)	Abel Xavier	Alexei Lalas
Dyed	Taribo West	Ian Wright	Romania, 2000
Outrageous	Abel Xavier	Carlos Valderrama	Alexei Lalas
Girlie	Charlie George	Barry Venison	Mario Kempes
AND THE WINNER IS:	Abel Xavier	Jason Lee	Alexei Lalas

KEY

Mullet: grievous 1970s rear overhang.
Comb-over: bald and in denial.
Perm: deliberate attempt to look like a show dog.
Dreadlocks: cool on Ruud, but pineapples were never in.
Pony-tail: old and in denial.
Beard: aerodynamically unsound, visually absurd.
Dyed: last resort of the immature.
Outrageous: says it all.
Girlie: 'La la la, superstar, he looks like a woman and he wears a bra.'

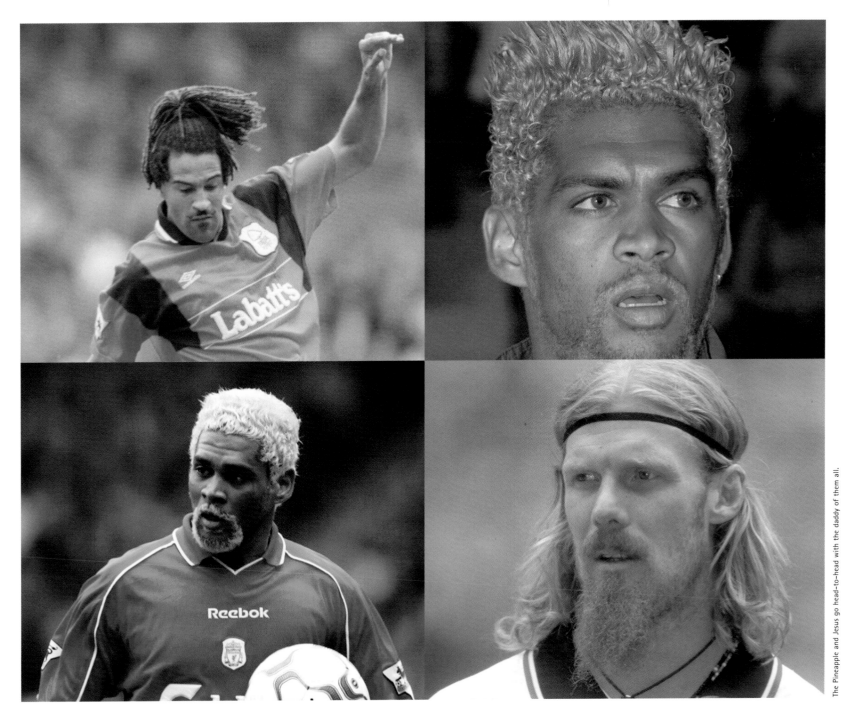

The Pineapple and Jesus go head-to-head with the daddy of them all.

↝ Xavier scores in two categories: outrageous hair and silly beard. He could easily have featured in dyed. Overall, a worthy winner.

↝ Jason Lee appeared confused and hurt when his coiffured 'pineapple' was met with derision from the terraces. His manager saw fit to defend him against a barrage of abuse from comedy duo Baddiel & Skinner, but that hair was indefensible.

↝ The 1970s was a shocking decade for haircuts in football. Starting with Charlie George looking like a big girl's blouse, the decade moved into bubble perms, ending with the mullet.

↝ The influence of style icons like Gullit and Batistuta has spawned a generation of wannabees. White men in dreads and sweaty Englishmen attempting windswept Latin locks. Yeeuch!

Fashion Victims, Part 2

IT WAS EASIER in the old days. Back then it was safe to rally your team with cries of 'Come on you blues/reds/whites'. Now it's not so simple. 'Come on you azures with the sienna trim, epaulettes and unfeasibly large logo', just doesn't have the same to ring to it does it? In the last 25 years, football kits have gone from simple, functional designs to the sort of garish tat normally peddled by the likes of Zandra Rhodes. The decline started in the late 1970s when manufacturers' logos joined club badges as a staple decoration on your standard jersey; these grew from discreet chest emblems to covering entire sleeves. Once clubs realised that fans would line up like sheep to part with £50 ever other year for a shirt with a minutely modified collar, filthy lucre instantly kicked tradition into touch. Nowadays, a successful performance in the club shop is more important than a Cup run. Manchester United have become the world's richest club by selling not just strips, but lampshades, duvet covers and credit cards. Traditionalists and parents may moan, but the biggest culprits are not the clubs but the fans. There is no law that states we have to buy a replica shirt, no one puts a gun to our heads. Guns to heads? Now there's an idea. Anyone know the way to Umbro's design department?

'For those of you watching in black and white, Spurs are the team in yellow.'

John Motson describes Tottenham's away strip

Clockwise from top left: Arsenal, Norwich, Chelsea and Forest employed the same two-year-old designer.

◁ Worst away-kit offenders? Chelsea. Jade green was offensive enough, while the 'tangerine and graphite' efforts in the mid-1990s were enough to trigger epilepsy.

◁ Manchester United famously changed their kit at half-time following a disastrous 45 minutes at the Dell. Alex Ferguson claimed their new grey strip made the players difficult to see.

◁ The pioneers of the silly strip were Coventry, who as early as the 1970s appeared in a chocolate-brown away kit.

◁ Shiny kits in the 1980s were a big mistake. The sight of Jan Molby and Paul Stewart squeezing their ample torsos into them rendered pre-match pies even more indigestible.

Fat Lady Forgets to Show

Spain 4 Yugoslavia 3, 2000

SPAIN DO NOT HAVE an impressive record at major finals, and at Euro 2000 they looked destined for yet another ignominious first-round exit. In their final group match they needed to beat Yugoslavia to ensure qualification for the second round, while their opponents required only a draw. After half an hour of frantic activity the first goal of the match finally arrived, Savo Milosevic bulleting a header past Canizares. But Yugoslavia could not hold their lead. Before half-time Raul, who had uncharacteristically spurned several chances of his own, set up Alfonso to equalise. Yugoslav substitute Govedarica restored their lead shortly after half-time, but again their lead was

short-lived, Munitis levelling for Spain just two minutes later. It was breathless stuff. Spain pounded the Yugoslavs, but left themselves open to the counter-attack, and were punished by Komljenovic with just 15 minutes left. So to the finale. Deep into injury time Abelardo was baulked in the box, and Mendieta kept his head with the penalty to draw Spain level at 3-3. Amazingly, there was still time for more. With the Yugoslavia fans whistling desperately for the ref to blow for full-time Alfonso, left unmarked by 10-man Yugoslavia (Jokanovic was sent off), waltzed through to score the winner. Cue chaos. A potential non-event had turned into drama of the highest order.

SCORERS: **Spain:** Alfonso (2), Munitis, Mendieta (pen)
Yugoslavia: Milosevic, Govedarica, Kremljenovic

EVENT: Euro 2000 group stage, Bruges, 21 June 2000

SPAIN
(Man: Jose Antonio Camacho)

1 Canizares	7 Paco
2 Salgado	8 Fran
3 Abelardo	9 Guardiola
4 Helguera	10 Alfonso
5 Sergi	11 Raul
6 Mendieta	

YUGOSLAVIA
(Man: Vujadin Boskov)

1 Kralj	7 Milosevic
2 Djorovic	8 Stojkovic
3 Jokanovic	9 Mihailovic
4 Djukic	10 Komljenovic
5 Jugovic	11 Drulovic
6 Mijatovic	

◁ The drama didn't end with the final whistle; the Yugoslavs dejection turned to joy as they discovered Slovenia had held Norway, and they too were through to the quarter-finals.

◁ This was Yugoslavia's second extraordinary game. In their opener against Slovenia they came from 3-0 down to draw 3-3 – with 10 men!

◁ To Aston Villa supporters' disbelief, Savo Milosevic was Yugoslavia's tournament star, scoring five goals in four matches.

◁ Jokanovic's sending off against Spain made it three in three for Yugoslavia. In the previous encounter against Norway, Kezman was sent off a minute after coming on as a substitute. Mihailovic saw red in their opening match against Slovenia.

Fergie's Generation

ROTATION HAS BEEN a key word at Manchester United in the last decade. Not just Alex Ferguson's much-publicised policy of resting players, but also his impeccable judgement in deciding when to bring players into Old Trafford and, just as crucially, when to let them go. Ferguson has recognised that to continue to compete in every tournament, every season, the team must evolve and improve. Jaap Stam was a cornerstone of the team that won the Treble in 1999, but a loss of form saw him moved on without the blink of an eye. Andrei Kanchelskis and Andy Cole were also offloaded while still first-team players. The genius of Eric Cantona seemed irreplaceable,

but after an indifferent start Teddy Sheringham began to exert a similarly talismanic influence. Others like Steve Bruce, Mark Hughes, Brian McClair and Denis Irwin were allowed to grow old with dignity at the club, and leave with full honours. Most of the recent changes have taken place in the defence and forward line; save the addition of Juan Veron the midfield has remained largely untouched. But then, when you can boast David Beckham, Paul Scholes, Roy Keane and Ryan Giggs in the centre of your formation, why change? Even Fergie can't improve on perfection.

Manager: Alex Ferguson

Key Players
Peter Schmeichel (G) Gary Neville (D) Jaap Stam (D)
David Beckham (M) Paul Scholes (M) Roy Keane (M)
Ryan Giggs (W) Eric Cantona (F) Andy Cole (F)
Teddy Sheringham (F)

Trophies
LT 1993, 1994, 1996, 1997, 1999 FAC 1990, 1994, 1996, 1999
LC 1992 CWC 1991 EC 1999

Ole-Gunnar Substitute does the job against Bayern in 1999.

◄¹⁾ Critics talk of luck in the European Cup final, but it's not over till it's over. United were missing both Keane and Scholes....

◄¹⁾ Andy Cole's improvement as a footballer under Ferguson and his coaches was remarkable, expunging memories of a disgruntled

Cantona scowling as his partner conducted an oral examination of the latest gift horse.

◄¹⁾ Others have taken a year or two to blossom at United, and the press have often been too quick to question Ferguson's

judgement. There have been very few dodgy signings at Manchester United in recent years.

◄¹⁾ Many doubted the wisdom of retaining Roy Keane ahead of Paul Ince. Not now.

Ferguson, Alex

Aberdeen, Manchester United, Scotland

RUTHLESS AS A PLAYER and driven as a manager, Alex Ferguson's record is one that only Bob Paisley can match. His background from the school of hard knocks in Govan served him well, requiring a commitment and self-discipline that he has always demanded, and received, from his players. Strange that such a professional started his footballing life with archetypal amateurs Queen's Park, but it was as Aberdeen manager that he really made his mark. For six years the Old Firm dominance was interrupted as three titles and a European trophy arrived at Pittodrie. Manchester United, desperate to escape Liverpool's shadow, broke the bank, and Aberdonian hearts, to get

their man. Although his 15-year tenure is the Premiership's longest and Ferguson's position is now unassailable, the first trophy did not arrive for four years amid mutterings that the Midas touch had vanished.

However, since landing United's first title in 26 years, the only competition has been for second place. Although he was widely expected to retire at the end of the 2002 season, Ferguson, apparently at the suggestion of his wife, surprised everyone by agreeing to a new contract to stay on as manager.

VITAL STATISTICS

Place of Birth: Glasgow, Scotland
Date of Birth: 31 December 1941
Died: n/a Caps: 0 Goals (International): 0
Clubs: As Player: Queens Park, St Johnstone, Dunfermline, Rangers, Falkirk, Ayr United; As Manager: East Stirling, St Mirren, Aberdeen, Scotland national side (as caretaker manager), Manchester United
Trophies: SLT 1980, 1984, 1985; SFAC 1982, 1983, 1984, 1986; CWC 1983, 1991; FAC 1990, 1994, 1996; LC 1992; LT 1993, 1994, 1996, 1997, 1999, 2000, 2001, 2003; EC 1999

LEGEND RATING

Achievement	10
Tactical Awareness	9
Motivation	9
Transfer Dealing and Team Selection	10
Personality	8
Overall Legend Rating	**46**

◁ A tearaway player, Ferguson was sent off seven times in the days when once was a rarity.

◁ 1978. St. Mirren sacked Ferguson for the only time in his career after 'unpardonable swearing at a lady on club premises'. The hair-drying technique was honed later.

◁ 1989. United fans called for Ferguson's head after a 5–1 defeat to local rivals City.

◁ 1999. Knighted following United's unique treble of League, FA Cup and European Cup.

◁ 2001. Won his seventh English league title to beat Bob Paisley's record.

THERE HAVE ALWAYS BEEN good football books. Hunter Davies' *The Glory Game* (1972) and Eamon Dunphy's *Only A Game* (1976), are examples of superb tomes published pre-Nick Hornby. Yet these books were released almost apologetically by publishers, as if they could never truly bring themselves to believe that football supporters actually had the ability to read. Hornby changed all that. *Fever Pitch* (1992) redefined football publishing. People with no interest in the game read and – often to their great surprise – even enjoyed it, impressed by Hornby's passion and insight. This was no journalist recounting his views from the press box, no retired player explaining why a fat has-been wasn't picked for the Cup final. This was a true fan, a terrace sweat, living out the triumph and the torture of the national game. Inevitably, the accelerating bandwagon was leapt upon enthusiastically, with publishers falling over themselves to print the memoirs of every two-bob sports journalist they could get their hands on. Wanabe Hornby's were rife, and the world was inundated with entries for soccer's 'Pseuds' corner'.

'A feminist colleague of mine literally refused to believe that I watched Arsenal, a disbelief that apparently had its roots in the fact that we once had a conversation about a feminist novel.'

Nick Hornby

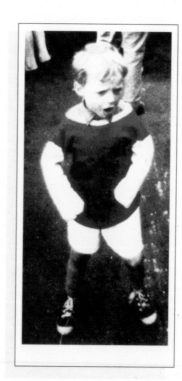

FEVER PITCH

Nick Hornby

'Funny, wise and true'
RODDY DOYLE

◄ *The Glory Game* is Hunter Davies' account of a year behind the scenes at Tottenham. An early insight into professional football, it remains an absorbing read.

◄ Recent footballing biographies have been written with greater care and consideration in the light of Hornby's achievement. Alex Ferguson's autobiography, by Hugh McIlvanney, and Tony Adams' searching *Addicted*, were bestsellers.

◄ Lesser players produce fascinating insights too. Gary Nelson's *Left Foot Forward*, and Steve Claridge's *Tales From The Boot Camp* are fine examples of this sub-genre.

◄ Splenetic and acerbic, *Only A Game* is a journeyman footballer's exploration of the whys and wherefores of the game.

FIFA

IF THE MANDARINS of the British game had won the argument, football would still be played only in its own backyard and the Home Internationals would be the World Cup. Hats off to the French for attempting to broaden its appeal. The Federation Internationale de Football Association was formed in Paris on 21 May 1904. The original signatories were seven European nations, but within 10 years Africa and South America were also represented.

Its third president, Jules Rimet, took the concept of togetherness even further, laying the foundations for the first World Cup in 1930. On his retirement in 1954, FIFA boasted 85 members.

The advent of television coverage, especially of the World Cup Finals, helped spread the gospel even further and by the 1960s even insular Britain had acknowledged FIFA's influence, providing Stanley Rous in 1961 as its sixth president. As World Cup tournaments grew, so did FIFA's income. The startling increase in the value of television rights has seen it rise from a small association into a major corporation. From its beginnings with a backroom staff of 12, FIFA now employs over 120 in its role as the game's international powerbroker.

'People are always kicking, old or young. Even an unborn child is kicking.'

Sepp Blatter, FIFA secretary-general, wobbles a few chins in 1990

FIFA President Sepp Blatter.

◄⁾ FIFA has more members than the United Nations.

◄⁾ The four UK nations, peeved at FIFA's growing influence, withdrew after the First World War. They returned only in 1946.

◄⁾ Most African countries have joined FIFA more recently, but

South Africa were its first non-European members, in 1909. They joined before any of the four British nations.

◄⁾ FIFA operates as a private institution. It receives no government grants or subsidies.

◄⁾ Increased power and money have brought the inevitable whiff of sleaze. President Joao Havelange's retirement in 1998 was tainted by allegations of corruption.

Figo, Luis

IN AN ERA when many top European footballers are fêted, paid king's ransoms and live life in a constant spotlight, some remain out in front of the chasing group. Luis Figo is one such player; no one stands taller in world football today. For all football's changes, it is comforting to find that Figo's origins and rise strike a familiar chord. Plucked from street football in a working-class district of Lisbon, he joined local club Sporting at 11, graduating from schoolboy to captain of the first team.

Figo is the complete midfielder, with a strong tackle, deft touch and deadly shot, and yet he failed to realise his full potential until being converted to a right winger by Johan Cruyff. Unlike some of Cruyff's tactical experiments it proved to be a masterstroke, though in truth such an embodiment of Total Football could probably play anywhere. Figo's world-record move to Real Madrid later saw him teamed with his only contemporary peer, Zinedine Zidane – a midfield partnership to excite everyone except possibly Catalans and Real's bank manager. At international level, he is the key reason for Portugal's rise from also-rans to serious world contenders (and back again at this year's World Cup).

VITAL STATISTICS

Place of Birth: Lisbon, Portugal

Date of Birth: 4 November 1972

Died: n/a   Caps: 92 (Portugal)

Goals (International): 28

Clubs: Sporting Lisbon, Barcelona, Real Madrid

Appearances: Club (Spanish League): 357

Goals: Club (Spanish League): 77

Trophies: PLA 1998, 1999, 2001; CWC 1997; EC 2002

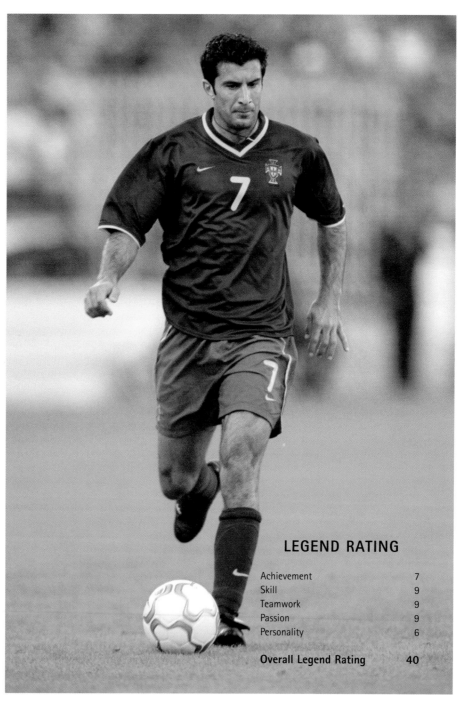

LEGEND RATING

Achievement	7
Skill	9
Teamwork	9
Passion	9
Personality	6
Overall Legend Rating	**40**

- He made his first-team debut for Sporting Lisbon at the age of 16.
- 1995/96. Banned from playing in Italy for two years after signing holding contracts with both Parma and Juventus. Serie A's loss was Barcelona's gain.
- Euro 2000. Figo was the Player of the Tournament but Portugal lost in the semi-finals.
- He was European Footballer of the Year 2000 and World Footballer of the Year 2001.
- 2000. Sold by Barcelona to deadliest rivals Real Madrid for £40 m, a then world record. Barcelona's profit was £38.6 m!

Finney, Tom

Preston North End, England

'TOM FINNEY WOULD HAVE been great in any team, in any match and in any age ... even if he had been wearing an overcoat.' So said Bill Shankly. Speculation as to how the great players of the 1940s and 1950s would have fared in the modern game is a favourite subject of bar-room, but it would take a brave man to dispute Shankly's assessment of his former Preston team-mate. There is no doubt that Finney's dribbling ability was the equal of his contemporary, Stanley Matthews, and many have argued that his reading of the game, and his shooting, were far superior. Whether he was better than Matthews will always be a matter of opinion.

After the war, Finney became the star of a great England side. His performances in a 10-0 demolition of Portugal and 4-0 thrashing of reigning World Champions Italy, were highlights of his early career. He continued playing for England until the age of 36, and his 30 goals for his country remained a record for many years. The maximum wage ruling meant Finney never earned the financial rewards his talents probably merited. It also tied him to Preston, which meant his medal collection was nothing to write home about either.

VITAL STATISTICS

Place of Birth:	Preston, England
Date of Birth:	5 April 1922
Died: n/a	Caps: 76 (England)
Goals (International): 30	
Clubs: Preston North End	
Appearances: Club (League): 433	
Goals: Club (League): 187	
Trophies: None	

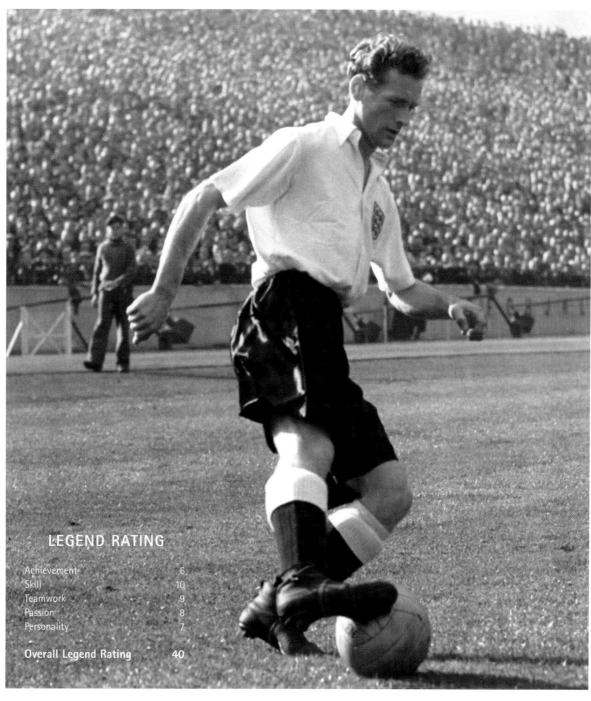

LEGEND RATING

Achievement	6
Skill	10
Teamwork	9
Passion	8
Personality	7
Overall Legend Rating	**40**

◀ Aged 40, Finney made a belated appearance in Europe. At the invitation of George Eastham he played for Irish club Distillery against Benfica in 1963. Distillery emerged with a heroic 3-3 draw.

◀ He was named Football Writers' Player of the Year in 1954 and 1957, the first player to win the award twice.

◀ Finney received an OBE in 1961 and a belated knighthood in 1999.

◀ Like Stanley Matthews, he was never booked in his career.

◀ Finney blew his one chance to win the FA Cup, having an uncharacteristically poor game in the 1954 final. North End lost 3-2.

Fists and Fury, Part 1

Racing Club 1 Celtic 0, 1968

THE BATTLES OF BERNE AND SANTIAGO may give it a run for its money, but all things considered this was probably the dirtiest game ever. It was an ill-advised match to begin with. The champions of Europe and South America had already battled it out (often literally) to a 2-2 stalemate over two legs, so setting up a final, decisive fixture was inviting trouble. After the Argentines had conducted a cynical campaign of thuggery in the first two matches, particularly against their tormentor Jimmy Johnstone, there were several outstanding scores to be settled. A neutral referee was appointed to officiate, probably in the hope that this would ease tensions. It didn't.

While the Argentines must shoulder most of the responsibility for setting the tone, it's fair to say that Celtic were no shrinking violets. Once Jock Stein's team snapped, the game developed into a free-for-all punctuated by occasional moments of football. Rulli's sending off in the 37th minute inspired a brawl bringing two more dismissals and the intervention of local riot police. Johnstone was the fourth player to go. Pushed beyond endurance, a flailing elbow saw him depart to the disappointment of the locals. The referee's humiliation was complete in the final minute, when Bertie Auld ignored his dismissal and completed the game. Oh, the score? Racing won 1-0.

SCORERS: Racing Club: Cardenas
EVENT: World Club Championship Final play-off. Estadio Centenario, Montevideo, Uruguay, 5 November 1967

RACING CLUB (Man: Juan José Pizzuti)		CELTIC (Man: Jock Stein)	
1 Cejas	7 Cardoso	1 Fallon	7 Johnstone
2 Perfumo	8 Maschio	2 Craig	8 Lennox
3 Chabay	9 Cardenas	3 Gemmell	9 Wallace
4 Martin	10 Rodriguez	4 Murdoch	10 Auld
5 Rulli	11 Raffo	5 McNeill	11 Hughes
6 Basile		6 Clark	

◁ Those five red cards: Rulli, Basile, Lennox, Johnstone, Auld.

◁ Celtic keeper Ronnie Simpson was felled by a bottle in the pre-match warm up before the second leg in Buenos Aires. He was led from the field bleeding and replaced by John Fallon.

◁ Under modern rules, a third game would never have taken place. Although they lost the second game 2-1, Celtic would have taken the trophy on away goals.

◁ Having qualified as Argentine champions, Racing Club failed to

win another title for 35 years, finally triumphing in 2001. Celtic's record in the same period was 16 league wins.

◁ Celtic won the first game 1-0 at Hampden Park in front of 103,000 with a Billy McNeill goal.

Fists and Fury, Part 2

Italy 1 Argentina 1, 1990

FOR HOSTS buoyed by fervent and total support, this was a bitter pill to swallow. Italy's progress had been a procession, a series of national celebrations in the wake of seemingly inexorable progress. Their awakening could not have been ruder.

Argentina didn't quite tie their victims to railway tracks while twirling their moustaches, but they played the part of tournament villains to the full. Cynical, defensive and dirty, they set out to spoil Italy from the outset. In fairness, dampening a fanatical home crowd is a legitimate tactic, but it looked to have backfired when the irrepressible Schillachi shot the home team into a 17th minute lead.

Even then, Argentina's tactics remained far from cavalier. They were saved by the honed striking instincts of Caniggia, who converted their one genuine opening mid-way through the second-half.

The goal was a cue for Argentina to retreat back into their shell, and the loss of Ricardo Giusti, sent off in extra-time, only hardened their defensive attitude. The penalty shoot-out came as a merciful relief. Both teams began the shoot-out in composed mood, with the first six attempts all finding their target. But the weight of expectation proved too much for the Italians, notably Donadoni and Serena who both cracked under the strain. A nation shared their grief.

SCORERS: Italy: Schillachi
           Argentina: Caniggia
EVENT: World Cup semi-final, Napoli, 3 July 1990

ITALY
(Man: Azeglio Vicini)

1	Zenga	8	De Napoli
2	Baresi	9	Giannini
3	Bergomi	10	Vialli
4	De Agostini	11	Schillachi
5	Ferri		
6	Maldini		
7	Donadoni		

ARGENTINA
(Man: Carlos Bilardo)

1	Goycoechea	8	Basualdo
2	Ruggeri	9	Calderon
3	Simon	10	Caniggia
4	Olarticoechea	11	Maradona
5	Serrizuela		
6	Giusti		
7	Burruchaga		

Italian keeper Zenga attempts to foil a cross despite having his nipple squeezed.

◄│▶ Penalty shoot-out: Italy; Baresi, Baggio, De Agostini, Donadoni (missed). Serena (missed). Argentina; Serrizuela, Burruchaga, Olarticoechea, Maradona.

◄│▶ At the ground where he had been such a favourite for Napoli Maradona's winning penalty was not well received. After the match Italians stoned his house.

◄│▶ Argentina were officially the dirtiest team of the tournament. They conceded 152 fouls, an average of one every four minutes.

Four of their players missed the final through suspension.

◄│▶ To the host nation's relief, Argentina were beaten 1–0 by Germany in the final. Two boorish and unattractive teams served up the World Cup's worst-ever final.

Five Times Champions!

Real Madrid 7 Eintracht Frankfurt 3, 1960

IT WAS A TREAT for the fans in Glasgow and is widely touted as the finest-ever display by a club side. Frankfurt, physical and formidable, arrived to challenge the mighty Real. Gone for Real were the smooth skills of Kopa and Rial, but they still had the two giants Puskas and Di Stefano who, even if the rest of the team were misfiring, could usually be relied upon to produce something special. At 1-0 down after 20 minutes the Spanish team began to find their rhythm, and soon it was clear that both Madrid's great players were on top form – which was just as well because Santamaria and his defence were being made to look ponderous by the quick German forwards.

By half-time Di Stefano had scored twice and Puskas once. Puskas completed a hat-trick before the hour to make it 5-1, and then two more goals for each side in a breathless four-minute spell completed a fine night's entertainment. It was to be the last of Real Madrid's run of five consecutive European Cup trophies. What a way to end an era.

SCORERS: Real: Di Stefano 3, Puskas 4
Frankfurt: Kress, Stein 2
EVENT: European Cup Final, Hampden Park, Glasgow, 18 May 1960, a crowd of 134,000!

REAL MADRID: (Man: Miguel Munoz)		EINTRACHT FRANKFURT (Man: Paul Osswald)	
1 Dominguez	7 Canario	1 Loy	7 Kress
2 Marquitos	8 Del Sol	2 Lutz	8 Lindner
3 Pachin	9 Di Stefano	3 Hofer	9 Stein
4 Vidal	10 Puskas	4 Weilbacher	10 Pfaff
5 Santamaria	11 Gento	5 Eigenbrodt	11 Meier
6 Zarraga		6 Stinka	

Di Stefano celebrates, the Frankfurt defence look on helplessly.

◀ Some claim Frankfurt were poor opposition, but Rangers probably wouldn't agree; in the semi-finals they went down to them 12-4 on aggregate.

◀ It was to be 14 years before another German team reached the final, Bayern Munich winning the first of their three consecutive victories in 1974.

◀ The Germans were also criticised for their tactics, but surely the only way to beat Real was to attack their vulnerable defence; it was hugely optimistic to hope for a clean sheet against that forward line.

◀ While they never attained this level again, Real reached three further finals in the 1960s, winning in 1966.

Flair and Failure

The Demise of the Gifted in the 1970s

THE 1970s, an otherwise dour period for English football, was enlivened by a handful of rebellious and talented individuals. They never seemed to feature much in the England set-up – perhaps that was why England were so poor – because Ramsey and Revie were mistrustful of their maverick talents.

Frank Worthington (eight caps), the strutting Elvis dress-a-like, won most of his caps under Joe Mercer. The conceited but gifted Alan Hudson (two caps) played two matches under Revie (both wins) and was discarded. Stan Bowles (five caps), a god at Loftus Road, was barely an apostle for England, much like his predecessor Rodney

Marsh (eight caps). The most capped of the 1970s entertainers was Tony Currie (17 caps), but his international career was spread over seven years. All these players, gifted as they were, invited criticism over their attitude. Hudson's career declined early, and Marsh always promised more than he delivered. By contrast, Bowles and Worthington, for all their flamboyance and apparent nonchalance, were fit and diligent players, with Worthington playing league football into his late 30s.

'I never seem to miss England quite enough. I might only be operating at about 30 per cent of my potential as a manager, but the lifestyle makes up for the rest.'

Rodney Marsh, comfortably ensconced at Tampa Bay Rowdies, reveals why he was such a perennial underachiever

Not Elvis with a beard, but the irrepressible Frank Worthington.

◁)) Bowles scored 11 goals in QPR's UEFA Cup campaign in 1976/77, playing brilliantly throughout the tournament. Three years later he walked out on Brian Clough and Nottingham Forest, and became a forgotten man.

◁)) Hudson's first cap was against World Cup holders West Germany in 1975. He orchestrated a 2–0 win, showing awesome confidence for a debutant. A 5–0 win over Cyprus followed, and then oblivion.

◁)) Asked which opponent he most feared, Worthington's answer was: 'My wife.' His autobiography was entitled *One Hump Or Two*. Frank was an entertaining footballer with a host of clubs, and remains an idol at Huddersfield, Leicester and Bolton.

135

Flower of Scotland

The Scotland Dream Team

THE KEEN-SIGHTED AMONG YOU will probably notice that we have not selected a goalkeeper. We make no apologies for this, reasoning that this team would have more chance of preventing goals with Alan Hansen as a sweeper cum rush-goalie than if we had selected any of the other clowns that have worn the Scottish number one jersey down the years. It also allows us to atone for the errors of various Scots managers and actually pick Hansen, who makes up a revolutionary back four with McLeish, Miller and Young. Apologies to John Greig, Martin Buchan, Richard Gough and Tom Boyd, who don't even make the 16.

The presence of the biting Bremner in midfield adds to the defensive cover, Baxter supplies enigmatic vision and Alex James combines ceaseless industry with neat footwork. On the wing Jimmy Johnstone provides flair out wide, so no place for Archie Gemmill who sits on the bench, ahead of other contenders Strachan and Souness.

The forward line picked itself. Skill, strength, imagination, pace and finishing – and that's just Kenny Dalglish! Craig Brown got a sympathy vote as manager, as he deserves the chance to work with some decent players. And because none of the truly great Scottish players have managed Scotland, at least not effectively.

Manager: Craig Brown

1-3-4-3

Alan Hansen (SW) (70s/80s) George Young (50s)
Alex McLeish (80s) Willie Miller (80s)

Jimmy Johnstone (60s/70s) Billy Bremner (C) (60s/70s)
Jim Baxter (60s) Alex James (20s/30s)

Kenny Dalglish (70s/80s) Hughie Gallagher (20s/30s)
Denis Law (60s/70s)

Subs: Dave Mackay (D/M) (60s/70s) Billy McNeill (D) (60s)
Archie Gemmill (M) (70s/80s) Billy Liddell (F) (00s) Andy Gray (F) (80s)

◁ George Young, the Rangers defender, won over 50 caps immediately after the war, and was the mainstay of Rangers' famous 'Iron Curtain' defence.

◁ Unlucky omissions? Talented wingers like Lennox, Cooke, Morgan and Robertson. Alex Jackson (a 1920s striker), Ally McCoist and also Danny McGrain, a fine attacking full-back.

◁ Deserving omissions? Paul McStay and Maurice Malpas – 77 and 55 caps respectively but neither fulfilled his potential.

◁ No current players make this team. Never before have Scotland had such a dearth of talent. Their current playmaker, Don Hutchison, is a Geordie.

Fontaine, Just

JUST FONTAINE, France's first genuinely great player, was actually a Moroccan who only moved to France in 1953 to start a career with Nice. His incisive forward play and goalscoring later saw him attract the attention of Reims, where he went on to win the League and Cup double in 1958.

It was his World Cup exploits the same year that shot him to international fame, though. His 13 goals in the Finals in Sweden set a record that still stands today. Fontaine scored six times in the group matches, including a hat-trick against Paraguay, and followed this with two more goals in the quarter-final win over Northern Ireland.

In the semis France met Brazil and, in truth, were overwhelmed in a 5-2 defeat. Fontaine scored only once in that match but, in the third-place play-off against defending champions Germany, he picked up the pace again, scoring four times as France ran out 6-3 winners. Despite France's semi-final defeat, Fontaine's place in World Cup history was assured. Tragically, the 1958 Finals proved to be his zenith as a player – a twice-broken leg forced him into premature retirement in 1962. In total Fontaine hit 30 goals in 21 appearances for France, the best ratio in the post-war era so far.

VITAL STATISTICS

Place of Birth: Marrakesh, Morocco
Date of Birth: 18 August 1933
Died: n/a   Caps: 21 (France)
Goals (International): 30 (record 13 goals in '58 Finals)
Clubs: AC Marrakesh, USM Casablanca, Nice, Reims
Appearances: Club (All matches): 213
Goals: Club (All matches): 200
Trophies: FLT 1956, 1958, 1960, 1962

LEGEND RATING

Achievement	6
Skill	8
Teamwork	7
Passion	8
Personality	6
Overall Legend Rating	**35**

‹)) Fontaine scored a hat-trick on his international debut in a 7-0 demolition of Luxembourg.
‹)) He became the first president of the French Football Union.
‹)) Fontaine only made his starting line-up in the first match against Paraguay because regular centre-forward Rene Bliard was injured.
‹)) Thirty goals in 21 internationals is the highest post-war ratio of any striker, apart from the odd one or two–cap wonder.
‹)) Fontaine scored 10 goals in Reims 1958-59 European Cup campaign, albeit against some poor sides.

Football's Coming Home

England 4 Holland 1, 1996

ENGLAND'S LAST GAME in the opening phase of Euro 96 promised to be a tight affair, as the two best teams in the group met with Terry Venables' men needing only a draw to progress to the quarter-finals. The first half was tight, with Alan Shearer's penalty the only difference between the teams, but the second period left fans open-mouthed as, in a glorious 11 minutes, England tore one of Europe's finest sides to shreds. The newly discovered combination of Sheringham and Shearer ran riot.

Holland's night was summed up by Van der Sar's fumble from Anderton's shot that allowed Sheringham to score England's fourth, although, in truth, the Dutch keeper didn't know what had hit him. With Gascoigne at his impish best, McManaman raiding down the flanks and Anderton finding space galore, England were irresistible, for once performing with the uninhibited style that has characterised so many of their successful club sides. If the Gazza-inspired victory over Scotland in the previous game had revived the hosts' expectations, this result raised them to euphoric levels.

SCORERS: England: Shearer 2 (1 pen), Sheringham 2
          Holland: Kluivert
EVENT: Group Stage, European Championship Finals,
          Wembley, 18 June 1996

ENGLAND (Man: Terry Venables)		HOLLAND (Man: Guus Hiddink)	
1 Seaman	8 Shearer	1 Van der Sar	7 Hoekstra
2 G. Neville	(Barmby)	2 Reiziger	(Cocu 72)
3 Pearce	9 Sheringham	3 Blind	8 Winter
4 Ince (Platt)	(Fowler)	4 Seedorf	9 Witschge
5 Adams	10 Anderton	5 De Boer	(De Kock)
6 Southgate	11 McManaman	(Kluivert)	10 Bogarde
7 Gascoigne		6 Bergkamp	11 Cruyff

Goal scorer Sheringham (centre) receives the congratulations of (from left) Anderton, Gascoigne and McManaman.

◄ At 4–0, England had inadvertently thrown Scotland a lifeline. Only Patrick Kluivert's late consolation for Holland prevented the Scots pipping the Dutch to a quarter-final place.

◄ This game formed part of Shearer's finest spell for England; he finished as top scorer in the tournament.

◄ As if this wasn't exciting enough, both England's quarter-final against Spain and semi-final versus Germany went to penalties.

◄ This result was sweet revenge for England, who had been eliminated by the Dutch during qualifying for the 1994 World Cup.

◄ Euro 96 was to end for England in familiar fashion, losing to Germany on penalties.

Forest

FOREST'S SUCCESSES were few and far between before the arrival of Brian Clough, FA Cup victories in 1898 and 1959 being all they had to show for nearly 100 years of endeavour. Perhaps not surprisingly then, players from the championship and European Cup winning team of the late 1970s and early 1980s dominate the line-up. Shilton, Anderson and Burns were the defensive backbone of that all-conquering side, and have been supplemented by two great players from a later generation: Des Walker and Stuart Pearce.

The midfield also pays homage to the European Cup winners, with Clough's wingers O'Neill and Roberston, plus Archie Gemmill taking three of the four places. Roy Keane gets the nod over McGovern and Bowyer for the final spot. Up front, alongside Trevor Francis, is Ian Storey-Moore, edging Woodcock on to the bench. Storey-Moore was one of the most talented forwards of his time, and may have achieved more had injury not ended his career prematurely.

Manager: Brian Clough

4-4-2

Peter Shilton (70s)

Viv Anderson (70s) Des Walker (80s/90s) Kenny Burns (70s)
Stuart Pearce (80s/90s)

Martin O'Neill (70s) Roy Keane (80s/90s) Archie Gemmill (70s)
John Robertson (70s)

Ian Storey-Moore (60s/70s) Trevor Francis (70s)

Subs: Mark Crossley (G) (90s) Bob McKinlay (D) (50s/60s)
Terry Hennessey (M) (60s) Tony Woodcock (F) (70s)
Arthur Grenville-Morris (1890s)

The stand is the financial legacy but the great team has long gone.

◁)) Bob McKinlay played 685 times for Forest over an 18-year career, so deserves his place on the bench ahead of Larry Lloyd, who was lucky to play in such a good side.

◁)) Bags of talent up front, but it's not the most robust forward line. Woodcock and Grenville-Morris would do well to keep warm on the bench.

◁)) 'If ever I felt off colour I'd sit next to him, because compared with this fat, dumpy lad I was Errol Flynn. But give him a ball and a yard of grass and he was an artist.' Brian Clough on John Robertson.

◁)) 'He's 19 and doesn't know where his talent comes from. Nobody does. It's just there.' Brian Clough on Roy Keane.

Forza Azzurri

The Italian Dream Team

MANAGER POZZO was one of the first genuine tacticians – a simple ploy of having his wingers switch positions every so often completely bamboozled the Czechs in the 1934 World Cup final.

Deploying the classic Italian sweeper formation, this would be an imposing defence (only an all-time German defence would be its equal). Get past the uncompromising attentions of Claudio Gentile and the timing of Scirea and Maldini, and you've still got to go through Baresi and Zoff. Maldini plays in his less-preferred position in the centre to accommodate Facchetti, the rampaging attacking back of the late 1960s.

If that weren't protection enough, the great playmaker from the 1930s Luis Monto sits in front of them – he made Claudio Gentile look like a pussy cat. Tardelli adds huge endeavour and Mazzola craft and subtlety.

Meazza is another from the great sides of the 1930s; he gets in alongside the great Luigi Riva ahead of substitutes Baggio and Piola, (a 1930s contemporary), leaving no room for Bettega, Boninsegna or Rossi.

Manager: Vittorio Pozzo

1-4-3-2

Dino Zoff (70s)

Franco Baresi (C) (80s/90s)

Claudio Gentile (80s)   Gaetano Scirea (80s)
Paolo Maldini (80s/90s)   Giacinto Facchetti (60s)

Marco Tardelli (80s)   Luis Monti (30s)   Sandro Mazzola (60s)

Guiseppe Meazza (30s)   Gigi Riva (60s)

Subs: Fabio Cudicini (G) (60s) Alessandro Costacurta (D) (90s) Gianni Rivera (M) (60s) Roberto Baggio (F) (90s) Vicente Piola (F) (30s)

- Baggio's inclusion in the starting line-up was jeopardised by his liking for fripperies – there's more to cool than a pigtail, Roberto.
- In Baresi, Maldini and Scirea, Italy have had three of the most accomplished defenders of the modern era.

- Roberto Bettega would have to be on standby in case a dodgy bookmaker managed to get to Rossi.
- The Italian public have great expectations of their team – if this lot failed they would get more than tomatoes chucked at them.

- In the 1990s many of the most skilful modern players were ignored by Italian managers. Zola has scandalously few caps and Di Canio has none. Others, like Del Piero and Lentini, have flattered to deceive.

Foulke, Bill

Sheffield United, Chelsea, Bradford City

AT 6 FT 3 IN and weighing over 22 stones, Bill Foulke attracted the inevitable nickname 'Fatty', but few were brave enough to use it to his face. After shooting to prominence in the Edwardian era, Foulke was not averse to chucking his considerable girth around, paying little heed to the ethics of the Corinthian age with his on-field antics. In an act of pique that would have upstaged even today's prima donnas, he once famously walked off the pitch during a match claiming that his defence wasn't trying hard enough. Opposing strikers who incurred his wrath were sometimes picked up and thrown into the goal, but his temper and stature belied a surprising

agility and skill. While it's fair to say he would never have got near a professional club in the modern era (dieticians and fitness trainers would have packed him off to the nearest park team), the game's history would be poorer for his absence. So too would the sepia-toned team photographs from his playing days, depicting Foulke freakishly dwarfing his team-mates.

VITAL STATISTICS

Place of Birth: Sheffield, England
Date of Birth: 12 April 1874
Died: 1916   Caps: 1 (England)
Goals (International): 0
Clubs: Sheffield United, Chelsea, Bradford City
Appearances: Club (League): 347
Goals: Club (League): 0
Trophies: FAC 1899, 1902; LT 1898

LEGEND RATING

Achievement
Skill
Teamwork
Passion   8
Personality   9

Overall Legend Rating   34

No prizes for spotting our hero.

◁ He cost Sheffield United £19 when signed from his local colliery team in Derbyshire.

◁ Despite his size, Foulke was a talented all-rounder, and also played county cricket for Derbyshire.

◁ Foulke was only 1 lb lighter than both Chelsea's full-backs put together.

◁ Foulke's strength was legendary; he once delayed a game by accidentally breaking the crossbar.

◁ 1905. Played in Chelsea's first-ever league game.

Francescoli, Enzo

River Plate, Uruguay

SOUTH AMERICAN FOOTBALLERS tend to be categorised into two stereotypes. One is the cynical hatchet-man defender, inscrutably taking out an opponent off the ball, and the other is the prima donna forward, locks streaming as he swallow dives in the box several metres from the nearest defender. But you can cast aside these impure thoughts when considering Enzo Francescoli Uriarte. The Gary Lineker of Uruguay is universally respected as one of the most gifted and honest forwards of the past 20 years. Idolised in Buenos Aires, his two spells at River Plate saw him sign off in 1987 with the most emotional farewell for a foreign player ever seen in

Argentina. The intervening years brought him a French title at Marseille and four seasons leading the line for less fashionable Cagliari and Torino in Serie A. His 40 per cent strike rate is remarkable considering he spent most of his career playing in some of the most sterile, defensive leagues in the world. Since retiring in 1987 'The Prince' has enhanced his nice-guy reputation yet further by becoming Uruguay's ambassador for the world children's charity, UNICEF.

VITAL STATISTICS

Place of Birth:	Montevideo, Uruguay
Date of Birth:	12 November 1961
Died: n/a	Caps: 122

Goals (International): 20

Clubs: Wanderers, River Plate, Matra Racing, Marseille, Cagliari, Torino

Appearances: Club (River Plate): 197

Goals: Club (River Plate): 115 Trophies: FLT 1990

LEGEND RATING

Achievement	7
Skill	8
Teamwork	8
Passion	8
Personality	7
Overall Legend Rating	**38**

◁))) Francescoli was playing for nursery club Real Cadys Junior at the age of six, and signed junior forms with Uruguayan team Wanderers at 14.

◁))) Three times Argentine Player of the Year, Francescoli won the South American award in 1985.

◁))) He has disappointed in World Cup Finals. Eight appearances in 1986 and 1990 brought only one goal.

◁))) Francescoli was hugely respected at Olympique Marseille,

winning the award for best foreign player in France in 1987.

◁))) Francescoli was Zidane's hero as a child, the Frenchman named one of his sons Enzo in his honour. When Juventus played River Plate in a 1996 friendly, Zidane swapped shirts with his hero.

Gallacher, Hughie

FOR A MAN standing only 5 ft 5 in tall, Hughie Gallacher was a mighty package; stocky, strong and quick, his low centre of gravity allowed him to evade centre-halves as easily as a mouse escapes the attentions of a three-legged cat. He could also dribble, tackle and packed a shot that could leave a dent in a ship's hull. And more often than not, he delivered.

All this made him not just a crowd favourite, but an idol. From his amateur days in his native Scotland he played for 10 clubs, never giving less than total commitment to them all. His glory days were at Newcastle, where he delivered the Magpies the league title in his

first full season. Not surprisingly, his sale to Chelsea for a then-massive £10,000 caused mass-protests on Tyneside. Gallacher continued to shine at Stamford Bridge, immediately overshadowing the Blues' top scorer George Mills, but by the late 1930s his star began to dip below the horizon and he retired in 1939. He dabbled in sports journalism but, without the structure and camaraderie that football provided, his life lost its purpose and in 1957 he created his own tragic headline by taking his own life.

VITAL STATISTICS

Place of Birth: Bellshill, Scotland
Date of Birth: 2 February 1903
Died: 1957   **Caps:** 19 (Scotland)
Goals (International): 22
Clubs: Queen of the South, Airdrieonians, Newcastle United, Chelsea, Derby County, Notts County, Grimsby Town, Gateshead
Appearances: Club (League): 541
Goals: Club (League): 387   **Trophies:** LT 1927

LEGEND RATING

Achievement	6
Skill	9
Teamwork	7
Passion	8
Personality	8
Overall Legend Rating	**38**

Nice shot of Hughie, but you can't take your eyes off those coppers: what a pair!

- In 174 games for Newcastle, his strike rate was 82 per cent.
- Gallacher's first game for Chelsea was away to his previous club, Newcastle. The record 68,386 crowd was all down to the wee man, with thousands more locked out.
- At Airdrie, he was a one-man team. They finished runners-up in four successive seasons and won the Scottish Cup in 1924. They have never threatened since.
- Gallacher put club before country, once ruling himself out of Scotland's team against England so he could play in a vital fixture for Newcastle.
- In 1928 Gallacher was one of the legendary 'Wembley Wizards', Scotland's finest-ever forward line that humiliated England 5-1.

Gallic Flair, Part 1

France, 1984

MUCH LIKE THE ALL-CONQUERING French team of recent years, the great French team of the 1980s thrived despite the absence of a quality striker. Their talents, again like the recent French team, were concentrated in midfield. Fernandez, a supreme fetcher and carrier, was a forerunner of Didier Deschamps, while Giresse and Tigana offered the power and athleticism currently provided by the likes of Vieria and Petit. Then there was was Platini, probably the most complete European footballer since Johan Cruyff. Zidane might be a world-class player, but Platini's gifts were not of this planet. He was a footballing god. And in the 1984 European Championships he played

like one, scoring eight goals as France won the competition on home soil. If St Etienne's Dominique Rocheteau, their one half-decent forward, had managed to stay fit they might easily have added a World Cup crown to their sideboard. But, in 1982 and 1986, their challenge foundered at the semi-final stage. France's elimination in the 1982 World Cup was particularly painful. Defeat by Germany on penalties was bad, but to see the German goalkeeper, Schumacher, escape unpunished for a foul on Battiston added injury to insult. It was Germany again in 1986, but this time a half-fit Platini failed to exert his influence. It was a last hurrah at the top level for this squad.

Managers: Michel Hidalgo and Henri Michel

Key Players
Joel Bats (G) Manuel Amoros (D) Patrick Battiston (D)
Max Bossis (D) Jean Tigana (M) Alain Giresse (M)
Luis Fernandez (M) Michel Platini (genius)
Dominique Rocheteau (F)

Trophies
EuroC 1984

⟨🔊⟩ Like Henry in 1998, Jean Pierre Papin was too raw to influence the 1986 World Cup campaign. Papin in his prime would have made this a formidable side indeed.

⟨🔊⟩ The opening game of Euro 84 was full of incident. Denmark's

Allan Simonsen was left screaming for over a minute by the referee after he broke his leg, while Amoros was sent off for an atrocious head-butt.

⟨🔊⟩ France failed to qualify for Euro 88; automatic qualification for

the holders didn't apply, and they were eliminated by a strong Soviet team in the groups.

Gallic Flair, Part 2

France were not highly fancied to win the 1998 World Cup, even on home soil. True, they had a solid-looking defence and an excellent midfield made up of wonderfully complimentary talents; Deschamps and Petit doing the donkey work with Djorkaeff and Zidane waving the wands. The reason no one fancied them was because their forwards were nondescript. The critics, not for the first time, were wrong. France won, although it has to be said Brazil did them a favour by not bothering to turn up for the final. France were indebted to Lilian Thuram for their 2-1 win over Croatia in the 1998 World Cup semi-final. Thuram had never scored for France before, but got two great goals to see his country through to the final.

Two years later at Euro 2000 the back four of Thuram, Desailly, Blanc and Lizarazu was still intact, the midfield had the added steel of Vieira, and Thierry Henry had blossomed into a convincing striker (not the lightweight winger he was at France 98). This time they were the favourites and justified it. Italy made a go of it in the final, but when David Trezeguet hit the golden-goal winner in extra-time it was no more than the French deserved.

Managers: Aime Jacquet (WC 1998) and Roger Lemerre (EC 2000)

Key Players
Fabien Barthez (G) Lilian Thuram (D) Bixente Lizarazu (D)
Marcel Desailly (D) Laurent Blanc (D) Zinedine Zidane (M)
Didier Deschamps (M) Youri Djorkaeff (M) Emmanuel Petit (M)
Patrick Vieira (M) Thierry Henry (F) Robert Pires (W)

Trophies

WorC 1998 EuroC 2000

Paris, 1998. Zidane holds the World Cup aloft.

◁ Barthez; Desailly; Blanc; Lebouef; Silvestre; Malbranque; Vieira; Petit; Pires; Henry; Saha. All Premiership players – we have been treated to the best in the world over the last few years.

◁ Full-back Lizarazu has been a key member of the powerful Bayern Munich side of the last five years, playing in the 1999 and 2001 European Cup finals.

◁ The 1998 strikers must rate as the worst to win the World Cup. Dugarry and Guivarc'h were barely international standard, while Henry still thought he was a winger and Trezeguet was raw.

◁ Many were sceptical when Wenger recruited Pires to replace Marc Overmars. He took some time to settle, but he has proved himself a better all-round player than the conceited Dutchman.

Game of Two Halves

Tottenham Hotspur 3 Manchester United 5, 2001

IT IS OFTEN SAID that football is a game of two halves, and on a bright London afternoon in September 2001, Tottenham and Man Utd endorsed the accuracy of this cliché in a match that will be talked about until young men are old. Spurs, keen to capitalise on United's uncertain start to the season, began brightly and took a 2-0 lead with goals from Dean Richards and Les Ferdinand. United were a shambles in defence and it was no surprise when, two minutes before half-time, Spurs claimed a third goal through Christian Ziege.

The heat from Alex Ferguson's team talk must have curdled the milk in the half-time tea. His practical response was to switch Irwin with Silvestre for more pace on the left flank, with Solskjaer providing a third attacker at Butt's expense. The effect was dramatic. Once Cole's header had reduced the deficit in the first minute after the break, Spurs played as if hypnotised. Blanc scored from a corner, and then Van Nistelrooy's head restored parity. United sensed Tottenham's anxiety and went for the kill. Solskjaer and Scholes combined sweetly for Veron to put them ahead 4-3 then, with four minutes remaining, Beckham hammered an emphatic swerving shot past a shell-shocked Sullivan to complete the greatest turnaround in Premier League history.

SCORERS **Tottenham:** Richards, Ferdinand, Ziege
United: Cole, Blanc, Van Nistelrooy, Veron, Beckham

EVENT: FA Premier League, White Hart Lane, 29 September 2001

TOTTENHAM (Man: Glenn Hoddle)		MAN. UTD. (Man: Alex Ferguson)	
1 Sullivan	7 Freund	1 Barthez	7 Butt
2 Richards	8 Anderton	2 G Neville	8 Veron
3 King	9 Poyet	3 Irwin	9 Cole
4 Perry	10 Ferdinand	4 Johnsen	10 Van Nistelrooy
5 Taricco	11 Sheringham	5 Blanc	
6 Ziege		6 Beckham	11 Scholes

Beckham celebrates becoming the game's eighth (and final) scorer.

- For £8 m new signing Dean Richards, it was a bitter-sweet debut. His move from Southampton produced a goal after eight minutes. If only it was a game of one half.

- For Teddy Sheringham, the game was a particular embarrassment. He had moved back to Spurs from United in the close season and was team captain for the day.

- One Spurs fan watched the second half with horror. He had bet £10,000 on a home win at half-time. The odds were 1-16.

- Hoddle was forthright: 'It looks like a Jekyl and Hyde performance from both sides.' Unfortunately it was his players who swallowed the wrong potion at half-time.

Garra

'OTHER COUNTRIES HAVE THEIR HISTORY, Uruguay has its football.' It's not known who first said this, or even if they said it at all, but it's a quote Uruguayans often use to explain the importance of the national football team to the inhabitants of their tiny nation.

Modern football enthusiasts have a tendency to overlook the abilities of players from earlier generations. For that reason it is often forgotten that for 30 years Uruguay were the undisputed daddies of world football. During their period of supremacy their 'garra' (a word used to signify determination, collective belief and strength of purpose) carried them over some significant hurdles.

In 1930 they came from behind to beat Argentina in the first World Cup Final (four of the selected players are from the 1930 team: Nasazzi, Jose Andrade, Scarone and Cea). Twenty years later in the Maracana they defeated Brazil 2–1 in the decisive match of the competition. In 1954 they came up against the Mighty Magyars in the semi-finals and, even with a weakened team, pushed the Hungarians all the way, eventually going down 4–2 in a fantastic match. Since those days Uruguay have had good players rather than good teams, and their 'garra' has too often mutated from grit and determination into spite and violence.

Managers: Alberto Suppici (1930s) and Juan Lopez (1950s)

Key Players
Roque Maspoli (G) Jose Nasazzi (D) Jose Santamaria (D)
Obdulio Varela (D) Jose Andrade (M) Victor Andrade (M)
Alcide Ghiggia (W) Julio Cesar Abbadie (W) Juan Schiaffino (F)
Pedro Cea (F) Hector Scarone (F) Omar Miguez (F)

June 26, 1954, Uruguay's keeper Maspoli breaks up an England attack during the 1954 World Cup. Uruguay won the match 4–2.

◁⍣ Ghiggia was a brilliant winger, blessed with pace, skill and clinical finishing ability. He overshadowed the great Schiaffino in the 1950 tournament, scoring the winner in the final.

◁⍣ Ghiggia's successor, Abbadie, was a more than decent replacement. Another quick, goalscoring winger he, along with Varela and Miguez, missed the semi-final against Hungary.

◁⍣ Centre-forward Miguez played in 1950 and 1954, scoring eight goals in the Finals. Though a top-class finisher, he was eclipsed by the genius of Schiaffino and Ghiggia.

◁⍣ Victor Andrade (of the 1950s team) was the nephew of Jose Andrade. Jose was one of the first successful black players, some years before Leonidas made his impact for Brazil.

Garrincha

Brazil

MANUEL DOS SANTOS FRANCISCO, otherwise known as Garrincha, was like a character from a fairytale. Born into poverty, and with a disability that meant his legs were bowed in opposite directions, he somehow managed to become one of the most feared attackers in the history of the game. Great balance and superb close control made him a deadly dribbler, and he was the first of the great Brazilian players to perfect the 'banana' shot.

He was 24 before he forced his way into the national side, but his exploits in three World Cups, particularly the successful 1958 and 1962 campaigns, earned him his place in Brazilian folklore. Perhaps his greatest moment was in 1962 when, after Pelé had bowed out of the tournament with injury, he took on the responsibility of leading the Brazilian attack. Garrincha destroyed England in the quarter-finals, then did the same to the violent hosts Chile in the semis and, despite his sending-off late in that game, he was allowed to appear in the final where he collected his second winner's medal. Unlike most modern Brazilian players, Garrincha played his domestic football in his home country, notably with Botafogo, whose rivalry with Pelé's Santos was a feature of the era.

VITAL STATISTICS

Place of Birth: Pau Grande, Brazil
Date of Birth: 28 October 1933
Died: 20 January 1983   Caps: 50 (Brazil)
Goals (International): 13   Clubs: Botafogo, Santos, Corinthians, Flamengo, Bangu, Portuguesa Santista, Olaria, AJ Barranquilla, Red Star Paris
Appearances: Club (Botafogo): 581   Goals: Club (Botafogo): 232
Trophies: BLT 1964, 1965; WorC 1958, 1962

LEGEND RATING

Achievement	9
Skill	10
Teamwork	8
Passion	8
Personality	9
Overall Legend Rating	**44**

- Garrincha means 'Little Bird', although not many defenders caught this pigeon!
- Garrincha wasn't a stranger to scandal. He had well-publicised pay rows with Botafogo, got in trouble with the tax authorities, and left his wife and eight children for a singer.
- When Brazil fell to Hungary in the 1966 World Cup it was Garrincha's first defeat in the yellow shirt in 60 games. No team ever defeated Brazil when Garrincha and Pelé were in the side.
- A fondness for the good life led to Garrincha's untimely death, aged only 49.
- Garrincha announced himself emphatically, scoring a hat-trick on his debut for Botafogo in 1953.

Gascoigne, Paul

Newcastle United, Tottenham Hotpsur, Rangers, England

IT IS A SAD FACT that the most talented footballer of his generation has also been the most self-destructive. 'He wears a No 10 jersey. I thought it was his position but it turns out to be his IQ,' said George Best in 1992 – and Georgie knew a drunken waster when he saw one. Gascoigne's excesses ranged from the endearingly playful to the crass and unpalatable, but his football, when fit, was sublime.

Blessed with superb control, Gascoigne also had a deceptive change of pace, a terrific shot and great vision. He could turn a game in an instant against opponents of the highest quality. The stunning free-kick he crashed past David Seaman in the 1991 FA Cup

semi-final and the cheeky goal against Scotland at Euro 96 stand out as two of his finest moments.

Despite his poor fitness and dodgy temperament, clubs queued up to sign him. Newcastle, Spurs, Lazio and Rangers all saw glimpses of Gascoigne at his most inspired, but later, notably at Middlesbrough and Everton, the physio saw a lot more of him than the fans.

In January 2003, Gazza appeared at desperation point. His signing by Gansu Tianma, then bottom of the Chinese second division, as player and coach, was almost certainly an ignominious end to his playing career.

VITAL STATISTICS

Place of Birth: Gateshead, England

Date of Birth: 27 May 1967

Died: n/a Caps: 57 (England) Goals (International): 10

Clubs: Newcastle United, Tottenham, Lazio, Rangers, Middlesbrough, Everton, Burnley

Appearances: Club (All Matches): 378

Goals: Club (All Matches): 81

Trophies: FAC 1991; SLT 1996, 1997; SFAC 1996

LEGEND RATING

Achievement	6
Skill	10
Teamwork	8
Passion	9
Personality	8
Overall Legend Rating	41

- 1990. Sports Personality Of The Year after fine performances in the World Cup, including well-documented tears after earning the booking that would have kept him out of the final.
- The reckless tackle that saw him carried off with a damaged knee in the 1991 Cup final delayed his move to Italy by a year and cost Spurs about £2 m in transfer fees.
- Once asked if he had a message for Norway prior to a World Cup qualifier, Gazza replied 'F*** off!'
- Gazza's best mate and drinking buddy, Jimmy 'Five Bellies' Gardner became a short-lived, cult micro-celebrity.
- He reached number two in the charts in 1990 with a reworking of Lindisfarne's Geordie anthem, 'Fog On The Tyne'.

Game of Two Halves

Tottenham Hotspur 3 Manchester United 5, 2001

IT IS OFTEN SAID that football is a game of two halves, and on a bright London afternoon in September 2001, Tottenham and Man Utd endorsed the accuracy of this cliché in a match that will be talked about until young men are old. Spurs, keen to capitalise on United's uncertain start to the season, began brightly and took a 2-0 lead with goals from Dean Richards and Les Ferdinand. United were a shambles in defence and it was no surprise when, two minutes before half-time, Spurs claimed a third goal through Christian Ziege.

The heat from Alex Ferguson's team talk must have curdled the milk in the half-time tea. His practical response was to switch Irwin with Silvestre for more pace on the left flank, with Solskjaer providing a third attacker at Butt's expense. The effect was dramatic. Once Cole's header had reduced the deficit in the first minute after the break, Spurs played as if hypnotised. Blanc scored from a corner, and then Van Nistelrooy's head restored parity. United sensed Tottenham's anxiety and went for the kill. Solskjaer and Scholes combined sweetly for Veron to put them ahead 4-3 then, with four minutes remaining, Beckham hammered an emphatic swerving shot past a shell-shocked Sullivan to complete the greatest turnaround in Premier League history.

SCORERS: **Tottenham:** Richards, Ferdinand, Ziege
United: Cole, Blanc, Van Nistelrooy, Veron, Beckham

EVENT: FA Premier League, White Hart Lane, 29 September 2001

TOTTENHAM
(Man: Glenn Hoddle)

1	Sullivan	7	Freund
2	Richards	8	Anderton
3	King	9	Poyet
4	Perry	10	Ferdinand
5	Taricco	11	Sheringham
6	Ziege		

MAN. UTD.
(Man: Alex Ferguson)

1	Barthez	7	Butt
2	G Neville	8	Veron
3	Irwin	9	Cole
4	Johnsen	10	Van Nistelrooy
5	Blanc	11	Scholes
6	Beckham		

Beckham celebrates becoming the game's eighth (and final) scorer.

◁ᴶᴼ For £8 m new signing Dean Richards, it was a bitter-sweet debut. His move from Southampton produced a goal after eight minutes. If only it was a game of one half.

◁ᴶᴼ For Teddy Sheringham, the game was a particular embarrassment. He had moved back to Spurs from United in the close season and was team captain for the day.

◁ᴶᴼ One Spurs fan watched the second half with horror. He had bet £10,000 on a home win at half-time. The odds were 1-16.

◁ᴶᴼ Hoddle was forthright: 'It looks like a Jekyl and Hyde performance from both sides.' Unfortunately it was his players who swallowed the wrong potion at half-time.

Gemmill, Archie

Derby County, Nottingham Forest, Scotland

HE WAS SHORT, stocky, balding, lacked pace and could easily have been mistaken for the secret, long-lost brother of Poland's Grzegorz Lato. In fact, on the face of it, Archie Gemmill didn't seem to have a lot going for him. But that did not stop him becoming one of the finest British midfield players of the 1970s.

Brian Clough and Peter Taylor were not bad judges, spotting Gemmill during a spying mission at Preston, and wasted no time bringing the diminutive playmaker to Derby County. At the Baseball Ground the young Scot flourished, his tireless running, tenacity and vision helping bring the Rams their first-ever First Division title. No

player was more inspirational, particularly when the going got tough. When Clough and Taylor moved on to Nottingham Forest, Gemmill joined them. More title glory followed at the City Ground, although Forest's two biggest triumphs, the European Cup victories of 1979 and 1980, were both in his absence. Gemmill had been injured in the 1979 European Cup semi-finals and, though he felt fit enough to play in the final, Clough left him on the bench. The decision so incensed Gemmill that he left for Birmingham the following season. Gemmill's passion and skill served Scotland well – his performances in the 1978 World Cup were deserving of better support from his abject colleagues.

VITAL STATISTICS

Place of Birth: Pailsey, Scotland

Date of Birth: 24 March 1947

Died: n/a **Caps:** 43 (Scotland) **Goals (International):** 8

Clubs: St Mirren, Preston North End, Derby County, Nottingham Forest, Birmingham City, Wigan Athletic

Appearances: Club (League: for Derby County): 261

Goals: Club (League: for Derby County): 17

Trophies: LT 1972, 1975, 1978; EC 1979

LEGEND RATING

Achievement	7
Skill	7
Teamwork	8
Passion	10
Personality	7
Overall Legend Rating	**39**

- Clough was so keen to capture Gemmill for Derby that he threatened to sleep in the car outside Gemmill's house until he signed. He ended up staying the night ... and got his man.
- In 1978 Gemmill scored the best goal of the World Cup Finals, dribbling through the entire Dutch defence to give Scotland a 3-2 win.
- 'Come on, let's take this lot. They cannae f***in' play.' Gemmill's assessment of UEFA Cup opponents Servette.
- Gemmill has since returned to Derby as the club's European scout.
- His son Scott is a chip off the old block, a current member of Everton's midfield.

MOST MODERN SUPPORTERS remember the 1970 team as the apotheosis of Brazilian football, but older supporters often claim that this was Brazil's second incarnation of greatness. Their first was in 1958. The World Cup Finals of that year were held in Sweden, and began with no clear favourites. Brazil had stuttered through qualification, and were thought of as a talented but disorganised side. That perception was quickly changed, though. In a flurry of attacking football, Brazil blew away the opposition, winning both the semi-final and final 5-2. The Brazilians played a new 4-4-2/4-2-4 system with two hard-working wingers supporting two forwards.

They chopped and changed the side throughout the tournament, and yet the end result was always the same: dazzling, winning football. The revelation of the tournament was Pelé, a 17-year-old whose talent and maturity astonished in equal measure. The strolling Didi was also a huge influence, waltzing his way through 90 minutes scarcely drawing a breath.

By the 1962 Finals Brazil were a settled and confident side who started the competition as clear favourites – and, despite an early injury to Pelé, they justified the bookmakers' faith in them, crushing the Czechs 3-1 in the final.

Manager: Vicente Feola

Key Players
Gylmar (G) Nilton Santos (D) Djalma Santos (D)
Didi (M) Zagallo (W) Garrincha (M) Pelé (F)
Mazzola – aka Jose Altafini (F) Vava (F)

World Cup Final, Stockholm, 1958. Swedish keeper Svensson dives in vain during his team's 5-2 defeat.

▸ Garrincha was a big influence in the latter stages of the 1958 tournament – a deputation of players, led by Nilton Santos demanded his inclusion. He saved his finest displays for 1962, when he was brought in as cover following an injury to Pelé.

▸ Both Nilton and Djalma Santos played in the 1958 and 1962 Finals. For the 1958 final Djalma was drafted in to combat the Swedish wingers Skoglund and Hamrin, forcing the unlucky de Sordi to miss out.

▸ Gylmar was probably the best keeper the Brazilians have ever had.
▸ The 1958 quarter-final against Wales was Mazzola's last game for Brazil. Reverting to his birth name, Jose Altafini, he represented his adopted country, Italy, in the 1962 Finals.

Genius, Part 2

THEY WERE PROBABLY the best football team ever. The fact that their goalkeeper would have struggled to make it as a park footballer, and that the rest of their defence was unconvincing at best, is irrelevant. When they got the ball they kept it. The movement and industry of the midfield and forwards was phenomenal, and those frail backs suddenly looked a whole lot better coming out to support the attacks.

1966 had been a hiccup, with Brazil eliminated in the group stage for the only time after the Portuguese cynically hacked Pelé out of the tournament. Now the great man was looking for a last hurrah on the big stage. Playing deeper than in the Finals of 1958 and 1962, he was the fulcrum of Brazil's play alongside the strolling Gerson, and the bustling, moustachioed Rivelino. The ball was played at speed with uncanny precision; man-marking was impossible as the flicks and tricks took out defenders with ease, and when the final ball was delivered, there was always Jairzinho or the selfless Tostao to receive. Four years later only Jairzinho and Rivelino remained, albeit with a better defence. Their football was disappointingly cautious, and they were easily brushed aside by the Dutch.

Manager: Mario Zagallo

Key Players
Carlos Alberto (D) Gerson (M) Rivelino (M) Pelé (M/F)
Jairzinho (F)

Trophies
WorC 1970 (Won World Cup for third time and kept Jules Rimet Trophy)

↖ Considering many of the Brazilians were heavy smokers, their fitness was impressive. Ignore the rose-tinted memories of them walking the ball around; these guys were like fluttering ribbons off the ball.

↖ Brazil's last goal in the final was not their only great goal of the tournament. Against Uruguay in the semi-final they scored three peaches: a one-two and finish from Clodoaldo; a tasty end to a passing move from Jairzinho; and a net-buster from Rivelino.

↖ Brazil's goalkeeping problems have never really gone away. Felix was awful, Waldir Peres an embarrassment in the great 1982 team, and Taffarel, the keeper throughout the 1990s, was only a marginal improvement.

Gentile, Claudio

Juventus, Italy

IF YOU WERE TO SELECT an all-time World XI from just two nations, Brazil could supply the forwards and most of the midfield, but the defence would have to be all Italian. And Claudio Gentile would have to be in it. Like all the best Italian defenders, he was comfortable at full-back, centre-half or sweeper. Gentile's reading of the game was such that he always seemed to appear in the right place at the most opportune moment; desperate lunges and last-ditch tackles just weren't his style. Intimidation, on the other hand, most definitely was.

In domestic football, like Roberto Bettega, Gentile was Juventus through and through, winning six Serie A titles in his 11 seasons

with the Turin giants. For Italy, his career highlight was an obvious one: the 1982 World Cup. Although Rossi's goals grabbed the headlines in the later stages, it was their back line, marshalled by Zoff and Gentile, that prevented an early flight home. (Italy's dismal group performances saw them scrape through with three draws, including an embarrassing 1-1 with Cameroon.) Sparkling victories over Argentina, Brazil and West Germany ensured they scaled Everest the hard way. Gentile played in every game.

VITAL STATISTICS

Place of Birth: Libya, Tripoli

Date of Birth: 27 September 1953

Died: n/a Caps: 71 (Italy) Goals (International): 1

Clubs: Arona, Varesse, Juventus, Fiorentina

Appearances: Club (League): 473

Goals: Club (League): 14

Trophies: SA 1975, 1977, 1978, 1981, 1982, 1984, 1986; UEFAC 1977; CWC 1984; WorC 1982

Gentile gets acquainted with Brazil's Zico at the 1982 World Cup.

LEGEND RATING

Achievement	9
Skill	8
Teamwork	9
Passion	8
Personality	6
Overall Legend Rating	**40**

- A World Cup winner in 1982, Gentile also played in the 1978 Finals, appearing in all six games as Italy finished fourth.
- Goals were a responsibility Gentile was content to leave with others. He failed to score in his last six seasons in Serie A.
- Best game? The 1982 World Cup clash with Argentina. Gentile's shadowing of Maradona verged on GBH, but a niggled Diego was subdued.
- Gentile's 13 games in World Cup Finals brought only two defeats.
- He was appointed coach of the Italian U-21s in December 2000.

Gento, Francisco

THERE HAVE ALWAYS BEEN quick players. Take Jackie Milburn, Jimmy Greaves and Ryan Giggs – all really quick and, it should be said, very good. Then there are the really, really quick players, like Tony Daley and Franz Carr who, to be honest, weren't very good at all. But occasionally a player comes along who is both really, really quick and very good. One such was Francisco Gento, the flying Spanish winger.

Blessed with frightening pace generated by his immense thighs (Jimmy Greaves considered him the fastest player he had ever seen), Gento also had great control, and could finish when called upon. Sadly, he was never seen at his best in the World Cup, but the European Cup was another matter. Gento was an integral component of the Real Madrid team that dominated the early years of the competition. Everyone remembers Di Stefano and Puskas, but it was Gento's pace that provided the team with that extra edge, especially when fed by the talented inside-left Rial. Even after five consecutive trophies, Gento wasn't done with the competition, returning for two more losing finals before winning for a sixth time in 1966. It was another 32 years before Real won the trophy again.

VITAL STATISTICS

Place of Birth: Guarnizo, Spain
Date of Birth: 22 October 1933
Died: n/a **Caps:** 43 (Spain) **Goals (International):** 5
Clubs: Nuevo Montana, Astillero, Rayo Cantabria, Real Santander, Real Madrid
Appearances: Club (Real Madrid): 605
Goals: Club (Real Madrid): 181
Trophies: EC 1956, 1957, 1958, 1959, 1960, 1966; PLA 1954, 1955, 1957, 1958, 1961, 1962, 1963, 1964, 1965, 1967, 1968, 1969

LEGEND RATING

Achievement	8
Skill	9
Teamwork	7
Passion	8
Personality	7
Overall Legend Rating	**39**

◁ Gento was always under pressure to maintain his form; Spain had another excellent left-winger in Atletico Madrid's Enrique Collar.
◁ Gento's six European Cup wins are still a record.
◁ Gento scored the winner in the 1958 European Cup final against Milan, in an unscheduled period of extra-time. This followed a goal in the previous year's final against Fiorentina.
◁ Twelve Spanish league titles wasn't a bad haul, either. Nor were his 800 appearances.
◁ Gento's Real career lasted 18 years (1953–71). Di Stefano, who joined the club in the same year, left four years before him.

Gers Decade

BEFORE 1986/87 being a Rangers fan meant living in the past. The title was a distant memory and Aberdeen were threatening to make the Old Firm irrelevant. Enter Graeme Souness. Although his combative style won him few friends outside Ibrox, particularly in the early days as player-manager, he deserves credit for ignoring the club's sectarian bigotry and picking players purely on ability. The effect was dramatic, as the Gers romped to nine straight Scottish titles.

They were not without their critics. Souness's policy of buying in players from outside Scotland led to Rangers being labelled an 'anglo' or foreign club. While it was true that imports were high, two of their best players were Scottish; Richard Gough formed a formidable partnership with Terry Butcher in central defence, while up front Ally McCoist wrote himself into the Scottish goalscoring record books.

The imported players were their prime inspiration. Paul Gascoigne, bought from Lazio, became a terrace hero but, despite his flickering genius, he was overshadowed by the brilliance of Brian Laudrup. Against the lesser lights in the SPL the Danish midfielder hardly broke sweat, and was their consistent performer in disappointing forays into the European Cup. After being Scotland's third club, Rangers reigned supreme. It took Celtic a decade to win back their crown.

Manager: Graeme Souness

Key Players
Graeme Souness Ally McCoist Brian Laudrup Richard Gough
Terry Butcher Paul Gascoigne Ian Durrant

Trophies
SLT 1990, 1991, 1992, 1993, 1994, 1995, 1996, 1997, 1999, 2000
SFAC 1992, 1993, 1996, 1999, 2000

◁◁ Rangers won nine successive Scottish championships (1989–97), equalling the record of Jock Stein's Celtic.

◁◁ Rangers' only poor record was their disciplinary one. Souness set the tone when he was sent off in his first match in charge.

◁◁ Despite being perennial entrants to the European Cup and later the Champions League, Rangers always struggled. One of their notable successes was a defeat of Leeds United in 1993.

◁◁ Before 1986/87 Rangers had gone nine years without a championship victory. And their record in the FA Cup wasn't much better, winning it only once in the 1980s.

◁◁ Other notable English signings included Chris Woods, Trevor Steven and Ray Wilkins. Oh, and Terry Hurlock. Whoops.

Giant Killers

CRAWFORD'S QUOTE SAYS IT ALL. For small clubs, struggling on meagre attendances with only the occasional local derby to lift the gloom, a major Cup scalp is talked about for years. Down the ages, the recipe for a giant-killing has remained the same. Combine a mudheap of a pitch, a freezing winter's afternoon and a ramshackle stadium jammed to the corner flags, and add complacent opposition who would rather be playing golf. Then sit back and watch the temperature rise. Yeovil Town and their famous sloping pitch created one of the biggest upsets, removing Sunderland in 1949. But the Mackems are just one of Yeovil's 17 league scalps – a record for a team outside the top four divisions. Scoring a goal in a Cup upset is a guaranteed ticket to enduring celebrity, even if it's the only achievement of note in your entire career. Ronnie Radford and Ricky George are still D-list celebrities more than 30 years after their strikes for Hereford knocked out Newcastle. Roy Essandoh answered an Internet advertisement to sign for Wycombe, scored the only goal to knock out Leicester in the 2001 quarter-final and promptly vanished. For technical ability, a clash between the world's best wins hands down. But for sheer excitement, nothing tops a Cup giant-killing.

'This was the match of a lifetime and a day I will never forget.'

Colchester hero Ray Crawford after their epic FA Cup win over Leeds in 1971

Top non-league giantkillers Yeovil Town fail on this occasion at home to Arsenal.

◄|► In the days before automatic promotion, many clubs achieved league status on the back of their giant-killing exploits. Peterborough, Hereford and Wimbledon all won promotion to the professional ranks this way.

◄|► Most giant killers win at home. Altrincham were the last non-leaguers to win at a top-flight ground, upsetting Birmingham 2–1 in 1986.

◄|► FA Cup giant killers rarely progress to the later stages but the League Cup has produced two Third Division winners – QPR and Swindon.

◄|► International shocks are rarer still. The USA's win over England in the 1950 World Cup was a shock of seismic proportions.

Giggs at the Gallop

Arsenal 1 Manchester United 2, 1999

TOWARDS THE END of an exhausting season, the last thing these two teams needed was for their FA Cup semi-final to extend to a replay, especially one that went to extra-time. But it did. And then the fun really started. Beckham had opened the scoring after 18 minutes, and Bergkamp's deflected second-half shot had squared things.

After Keane was dismissed the Arsenal pressure was relentless, and Gary Neville brought down Parlour in injury time – penalty. Schmeichel, not for the first time, came to United's rescue, saving Bergkamp's tame effort. In extra-time Arsenal continued to turn the screw against 10-man United, but it was the Old Trafford men who stole victory. Deep into injury time Ryan Giggs, who had been introduced as a sub just past the hour, collected the ball in his own half and sprinted forward. He evaded Vieira, swerved past Dixon, deceived Keown, brushed off another challenge from Dixon and thrashed the ball past the suddenly exposed Seaman. Giggs had the courage to take the game into his own hands and the skill to skip through the country's meanest defence. Pure and undiluted genius.

SCORERS: Arsenal: Bergkamp
Manchester United: Beckham, Giggs
EVENT: FA Cup semi-final replay, Villa Park, 14 April 1999

ARSENAL (Man: Arsène Wenger)		MANCHESTER UNITED (Man: Alex Ferguson)	
1 Seaman	8 Bergkamp	1 Schmeichel	8 Keane
2 Dixon	9 Anelka	2 Neville, G	9 Solskjaer
3 Winterburn	10 Vieira	3 Neville, P	10 Sheringham
4 Parlour	11 Petit	4 Butt	11 Blomqvist
5 Adams		5 Johnsen	
6 Keown		6 Stam	
7 Ljungberg		7 Beckham	

Giggs caps an incredible run by shooting the winner past Seaman.

◁))   This was one of two crucial matches in United's drive for the Treble; the other being the European Cup final. Both were games of memorable late drama and emotion.

◁))   Jesper Blomqvist was bought as cover for the injury-prone Giggs. Ironically, the Welshman's fitness has since improved while Blomqvist has had to resurrect his career at Everton after 18 months out with a knee injury.

◁))   It was a game of two remarkable goals. For the opener David Beckham drove a 30-yard dipper over David Seaman after a perfect tee-up from Teddy Sheringham.

◁))   The FA Cup final against Newcastle was an anti-climax. Newcastle froze, and United won at a canter.

Giggs, Ryan

Manchester United, Wales

THE PARALLEL GROWTH of Ryan Giggs and Manchester United since 1991 is no coincidence. The best left winger in British football burst on to the scene as a 17-year-old, scoring the only goal in a Manchester derby. Although success appeared to come easy, it is to his credit that the tabloid mud accurately thrown at his peers has never stuck. Nurtured and protected by Alex Ferguson he has developed into an indispensable player; only Roy Keane or David Beckham can claim a similar influence.

Like George Best, with whom he has often been compared, Giggs seems destined never to play at a major international tournament.

Wales again failed to qualify for the 2002 World Cup Finals, and there is a growing suspicion that Giggs is now more concerned with channelling his efforts into club football – indeed, his propensity for crying off with minor injuries before international fixtures has already prompted many fans to accuse of him of lacking commitment to his country.

Despite his loyalty to United over many seasons, indifferent form in 2002/3 provoked disquiet amongst some fans and rumours persisted of a move to Italy. He would be a tough act to follow.

VITAL STATISTICS

Place of Birth: Cardiff, Wales

Date of Birth: 29 November 1973

Died: n/a   Caps: 40 (Wales)

Goals (International): 8

Clubs: Manchester United   Appearances: Club (All Matches): 543

Goals: Club (All Matches): 116

Trophies: LC 1992; LT 1993; 1994, 1996, 1997, 1999, 2000, 2001, 2003; FAC 1994; 1996; 1999; EC 1999

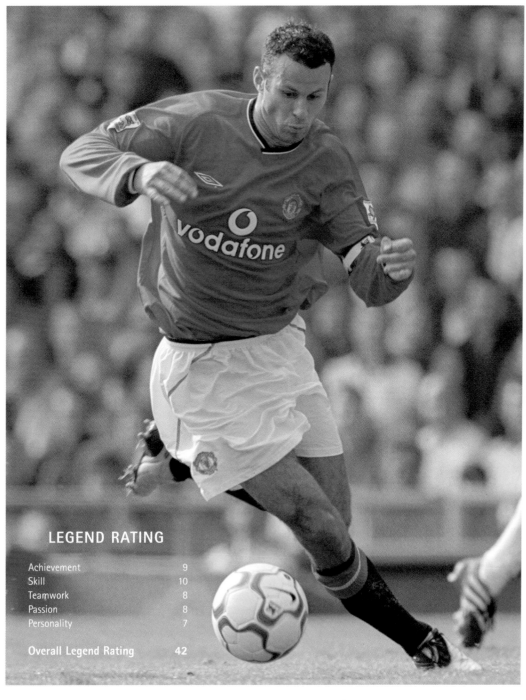

LEGEND RATING

Achievement	9
Skill	10
Teamwork	8
Passion	8
Personality	7
Overall Legend Rating	**42**

◁» He made his professional and full international debut at 17.

◁» He played for England schoolboys but adopted his mother's Welsh homeland. What would England now give for Giggs to fill a left-sided gap?

◁» He had won seven League titles before his 28th birthday.

◁» 1999. His best goal ever, a dribble from the half-way line, destroyed England's meanest club defence and won United the FA Cup semi-final against Arsenal.

◁» 2001. A great disciplinary record is blemished when Giggs was sent off for the first time in his career, as Welsh captain.

Giles, Michael John, 'Johnny'

Leeds United, Republic of Ireland

DON REVIE PAID Manchester United £35,000 for the young Irishman Johnny Giles in 1963. Revie had obviously seen something Sir Matt Busby had missed, and quickly converted Giles from outside-right to central midfield where, within a few years, he developed into the complete midfielder. A superbly accurate passer with great vision allied to a tough streak – the Leeds side of that era took no prisoners – he was rarely injured and became a key member of a great midfield: Bremner's aggression, Lorimer's explosive shooting, Gray's dribbling, and, at the core, Giles, prompting and coaxing those around him.

In 1973 Giles was introduced to management when he was appointed player-manager of the Republic of Ireland. He introduced a young Liam Brady and David O'Leary to international football, but his squad lacked the depth that Jack Charlton was to enjoy in the following decade. He remained in the post until 1980, by which time he'd had enough of management, having earlier endured a tough couple of years at West Bromwich Albion.

VITAL STATISTICS

Place of Birth: Dublin, Ireland
Date of Birth: 1940
Died: n/a Caps: 59 (Republic of Ireland)
Goals (International): 5
Clubs: Manchester United, Leeds United, West Bromwich Albion, Shamrock Rovers, Vancouver Whitecaps
Appearances: Club (League): 702
Goals: Club (League): 128
Trophies: LT 1969, 1974; FAC 1972; LC 1968; EUFAC 1968, 1971

LEGEND RATING

Achievement	7
Skill	8
Teamwork	9
Passion	7
Personality	6
Overall Legend Rating	**37**

◄)) He made his debut for the Republic at 18, scoring after 16 minutes against Sweden.

◄)) Giles is Nobby Stiles' brother-in-law.

◄)) He missed one penalty in his career, and scored 78.

◄)) Crucially, Giles missed the European Cup Winners' Cup final in 1973 when Leeds were robbed by AC Milan.

◄)) Giles on management: 'The government should issue a health warning to managers: the only certain thing is the sack.'

Glory Game

The Tottenham Hotspur Dream Team

IT REALLY WOULDN'T BE SPURS if they didn't have mesmerising attacking players and a mundane defence would it? Starting at the back they do have an all-time great in Jennings, but full-backs Stephen Carr (promising) and 'Nice One' Cyril Knowles (functional) would surely find George Best and Ryan Giggs a bit of a handful.

The choice of Sol Campbell might rankle, but loyalists Gary Mabbutt and Steve Perryman were just not that good. Dave Mackay wasn't really an orthodox centre-half but, on the basis of his spell at Derby, where he briefly occupied the position, he wins selection thus freeing up space in midfield where Spurs have traditionally enjoyed

an embarrassment of riches. Who to leave out? After much soul-searching it was Mullery and Gascoigne who had to settle for the bench, leaving Ardiles, Hoddle, Blanchflower and winger Jones to strut their stuff.

The choice of forwards was mouth-watering, with Bobby Smith, Alan Gilzean, Martin Chivers, Steve Archibald and Herr Klinsmann not even making the bench. Sheringham got the nod ahead of Lineker on the grounds of longevity, and our hunch that he would be a better foil for Jimmy Greaves.

Manager: Bill Nicholson

4-4-2

Pat Jennings (60s/70s)

Stephen Carr (90s) Sol Campbell (90s)
Dave Mackay (C) (60s) Cyril Knowles (60s)

Danny Blanchflower (50s/60s) Ossie Ardiles (80s)
Glenn Hoddle (80s) Cliff Jones (60s)

Jimmy Greaves (60s) Teddy Sheringham (90s)

Subs: Ted Ditchburn (G) (40s/50s) Alan Mullery (M) (60s) John White (M) (60s) Paul Gascoigne (M) (90s) Gary Lineker (F) (90s)

Spurs' mascot shows a balance worthy of Greaves himself.

◁ Cyril Knowles and Joe Kinnear were Spurs' full-backs for most of the 1970s.

◁ No one from the 1901 Cup winning side makes the team – Spurs were a non-league club at the time! This victory started the 'year ends in one' tradition. Trophies followed in 1921, 1951, 1961, 1971, 1981 and 1991. In 2001 Alan Sugar relinquished control of the club, which was a triumph of sorts.

◁ Stephen Carr missed most of the 2000/01 season with injury.

◁ Tottenham's first meeting with (Royal) Arsenal was abandoned 15 minutes from the end 'owing to darkness'.

◁ Steve Perryman made the most appearances for Tottenham, but was never more than a competent honest pro.

Glory Glory Man United

AS THE DARK MEMORIES of the Munich air crash receded, a revitalised Manchester United swung into the 1960s with a rebuilt team and new stars. Crash survivors Bill Foulkes and Bobby Charlton were retained, with Foulkes forming a redoubtable defensive barrier alongside David Sadler, while Charlton formed an effective midfield partnership with arch-stroller, Paddy Crerand. Up front Denis 'The Law-man' Law was racking up the goals, and George Best was in his pomp.

Marking Best was like trying to catch soap in the bath. Twice in the European Cup he destroyed Benfica; first in the 1966 quarter-final, and then again two years later in the Final at Wembley. But the big prize represented the beginning of the end for this United side. The team was ageing and Busby, memories of the air crash still fresh in his mind, had been looking to bury ghosts rather than build for the next decade. The following year they suffered the indignity of losing the First Division title to rivals Man City, presaging a few years of mediocrity before their tumble into Division Two in 1974. Busby had retired by then so didn't preside over the club's decline. Arguments rage over which is the best United side ever: the original Busby Babes, the 1968 European champions, or Ferguson's 1999 Treble winners? A debate that will continue long after we have kicked our last ball.

Manager: Matt Busby

Key Players:
Alex Stepney (G) Bill Foulkes (D) Tony Dunne (D)
Paddy Crerand (M) Bobby Charlton (M/F)
Dennis Law (F) George Best (genius)

Trophies
LT 1967 EC 1968 (First English side to win European Cup)

Law, Charlton and Best show off awards to a new generation at Old Trafford.

⇨ Foulkes and Sadler got United to Wembley for their encounter with destiny, scoring a goal apiece in the second half in Madrid to see off Real.

⇨ Some believe that had Busby replaced his ageing stars and relied on Best, he might have maintained the success and saved the errant maverick's soul.

⇨ Law on Crerand: 'I used to say he was a great asset to television, because they didn't need slow-motion when he was on the ball.'

⇨ Law was leading scorer in both United's title-winning seasons in the 1960s but, playing for Man City in 1974, he scored the goal that sent United into Division Two.

Goal!!!

EVERY SEASON there are special goals; curled free kicks, overhead kicks, almighty 30-yarders, ribbons of passing finished with a tap-in. But every now and then one stands out from the crowd – a goal tinged with genius. Le Tissier, Beckham, Bergkamp – all seem incapable of scoring boring goals, probably because they are the sort of players who have innate confidence in their ability to do outrageous things.

But, occasionally, players with more parochial gifts produce crackers too. Blackpool's Micky Walsh was a nondescript Division Two player who earned his place in history with a blistering strike,

while Justin Fashanu secured himself a £1 m move to Nottingham Forest on the basis of a stunning turn and volley for Norwich against Liverpool in the 1980s. Perhaps the most memorable of all was the 'donkey kick' goal scored by Coventry's Ernie Hunt against Everton in the 1970s; Hunt cracked a dipping volley over the wall and into the net after his team-mate, Willie Carr, had flicked the ball up to him with his heels. Great concept, even better execution.

> 'I went up to him afterwards, shook his hand and called him a b*****d.'
>
> Neil Sullivan, then Wimbledon goalkeeper, after David Beckham beat him from the half-way line

Zidane's winning wonder goal against Bayer Leverkusen in the 2002 Champions League final.

◁ The best goal involving Beckham was scored by Paul Scholes; an edge-of-the-box volley direct from a pinpoint Beckham corner.

◁ Dennis Bergkamp once filled the top three positions in the *MOTD* Goal of the Month competition. A special effort against Leicester eventually won goal of the season, but a sand wedge against Bayern Leverkusen in 2002 wasn't far behind.

◁ Trevor Sinclair is known for spectacular acrobatics; an overhead kick playing for QPR flew into the net from all of 25 yards. He's done it consistently enough since to prove it was no fluke.

◁ Personal favourite? Frank Worthington teeing the ball up, flicking it over his head between two defenders and volleying it in for Bolton against Ipswich in 1978.

Golden Gods

The Wolverhampton Wanderers Dream Team

NO ARGUMENTS HERE about the manager. As the man who led Wolves to three league titles in the 1950s, Stan Cullis had very little competition. He also makes it into this team as a player, forming a fierce central defensive pairing with Billy Wright. Peter Broadbent and Ron Flowers in midfield, and Jimmy Mullen, the tricky outside-left, also played in that fine team, as did Bert Slater and the other wide player, Johnny Hancocks. Good players in a strong and disciplined team, they brought the kind of success current Wolves fans ache for.

Mike Bailey was a stalwart and captain of the side in the late 1960s and 1970s, and Kenny Hibbitt was the best of a decent

midfield in that era. This later era of top-flight football featured some powerful forwards. Andy Gray, a folk hero at Wolves, plays alongside the rampaging Steve Bull. 'The Tipton Terror' won 13 caps for England, despite never playing in the top division, but his loyalty to Wanderers probably did him no favours; a move to a better side would have improved his touch and enhanced his performances on the international stage, where he tended to look clumsy and out of his depth. This team serves as a painful reminder of how little Wolves have achieved in recent years. At last, in Dave Jones, they have a manager who looks capable of bringing back some pride to Molineux.

Manager: Stan Cullis

4-4-2

Bert Williams (40s/50s)

Bill Slater (50s) Stan Cullis (30s/40s)
Billy Wright (C) (50s/60s) Mike Bailey (60s/70s)

Kenny Hibbitt (70s) Peter Broadbent (50s/60s)
Ron Flowers (50s/60s) Jimmy Mullen (40s/50s)

Derek Dougan (60s/70s) Steve Bull (80s/90s)

Subs: Phil Parkes (G) (70s) Tommy Galley (D/M/F) (30s)
Johnny Hancocks (W) (50s) John Richards (F) (70s) Andy Gray (F) (80s)

Woolly-Bully, The Tipton Terror.

◁▷ The midfielders may not be household names, but they were all first-rate players. Flowers, an unheralded rock, won 49 caps, Mullen 12 and Broadbent seven. Far worse players than Hibbitt won caps for England.

◁▷ Bert Williams played for Wolves immediately after the war, and was good enough to win 24 caps for England.

◁▷ Reserve strikers Dougan and Richards played together in the early 1970s; Richards scored the winner in the 1974 League Cup final.

◁▷ Gray won most of his 20 Scottish caps while with Wolves, and his goal brought Wolves their last major trophy, the 1980 League Cup.

Gough, Richard

IN THE MID-1980s, Rangers were at an all-time low. Years of watching Celtic rattle up trophies throughout the 1960s and 1970s, then to see Aberdeen supplant them in the 1980s was hard to bear for the blue half of Glasgow.

It was Graeme Souness's arrival that started a run of nine consecutive league championships, the equal of Celtic's coveted record. His most important signing was one of Scotland's most cultured central defenders and a natural captain. Dundee United had already recognised his worth by refusing to sell him to an SPL rival, but following a year's sabbatical with Spurs, Rangers got their man.

Initially a right-back at Ibrox, his conversion continued a Scottish central defensive pedigree that saw Gough elevated to the status of bygone defensive pillars such as Alan Hansen, Alex McLeish and Willie Miller. His departure from Glasgow at 35 appeared to be the end, but his fitness and appetite for the game made him good enough to play in the English Premier League at 38 with Everton, before he finally retired in 2001.

VITAL STATISTICS

Place of Birth: Stockholm, Sweden
Date of Birth: 5 April 1962
Died: n/a Caps: 61 (Scotland) Goals (International): 6
Clubs: Dundee United, Tottenham, Rangers, Kansas City Wizz, San Jose Clash, Nottingham Forest, Everton
Appearances: Club (League): 590 Goals: Club (League): 48
Trophies: SLT 1983, 1989, 1990, 1991, 1992, 1993, 1994, 1995, 1996, 1997; SFAC 1992, 1993, 1996

LEGEND RATING

Achievement 8
Skill 7
Teamwork 8
Passion 9
Personality 6

Overall Legend Rating 38

↙ The only Rangers player to win nine consecutive league winner's medals in the great teams of the 1980s and early 1990s.
↙ 1987. Scored the winning goal in 1987 Cup Final. Unluckily for Gough, it was a deflection at the wrong end.

↙ Gough attended a trial for Rangers at 18, but was turned away. Seven years later it cost them £1.1 m to buy him back and rectify their error.
↙ Born in Stockholm to a Swedish mother and an English father

(who played for England), Gough was brought up in South Africa. Nonetheless, he remains a true Scottish legend.
↙ 1997. Emotional end-of-season 'farewell' to Ibrox after announcing a move to the US, only to return in October.

Graham, George

SCOTTISH MIDFIELD PLAYMAKER, George Graham was the pivot of the 1971 Arsenal double-winning side. His performances at his next club, Manchester United, were generally considered to be a disappointment and Graham's playing career was judged past its zenith.

A four-year spell as manager of Millwall led to his appointment as manager of his old club, Arsenal, in 1986. Nine years of consistent success followed, as Graham built the formidable outfit that became known as 'boring, boring Arsenal'. A solid defence, hard-working midfield and quick strikers became legend for nicking games 1-0 after their opponents had foundered on their obduracy.

Unfortunately sly victories weren't the only thing George pocketed, and he resigned as Arsenal manager in disgrace when he was found guilty of taking cash as a sweetener in two transfer deals.

Banned for 12 months, Graham returned as manager of Leeds, and rapidly began rebuilding the Yorkshire club in his own image. Despite relative success he was tempted back to London by the vacant manager's job at Spurs. Graham and Tottenham never sat easily and he was sacked in 2001 to make way for Glenn Hoddle's return. Graham remains a cogent and cool analyst of the game, making frequent appearances as a TV pundit.

VITAL STATISTICS

Place of Birth: Bargeddie, Fife
Date of Birth: 30 November 1944
Died: n/a   Caps: 12 (Scotland)
Goals (International): 3
Clubs: As Player: Aston Villa, Chelsea, Arsenal, Man United, Portsmouth, Crystal Palace; As Manager: Millwall, Arsenal, Leeds United, Tottenham Hotspur
Trophies: LT 1989, 1991; FAC 1993; LC 1987, 1993, 1999; CWC 1994

LEGEND RATING

Achievement	9
Tactical Awareness	9
Motivation	7
Transfer Dealing and Team Selection	7
Personality	6
Overall Legend Rating	**38**

Graham's blazer was trademark but Spurs' cockerel motif never suited him.

◁ Graham claimed the equaliser in the 1971 FA Cup final, but TV replays showed his heel did not make contact with the ball after team-mate Eddie Kelly's shot, and was denied credit for the goal.

◁ Graham's uncompromising discipline earned him the nicknames 'Ayatollah' and 'Gadaffi'. Internal discipline wasn't always mirrored on the pitch; Graham's tenure saw the start of the trend for on-field naughtiness that has dogged Arsenal in recent years.

◁ Arsenal became the first team to win both domestic cups in 1993, bizarrely playing the same team, Sheffield Wednesday, in both finals.

◁ In 1991 Graham's Arsenal conceded just 18 goals and lost only one game in winning the title.

Gray, Andy

Wolverhampton Wanderers, Aston Villa, Everton, Scotland

MEMORIES OF ANDY GRAY as a player conjure up images of a fearless battering ram throwing himself into the fray, diving in with his head amongst flailing feet. It was no wonder Gray was so often injured; few men have played the game with such scant regard for their own safety. Gray was not just a big bloke who put himself around, though. He was a prodigious header of the ball and, while not dazzling with the ball at his feet, his touch was still the equal of most of his contemporaries.

All his clubs enjoyed successful periods with him as their spearhead in attack, but it was his spell at Everton that brought him the rewards he deserved. Toffees boss Howard Kendall took a gamble purchasing Gray (at the time many regarded him to be past his best, and with dodgy knees to boot) but his partnership with his young countryman and acolyte, Graeme Sharp, provided the goals that brought the title back to Goodison. The purchase of Gary Lineker two years later saw Gray exit to Aston Villa, and retirement soon followed. Through the last decade Gray has worked as a pundit for Sky television, where his enthusiasm and entertaining use of high-tech graphics have done much to help the Rupert Murdoch-funded operation overcome initial antagonism towards their franchise.

VITAL STATISTICS

Place of Birth: Glasgow, Scotland
Date of Birth: 30 November 1955
Died: n/a Caps: 20 (Scotland) Goals (International): 6
Clubs: Dundee United, Aston Villa, Wolves, Everton, West Bromwich Albion, Rangers, Cheltenham Town
Appearances: Club (All Matches): 593
Goals: Club (All Matches): 202
Trophies: LC 1980; FAC 1984; LT 1985; CWC 1985; SLT 1989

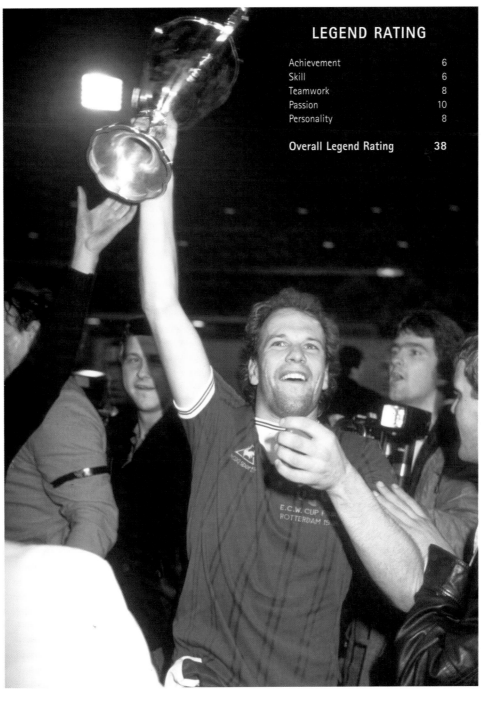

LEGEND RATING

Achievement	6
Skill	6
Teamwork	8
Passion	10
Personality	8
Overall Legend Rating	**38**

Gray shows off the European Cup Winner's Cup for Everton in 1985.

◄)) Gray and Sharp scored the goals that won the 1984 FA Cup Final.
◄)) He scored the winner for Wolves in 1980 League Cup final.
◄)) Voted PFA Player of the Year and Young Player of the Year, 1977.

◄)) Wolves paid Villa a then British record fee of £1,469,000 for Gray in 1979.
◄)) Gray was a surprising omission from Ally McLeod's 1978 World Cup squad. Oh, how they missed him.

FOR ALL ARSENAL'S modern flair and expensive foreign talent, the bedrock of this team is steeped in history. Herbert Chapman's team was Arsenal's first great one, sweeping all before them in the 1930s, and it's from this side that we have selected both full-backs, Eddie Hapgood and George Male (Dixon and Winterburn have racked up the appearances but don't possess the same pedigree).

In central defence, the newer guard holds sway. Both O'Leary and Adams possess the talent and leadership, and have the happy knack of rising to the big occasion. The midfield combination is both a league of nations and a rock of ages. Armstrong's inclusion is not just for his loyalty, but for the accuracy of his crossing, which should lend this team an extra dimension. Vieira and Alex James are a fascinating blend, and Cliff Bastin would provide goal-scoring support for the two strikers. Not that the front two would be liable to dry up. Drake's direct approach and Henry's subtle skills would always boost the goal difference – the pair provide a dream combination of aerial power and blinding pace.

Manager: Herbert Chapman
4-4-2

Pat Jennings (70s/80s)

George Male (30s) Tony Adams (80s/90s) David O'Leary (70s/80s)
Eddie Hapgood (C) (30s)

George Armstrong (60s/70s) Patrick Vieira (90s) Alex James (30s)
Cliff Bastin (30s)

Ted Drake (30s) Thierry Henry (90s/00s)

Subs: Bob Wilson (G) (60s/70s) Frank McLintock (D) (70s)
Liam Brady (M) (70s) Joe Mercer (M) (40s/50s)
Dennis Bergkamp (F) (90s)

◄ Hardest man to leave out? Liam Brady. The man with the sweetest left foot ever seen at Highbury would undoubtedly play a part as a substitute.

◄ The sight of Pat Jennings in goal will continue to stick in the throat of any Spurs fan. Blame Keith Burkinshaw for selling him.

◄ Frank McLintock fails to make the first team despite captaining the 1971 double winners and collecting the Footballer of the Year award.

◄ Herbert Chapman is the least contentious choice of manager. Not only did his Arsenal team win three successive titles, he set new standards in tactics, professionalism and commercial awareness.

Greatest Game Ever?

Hungary 4 Uruguay 2 (aet), 1954

THE REIGNING CHAMPIONS against the favourites. Hungary had scored 21 goals in their first three matches, Uruguay a mere 13 (including four against a disappointing England), but both sides were missing key players, notably Puskas for Hungary and Varela for Uruguay. Yet still one sensed the game would provide thrills and spills aplenty.

Hungary dominated early on, taking a 2-0 lead early in the second half through Czibor and Hidegkuti, the second a wonderful diving header to finish a typically clinical move. In the last quarter of normal time Uruguay, driven on by the dribbling skills of their great

forward Juan Schiaffino, again showed the gutsy spirit that had brought them the trophy four years previously, and equalised with two goals from Hohberg, making his first appearance of the tournament. So to extra time, and with Schiaffino carrying a knock the Hungarians regained the upper hand. Pinpoint crosses from first Budai and then Bozsik found Sandor Kocsis, and the man they called 'Golden Head' duly put them away. Hungary were through to the final – and surely couldn't lose to a side they had beaten 8-3 in the group stage.

SCORERS: Hungary: Czibor, Hidegkuti, Kocsis (2)
Uruguay: Hohberg (2)
EVENT: World Cup semi-final, Lausanne, 1954

HUNGARY		URUGUAY	
(Man: Gustav Sebes)		(Man: Juan Lopez)	
1 Grosics	8 Kocsis	1 Maspoli	8 Ambrois
2 Buzansky	9 Palotas	2 Santamaria	9 Schiaffino
3 Lantos	10 Hidegkuti	3 Martinez	10 Hohberg
4 Bozsik	11 Czibor	4 Andrade	11 Borges
5 Lorant		5 Carballo	
6 Zakarias		6 Cruz	
7 Budai		7 Souto	

Hidegkuti gets down and dirty in the Hungarian cause.

⟨⟩ Only three of the Uruguayan team had played in the 1950 final – Maspoli, Andrade and Schiaffino.

⟨⟩ Happily, concerns that the game would descend into a brawl like Hungary's quarter-final against Brazil proved ill-founded.

⟨⟩ Just as at the Olympics two years earlier, Kocsis scored in every round except the final.

⟨⟩ The Uruguayan number two is the same Santamaria who played at the heart of the great Real Madrid side later that decade.

⟨⟩ Hungary, of course, did lose the final, 3-2 to West Germany.

Greaves, Jimmy

Tottenham Hotspur, England

ONE OF THE GREAT GOAL SCORERS, Greaves scored at a similar rate to strikers of the 1930s in the more defensive 1960s and 1970s. Although small for a forward, at only 5 ft 8 in and 10 stones wet through, he was fast and had quicksilver feet.

The sight of Greaves dancing around defenders and smacking in yet another hat-trick was one of the treats of the time. Like many natural-born goal scorers he could be selfish, when he received possession he rarely had more than one thought on his mind, and if his team were under pressure he had a tendency to go missing. Greaves maintained his scoring record in internationals, but never really fired in World Cup Finals (only one goal in seven appearances). His greatest disappointment was missing the 1966 World Cup final; he started the tournament but got injured and was unable to win back his place from Geoff Hurst.

Greaves started drinking heavily at the end of his career, but recovered well and later formed a successful TV double-act with Ian St John on ITV's *The Saint & Greavsie Show*. Greaves made an entertainingly informal pundit (St John was wooden and unfunny).

VITAL STATISTICS

Place of Birth: London, England
Date of Birth: 20 February 1940
Died: n/a Caps: 57 (England) Goals (International): 44
Clubs: Chelsea, AC Milan, Tottenham, West Ham
Appearances: Club: 528
Goals: Club: 366
Trophies: FAC 1962, 1967; CWC 1963

LEGEND RATING

Achievement	6
Skill	10
Teamwork	6
Passion	8
Personality	8
Overall Legend Rating	**38**

◀ᴵᴵ Greaves scored on his debut for every club (including a hat-trick on his Spurs debut), and for England.

◀ᴵᴵ He still holds the Spurs record for league goals in a season, 37 in 1963.

◀ᴵᴵ He became the first player to score 100 goals before he was 21.

◀ᴵᴵ Bill Nicholson, unwilling to saddle Greaves with the label of the first £100,000 player, paid Milan £99,999 for his services.

◀ᴵᴵ Greaves once bemoaned, in his role as a pundit, the absence in the modern game of 'the old hey-diddle-diddle-down-the-middle and stick it in the net'.

Greenwood, Ron

West Ham United, England

AS THE MANAGER who restored pride to the England team, Ron Greenwood's stock remains high with a press and public not noted for their kid-glove treatment of the national boss. A genial exterior belied a deep knowledge of the game, while a steely interior, honed during his centre-half playing days, was hardly ever revealed in public.

Greenwood was drifting out of the game as boss of non-league Eastbourne before West Ham resurrected his career, but his 13-year tenure continued the stylish traditions of the Upton Park 'academy'. He had already served England by nurturing the likes of Hurst and Peters for the 1966 World Cup squad, before his appointment as national manager restored respectability to a position tarnished by the sordid exit of Don Revie. Despite notable slip-ups, England qualified for the 1982 World Cup Finals (the first they had reached for 20 years) but, hampered by the loss of Kevin Keegan and Trevor Brooking, they failed to make the knockout stages despite exiting the tournament with an unbeaten record.

VITAL STATISTICS

Place of Birth: Burnley, England

Date of Birth: 11 November 1921

Died: n/a   Caps: 0

Goals (International): 0

Clubs: As Player: Bradford Park Avenue, Brentford, Chelsea, Fulham; As Manager: West Ham, England national side

Trophies: FAC 1964; CWC 1965

LEGEND RATING

Achievement	6
Tactical Awareness	9
Motivation	8
Transfer Dealing and Team Selection	7
Personality	7
Overall Legend Rating	**37**

◄)) 1955. Greenwood won a Championship medal with Chelsea.

◄)) 1964 & 1965. Managed West Ham to successive Wembley victories in the FA Cup and the European Cup Winners' Cup.

◄)) 1971. Greenwood dropped Bobby Moore at West Ham after he broke a club curfew.

◄)) 1977. Picked seven Liverpool players for England in an early experiment, the most from one club since before the war.

◄)) 1977. Had to overcome press hostility on his appointment as England manager (Brian Clough was the 'people's' choice).

Greig, John

ONE OF AN ELITE BAND to have won the league with the same club as both player and manager, no individual contributed more to the success of the post-war Rangers team than John Greig. An inspiration at centre-half after moving from right-half early in his career, he became, in 1964, only the second Scot to captain a treble-winning side, but Celtic's later dominance frustrated his title ambitions for a further 11 years. His consolation was becoming the only Rangers captain to lift a European trophy, the Cup Winners Cup in 1972.

Greig's move, during a whirlwind three weeks, from captain to the manager's desk in 1978 seemed a natural one, but in five seasons he failed to bring the title to Ibrox. It was an indication of his reputation among the fans that he kept his job for so long; an outsider with a similar record would have been dismissed without hesitation. Greig's commitment, strength and leadership, plus his telepathic understanding with playmaker Jim Baxter, served Scotland well too, never more so than in the famous 3-2 defeat of England at Wembley in 1967.

VITAL STATISTICS

Place of Birth: Edinburgh, Scotland
Date of Birth: 11 September 1942
Died: n/a Caps: 44 (Scotland) Goals (International): 3
Clubs: Rangers
Appearances: Club (All Matches): 755
Goals: Club (All Matches): 120
Trophies: SLT 1963, 1964, 1975, 1976, (1978); SFAC 1963, 1964, 1966, 1973, 1976, (1978), (1979), (1981); CWC 1972

LEGEND RATING

Achievement	7
Skill	7
Teamwork	8
Passion	9
Personality	6
Overall Legend Rating	**37**

Bet you're glad we used this one, Greigy!

◁▷ His 44th and final cap against Denmark in 1976 came five years after his previous Scottish appearance.

◁▷ He was twice Scottish player of the year and received an MBE in 1997.

◁▷ He played a record 496 league games for Rangers, and scored a remarkable 120 goals from defence and right-half.

◁▷ Greig endeared himself to the community by tirelessly leading his team to funerals and services after the Ibrox disaster in 1971.

◁▷ In 1999 Greig was voted 'Greatest Ever Ranger' in a fans' poll. Greig actually supported Hearts as a boy.

Gre-No-Li

WHEN SWEDEN WON the Olympic football tournament in 1948, the wealthy Italian clubs ran their covetous eyes over the victorious squad and reached for their wads of lire. As a result, three of the best players – inside-forward Gunnar Gren, striker Gunnar Nordahl and wing-half Nils Liedholm – ended up at AC Milan. At the San Siro, playing in an exciting Milan team, the trio, dubbed Gre-No-Li by the fans, settled well and were instrumental in the Rossoneri's League title win in 1951 – the club's first Scudetto since 1907.

Nordahl, the most successful of the three in Italy, retired in 1957, but the other two, veterans by now, were at the heart of the Swedish team that exceeded expectations in the 1958 World Cup. Liedholm, Gren and the rest of an ageing side played at walking pace at times, but they had enough skill and wit to see them through to the final, after the maverick winger Kurt Hamrin destroyed West Germany's hopes with two late goals in the semis.

But there was to be no fairytale. Despite an early goal from Liedholm, now a prototype attacking sweeper, Sweden were swept away by the awesome Brazilians.

VITAL STATISTICS

GUNNAR GREN

Place of Birth: Gothenburg, Sweden

Date of Birth: 31 October 1920

Died: 10 November 1991 **Caps:** 57 (Sweden)

Goals (International): 33

Clubs: Garda, IFK Gothenburg, AC Milan, Fiorentina, Genoa, Orgryte, Gais, Skogens

Appearances: Club (League: in Serie A): 217

Goals: Club (League: in Serie A): 35

Trophies: SLT 1942; SA 1951

NILS LIEDHOLM

Place of Birth: Sweden

Date of Birth: 8 October 1922

Died: n/a **Caps:** 23 (Sweden)

Goals (International): 10

Clubs: Valdemarsvik, Sleipner, IFK Norrkoping, AC Milan

Appearances: Club (All matches for AC Milan): 359

Goals: Club (All matches for AC Milan): 81

Trophies: SLT 1947, 1948; SA 1951, 1955, 1957, 1959

GUNNAR NORDAHL

Place of Birth: Hornefors, Sweden

Date of Birth: 8 October 1922

Died: 15 September 1995 **Caps:** 33 (Sweden)

Goals (International): 43

Clubs: Hornefors, Degerfors IF, IFK Norrkoping, AC Milan, Roma, Karlstad BIK

Appearances: Club (League: in Serie A): 291

Goals: Club (League: in Serie A): 225

Trophies: SLT 1945, 1946, 1947, 1948; SA 1951, 1955

LEGEND RATING

Achievement	7
Skill	7
Teamwork	9
Passion	7
Personality	6
Overall Legend Rating	**36**

Gunnar Gren sets the style template for Sven Goran Eriksson.

- Nordahl chalked up 225 goals in Italian football (almost a goal per game) and finished as the Serie A's top scorer five times.
- Liedholm stayed in Italy, eventually becoming manager of Milan, Fiorentina and Roma.
- Gren's premature baldness and thoughtful style earned him the inevitable nickname 'The Professor'.
- Gunnar Nordahl's four brothers all played First Division football in Sweden.
- Nordahl and Liedholm played in championship-winning sides in Sweden at Norrkoping, for whom Nordahl scored 93 goals in 92 games.

Gullit, Ruud

AC Milan, Holland

ONE OF THE GREAT PLAYERS of the modern generation, Ruud Gullit had the lot – heading, shooting, passing, and tackling all came so easily to him that he was like four players rolled into one. After starting his career as a sweeper at Feyenoord, Gullit moved on to PSV where he was quickly converted to striker, a position he also later occupied at AC Milan alongside his Dutch colleague Marco van Basten.

For his country though, Gullit turned out mostly in midfield and it was from here that he skippered the Dutch to their European Championship victory in 1988. Glenn Hoddle brought him to Chelsea in 1994, and after one season he succeeded the former Spurs midfielder as player-manager. Although he introduced some exciting overseas players to the Premiership and brought Cup success, the league championship evaded him and, after Ken Bates accused him of being a greedy playboy, he was eventually sacked in 1998. A dire spell as manager of Newcastle, where Gullit failed to adjust to the Geordie culture, left an impression that here was a man not prepared for compromise – it was his way or, er, his way. Sadly, his way didn't work.

VITAL STATISTICS

Place of Birth: Surinam

Date of Birth: 1 September 1962

Died: n/a Caps: 65 (Holland) Goals (International): 16

Clubs: Harlem, Feyenoord, PSV Eindhoven, AC Milan, Sampdoria, Chelsea

Appearances: Club (League): 465 Goals: Club (League): 175

Trophies: EuroC 1998; DLT 1984, 1986, 1987; SA 1988, 1992, 1993; EC 1989, 1990; FAC (1997)

LEGEND RATING

Achievement 9
Skill 9
Teamwork 9
Passion 7
Personality 9

Overall Legend Rating 43

◀)) The £5.5 m Milan paid PSV for Gullit was a world record at the time.

◀)) Gullit was the first overseas coach in England to win a domestic trophy (the FA Cup with Chelsea in 1997).

◀)) The distinctive dreadlocks worn as a player won admirers of both sexes, and were copied by many of his younger contemporaries.

◀)) He was voted European Player of the Year in 1987.

◀)) He scored in Holland's win over Russia in the 1988 European

Championship final, and repeated the feat for Milan in their 4–0 win over Steaua Bucharest in the European Cup final a year later.

Hagi, Gheorghe

Romania

MADDENINGLY VOLATILE but sublimely talented, the list of great Romanian footballers can be headed by only one man. Gheorghe Hagi remained untamed by a succession of club and international managers, continuing in his mid-30s to explode the myth that one mellows with age.

Short and stocky, he was as much at home leading the attack as he was leaving full-backs for dead on the wing. Such was his hunger for the ball he would often drop back into his own half to start moves that he would sometimes finish himself, making him virtually impossible to man-mark.

The star of the Romania team in five European and World Cup Finals tournaments, his 17-year international career came to a peak in USA 94. Improbably, Romania reached the quarter-finals, a run that included a memorable defeat of Argentina that was inspired by the man they used to call the 'Maradona of the Carpathians'. Only penalties denied Hagi's team a place in the last four.

Fittingly, his last major club side was Galatasaray, where his passion and volatility was more than matched by the Turkish supporters. Whether being booked for dissent or turning a game with a moment of brilliance, you ignored him at your peril.

VITAL STATISTICS

Place of Birth: Constanta, Romania

Date of Birth: 5 February 1965

Died: n/a **Caps:** 125 (Romania) **Goals (International):** 34

Clubs: Farul Constanta, Sportul Studentesc, Steaua Bucharest, Real Madrid, Brescia, Barcelona, Galatasaray

Appearances: Club (All Matches): 550

Goals: Club (All Matches): 269

Trophies: RLT 1987, 1988, 1990; TLT 1997–2000; UEFAC 2000

LEGEND RATING

Achievement	6
Skill	10
Teamwork	8
Passion	10
Personality	7
Overall Legend Rating	**41**

◀ᴊᴵᴵ He is the most-capped Romanian and his country's top goalscorer with 35.

◀ᴊᴵᴵ He came equal 12th in the most-capped world list; he shares his tally of 125 with Peter Shilton.

◀ᴊᴵᴵ Best goal? His 30-m scorcher against Colombia in the 1994 World Cup Finals.

◀ᴊᴵᴵ He was sent off for an outrageous dive against Italy in the quarter-finals of Euro 2000.

◀ᴊᴵᴵ He has been voted Romanian Player of the Year six times.

Hamm, Harkes & Lalas

Stars in Stripes

JOHN HARKES is one of the few American-born players to make an impact abroad. He became the first American to appear in an FA Cup final, with Sheffield Wednesday in 1993, and scored in the League Cup final that year. A hard-working, if unspectacular, midfield player, he won 89 caps for the USA, appearing in two World Cup Finals.

Alexei Lalas was another pioneer; after some decent performances in the 1994 World Cup he was snapped up by Padova and became the first American player to appear in Serie A. He was not a conspicuous success in Italy, but he went on to win 98 caps for the USA, and is now the main soccer commentator for NBC.

Arguably America's finest player of the last 20 years has been Mia Hamm, the skilful goal scorer in their successful women's team. First capped at the age of 15, the gifted, two-footed forward formed an exciting attacking combination with Kristine Lilly. Glamorous, and with a following and sponsorship worthy of a rock star, Mia Hamm is the superstar of women's football.

Another American star, Michelle Akers, was top scorer at the 1991 World Cup, and remained a major force in 1999 as a driving midfielder. As influential a player as Hamm, she lacks her colleague's looks and panache.

'I thought I knew everything about British soccer, but I had never heard of a team called Wednesday or a place called Sheffield. I had to look them up pretty quickly. Then I imagined I might be able to pop back and see my folks at Christmas. I had to tell them the bad news on the 'phone. They'd never heard of Boxing Day.'

John Harkes

Tiffeny Milbrett (right), leading scorer for USA in 1999 Women's World Cup.

◄ John Harkes' wife, Cindy, was also an excellent footballer, but never quite made the national team.
◄ Harkes scored the 1990 Goal of the Season, a 35-yard thunderbolt past, of all people, Peter Shilton.

◄ Few North American stars have made the grade in the Premiership; many of the exceptions have been goalkeepers – Kasey Keller and Brad Fiedel have been consistently high-quality performers over the past few years.

◄ The US remain a fit, athletic squad, but lack a superstar to elevate the team to new levels of creativity. One day, inevitably, a top-class ball player will eschew gridiron and basketball, and become the USA's first world-class soccer player.

Hampden Park

Glasgow, Scotland

HAMPDEN PARK has been the home of the Scottish international side since 1903. Its unique bowl has been the scene of some of football's most epic encounters.

In 1960 what is regarded by many as the best match of all time took place as Real Madrid beat Eintracht Frankfurt 7-3 in front of 134,000 fans in the European Cup final. Alfredo di Stefano became the toast of Glasgow, his masterly display included a superb hat-trick.

Its many confrontations between England and Scotland include the 1937 encounter which attracted a record attendance of 149,415.

Hampden Park was rebuilt in 1998 at a cost of £65 m. The renovation of the crumbling terraces was long overdue, but the all-seater capacity of 52,000 has robbed the stadium of its imposing and intimidating qualities.

While the ground has hosted Scotland's biggest international matches in front of vast attendances, it has remained the home ground of amateur minnows Queen's Park. Scotland's original club was once regarded as the best team in the world but now play their home games in front of a few hundred spectators.

VITAL STATISTICS

Local Club:	Queen's Park
Date Built:	1903
Current Capacity:	52,000
Max. Capacity:	150,000

The modern Hampden hosts another Old Firm Cup Final, May 2002.

◁ᴵᴵ The stadium was designed by Archibald Leitch and remained the largest ground in the world until 1950, when Brazil's Maracana was built.

◁ᴵᴵ The ground was so packed during big games that the terraces became known as the Nodding Gallery. Fans were unable to celebrate by any movement more animated than moving their heads, although the Hampden roar remained undiminished.

◁ᴵᴵ Biggest club game: the 1970 European Cup semi-final epic between Celtic and Leeds. Celtic edged through the 'battle of Britain' with the only goal of the tie.

◁ᴵᴵ Hampden Park hosted its third European Cup final in 2002. Apart from the monumental 1960 affair, the other was in 1976.

Hansen, Alan

ONE OF THE MOST elegant defenders in the game's history. Hansen played over 600 matches for Liverpool without appearing to break sweat, a trait that prompted colleague Phil Neal, at the end of every game, to ask, jokingly: 'Did Hansen get dirty today?' His reading of the game was so good that he never appeared stretched but, when required, his tackling and heading were sound, and his distribution was more reminiscent of a foreign sweeper than a British stopper.

Bought for £100,000 from Partick Thistle, Hansen was eased into the Liverpool side as a replacement for Emlyn Hughes. His partnerships over 13 seasons at Anfield, with Phil Thompson, Mark Lawrenson and Gary Gillespie coincided with the most successful period in the club's history.

Why successive Scottish managers chose to award Hansen only 26 caps between them remains a mystery. He would have walked into most other national teams, and Scotland were hardly blessed with high-calibre defenders. Eschewing the managerial career many predicted for him upon retirement, Hansen became a TV pundit where his scathing dismissals of Jimmy Hill's opinions on the BBC enlivened many a dull match. Ironically, as a pundit he has achieved more fame and recognition than he ever enjoyed as a player.

VITAL STATISTICS

Place of Birth: Clackmannanshire, Scotland

Date of Birth: 13 June 1955

Died: n/a **Caps:** 26 (Scotland) **Goals (International):** 0

Clubs: Partick Thistle, Liverpool

Appearances: Club (Liverpool): 623

Goals: Club (Liverpool): 13

Trophies: LT 1979, 1980, 1982, 1983, 1984, 1986, 1988, 1990; FAC 1986, 1989; LC 1981, 1983, 1984; EC 1978, 1981, 1984

LEGEND RATING

Achievement	9
Skill	9
Teamwork	8
Passion	8
Personality	6
Overall Legend Rating	**40**

◄❱ Like his pal, Kenny Dalglish, Hansen is a top-class golfer and also played volleyball, basketball and squash to a high standard.

◄❱ Hansen wasn't a frequent goal scorer, but he did hit the winner against West Ham in the 1981 League Cup Final replay.

◄❱ He memorably uttered the famous line: 'You'll never win anything with kids.' The kids in question, Man United's young side of the mid-1990s, proceeded to waltz away with the Premiership title.

◄❱ The Aberdeen pairing of McLeish and Miller kept Hansen out of the Scotland side – a modern coach would have played five at the back with Hansen as an attacking sweeper.

◄❱ Hansen won eight league titles, a record he shares with Liverpool colleague Phil Neal.

Happel, Ernst

Austria, Holland

ERNST HAPPEL WAS ONE of the cornerstones of the tip-top Austrian side of the early 1950s. In a methodical passing team, organised by the midfield maestro Ernst Ocwirk he and Gerhard Hanappi provided the backbone of the defence. A tough, uncompromising stopper and a formidable striker of a dead ball Happel also starred for Rapid Vienna, the finest Austrian club side of their generation.

Already assured of greatness as a player, his management career increased his reputation still further. An early advocate of 'Total Football', he led Feyenoord to victory in the 1970 European Cup final, depriving Celtic of a second triumph. The trophy was magnetic for Happel; he reached the final with Bruges, losing to Liverpool in 1978, and won the competition again with Hamburg in 1983. Succeeding Rinus Michels as Holland coach, he emulated the great man by taking the Dutch to the Final of the World Cup in 1978. And that was without Cruyff and Van Hanegem who, in typical Dutch style, chucked their toys from the pram on the eve of the tournament and refused to play in it.

VITAL STATISTICS

Place of Birth: Vienna, Austria

Date of Birth: 29 June 1925

Died: 14 November 1992   **Caps:** 51 (Austria)

Goals (International): 5   **Clubs:** As Player: Rapid Vienna, Racing Club de Paris; As Manager: Rapid Vienna, Feyenoord, Sevilla, Club Bruges, Standard Liege, Hamburg, Innsbruck

Trophies: ALT 1946, 1948, 1951–52, 1954, 1957, (1960, 1989–90); DLT (1969); BLT (1976–78); BLG (1982–83); EC (1970, 1983)

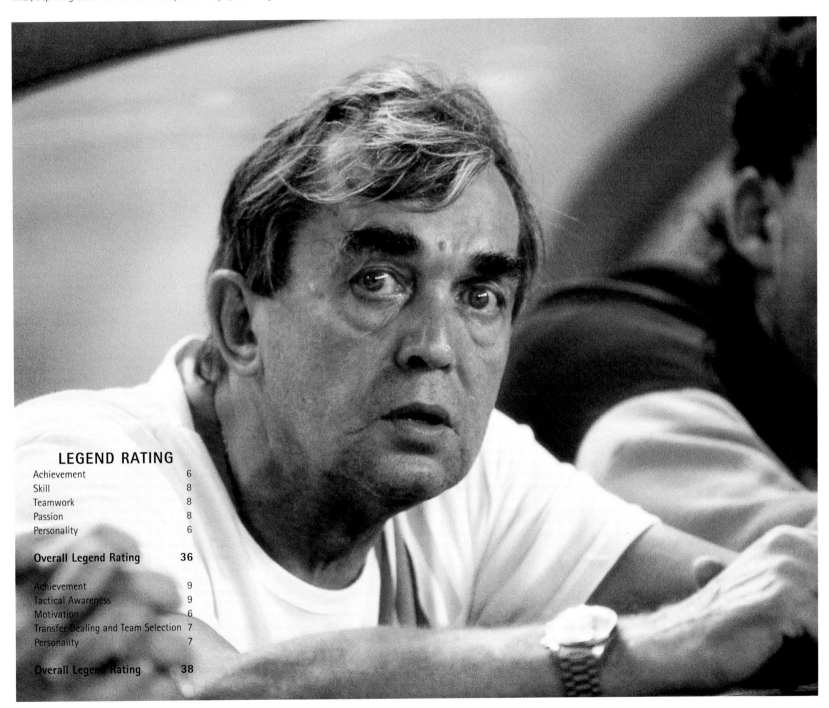

LEGEND RATING

Achievement	6
Skill	8
Teamwork	8
Passion	8
Personality	6
Overall Legend Rating	**36**
Achievement	9
Tactical Awareness	9
Motivation	6
Transfer Dealing and Team Selection	7
Personality	7
Overall Legend Rating	**38**

- He played for a FIFA World XI in 1953.
- He scored a hat-trick in the European Cup in 1957 against Real Madrid – two free-kicks and a penalty.
- In the 1954 World Cup for Austria his defence conceded three goals in three minutes against Switzerland, but went on to win 7–5, despite missing a penalty. Typically, they lost 6–1 to West Germany in the next round.
- Happel returned to the Finals in Sweden in 1958, but the team were past their best and went out early.
- Rapid Vienna renamed their Prater stadium the 'Ernst Happel-Stadion' in his honour when Happel died in 1992.

Happiest Hammers

OF ALL THE DREAM TEAMS, this was the easiest to pick; West Ham legends tend to have that longevity of service that stamps them with the mark of a Hammer. Parkes was comfortably West Ham's most able goalkeeper, and was unlucky to play in an era when Clemence and Shilton traded the England number one jersey between them.

The back four played over 2,500 matches for the club, an outstanding level of passion and commitment (only Moore, in his swansong at Fulham, played for another club), but they will need to be on their mettle in this team. The ball artists ahead of them are not noted for their ability to track back.

The attacking players are so very West Ham; subtlety (Peters), touch (Brooking), pace (Devonshire), tricks (Di Canio), power (Watson) and finishing (Hurst). They might lose to some of the bigger clubs' all-time teams, but it would be glorious stuff.

A new seam has been tapped in recent years: Rio Ferdinand, Frank Lampard jnr, both now departed, have been followed by Joe Cole, Michael Carrick and Jermaine Defoe, all surely destined for England glory.

Manager: Ron Greenwood

4-3-3

Phil Parkes (80s/90s)

Billy Bonds (C) (70s/80s) Bobby Moore (60s/70s) Alvin Martin (80s/90s) Frank Lampard (70s/80s)

Alan Devonshire (80s/90s) Trevor Brooking (60s/70s)
Martin Peters (60s/70s)

Geoff Hurst (60s/70s) Vic Watson (20s/30s) Paolo Di Canio (90s)

Subs: David James (G) (00s) Ray Stewart (D) (80s/90s) Len Goulden (M) (30s) Jimmy Ruffell (W) (20s/30s) Tony Cottee (F) (80s/90s)

Billy Bonds. He spits in claret and blue.

◄ Appearances: Watson (505), Moore (642), Martin (586), Lampard (665), Hurst (502), Devonshire (446), Brooking (632), Bonds (793).

◄ Harry Redknapp was a good player and an excellent manager, but lost out to Greenwood because he bought Marco Boogers and Paulo Futre.

◄ Jimmy Ruffell and Vic Watson played in the first FA Cup final at Wembley, the Hammers losing 2-0 to Bolton.

◄ Len Goulden played 14 times for England. It would have been more but his career was cut short by the war.

◄ Brooking, Bonds and Lampard played in both West Ham's FA Cup wins in 1975 and 1980.

Hard Men

THERE IS A DIFFERENCE between hard and dirty. A genuinely hard player can freeze an opponent out of the game purely on his reputation, whereas a dirty player who fancies himself simply gets wound up and sent off (think Dennis Wise or Alan Smith).

Higuita's conviction for kidnapping demands his inclusion; we're talking serial nutter here. Ron 'Chopper' Harris was the daddy of 1970s thuggery, and Ron Yeats easily eclipsed Tommy Smith as the hard man of Liverpool (Smith talked too much). Monti was the granddaddy, a ball-playing thug long before it was cool, and Gentile is the modern game's greatest man-marker, a man who turned

wingers' bowels to water. Mackay was a legend – he would captain this side. Benetti was a vicious, cynical assassin who stood out even in a brutal Italian team. Neeskens was a great player but he wasn't afraid to leave a foot in, and Giles edges out Souness as the sly, provocative element. Up front we have Joe Jordan, all flailing elbows and tungsten head, toothless only in the literal sense. And Lineker. A decade of being hacked and harassed by the toughest defences in the world and never booked. That's hard.

Manager: Lorenzo (Argentina)

4-4-2

Rene Higuita

Ron Harris   Ron Yeats   Luis Monti   Claudio Gentile

Dave Mackay   Romeo Benetti   Johan Neeskens   Johnny Giles

Joe Jordan   Gary Lineker

Clockwise from top left: Lineker, Yeats, 'Chopper' Harris, Gentile.

◁» Unlucky omissions (defenders): Norman 'Bites Yer Legs' Hunter, Antonio Rattin, Dmitri Kuznetsov and Karl–Heinz Schnellinger.

◁» Deserved omissions: Terry Hurlock (hirsute pedestrian laughing stock), Neil Ruddock (Phil Mitchell in shorts), Robbie Savage (can't see Ron Yeats tolerating that hairstyle).

◁» Unlucky omissions (others): Andy Gray, Ted Drake, Bruce Rioch and John Fashanu.

◁» What, no place for Vinnie Jones? Sorry, not good enough. With the exception of Harris this lot are all quality internationals.

Haynes, Johnny

Fulham, England

IT IS RARE FOR ONE PERSON to dominate a club's history so totally, but the bar-room discussions in Fulham begin and end with a collective nod: Johnny Haynes was the greatest player ever to pull on the black and white. An inside forward of immense technique, his confidence on the ball made him a London role model for a later generation of pretenders, including Terry Venables, Rodney Marsh and Stan Bowles.

Until the return of the Cottagers to the Premier League in 2001 the era of Haynes represented Fulham's only golden age and, while today's team is good to watch, it pales compared to the one of Haynes, Hill and Jezzard. Good enough to represent England at the 1958 World Cup when still a Second Division player, Haynes remained at Fulham throughout his career. It was a measure of his importance to them that, despite modest revenues, they were always prepared to meet his salary demands following the abolition of the maximum wage (Haynes was the first £100-a-week footballer). Successive relegations in 1968 and 1969 were a sad end to his career, but even while the team around him floundered, Haynes could never do any wrong in the eyes of Fulham fans.

VITAL STATISTICS

Place of Birth: London, England

Date of Birth: 17 October 1934

Died: n/a Caps: 56 (England) Goals (International): 18

Clubs: Fulham, Durban City

Appearances: Club (League): 594

Goals: Club (League): 145

Trophies: None

LEGEND RATING

Achievement	4
Skill	9
Teamwork	8
Passion	8
Personality	8
Overall Legend Rating	**37**

◁)) 1954. Scored on his England debut in a 2–0 win over Northern Ireland in Belfast.

◁)) 1958. Hit an international hat-trick as USSR were thrashed 5–0.

◁)) 1961. The first player to earn £100 per week at a British club.

◁)) 1962. Seriously injured his knee in a road accident and is never picked again for England.

◁)) His 594 league appearances for Fulham are a club record.

NEWSPAPERS HAVE ALWAYS performed a role greater than simply printing results and match reports. The England job has become progressively less glamorous following concerted and often vitriolic campaigns against previous managers. Nothing hits the mark more than a headline.

Lest we forget, the now near-sainted Bobby Robson was pilloried during the late Eighties. 'In the name of Allah, Go!' screamed the *Daily Mirror* after England drew a friendly in Saudi Arabia. 'Bring 'Em Home Mrs T.' was the *Sun*'s preposterous plea to Margaret Thatcher after England drew with Ireland at Italia 90. Three weeks later, this was conveniently forgotten as 'our boys' reached the semi-finals.

With the hindsight of tabloid treatment of Graham Taylor, this was genteel stuff. 'Swedes 2 Turnips 1' greeted England after their Euro 92 exit. In case we didn't fully comprehend the allusion, an image of Taylor's head was superimposed on the vegetable in question.

Headline writers work to a tried and tested formula, find a pun and make it as excruciating as possible. Some events are the stuff of journalistic dreams. Below are some of the best.

'Increible' (sic)

Spanish newspaper headline captures the drama, but not the grammar, of Manchester United's 1999 Champions League triumph.

⮐ 'Super Cally Go Ballistic Alloa Atrocious' magnificent local paper headline following Inverness Caledonian Thistle's drubbing of Alloa. Adapted by the *Sun* following the same team's Cup victory at Celtic.

⮐ 'Swollen Dicks Out'. The *Sun* incurs the displeasure of proprietor Rupert Murdoch after their interpretation of an injury to West Ham's Julian Dicks.

⮐ 'Bergy: I'll Linger Longa for Wenger's Wonga'. The *Sun* (again) describe Dennis Bergkamp's satisfaction with his package at Highbury.

⮐ 'March of the Dai'. The *Sunday People* describe Wrexham keeper Dai Davies' sending off during an FA Cup tie at Upton Park.

Henry, Thierry

Arsenal, France

WHEN THE TROUBLESOME and disruptive Nicolas Anelka left Arsenal in 1998, Arsène Wenger turned to another quick French attacker to replace him. Thierry Henry had emerged as a wide attacking player at Monaco under Wenger's tutelage, and won a league title there in 1998. A lucrative move to Juventus followed, but, like many others in Serie A, Henry spent more time on the bench than the pitch, and left after less than a year.

So to Arsenal, and a difficult start, when both manager and player seemed unsure as to the most satisfactory use for all that skill and speed. Only when Wenger consistently used Henry in a central striking role, an opportunity afforded by Dennis Bergkamp's injuries and loss of form, was his true potential unearthed. Henry's second and third seasons at Arsenal brought him a torrent of goals in a classy side. The discovery that he could play as an orthodox front man was of equal benefit to France, for whom the addition of a world-class striker proved to be the missing piece in their attacking jigsaw.

The 2002 World Cup suggested Henry still has much to prove as an international player, but his subsequent league form in 2002/3 proved little short of sensational.

VITAL STATISTICS

Place of Birth: Paris, France
Date of Birth: 17 August 1977
Died: n/a   Caps: 46 (France)
Goals (International): 18
Clubs: Monaco, Juventus, Arsenal
Appearances: Club (League): 257 Goals: Club (League): 105
Trophies: WorC 1998; EuroC 2000; FLT 1997; LT 2002; FAC 2002, 2003

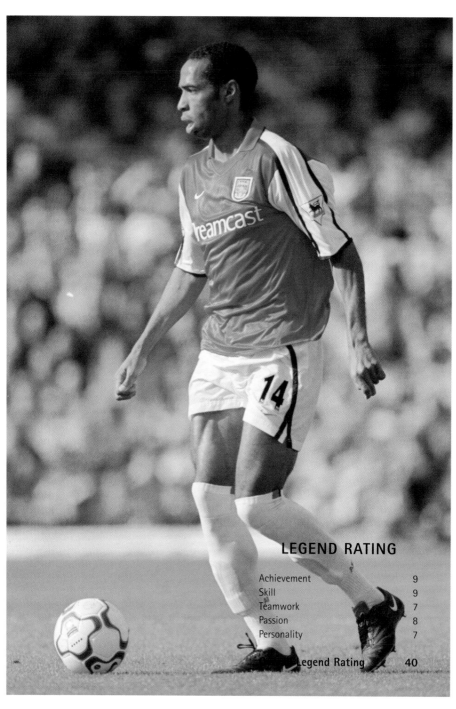

LEGEND RATING

Achievement	9
Skill	9
Teamwork	7
Passion	8
Personality	7
Legend Rating	40

- He made his Monaco debut aged 17 and still looks as if he is about 17.
- Scored three goals in six games at the 1998 World Cup, but never wholly convinced, remaining on the bench for the final.
- Henry has a fiery streak, his browbeating of an official after a home defeat by Newcastle late in 2001 resulted in an FA disrepute charge.
- Intelligent and articulate, Henry is another player who adds substance to the notion that the best English spoken in the Premiership is by the overseas players.
- Won the PFA's Player of the Year award for 2002/3.

Herbert, Herbert What's the Score?

Walsall 2 Arsenal 0, 1933

AFTER NEARLY 70 YEARS this match is still talked about in Walsall. Like all Cup upsets it defied logic; Arsenal were in the first season of what was to be a championship winning hat-trick, while the Saddlers were muddling around in the Third Division and approached the match with little more than the hope of making some quick cash. Arsenal's line-up included the Scottish 'Wembley wizard' Alex James, Britain's costliest player David Jack and the winger who became the club's record goalscorer, Cliff Bastin. Their manager, Herbert Chapman, had already made his name by leading Huddersfield to three league title wins.

But reputations meant little to the Walsall players who were intent on proving they were the physical (if not footballing) equals of the Gunners. Two Arsenal players had already been kicked into the stand before Gilbert Alsop's header gave Walsall a second-half lead, then, illustrating that the Corinthian spirit wasn't always prevalent despite those Pathé newsreel images, a kick by Arsenal's Tommy Black on Alsop led to a mass brawl and a penalty to the home side. Bill Sheppard duly converted; a rattled Arsenal had been well and truly outgunned.

SCORERS: Walsall: Alsop, Sheppard (pen.)
EVENT: FA Cup Third Round., Fellows Park, 14 January 1933

WALSALL (Man: Sid Scholey)		ARSENAL (Man: Herbert Chapman)	
1 Cunningham	8 Ball	1 Moss	8 Jack
2 Bennett	9 Alsop	2 Male	9 Walsh
3 Bird	10 Sheppard	3 Black	10 James
4 Reed	11 Lee	4 Hill	11 Bastin
5 Leslie		5 Roberts	
6 Salt		6 Sidley	
7 Coward		7 Warnes	

Gilbert Alsop: toast of the Black Country.

◁ Flushed with this goalscoring success, Gilbert Alsop scored 40 league goals in each of the next two seasons, a club record.

◁ Chapman, who was a strict disciplinarian, never picked Tommy Black again.

◁ Scorer Bill Sheppard had a keen sense of timing; it was his first goal for the club.

◁ Arsenal ended the season as League Champions, Walsall finished fifth in Division Three (North).

◁ Walsall's dream ended in round four, where they lost 2-0 at Manchester City.

Heysel Stadium

29 MAY 1985 SHOULD HAVE BEEN a red-letter day for fans of Liverpool and Juventus. More than 60,000 of them were massed in Brussels' Heysel stadium before the European Cup final. But misguided ticket arrangements had allocated Liverpool a terrace behind one goal separated only by a thin chicken wire fence from 'neutrals' in the other half. The majority of these 'neutrals' turned out to be Juve fans who had snapped up tickets from locals when their own allocation ran dry.

How it all started will always be debatable. Some Liverpool fans claimed they reacted to missile throwing, while the Italians talk of a drunken English charge. The outcome was all too apparent. Fans fleeing from the trouble attempted to scale a wall in the now infamous sector Z, which collapsed under increasing pressure.

Thirty-nine Italians and Belgians died in the carnage and hundreds were injured, their fear and pain going out live to horrified television audiences watching across the world. Recriminations continued for years. Fingers were pointed at fans, local bar-owners, ticket allocators, Belgian police and the stadium authorities. All were a factor but the lessons were not learned, as Liverpool fans were to discover only four years later at Hillsborough.

'If I had known about the fatalities I wouldn't have wanted to play. You go along to watch a game.'

Kenny Dalglish

⏴» The stadium's age was cited as a factor but, built in 1930, it was actually seven years younger than Wembley and not unusually old for the time.

⏴» Following the tragedy UEFA banned English clubs from Europe indefinitely. Ironically, the first club prevented from entering the European Cup were Liverpool's rivals, Everton. The ban was lifted after five years.

⏴» Disgracefully, no memorial or plaque commemorates the disaster.

The only reminder is a gate left for posterity when the stadium was razed to the ground.

⏴» After the chaos, UEFA officials insisted the game should take place that evening, fearing further disturbances if they cancelled.

Hidegkuti, Nandor

IN WINNING THE WORLD CUP in 1966 Alf Ramsey deployed Bobby Charlton as a deep-lying centre forward. It would not be overstating the case to say that, without Nandor Hidegkuti, the thought would probably never have entered his head. In 1953 Ramsey played in the England team that were slaughtered by the Hungarians at Wembley, and from his position at right-back he had the perfect viewpoint to admire the skills of the Hungarian striker.

It helped that Hidegkuti was a hugely gifted player. He used the space behind his forwards to probe at the opposition, always looking for opportunities to shoot with either foot. Teams simply did not know how to contain him. The rigid formations of the 1950s could not be easily adapted to negate his threat, nor that of his interchanging team-mates Puskas, Kocsis and Czibor. That said, Hidegkuti's achievements were limited – his side failed to take a golden opportunity to win the World Cup, and, unlike Puskas, Kocsis and Czibor, he stayed in Hungary after the Soviet revolution, eschewing the riches of western Europe. But his legacy to the game endures. Cruyff might have patented his own turn, but Hidegkuti invented a whole new position.

VITAL STATISTICS

Place of Birth:	Budapest, Hungary
Date of Birth:	3 March 1922
Died: n/a	Caps: 68 (Hungary)

Goals (International): 39

Clubs: MTK Bucharest (then known as Voros Lobogo)

Hidegkuti's efforts (left) in the 1954 World Cup Final proved in vain as Hungary lost to West Germany.

LEGEND RATING

Achievement	7
Skill	9
Teamwork	8
Passion	8
Personality	7
Overall Legend Rating	**39**

◁ Hidegkuti scored a hat-trick in the mauling of England at Wembley.

◁ In the 'Battle of Berne' against Brazil in the 1954 World Cup, he scored after four minutes, losing his shorts in the process.

◁ Hidegkuti became a successful coach at Fiorentina, winning the 1961 European Cup Winners' Cup.

◁ Hidegkuti won an Olympic Gold medal in 1952, in the middle of the team's four-year unbeaten run.

◁ On Hidegkuti's death in 2002, his club, MTV Budapest, announced that their stadium would be re-named in his honour.

Highbury

HIGHBURY'S HALLOWED MARBLE HALLS have been a symbol of Arsenal's power and success through the decades. Since opening in 1913, the stadium has become one of the most aristocratic grounds in the game.

It underwent major redevelopment during Herbert Chapman's era in the 1930s and the remaining Art Deco exterior is unique. The stadium's east and west stands have the unusual accolade of being classed as buildings of special architectural merit. In recent years the ground has been transformed into an all-seater modern arena, while retaining the traditional features of the Clock End and the east and

west stands. The record attendance of 73,296 against Sunderland in 1935 is now a distant memory, with the current capacity cut back to just 38,500. This lack of space has prompted the club to seek alternative accommodation, and they have recently won planning permission from the local council to build a 60,000 all-seater stadium in nearby Ashburton Grove. If all goes according to plan Highbury will see its last game in the next few seasons, and the club will relocate to the new complex, ending 90 years of football on the site.

VITAL STATISTICS

Location:	London, England
Local Club:	Arsenal
Date Built:	1913
Current Capacity:	38,500
Max. Capacity:	73,295

◁ Arsenal moved to Highbury from their original location in South London, when they were known as Woolwich Arsenal.

◁ Despite the universal name of Highbury, the ground's official name is The Arsenal Stadium.

◁ Highbury staged 12 full England internationals between 1920 and 1961, including the infamous 'battle of Highbury' against Italy in 1934.

◁ The 1939 film, *The Arsenal Stadium Mystery*, was a detective story, involving the murder of an opposition centre-forward, and featured many of the actual Arsenal team.

◁ The Highbury pitch, at 101 x 67 m, is the smallest in the Premiership.

Hill, Jimmy

Coventry City, BBC TV

JIMMY HILL CAN LAY CLAIM to being the first renaissance man of English football. Player, linesman, employment-rights activist, PFA and club chairman, media pundit ... there are few areas of the modern game in which Jimmy Hill has not exerted an influence. A competent player in average sides, his most lasting achievement came in his role as PFA chairman when, leading a case on behalf of George Eastham in 1961, he brought about the abolition of football's maximum-wage system.

As a manager and then chairman, Hill transformed Third Division Coventry City, laying the foundations for a 34-year membership of the league's elite and pioneering the movement for the abolition of terracing (Highfield Road was an all-seater stadium 15 years before the Taylor Report made them compulsory).

In the media, he embraced the new culture of television coverage and became a national figure as a presenter and summariser for both ITV and the BBC. He irritates many, the Football League has never quite forgiven him for taking them on over 40 years ago, but the shadow of the most famous chin in football has cast a lasting influence.

VITAL STATISTICS

Place of Birth:	Balham, London
Date of Birth:	22 July 1928
Died:	n/a
Caps:	0
Goals (International):	0
Clubs:	As Player: Brentford, Fulham;
	As Manager: Coventry City
Trophies:	None

LEGEND RATING

Achievement	7
Tactical Awareness	8
Motivation	8
Transfer Dealing and Team Selection	7
Personality	8
Overall Legend Rating	**38**

◁ 1961. First PFA chairman to call for a players' strike over the maximum wage.

◁ 1972. Deputised for an injured linesman at Highbury. Hill was originally attending as a commentator.

◁ 1978. Key negotiator in the threatened strike over freedom of contract. This nut didn't crack until the Bosman case nearly 20 years later.

◁ 1982. Organised a rebel tour to South Africa, infuriating the FA and breaching the Gleneagles agreement not to play sport with a land still under the apartheid regime.

◁ 'Jimmy Hill is to football what King Herod is to babysitting,' Tommy Docherty once said.

Hillsborough

PERHAPS THE MOST sickening aspect of the worst disaster in British football was that it contained so many chilling echoes of previous tragedies. Like the crowd-related disasters at Ibrox and Heysel, it unfolded in a few minutes and was the result of sudden overcrowding. What made 10 April 1989 worse, apart from the unprecedented loss of 96 lives, were the terrifying images of fans – men, women, children and even whole families – struggling for life in the chaos. Reporting of a disaster normally contains scenes of the aftermath, the venue cleared and the dead removed, but with the media already gathered for the FA Cup semi-final between Liverpool

and Nottingham Forest, the camera lenses quickly turned to the Leppings Lane terrace. The central pen was filling with Liverpool fans misdirected into an area too small to contain them, while outer sections remained relatively free. The pictures of helpless fans sparked a grief that went far beyond the boundaries of football. The following days were incredibly moving: the Kop was a sea of flowers, and players mingled with fans at funerals. The legacy was the Taylor Report, resulting in all-seater stadiums and an overhaul of crowd-control measures at all British events. The tragedy is that 96 innocent lives were lost before anyone would admit there was a problem.

'Football is irrelevant now.'

Kenny Dalglish

'The only safe stadium in my view is an empty one.'

South Yorkshire coroner Stefan Popper, at the inquest

IN MEMORY OF THE
96
EN, WOMEN AND CHILDREN WHO TRAGICALLY DIED
AN   COUNTLESS PEOPLE WHOSE LIVES WERE CHANGED FOREVER.
.A. CUP SEMI-FINAL. LIVERPOOL v NOTTINGHAM FOREST.
15TH APRIL 1989.
"You'll never walk alone."

Although 95 people died as an immediate result of Hillsborough, the toll was to rise several years later after one young man's failure to recover from a coma.

The Sun newspaper claimed outrageously that some Liverpool fans had stolen personal items from the dead. Copies of the paper were ritually burned on Merseyside.

A national service of remembrance was held in Liverpool's Anglican Cathedral on 29 April 1989.

The Hillsborough Justice Campaign still fights for the bereaved and their families. The authorities have escaped punishment and compensation for victims' families has been tiny, contrasting with the large awards given to police officers affected by 'stress'.

Hoddle, Glenn

Tottenham Hotspur, Chelsea, England

GLENN HODDLE WAS A continental footballer who had to overcome the misfortune of being born in Hayes, Middlesex. Not overly concerned with pace and aggression, Hoddle rose above the hurly-burly of English football. The radar-equipped right foot bent and curled some classic goals in a long career.

Hoddle spent 12 years at Tottenham before he tried his luck abroad with Monaco, where he was hugely appreciated. His performances for England were patchy – occasionally inspired, too often anonymous. To be fair, no one built a side around his talent, which was what was needed.

He was lured back to England as player-manager of Swindon Town. His understanding of the game and tactical acumen were immediately evident as he took an ordinary side into the top flight for the first time in their history. Those instincts served him equally well at Chelsea, and earned him a call from the FA who appointed him England manager as successor to Terry Venables. He made a decent fist of the job and it was his strong, and sometimes quirky, personal views that saw him eased out. His abilities as a manager have been confirmed by sound work at Southampton and more recently following an emotional homecoming, at Spurs.

VITAL STATISTICS

Place of Birth:	Hayes, Middlesex, England
Date of Birth:	27 October 1957
Died: n/a	Caps: 53 (England)

Goals (International): 8

Clubs: Tottenham, Monacco, Swindon Town, Chelsea

Appearances: Club (League: for Tottenham): 377

Goals: Club (League): 88

Trophies: FAC 1981, 1982; EUFAC 1984; FLT 1988

LEGEND RATING

Achievement	7	Achievement	8
Skill	9	Tactical Awareness	9
Teamwork	7	Motivation	7
Passion	7	Transfer Dealing and Team Selection	7
Personality	7	Personality	8
Overall Legend Rating	**37**	**Overall Legend Rating**	**39**

▸ He scored the only goal in 1982's FA Cup Final replay against QPR.
▸ He started Chelsea's rush of foreign imports when he persuaded Ruud Gullit to come to Stamford Bridge. Gullit was to succeed him as manager.

▸ Hoddle's debut for England against Bulgaria was awesome; he scored in a 2-0 win and oozed class.
▸ Played well in the 1986 World Cup, until he confirmed his propensity for disappearing in big games during the 'Hand Of

God' match against Argentina.
▸ A bizarre trust in Eileen Drewery, a faith healer, started the decline in Hoddle's relationship with the FA and the media that ultimately led to his demise as England manager.

Holy Trinity

THEIR FAILURE TO QUALIFY for the Finals of the 1982 and 1986 World Cups prompted Holland to call once again for the services of their greatest coach, Rinus Michels. Michels' 'Total Football' philosophy, born at Ajax in the late 1960s, was to serve Holland well yet again. The core of the team was Koeman, the captain, along with the Holy Trinity of Gullit, Rijkaard and Van Basten. Koeman was a decent defender who also happened to be a terrific attacking playmaker, and almost every Dutch move seemed to start with his precision passing from the back. Be it a short ball to the ever-willing Rijkaard or a longer pass to meet the run of an attacker, Koeman

rarely missed his target. Gullit could attack or defend with equal aplomb, and Van Basten was a brutally efficient finisher. And for once a Dutch team delivered what it promised. At Euro 88 they produced the fluent, attacking football for which they were famous, and a first victory for 32 years over hosts West Germany won them a place in the final. A terrific game saw them wear down a skilful USSR team – a trophy had come home at last.

Manager: Rinus Michels

Key Players
Hans Van Breukelen (G) Jan Wouters (D) Ronald Koeman (D)
Frank Rijkaard (M) Ruud Gullit (M/F) Marco Van Basten (F)

Trophies
EuroC 1988

Van Basten shows off the European Championship trophy after Holland's victory in 1988.

◁❱ Van Breukelen saved a penalty that would have brought Russia back into the game in the final – he was a superior keeper to any of the 1970s custodians.

◁❱ The second goal in the final was a masterpiece, Van Basten

volleying a deep cross with stunning power past Rinat Dasaev.

◁❱ Even this squad had its internal ructions. There were rumours of a racial divide in the camp.

◁❱ The Dutch performance at the 1990 World Cup Finals was a

sad coda to these heroics. With virtually the same team, they managed three dreary draws and were eliminated by Germany.

Home Internationals

BY 1884 ENGLAND, Scotland, Wales and Ireland were all playing international football. So the idea that they should all play each other in an annual league was a logical step, and thus the Home Internationals were born. Scotland quickly gained the upper hand, winning three and sharing one of the first four tournaments, but it wasn't long before England rose to the challenge and, bar the occasional triumph for Wales and N. Ireland, it was the auld enemies that grew to dominate the event. For fans north of the border a visit to Wembley was always a trip to savour. Indeed, such was their enthusiasm for the fixture they were even known to outnumber the home fans on occasion. But after nearly a century, the Home Internationals began to fall apart. England and Wales refused to play in Belfast, wary of the political situation, and when Scotland and England cancelled games against the other home nations after 1984, the tournament was effectively over. Although the England/Scotland fixture continued for another five years, the extended season and the importance of other tournaments had finally taken its toll.

'It meant more for the Scots to beat the English than it did for the English to beat the Scots.'

Bobby Charlton makes a dubious claim after the Scots win at Wembley in 1967

Coppell and Hansen attempt a pas de deux in 1982.

◁ Best English game? A 9-3 drubbing of Scotland in 1961. Jimmy Greaves helped himself to a hat-trick. Scottish keeper Frank Haffey never played for his country again.

◁ Best Scottish game? The 3-2 win at Wembley in 1967, England's first defeat since winning the World Cup.

◁ Best Welsh game? A 4-1 drubbing of England at Wrexham in 1980. Leighton James and Mickey Thomas put paid to Larry Lloyd's England career.

◁ Best Irish game? A 1-0 win against Wales in 1980 earned them their first outright championship victory for 66 years.

◁ The final tally of outright wins reads: England 34, Scotland 24, Wales 7, Northern Ireland 3.

Hooligans

FOOTBALL HOOLIGANISM: a disease cultivated by the game itself or merely the reflection of a violent society? Your opinion on this subject tends to depend on whether you love or despise the game. One undeniable truth is that football violence is nothing new.

Rivalry, large crowds and a contact sport have provided a violent cocktail as long as the game has been played. In 1909, a major riot took place in Glasgow after officials unwisely refused to play extra-time to settle an Old Firm derby. The result was a burned stand, a ruined pitch and widespread damage to local property.

Even in the golden age of the 1940s, Millwall fans pelted the referee and linesmen during a routine match against Exeter. The late 1960s saw the dawn of organised gangs, with premeditated 'taking' of away ends and railway stations setting an unwelcome trend. As police tactics grew more sophisticated in the 1980s, so did the hooligans. Sharply dressed casuals with Stanley knives replaced the skinheads and their Dr Martens. Today the problem is controlled at league games with more season tickets and all-seater stadiums but away from the stadiums, in city centres, car parks and even on cross-channel ferries, the threat of hooliganism still lingers.

'These people are society's problems and we don't want your hooligans at our sport.'

FA Secretary Ted Croker bites back at Prime Minister Thatcher, 1985

A Liverpool fan gets some far too literal stick.

◀》 1972. Chelsea became the first British club to erect a perimeter fence. Although Hillsborough brought their eventual removal, they are still a common sight in grounds throughout the world.

◀》 In 1975/76 the Police Superintendents' Association suggested a

film-style classification system for fixtures, with under-16s banned from certain matches. Similarly barmy calls for the birch and national service have been routinely suggested.

◀》 In 1985 televised rioting at a match between Luton and Millwall

led to the introduction of an ill-fated identity card scheme.

◀》 February 2002. A reconciliatory football match in Kabul following the Afghan War sparked a riot. The stadium had a more grisly recent history as a Taliban execution venue.

WITH A CLUB LIKE CELTIC, who have been winning domestic trophies hand over fist since their formation, the list of potential Dream Team candidates is long. One could easily select a squad that would require a convoy of team coaches to get to away games.

Inevitably, the Lisbon Lions feature heavily: McNeill, Gemmell, Johnstone, Murdoch and Lennox are all represented. Perhaps the most interesting blend is up front. The prolific Jimmy McGrory scored nearly 400 goals over 17 seasons – a club record that may never be beaten – while his striking partner, Kenny Dalglish, is one of the most complete forwards Britain has produced since the war. The

midfield is as perfect as they come, a unit capable of turning from intricate ball-juggling to biting tackles at the flick of a tactical switch. There was only ever going to be one winner in the competition for the managerial hotseat. Jock Stein won nine championships in a row, and was the first manager to lead a British team to victory in the European Cup.

Manager: Jock Stein

4-4-2

Pat Bonner (80s/90s)

Danny McGrain (70s) Billy McNeill (60s/70s)
John Clark (60s) Tommy Gemmell (60s)

Jimmy Johnstone (60s/70s) Paul McStay (80s/90s)
Bobby Murdoch (60s) Bobby Lennox (60s)

Kenny Dalglish (70s) Jimmy McGrory (20s/30s)

Subs: John Thomson (G) (20s/30s) Tom Boyd (D) (90s) Paul Lambert (M) (90s) Henrik Larsson (F) (90s/00s) Frank McAvennie (F) (80s)

◄)) John Thomson might easily have become Celtic's greatest-ever keeper. Sadly, aged just 22, he was killed from injuries sustained in an Old Firm game.

◄)) Tom Boyd deserves a place on the bench for his loyalty during the 1990s, a decade dominated by Rangers.

◄)) Frank McAvennie wins the cheeky chappie award ahead of Charlie Nicholas: he could drain a mini-bar quicker.

◄)) Unlucky omissions? Collins and Auld. Celtic's midfield is so strong that even these club legends from the 1950s and 1960s fail to get a look in.

◄)) These boys would surely add a second European Cup to their 1967 success in Lisbon.

Houllier, Gerard

Liverpool

GERARD HOULLIER IS ONE of the modern breed of coaches – a professional tactician and man-manager, not a wily ex-pro imparting his experience and knowledge. After qualifying as a coach Houllier worked for a number of years in French domestic football, winning the title with Paris Saint-Germain in 1986. This earned him an appointment as France's technical director, assisting then-manager Michel Platini in plotting the direction of the national team. A brief tenure as manager of the national side followed. In July 1998 Houllier was appointed joint-manager of Liverpool in a bizarre collaboration with Roy Evans. This was never going to work, and it was Evans who was released in November of that year. It has taken Houllier time to make an impact, and the team he built has earned a reputation for functionality without flourish.

Three cups in 2001 restored some pride to the club and won over the fans, and better may have followed the year after but for his sudden heart attack. Now restored to health, and with a side containing world-class players, Houllier needs to recover the style and success of former sides to completely win over the fans.

VITAL STATISTICS

Place of Birth: Therouanne, France

Date of Birth: 3 September 1947

Died: n/a   Caps: 0

Goals (International): 0

Clubs: As Player: Le Tourquet; As Manager: Le Tourquet, Neoux Les Mines, Lens, Paris Saint Germain, France national side, Liverpool

Trophies: FLT 1986, FAC 2001, LC 2001, 2003; UEFAC 2001

Houllier with the UEFA Cup, 2001.

LEGEND RATING

Achievement	7
Tactical Awareness	8
Motivation	7
Transfer Dealing and Team Selection	8
Personality	8
Overall Legend Rating	**38**

- He is credited with laying the groundwork for the French national team's recent period of international dominance.
- Houllier was an avid follower and admirer of the great Liverpool teams of the 1970s and 1980s.

- Houllier's heart attack in 2001 led to serious concerns about the levels of stress endured by football managers in the modern game.
- For the record, the world-class players alluded to are Jerzy

Dudek, Sami Hyppia, Steven Gerrard and Michael Owen (sorry, Emile).
- Shankly, Paisley, Fagan, Dalglish, Souness, Evans ... embarrassing to think that Houllier speaks better English than any of them!

Howlers

WE'VE ALL DONE IT. Fortunately for the rest of us, the repercussions of shanking an open goal or letting a tiddler through the legs are restricted to the banter of team-mates in the pub after the game.

Imagine if you can the misery of making the same error in front of a thirty-thousand crowd and a sniggering armchair audience of millions. How Villa's Peter Enckelman must look forward to visiting St. Andrew's again. In 2002, during the first Birmingham derby for sixteen seasons, he let a throw-in from one of his own players gently caress his studs as a near air-shot trickled past him and into the net.

Goalkeepers are in a unique position regarding howlers but strikers too have their own hall of infamy. Ryan Giggs can point to a groaning, personal trophy cabinet as proof of his talent but his pass into the Stretford End, when an open-goal beckoned during an FA Cup tie against Arsenal in 2003, will be replayed on out-take compilations for years to come. The bigger they are...

'David James. Superstar. Drops more b******s than Grobelaar'

Manchester United fans at Anfield point out 'Calamity' James' propensity for dropping the occasional clanger.

Seaman misses Ronaldinho's free kick. England vs Brazil, 2002 World Cup quarter-final.

◥ David Seaman. Being beaten by Nayim from the halfway line in 1995 had finally become a distant memory. Then Ronaldinho approached an innocuous-looking free kick in Shizuoka seven years later...

◥ Paul Gascoigne. Fame and fortune in Italy should have awaited Gascoigne after the 1991 FA Cup Final, his last appearance for Tottenham. The worst tackle of the decade left him the poorer by one cruciate ligament and with a career that never recovered.

◥ Gary Sprake. But for the ex-Leeds and Wales keeper, Elland Rd. would have bulged with trophies in the Sixties and Seventies. The jewel in his tarnished crown was an own goal caused by his throwing the ball backwards.

Hughes, Emlyn

Liverpool, England

WHEN BILL SHANKLY was looking around for a passionate, call-to-arms leader for his Liverpool side, he spotted a young wing-half at Blackpool. The player in question, Emlyn Hughes, went on to play over 650 games for the Anfield club, reinforcing Shankly's reputation as one of the game's shrewdest judges.

'Crazy Horse,' as he became known, missed only three games through injury in his first nine seasons at Liverpool, and in 12 years at Anfield he was never asked to play in the reserves.

Although not remarkably gifted, Hughes showed great understanding, was difficult to knock off the ball, and possessed almost boundless reserves of energy and heart. He was also an immensely disciplined player, and his commitment never crossed the line into nastiness. Even after leaving Liverpool with arthritic knees, Hughes gave unstinting service to a variety of clubs lower down the leagues. There are many who feel his 62 caps flatter him but, like cricket captain Mike Brearley, Hughes' value to a side as a leader more than compensated for his shortcomings as a player.

VITAL STATISTICS

Place of Birth: Barrow-in-Furness, England

Date of Birth: 28 August 1947

Died: n/a   Caps: 62 (England)   Goals (International): 1

Clubs: Blackpool, Liverpool, Wolverhampton, Rotherham United, Hull City, Mansfield Town

Appearances: Club (for Liverpool): 665   Goals: Club (for Liverpool): 48

Trophies: LT 1973, 1976, 1977, 1979; FAC 1974; EC 1977, 1978; EUFAC 1973, 1976

LEGEND RATING

Achievement	9
Skill	5
Teamwork	8
Passion	10
Personality	8
Overall Legend Rating	**40**

Rome, 1977. Hughes brandishes Liverpool's first European Cup.

◁〕 On retirement, Hughes made a career as a motivational speaker, and was a popular team captain on TV's *A Question Of Sport*.

◁〕 He was Football Writers' Player of the Year in 1977.

◁〕 Hughes scored both goals in a Merseyside derby victory at Goodison Park in the 1973 title-winning campaign. And duly celebrated both goals by running around like a madman.

◁〕 1972. Hughes scored his only international goal against Wales in a 3-0 win.

◁〕 1977-78. Scored the winning goal in a European Cup tie in Lisbon that ended Benfica's 46-match unbeaten run.

Hughes, Mark

WITH HIS FEARLESS, lion-hearted approach to striking, Mark Hughes could have easily made his mark in the era of Nat Lofthouse and Tommy Lawton. 'Sparky' was a powerful forward with legs like tree trunks and, though less than 6 ft tall, he was huge in stature. To judge him by his goal scoring record alone is a mistake, as his phenomenal work-rate made him a favourite of fans and colleagues alike wherever he has played. His shielding of the ball brings grateful tributes from fellow strikers, while his waist-high volleys and control of a bouncing ball have produced countless goals from half-chances.

Despite his frequent later moves, he remains a son of Manchester United, who performed canny business by buying him back from Barcelona for a profit. His combative nature has inevitably brought dismissals, but he was never a dirty player. It is unlikely that anyone else would have been appointed Welsh national boss with no previous managerial experience, but his inspiration as a Red Dragon as well as a Red Devil made him a popular choice. Wales's roaring start to the Euro 2004 qualifiers has ensured Hughes a much-improved five-year contract.

VITAL STATISTICS

Place of Birth: Wrexham, Wales

Date of Birth: 1 November 1963

Died: n/a Caps: 72 (Wales) Goals (International): 16

Clubs: Manchester United, Barcelona, Bayern Munich, Chelsea, Southampton, Everton, Blackburn

Appearances: Club (League): 646   Goals: Club (League): 164

Trophies: FAC 1985, 1990, 1994, 1996, 1997; CWC 1991; LC 1992; LT 1993, 1994

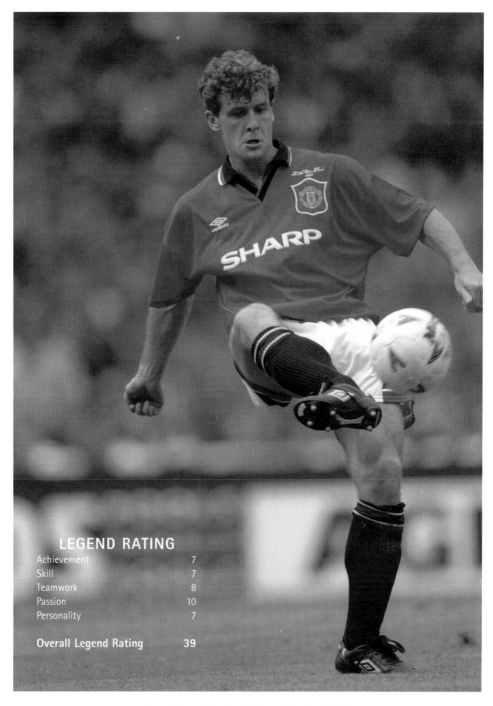

LEGEND RATING

Achievement	7
Skill	7
Teamwork	8
Passion	10
Personality	7
Overall Legend Rating	**39**

◀))) Hughes' physique inspired the epithets 'Sparky' (the battery boy) in England and 'El Toro' (the bull) at Barcelona.

◀))) 1990. Scored twice in the FA Cup final versus Crystal Palace.

◀))) 1994. Scored another FA Cup final goal against Chelsea, with whom he later enjoyed another Cup win in 1997, his fifth victory in the competition.

◀))) 1998. He was awarded MBE for services to football.

◀))) 1999. Appointed Welsh manager while a player at Southampton.

Hunt, Roger

AS THE LIVERPOOL TEAM was re-built in the early 1960s, Roger Hunt emerged as a key player in Shankly's new order. At only 5 ft 9 in Hunt wasn't the tallest striker, but his pace and the timing of his runs made him a difficult player for defenders to keep track of while his fierce shot ensured that he rarely needed a second invitation to find the target.

His strike-rate for Liverpool was stunning, better than a goal every two matches, and the club struggled to replace him before raiding Scunthorpe for a long-haired prospect called Kevin Keegan. A year after he left Liverpool for a spell at Bolton, 'Sir' Roger, as the Kop dubbed him, returned to Anfield for a testimonial attended by a capacity 55,000 fans. Hunt was a member of England's World Cup winning side of 1966, although he was resented by many fans for keeping Jimmy Greaves out of the side in the latter stages of the competition. Actually, Hunt played in every game during the tournament; it was hat-trick hero Geoff Hurst who was preferred ahead of Greaves.

VITAL STATISTICS

Place of Birth: Golborne, Lancashire, England
Date of Birth: 20 July 1938
Died: n/a   Caps: 34 (England)
Goals (International): 18
Clubs: Liverpool, Bolton Wanderers
Appearances: Club (for Liverpool): 492
Goals: Club (for Liverpool): 245
Trophies: LT 1964, 1966; FAC 1965; WorC 1966

LEGEND RATING

Achievement	8
Skill	8
Teamwork	7
Passion	7
Personality	6
Overall Legend Rating	**36**

⤜ Hunt scored 41 goals in Liverpool's 1962 promotion campaign, a club record.

⤜ His 245 league goals remains a club record, although Ian Rush scored more overall.

⤜ He was awarded the MBE in 1999, along with the other 'forgotten' members of the World Cup winning side.

⤜ He scored one of the goals in extra-time as Liverpool beat Leeds 2-1 to win the FA Cup for the first time in 1965.

⤜ Hunt on his manager, Bill Shankly: 'He was dynamic. If you lost a game you lost to rubbish. If you won, you had beaten a great team.'

Hurst, Geoff

West Ham United, England

THE SIGHT OF an airborne Geoff Hurst smashing his hat-trick to seal England's World Cup final victory is one of the country's indelible post-war images. Inevitably, it dwarfed the rest of his career, but at the beginning of the tournament Hurst was a squad player, drafted in by Sir Alf Ramsey merely as cover for the more experienced Roger Hunt and Jimmy Greaves (Hurst had only made his debut for England earlier that year). But an injury to Greaves in the group stage provided Hurst with his opportunity. It was one he seized, scoring the only goal against Argentina in the quarter-finals.

Hurst was groomed as a striker by Ron Greenwood at West Ham; along with England team-mates Martin Peters and skipper Bobby Moore, he was a graduate of the Upton Park academy. After tasting the ultimate success at 24, Hurst's career rather stagnated and by the time he left the Hammers for Stoke at the age of 30 it was all but over. Like nearly all the 1966 England team, he was a managerial failure and excused himself from football for 15 years before returning as a promotional figurehead for England's successful Euro 96 bid. More recently he was part of the team that fought Germany for the right to host the 2006 World Cup Finals. On this occasion he lost.

VITAL STATISTICS

Place of Birth: Ashton, England
Date of Birth: 8 December 1941
Died: n/a   Caps: 49 (England)
Goals (International): 24
Clubs: West Ham, Stoke, West Bromwich
Appearances: Club (League: for West Ham): 410
Goals: Club (League: for West Ham): 180
Trophies: FAC 1964; CWC 1965; WorC 1966

LEGEND RATING

Achievement	8
Skill	8
Teamwork	7
Passion	7
Personality	6
Overall Legend Rating	**36**

◄ Hurst is still the only man to score a hat-trick in a World Cup final. It was Hurst's third different winner's medal at Wembley in successive seasons, having earlier won the FA Cup and European Cup Winners' Cup with West Ham.

◄ In the 1964 FA Cup final Hurst scored via the underside of the crossbar, a Wembley precursor to his more famous effort two years later in the World Cup final.

◄ 1998. Hurst was made a Knight of the Realm.

◄ In 2001 Hurst finally published his long-awaited autobiography, *1966 And All That*.

◄ A talented all-round sportsman, Hurst considered becoming a professional cricketer.

Hwan Nation Under A Groove

DEFENDING ONE-NIL LEADS, this one courtesy of Vieiri's near-post header from an eighteenth-minute corner, is the Italians' stock-in-trade. After 88 minutes, their defence filed back in textbook fashion to repel a final Korean attack before taking their accustomed place in the quarter-finals. A seemingly harmless cross rebounded from the flailing Panucci; Seol-Ki-Hyeon picked his spot from ten yards and the game was turned on its head.

Extra time continued the air of unreality. Korea were possessed, Italy were rattled. With penalties three minutes away, Lee Young-Pyo's hopeful cross was apparently aiming for Maldini's head. The ageing maestro's legs finally failed, and he scarcely left the turf as Ahn Jung-Hwan's glancing header edged past Buffon into the far corner.

It didn't end there; with the Italian recriminations still ringing through the media, Spain were the next team to drown in the Red Sea. Negative and uninspired as they had been against Ireland, Spain allowed themselves to be taken to penalties. The nerve of the inexperienced Koreans held as they scored their first four penalties. Joaquin missed and Hong Myung-Bo stepped up to take his side into the semis.

SCORERS:
South Korea: Seol Ki-Hyeon; Ahn Jung-Hwan
Italy: Vieri

EVENT:
Second Round, World Cup Finals, Seoul, 18 June 2002

S. KOREA
(Man: Guus Hiddink)

1 Lee Woon-Jae	6 Yoo Sang-Chul
2 Choi Jin-Chul	7 Lee Young-Pyo
3 Hong Myung-Bo	8 Park Ji-Sung
4 Kim Tae-Young (Hwang Sun-Hong)	9 Song Chong-Gug
5 Kim Nam-Il (Lee Chun-Soo)	10 Seol Ki-Hyeon
	11 Ahn Jung-Hwan

ITALY
(Man: Giovanni Trapattoni)

1 Buffon	8 Tommasi
2 Panucci	9 Totti
3 Iuliano	10 Del Piero
4 Coco	11 Vieri
5 Maldini	
6 Zanetti	
7 Zambrotta (Di Livio)	

South Korea sprint from the centre circle after knocking out Spain on penalties.

◁ South Korea could afford the luxury of a fifth-minute penalty miss. Ahn Jung-Hwan's low kick to Buffon's right lacked power, and the Italian keeper made an excellent save. Ahn made amends.

◁ Italy had Totti sent off for a nonsensical second offence. Tommasi was pulled back for a dubious offside when clear. Cue moaning. In the end they were the victims of their own negative approach; at 1–0 up they had the players to roast Korea, but not the will.

◁ Guus Hiddink became the toast of Korea. He had a street named in his honour, and amongst the many gifts showered upon him was four years of first-class air travel from Korean Air.

Immovable Object

PRIOR TO 1974 the closest a German team had come to winning the European Cup was in 1960, when Eintracht Frankfurt were walloped by a rampant Real Madrid. Atletico Madrid were their opponents in the 1974 final and the Spaniards put up stern resistance, holding them to a 1-1 draw in the first game before succumbing 4-0 in the replay. Once Bayern had taken possession of Europe's biggest prize they were not keen to let go. Cajovski's team won the next two finals, overcoming Don Revie's Leeds in 1975, and then seeing off the challenge of St Etienne in 1976, emulating Ajax and Real Madrid in the process. The team was gradually dismantled after the 1976 win at

Hampden Park; Beckenbauer and Maier retired and Breitner tried his luck abroad. As they faltered the Borussia Monchengladbach team of Vogts, Bonhof and Simonsen took control in Germany, while Liverpool became the new masters of Europe. A domestic revival saw Bayern win the Bundesliga fairly regularly in the 1980s, but the wait for another European Cup would last longer, defeats in the finals of 1982 and 1987 adding to their frustration before their triumph in 2001.

Manager: Tschik Cajovski

Key Players
Sepp Maier (G) Franz Beckenbauer (D)
Georg Schwarzenbeck (D) Paul Breitner (D)
Uli Hoeness (M) Franz Roth (W/F) Gerd Müller (F)

Trophies
BLG 1972, 1973, 1974 EC 1974, 1975, 1976 WCC 1976

Bremner and Beckenbauer shake hands before the 1975 European Cup final.

◀◗ The 1975 final was played to a backdrop of appalling crowd trouble in Paris, as riot police struggled to contain Leeds fans in the stadium. Leeds were later banned from Europe for four years.

◀◗ Aston Villa beat Bayern 1-0 in the 1982 European Cup final;

Breitner, Hoeness and Durnberger were still in the team, but past their best.

◀◗ Coach Cajovski was the man who led Bayern out of the darkness in the 1960s, building a team around Franz Beckenbauer.

◀◗ A young Karl-Heinz Rummenigge played in the 1976 European Cup final.

◀◗ Six Bayern players played in the 1974 World Cup final; all the seven listed above except Roth, a winger with a vicious shot.

Indiscipline

THERE ARE FAR MORE RED CARDS these days, so football must be a dirtier game, right? Nothing could be further from the truth.

Yes, we know that neither Stanley Matthews or Bobby Charlton were cautioned during their careers, but in those days the referee sharpened his pencil just about once every 10 years. In the days of black-and-white TV, a player had to clock up two falls and a submission to warrant a red card. Nowadays, a dozen red cards is a standard haul on any given Saturday. And yet there are still players with unblemished records. In a recent season at Spurs Sol Campbell managed to complete an entire campaign without a collecting a single booking, while Gary Lineker, like Matthews and Charlton, kept his nose clean throughout his career.

Of course there are players whose middle names might as well be Trouble. In the modern era Mark Dennis, Vinnie Jones and Alan Smith have all periodically forgotten what it feels like to shower with the rest of the team. But do footballers behave any worse today than they did 40 years ago? Not in our view.

> 'The lad was sent off for foul and abusive language, but he swears blind he didn't say a word.'
>
> Oldham manager Joe Royle tries unsuccessfully to explain his player's dismissal

Andy D'Urso points and Leicester are reduced to ten.

↶ Take a bow Vinnie Jones. His booking for Chelsea after three seconds remains the quickest ever in the game's history

↶ It was 96 years before a player was sent off playing for England. Alan Mullery achieved this distinction against Yugoslavia in 1968.

↶ Red and yellow cards were invented by an ex-referee, Ken Aston. He must have got the idea after taking charge of Brazil versus Chile in the 1962 World Cup. The 'Battle of Santiago' was one of the dirtiest games ever played.

↶ If more than four members of one team are dismissed, the match is abandoned and awarded to the opposition. America Tres Rios managed this dubious feat in a 1991 Brazilian cup tie after losing their fifth player.

Injuries

Ow!

INJURY is a professional footballer's greatest dread, even worse than being a full-back and discovering that Ryan Giggs has passed a fitness test. At their worst, they can make even spectators wince. Coventry's David Busst, sandwiched in a tackle at Old Trafford, snapped a leg at such a hideous angle that it made Peter Schmeichel physically sick and moved him to attend a post-match counselling session. But not all injuries are career threatening. Dave Beasant once missed several games after dropping a bottle of salad cream on his foot. (Sadly for Chelsea, his handling didn't improve noticeably on his return to the first team.)

It is one of the quirks of the game that some players can tackle their way through seasons of campaigning without collecting a scratch, while others can limp off after a pre-match kickabout with the club mascot. For his frequent absences from the first team during his spell at Aston Villa, Dalian Atkinson acquired the unenviable nickname of 'Sick Note' from sections of the Holte End. This tag has recently been inherited by Tottenham's Darren Anderton. Any career can be ended at a stroke by a mistimed tackle or an awkward landing. Despite the money, adulation and glamour, job security is not one of the benefits offered by professional football.

'He'll probably injure himself getting off the bus.'

TV summariser Brian Clough has harsh words for Stuart Pearson before the 1977 FA Cup final

An innocuous but sickening clash shatters David Busst's leg.

◁⁾ Injuries can cost a team in more ways than one. In 1996 Middlesbrough were deducted three points after cancelling a fixture against Blackburn in 1996. Boro claimed most of their players were injured or had flu.

◁⁾ Wembley acquired a hoodoo after players were badly injured in Cup finals during the 1950s and 1960s. In these pre-substitute times, they often changed the course of the match.

◁⁾ 1980. Proving that danger lurks round many corners, Charlie

George lost one finger and mangled two more after a run-in with a lawn mower.

◁⁾ An injury crisis once forced Man City to name Tony Book and Glyn Pardoe as 'A' team substitutes. Their combined age was 92.

Introducing Michael Owen

England 2 Argentina 2, 1998

ENGLAND'S PROGRESS through the opening phase of France 98 saw them face a formidable and familiar foe in the first knockout stage. It proved to be one of the tournament's best games. Argentina were favourites, and when Batistuta converted a penalty after six minutes, they looked likely to win. Eleven minutes later, they were behind.

Owen's innocuous fall in the box produced a harsh penalty that Shearer, in typically nerveless style, tucked away. Owen's next contribution was as emphatic as it was startling, the 18-year-old reducing Chamot and Ayala to bemused spectators before drilling an unstoppable shot into Roa's top corner from the edge of the area.

England's lead was not to last, though. A lapse in concentration let in Zanetti who, after an intricate passing move from a free-kick, made it 2-2 two minutes before the break. The second half, although goalless, turned on Beckham's petulant kick on Simeone. Hardly venomous, but an inevitable red card followed. England fought a rearguard action for nearly an hour, bravely holding out for penalties. But it was all in vain. This time it was the hand of Roa (not God) that did England, the Argentine keeper turning aside Batty's weak strike. For the third time in the 1990s, England had gone out of a major tournament on penalties.

SCORERS: **England:** Shearer (pen.); Owen
Argentina: Batitusta (pen.); Zanetti
EVENT: World Cup second round, St Etienne, 30 June 1998

ENGLAND
(Coach: Glenn Hoddle)

1	Seaman	8	Scholes
2	G. Neville	9	Sheaer
3	Adams	10	Owen
4	Campbell	11	Anderton
5	Le Saux		
6	Beckham		
7	Ince		

ARGENTINA
(Man: Daniel Passarella)

1	Roa	8	Ortega
2	Vivas	9	Simeone
3	Ayala	10	Batistuta
4	Chamot	11	Lopez
5	Zanetti		
6	Almeyda		
7	Veron		

Michael Owen tormented the Argentine defence throughout.

◁┊ Both England's previous World Cup matches against Argentina had been controversial affairs, producing the Rattin sending-off in 1966 and the 'Hand of God' goal 20 years later.

◁┊ Despite being reduced to 10 men, England nearly won it in the 82nd minute. Campbell's header was unluckily chalked off after Shearer was adjudged to have pushed Roa.

◁┊ Penalty takers: Argentina: Crespo (missed); Berti, Veron, Gallardo, Ayala.

◁┊ England: Ince (missed), Shearer, Merson, Owen, Batty (missed).

◁┊ Beckham was made a scapegoat for the defeat, and suffered terrible abuse including death threats. A picture of fans burning him in effigy made the front pages of the newspapers.

Jack, David

Bolton Wanderers, Arsenal, England

LIKE ALF COMMON (the first £1,000 player) and Trevor Francis (the first £1 m player), David Jack's name is a favourite point of reference for pub quizmasters up and down the country. A star of Bolton's 1923 and 1926 FA Cup winning sides, Jack was a primary target for Herbert Chapman, manager of Arsenal. Legend has it that during the lengthy negotiations, Chapman plied the Bolton board with strong gin while he sipped enthusiastically from a glass of tonic water. True or not, Chapman was successful in persuading a reluctant Bolton board to part with Jack. But it would cost him an unprecedented £10,750, a landmark first-ever five-figure transfer fee. Actually, it could have been more; initially Bolton had demanded £13,000. The money proved well spent. Jack was to return to Wembley twice with the Gunners, once as a winner, and was a vital component of the side that won three league championships in the early 1930s. A clever inside forward with a good shot, Jack was part of the legendary Arsenal forward line of Hulme, Jack, Lambert, James and Bastin. Like many of his team-mates, Jack was shocked by Chapman's premature death in 1934, and was one of the pallbearers at the great man's funeral.

VITAL STATISTICS

Place of Birth: Bolton, England
Date of Birth: 3 April 1899
Died: 1958   Caps: 9 (England)
Goals (International): 0
Clubs: Plymouth Argyle, Bolton, Arsenal
Appearances: Club (League: for Arsenal): 181
Goals: Club (League: for Arsenal): 113
Trophies: FAC 1923, 1926, 1930; LT 1931, 1933, 1934

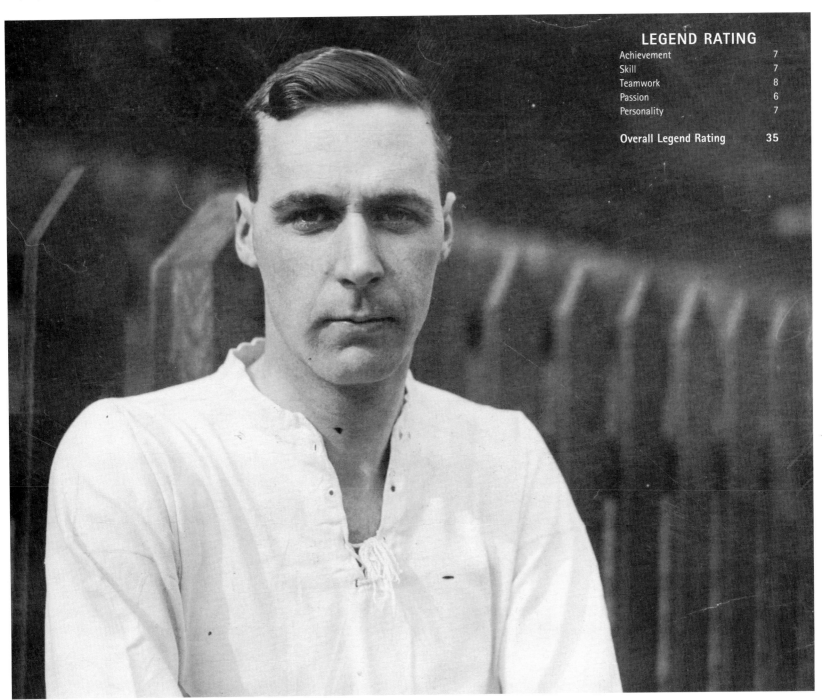

LEGEND RATING

Achievement	7
Skill	7
Teamwork	8
Passion	6
Personality	7
Overall Legend Rating	**35**

◁» Jack won his first two caps in 1924, but had to wait four years to be given another.

◁» Jack scored the opening goal in the first Wembley FA Cup final, as Bolton beat West Ham 2-0.

◁» Three years later he repeated the feat, this time scoring the only goal of the game against Manchester City.

◁» Jack's brother Rollo also played professional football, following David from Plymouth to Bolton.

◁» 'No player in the world is worth £10,000.' Sir Charles Clegg, FA President.

Jairzinho

Brazil

BORN JAIR VENTURA FILHO, the young Jairzinho cut his footballing teeth as a dashing left winger with Botafogo. Less tricky, but more direct than his great predecessor Garrincha, his weapons were a deceptive change of pace and a fierce shot, but it was only when he emerged from Garrincha's shadow and moved to the right that Brazil got the best from him. A key member of the fabulous 1970 World Cup winning side, Jairzinho was an ideal outlet for the Brazilians, bringing the ball forward at high speed and feeding passes inside to Pelé and Gerson. He was also a consistent goal threat, and scored in every round of the tournament including the final (one of only two players to do so in the history of the game). Four years later Brazil were no longer the beautiful team and Jairzinho failed to make the same impact. A spell in European football with Olympique Marseille wasn't a great success and Jairzinho returned to his homeland, where he earned the last of his 98 caps for Brazil aged 38.

VITAL STATISTICS

Place of Birth: Rio de Janeiro
Date of Birth: 25 December 1944
Died: n/a   Caps: 98 (Brazil)
Goals (International): 37
Clubs: Botafogo, Marseille, Cruzeiro, Portuguesa, Caracas
Trophies: WorC 1970

LEGEND RATING

Achievement	9
Skill	9
Teamwork	8
Passion	8
Personality	7
Overall Legend Rating	**41**

Jairzinho confuses Peru at the 1970 World Cup.

- ◁ He scored the winner in Cruzeiro's 1976 Copa América win.
- ◁ The 1966 World Cup saw Jairzinho playing on his less-favourite left side to accommodate Garrincha. He was twice the player on the right.
- ◁ Jairzinho recovered from a twice-broken leg to play in the 1970 World Cup Finals.
- ◁ Jairzinho had a somewhat ungainly running style, appearing never to be quite in control. Trust us, he was.
- ◁ The other player to score in every round at a World Cup Finals tournament was Alcide Ghiggia for Uruguay in 1950 – but his streak spanned just four games.

James, Alex

THE ARSENAL SIDE of the 1930s was brimming with fantastic players, but Alex James was probably its most gifted. James was short and wiry and the baggy shorts of the day made him look almost Chaplinesque, but there was nothing slapstick about his football. Like his manager, the legendary Herbert Chapman, James was ahead of his time and, as a natural reader of the game, he adapted well to Chapman's innovative tactics. Arsenal fought off fierce competition to sign him from Preston, beating Liverpool, Aston Villa, Birmingham and Manchester City, although initially they may have wondered if it had been worth the trouble; James struggled to settle and was even dropped for a spell. Then one day, in a typically unconventional move, Chapman turned up at James's house and hauled him out of bed to play in an FA Cup replay at Birmingham. From thereon James never looked back, forming a successful partnership with the prolific Cliff Bastin on the left side of Arsenal's 3-4-3 formation. Both were consistently inspirational as Arsenal walked away with trophy after trophy. Eight caps for Scotland was a scandalous waste of his talent, especially as he was one of the architects of their finest pre-war hour: the 5-1 thrashing of England by the 'Wembley Wizards' in 1928.

VITAL STATISTICS

Place of Birth: Mossend, Scotland

Date of Birth: 14 September 1901

Died: 1953 Caps: 8 (Scotland)

Goals (International): 4

Clubs: Raith Rovers, Preston North End, Arsenal

Appearances: Club (League: for Arsenal): 231

Goals: Club (League: for Arsenal): 26

Trophies: FAC 1930, 1936; LT 1931, 1933, 1934, 1935

LEGEND RATING

Achievement	8
Skill	9
Teamwork	8
Passion	7
Personality	7
Overall Legend Rating	39

- Arsenal paid Preston £8,750 for James in 1929 – a huge fee at the time.
- Preston were frequently referred to as 'Alex James and 10 others'.
- James's eight Scotland caps were spread over seven years, and included four goals, two of them in the annihilation of England in 1928.
- James's obituary appeared in *The Times*, a rare accolade for a footballer in 1953.
- James scored a cracking goal in the 1930 FA Cup final. Taking a free-kick quickly, he played a one-two with Bastin and smashed the ball into the roof of the net.

Jargon and Gibberish

The Thoughts of Chairman Ron

FOOTBALL IS NOT UNIQUE in having its own 'trade' vocabulary. All professions like to shroud themselves with an air of mystery by inventing a language that confuses and belittles outsiders. Computer programmers, financiers, doctors – all rely on our fear of their superior knowledge to protect their interests. Football is unique in having a language that is lacking in poetry and invention, but what it lacks in these departments it makes up for in sheer and utter nonsense. Without further ado, here are some favourites:

'Well we got nine ... and you can't score more than that.' Bobby Robson.

'That would have been a goal if the goalkeeper hadn't saved it.' Kevin Keegan

'When a player gets to 30, so does his body.' Glenn Hoddle

'I think we just ran out of legs.' David Pleat

'Hagi could open a tin of beans with his left foot.' Ray Clemence

Masterpieces of verbal effluvium we're sure you'll agree, but all are competing for the best supporting role. Not even Keegan's bumbling inanities threaten the pre-eminence of Ron 'Early Doors' Atkinson. By turns irritating and amusing, Big Ron is the nonpareil of football jargon-merchants.

> 'We must have had 99 per cent of the game. It was the other three per cent that cost us the match.'
>
> **The normally coherent Ruud Gullit forgets his calculator**

Big Ron (right) laughs at one of his own jokes. Someone has to.

The thoughts of Big Ron:

◀🎙 On Gordon Strachan: 'There's nobody fitter at his age, except maybe Raquel Welch.'

◀🎙 'Well, either side could win it, or it could be a draw.'

◀🎙 'You half fancied that to go in as it was dipping and rising at the same time.'

◀🎙 'They've picked their heads up off the ground and they now have a lot to carry on their shoulders.'

◀🎙 In Ron's defence he can occasionally be very funny. Witness this 1993 gem: 'I always make sure I write Atkinson D (for Dalian) on the team-sheet. Sometimes I wonder if I'm making a mistake.'

Jennings, Pat

Tottenham Hotspur, Arsenal, Northern Ireland

WHEN TOTTENHAM sold the 32-year-old Pat Jennings for a paltry £40,000 in 1977 their fans were deeply unhappy. So imagine how they felt when, shortly after, it was revealed that the team who had bought him were Arsenal. On second thoughts, don't even go there....

Jennings played for a further seven seasons at Arsenal, and continued playing for Northern Ireland for a couple of years after that, before returning to Spurs in 1993 as goalkeeping coach.

In an era when British football was littered with great goalkeepers (except Scotland, of course), Jennings was up there with the best of them. A big man, with almost comically large hands, he exuded a comforting presence behind the defence not unlike Peter Schmeichel, although he was less inclined to fits of apoplectic rage than the excitable Dane. 'Big Pat' was perhaps marginally less acrobatic than one or two of his contemporaries, but his handling was impeccable. Jennings was a fixture in the Northern Ireland team in an international career spanning an amazing 22 years. He played in two World Cup Finals, making his final appearance in the 1986 Finals against Brazil in Mexico – on his 41st birthday.

VITAL STATISTICS

Place of Birth: County Down, Northern Ireland
Date of Birth: 12 June 1945
Died: n/a   Caps: 119 (Northern Ireland)
Goals (International): 0
Clubs: Watford, Tottenham, Arsenal
Appearances: Club (League): 757
Goals: Club (League): 0
Trophies: FAC 1967, 1979; LC 1971, 1973; EUFAC 1973

LEGEND RATING

Achievement	7
Skill	9
Teamwork	8
Passion	9
Personality	7
Overall Legend Rating	**40**

- Probably his finest moment was a brilliant performance in Northern Ireland's 1-0 win over hosts Spain at the 1982 World Cup Finals.
- Jennings scored a freak goal in the 1967 Charity Shield, a huge punt bouncing over Alex Stepney into the Manchester United goal.
- He was Football Writers' Player of the Year, 1973 and PFA Player of the Year in 1976.
- Undoubtedly, Jennings' most embarrassing moment was being dressed as a car battery in a ludicrous 1970s TV advertisement.
- He received an MBE in 1976 and an OBE in 1987.

211

Jock's Delight

Celtic 2 Internazionale 1, 1967

IN THE TUNNEL it looked like a mismatch. Favourites Internazionale stood tall, tanned and experienced, and numbered Facchetti, Mazzola and Domenghini amongst their team of European all-stars. Celtic, in comparison, appeared pale, undersized and more used to scrapping in a frost-bound Glasgow than the Portuguese sunshine, and when Mazzola converted a penalty on six minutes after Craig had fouled Cappellini, few gave the Scots an earthly chance against Inter's famous *catenaccio* ('doorbolt') defence. Led by the peerless Facchetti, the Milan side were pioneers of the cagey game, defending in numbers and countering with speed.

But the turning-point came on the hour; making amends for his earlier indiscretion, Craig combined with Murdoch to create a chance that Gemmell converted with aplomb. A rattled Inter had been hustled into altering their game plan, but couldn't raise the pace. The match was heading for extra-time when a speculative cross-shot from the edge of the box was swept in by Chalmers with six minutes to go. Lucky perhaps, but no more than the Bhoys' performance merited. Inter had been sunk by Glaswegian passion, the Cup belonged to Celtic.

SCORERS: Celtic: Gemmell; Chalmers
Inter: Mazzola (pen.)
EVENT: European Cup Final, Lisbon, 25 May 1967

CELTIC (Man: Jock Stein)
1 Simpson
2 Craig
3 Gemmell
4 Murdoch
5 McNeill
6 Clark
7 Johnstone
8 Wallace
9 Chalmers
10 Auld
11 Lennox

INTERNAZIONALE (Man: Helenio Herrera)
1 Sarti
2 Burgnich
3 Facchetti
4 Bedin
5 Guarneri
6 Picchi
7 Bicicli
8 Mazzola
9 Cappellini
10 Corso
11 Domenghini

Friends, Glaswegians...

- Celtic were the first British team ever to win the European Cup, beating Manchester United to it by a year.
- Tommy Gemmell also scored in the 1970 final, but Celtic lost 2-1 to Feyenoord
- The match proved to be third time unlucky for Inter (they had won the trophy in 1964 and 1965).
- A genuine triumph for the city: all of Celtic's team were born within 15 miles of Glasgow.
- For Celtic the match completed a clean sweep; they had already won a domestic treble.

212

Johnstone, Jimmy

Celtic, Scotland

IF JOCK STEIN was the architect of Celtic's greatest-ever team and Billy McNeill its keystone, then Jimmy 'Jinky' Johnstone was its magician-in-chief. A small, mercurial winger from a rich Scottish tradition of natural ball-players, Johnstone could win a game in a moment and was dubbed the 'flying flea' by a laudatory French press after a European tie against Nantes.

Although a member of the 1967 European Cup winning team, his most memorable games were Celtic's most infamous, namely the two ties against Racing Club in the 1967 World Club Championship. Johnstone's reputation saw him cynically hacked and abused in the first-drawn game (he had to wash opponents' spittle from his hair at half-time) and, determined to give as good as he got in the replay, he eventually received a red card for elbowing an opponent.

His greatest game came in 1970 when, against Leeds in a European Cup semi-final, he teased and tormented the English team's defence in a famous victory. He was ineffective in the final though, well shackled by an impressive Feyenoord rearguard.

Despite his success, the game failed to make him his fortune and he was later forced to take jobs as a lorry driver and construction worker.

VITAL STATISTICS

Place of Birth: Viewpark, Lanarkshire, Scotland
Date of Birth: 30 September 1944
Died: n/a Caps: 23 (Scotland)
Goals (International): 4
Clubs: Celtic, San Jose Earthquakes, Sheffield United, Dundee
Trophies: EC 1967

LEGEND RATING
Achievement 7
Skill 9
Teamwork 6
Passion 8
Personality 7

Overall Legend Rating 37

- Johnstone would have won more than 23 Scottish caps but for a lifelong fear of flying.
- His debut in 1963 was also his heaviest defeat as a player; a 6-0 trouncing by Kilmarnock.
- The line of skilful Scottish wingers continued through Willie Johnston, Charlie Cooke, John Robertson, Pat Nevin and Davie Cooper, but died out in the last decade.
- Johnstone once scored twice in a 5-1 drubbing of Red Star Belgrade. Before the match Jock Stein had promised him he would not have to fly to the return leg if Celtic won easily.
- Johnstone wasn't the only player sent off against Racing Club – three Celtic players were dismissed along with two opponents.

Jones, Vinnie

VINNIE JONES does not appear in this volume for his ability with a ball (just as well, we hear you shout), but rather for his status as a footballing personality. There are myriad examples of footballers being exploited by the media, but Jones was one of the first to manipulate the media to further his own non-footballing career.

After making his mark as a player in the Wimbledon 'crazy gang' (he was a member of their famous 1988 FA Cup winning side), Jones built up a deserved reputation as a hard man, collecting red and yellow cards with a rare enthusiasm. That said, he was probably a better player than people would care to admit; he hit a mean long ball and was a threat in the air at set-pieces. As the famous Wimbledon team broke up, Jones began his wanderings around the league, including spells at Chelsea and Leeds and even a brief flirtation with international football after he discovered some ancient Welsh blood in his family tree. Now firmly established in green-belt Hertfordshire, country squire Jones made his movie debut in 1998 in Guy Ritchie's landmark Brit-gangster movie *Lock, Stock and Two Smoking Barrels*. Hollywood beckoned, and Vinnie was a made man.

VITAL STATISTICS

Place of Birth: Watford, England
Date of Birth: 5 January 1965
Died: n/a Caps: 9 (Wales) Goals (International): 0
Clubs: Wimbledon, Leeds, Sheffield United, Chelsea, Queens Park Rangers
Appearances: Club (League): 393
Goals: Club (League): 33
Trophies: FAC 1988

It's been emotional....

LEGEND RATING

Achievement	5
Skill	5
Teamwork	7
Passion	9
Personality	9
Overall Legend Rating	**35**

◁))) Jones holds the record for the fastest booking in British football. Playing for Chelsea against Sheffield United he received a yellow card after only three seconds, breaking his own record of five seconds playing for Sheffield United the year before.

◁))) 'He wouldn't have lasted five minutes in my day,' said Tommy Smith, still the macho braggart years after his retirement.

◁))) 'I'm 27 years old and the referee tells me I'm not allowed to swear.' Vinnie never really got to grips with the rules.

◁))) 2002. Jones turns recording artist and sings on BBC's *Later* with Jools Holland.

Jules Rimet Trophy

THE WORLD CUP was the brainchild of the president and the secretary of FIFA, Jules Rimet and Henri Delaunay. The only global tournament at the time was the strictly amateur Olympics, so Rimet persuaded FIFA to fund its own tournament. On their formation in 1904, FIFA had reserved the right to organise just such an event. Uruguay was the venue for the first tournament in 1930, but only four European teams travelled (due to a dispute with FIFA none of the British home nations bothered turning up). It would be 1950 before England competed in a Finals tournament, and it was not until 1958 that all four home nations reached the Finals.

Qualification has become more difficult since the early days, largely because of the improvements made by some of the so-called lesser nations. Wales and Northern Ireland no longer enjoy success at international level, while the likes of Denmark and Turkey, once no-hopers, are now among the top seeded teams in Europe. Many observers were critical of the expansion of the Finals from 16 to 24, and then 32 teams. True, the reasons were principally commercial, and it has led to the inclusion of a higher proportion of weak sides, but the developing nations will only improve from exposure to a high level of competition.

'To say that these men paid their shillings to watch twenty-two hirelings kick a ball is merely to say that a violin is wood and catgut, that *Hamlet* is so much paper and ink.'

J. B. Priestley, a rare example of a literary giant with a good word for the beautiful game

- Brazil were allowed to keep the original trophy after winning for the third time in 1970.
- In a table based on results in World Cup Finals, the top sides are Brazil, Germany, Italy, Argentina and England.
- The 2002 World Cup in Japan and Korea was the first tournament outside Europe or the Americas. The 2010 finals will almost certainly take place in Africa.
- In 1986 Morocco became the first African team to get beyond the initial groups at the Finals. Cameroon went one better in 1990, reaching the quarter-finals and scaring England before losing on penalties.

Juventus

STRANGELY, given that they were one of the dominant sides of the 1990s, none of Juventus' 1996 European Cup winning side makes it into our Dream Team. This is largely down to the rapidity with which players have come and gone in recent years; great players like Zidane, Baggio and Ravanelli have passed fleetingly through Turin. To be fair, Gianluca Vialli stayed a little longer, but the competition for places up front means that even he fails to make the grade. Boniperti is the club's leading scorer, and leaving Bettega out of any Juve side would be considered a lynching offence by fans of the Old Lady.

The midfield is made up of the 1980s trio, supplemented by the Argentinian genius, Sivori. The moustachioed winger Causio and Ferrari, one of the greats from Juve's pre-war successes, keep the likes of Brady and Dino Baggio in the stand. Defensively, in true Italian tradition, this team is formidable. In goal the great Dino Zoff would probably be bored, hoping for a rare error from Scirea or Cabrini to help keep his fingers warm. Then again, with the merciless Gentile and Monti kicking lumps out of their opponents in front of him, he would inevitably have the occasional free-kick to deal with.

Manager: Carlo Carcano

4-4-2

Dino Zoff (70s/80s)

Claudio Gentile (70s/80s) Gaetano Scirea (70s/80s) Luis Monti (30s)
Antonio Cabrini (80s)

Zbigniew Boniek (80s) Michel Platini (80s) Marco Tardelli (80s)
Omar Sivori (50s/60s)

Roberto Bettega (70s) Giampiero Boniperti (40s/50s)

Subs: Giampieri Combi (G) (30s) Carlo Parola (D) (50s) Franco Causio (M) (70s) Giovanni Ferrari (M/F) (30s) John Charles (F) (50s/60s)

Juve line up before the 1983 European Cup final.

◁ Manager Carlo Carcano set the tone for future decades by winning five consecutive championships in the 1930s.

◁ Even in the 1930s Juve were known for importing players; Monti was Argentinian, as was his colleague Raimundo Orsi.

In the 1950s and 1960s this trend was continued with the purchase of John Charles and the Danes Karl and John Hansen.

◁ Sivori, who scored nearly 150 goals for Juve, was named European Footballer of the Year in 1961. Internationally he played for both Argentina and his adopted Italy, spearheading their attack along with the Brazilian-born Altafini in the 1962 World Cup.

216

Kanu, Nwankwo

Ajax, Arsenal, Nigeria

WHEN A PLAYER ACHIEVES so much at an early age, there is a danger that the rest of his career will become an anti-climax. But, after being diagnosed with a life-threatening heart condition at the age of 21, every day that Nwankwo Kanu gets to kick a ball is a bonus.

Kanu was lured to Ajax along with Finidi George, the two having been spotted playing in Nigeria. His natural touch and balance were surprising in such a big youth, and he possessed good vision and passing ability. He was still 18 when he came on as a substitute in the European Cup final, and was not yet 21 when he captained Nigeria to Olympic glory in 1996. A dream move to Inter Milan turned into a personal nightmare but his return to fitness, aided by an operation to repair a defective heart valve, is testimony to his great strength of character. Since joining Arsenal his form has been fitful. But there have been occasional flashes of genius, including a stunning performance against Chelsea in 1999 when he completed a hat-trick with a curling shot from an angle so acute Pythagoras would have struggled to measure it.

VITAL STATISTICS

Place of Birth: Owerri, Nigeria
Date of Birth: 1 August 1976
Died: n/a Caps: 35 (Nigeria) Goals (International): 12
Clubs: Federation Works, Iwuanyanwo Nationale, Ajax, Inter Milan, Arsenal
Appearances: Club (League): 234
Goals: Club (League): 58
Trophies: DLT 1994–6; LT 2002; FAC 2002, 2003; EC 1995

LEGEND RATING

Achievement	7
Skill	9
Teamwork	7
Passion	8
Personality	7
Overall Legend Rating	**38**

- A year after picking up his winner's medal in the European Cup, Kanu played in a second final, but a disappointing performance from Ajax meant no second medal.
- Nigeria beat a full Brazilian team 4-3 in the semi-finals at the Olympics, with Kanu scoring the golden-goal winner. They went on to beat Argentina 3-2 in the Final.
- The African Nations Cup has proved elusive for Nigeria. They pulled out of the 1996 tournament, lost on penalties to Cameroon in 2000, and were knocked out in the semi-finals by Mali in 2002.
- Kanu has twice been named African Footballer of the Year, in 1996 and 1999.

Keane, Roy

ROY KEANE WAS PLAYING for Cobh Ramblers when he was spotted by a Nottingham Forest scout and brought to England by Brian Clough in 1990. Three years later Forest turned their £10,000 investment into £3.75 m from Manchester United. What seemed an extraordinary fee in 1993 now looks a snip, as Keane has been the driving force behind the Old Trafford club's recent run of success.

In the 2000/01 season Keane was vociferous in his criticism of his team-mates, accusing them of failing to maintain their hunger for success after the treble-winning season. Keane could justifiably lay claim to being the most complete midfielder currently playing in the Premiership. Only Patrick Vieira runs him close and, like Vieira, Keane has a dark side to his game. Fans will remember sendings-off for vicious tackles and violent outbursts alongside the dominant, driving performances.

Keane's influence was also strong at international level. In a team big on passion but short on world-class players, it is the United man who is frequently asked to stand tall in crucial games. Unlike club colleague Ryan Giggs, Keane had always been there for his country, before his ill-judged outburst in the 2002 World Cup Finals and subsequent retirement from international football.

VITAL STATISTICS

Place of Birth: Cork, Ireland

Date of Birth: 10 August 1971

Died: n/a Caps: 58 (Republic of Ireland) Goals (International): 9

Clubs: Nottingham Forest, Manchester United

Appearances: Club (League): 374

Goals: Club (League): 51

Trophies: EC 1999; LT 1994, 1996, 1997, 1999, 2000, 2001, 2003; FAC 1994, 1996, 1999

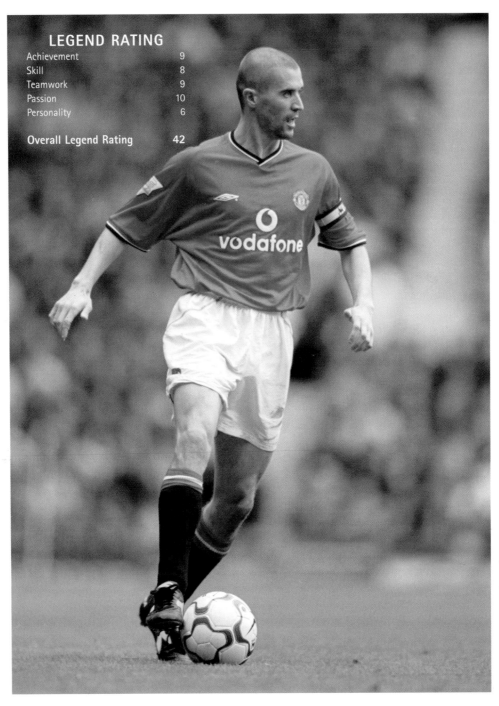

LEGEND RATING

Achievement	9
Skill	8
Teamwork	9
Passion	10
Personality	6
Overall Legend Rating	**42**

- A new United contract in 2000, worth a reputed £52,000 per week, made him the highest-paid player in the Premiership, and destroyed Old Trafford's established wage structure.
- He was the 2000 PFA and Football Writers' Player of the Year.
- In 1999 Keane missed United's famous Champions League final triumph over Bayern Munich through suspension.
- From 1996–2001 United won the title every year, except the one Keane spent sidelined with cruciate ligament damage to his knee.
- Keane was an amateur boxer in his youth and, as many opponents will testify, he still packs a punch.
- Keane has been critical of United's passionless corporate fans, once famously dismissing them as the 'prawn sandwich' brigade.

Keegan, Kevin   Liverpool, Hamburg, Southampton, Newcastle United, England

HUGELY COMMITTED, deeply passionate – and, at times, comically naive – Kevin Keegan is one of the great characters of the modern game. Plucked from obscurity at Scunthorpe by Bill Shankly, Keegan became the focal point of Liverpool's attack, and his almost telepathic understanding with John Toshack proved to be one of the club's most successful striking partnerships. Never afraid of a new challenge, Keegan later moved to Hamburg, where his enthusiasm won colleagues and fans over after a shaky start. Back to England and another successful spell at Southampton under Lawrie McMenemy, and a final flourish at Newcastle.

Twenty-one goals in 63 internationals was a decent return for a striker, but Keegan rarely got the opportunity to shine in major tournaments – a 20-minute stint as a substitute against Spain in 1982 was his only appearance at a World Cup Finals.

As a club manager Keegan has always sent out teams with one objective in mind: to attack. This approach has made his teams popular but has not seen him collect any major silverware. He was an absurd choice as England manager, clearly lacking the tactical wherewithal for international football, but he does deserve credit for reviving the fortunes of Newcastle, Fulham and Manchester City.

VITAL STATISTICS

Place of Birth: Armthorpe, Yorkshire, England
Date of Birth: 14 February 1951
Died: n/a   Caps: 63 (England)   Goals (International): 21
Clubs: Scunthorpe United, Liverpool, Hamburg, Southampton, Newcastle
Appearances: Club (for Liverpool): 323
Goals: Club (for Liverpool): 100
Trophies: LT 1973, 1976, 1977; FAC 1974; EUFAC 1976; EC 1977; BLG 1979; European Player of the Year 1978, 1979

LEGEND RATING

Achievement	9	Achievement		5
Skill	7	Tactical Awareness		5
Teamwork	9	Motivation		9
Passion	9	Transfer Dealing and Team Selection		9
Personality	8	Personality		8
Overall Legend Rating	**42**	**Overall Legend Rating**		**36**

◁ᴵᵂ He was Footballer of the Year, 1976 and European Footballer of the Year, 1978 and 1979.

◁ᴵᵂ He is famous for emotional outbursts, most notably when wound up by Alex Ferguson in the race for the 1997 league title.

◁ᴵᵂ He retired from international football when he was left out of Bobby Robson's first squad in 1982.

◁ᴵᵂ His song, 'Head Over Heels', was a minor hit in both England and Germany.

◁ᴵᵂ He resigned as England manager after a home defeat by Germany in 2000, and was honest enough to admit to his tactical shortcomings.

Kempes, Mario

Argentina

THERE HAVE ALWAYS been players whose flames have flickered brilliantly one minute, only to be put out with an industrial-strength fire extinguisher the next. Mario Kempes fits into this category. A short purple patch elevated what would have been a worthy career into a memorable one, when Kempes fired Argentina to victory in the 1978 World Cup.

Kempes broke through into the national team early, but showed little sign of the success to come; in the 1974 World Cup Finals he failed to score a single goal. A move to Valencia in Spain helped improve his game against better defenders, and he succeeded in adding more disciplined finishing to the pace, balance and close control he already possessed. Suitably honed, Kempes cut a dash at the 1978 World Cup, his six goals in a tight tournament proving decisive, especially his excellent brace in the final against Holland. The winning goal, the finale to a burst through the Dutch defence, epitomised his determination, persistence and exquisite balance. Thereafter though, Kempes retreated into mediocrity, flitting between Europe and Argentina and failing to make an impact, or even score a goal, in the 1982 World Cup.

VITAL STATISTICS

Place of Birth: Bellville, Cordoba, Argentina
Date of Birth: 15 July 1952
Died: n/a   Caps: 43 (Argentina)
Goals (International): 20
Clubs: Insituto de Cordoba, Rosario Central, Valencia, River Plate
Trophies: CWC 1980; WorC 1978

LEGEND RATING

Achievement	8
Skill	8
Teamwork	6
Passion	7
Personality	8
Overall Legend Rating	**37**

- He scored a penalty in the shoot-out against Arsenal in Valencia's 1980 European Cup Winners' Cup victory.
- He was South American Footballer of the Year in 1978.
- Kempes scored 24 goals in his first season in La Liga, and 28 the following year, the highest return since the great Di Stefano in 1957.
- He is known as 'El Matador' for his Latin good looks and fashionable long hair.
- He was the only player in Argentina's 1978 squad playing outside South America.

Kennington Oval

London, England

THE HOME OF CRICKET was football's first-ever major venue. What is regarded as the first unofficial international was played at the Kennington Oval on 5 March 1870.

The game was organised between England and Scotland by the English FA, who chose the visiting team predominantly on the basis of their Scottish-sounding names or family connections. As both sides were chosen by the English, the game is not recognised as an official international. A further four 'unofficial' games were staged at the Kennington Oval before the first official international between England and Scotland took place at Partick in 1872.

The Oval was also the venue for the first FA Cup final in 1872, when 2,000 spectators watched the Wanderers beat the Royal Engineers 1-0, the winning goal being struck by Matthew P. Betts after the Royal Engineers lost a player with a fractured collarbone.

The Oval staged a further eight finals between 1874–92 before the venue was switched to Fallowfield in Manchester. Since then, its dramas and heroes have been cricketing ones, but English football's development owes much to the amateur enthusiasm of Kennington.

VITAL STATISTICS

Location:	London, England
Local Club:	None – as far as football clubs are concerned. (The Oval remains the home of Surrey County Cricket Club)
Date Built:	1845
Current Capacity:	17,500 (as cricket venue)
Max. Capacity:	25,000

◁⑲ The spectators at the 1872 FA Cup final each paid a shilling to get in. At that time, the average weekly wage was less than £1.

◁⑲ International cricket came later. The first cricket test match in England took place against Australia in 1880.

◁⑲ The largest crowd to watch an FA Cup final at The Oval was the last to be staged there in 1892, when 25,000 watched West Bromwich Albion beat Aston Villa 3-0.

◁⑲ After the first final of 1872, the final did not return to the Oval for two years. The Wanderers chose Lillie Bridge in 1873, the rules then stated that the holders could nominate the venue.

◁⑲ The most sucessful Oval team were The Wanderers, with four victories in nine finals.

Kewell, Harry

HARRY KEWELL IS NOT the first Australian to excel in a Leeds sporting arena; legendary cricketer Don Bradman was thrilling Yorkshire crowds 30 years before Kewell was even born. Unlike Bradman, though, Kewell has not yet established himself as a sporting hero in his home nation where cricketers, stars of Aussie Rules and both rugby codes still dominate the affections of the public.

He is, nevertheless, the first world-class footballer to emerge from Australia, and could become the inspiration that establishes them as a world power. A fleet-footed attacking midfielder with a deadly shot and a goal-to-game ratio that is the envy of many strikers, Kewell has impressed increasingly since signing as a 17-year-old in 1995 and was an indispensable component of David O'Leary's young team.

Already a veteran of six Premier League campaigns, his maturity and coolness under pressure are qualities that some of his team-mates would do well to copy. All that remains is silverware, but that is surely a formality if he can maintain his motivation with the lack of international football. Leeds' parlous financial state and recent fall from grace may mean a change of club before Kewell's sideboard fills with winner's medals.

VITAL STATISTICS

Place of Birth:	Sydney, Australia
Date of Birth:	22 September 1978
Died: n/a	Caps: 14 (Australia)
Goals (International): 4	
Clubs: Leeds United	
Appearances: Club (League): 184	
Goals: Club (League): 45	
Trophies: None	

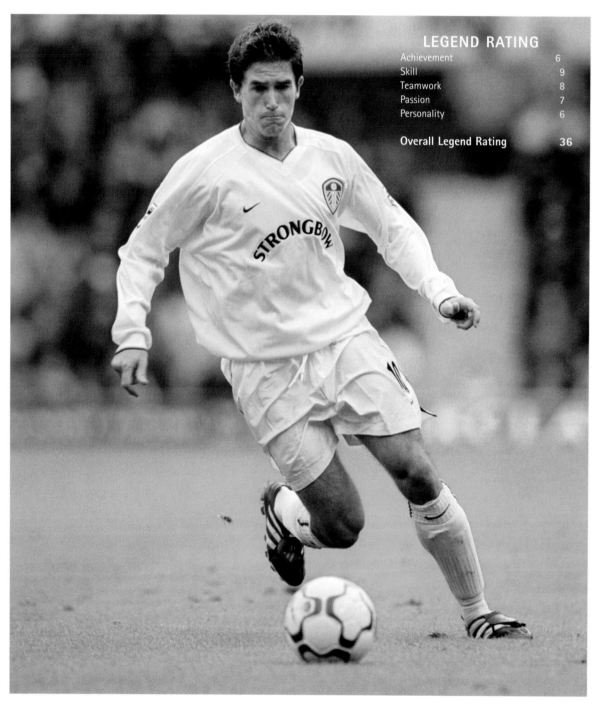

LEGEND RATING

Achievement	6
Skill	9
Teamwork	8
Passion	7
Personality	6
Overall Legend Rating	**36**

◁ᴵᴵᴵ A graduate of the Australian Academy of Sport, Kewell arrived in Yorkshire on a scholarship from the NSW soccer foundation.

◁ᴵᴵᴵ 1998. In a familiar club-versus-country dispute, Leeds withdrew Kewell from international duty, citing injury. Australia appealed to FIFA, who ordered Leeds to release him.

◁ᴵᴵᴵ 2000. PFA Young Player of the Year and Leeds United Player of the Year.

◁ᴵᴵᴵ 2000/01. Kewell was absent through injury as Leeds made a poor start to the season. Coincidence? We think not.

◁ᴵᴵᴵ August 2000. To the relief of Leeds' fans, Kewell signs a lengthy new contract at Elland Road.

Klinsmann, Jurgen

Tottenham Hotspur, Germany

JURGEN KLINSMANN has always been keen to embrace new challenges, and when he returned to Tottenham Hotspur for a second spell in December 1997 he faced one of his biggest. Under the inept management of Christian Gross, an unpopular appointment by an unpopular chairman, Alan Sugar, the club were facing relegation. That they avoided this fate was largely down to the German striker who, repeating his success of the 1994/95 season, lit up White Hart Lane with his leggy athleticism and, more crucially, goals.

Klinsmann's appetite for new adventures is evidenced by his willingness to play in Italy, France and England, as well as his native Germany. Quick and incisive in the box, as well as good in the air, Klinsmann has been a consistent goal scorer at every one of his clubs, even maintaining an impressive ratio in the notoriously defensive Serie A with Inter. Adaptable and intelligent (while at Spurs he spoke English more eloquently than most of his colleagues), he appeared in three World Cups, scoring 11 goals in 17 games. Sometimes criticised for diving, it was a foul on him that won the penalty from which Andreas Brehme scored to win the 1990 World Cup final for Germany.

VITAL STATISTICS

Place of Birth: Goppingen, Germany

Date of Birth: 30 July 1964

Died: n/a Caps: 108 (Germany) Goals (International): 47

Clubs: Stuttgart Kickers, VfB Stuttgart, Inter Milan, Monaco, Tottenham, Bayern Munich, Sampdoria

Appearances: Club (League): 491 Goals: Club (League): 194

Trophies: SA 1989; WorC 1990; BLG 1997; EuroC 1996; EUFAC 1996

LEGEND RATING

Achievement 9
Skill 8
Teamwork 9
Passion 8
Personality 7

Overall Legend Rating 41

◄ The much-travelled Klinsmann spent 15 years in search of a league title before he finally won one – in the Bundesliga with Bayern Munich in 1997.

◄ He arrived at Spurs in 1994 amidst media furore about his penchant for diving. A headlong plunge towards the corner flag on scoring his first goal for the club revealed a sense of humour.

◄ Klinsmann ended the 1994/95 season having turned the media around sufficiently for the Football Writers' Association to vote him their Player of the Year.

◄ In the 1990 World Cup Klinsmann gave one of the great individual performances, seeming to beat Holland almost single-handed after the early dismissal of his strike partner Voller.

◄ His 15 goals in Bayern's successful 1996 UEFA Cup campaign remains a record for European competition.

Kocsis, Sandor

FOR HIS EXPLOITS in the great Hungarian side of the 1950s, Sandor Kocsis became known as 'The Man With The Golden Head'. Kocsis had one role in the team: to score goals. This he did with huge aplomb, especially with his head. Although only 5 ft 9 in, he had a neck like a bull and could head the ball with tremendous power, often scoring from beyond the penalty spot.

He played alongside Ferenc Puskas in the Honved side of the early 1950s and developed a tremendous understanding with 'The Galloping Major'. His Honved career ended in a bizarre manner, however, as he and the rest of his team refused to fly home after a

match in Spain during the Hungarian uprising. The Spanish wasted little time taking advantage of this situation: shortly after, Puskas signed for Real Madrid while Kocsis moved to their great rivals, Barcelona, where he spent eight years before retiring in 1966.

The Hungarian international side, with Kocsis, Puskas, winger Zoltan Czibor and the great playmaker Nandor Hidegkuti, were the first exponents of what became known as 'Total Football'. Their breathtaking movement and passing made chance after chance for Kocsis, who was more than equipped to apply the finishing touch – a fact supported by his record of 75 goals in 68 internationals.

VITAL STATISTICS

Place of Birth: Budapest, Hungary

Date of Birth: 30 September 1928

Died: 22 July 1979   Caps: 68 (Hungary)

Goals (International): 75

Clubs: Fernecvaros, Honved, Young Boys Berne, Barcelona

Trophies: EUFAC 1960; HLT 1949, 1952, 1954; PLA 1959

LEGEND RATING

Achievement	7
Skill	8
Teamwork	8
Passion	7
Personality	6
Overall Legend Rating	**36**

- Kocsis scored a record seven hat-tricks for Hungary.
- He played in the legendary Hungarian team that crushed England 6–3 at Wembley in 1953. They followed this up with a 7–1 hammering the following year.
- Hungary, technically amateurs, competed in and won the 1952 Olympics.
- Sadly, Kocsis died in 1978, aged only 49, and missed the hero's return to a free Hungary enjoyed by Puskas and others.
- In the 1954 World Cup, Kocsis finished as top scorer with 11 goals, but Hungary threw away a 2–0 lead to lose 3–2 in the final to Germany.

Kopa, Raymond

PRIOR TO THEIR GREAT TEAM of the 1980s, France had only previously produced one side worthy of international acclaim. In the 1958 World Cup an unfancied French team produced some scintillating attacking football and their striker, Just Fontaine, earned a place in history by scoring 13 goals, a tournament record. Yet, while Fontaine took the plaudits, it was a first-generation Polish émigré, Raymond Kopaszewski, or Kopa, who was their true inspiration.

A traditional inside forward Kopa was a dazzling player; light on his feet, inventive and at the heart of everything the French created. The team piled on the goals, but a shaky defence was unable to cope against Brazil in the semi-final – an early goal from Fontaine merely stung the Brazilians into action. By this time Kopa had moved from Stade de Reims to Real Madrid to play alongside Di Stefano and Puskas. He was somewhat wasted on the wing, but his reward was a string of medals. The prodigal son later returned to Reims where he is lionised to this day, still remembered for his 13 years of exemplary service.

VITAL STATISTICS

Place of Birth: Noeux-les-milnes, France
Date of Birth: 13 October 1931
Died: n/a
Caps: 45 (France)
Goals (International): 18
Clubs: Angiers, Reims, Real Madrid
Trophies: EC 1957, 1958, 1959; PLA 1957, 1958

LEGEND RATING

Achievement	7
Skill	8
Teamwork	8
Passion	7
Personality	7
Overall Legend Rating	**37**

- ◁〕 In the very first European Cup in 1956, Kopa played against Real Madrid for Stade de Reims. Before the game Kopa already knew he was on his way to Real. Reims lost 4–3.
- ◁〕 Kopa played against Reims in the 1959 final, and again this presaged a move from one club to the other, this time the other way.
- ◁〕 Kopa masterminded a French slaughter of England in a preliminary match for the 1964 European Championships.
- ◁〕 He was voted European Footballer of the Year in 1958.
- ◁〕 He was also awarded the *Legion d'Honneur* in 1970.

Larsson, Henrik

Celtic, Sweden

SWEDEN'S FINEST EXPORT since Abba got a boyhood taste for football watching English league matches live on television, but it is north of the border where Henrik Larsson has made his name, becoming the biggest Celtic icon of the past 10 years.

Eye-catching both for his striking ability and fashionable dreadlocks, his 16 goals were a major factor in the title coming home to Parkhead after nine years of Rangers domination. It nearly ended there, though. After breaking his leg during a UEFA Cup match against Lyon in October 1999, there were fears that Larsson would never play again. But he battled back and, after a gradual comeback

programme, soon began to find the net again. Following the arrival of Martin O'Neill as manager, Larsson's 42-goal season helped Celtic sweep all before them in 2001, and he followed that with an almost identical campaign in 2002.

Already a seasoned international, he was one of the scorers in USA 94 as Sweden edged out Romania in a quarter-final shoot-out, and did his reputation no harm in the Far East in 2002, before announcing his retirement from internationals.

VITAL STATISTICS

Place of Birth: Helsingborg, Sweden

Date of Birth: 20 September 1971

Died: n/a   Caps: 73 (Sweden)

Goals (International): 24

Clubs: Hogabog BK, Helsingborgs BK, Feyenoord, Celtic

Appearances: Club (League – for Celtic): 183

Goals: Club (League – for Celtic): 143

Trophies: SLT 1998, 2001, 2002; SFAC 2001, 2002

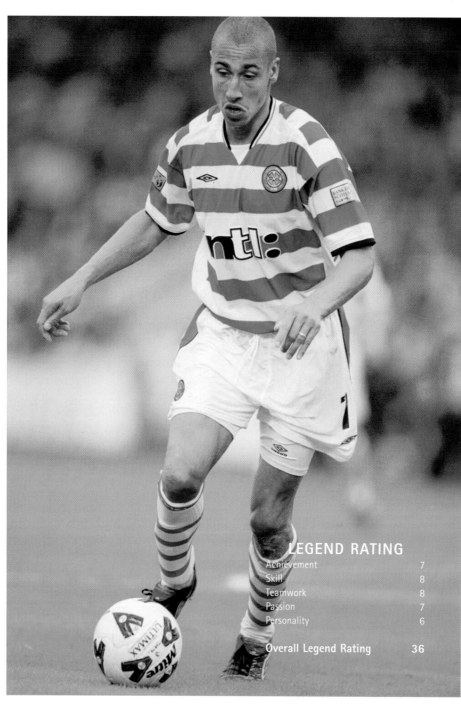

LEGEND RATING

Achievement	7
Skill	8
Teamwork	8
Passion	7
Personality	6
Overall Legend Rating	**36**

- His 2001 European Golden Boot award was the first made to a Scottish-based player since Ally McCoist in 1993.
- He scored on his international debut as Sweden qualified for USA 94.
- Larsson was signed twice by Wim Jansen, for Feyenoord and Celtic.
- His son Jordan is named after his hero, basketball star Michael Jordan
- He holds his strike partner Chris Sutton in high regard. Unlike Chelsea fans.
- He retired from internationals after the 2002 World Cup, but changed his mind to help Sweden in their Euro 2004 qualifiers.

Last Gasp Title

Liverpool 0 Arsenal 2, 1989

IT REMAINS THE MOST dramatic finish to a championship race in history. A rearranged fixture had inadvertently brought the top two together for the season's final game. Liverpool held all the aces; only a two-goal Arsenal victory would bring the title to Highbury.

A goalless first-half suited Liverpool, but the home crowd's celebrations were put on ice at 52 minutes, when Alan Smith, applying the faintest of touches to a Nigel Winterburn free-kick, gave Arsenal the lead. The goal made Liverpool edgy, and as the final whistle drew closer they retreated towards their own goal, inviting pressure from the Gunners.

Deep into injury time the score remained 1-0 and the Kop's volume was increasing. Steve McMahon rallied the Liverpool ranks, gesturing frantically to his team-mates that there was just one minute to go. But a minute was all Arsenal needed. Dixon pumped a hopeful last effort to Smith, who spotted the desperate gallop of Michael Thomas. The pass was precise, the flick over Grobbelaar ice-cool. On 91 minutes and 22 seconds, Arsenal had won it.

SCORERS: Smith, Thomas
EVENT: Division One, Anfield, 26 May 1989

LIVERPOOL		ARSENAL	
(Man: Kenny Dalglish)		(Man: George Graham)	
1 Grobbelaar	9 Rush	1 Lukic	9 Smith
2 Ablett	10 Barnes	2 Dixon	10 Bould
3 Staunton	11 McMahon	3 Winterburn	11 Merson
4 Nicol		4 Thomas	
5 Whelan		5 O'Leary	
6 Hansen		6 Adams	
7 Houghton		7 Rocastle	
8 Aldridge		8 Richardson	

Michael Thomas (yellow shirt) lifts the ball over a prone Grobbelaar for Arsenal's clincher.

◁ Ray Kennedy's goal at White Hart Lane to clinch the 1971 title and Alan Sunderland's winner in the FA Cup final eight years later had brought Arsenal fans to the brink. This result reduced them to gibbering wrecks.

◁ Both teams finished with virtually identical records: W22 D10 L6 GD +37. Arsenal won by scoring 73 goals to Liverpool's 65.
◁ Arsenal's task had looked impossible after Liverpool beat West Ham 5-1 in their previous home game to create a two-goal

cushion. The *Daily Mirror* headline the following day was typical: 'You Haven't Got A Prayer, Arsenal'.
◁ Brian Moore's commentary is familiar to Arsenal fans: 'Thomas ... it's up for grabs now ... Thomasss!'

Lato, Grzegorz

Poland

STOCKY AND BALDING, Grzegorz Lato cut an unlikely looking sporting hero, but his three World Cup Finals and 10 goals made him one of Poland's most celebrated sons. Lato's whippet-like pace and tireless running proved a handful for most defenders, including Norman Hunter, whose missed tackle resulted in Lato's assist for Poland's goal at Wembley in 1973 – a goal that ensured their qualification for the Finals at England's expense.

In Germany a year later, where his combination with the dashing Andrej Szarmach was a feature of the tournament, Lato (who spent most of his career with Polish outfit Stal Mielec)

finished as top scorer, his seven goals ensuring little-fancied Poland took third place.

Four years later the Poles disappointed, but 1982 provided Lato with a swansong as he and Szarmach were re-united alongside the new superstar, Zbigniew Boniek. Older, and with even less hair, he helped Poland to yet another third-place finish. Lato briefly played alongside his compatriot Wlodek Lubanski, for KSC Lokeren in Belgium, before a spot of belated globetrotting saw him wind up his career in Mexico and Canada.

VITAL STATISTICS

Place of Birth:	Malbork, Poland
Date of Birth:	8 April 1950
Died: n/a	Caps: 100 (Poland)

Goals (International): 42

Clubs: Stal Mielec, KSC Lokeren, Atlante

Trophies: PLT 1973, 1976

LEGEND RATING

Achievement	7
Skill	8
Teamwork	8
Passion	9
Personality	6
Overall Legend Rating	**38**

◁﹚ Lato's 10 World Cup Finals' goals have been bettered only by Pelé, Gerd Müller and Just Fontaine.

◁﹚ Lato won his 100th cap in Poland's Boniek-inspired destruction of Belgium in the 1982 tournament.

◁﹚ In 1976 a crowd of 106,000 in Warsaw saw Poland beat the mighty Dutch team of Cruyff and Neeskens 4-1 in a European Championship qualifier. Lato was among the scorers.

◁﹚ His final goal tally (42) for Poland was second only to Lubanski.

◁﹚ Lato has recently renewed his links with football, becoming a FIFA ambassador for childrens' charities.

Laudrup, Brian & Michael

Denmark

DENMARK'S EMERGENCE as a major force in European football is a relatively recent phenomenon, roughly starting around 25 years ago with the arrival of Allan Simonsen. Since then they have produced a string of talented players, not least the brothers Michael and Brian Laudrup. Michael, the elder by nearly five years, was the bright young thing in the side that helped illuminate Mexico 86 before their disappointing capitulation to Spain in the second round. A modern attacking midfielder with pace and touch, Michael's list of clubs (Juventus, Barcelona, Real Madrid, Ajax) bears witness to his quality. And yet, ironically, he was to miss his country's finest hour;

a dispute with coach Richard Moller Nielsen led to him being left out of Denmark's stunning victory at Euro 92.

His brother, Brian, did win a medal at that tournament and went on to follow in his brother's footsteps, enjoying spells at several of Europe's finest club teams. His best days were probably at Ibrox where, after a spellbinding first season, he won over a sceptical Rangers crowd. It was often said that the brothers rarely played well together but on Michael's international finale, a memorable quarter-final at France 98 that Denmark narrowly lost 3-2 to Brazil, they made a mockery of this theory. Both played out of their proverbial skins.

VITAL STATISTICS

BRIAN LAUDRUP
Place of Birth: Vienna, Austria
Date of Birth: 22 February 1969
Died: n/a Caps: 82 (Denmark) Goals (International): 21
Clubs: Brondby, Bayer Uerdingen, Fiorentina, AC Milan, Rangers, Chelsea, Copenhagen
Appearances: Club (For Rangers): 151
Goals: Club (Rangers): 45
Trophies: SLT 1995, 1996, 1997; SFAC 1996; DLT 1987, 1988; SA 1994; EuroC 1992

MICHAEL LAUDRUP
Place of Birth: Copenhagen
Date of Birth: 15 June 1964
Died: n/a Caps: 104 (Denmark) Goals (International): 37
Clubs: KB Copenhagen, Brondby, Juventus, Lazio, Barcelona, Real Madrid, Vissel Kobe, Ajax
Trophies: EC1992, PLA 1991, 1992, 1993, 1994, 1995; SA 1986; DLT 1998

LEGEND RATING

Achievement	8
Skill	9
Teamwork	8
Passion	6
Personality	7
Overall Legend Rating	38

Brian (left) holds the 1992 European Championship trophy.

◁ Between them the Laudrup brothers have turned out for most of the great European clubs.

◁ Brian is the first foreign player to be voted Scottish Footballer of the Year.

◁ Unlike the Rangers faithful, Chelsea fans do not have fond memories of Brian Laudrup. He left the club in bizarre circumstances to return to Denmark after only a few games.

◁ After the quarter-final with Brazil at France 98 Michael threw his boots into the crowd to signal his retirement. Brian's retirement from internationals followed soon after.

◁ Michael is now assistant coach to Bo Johansson with the Danish national team.

Law, Denis

HE SQUINTED, was scrawny and his unkempt, spiky hair gave him the appearance of a toilet brush. Yet, all this appeared little hindrance to Denis Law, who emerged as one of Manchester United's and Scotland's finest-ever strikers. The 'flying Scot' was as quick as a greyhound and with an aerial game few have surpassed.

He owes a huge debt to Bill Shankly, his first manager at Huddersfield, who moulded a novice schoolboy into an 18-year-old international. Like Jimmy Greaves, he failed to settle in Italy and it was only his return to Manchester, swapping a blue shirt for a red one, that revived his career. His forward combination with George Best and Bobby Charlton was the finest in English club football. Law left Old Trafford after being kicked out of the club by Tommy Docherty who, keen to assert his authority on his arrival in 1972, made an example of him. Law joined Man City and came back to haunt Docherty the following season when his back-heeled goal for City in the Manchester derby contributed to United's relegation to Division Two. Famously, Law did not celebrate the goal. Head bowed, he simply turned round and walked solemnly back to the centre-circle. Since his retirement, his partnership with former team-mate Paddy Crerand, has made him one of the circuit's most popular after-dinner speakers.

VITAL STATISTICS

Place of Birth: Aberdeen, Scotland
Date of Birth: 24 February 1940
Died: n/a Caps: 55 (Scotland) Goals (International): 30
Clubs: Huddersfield Town, Manchester City, Torino, Manchester United
Appearances: Club (All Matches): 566
Goals: Club (All Matches): 301
Trophies: FAC 1963; LT 1965, 1967

LEGEND RATING

Achievement	7
Skill	9
Teamwork	8
Passion	8
Personality	9
Overall Legend Rating	**41**

◀ Law broke three transfer records; £35,000 to Man City (UK); £100,000 to Torino (world); £115,000 to Man United (world).
◀ He was voted European Footballer of the Year, 1964.
◀ 1968. Missed United's European Cup final victory through injury.
◀ His 30 goals for Scotland set a national record, now jointly held with Kenny Dalglish.
◀ Law retired with over 300 goals in club football.

Lawton, Tommy

ASK THE OLD BOY in the pub, the one who always sits at the bar with a pint of mild and a copy of *The Sporting Life* (there's always one), why he thinks players in the old days were superior to their modern counterparts, and the name of Tommy Lawton is guaranteed to crop up within five seconds. Brave, strong, supreme in the air and with a cannonball shot, Lawton was the archetypal English centre-forward. Bought to replace the immortal Dixie Dean at Everton, he took on and achieved the daunting task of filling the great man's shoes. In the days of five forwards, goal scoring comparisons with

today are unwise, but a career record of nearly two goals every three games, plus 22 goals from 23 England caps are a reliable indicator of his quality. Strangely, for a man whose prime years were taken by the war, he opted to play most of his career in the lower divisions, even dropping into the Third Division with Notts County before Second Division Brentford offered him a player-manager role. Due to wage restrictions Lawton made little money from the game, and spent his later years living close to poverty until his death in 1996.

VITAL STATISTICS

Place of Birth: Bolton, England
Date of Birth: 6 October 1919
Died: 6 November 1996
Caps: 23 (England) **Goals (International):** 22
Clubs: Burnley, Everton, Chelsea, Notts County, Brentford, Arsenal, Kettering Town
Appearances: Club (League): 390
Goals: Club (League): 231 **Trophies:** LT 1939

LEGEND RATING
Achievement 5
Skill 8
Teamwork 8
Passion 9
Personality 5

Overall Legend Rating 36

Griffin Park, Brentford. Lawton rounds the keeper to score for the Bees.

◄)) He managed Notts County and Brentford but was never a success in this role.
◄)) He scored a hat-trick on his debut, aged 16.
◄)) His 28 goals in the 1946/47 season was a Chelsea club record.

◄)) John Arlott on Tommy Lawton: 'I have faith in genius'.
◄)) 1948. His £20,000 move to Notts County set a British record; Third Division County saw gates rocket.

Le Tissier, Matthew

PERHAPS THE GREATEST ENIGMA of the modern English game, Matt Le Tissier's achievements do not merit him an entry into the hall of fame, but in many ways it is his lack of success that marks him out. His touch, and his use of the ball were reminiscent of Glenn Hoddle, his free-kicks were Beckhamesque, and his dribbling was worthy of any of the 1970s mavericks with whom he is often compared.

Le Tissier's natural diffidence off the field may explain why he stayed with Southampton, then an unfashionable and struggling club, throughout his career, although many have argued that fear of failure was his prime motivation in not seeking a move to a bigger one. There may be an element of truth in this, but it would be churlish not to give Le Tissier credit for his loyalty. There have been numerous campaigns for his inclusion in the England side, but on the rare occasions he appeared he seemed to lack the confidence to express himself. Maybe, in a parallel universe, Le Tissier did move to Chelsea, win the Cup and captain England. But if he did, that means that out there somewhere is another Ken Bates. And that's not something we should even joke about.

VITAL STATISTICS

Place of Birth: Guernsey
Date of Birth: 14 October 1968
Died: n/a   Caps: 10 (England)
Goals (International): 0
Clubs: Southampton
Appearances: Club (League): 443
Goals: Club (League): 163
Trophies: None

LEGEND RATING

Achievement	5
Skill	10
Teamwork	6
Passion	8
Personality	6
Overall Legend Rating	**35**

◁ Glenn Hoddle had the excellent idea of holding a couple of B internationals to check out some fringe players. Le Tissier scored a hat-trick, but was still left out of the World Cup squad. Go figure....

◁ He scored 24 goals in 1989/90 and was voted PFA Young Player of the Year.

◁ He has only missed one penalty in over 50 attempts.

◁ He scored some astonishing goals, including one against Blackburn where he waltzed through the defence playing keepy-uppy and stroked the ball into the net.

◁ Appropriately, as their greatest contemporary player, Le Tissier scored the last-ever goal at The Dell in a 3-2 win over Arsenal.

League Cup

IT TOOK AN AGE to get going, and but for the persistence of league secretary Alan Hardaker it would never have got off the ground. The idea of a Cup purely for the top four divisions had been mooted for years but it didn't exactly arrive with a fanfare.

Most top clubs viewed 'Hardaker's folly' as an irrelevance and refused to enter, and Rochdale's appearance in the second final was indicative of its lack of cachet.

It was not until the final was switched to Wembley in 1967 that the tournament acquired the respect it so desperately needed, and QPR and Swindon provided further interest by winning it as Third Division sides, both beating First Division opposition in their respective Finals against WBA and Arsenal. The award of a UEFA Cup place for the winners has helped maintain its importance over the years, but the recent growth of the Champions League has eroded its importance to the big clubs who now regularly field weakened teams in the competition.

Q: What is taken to Wembley every year and never used?

A: Malcolm McDonald

Sunderland quip after the 1976 League Cup final; it was his second Wembley disappointment in three seasons

Cardiff, 2002. Blackburn celebrate after beating Spurs in the final.

- The League Cup has been through several incarnations. Bizarrely known as the Milk Cup for a while, it has also lent its name to sponsors Rumbelows, Coca-Cola, Littlewoods and Worthington's.
- The 1967 and 1969 finals were the making of Rodney Marsh and Don Rogers. Both scored winners and moved to bigger clubs.
- Liverpool fans were particularly scathing about the League Cup, mainly because it took them 20 years to win it. After four straight wins (1981–84) the 'tea kettle' jibes disappeared.
- The Aston Villa v Everton final went to a third game in 1977. After two dull encounters, Villa won 3–2 after extra-time.
- Oxford and Luton won the trophy in the late 1980s. Both subsequently played in the bottom division.

Leeds United

A TEAM THAT TAKES no prisoners. The defence is entirely from the great Revie team of the 1960s and 1970s, one of the meanest in domestic history, and two players from that era, Bremner and Giles, also occupy the central midfield positions. The sixth and final member of the Revie side to make this Dream Team starting XI is Alan 'Sniffer' Clarke, a striker who rarely failed to live up to his nickname.

Lest these players are not considered combative enough, Gordon Strachan adds more bite in midfield, leaving Harry Kewell free to link with the front two. The sole representative of Corinthian sportsmanship is provided by the Gentle Giant himself at centre-forward, John Charles. One shudders to think what he would have made of Revie's team talks, the shin-high tackles or the incessant baiting of the officials, but if his sensibilities were too offended, he could always be replaced by toothless assassin Joe Jordan. Make no mistake, this team will autograph a few shins. The referee will need an A4 notebook.

Manager: Don Revie

4-4-2

Nigel Martyn (90s/00s)

Paul Madeley (60s) Jack Charlton (60s/70s)
Norman Hunter (60s/70s) Terry Cooper (60s/70s)

Gordon Strachan (80s) Billy Bremner (C) (60s/70s)
Johnny Giles (60s/70s) Harry Kewell (00s)

John Charles (50s) Alan Clarke (70s)

Subs: David Harvey (G) (70s) Rio Ferdinand (D) (00s)
David Batty (M) (90s) Eddie Gray (W) (60s/70s) Joe Jordan (F) (70s)

The last decade — prior its unravelling during the 2002/3 season following disastrous financial results.

◄)) If Revie's team had enjoyed the benefit of Nigel Martyn in goal rather than the accident-prone Gary Sprake, they may have finished runners-up less often.

◄)) Despite less than two full seasons, Rio Ferdinand deserves his place on the bench for his improvement and increased maturity. It also means we don't have to pick Gordon McQueen.

◄)) The dependence on the modern era is entirely justified. Leeds won nothing prior to the Revie years.

◄)) Two great flair players are not included: Eric Cantona and Tony Currie both enjoyed better spells with other clubs.

Leeds United – The Revie Years

THE WORD PROFESSIONAL has several shades of meaning, and Don Revie's Leeds knew them all. Fit, organised and skilful they were the epitome of mechanical excellence but, at Revie's behest, they were also hard, ruthless and prone to bending the rules when it suited them. None of this should disguise their ability, though. Leeds lost only twice in winning the league in 1969, the lowest total in a 42-game season, and when they won the league again five years later it was with essentially the same team – togetherness was undoubtedly a factor in their success. Yet, at times, they could be their own worst enemy, and often failed at the final hurdle. They were league runners-up five times and blew two FA Cup finals, notably against Second Division Sunderland in 1973. They weren't always the prettiest or most popular team, but few sides got the better of them.

Manager: Don Revie

Key Players

David Harvey (G) Jack Charlton (D) Norman Hunter (D)
Paul Reaney (FB) Terry Cooper (FB) Billy Bremner (M)
Johnny Giles (M) Peter Lorimer (F) Eddie Gray (W)
Allan Clarke (F) Mick Jones (F)

Trophies

LT 1969, 1974 FAC 1972 LC 1968 UEFA 1968, 1971

◁ Harvey's emergence as a replacement for the error-prone Gary Sprake was a major improvement to the side.

◁ The downside of the close-knit team was that they aged together; Leeds fell into sharp decline after this team broke up,

and only re-emerged as a force in the early 1990s.

◁ Cooper was a great attacking full-back who ought to have won more than his 20 caps. He scored the goal that won the 1968 League Cup, bringing the squad their first trophy.

◁ Even in their title winning seasons Leeds weren't prolific scorers; Jones top scored in both campaigns with just 14.

Leonidas

Brazil

WHEN LEONIDAS DA SILVA appeared in the 1934 World Cup Finals for Brazil, he was the only black player in the side and scored his country's only goal as a transitional team were easily brushed aside by Spain. His next appearance was at the 1938 Finals, in the extraordinary 6-5 extra-time win over Poland. Leonidas scored a hat-trick and scored in both games against Czechoslovakia in the next round. For the semi-final against Italy, Brazil made one of the most bizarre selection decisions in football history and left him out, a ploy designed to keep him fit for the final. Bet you can guess what happened next. Sure enough, they lost (2-1 to Italy), and Leonidas'

chances of ever playing in a World Cup final were swept away by Hitler's armies just a few months later.

Leonidas was a major draw in his home country, appearing for many of the great sides, as well as for Penarol in Uruguay.

Diminutive and pugnacious, he was a well-balanced player with a reputation for scoring with extravagant bicycle kicks. In many ways he was the forefather of the great Brazilian sides to come – an early hint to the white-dominated footballing authorities that the black population harboured their game's true soul.

VITAL STATISTICS

Place of Birth: Sao Cristovao, Brazil

Date of Birth: 11 November 1912

Died: n/a **Caps:** 25 (Brazil) **Goals (International):** 25 (Top scorer in 1938 World Cup Finals with 8 goals)

Clubs: Havanesa, Barroso, Sul Americano, Sirio Libanes, Bomsucesso, Nacional, Vasco da Gama, Botafogo, Flamengo, Sao Paulo

LEGEND RATING

Achievement	6
Skill	9
Teamwork	7
Passion	8
Personality	
Overall Legend Rating	**37**

◁ Many accounts credit Leonidas with four goals in the win over Poland, but this is inaccurate. The Polish centre-forward Willimowski did score four, but in vain.

◁ He became known as 'The Black Diamond' in Brazil, and sometimes 'The Rubber Man' due to his acrobatic attempts on goal.

◁ Leonidas scored twice on his international debut against the powerful Uruguayans.

◁ Leonidas started a World Cup match in socks on a boggy pitch, but was told by the referee to put on some boots.

◁ Leonidas' replacement Peracio missed two sitters in the 1938 World Cup semi-final.

L'Equipe

THE STORY OF FRENCH FOOTBALL begins at the 1958 World Cup when, inspired by Just Fontaine's 13-goal burst (still a Finals record), *Les Bleus* finally emerged from the shadow of their illustrious European neighbours, Italy and Germany. But it took them a further 26 years to claim their first international honour, the European Championship in 1984.

The peerless Platini and Giresse, two-thirds of that team's irresistible midfield, are included here. Jean Tigana, the third member of that celebrated midfield triumvirate, must wait on the bench though, forced out by Kopa and Zidane.

The backline is almost exclusively drawn from the team that won the 1998 World Cup and Euro 2000 titles. The exception is Marius Tresor, who is good enough to relegate Laurent Blanc to the bench.

Up front, as well as Fontaine's prodigious goal scoring, the pace of Papin will open up defences leaving gaps for the forward surges of Platini and Zidane. And, in the unlikely event that goals are not forthcoming, player-manger Platini can turn to the bench and order Thierry Henry to strip for action.

Player-Manager: Michel Platini
4-4-2

Fabien Barthez (90s)

Lilian Thuram (90s) Marcel Desailly (90s)
Marius Tresor (70/80s) Bixente Lizarazu (90s)

Alain Giresse (80s) Raymond Kopa (50s)
Zinedine Zidane (90s) Michel Platini (C) (80s)

Just Fontaine (50s) Jean-Pierre Papin (80s)

Subs: Joel Bats (G) (30s) Laurent Blanc (D) (80s) Jean Tigana (M) (80s)
Thierry Henry (F) (90s) Dominique Rocheteau (F) (80s)

Traditional French enthusiasm for football when they're not winning.

◀ Platini has performed the roles of midfield general, captain, player-manager and French ambassador to FIFA.

◀ Four of this squad play in the Premier League: Barthez and Blanc with Man United; Henry with Arsenal; and Desailly with Chelsea.

◀ Fontaine scored 30 goals in only 21 internationals for France, the best strike-rate in international football history.

◀ Both goalkeepers are noted for their eccentricity, combining flashes of brilliance with occasional dashes outside the box.

◀ Despite founding FIFA and the World Cup, France have taken their time to establish their international dominance. But, for their fans, the wait has been worth it. No other nation has held the World Cup and the European Championship simultaneously.

Liddell, Billy

Liverpool, Scotland

THERE HAVE ARGUABLY been better Liverpool players, and there have certainly been players who won far more at Anfield, particularly in the glory days of the 1970s and 1980s, but the more decorated names of Neal, McDermott or Souness are not the ones that Liverpool fans are currently campaigning to have inscribed on the Shankly Gates. That honour is reserved for one man: Billy Liddell. A hugely versatile player, his favourite role was as a marauding striker with a wicked shot in either foot. He signed for Liverpool as an amateur in 1938, but his name was made as a winner of the first post-war league title nine years later. Ironically, this lone league medal came courtesy of Manchester United, whose 2-1 defeat of Stoke on the final day handed Liverpool the championship. Older Kopites still maintain that Liddell's injury in the 1950 FA Cup final robbed them of victory against Arsenal, and he remained their only hope during wilderness years that saw them relegated in 1954. Despite his efforts, he never again played in the First Division. His death, at 79 in July 2001, prompted grief on a scale not witnessed since the passing of Shankly.

VITAL STATISTICS

Place of Birth: Dunfermline, Scotland
Date of Birth: 10 January 1921
Died: 3 July 2001   Caps: 28 (Scotland)
Goals (International): 6
Clubs: Liverpool
Appearances: Club (League): 537
Goals: Club (League): 229
Trophies: LT 1947

LEGEND RATING

Achievement	5
Skill	8
Teamwork	8
Passion	9
Personality	6
Overall Legend Rating	36

◁)) The club was dubbed 'Liddellpool' due to his huge influence.

◁)) The archetypal 'Boys Own' hero had an unlikely beginning, training as an accountant.

◁)) Liddell played in every outfield position for Liverpool.

◁)) Liddell and Stanley Matthews are the only players to have twice appeared in a United Kingdom XI.

◁)) A true Corinthian, Liddell was never booked despite his tenacious attitude.

Lineker, Gary

Leicester City, Everton, Tottenham Hotspur, England

THE GOLDEN BOY. Lineker is a man it is hard to dislike, even if you find his personality a little anodyne. A model professional with all his clubs, not a season went by without Lineker delivering his quota of goals; he was top scorer in England three times, each time with different clubs. Despite recent gags regarding a longstanding toe problem, Lineker was rarely injured until moving to Japan and, incredibly for a player who regularly suffered intense provocation, went through his entire career without receiving a yellow card.

Following success in England with Leicester and Everton, Lineker moved to Barcelona, and soon proved he was capable of rising to the challenges of life in a foreign country. Indeed, but for a disagreement with Johan Cruyff who, bafflingly, decided that Lineker's best position was on the right wing, he could well have spent the rest of his career at the Nou Camp. As it was he returned to England to play for Terry Venables at Spurs with whom, at the age of 30, he finally collected his first domestic trophy, the FA Cup in 1991.

Since retiring, Lineker has enjoyed a successful media career, succeeding Des Lynam as the anchor on *Match Of The Day*. He had an outstanding 2002 World Cup in this capacity.

VITAL STATISTICS

Place of Birth: Leicester
Date of Birth: 30 November 1960
Died: n/a Caps: 80 (England)
Goals (International): 48
Clubs: Leicester City, Everton, Barcelona, Tottenham, Nagoya Grampus
Appearances: Club (All Matches): 447
Goals: Club (All Matches): 236
Trophies: CWC 1989; FAC 1991

LEGEND RATING

Achievement 8
Skill 9
Teamwork 8
Passion 9
Personality 7

Overall Legend Rating 41

- He scored 10 goals in two World Cup Finals, winning the Golden Boot at Mexico 86 with six goals.
- He scored after four minutes of the first all-Merseyside FA Cup Final in 1986, but Everton lost.
- He scored all four goals for Barcelona against Real Madrid in 1987.
- Lineker was controversially substituted by Graham Taylor during England's defeat to Sweden at the 1992 European Championships. It was to be his last appearance for his country.
- He was voted PFA Player of the Year, 1986 and 1992.

Lisbon Lions

GREAT SIDES TODAY are usually the product of a large chequebook and a worldwide scouting network. What made Celtic special was that their great teams were all home-grown, a collection of local lads with local roots; nearly all the players had stepped from the terraces to the pitch. Their mentor was manager Jock Stein. In Scottish footballing terms, Celtic were a big club with large resources when Stein joined them in 1965. But they were not successful. At the time the Scottish league belonged to the Rangers team of Greig and Baxter. Not only did Stein make them league champions within a year, he took the team beyond their parochial confines to make them Champions of Europe. The local lads became the 'Lisbon Lions' in 1967.

Like the great Liverpool teams, Celtic's continuity ensured a decade of success, including nine consecutive league titles. Players left and retired without disrupting the club's rhythm, a testimony to the conveyor belt of talent the club had created. Craig became McGrain and Auld became Dalglish. The result was the same: total domination.

Manager: Jock Stein

Key Players
Billy McNeill (D) Tommy Gemmell (D) Danny McGrain (D)
Bobby Lennox (M) Jimmy Johnstone (W) Bobby Murdoch (M)
Steve Chalmers (M) Kenny Dalglish (F)

Trophies
SLT 1966, 1967, 1968, 1969, 1970, 1971, 1972, 1973, 1974 SFAC 1967, 1969, 1971, 1972, 1974 EC 1967

The Bhoys are Back in Town. Celtic bring home the European cup in 1967.

- Stein had also been a Celtic player, winning the league and Cup double in 1954.
- In 1970 Celtic reached a second European Cup final, losing 2-1 to Feyenoord.
- In 1967 Celtic won every competition they entered. The European Cup, the Scottish Cup, the Scottish League Cup and the Glasgow Cup.
- Celtic declined after Stein's departure in 1978, and the manager's only venture into English club management lasted 44 days at Leeds.
- Before Stein's first title in 1966, Celtic had not won the league for 11 years.

Litmanen, Jari

ONE CAN SAY without fear of contradiction that Jari Litmanen is the best thing to come out of Finland since roll-mop herring. During his international career Finland have gone from being cannon fodder to dangerous floaters, albeit without making the major breakthrough and qualifying for a major tournament. Litmanen is an ideal player to build a team around. A subtle, deep-lying forward, his vision and passing ability are perfect assets for bringing others into the game, and his goal-scoring record is none too shabby either.

After several successful years in Finland, Litmanen made the switch to Ajax where, following the departure of Dennis Bergkamp

to Inter, he won a regular starting place in his preferred role as a slightly withdrawn front man. Once established he became a revelation, inspiring Ajax to three successive titles and successive European Cup Finals in 1995 and 1996, winning the first. A move to Barcelona proved disappointing as Litmanen spent most of his time on the bench. More recently Liverpool, too, have chosen to squander his talents, using him only sparingly as cover for Michael Owen and Emile Heskey.

VITAL STATISTICS

Place of Birth: Lahti, Finland
Date of Birth: 20 February 1971
Died: n/a Caps: 82 (Finland) Goals (International): 22
Clubs: Reipas Lahti, HJK Helsinki,MyPa, Ajax, Barcelona, Liverpool
Appearances: Club (League): 346
Goals: Club (League): 147
Trophies: DLT 1991, 1994, 1995, 1998; EC 1995

LEGEND RATING

Achievement	8
Skill	9
Teamwork	8
Passion	6
Personality	6
Overall Legend Rating	**37**

- Injuries have hampered Litmanen in recent years – he was devastated to miss out on Liverpool's Cup treble in 2001.
- Thirty-four goals in his first full season solidified his reputation at Ajax, and his 24 goals in Europe is a club record.
- Litmanen scored Ajax's goal in the 1996 European Cup final, but Juventus triumphed on penalties.
- He was voted Finnish Footballer of the Year for seven successive years (1992–98).
- Gerard Houllier's reluctance to pick Litmanen is strange; whenever he plays he adds a creative edge to a largely unimaginative side.

Loadsabentmoney

IN A PROFESSIONAL GAME where millions, and now billions, change hands in transfer fees and sponsorship deals, it was always hoping against hope to assume that a sporting spirit would prevail.

The maximum-wage system has got a lot to answer for. During its existence players would routinely supplement their income with under-the-counter cash payments, often surreptitiously placed in a pocket or shoe after the game. And old habits die hard. Even in the modern era, several clubs and individuals have been relegated, fined or expelled for conducting their financial business in a less than honest fashion.

Betting has brought the most severe problems. In 1964 tabloid revelations exposed three Sheffield Wednesday players in a match-fixing scandal. This proved to be the tip of a decidedly sleazy iceberg. The spiralling transfer fees and use of third-party agents in recent times have also led to some high-profile cases of skulduggery, the most notorious example being that of George Graham and agent Rune Hauge. For every one found guilty, you can be almost certain there are at least a dozen getting away with it.

'What I know most surely about morality and the duty of man I owe to sport.'

Albert Camus, novelist and Philosopher (1913–60); Camus briefly played professional football as a goalkeeper

If you've just been convicted of a crime, why not look like a criminal for good measure? Bruce Grobbelaar leaves court.

◄)) Match officials are not whiter than white. In 1979, a Scottish referee and both linesmen were banned for three years after accepting gifts from Milan before taking charge of their UEFA Cup tie against Levski Spartak.

◄)) 1982. A major Italian betting scandal claimed several high-profile casualties, including Paolo Rossi.

◄)) In a 1990s match-fixing scandal, Bruce Grobbelaar and Hans Segers faced court action after they were alleged to have accepted cash for conceding goals. Grobbelaar's case started a legal storm as his acquittal was quashed by an appeal court.

◄)) Corruption isn't a modern preserve. In 1919 Leeds City were expelled from the league for making irregular payments.

Loadsamoney

CHAIRMEN TEND TO FALL into two categories. The first are the local businessmen who, made wealthy by their acumen in scrap metal or toilet paper, wish to realise a childhood dream, while the second are a disparate bunch of entertainers and media puppies who have nothing better to do with their money.

That said, many are genuine fans whose input is far more than financial; Elton John racks up enormous international phone bills and charters private jets in his desire to follow Watford, while Jasper Carrott stood on the St Andrews terraces for years before his fame brought him greater influence in the affairs of Birmingham City.

Delia Smith, although a director rather than chairwoman, brings more than a decent half-time pie to Norwich City. Some of them are in it simply for the dough, though. Take Stan Flashman, whose principal interest at Barnet was never anything other than to turn a fast buck. 'Why sleep when you can make money', reflected an attitude that many of his peers share but dare not utter in public.

> 'Maxwell Chairman? We may as well have Max Wall.'
>
> Derby County fanzine *The Sheep* gets justifiably splenetic

Elton John laments on what Watford have done with his cash.

◀)) 'He's fat, he's round, he's never in the ground, Cap'n Bob.' Like their fanzine's editors, Derby fans fail to join the Robert Maxwell fan club.

◀)) Elton John has always retained a philosophical attitude to some unacceptable homophobic chanting from opposing fans.

◀)) Uri Geller's 'positive energy' had the opposite effect on Reading, who finished bottom of Division One in 1998. If he'd bent the goalposts instead of spoons they might have scored more often.

◀)) Visiting fans at Craven Cottage (and now Loftus Road) collectively wave British passports at Mohamed al Fayed. It takes more than ownership of Fulham to obtain one, apparently.

LoadsaMurdochmoney

Sky TV

WHEN RUPERT MURDOCH'S satellite network joined the TV rights arena the rules suddenly changed. Here was a multi-billion dollar organisation prepared to use football as a loss-leader to accelerate subscription. How could the BBC, or even the commercial channels compete with that kind of spending power? Answer: they couldn't. Overnight we entered an era of saturation coverage. Live games were shown on Friday, Sunday and Monday. Now even Saturday morning games have begun to creep in. On top of the matches, endless magazine programmes have also been rolled out, featuring the exclusive insights of opinionated has-beens like Rodney Marsh and

overweight tabloid journalists. Thank heavens for Andy Gray. Complete with his state-of-the-art graphics, Gray has brought boundless enthusiasm and optimism to Sky's live broadcasts. Yes, he tries to talk up a dour stalemate as a minor classic, but here is a man who earned respect for his achievements in the game talking to the viewer as an equal, another fan. Gray's computers were a bit of a standing joke at first, but the technology is excellent – those extra camera angles and graphics enhance, rather than detract from, the armchair experience.

'The governing body of football: television.'

Mike Ingham, 1991

Andy Gray (foreground) has found more fame as a summariser than most commentators.

◁ Sky feature great graphics and camera angles. But does anyone really care about 'player-cam'?

◁ 'The biggest advance in TV football since the invention of the camera.' David Hill, 1992.

◁ 'The most ludicrous and backward step football has taken in a long time.' Alex Ferguson, 1992.

◁ Thus far Sky hasn't had the negative effect on attendances many expected; beware pay-per-view.

◁ For all the criticism heaped upon them, Sky have given audiences significantly more opportunity to watch teams outside the Premiership than the terrestrial channels ever did.

Lofthouse, Nat

Bolton Wanderers, England

'IL BANDIERA' is an Italian expression used to describe a player whose career is so intertwined with the fortunes of his club he becomes a symbol of its very soul. Nat Lofthouse is the 'Il Bandiera' of Bolton Wanderers. By far their most famous and successful player, he was the inspiration behind their most recent success, and as president still retains close ties with the Trotters.

Bolton were a robust Division One club in the 1950s and Lofthouse's battering-ram style suited them; powerful and dominant in the air he was the sort of player that coaches and pundits like to describe as 'a real handful'. In the 1958 FA Cup final against Manchester United, who were fielding a team weakened by the Munich air crash, he was able to put sentiment aside and scored both goals in a 2-0 win.

In a fine England career Lofthouse's greatest moment came in a 3-2 win against an Austrian team who were one of the best in Europe. A scratch England team had done well to stay level and, with just 10 minutes left, Lofthouse broke from inside his own half and finished in style. From that day forward he was universally referred to as 'The Lion of Vienna'.

VITAL STATISTICS

Place of Birth: Bolton, England
Date of Birth: 27 August 1925
Died: n/a Caps: 33 (England)
Goals (International): 30
Clubs: Bolton Wanderers
Appearances: Club (For Bolton): 485
Goals: Club (For Bolton): 285
Trophies: FAC 1958

LEGEND RATING

Achievement 6
Skill 8
Teamwork 9
Passion 9
Personality 6

Overall Legend Rating 38

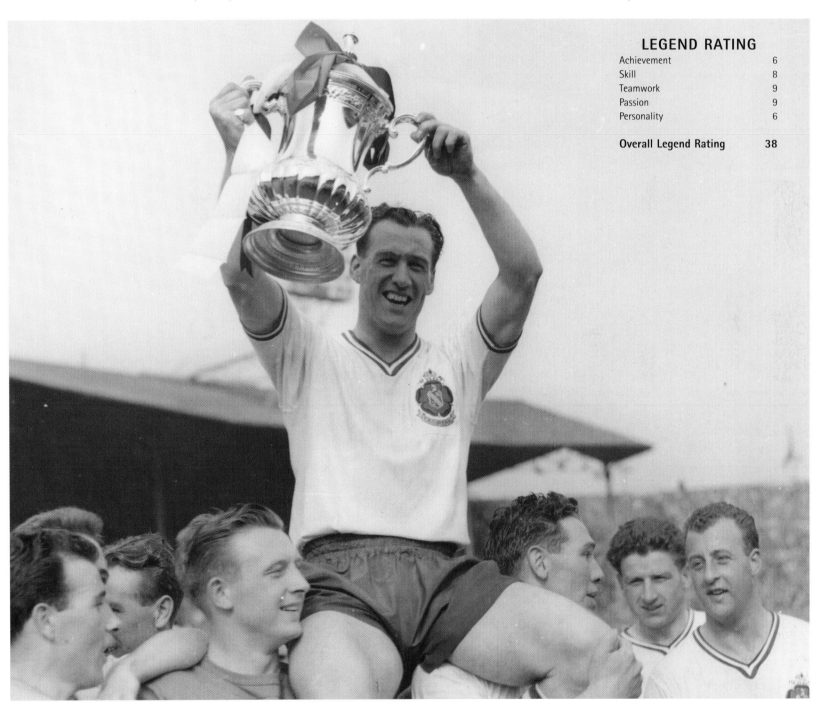

- Lofthouse scored the opening goal in the 1953 'Matthews Final'.
- The second goal in the 1958 FA Cup final was highly controversial; Lofthouse barged United keeper Harry Gregg into the net with the ball.
- Lofthouse was the First Division's top scorer with 33 goals in 1956.
- He scored twice in a 2-2 draw on his England debut against Yugoslavia in 1950.
- Lofthouse displaced Jackie Milburn in the England team, and his impressive scoring rate saw him retain his place until the emergence of Tommy Taylor.

245

Losing it in Leon

England 2 West Germany 3, 1970

HARD DONE BY after the 1966 World Cup final when, but for the intervention of that famous Russian linesman, they would have almost certainly taken home the trophy, Germany were eager for revenge against England. And, in the sweltering heat of Leon in 1970, they extracted it with great relish.

England approached the game confidently. They were, after all, defending champions and had progressed through a group in which they were only narrowly defeated by the brilliant Brazilians. With 21 minutes left they were comfortably holding a 2-0 lead and their progress to the semi-finals looked assured but, proving that a chain is only as strong as its weakest link, stand-in keeper Peter Bonetti dived over a speculative effort from Beckenbauer and the match was suddenly back in the balance. Then, with the hapless Chelsea keeper a stranded spectator, Uwe Seeler's bizarre back-header looped agonisingly into the net with eight minutes remaining to send the match into extra-time. The German swagger had returned, while England looked exhausted. Gerd Müller had had a quiet game thus far, so quiet that it's doubtful if he had even broken sweat, but, great striker that he was, 'Der Bomber' took his only chance and England were out.

SCORERS: **England:** Mullery, Peters
West Germany: Beckenbauer, Seeler, Muller
EVENT: World Cup Quarter-Final, Leon, Mexico, 14 June 1970

ENGLAND (Man: Sir Alf Ramsey)		WEST GERMANY (Man: Helmut Schoen)	
1 Bonetti	9 R Charlton	1 Maier	9 Libuda
2 K Newton	10 Hurst	2 Schnellinger	10 Müller
3 Cooper	11 Peters	3 Vogts	11 Löhr
4 Mullery		4 Fichtel	
5 Labone		5 Höttges	
6 Moore		6 Beckenbauer	
7 F Lee		7 Overath	
8 Ball		8 Seeler	

Gerd Müller fires the killer third past Bonetti.

◄)) With England 2-0 up, Alan Mullery missed a sitter and the chance to put the game beyond Germany's reach.

◄)) For the substituted Bobby Charlton, it was to be a sad end to his 106th and final England game.

◄)) Peter Bonetti was also never to play for England again.

◄)) It has been claimed that England's loss altered the mood of the nation and contributed to Labour's defeat in the British General Election that took place a few weeks later.

◄)) This match helped set up an Italy versus West Germany classic in the semi-final that the Germans lost.

Lucky (?) Arsenal

NOT WISHING TO BE OUTDONE by their neighbours, Arsenal became the fourth English team to win the League and Cup double 10 years after Spurs achieved the feat in 1961. Unlike Tottenham, who sauntered through the season without a hitch, Arsenal's double required every ounce of their famous resilience; they overhauled Leeds Utd's huge lead to win the title in the last game of the season, and twice came back from the dead in the FA Cup.

Man for man, Arsenal were not the best team in Division One, but their team spirit and organisation made up for their technical shortcomings, much in the way Ipswich had done in winning the title nine years earlier. The assured McLintock was the pick of the defence, Radford was a tireless worker up front, George Armstrong provided pace and width, while Ray Kennedy was their youthful spark, linking attack with midfield. Their sole concession to fancy dan-dom was local lad Charlie George, a maverick genius long on talent and sideburns. Arsenal's constant ability to extricate themselves from the mire led to them being tagged 'lucky Arsenal'. But that was unfair. In truth, no side could have been that lucky for that long.

Manager: Bertie Mee

Key Players

Bob Wilson (G) Frank McLintock (D) Charlie George (F)
John Radford (F) George Armstrong (W) Ray Kennedy (M)
George Graham (M)

Trophies

LT 1971 FAC 1971

Cup final winner. Lying prone on the ground, long hair flowing like a nymph. Team-mates leaping on you without any fear of accusations of homosexuality. Enduring image, isn't it? (Apologies to Mr Whitehouse.)

◁⟩ Arsenal's Fairs Cup win of 1970 laid the foundations and ended a long drought: their first trophy since the league title of 1953.

◁⟩ Arsenal won the 1971 FA Cup the hard way. They were drawn away in every round, snatched a replay in the semi-final with an injury-time penalty, then came from behind in extra-time to beat Liverpool in the final.

◁⟩ In 1970/71 Arsenal played 64 matches. When Preston won the first double in1889, they wrapped up both trophies in just 27.

◁⟩ Bertie Mee had been a reluctant manager in 1966. He asked for a get-out clause in his contract, allowing him to return to his previous position of physio if he wasn't successful.

Machine Dream

LIKE ALL THE BEST German teams it is strong in every position. Schoen was a disciplined manager with great tactical ability and a habit of getting the best out of his players. The balance of the side is tremendous – no midfield packed with fancy dans for Germany. We start with a world-class keeper in Sepp Maier, and a simply superb defence. The flair and brilliance of Franz Beckenbauer, with the taller, physically imposing Matthias Sammer alongside him is a partnership made in heaven. Outside them we have two conventional full-backs: on the right the tough-tackling Bertie Vogts and on the left the unflappable Andreas Brehme.

Lothar Matthaus is in his best position, that of a ball-carrying midfielder not ponderous sweeper. Walter, captain of the 1954 World Cup winning side, was a complete player – hard and skilful – and Rahn and Overath add pace and power to the flanks.

Up front the skills and industry of the durable Seeler sit well alongside the rapier thrusts of Gerd Muller, and Karl-Heinz Rummenigge provides back up on the bench alongside a certain J. Klinsmann.

Manager: Helmut Schon (60s/70s)

4-4-2

Sepp Maier (70s)

Berti Vogts (70s) Franz Beckenbauer (C) (70s)
Matthias Sammer (90s) Andreas Brehme (80s)

Helmut Rahn (50s) Lothar Matthaus (80s/90s)
Franz Walter (50s) Wolfgang Overath (70s)

Uwe Seeler (60s) Gerd Muller (70s)

Subs: Oliver Kahn (G) (90s) Paul Breitner (D) (70s) Gunter Netzer (M) (70s) Karl-Heinz Rummennigge (F) (80s) Jurgen Klinsmann (F) (90s)

Munich, 1974. The peerless Beckenbauer lifts the World Cup.

◁ Only Matthias Sammer hails from the former East Germany.
◁ Beckenbauer made a strong case for player/manager, but we spared him the agony of having to leave out team-mate Paul Breitner.

◁ Gunther Netzer only made it to the bench, just like in 1974. Considering West Germany appeared in every Finals, it is extraordinary that such a good player played only 20 minutes in a World Cup tournament.

◁ Only Oliver Kahn of the current squad features in the 16 – a reflection of the current poverty of talent in German football. Hassler, Moller (Andreas), Voller and Scholl are just not in this league.

Mackay, Dave

Tottenham Hotspur, Derby County, Scotland

EVERY TEAM NEEDS a hard man and Dave Mackay filled that role with distinction for his various clubs, and for Scotland. Indeed, the image of Mackay taking exception to a tackle by a young Billy Bremner is one of the most enduring football photographs.

Mackay shot to fame in the midfield of the Hearts side that won the Scottish League in 1958, before moving to Spurs, where he became the cornerstone of the side that won the double in 1961.

After nearly a decade at White Hart Lane, Brian Clough persuaded Mackay to move to Derby County, where he captained the side that won promotion to the First Division. He then enjoyed spells as a

manager at Swindon and Nottingham Forest, before returning to the Baseball Ground to help his old side through the aftermath of Clough's sudden departure to Leeds. With Mackay at the helm Derby won a second league title in 1975, but the suspicion that he was merely enjoying the fruits of Clough's earlier groundwork were borne out by his inability to start rebuilding the team effectively, and he was dismissed in 1976.

VITAL STATISTICS

Place of Birth: Edinburgh, Scotland
Date of Birth: 14 November 1934
Died: n/a Caps: 22 (Scotland) Goals (International): 4
Clubs: As Player: Heart of Midlothian, Tottenham Hotspur, Derby County, Swindon Town; As Manager: Swindon Town, Nottingham Forest, Derby County, Walsall, Birmingham City
Appearances: Club (All Matches): 669
Goals: Club (All Matches): 88
Trophies: SFAC 1956, 1957; SLT 1958, 1959; LT 1961 (1975); FAC 1961, 1962, 1967

LEGEND RATING

Achievement	8
Skill	6
Teamwork	8
Passion	10
Personality	7
Overall Legend Rating	**39**

- He was joint (with Tony Book) Football Writers' Player of the Year in 1969.
- He had a reputation as a fearsome drinker, matched only by Alan Gilzean at Spurs.
- Battled back from two broken legs in 1963-64 (not so easy then, no micro-surgery).
- Missed the European Cup Winners' Cup final in 1963 with a stomach upset.
- Mackay played in the Hearts that who won the title with 132 league goals (a Scottish record), and a Spurs side that won the title with 115 goals (a joint English record).

Magyar Magic

Hungary, 1950s

GOING INTO the 1954 World Cup, Hungary had the footballing world at its feet. They were unbeaten since 1950 and had left a trail of strong sides in their wake, many of whom were still coming to terms with the humiliating nature of their defeats.

Like most great teams, the key to their success lay in the quality of their personnel. They had the best goalkeeper in the world in Grosics, a decent defence, a good prompter in half-back Bozsik and the best forwards the planet had ever seen. Kocsis, the bull-headed bomber, Hidegkuti, a subtle and deep-lying centre forward, and Czibor their flying winger were all outrageous technicians. And then

there was Puskas, the dumpy maestro, tormenting defenders with his trademark dragbacks, and scoring goals for fun.

They were the best side in the tournament in 1954, surviving a 22-man battle in the quarter-final against Brazil and a classic semi-final against Uruguay, to reach their first and only major final. They blew it, throwing away a 2-0 lead to hand a workaday West German team the trophy. Two years later the Soviets invaded Hungary and within a year Puskas, Kocsis and Czibor had all fled to Spain, never to be reunited in the colours of their country.

Manager: Gustav Szebes

Key Players
Gyula Grosics (G) Jozef Bozsik (H/B) Sandor Kocsis (F)
Ferenc Puskas (F) Nandor Hidegkuti (F) Zoltan Czibor (F)

Trophies
They did not win a professional trophy (surprisingly they were beaten in the 1954 World Cup final by West Germany), but they did win the 1952 Olympic title in Helsinki and were also the first overseas country to beat England at home (they won 6-3 at Wembley on 25 November 1953). To prove that was not a one-off, they beat England 7-1 in Budapest on 23 May 1954.

Max Morlock of West Germany scores the first for his country to get them back in the game during the 1954 World Cup final against Hungary.

- Having hammered South Korea 12-0 in the 1952 Olympics, Hungary restricted themselves to nine goals in the 1954 World Cup. One of the Korean players, suffering from cramp, was given a massage by the Hungarian full-back, Buzansky.
- Puskas went on to European Cup fame with Real Madrid as a member of their all-conquering side, and Kocsis played in a European Cup Final for Barcelona.
- The World Cup final against Germany was painful; Hungary were

2-0 up, but Morlock and Rahn got Germany back level, then Rahn settled the game with a late breakaway.
- Puskas missed most of the 1954 World Cup Finals. He was injured in the first game against Germany.

250

Maier, Sepp

THANKS TO the widening influence of television during the 1960s and 1970s, Josef-Dieter Maier was one of the most recognisable footballers in the world. His enormous black shorts belonged to another age, while his outsize gloves made him a hero to sportswear manufacturers and set a trend. (Today, it is unbelievable to think that goalkeepers once played with their bare hands.)

His 19 years as a member of Bayern Munich's greatest-ever side brought him 13 major trophies, including three consecutive European Cups, but it was as national goalkeeper that 'die Katze' caught the eye, and not always for the right reasons; TV viewers of the 1970 World Cup Finals were as maddened by his habit of falling over at the slightest contact as they were impressed by his spectacular agility. Maier's crowning glory was during the 1974 World Cup when, despite conceding the Final's quickest-ever goal (a Neeskens penalty), he helped West Germany claim the world crown with victory over Holland. A car accident in 1979 brought an untimely end to a career that might otherwise have reaped him a century of international caps.

VITAL STATISTICS

Place of Birth: Haar, Germany

Date of Birth: 28 February 1944

Died: n/a Caps: 95 (West Germany) Goals (International): 0

Clubs: TSV Haar, Bayern Munich

Appearances: Club (League): 473

Goals: Club (League): 0

Trophies: CWC 1967; BLG 1969, 1972, 1973, 1974; EC 1974, 1975, 1976; EuroC 1972; WorC 1974

LEGEND RATING

Achievement	9
Skill	8
Teamwork	8
Passion	8
Personality	6
Overall Legend Rating	**39**

Sepp swaps his cap for the 1974 World Cup.

◄ Maier was an ever-present at Bayern for 11 years and nearly 400 games.

◄ He was a squad member in four World Cup Finals, but failed to start a match in 1966.

◄ He was three-time German Player of the Year.

◄ Still a Bayern man, Maier remains on the coaching staff.

◄ At the 1974 World Cup Finals, Maier conceded just four goals in seven matches.

Maldini, Paolo

AC Milan, Italy

ARGUABLY THE FINEST LEFT-BACK ever to play the game, Paolo Maldini's class was emphasised early when, at 16, he became one of Serie A's youngest-ever debutants in 1985. Accomplished on the ball and decisive in the tackle, Maldini has been the immovable object of world football, equally comfortable on the left or in the centre where he has spent much of the latter part of his career.

Unusually for someone who could have commanded huge signing-on fees, he has played his club football only with Milan. His six league titles, four Italian Cups and three European Cups are a deserving reflection of his talent and loyalty.

Ultimate international success continues to elude Maldini, though. He was a member of the Italian teams that failed to secure the world crown at Italia 90, USA 94 and France 98, each time going out on penalties (most crushingly in 1994 when they were beaten by Brazil in the final). Maldini has played in some of the tightest defences the game has known, the foursome he made up with Antonio Benarrivo, Franco Baresi and Alessandro Costacurta in USA 94 being perhaps the finest of all. In 2003 he lifted the European Cup at Old Trafford as Milan's captain. Father Cesare performed the same task for the same club in the same country 40 years earlier.

VITAL STATISTICS

Place of Birth: Milan, Italy

Date of Birth: 26 June 1968

Died: n/a Caps: 126 (for Italy) Goals (International): 7

Clubs: AC Milan

Appearances: Club (All Matches): 521

Goals: Club (All Matches): 25

Trophies: SA 1988, 1992, 1993, 1994, 1996, 1999;
EC 1989, 1990, 1994, 2003

LEGEND RATING

Achievement	9
Skill	10
Teamwork	8
Passion	9
Personality	8
Overall Legend Rating	**44**

- Maldini's international caps are an Italian record to which he is still adding.
- He was World Player of the Year in 1994.
- In the 1994 World Cup Finals, when Franco Baresi was injured, Maldini moved into the middle for the first time, and immediately looked as accomplished as any centre-half in the tournament.
- Maldini's loyalty to Milan stemmed from his father, Cesare, who captained the team and was Paolo's boyhood coach.
- Cesare and Paolo formed a unique father-son, manager-captain combination at the 1998 World Cup Finals; no one complained about Cesare picking Maldini junior.

Mannion, Wilf

DESPITE MIDDLESBOROUGH'S RELIANCE on expensive, overseas imports in recent years, it is the homeboy who made his debut in 1937 who is considered to be their best-ever player. A wonderful dribbling forward, he never won the acclaim of his contemporary Stanley Matthews, but to Teessiders there was no finer sight than Wilf Mannion in full flow. Like Matthews, his prime years were interrupted by the Second World War, during which Mannion was one of thousands dramatically evacuated from Dunkirk.

The absence of top-flight football during the war meant that an England cap didn't materialise until he was nearly 29, but he quickly made up for lost time. His 26 caps included a hat-trick against the Republic of Ireland, and a trip to Brazil as a member of England's first World Cup Finals' squad in 1950. In 1954, his last season at Middlesborough brought the anti-climax of relegation, and effectively signalled the end of his career. A brief flurry with Hull followed but his heart was never truly in it, and he soon returned to Middlesbrough, where he remained until his death in April 2000.

VITAL STATISTICS

Place of Birth:	Middlesbrough, England
Date of Birth:	16 May 1918
Died: 14 April 2000	Caps: 26 (England)

Goals (International): 11

Clubs: Middlesbrough, Hull City

Appearances: Club (For Middlesbrough): 368

Goals: Club (For Middlesbrough): 110

Trophies: None

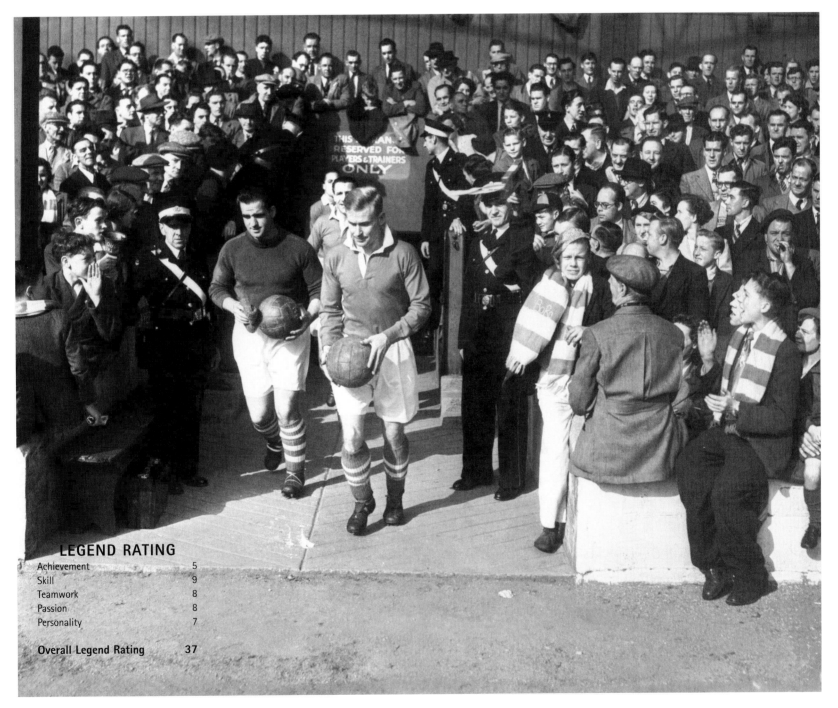

LEGEND RATING

Achievement	5
Skill	9
Teamwork	8
Passion	8
Personality	7
Overall Legend Rating	**37**

- Mannion is still Middlesborough's most-capped player.
- He scored Boro's first post-war goal in 1946.
- He was once suspended by the Football League for a controversial newspaper article.
- 'Can't we play them again tomorrow?' Mannion after England's 1–0 defeat by the USA in the 1950 World Cup.
- 'Hello. I'm Wilf Mannion.' Made occasional appearances on Baddiel and Skinner's *Fantasy Football League* TV show.

Maracana

Rio De Janeiro, Brazil

THE ONCE-MAGNIFICENT Maracana in Rio de Janeiro is officially the biggest football stadium in the world, and still holds the record for the largest-ever officially counted attendance.

The stadium was built in readiness for the 1950 World Cup and it was the deciding fixture at the Finals between Uruguay and Brazil that attracted the landmark crowd, a colossal 199,854. Due to modern safety regulations it's a crowd record that is unlikely to be beaten.

In its time, the Maracana set a procession of records and innovations. The cantilevered roof was the world's largest. The lifts to the VIP boxes, the luxurious dressings rooms, complete with oxygen masks, set standards that dingy wooden English grounds took two generations to match.

Sadly the stadium, which will be forever associated with the great days of Brazilian soccer, is now in a poor state of repair and major refurbishment work is urgently required. At present, much of the stadium, which still has a capacity of 80,000, has been declared unsafe and crowds of less than 10,000 are now common.

VITAL STATISTICS

Location:	Rio De Janeiro, Brazil
Local Club:	Botofago, Vasco da Gama, Flamengo, Fluminense
Date Built:	1950
Current Capacity:	120,000
Max. Capacity:	199,854

◀ Originally called Estadio Municipal, it was renamed in 1964 after Mario Filho, the mayor of the city who masterminded the project. It became known as the Maracana after the little river that runs close by the stadium.

◀ The famous 1950 World Cup encounter with Uruguay proved Brazil's most bitter defeat. Their national team fell to a shock 2-1 defeat and Uruguay were crowned champions.

◀ The temperature in the dressing rooms is regulated to reflect precisely the air temperature at pitch level. In many cases this is over 35° C.

◀ The Maracana also holds the world record for a club game, Flamengo and Fluminese drew 177,656 in August 1963.

Maradona, Diego

THE MOST NATURALLY GIFTED PLAYER football has ever seen, or a despicable drug-ridden cheat? Whatever your opinion, Maradona's talent was undeniable. After emerging in his native Argentina with Argentinos Juniors, for whom he made his league debut aged only 15, Maradona quickly attracted the attention of European scouts.

A move to Spain for £4.2 m should, in theory at least, have made him the jewel in Barcelona's star-studded crown, but the young and immature Diego failed to settle and, in 1984, joined Napoli in Italy's Serie A for £6.9 m. Maradona brought unprecedented success to Naples, single-handedly shifting the powerbase of Italian football from north to south, but he also fell in with the wrong crowd. Throughout his time at the club he was repeatedly seen in the company of local mobsters, and rumours of his cocaine addiction were rife.

The 1986 World Cup quarter-final versus England provided an insight to his personality: a flagrant punch past Peter Shilton for Argentina's first goal was followed by a 60-yard run and wonder-goal minutes later. Maradona's personal flaws make him an unattractive figure, but should not obscure his vast talents as a footballer. His poor origins and volatility made him susceptible to bad advice off the pitch and provocation on it, compounded by his failure to ignore either.

VITAL STATISTICS

Place of Birth: Lanus, Argentina
Date of Birth: 30 October 1960
Died: n/a Caps: 91 (Argentina) Goals (International): 34
Clubs: Argentinos Juniors, Boca Juniors, Barcelona, Napoli, Seville, Newell's Old Boys
Appearances: Club (All Matches): 749
Goals: Club (All Matches): 311
Trophies: WorC 1986; SA 1987; EUFAC 1988

Maradona snakecharms the Belgians during the 1982 World Cup in Spain.

LEGEND RATING

Achievement	9
Skill	10
Teamwork	8
Passion	10
Personality	6
Overall Legend Rating	**43**

◁╗ Maradona was the subject of three world-record transfer fees, and was the first £1 m teenager.

◁╗ Maradona inspired Napoli to their first *Scudetto*. When he left, their fortunes immediately declined.

◁╗ Maradona was banned twice for drug use and is still battling against cocaine addiction.

◁╗ He was South American Player of the Year in 1979 and 1980 and was voted FIFA's Player of the 20th Century.

◁╗ A tackle, by the 'Butcher of Bilbao' Andoni Goicochea, that ruled Maradona out for four months, sparked an attempted storming of Bilbao's team hotel by enraged Catalans.

Masters of the Maracana

The Brazil Dream Team

THIS BEING BRAZIL, the defence isn't particularly impressive (we certainly weren't agonising over who to leave out). Julio Cesar and Edinho got the vote because they were the only proven combination we could find. The Branco we selected is the fulminating attacking back of the 1986 and 1990 World Cups, not the has-been who turned out for Middlesbrough. Djalma Santos was scary and aggressive, and adds serious bite, while the goalkeeper, Gylmar, was the best of a pretty ordinary bunch.

'Not that amazing' could not be said of the midfield – numerous world-class players didn't even make the 16 (Zagallo, Falcao, Dunga, Didi, Cerezo, Zico). We went for Rivaldo for a bit of bite and movement as well as skill, as Socrates wasn't overfond of running.

The 1950s' legends Ademir and Leonidas, both on the bench, got the vote up front as big, powerful strikers who would score shed-loads with the service from Garrincha and Jairzinho. Ronaldo, after his comeback in the 2002 World Cup Finals, gets a place ahead of Romario, Tostão and and 1950s legend Vava.

But then does it really matter how good the rest of them are? Any team containing Pelé has to be awesome.

Manager: Mario Zagallo

4-4-2

Gylmar (50s)

Djalma Santos (50s/60s) Junior Cesar (80s)
Edinho (80s) Branco (80s/90s)

Garrincha (50s/60s) Socrates (80s)
Rivaldo (90s) Jairzinho (60s/70s)

Pelé (C) (50s/60s) Ronaldo (90s/00s)

Subs: Nilton Santos (D) (50s/60s) Gerson (M) (60s/70s)
Rivelino (M) (70s) Ademir (F) (50s) Leonidas (F) (30s)

◄ Gylmar was Brazil's goalkeeper in the 1958, 1962 and 1966 World Cups.
◄ Socrates and Gerson had to be kept apart in training to stop them nicking each other's cigarettes.

◄ Julio Cesar and Edinho were the excellent central defensive combination in the dour 1986 side.
◄ No space for Bebeto (that baby-cradling nonsense was unforgivable).

◄ No substitute goalkeeper, most of the recent ones have been pretty awful – odd that such a fabulous team has such a dearth of decent 'keepers.

Matthaus, Lothar

Bayern Munich, Germany

A CENTRAL FIGURE in German football for two decades, Lothar Matthaus was the natural successor to Franz Beckenbauer. Though not as good defensively as Beckenbauer, he possessed the same ability to launch attacks from deep, and scored more goals than 'The Kaiser'. Matthaus also had admirable stamina, was rarely injured and managed to continue playing at the highest level until the age of 38 without looking silly, except maybe once or twice when he started to fancy himself as a sweeper.

Matthaus' enjoyed a club career that saw him win countless trophies in Germany, with Bayern Munich, and Inter Milan in Italy,

although the closest he came to European Cup success was the heart-stopping 1999 Champions League final against Man United.

For all his club achievements, though, it was in the international arena that Matthaus marked himself out as an all-time great. He was the lynchpin of the German national team for the best part of a decade, and scored the penalty that won them the World Cup final against Argentina in 1990. Possessed of a self-belief that often spilled over into arrogance, Matthaus has never been the most popular player and has been involved in several run-ins with team-mates, including the normally docile Jurgen Klinsmann.

VITAL STATISTICS

Place of Birth: Erlangen, Germany

Date of Birth: 21 March 1961

Died: n/a Caps: 144 (Germany) Goals (International): 22

Clubs: Borussia Monchengladbach, Bayern Munich, Inter Milan, New Jersey Metrostars

Appearances: Club (League): 581 Goals: Club (League): 160

Trophies: BLG 1985, 1986, 1987, 1994, 1997; SA 1989; EUFAC 1991, 1996; WorC 1990

LEGEND RATING

Achievement	10
Skill	8
Teamwork	9
Passion	8
Personality	6
Overall Legend Rating	41

◄ He had retired from international football, but returned to the squad for France 98 when Matthias Sammer was injured.

◄ He was voted European player of the year in 1990, and was named as the first World Player of the Year in 1991.

◄ In the 1999 European Cup final Matthaus was substituted after 80 minutes, and watched in horror as Man United scored the two late goals that denied him a full set of European medals.

◄ He played in a record 25 games at the World Cup Finals, and

jointly holds the distinction of playing in five Finals' tournaments with Antonio Carbajal of Mexico.

◄ Matthaus currently manages Rapid Vienna, and was briefly linked with the vacancy at Aston Villa in 2002.

Matthews' Final

Blackpool 4 Bolton Wanderers 3, 1953

ONE OF WEMBLEY'S most sentimental occasions, the 'Matthews Final', saw the nation's favourite balding winger with baggy shorts finally win an FA Cup final at 38.

The drama was perfectly scripted. Blackpool, 3-1 down after an hour, were heading for their third final defeat in six seasons when, as if on cue, Stanley Matthews embarked on a trail of destruction down the right wing, setting up Stan Mortensen to score. With only three minutes left, it still looked like mere consolation, but a Mortensen free-kick to complete his hat-trick set up the FA Cup's most memorable finale. Again, it was a dribble from Matthews, who

seemed to lose his footing before squaring for Bill Perry to smash the winner.

For the nation it was all part of the 1953 pageantry that inspires images of the Coronation, Everest and Compton's Ashes. For Bolton, it could have been so different had an injury not reduced England left-back Banks to the role of passenger for the last, vital half an hour. But the enduring image is that of Matthews standing proud, finally holding the FA Cup.

SCORERS: Blackpool: Mortensen 3, Perry
Bolton: Lofthouse, Moir, Bell

EVENT: FA Cup Final, Wembley, 2 May 1953

BLACKPOOL (Man: Joe Smith)		BOLTON WANDERERS (Man: Bill Ridding)	
1 Farm	8 Taylor	1 Hanson	8 Moir
2 Shimwell	9 Mortensen	2 Ball	9 Lofthouse
3 Garrett	10 Mudie	3 Banks	10 Hassall
4 Fenton	11 Perry	4 Wheeler	11 Langton
5 Johnston		5 Barrass	
6 Robinson		6 Bell	
7 Matthews		7 Holden	

Matthews (left) on England duty.

◁» This was Matthews' third FA Cup Final; he was a loser in 1948 and 1951.

◁» Blackpool nearly didn't make it to Wembley. Outplayed by Spurs, they won their semi-final in the last minute.

◁» Hat-trick hero Stan Mortensen scored in every round.

◁» Mortensen later managed the club, from 1967–69.

◁» Like many north-west clubs, both Blackpool and Bolton faded in the 1960s.

Matthews, Stanley

Blackpool, Stoke City, England

ASK ANY LEFT-BACK between 1930 and 1965 who was the opponent they most feared and the answer would have been instant: Stanley Matthews. One of the quickest players ever over 10 yards, Matthews defined modern wing play and pioneered standards of fitness that enabled him to play beyond his 50th birthday. Pointless arguments still rage about how he would have fared in the modern game, but there have been few bigger draws. Stoke's attendance leapt from 8,000 to 35,000 when he re-signed in 1961, returning to his hometown club after 13 years away. His defining match was with Blackpool, whom he joined after a clash with management at Stoke

in 1947. The sight of Matthews transforming the 1953 FA Cup final by laying on three late goals for a 4-3 win is now as much a part of Wembley folklore as the twin towers and Billy the white horse. Yet, for all his ability, that game produced his only major trophy. Still, trophies and medals were not what made Matthews popular. He won his acclaim as the people's champion for his innate modesty and sportsmanship. His death, in February 2000, solicited immaculate one-minute's silences at grounds throughout the country.

VITAL STATISTICS

Place of Birth: Stoke-on-Trent, England
Date of Birth: 1 February 1915
Died: 23 February 2000 Caps: 54 (England)
Goals (International): 11
Clubs: Stoke City, Blackpool
Appearances: Club (League): 698
Goals: Club (League): 71
Trophies: FAC 1953

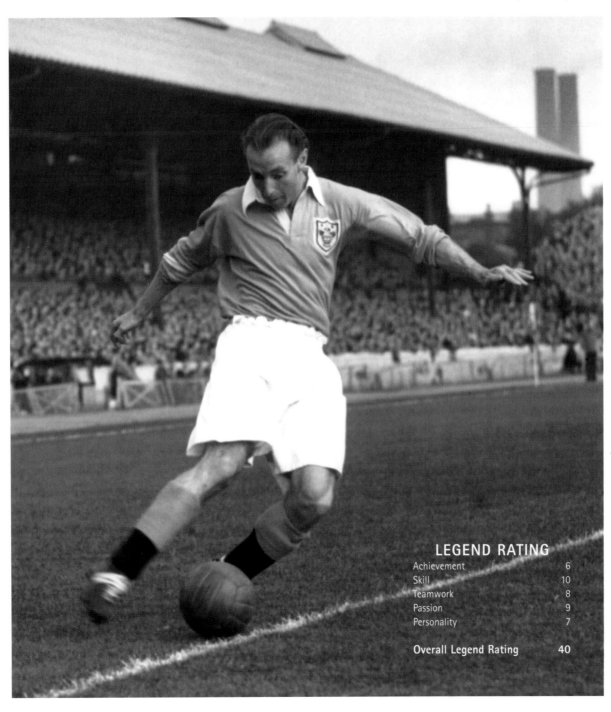

LEGEND RATING

Achievement	6
Skill	10
Teamwork	8
Passion	9
Personality	7
Overall Legend Rating	**40**

- Matthews was the inaugural European Footballer of the Year in 1956 and Football Writers' Player of the Year in 1948 and 1963.
- 1965. He became the first footballer to be knighted.
- He was the oldest ever First Division player at 50 years, 5 days.
- He never earned fortunes, taking home a basic £50 per week on his retirement.
- The ultimate gentleman, Matthews was never booked in a 35-year career.

Maximum Wage

ROY KEANE IS REPORTED to earn £200,000 every month. Yet, just over 40 years ago, players nearly came out on strike over the less than princely sum of £20 per week. The argument had been rumbling for years. The legendary Billy Meredith had led a players' revolt as early as 1907 over a £4 per week ceiling and a contract that tied players to a club effectively for an entire career. He succeeded in establishing a players' union, but the maximum wage remained. It was not until 1961 that the next instalment of this saga erupted. PFA Chairman Jimmy Hill had successfully managed to get the maximum wage abolished when he took up the case of George

Eastham. Eastham's contract had expired at Newcastle and though Arsenal were keen to sign him the Magpies refused to release him. The case went to the Ministry of Labour, who ruled in Eastham's favour. The days of the tied contract were over. Today's complaint that all players earn too much misses an important point. For every Keane, there are 10 YTS lads at Halifax scraping a living.

'A slave contract.'

Jimmy Hill defines the maximum wage system

George Eastham.

◄❯ The first beneficiary of the maximum wage's demise was Johnny Haynes. Fulham made him the country's first £100 per week player.

◄❯ 1950. Following the post-war boom in attendances, players threatened to strike unless their pay was increased. They won a rise but the maximum wage was to remain for another 11 years.

◄❯ The rise of agents has helped inflate players' pay packets. Some, like Eric Hall, admit only a passing interest in football.

◄❯ Most former players are philosophical about the riches they missed out on. As Stanley Matthews remarked in 1987: 'People say the wages are too high, but it's a short career.'

◄❯ For top players today, merchandising rights are as important as salary. 'Image rights' is the latest phrase in contract negotiations.

Mazzola, Sandro & Rivera, Gianni

TWO GREAT PLAYERS born less than a year apart, the careers of Alessandro Mazzola and Gianni Rivera ran almost in parallel. Which of them was the better player remains a source of debate even today amongst Italian football followers. Rivera was the first to shine, earning himself the nickname *Bambino d'Oro* ('Golden Boy') when he first shot to prominence playing for AC Milan in the early 1960s. Handsome and cavalier, he immediately became the darling of the Italian football press, a status he enhanced when, aged just 19, he was a member of the Milan side that won the European Cup in 1963. Rivera went on to collect a sackful of medals, picking up his final

Scudetto at the age 35 in 1979. Milan's great rivals Inter had also forged a European Cup winning side based around their great homegrown talent. Though Sandro Mazzola did not break through with the fanfare of Rivera, he nonetheless developed into an equally gifted and influential playmaker.

At international level again it was Rivera who shone first, but Mazzola forced his way into the side in the late 1960s, and from thereon most judges agree he made the greater impact. Curiously, no coach ever attempted to build a side around them both.

VITAL STATISTICS

SANDRO MAZZOLA

Place of Birth:	Torino, Italy
Date of Birth:	8 November 1942
Died: n/a	Caps: 70 (Italy)
Goals (International): 22	Clubs: Inter Milan

Appearances: Club (For Inter): 561

Goals: Club (For Inter): 157

Trophies: EC 1964, 1965; SA 1963, 1965, 1966, 1971; EuroC 1968

GIANNI RIVERA

Place of Birth:	Allessandria, Italy
Date of Birth:	8 August 1943
Died: n/a	Caps: 60 (Italy)
Goals (International): 14	Clubs: Allessandria, AC Milan

Appearances: Club (League): 527

Goals: Club (League): 128

Trophies: EC 1963, 1969; CWC 1968, 1973; SA 1962, 1968, 1979; EuroC 1968

LEGEND RATING

Mazzola:		Rivera:	
Achievement	9	Achievement	8
Skill	8	Skill	8
Teamwork	8	Teamwork	7
Passion	7	Passion	8
Personality	6	Personality	7
Overall Legend Rating	**38**	**Overall Legend Rating**	**38**

Gianni Rivera and Alessandro Mazzola.

‹⁀ Mazzola's father, Valentino, played for Italy, but was killed along with the rest of his Torino colleagues in an air crash in 1949.

‹⁀ In the 1970 World Cup, Italian coach Valcareggio could not decide who to pick, so played Mazzola and Rivera 45 minutes each. But Mazzola played so well in the final Rivera was only given a paltry six minutes to shine.

‹⁀ Rivera's feats for Milan led to him being voted European Footballer of the Year in 1969.

‹⁀ Mazzola scored Inter's goal in the 2–1 defeat by Celtic in Lisbon in the 1967 European Cup final.

‹⁀ One of the few occasions both appeared in a World Cup game was in 1966, when the *Azzurri* were eliminated by North Korea.

McCoist, Ally

PERHAPS MORE than any other player, Ally McCoist was responsible for the transformation of Rangers from football Cinderellas into Scotland's dominant force of the 1980s and 1990s. In that period the Gers collected nine league titles on the bounce, equalling the record held by their Glasgow neighbours, Celtic.

McCoist, Rangers' highest-ever goal scorer, was the attacking spearhead of the team, a man whose confidence in front of goal seemed to invest his colleagues with added belief in their own abilities. But success was not immediate for McCoist. Three inauspicious years at St Johnstone saw him offloaded to Sunderland in 1981, where two indifferent seasons followed before his life-changing move to Rangers.

McCoist introduced himself to the Ibrox faithful by scoring within one minute of his debut in an Old Firm derby and went on, in his 15-year association with the club, to become the most decorated player of his generation. An easy-going nature and confidence on camera saw him recruited to BBC's *A Question of Sport* as a team captain, and this has led to further TV roles, his latest being as a wisecracking analyst on ITV's *The Premiership*.

VITAL STATISTICS

Place of Birth: Glasgow, Scotland
Date of Birth: 24 September 1962
Died: n/a **Caps:** 61 (Scotland) **Goals (International):** 19
Clubs: St Johnstone, Sunderland, Rangers, Kilmarnock
Appearances: Club: 637
Goals: Club: 363
Trophies: SLT 1987, 1989, 1990, 1991, 1992, 1993, 1994, 1995, 1996, 1997; SFAC 1992, 1993, 1996

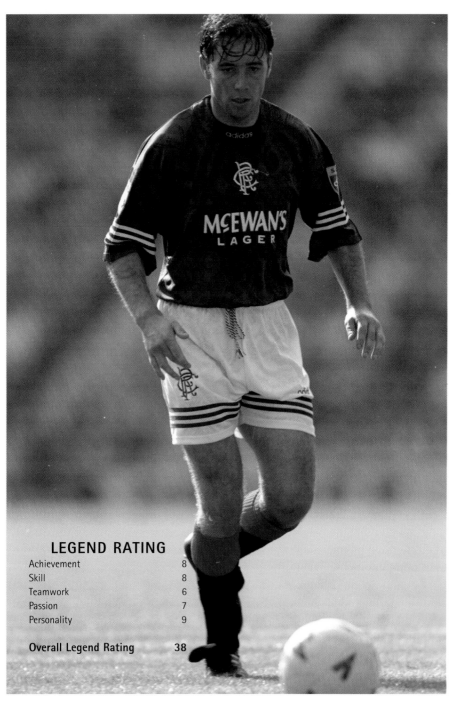

LEGEND RATING

Achievement	8
Skill	8
Teamwork	6
Passion	7
Personality	9
Overall Legend Rating	**38**

◁ Despite a Rangers record of 355 goals, McCoist's first league strike was in England against no less a keeper than Peter Shilton.

◁ He was the first Scottish player to win Europe's golden boot for most league goals in a season.

◁ In his last years as a player McCoist became known as 'The Judge', due to the amount of time he spent on the bench.

◁ He scored the crucial goal against Norway that gave Scotland entry to the 1990 World Cup Finals.

◁ At the 1990 Finals he was left on the bench for most of the defeat by Costa Rica.

McGrath, Paul

AS ONE OF THE FIRST black players to emerge from Ireland, Paul McGrath knows a thing or two about defying the odds. His ability to fight a battling rearguard was evident on a football pitch too. McGrath was one of the bravest players of the last 20 years, and a defiant example to those who maintain that all contemporary players burst into tears at the first sign of a blister. McGrath's bravery brought a catalogue of injuries that would have forced lesser men into retirement but, defying the pain and the doctors, he continued to play at a high level well into his 30s. Later in his career, at Aston Villa, he was scarcely able to train due to the strain on his battered knees, but his level of performance rarely deviated beyond the exceptional.

Having signed for Man United in 1982 after schoolboy and club football in Ireland, his seven years at Old Trafford made him a terrace hero. In 1985, that status was cemented when, following the sending off of Kevin Moran, McGrath single-handedly kept out Everton to set up United's unlikely FA Cup final victory. Throughout his career he was the backbone of the Republic of Ireland's side, underpinning their charge to the World Cup quarter-finals in 1990, and is a player for whom the Republic have yet to discover a worthy replacement.

VITAL STATISTICS

Place of Birth: Greenford, England
Date of Birth: 4 December 1959
Died: n/a Caps: 83 (Republic of Ireland)
Goals (International): 8
Clubs: Manchester United, Aston Villa, Derby County
Appearances: Club (All Matches): 519
Goals: Club (All Matches): 25
Trophies: FAC 1985; LC 1994, 1996

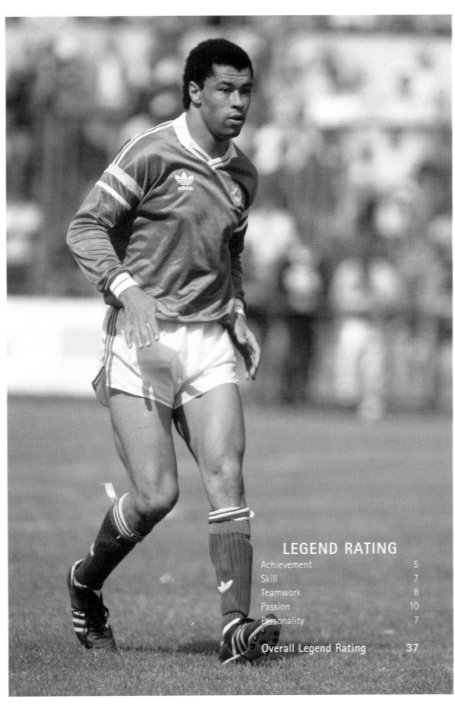

LEGEND RATING

Achievement	5
Skill	7
Teamwork	8
Passion	10
Personality	7
Overall Legend Rating	37

• Hugely respected by colleagues, McGrath was PFA Player of the Year in 1983.
• Surprisingly, he gained only one FA Cup medal and no championship medal despite seven years at Old Trafford.

• Always a transfer bargain, McGrath cost Manchester United only £30,000 and Villa £400,000.
• McGrath has re-emerged recently as an occasional TV pundit, making engaging contributions with a wry grin and soft accent.

• He is Villa's most capped player with 51 full internationals.

McLeish, Alex & Miller, Willie

Aberdeen, Scotland

NEITHER ALEX McLEISH nor Willie Miller was ever short-listed for the European Footballer of the Year award, but together they formed a central defensive partnership that was the equal of any in Europe. McLeish was the dour one, an unflappable stopper and tackler, while Miller was the more elegant playmaker, sometimes fancying his chances with Beckenbauer-style forays into opposition territory. Their 10 years at Pittodrie spanned the entire decade of the 1980s, and coincided with the most successful period in Aberdeen's history.

Both have tried their hand in management, with McLeish proving to be the more successful. Miller was an ordinary boss of the club where he played with such distinction, and was eventually sacked in 1995 after three seasons. McLeish wisely chose to make a clean break from Aberdeen, and performed impressively at Motherwell and Hibs before taking the hot seat at Ibrox in December 2001.

VITAL STATISTICS

ALEX McLEISH

Place of Birth:	Glasgow, Scotland
Date of Birth:	21 January 1959
Died: n/a	Caps: 77 (Scotland)

Goals (International): 1

Clubs: Aberdeen **Appearances:** Club (League): 492

Goals: Club (League): 25

Trophies: SLT 1980, 1984, 1985; SFAC 1982, 1983, 1984, 1986, 1990, (2002); CWC 1983

WILLIE MILLER

Place of Birth:	Glasgow, Scotland
Date of Birth:	2 May 1955

Died: n/a

Caps: 65 (Scotland)

Goals (International): 1

Clubs: Aberdeen

Appearances: Club (League): 556

Goals: Club (League): 21

Trophies: SLT 1980, 1984, 1985; SFAC 1982, 1983, 1984, 1986; CWC 1983

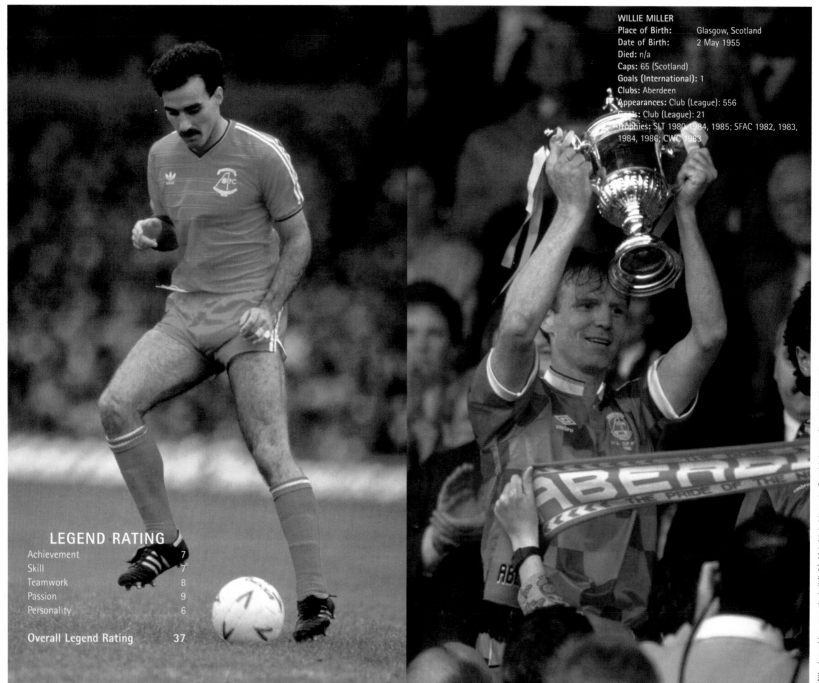

LEGEND RATING

Achievement	7
Skill	7
Teamwork	8
Passion	9
Personality	6
Overall Legend Rating	**37**

Miller keeps his eye on the ball (left). McLeish holds up the Scottish League Championship trophy.

◁ Miller was signed by Aberdeen as a striker in 1971, and was not converted into a centre-back for several years.

◁ McLeish is Aberdeen's most capped player with 77, while Miller holds the club record for league appearances (556).

◁ Both have played under Alex Ferguson for club and country. All three represented Scotland at the 1986 World Cup Finals.

◁ Miller was Scottish Player of the Year in 1984, and McLeish won the same award six years later.

◁ McLeish's managerial career had a stuttering start. Motherwell were relegated in his first season, but bounced straight back with the First Division title in 1999.

McNeill, Billy

Celtic, Scotland

ON HIS 17TH BIRTHDAY in 1957, Billy McNeill began a 34-year association with Celtic that eventually made him the club's most decorated captain and one of its most popular figures. McNeill was the centre-half keystone around which Jock Stein built Celtic's famous 'Lisbon Lions', the European Cup winners of 1967. He won his first league title with Celtic in 1966, and went on to win it a further eight years in a row, setting a record that remained in tact until Rangers enjoyed an identical period of domination in the 1980s and 1990s.

Like his mentor Jock Stein, he won the double with Celtic both as player and manager. Unlike Stein, however, he lasted longer in

English management, although his four years with Aston Villa and Manchester City were undistinguished. Rejoining his alma mater, he was fired unsentimentally in 1991 after two trophy-less seasons. A triple heart bypass has since curtailed his public appearances, but the family-run McNeill's bar in the city centre stands both as a testament to his Glasgow roots and a museum to his achievements.

VITAL STATISTICS

Place of Birth: Blantyre, Scotland

Date of Birth: 2 March 1940

Died: n/a   Caps: 29 (Scotland)   Goals (International): 3

Clubs: Celtic   Appearances: Club (League): 486

Goals: Club (League): 22

Trophies: EC 1967; SLT 1966, 1967, 1968, 1969, 1970, 1971, 1972, 1973, 1974; SFAC 1965, 1967, 1969, 1971, 1972, 1974, 1975

1967. McNeill poses with the European Cup.

LEGEND RATING

Achievement	8
Skill	7
Teamwork	9
Passion	9
Personality	7
Overall Legend Rating	**40**

◁ On McNeill's international debut Scotland lost 9–3 to England.

◁ McNeill's 486 league appearances are a Celtic record.

◁ He scored the opening goal in a 4–0 thrashing of Rangers in the 1969 Scottish Cup final.

◁ McNeill also scored the winner in the 1965 Scottish Cup final.

◁ He earned the nickname 'Caesar' (presumably due to his commanding leadership rather than fondness for wearing a toga).

Meazza, Giuseppe

Internazionale, Italy

GIUSEPPE MEAZZA WAS THE FIRST international footballer to shine on the world stage. The original World Cup Finals in 1930 had fired the imagination of the elite nations – England apart – and Italy seized the European initiative by winning the 1934 and 1938 competitions. The brawny 'Peppino' Meazza was their attacking focal point and goalscorer, although his versatility meant he was comfortable at either centre or inside-forward.

Good enough to play for Inter at 17, he scored 33 goals in the 1929/30 season while still a teenager, and his athleticism and fitness meant that Inter continued to rely on him until way past his 35th birthday. His most successful period was during the 1930s; following his international debut at the start of the decade he remained Italy's undisputed first-choice striker until the outbreak of the Second World War. After wartime spells with Milan, Juventus and Varese, he later returned to his spiritual home at Inter as player-manager. His death, at 69 in 1979, united fans of the rival Milanese teams in common grief.

VITAL STATISTICS

Place of Birth: Milan, Italy
Date of Birth: 23 August 1910
Died: 21 August 1979   Caps: 53 (Italy)
Goals (International): 33 Clubs: Ambrosiana, AC Milan, Juventus, Varese, Atalanta, Inter Milan
Appearances: Club (League): 439
Goals: Club (League): 264
Trophies: WorC 1934, 1938; SA 1938, 1940

LEGEND RATING

Achievement	8
Skill	8
Teamwork	7
Passion	9
Personality	7
Overall Legend Rating	**39**

COUPE DU MONDE 1938

Meazza (left) captains Italy in the 1938 World Cup Final.

◄)) Thirty-three goals in 53 internationals made him Italy's leading scorer until Luigi Riva.

◄)) 1930. Scored twice on his international debut versus Switzerland.

◄)) 1938. Captained Italy to second successive World Cup final triumph.

◄)) Italy scored six goals in the two World Cup Finals of the 1930s. Surprisingly, not one came from Meazza.

Mercer, Joe

Everton, Arsenal, Manchester City, England

AS A PLAYER Joe Mercer was the heartbeat of two formidable sides. He played left-half in the Everton team that won the last pre-war championship and, at the end of the war when Arsenal were looking to shore up their ranks with some experience and know-how, he added to his medal collection as the Gunners claimed league titles in 1948 and 1953. Mercer had been expected to stay at Arsenal for no more than a couple of seasons, but eventually stayed eight years, only retiring in 1953 when, after skippering them to the title, he received a rousing final ovation from the Highbury faithful.

Managerial spells with Sheffield United and Aston Villa were followed by a successful period at Manchester City, where he teamed up with Malcolm Allison. Mercer's genial man-management and Allison's tactical inventiveness proved to be a potent combination, and they duly delivered the FA Cup and the club's first and only league title. When England sacked Alf Ramsey after he failed to take England to the 1974 World Cup Finals, Mercer was appointed caretaker boss. But he had no desire to inherit the job permanently, and his brief tenure served as little more than light relief before the appointment of Don Revie.

VITAL STATISTICS

Place of Birth: Ellesmere Port, Cheshire

Date of Birth: 9 August 1914

Died: 9 August 1990

Caps: 5 (England)

Goals (International): 0

Clubs: As Player: Everton, Arsenal; As Manager: Sheffield United, Aston Villa, Manchester City, Coventry City

Trophies: LT 1948, 1953, (1968); FAC 1950, (1969); LC (1970)

LEGEND RATING

Achievement	8	Achievement	7
Skill	6	Tactical Awareness	8
Teamwork	8	Motivation	8
Passion	9	Transfer Dealing and Team Selection	6
Personality	7	Personality	8
Overall Legend Rating	**37**	**Overall Legend Rating**	**37**

- City axed Mercer in 1972. Allison stayed, amid rumours of political dirty tricks.
- England lost only one of Mercer's seven games in charge, despite his apparently carefree approach.
- He was voted PFA Player of the Year in 1950.
- Joe Mercer to newly-appointed Stoke boss, Tony Waddington: 'My advice is never to trust anyone in the game, and when I put down this phone, don't trust me either.'

Meredith, Billy

ONE OF WALES' greatest internationals, the original 'wizard of the wing' dazzled crowds in an amazing career lasting 30 years. An adopted son of Manchester, his two spells with City and one for United made him the forerunner of Ryan Giggs, Peter Barnes and co. Not surprisingly, since he played until he was nudging 50, most of Meredith's records surround his incredible longevity, although his own claim to have played in over 1,500 games and scored 470 goals has never been convincingly validated.

However, the stocky ex-miner's legacy was more enduring than his mighty playing career. As a feisty chairman of the maverick player's union, Meredith and his United sidekick, Charlie Roberts, eventually persuaded the FA to recognise them as an official body in 1908 and, though their fledgling union collapsed following a revolt a year later, their work is now acknowledged to have been a significant step in the advancement of player's rights.

VITAL STATISTICS

Place of Birth: Black Park, Chirk, Wales
Date of Birth: 30 July 1875
Died: 19 April 1958   Caps: 48 (Wales)
Goals (International): 11
Clubs: Northwich Victoria, Manchester City, Manchester United
Appearances: Club (League: for Man Utd): 303
Goals: Club (League: for Man Utd): 35
Trophies: LT 1908, 1911; FAC 1904,1909

LEGEND RATING

Achievement	7
Skill	8
Teamwork	7
Passion	8
Personality	9
Overall Legend Rating	**39**

Suits you sir. Style guru Meredith (left) sports a new neckwear range.

- His 48 caps for Wales was an astonishing total for a team playing scarcely more than home internationals.
- 1920. He became the oldest man to play international football at 45 years and 229 days.
- 1924. Became the oldest player to play in the FA Cup aged 49.
- Meredith's maximum wage was £4 per week in 1907. Roy Keane earns the same today in just over 46 seconds.
- He captained Wales to their first Home International title in 1907.

Mighty Maccams

The Sunderland Dream Team

SUNDERLAND'S GREATEST DAYS were long ago, when they won four championships between 1891 and 1902. Jimmy Millar, an inside forward, played in all of them, alongside another Scot, Johnny Campbell. Sunderland's next title came in 1913, when the opposition was a bit stiffer. Their playmaker was the great Charlie Buchan, and it was his right-sided partnership with half-back Cuggy and winger Jackie Mordue that was regarded as the key to their success.

Perhaps the club's greatest achievement was wrestling the title from Herbert Chapman's Arsenal in 1936, after the Gunners had won the previous three. Sunderland scored a marvellous 109 goals that season, with 31 each for Raich Carter and Bobby Gurney. The same squad won the FA Cup the following season, but it was 36 years before the club won another major trophy. In 1973, Sunderland, by now a Division Two side, pulled off a shock FA Cup win, beating Don Revie's Leeds 1-0 in the final with a goal from Ian Porterfield. An unsuccessful return to Wembley in 1992 was the closest they have come since. Peter Reid's modern team flirted with success without quite delivering. In 2002, he paid the price and was sacked. Sunderland's spectacular fall from grace in 2002/3 means that it could be some time yet before the good times return.

Manager: Johnny Cochrane

4-4-2

Jimmy Montgomery (70s)

Charlie Gladwin (10s) Dave Watson (C) (70s) Charlie Hurley (50s/60s)
Michael Gray (90s)

Jackie Mordue (10s) Charlie Buchan (10s/20s) Raich Carter (30s)
Gary Rowell (80s/90s)

Len Shackleton (50s) Kevin Phillips (90s)

Subs: John Doig (G) (1890s) Frank Cuggy (D/M) (10s)
Bobby Kerr (M) (70s) Bobby Gurney (F) (30s) Jimmy Millar (F) (1890s)

◁ Goalkeepers Jimmy Montgomery and John Doig totted up over 1,000 first-team appearances between them. Montgomery is the club's longest-serving player. His finest moment was the 1973 Cup final, where he made one breathtaking double save.

◁ Bobby Kerr, the lively moustachioed Scottish winger, is the only other representative of the Cup-winning team here.

◁ Charlie Hurley won the most caps while at the club; 38 of his 40 caps for the Republic of Ireland were as a Sunderland player.

◁ The consistent Gary Rowell is the only representative of the modest 1980s teams. A frequent scorer from midfield, Rowell was a much underrated performer.

Milburn, Jackie

Newcastle United, England

JOHN EDWARD THOMPSON MILBURN, or 'Wor Jackie', was the son of Alec Milburn. Alec's brother Tanner had four sons, all of whom played league soccer, while Tanner's daughter, Cissie, had two more sons, Jackie and Bobby Charlton. On these grounds, it is probably safe to say that Jackie Milburn came from decent footballing stock.

In his long career at St James's Park, Milburn's name became synonymous with Newcastle United. On his death, thousands poured on to the streets to pay their respects, and a statue has been erected in his memory in the city centre. Milburn started his professional career late due to the war, and played initially as an inside-forward,

then on the wing before moving to centre-forward in 1947. He wasn't tall, but he terrorised defences with his speed and quick feet, and his 13 England caps were a meagre reflection of his ability. Had he been a little more selfish, his goals tally may have been even more impressive than the 177 league goals he notched for the Magpies.

Upon his retirement Milburn briefly tried his hand as a manager, notably taking over an ageing Ipswich team from Alf Ramsey. They were relegated two years after winning the title, and Milburn moved back to the north-east to work in the local media.

VITAL STATISTICS

Place of Birth: Ashington, England
Date of Birth: 11 May 1924
Died: 9 October 1988   Caps: 13 (England)
Goals (International): 10
Clubs: Newcastle United
Appearances: Club (League): 354
Goals: Club (League): 177
Trophies: FAC 1951, 1952, 1955

LEGEND RATING

Achievement	6
Skill	9
Teamwork	7
Passion	9
Personality	7
Overall Legend Rating	**38**

◁ 46,000 turned out for Milburn's testimonial – 10 years after he left Newcastle.

◁ His tally of 177 league goals for Newcastle remains a record.

◁ He scored both goals in a 2–0 FA Cup Final defeat of Blackpool in 1951, and after 45 seconds in the 1955 final against Manchester City.

◁ He scored on his debut for England and got one hat-trick, against Wales.

◁ Milburn left Newcastle for a successful spell as player-manager at Linfield in Northern Ireland. He even appeared in the European Cup for the club.

Milla, Roger

ALTHOUGH ROGER MILLA'S World-Cup goal scoring exploits for Cameroon are a matter of record, reliable information regarding his date of birth and even his name is harder to come by. The family name is written Miller, so Roger's own spelling is baffling while his age has proved so difficult to pin down journalists have been forced into guesswork. Even Joan Collins has guarded her date of birth less zealously than this player.

After nine years with top Cameroon side Tonerre Yaounde, Milla moved to France, where he entertained fans across the country with his brio and humour. The 1982 World Cup Finals in Italy finally provided him with an international stage 15 years after his professional debut, and he was still around for the 1994 Finals despite being well over 40. His, and Cameroon's, best tournament was Italia 90, where the outsiders stunned the world in the opening game by beating holders Argentina, and eventually forced their way through to the quarter-finals where they were only despatched by Gary Lineker's penalties. His style, enthusiasm and trademark cornerflag dance brought some levity to what was largely a brutal and disappointing tournament.

VITAL STATISTICS

Place of Birth: Yaounde, Cameroon
Date of Birth: 20 May 1952
Died: n/a   **Caps:** 81 (Cameroon)
Goals (International): 42
Clubs: Leopaerd Douala, Tanerre Yaounde, Valenciennes, Monaco, Bastia, Saint Etienne, Montpellier, Saint Pierre
Trophies: African Player of the Year 1976, 1990

LEGEND RATING

Achievement	5
Skill	7
Teamwork	7
Passion	9
Personality	10
Overall Legend Rating	**38**

◁♪ Aged 42 (allegedly) at USA 94, Milla became the oldest player in World Cup Finals history.

◁♪ Twice African Footballer of the Year, his 1976 award wasn't repeated until 14 years later.

◁♪ Fittingly, the 42-year-old scored in his 1994 swansong appearance, albeit in a 6-1 thrashing by Russia.

◁♪ Milla scored two goals against Romania to take Cameroon past the group stage for the first time in 1990.

◁♪ He followed that with two more, as Cameroon became the first African side to reach the quarter-finals with a 2-1 win over Colombia.

Millennium Stadium

Cardiff, Wales

THE MILLENNIUM STADIUM in Cardiff opened in October 1999. Funded in part by the Millennium Commission and the Welsh Rugby Union, the stadium took over two years to construct. Unlike most other large constructions with public investment, it was completed on time.

Its unique feature is the retractable roof, a feather in the cap for architects the Lobb Partnership. It thus became the first stadium in Britain to enjoy this luxury (and the largest such stadium in the world), allowing games to be played under cover when weather conditions are poor, which in South Wales means most of the year.

Although primarily intended as a rugby venue, the stadium has come to the fore as a perfect stand-in for Wembley while the debacle of English football's national stadium grinds to a conclusion. It hosted the first FA Cup final outside London since 1915 when Liverpool beat Arsenal in 2001, altering a host of football chants in the process.

With a new national football stadium remaining stubbornly on the drawing board, the Millennium Stadium looks set to continue as the sport's premier ground for some years to come.

VITAL STATISTICS

Location:	Cardiff, Wales
Local Club:	None
Date Built:	1999
	The Lobb Partnership were the architects and Laing Plc constructed the stadium

Current Capacity: 72,500
Max. Capacity: 72,500

- Despite weighing 8,000 tonnes, the retractable roof takes just 20 minutes to open.
- Although the new stadium is on the site of the old Arms Park, the Millennium Stadium is at right-angles to its predecessor.
- Football becomes the third major sport to be played on the site. As well as being the cathedral of Welsh rugby, the original game was cricket, played on the Arms Park as early as 1848.
- Besides the FA Cup final, the stadium is also the temporary venue for the Worthington Cup final and the end-of-season English play-offs.
- It is used for Welsh national home games, a vast improvement on the club grounds of Cardiff, Swansea and Wrexham.

Mine's A Treble!

Manchester United 2 Bayern Munich 1, 1999

IT WAS FAR FROM the greatest European Cup final, and a much inferior game to Man United's previous final appearance in 1968. But for late, jaw-dropping drama there will probably never be another game like it. Bayern scored after six minutes and after 90 minutes United were still 1-0 down. The referee's assistant held up a board showing three minutes of injury time. Up in the stand the ribbons of Bayern Munich were being attached to the giant trophy. Then, a minute later, United won a corner. Maybe Bayern were distracted by the sight of Peter Schmeichel haring into the penalty area. If so the great Dane proved to be an ideal decoy, leaving

Sheringham to sweep the ball past Oliver Kahn for the equaliser. It was more than United had dared hoped for, and a minute later their wildest dreams had been realised. Beckham curled in another corner, Sheringham flicked on and supersub Ole Gunnar Solskjaer volleyed past a disbelieving Kahn. The Bayern team sank to their knees as United capered back to the half-way line.

SCORERS: United: Sheringham; Solskjaer
Bayern: Basler

EVENT: European Champions League Final, Nou Camp, Barcelona, 26 May 1999

MANCHESTER UNITED (Man: Alex Ferguson)		BAYERN MUNICH (Man: Ottmar Hitzfeld)	
1 Schmeichel	8 Blomqvist	1 Kahn	8 Effenberg
2 Neville (G)	(Sheringham,	2 Babbel	9 Jancker
3 Irwin	67)	3 Tarnat	10 Basler
4 Butt	9 Cole	4 Linke	11 Zickler
5 Johnsen	(Solskjaer, 81)	5 Matthaus	
6 Stam	10 Yorke	6 Kuffour	
7 Beckham	11 Giggs	7 Jermies	

Supersub Solskjaer basks after his late, late winner.

- The game was won on the 90th anniversary of Matt Busby's birth.
- United played poorly. To cover the loss of Keane and Scholes (both suspended) Beckham was forced inside and Giggs played on the right, where he failed to offer his customary threat.
- The referee was Pierluigi Collina, who would witness another English triumph over German opposition in Munich in 2001.
- There was sympathy for most of the German team, but not for Mario Basler, whose triumphal exit as he was substituted in the last minute was premature and presumptuous.
- Consolation came two years later for Bayern, as they beat Valencia on penalties to win the Cup, having beaten Man United home and away in the quarter-finals.

273

Modern Classic

LIVERPOOL WERE HUNTING a unique treble. They had already won the Worthington Cup, and Michael Owen had stolen the FA Cup from under Arsenal's noses the previous Saturday. Alaves provided almost unknown opposition. They had been Spain's surprise package for a couple of seasons and, in striker Javi Moreno, boasted the top scorer in La Liga.

The entire game was played at breakneck pace. Liverpool seemed to sense a weakness in the Alaves defence and went for the jugular, while Alaves, perhaps mindful of their defensive frailties, went for all-out attack. But then, after going two goals behind in the first

16 minutes they didn't really have much choice. Coach 'Mane' abandoned three at the back early, adding an extra forward and moving to 4-3-3. The substitute, Ivan Alonso, scored almost immediately. After coming on for Emile Heskey, Robbie Fowler looked to have scored the winner but Jordi Cruyff popped up with a last-gasp header to tie the scores at 4-4.

Alaves had two players sent off in extra-time but fought doggedly until, with just three minutes remaining, Geli put through his own net to hand victory, and a unique Cup treble, to Liverpool. They had won it with a Golden Goal.

SCORERS:	Liverpool: Babbel 4, Gerrard 16, McAllister (p) 40, Fowler 73, Geli (og) 117.
	Alaves: Ivan Alonso 27, Moreno 48, Moreno 50, Cruyff 90
EVENT:	UEFA Cup Final, Dortmund, 16 May 2001

LIVERPOOL (Man: Gerard Houllier)		ALAVES (Man: Jose Manuel Esnal)	
1 Westerveld	7 Murphy	1 Herrera	7 Tellez
2 Babbel	8 Gerrard	2 Karmona	8 Desio
3 Carragher	9 Heskey	3 Tomic	9 Javi Moreno
4 Hamann	10 Owen	4 Geli	10 Astudillo
5 Hyypia	11 McAllister	5 Contra	11 Cruyff
6 Henchoz		6 Eggen	

Geli's wobble gives Liverpool a dramatic Golden Goal.

◄» There were some curious substitutions in this match. Alaves withdrew their best player, Moreno, after he had scored twice while Liverpool took off Henchoz, whom Moreno had tormented, and used Steven Gerrard at right-back.

◄» Alaves came into the tournament with no European pedigree, but they beat Rosenborg, the perennial Norwegian champions, Inter Milan and Kaisersalutern on the way to the final.

◄» Spain had seven quarter-finalists, four semi-finalists and two finalists in the two European competitions in 2001. Italy's teams were all knocked out before the quarter-finals.

◄» Westerveld's performance suggested he wasn't quite up to the mark. He, too, was replaced the following year.

Monti, Luis

LUISITO MONTI WAS BORN in Buenos Aires and played most of his early football in South America. He appeared for Argentina in the inaugural World Cup, playing in the ill-tempered final that saw his team defeated 4-2 by the ruthless Uruguayans. Four years later, and playing for Juventus, Monti, along with many other *Oriundi* (foreigners of Italian descent), was invited to represent Italy in the 1934 tournament. This time he won a winner's medal as the hosts, aided by some supine refereeing, battered their way to victory.

Monti personified the Italian team. Though a gifted player, his talents included a great ability to spread the play with raking passes,

he was more than happy to mix it when necessary. In the semi-final he intimidated the Austrian playmaker Sindelar, and handed out similar bad office to the Czech, Nejedly, in the final.

The tournament, intended as a showpiece for Mussolini's Italy, instead became a symbol of its ugliness and corruption. In a different era Monti may have been encouraged to show more of his footballing skill and less of his cynicism, but as it is he will be remembered as the prototype brutal footballer – a Vinnie Jones in baggy shorts.

VITAL STATISTICS

Place of Birth: Buenos Aires, Argentina
Date of Birth: 15 May 1901
Died: 9 September 1983　Caps: 18 (Italy) He also played for Argentina in the 1930 World Cup
Goals (International): 1 (for Italy)
Clubs: Huracan, Boca Juniors, San Lorenzo, Juventus
Appearances: Club (League: for Juventus): 225
Goals: Club (League: for Juventus): 24
Trophies: ALT 1923, 1924, 1927; SA 1932, 1933, 1934, 1935; WorC 1934

Luis Monti, back row, second from left.

LEGEND RATING

Achievement	9
Skill	6
Teamwork	7
Passion	8
Personality	6
Overall Legend Rating	**36**

- He won four successive Italian league titles at Juventus (1932–35).
- Monti won a major trophy before the World Cup was even invented, leading Argentina to the South American championship in 1927.
- Monti played in the 1930 World Cup final despite receiving a death threat before the match; the police searched all spectators for revolvers at the gates.
- Monti was instrumental in turning a friendly against England

into the 'Battle Of Highbury.' When he limped off after a tackle by Ted Drake, the Italian team went berserk.
- Monti is the only player to have appeared in World Cup Finals for two different nations.

Moore, Bobby

West Ham United, England

'WORDS CANNOT SUM UP the grief I feel for my great friend. He was one of the world's finest defenders and a great sportsman.' So said Pelé after the sudden death, from cancer, of Bobby Moore in 1993.

Moore was the ultimate example of mind over body. He appeared to possess few of the physical attributes required in a great defender, but made up for his lack of muscle with an ability to read the game that bordered on the psychic. Moore took the ball by stealth rather than power and, though he rarely needed to resort to tackling, when he did so it was always surgical and clean. Rattling bones wasn't his style. He was loyal too; with the exception of a swansong alongside

George Best and Rodney Marsh at Fulham, Moore spent his entire career at West Ham. Upton Park now has a stand named after him, and the ground is home to a bust and plaque honouring his achievements.

His England career started in 1962, and continued almost unbroken until his retirement from internationals in 1973. He competed in three World Cups, winning the Player of the Tournament award in 1966 when he captained England to a 4-2 victory over Germany in the final.

VITAL STATISTICS

Place of Birth: Barking, Essex, England
Date of Birth: 12 April 1941
Died: 24 February 1993 Caps: 108 (England)
Goals (International): 2
Clubs: West Ham United, Fulham, Seattle Sounders, San Antonio Thunder
Appearances: Club: 823
Goals: Club: 29
Trophies: WorC 1966; FAC 1964; CWC 1965

LEGEND RATING

Achievement	9
Skill	10
Teamwork	9
Passion	9
Personality	6
Overall Legend Rating	**43**

◄ Moore was outstanding in the 1970 World Cup Finals, despite having spent four days in a Colombian jail after a woman falsely accused him of stealing a bracelet.

◄ Moore nearly missed the 1966 World Cup as he was in

contractual dispute with West Ham. Under FA rules this made him ineligible for England, so a temporary contract was arranged to see him through the tournament.

◄ Moore was not the saint he is often made out to be. He was

twice reprimanded for breaking pre-match curfews for West Ham and England.

◄ He was PFA Player of the Year in 1964, and received an OBE in 1967.

Mortensen, Stanley

THE NORTH-EAST has been a fertile breeding ground for traditional English centre-forwards, but one who slipped through the local net was Stan Mortensen. Initially, timing was not on his side. He signed as a professional for Blackpool in May 1939, but the Second World War ensured that his league career didn't start until he was past 25. Mind you, once he got going, there was no stopping him. Mortensen's height and strength made him a natural target man. Unlike some tall players, he was a natural jumper and deadly in the air. The combination of Stanley Matthews' accurate crosses and Mortensen's aerial strength was fully exploited. The result was three FA Cup finals in six seasons, though Mortensen's efforts rank amongst the most ignored in Wembley history; despite scoring a hat-trick in 1953 the match became universally celebrated as 'The Matthews Final'. Shabbily treated by Blackpool, he left under a cloud for Hull City in 1955. He continued playing until the age of 40, dropping into non-league football before returning to Blackpool as manager where, after two competent seasons, he was sacked. Blackpool did not deserve him.

VITAL STATISTICS

Place of Birth: South Shields, England
Date of Birth: 26 May 1921
Died: 7 May 1991   Caps: 25 (England)
Goals (International): 23
Clubs: Blackpool, Hull City, Southport
Appearances: Club (League: for Blackpool): 316
Goals: Club (League: for Blackpool): 197
Trophies: FAC 1953

LEGEND RATING

Achievement	6
Skill	8
Teamwork	8
Passion	7
Personality	6
Overall Legend Rating	**35**

◄》 Mortensen's career almost never saw the light of day. He cheated death in a practice parachute jump in 1943 and, as an RAF pilot, was seriously injured in active service.

◄》 He scored four times on his international debut as England trounced Portugal 10–0 in 1947. His 25 caps produced 23 goals, a record to compare with the best.

◄》 Mortensen's first season as manager saw Blackpool finish third, missing out on promotion to Division One on the final day of season 1967/68.

◄》 Wag on Mortensen's death: 'I suppose they'll call it the Matthews funeral'.

Müller, Gerd

Bayern Munich, West Germany

GERD MÜLLER, 'Der Bomber', was arguably the most lethal finisher in the history of the game. Like many out-and-out goal scorers, he did little outside the penalty area, and looked unremarkable in open play, but in the box his reflexes were cobra-like. Powerful, and with terrific balance, he was always in the right position to receive the ball, his body always shaped in readiness for a strike on goal.

Müller was drafted into the German team in 1966 immediately after the World Cup final, and surprisingly retired after scoring the winner against Holland in the 1974 final, aged only 28. The eight years in between were a one-man goal-fest as Germany swept aside lesser opposition, and even proved themselves a match for the inspired Dutch. At club level Müller spent 15 years with Bayern Munich, scoring at a ratio of better than one goal per game for a remarkable seven seasons.

VITAL STATISTICS

Place of Birth: Zinsen, Bavaria, Germany

Date of Birth: 3 November 1945

Died: n/a Caps: 62 (Germany) Goals (International): 68

Clubs: TSV Nordlingen, Bayern Munich, Fort Lauderdale Strikers

Appearances: Club (League: for Bayern Munich): 427

Goals: Club (League: for Bayern Munich): 365

Trophies: WorC 1974; EC 1974, 1975, 1976; BLG 1969, 1972, 1973, 1974; CWC 1967

LEGEND RATING

Achievement	10
Skill	10
Teamwork	6
Passion	8
Personality	8
Overall Legend Rating	**42**

◁)) He was European Footballer of the Year in 1970, and twice winner of the Golden Boot.

◁)) He scored a phenomenal 14 goals in 13 games in two World Cup final tournaments, including successive hat-tricks in 1970.

◁)) Müller was top scorer at the World Cup in 1970 and the European Championships in 1972.

◁)) Hampered by an injury in 1978, Müller saw out his career in the NASL with Fort Lauderdale.

◁)) He won a hat-trick of European Cups with Bayern Munich.

Munich Air Disaster

6 FEBRUARY 1958 is a date that will remain a black-letter day in the world of football. A plane crash with fatalities was a tragic event in itself, but that the airliner involved should also include most of English football's finest post-war club side was headline news that numbed fans across the globe. In the freezing conditions at Munich airport the plane had already made one abortive attempt at a take-off but, undeterred, the pilot made the decision to try again. On the second attempt the plane left the ground but could not climb high enough to avoid hitting a fence and airport building, whereupon it broke in two and burst into flames.

Although eight players died, some miraculously managed to escape the wreckage alive. They included manager Sir Matt Busby and a young Bobby Charlton, who was to continue playing for another 15 years after the crash. Charlton's long career served as a poignant reminder of what may have lain ahead for his less fortunate colleagues. The names of the dead are a roll-call of unfulfilled talent:

Geoff Bent; Roger Byrne; Eddie Colman; Duncan Edwards; Mark Jones; David Pegg; Tommy Taylor; Bill Whelan.

'People still haven't forgotten. Strangers come up and tell me: "He were a good 'un."'

Anne Edwards, mother of Duncan, 1993

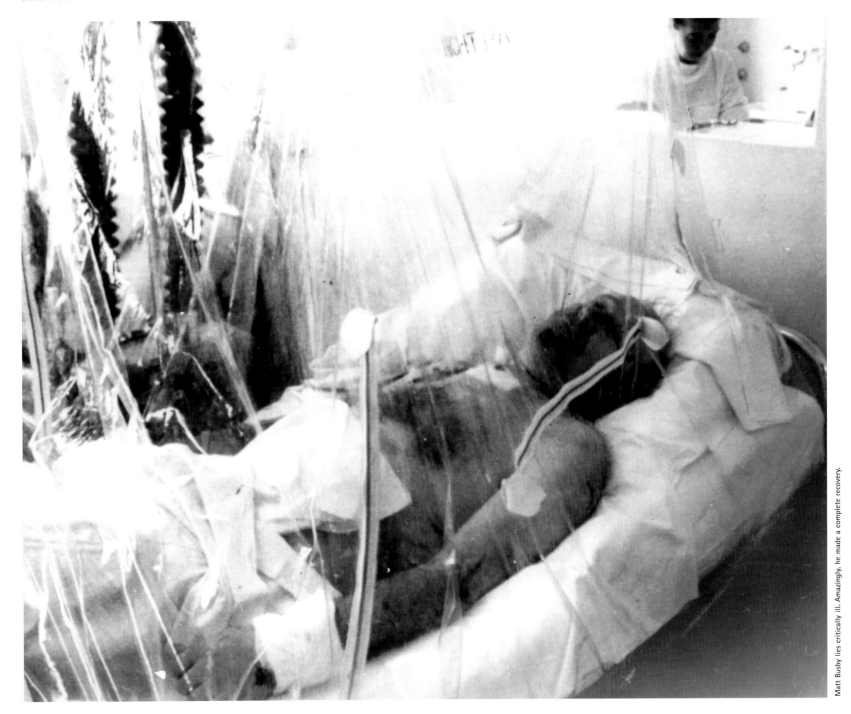

Matt Busby lies critically ill. Amazingly, he made a complete recovery.

- Duncan Edwards was not killed in the crash, but died from his injuries on 21 February 1958.
- Seven of the dead were 25 or younger; Busby's famous Babes had been almost totally wiped out.
- Three members of United's staff also died, plus the journalist Frank Swift, an ex-Manchester City and England goalkeeper.
- A memorial clock was erected at Old Trafford. It contains the date of the crash and is a popular meeting point for fans.
- The programme for United's next league match contained 11 blank spaces where the players' names would normally have been inserted.

Mussolini's Muscle

VITTORIO POZZO COACHED the Italian squad at the 1912 Olympics as a young man. He was hugely impressed by what he saw of the great Austrian coach, Hugo Meisl, and when he was given control of the Italian national side, he determined to build a side to match Weisl's 'Wunderteam'.

Pozzo introduced a discipline not previously seen in a national team, along with some deeply innovative tactics. By the time the 1934 World Cup Finals came along, the Italians had a strong squad. Add to this their home advantage, and a propensity for intimidating both opponents and weak referees, and it was little surprise to see

them emerge as winners of a deeply unsatisfactory tournament. They won again four years later – same manager, same tactics and yet more aggro. But we shouldn't be too cynical; Schiavio, Meazza, Ferrari and Piola were super players and Monti, however brutal, was a card-carrying colossus. Still, for many their 1938 victory will always be tarnished; not because of their underhand approach, but because of Giuseppe Meazza's unfortunate decision to celebrate with a fascist salute after being presented with the trophy.

Manager: Vittorio Pozzo

Key Players

Gianpero Combi (G) Luis Monti (D) Giovanni Ferrari (F)
Raimundo Orsi (W) Gino Colaussi (W) Giuseppe Meazza (F)
Angelo Schiavio (F) Silvio Piola (F)

A victorious Italy chair Pozzo from the field.

◁ Pozzo used Monti as an attacking centre-half, an innovation to help combat the changes made to the offside laws in 1926.

◁ Between their two World Cup triumphs, Italy also won at the Olympics.

◁ Pozzo fortified the team with the *oriund*, nationalised South Americans like Monti and Orsi (both former Argentines).

◁ Tactics were very rigid in the 1930s; Pozzo confounded the Czechs in 1934 by simply asking his wide players to swap wings.

◁ Pozzo remains the only manager to have won two World Cups.

FOOTBALL HAS BEEN PLAYED in the States since the original settlers arrived from Britain in the 1600s. Historically however, the game has struggled to compete with the traditional stateside passions of American football and baseball. Although millions of youngsters now play the game, professional 'soccer' has consistently failed to make an impact. The first national league in the States was actually formed in 1895, but it was not until the mid-1970s that football began to capture the hearts and minds of the wider public. The arrival of the great Pelé at the New York Cosmos in 1975 was the catalyst for a golden era, and other soccer greats such as Franz Beckenbauer, George Best, Rodney Marsh and Zico also made their way out to the North American Soccer League before it folded in 1984. A decade of decline followed until America was chosen to host the 1994 World Cup. This sparked new interest and Major League Soccer was launched two years later. It attracted the major TV companies and sponsorship, and continues to thrive today.

'If the American League of Association Football of 1895 had been a success the sports landscape in America might be much different today.'

US sports historian
Steve Holroyd

Alan Biley's hair provided a major inspiration for US cheerleaders.

◁ᴵ⁾ The Oneida Football Club was formed in 1862 in Boston and is widely regarded as the first team to be formally established in the States. It was made up of youngsters from public schools in the Boston area.

◁ᴵ⁾ The American Football Association was founded in 1895, only the fourth national association to be formed worldwide. It helped establish the first national competition – the American Cup.

◁ᴵ⁾ The United States' 1-0 victory over England in the 1950 World Cup is regarded as one of the biggest international upsets in history. England were one of the best sides in the world at the time.

Neeskens, Johan

JOHAN CRUYFF WAS THE CUTTING EDGE of the great Holland team of the 1970s, but Johan Neeskens (or 'Johan Two' as he became known) was the conductor of the orchestra. An ideal midfield fulcrum, his accurate passing and shooting underpinned the movement and pace of his colleagues. Neeskens made the transition from Ajax star to international star in 1970, and went on to play in both the 1974 and 1978 World Cup Finals. By the time the latter came he had left Ajax for Barcelona, spending five years with the Catalan club. Perhaps Neeskens' defining moment came against Brazil in 1974 when, ignoring all his colleagues, he casually chipped the goalkeeper like a golfer holing out from a bunker. Like many other stars of his generation, Neeskens finished his career in the NASL with New York Cosmos. He has assisted later Dutch teams in a coaching capacity and remains active in the game.

VITAL STATISTICS

Place of Birth: Heemstede, Holland

Date of Birth: 15 September 1951

Died: n/a   Caps: 49 (Holland)   Goals (International): 17

Clubs: Haarlem, Ajax, Barcelona, New York Cosmos, Groningen, Fort Lauderdale Strikers, Baar

Appearances: Club (League): 481

Goals: Club (League): 92

Trophies: DLT 1972, 1973; EC 1971, 1972, 1973; CWC 1979

LEGEND RATING

Achievement	7
Skill	9
Teamwork	9
Passion	7
Personality	6
Overall Legend Rating	**38**

- In 1974 Neeskens scored with a second-minute penalty in the World Cup final.
- Scored five times from midfield in World Cup 1974: impressive for a player not known for getting into the opposition box.
- In 1976 Holland lost to Czechoslovakia in a violent European Championship semi-final. Again Neeskens showed his dark side and was one of two Dutch players sent off.
- Although talented, Neeskens was no angel. In a notoriously bitter match against Brazil in 1974 he played the role of midfield hard-man to great effect.
- Neeskens' move to Barcelona was orchestrated by former Dutch coach Rinus Michels, anxious to reunite him with Cruyff.

Nerazzurri – The Finest

The Internazionale Dream Team

IN 1930 the first national championship of Italy was won by Ambrosiana-Inter, as Internazionale were first known. Their leading scorer, and the top scorer in the country that year, was Giuseppe Meazza. Inter have continued to win trophies throughout their history, but only one of their teams has enjoyed total domination of Serie A.

In the 1960s, led by their controversial coach Helenio Herrera, Inter, with a team built on a rock-like defence including Burgnich, Guarneri and the formidable attacking back Facchetti, were out on their own. Yet, while their defence might have taken most of the plaudits, their midfield, boasting the talents of Sandro Mazzola, the Spaniard Suarez and the young Angelo Domenghini, was not short on ability either. Try as they might, subsequent Inter coaches have failed to match that synthesis of efficient defending and rapid counter-attack. Perhaps the problem is that players in the modern Serie A come and go too fast; Inter have had great players like Baggio, Matthaus, Ronaldo, Bergkamp and Klinsmann, but no great team.

Manager: Helenio Herrera
4-3-1-2

Walter Zenga (80s/90s)

Tarcisio Burgnich (60s/70s) Riccardo Ferri (80s)
Giuseppe Bergomi (80s/90s) Giacomo Facchetti (C) (60s/70s)

Sandro Mazzola (60s) Luis Suarez (60s) Angelo Domenghini (60s/70s)

Roberto Baggio (90s)

Roberto Boninsegna (60s/70s) Giuseppe Meazza (30s)

Subs: Giorgio Ghezzi (G) (50s) Aristide Guarneri (D) (50s/60s)
Lothar Matthaus (D/M) (90s) Jair (M/F) (60s) Jurgen Klinsmann (F) (90s)

The 1960s Inter was the

◄» 1950s goalkeeper Ghezzi was known as Kamikaze. Brave and agile, he is a legend at Inter.

◄» Facchetti remains Inter's most-capped player, with 94 appearances for Italy.

◄» Bergomi is Inter's most loyal player of recent years. No flitting about for him, as just over 750 appearances show.

◄» Meazza remains Inter's top scorer with 264 goals from 439 matches.

◄» Three UEFA Cup wins in the 1990s merely offered tantalising glimpses of the European success the club craves. Two of the final victories were over Italian opposition.

283

Netzer, Gunter

Borussia Monchengladbach, West Germany

A GERMAN GASCOIGNE without the boozing, belching and domestic violence; for a brief period Gunter Netzer could lay claim to being the finest midfield player in the world. After missing out on the 1970 World Cup, Netzer came to the fore in the 1972 European Championships when he was instrumental in his country's victory over England in the quarter-final. Despite being several players short, West Germany won at a canter. Beckenbauer was magnificent at the back, Müller unstoppable in the box, and Netzer, long hair flowing, linked the two with aggression and immaculate distribution. The Germans went on to win the tournament with ease. For years the mainstay of a strong Borussia Monchengladbach team, Netzer later made a high-profile move to Real Madrid in 1973, only to suffer a grievous loss of form that impacted on his international career. At the 1974 World Cup Finals he made just one appearance, briefly figuring as a substitute against East Germany. Few players looked as good as Netzer did for those few years, but few have faded so dramatically either.

VITAL STATISTICS

Place of Birth: West Germany

Date of Birth: 14 September 1944

Died: n/a   Caps: 37 (West Germany)   Goals (International): 6

Clubs: Borussia Monchengladbach, Real Madrid, Grasshopper

Appearances: Club (League: For Borussia): 230

Goals: Club (League: For Borussia): 82

Trophies: BLG 1970, 1971 (1979 as manager of Hamburg); EuroC 1972; PLA 1975, 1976

LEGEND RATING

Achievement   8

Skill   9

Teamwork   8

Passion   7

Personality   7

Overall Legend Rating   39

Netzer takes on the Soviet Union in the European Nations Cup Final, 1972.

- Netzer was in Hennes Weiweiler's Monchengladbach side that won the club their first Bundesliga title in 1970.
- Netzer's replacement in the German team, Monchengladbach team-mate Rainer Bonhof, was a strong, hard-running player, less skilful than Netzer, but an easier player to fit into Helmut Schoen's pattern.
- Monchengladbach lost the 1973 UEFA Cup final to Liverpool. Shankly's team were grateful for a 3-0 lead from Anfield, as Monchengladbach pummelled them in the return, winning 2-0.
- Netzer became manager of Hamburg on his retirement, inheriting a strong team including Kevin Keegan. He duly brought them their first Bundesliga title for 19 years.

New Theories

A PACKED HOUSE arrived at Wembley confidently expecting an easy England victory. A bullish press had led the nation to believe that England were unbeatable, largely on the basis that no overseas team had won at Wembley before. The England team, ageing and complacent in their heavy boots, scoffed at the men wearing 'carpet slippers', especially the 'little fat chap' leading them out. It is unthinkable that a modern coach would be so badly prepared (England's opponents were a highly dangerous outfit, unbeaten for 20 games). Hungary scored in the first minute, a precise angled strike from Nandor Hidegkuti. An England equaliser offered false

hope before Hidegkuti scored again and 'the little fat chap', Ferenc Puskas, added two more.

The rest of the detail is irrelevant. Hungary went into cruise mode, giving the impression they could score at will. Their passing triangles and sudden sprints forward into space completely flummoxed an unimaginative England defence. Puskas had breezed past Billy Wright, England's best defender, on numerous occasions, and the use of the deep-lying centre forward Hidegkuti had given prosaic England untold problems.

SCORERS:	England: Sewell, Mortensen, Ramsey (pen)
	Hungary: Hidegkuti (3), Puskas (2), Bozsik
EVENT:	Friendly International, Wembley,
	25 November 1953

ENGLAND		HUNGARY	
(Man: Walter Winterbottom)		(Man: Jimmy Hogan)	
1 Merrick	7 Matthews	1 Grosics	7 Budai
2 Ramsey	8 Taylor	2 Buzansky	8 Kocsis
3 Eckersley	9 Mortensen	3 Lantos	9 Hidegkuti
4 Wright	10 Sewell	4 Bozsik	10 Puskas
5 Johnston	11 Robb	5 Lorant	11 Czibor
6 Dickinson		6 Zakarias	

Puskas (No. 10) celebrates another Hungary goal.

- The headlines next day compared Hungary to the Scottish 'Wembley Wizards' of 1928, who had embarrassed England at Wembley in much the same fashion.
- The England side featured Matthews and Mortensen fresh from

their heroics at the FA Cup final. Mortensen got a consolation but Matthews hardly saw the ball.
- The sides played again six months later as a last warm-up for Hungary's World Cup campaign. England made seven changes in

an effort to counter the Hungarian tactics. The plan failed dismally as Hungary won 7–1. Back to the drawing board, chaps.

Nicholson, Bill

WHEN BILL NICHOLSON RESIGNED as manager of Spurs in 1974, it brought a 36-year love affair to an end. With Bill Shankly retiring the same year it also marked the passing of the last remaining manager from the old school. 'I am abused by players, there is no longer respect', lamented Nicholson, announcing his decision to step down.

If anyone deserved respect it was Nicholson. As a player he had served the club well in the post-war years; starting at full-back, he later switched inside to centre-half, then moved again, this time to half-back, in the 1951 league title winning side. As manager he brought success and consistency to the club, while always remaining mindful of his obligation to play exciting football. The 1961 double-winning team scored over 100 goals, playing scintillating football at odds with Nicholson's dour, uncompromising demeanour.

Under his tutelage, after a difficult first season, Spurs only once finished in the bottom half of the First Division. They were a notable cup team, too, becoming the first British side to win a European trophy. Nicholson was incensed when the club appointed an Arsenal man, Terry Neill, to replace him, arguing that Danny Blanchflower would have been a better choice. His instincts proved right. Neill took Spurs into Division Two within three years.

VITAL STATISTICS

Place of Birth: Scarborough, England

Date of Birth: 26 January 1919

Died: n/a   Caps: 1 (England)

Goals (International): 1

Clubs: As Player: Tottenham Hotspur; As Manager: Tottenham Hotspur

Trophies: LT (1951) 1961; FAC 1961, 1962, 1967; LC 1971, 1973; CWC 1963; UEFAC 1972

LEGEND RATING

Achievement	9
Tactical Awareness	8
Motivation	8
Transfer Dealing and Team Selection	9
Personality	8
Overall Legend Rating	**42**

- In Nicholson's first game as a manager, Tottenham was a 10-4 winner against Everton.
- Nicholson scored after 19 seconds of his England debut, but was never picked again.
- He won a PFA merit award in 1984 for his services to the game.
- In 1961, the Spurs double-winning team had just one player booked all season.
- Nicholson was a contributor to Soccer – The Fight For Survival, A Blueprint For The Future, a 1980/81 review of a game in crisis.

Nicknames

TEAM NICKNAMES are a proud tradition in football, with most teams having an official alternative to their full title. Some are derivations of the name of the team, like The O's (Orient) or The Gills (Gillingham), while some reflect the team's traditional colours, such as The Canaries (Norwich) or The Clarets (Burnley). Others take their inspiration from the local community, reflecting the working traditions of a town or city; The Cobblers (Northampton – a traditional shoe-making town), The Hatters (Luton – a millinery centre) or The Mariners (Grimsby – a fishing port). Some of the names become indistinguishable from the team, like Wolves or Spurs,

and others are used just as frequently as the team's real name. For instance, a match between The Saints and Pompey means a local derby in Southampton or Portsmouth.

Players have nicknames too, although these tend to be less official and often uncomplimentary. In Brazil players rarely go by their real names, preferring to abbreviate their long-winded Portuguese surnames to a single, lyrical word. Zico would never have seemed as cool if commentators had referred to him by his real name: Arthur just doesn't have the same ring to it.

> 'A nickname is the heaviest stone that the devil can throw at a man.'
>
> William Hazlitt, Sketches And Essays, 1839

'Ronaldo' trips off the tongue easier than Ronaldo Luis Nazario de Lima, doesn't it?

◁▷ The most literal use of a colour-derived name must be the team from Essen. They play in red and white and their name is Rot Weiss Essen.

◁▷ Chelsea used to be known as The Pensioners, but dropped it as it seemed a little inappropriate to a football team. Seats for the uniformed veterans are still reserved at Stamford Bridge.

◁▷ Players occasionally adopt self-styled nicknames. Paul Ince adopted the absurd moniker 'The Guv'nor' because he thought it made him sound hard. He was wrong.

◁▷ Some nicknames are derived from players' names, (Gordon 'Jukebox' Durie), 'Lambchop' (Paolo Wanchope); or their playing style ('The Lawnmower' – Stig Tofting: he covers so much grass!).

Non-League Glory

Sutton United 2 Coventry City 1, 1989

DAGENHAM AND REDBRIDGE came within four minutes of putting out Charlton in 2000, but these days non-league teams appearing in the third round of the FA Cup generally have to content themselves with scalps from the Second and Third Divisions. Not so Sutton United who, for one glorious Saturday in 1979, turned the *Match Of The Day* cameras away from the likes of Old Trafford and Anfield to a backwater suburb of Surrey.

Coventry were in good form, fresh from a 5-0 thrashing of Sheffield Wednesday five days earlier, but on a muddy pitch in front of a tightly-packed 8,000 crowd they seemed to freeze.

At half-time they went in 1-0 down courtesy of a Tony Rains header and, though David Phillips managed to draw them level shortly after the break, on 60 minutes Matthew Hanlan restored Sutton's advantage, referee Alf Buksh having conveniently missed a blatant foul on Coventry keeper Steve Ogrizovic. The expected siege from Coventry produced only near misses and agonising 'oohs' from the crowd: cue chaos, clichés and Sutton into round four.

SCORERS: Sutton: Rains, Hanlan
Coventry: Phillips

EVENT: FA Cup Third Round, Borough Sportsground, Gander Green Lane, 7 January 1989

SUTTON UNITED
(Man: Barry Williams)

1 Roffey   7 Stephens
2 Jones   8 Dawson
3 Rains   9 Hanlan
4 Golley   10 Dennis
5 Pratt   11 McKinnon
6 Rogers

COVENTRY CITY
(Man: John Sillett)

1 Ogrizovic   7 Bennett
2 Borrows   8 Speedie
3 Phillips   9 Regis
4 Sedgely   10 McGrath
5 Kilcline   11 Smith
6 Peake

Scorers Rains (left) and Hanlan toast victory with a postmatch...er...water.

- This is the most recent incident of a non-league team knocking out a club from the top division in the FA Cup.
- Coventry included seven players who had won them the Cup two seasons earlier.
- Sutton had reached the third round the previous year, unluckily losing a replay to Second Division Middlesbrough.
- Sutton lost 8-0 at Norwich in the next round.
- The sister of winning goalscorer Matthew Hanlan achieved her own celebrity; her tearful reaction at the final whistle was part of *Match Of The Day's* opening credits for the following season.

Nou Camp

THE NOU CAMP is rightly regarded as one of the great stadiums of world soccer and enjoys the rare and coveted UEFA five-star rating.

Home to Barcelona and its passionate fans, the stadium opened in 1957 and is seen as a monument to Catalan pride. It is regularly packed to capacity. Even today, with a slightly reduced capacity of 109,000, the stadium is the biggest in Europe and attendances for league matches regularly top the 100,000 mark.

The pitch is built eight metres below street level and its towering stands make it one of the most intimidating theatres in the game. The word cauldron has been used to the point of cliché by commentators but it describes the shape and atmosphere of the Nou Camp in a nutshell.

The Nou Camp underwent a major refurbishment in readiness for the 1982 World Cup Finals, increasing the capacity from a scarcely snug 90,000 to an immense 120,000. It played host to the opening game of the competition between Argentina and Belgium. Due to the Bernabeu's lure in the nation's capital, the Nou Camp remains the finest ground never to have staged the final.

VITAL STATISTICS

Location:	Barcelona, Spain
Local Club:	Barcelona
Date Built:	1957
Current Capacity:	109,000
Max. Capacity:	120,000

◄▮ Despite the increased capacity, the curtain-raiser of the 1982 World Cup is the only time that the opening match has not been watched by a capacity crowd. A mere 85,000 turned up.

◄▮ The first-ever match in 1957 at the Nou Camp was a curious choice. Barcelona's opponents were Poland – the home side winning 4-2.

◄▮ The formal name is El Nou Estadi del Futbol Club Barcelona. No wonder they stick to Nou Camp.

◄▮ The Nou Camp has staged four major European club finals; the European Cup in 1989 and 1999, plus the Cup Winners' Cups of 1972 and 1982.

Now Listen To Me, Young Man!

Nottingham Forest, late 1970s

WHEN BRIAN CLOUGH and Peter Taylor joined Nottingham Forest in 1975, no one could have anticipated the success the next five years would bring. Upon winning promotion in 1977 they added the great Peter Shilton to their side, went top of the First Division after three opening wins, and stayed there. A tight defence, a midfield with an unparalleled work rate, and mobile strikers were the key ingredients – plus a little bit of that Cloughie *je ne sais quoi* sprinkled on top.

Even greater things followed in Europe, courtesy of two contrasting European Cup finals. The first in 1979, won by a single Trevor Francis goal, was reward for a sparkling performance against Malmo while the second, another 1-0 win over Kevin Keegan's Hamburg in 1980, showed the more dogged side of their nature. Despite unceasing pressure from the German team Forest stood firm, with Kenny Burns outstanding at the heart of their defence. That was the last of their major titles, but under Clough they remained a significant force in the top flight for another decade, as new stars like Neil Webb, Stuart Pearce and Clough's own son, Nigel came to the fore.

Manager: Brian Clough

Key Players

Peter Shilton (G) Larry Lloyd (D) Viv Anderson (D)
Kenny Burns (D) John McGovern (M) Ian Bowyer (M)
Archie Gemmill (M) Martin O'Neill (W) John Robertson (W)
Trevor Francis (F) Tony Woodcock (F)

Trophies

LT 1978 EC 1979, 1980 LC 1978, 1979

Forest celebrate their first European Cup in 1979.

◁ Robertson made the goal in the 1979 European Cup final, and scored the winner in 1980.

◁ Forest ousted reigning champions Liverpool in the first round of the 1979 European Cup.

◁ Forest also won the League Cup in 1979, Gary Birtles scoring twice in a 3-2 win.

◁ Forest won the League Cup twice more under Clough, in 1989 and 1990. Alas though, the FA Cup eluded him.

◁ Birtles is best remembered for a nightmare spell at Man United, but his performance as a lone striker in the 1980 European Cup final for Forest was outstanding.

Numbers

AT THE START of the 1928/29 season, the players of Chelsea and Arsenal wore shirt numbers for the first time. The experiment proved popular, not least because it was a crude ploy to make fans buy the match programme. In 1933 numbers made their first appearance at the FA Cup final, and six years later they were voted in as a permanent fixture. This meant that, for the first time, players' positions became synonymous with the numbers they wore; the centre-forward became simply 'the number nine', while it was unthinkable that the number seven would not hug the right touchline for most of the game.

In 1993/94 numbering was replaced by the squad system in the Premier League. This saw players keep their number for an entire season and, in most cases, even longer, usually until they move to another club. This has enabled the introduction of the players' names to be printed above the number; a feature that clubs quickly learned the value of when selling replica shirts. Who wants a plain old number nine jersey when you can have 'Lua Lua 20' instead?

'When he gets mine home he'll wonder who the bloody hell's it is.'

Ireland's Mick McCarthy after swapping shirts with Ruud Gullit at the 1988 European Championships

One of Pelé's Brazilian shirts goes on display.

◀ In the 1933 FA Cup final, the teams were numbered one to 22, each player having his own number. The goalkeepers wore one and 22.

◀ Some players are synonymous with their numbers. Who can imagine Pelé without the number 10 shirt on his back, or Bobby Moore walking out in anything but his famous number six?

◀ The number 13 remains unpopular for superstitious reasons. If used at all, it usually goes to the substitute goalkeeper.

◀ Ade Akinbiyi selected the preposterous 55 as his squad number after moving to Crystal Palace in 2002. Denied his favourite number 10 shirt, he selected a sum of 10 instead.

Offside

Oi, linesman, get that flag up!

FOOTBALL IN THE 1920s was becoming defensive and stale, with as many as 40 offside decisions per game, so the authorities introduced a simple but effective antidote. They decided, from that point on, that an attacker needed just two (rather than three) players between him and the goal to be called onside. Immediately teams had to rethink their tactics, with many sides introducing a withdrawn centre-half as a third defender to combat the new ruling. Recently the offside law was once again changed in favour of the attacking side; where previously an attacking player who was level with the opposition's last defender was considered offside, he is now free to

continue (in other words he's onside). This makes defending against players with the pace of Ronaldo, Thierry Henry or Michael Owen very difficult. Less satisfactory is the 'not interfering with play' rule affecting players in 'secondary' and 'non-active' areas. This is blurred and confusing, and leads to the sort of inconsistency that gives managers premature heart attacks.

'There's a big misconception. We never actually played offside. You'll see countless pictures of us standing in a line with our hands up appealing, but we were not actually going out to get sides offside.'

Lee Dixon

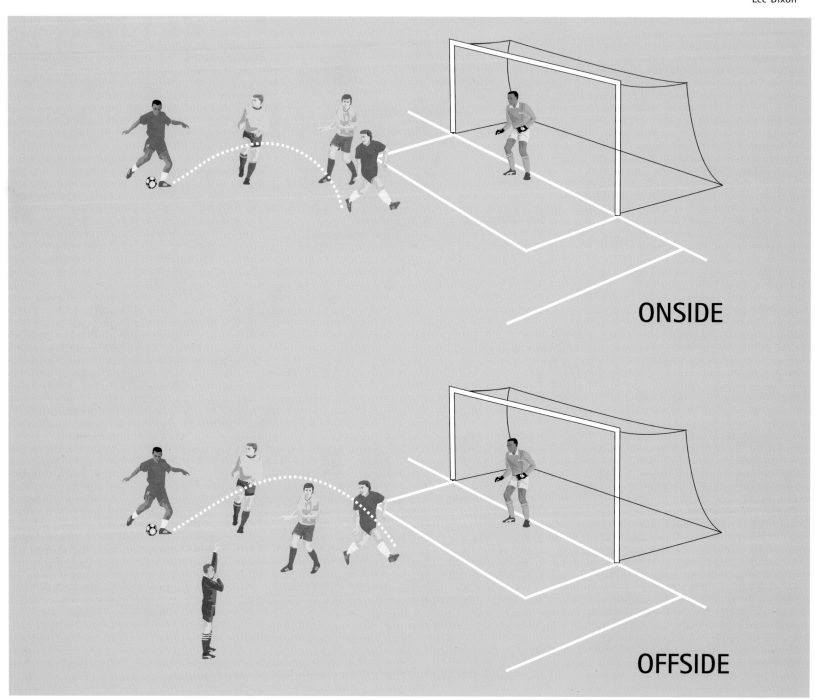

ONSIDE

OFFSIDE

◁ Combined with the back-pass rule, the 'level' ruling has spawned a generation of goalkeepers adept at coming off their line and playing the ball with foot or head. Fabien Barthez and David James are both able to operate as a sweeper when required.

◁ The ability to stay onside is a good measure of a striker's awareness and timing, and a handy guide to the intelligence of a footballer. Alan Shearer hardly ever gets caught offside. Craig Bellamy does. We rest our case.

◁ Arsenal are the masters of the offside trap. Their 'fab five' of Seaman, Dixon, Winterburn, Adams and Bould were great defenders, and played the tactic to near-perfection.

THE GREAT WOLVES TEAM of the 1950s nearly ended the decade by winning the double; had they done so they would have emulated the feats of Huddersfield and Arsenal in winning three consecutive titles. That they stumbled just short shouldn't obscure the fact that this was a more than tidy team, and one that had dominated for the best part of 10 years despite formidable challenges from Blackpool, Manchester United and big-spending Arsenal.

Wolves managed by Stan Cullis were the masters of harrying teams out of their stride. They didn't have the inspirational individuals that some of the other teams could boast, but they had a tried-and-trusted system and a collection of players who knew precisely what their roles were within it. An excellent keeper in Bert Williams, and a defence augmented in later years by Billy Wright's move to centre-half, gave them a solid base at the back. In midfield their half-backs Eddie Clamp and Ron Flowers were industrious and tenacious, and wasted little time dwelling on the ball, preferring instead to release the wingers, Mullen and Hancocks. Once in the possession of the wide players the ball would be taken to the byline and crossed, hopefully finding the head or boot of Peter Broadbent. 'Total Football' it wasn't, but it worked, and few opponents had an answer to it.

Manager: Stan Cullis

Key Players
Bert Williams (G) Ron Flowers (HB) Billy Wright (HB/D)
Bill Slater (HB) Johnny Hancocks (W) Jimmy Mullen (W)
Peter Broadbent (F)

Trophies
LT 1954, 1958, 1959 FA Cup 1960

Wembley, 1960. Billy Wright and the FA Cup enjoy a couple of helping hands.

◄ Apart from Wright and Flowers, few of these were great internationals; they were a team, not a collection of individuals.
◄ Cullis started the great post-war era as Wolves' captain, but never won a major trophy as a player.

◄ Bill Slater was one of the last successful amateurs, mixing work at Birmingham University with football. He played for England as a semi-professional.
◄ Slater was voted PFA Player of the Year in 1960, and later

received an OBE and CBE for his services to sport.
◄ Billy Wright and Jimmy Mullen were awarded a joint testimonial in 1962. Stan Cullis had to wait until 1992, when a new stand at Molineux was also opened in his honour.

O'Leary, David

Arsenal, Leeds United, Republic of Ireland

WHEN HE FIRST APPEARED in Arsenal's first team as a skinny, gangling teenager, David O'Leary looked too fragile to last 90 minutes. But in a distinguished career at Highbury he eventually managed over 600 appearances for the club, including 558 in the league. O'Leary became one of the best defenders in Europe during his 20-year career. Good in the air, comfortable on the ground, and an excellent reader of the game, he was the rock at the heart of the Arsenal team, much in the way Tony Adams has been in the last decade.

O'Leary picked up 67 caps for the Republic of Ireland, and would surely have played many more internationals but for a long spell in the wilderness following a row with Jack Charlton. But the two did patch up their differences sufficiently for O'Leary to be picked in the squad for the 1990 World Cup Finals in Italy.

O'Leary served his management apprenticeship under George Graham at Leeds, stepping up to the top job when Graham left for Tottenham. Pitching youngsters like Alan Smith and Jonathan Woodgate into the first team, Leeds made progress, reaching the semi-final stage of the Champions League in 2001. Despite expensive purchases in the transfer market, O'Leary was eased out in 2002 as Leeds failed to make the Champions League.

VITAL STATISTICS

Place of Birth: Dublin, Ireland

Date of Birth: 2 May 1958

Died: n/a Caps: 68 (Republic of Ireland)

Goals (International): 1

Clubs: As Player: Arsenal; As Manager: Leeds United

Appearances: Club (League): 558

Goals: Club (League): 10

Trophies: LT 1989, 1991; FAC 1979; LC 1987

LEGEND RATING

Achievement	7
Skill	8
Teamwork	8
Passion	8
Personality	7
Overall Legend Rating	**38**

◁❯ David's brother Pierce was capped seven times by Ireland. He once came on for David in a Wembley international.

◁❯ Gangling appearance earned him the nickname 'Spider' at Arsenal.

◁❯ Leeds came through tough groups to reach the semi-final of the 2001 Champions League. They beat Milan, Lazio and Deportivo La Coruna along the way, and eliminated Barcelona in the initial group stages.

◁❯ O'Leary's departure from Leeds in 2002 was followed by months of dispute over his severance package.

◁❯ Scored the winning spot-kick in a penalty shoot-out against Romania in the second round of the 1990 World Cup Finals.

Olympiastadion

THE OLYMPIASTADION IN BERLIN won its place in the history books when it played host to the 1936 Olympic Games. Designed by Werner March, it had been specially built for the Games by the Nazis and was intended as a demonstration of Aryan superiority. Happily, it was black athlete Jesse Owens who stole the show.

Since then, the stadium has been home to Hertha Berlin, who have never matched its splendour in footballing terms, as the greater glory has gone to Munich and Hamburg. Two World Cup matches were staged at the ground in 1974, but these proved rare glimpses of the big time as Hertha struggled on the pitch and sunk out of

top-flight German football. Their fortunes have since revived, they appeared in the Champions League as recently as 1999.

In 1995 the stadium, a regular venue for international athletics matches, hosted its first international football for seven years. Germany overcame Bulgaria in a European Championship qualifier. Such was the support from the crowd that day, the German FA decided to include the stadium in their successful bid for the 2006 World Cup.

VITAL STATISTICS

Location:	Berlin, Germany
Local Club:	Hertha BSC, Blau-Weiss
Date Built:	1936
Current Capacity:	76,006
Max. Capacity:	88,000

Jesse Owens makes history at the Olympiastadion in the 1936 Berlin Olympics.

◄ᴺ A reported 100,000 crammed into the stadium when Hitler opened the 1936 Olympic Games

◄ᴺ Still holds the attendance record for a Bundesliga match – 88,000 for Hertha Berlin against Cologne in 1969.

◄ᴺ The stadium is used annually for the German Cup final.

◄ᴺ The Olympiastadion remained one of the few German public buildings and virtually the only major sports venue to survive the Second World War.

◄ᴺ Work is now underway to transform the stadium – complete with a retractable stand – into a 77,000 capacity venue for the 2006 World Cup Finals.

◄ᴺ Work is now underway to transform the stadium – complete

O'Neill, Martin

Nottingham Forest, Celtic, Northern Ireland

ONE OF THE MORE ENTERTAINING features of Leicester City and Celtic matches in recent years has been the sight of a slender, curly-haired man hopping up and down manically on the touchline. Martin O'Neill wears his heart on his sleeve; if a referee or player has incurred his wrath, there's no need to wait for the press conference.

O'Neill was a fine player, winning trophies at home and in Europe under Brian Clough at Nottingham Forest. The width provided by O'Neill and John Robertson were crucial to that side's success. Playing for Northern Ireland, his chances of winning international trophies were limited, but he captained the side in one of their proudest

moments when they defeated hosts Spain in the 1982 World Cup. As a manager O'Neill has been able to combine the qualities he brought to that Irish side – namely spirit and determination – with the tactical and motivational lessons learned under his former boss, Brian Clough. An excellent record in the lower divisions with Wycombe took him eventually to Leicester, where he made the club competitive in the Premier League. At Filbert Street the press speculated furiously about where O'Neill was heading next, and what he would or would not achieve when he got there. He eventually opted for Celtic, and won the Scottish League in his first two seasons.

VITAL STATISTICS

Place of Birth: Kilrea, County Derry, N. Ireland

Date of Birth: 1 March 1952

Died: n/a Caps: 64 (Northern Ireland) Goals (International): 8

Clubs: As Player: Distillery, Nottingham Forest, Norwich City, Manchester City, Notts County. As manager: Wycombe Wanderers, Norwich City, Leicester City, Celtic

Trophies: EC 1979, 1980; LT 1978; LC 1978, 1979, (1997, 2000); SLT (2001, 2002); SFAC (2001)

LEGEND RATING

Achievement	8	Achievement	8
Skill	7	Tactical Awareness	7
Teamwork	8	Motivation	10
Passion	7	Transfer Dealing and Team Selection	7
Personality	7	Personality	9
Overall Legend Rating	**37**	**Overall Legend Rating**	**41**

O'Neill has earned respect for the honourable way he has conducted himself in his managerial career; he turned down a huge job at Leeds in order to honour his commitments with Leicester.

O'Neill took Wycombe Wanderers into the league for the first time in their history, overcoming huge local apathy in commuter-belt Buckinghamshire.

O'Neill won the title in his first season at Celtic, his purchase

of Chris Sutton providing the perfect foil for the lethal Henrik Larsson.

O'Neill missed Forest's first European Cup Final in 1979 through injury, but played in the win over Hamburg a year later.

One Keane In Ireland

Germany 1 Republic of Ireland 1, 2002

The Republic of Ireland had fought mightily to come back from a goal down against Cameroon in their previous match. Germany had had a stroll in the park against Saudi Arabia (an appropriate metaphor since the Saudis defended like a park team). The Germans seemed to be giving the lie to the suggestion that they were not going to threaten at this World Cup. The Irish were determined to give the lie to the allegations that they were a one-man team.

After an hour-and-a-half of manful struggle it seemed that the best efforts of Staunton, Holland, Keane and the brilliant Damien

Duff would prove in vain. One last punt into the German box, a flick on from giant substitute Niall Quinn and there was Keane (no, not that one!) to chest the ball on and belt it into the roof of the goal. The sea of green at one end of the stadium erupted into a storm of fervent celebration.

In patches Germany showed their habitual resilience and efficiency, but in truth they only held on until Ireland's late equaliser because of Kahn's superb presence and anticipation. Three or four outstanding saves kept the Irish at bay until that roof-raising finish.

SCORERS:	Germany: Klose
	Republic of Ireland: Keane
EVENT:	Group E, second match, World Cup Finals, Ibaraki, 5 June 2002

GERMANY
(Man: Rudi Voller)

1	Kahn	8	Ballack
2	Frings	9	Hamann
3	Linke	10	Klose
4	Metzelder	11	Jancker
5	Ramelow		
6	Ziege		
7	Schneider		

REPUBLIC OF IRELAND
(Man: Mick McCarthy)

1	Given	6	Kelly
2	Finnan		(Reid)
3	Breen	7	Holland
4	Staunton	8	Kinsella
	(Cunningham)	9	Kilbane
5	Harte	10	Duff
	(Quinn)	11	Keane

Robbie Keane in trademark celebration after his late, late strike.

▸ Steve Staunton became the first player to make 100 appearances for Ireland 14 years after his debut. What a game to choose!

▸ This was the last goal Germany conceded as they notched up four clean sheets before succumbing to Brazil in the final.

▸ Mick McCarthy's face as the goal went in was a picture. His mouth seemed to hang for an age in slack-jawed disbelief as he watched Keane gather the ball, before he exploded into an ungainly jig of delight. Fortune favours the brave, Mick.

▸ New scoring-sensation Klose, fresh from a hat-trick against Saudi Arabia, was a threat in the first half but faded along with strike-partner Carsten Jancker.

Outsiders Meet In Final

Brazil 2 Germany 0, World Cup Final, 2002

CLASH OF THE TITANS. Battle of the Giants. Whichever cliché you turned to revealed the simple fact that this match was a confrontation between the two pre-eminent footballing powers in the modern game. The purity and ebullience of Brazil against the professionalism and indomitability of the Germans.

As befitted a tremendously entertaining tournament it was an open contest, with Germany surprising many observers by their willingness to press forward and exploit Brazil's supposed weakness at the back. That weakness never materialised, and Brazil's determination and resilience was exemplified by two super-saves

from their under-rated goalkeeper, Marcos. A tip onto the post from Neuville's fierce free kick was top-drawer.

At the other end Kahn looked as competent and formidable as he had all tournament, and when Ronaldo missed a couple of chances, and Kleberson's fine strike came back off the bar, it began to look like a classic 1-0 victory for Germany. Fate conspired against Kahn in the end. Just about his first major error of the tournament, spilling Rivaldo's less-than-venomous shot, was punished ruthlessly by the predatory Ronaldo. A high-class second confirmed that the Brazilian's nightmare of four years ago would no longer keep him awake.

SCORERS: **Brazil:** Ronaldo (2)
EVENT: World Cup Final 2002, Yokohama, 30 June 2002

BRAZIL (Man: 'Big Phil' Scolari)		GERMANY (Man: Rudi Voller)	
1 Marcos	7 Gilberto	1 Kahn	8 Jeremies
2 Cafu	8 Silva	2 Frings	(Asamoah)
3 Roque	9 Kleberson	3 Linke	9 Hamann
Junior	10 Ronaldinho	4 Ramelow	10 Klose
4 Lucio	(Juninho)	5 Metzelder	(Bierhoff)
5 Edmilson	11 Ronaldo	6 Bode	11 Neuville
6 Roberto	(Denilson)	(Ziege)	
Carlos	12 Rivaldo	7 Schneider	

Remarkably, this was the first World Cup meeting between Brazil and Germany. Maybe Sepp Blatter has been at work longer than we thought....

Ronaldo's goals earned him the Golden Boot award for the top scorer in the tournament. Not since Paolo Rossi in 1982 had a Golden Boot winner got his hands on the trophy. His comeback from the torment of 1998 and terrible injury troubles was most heartwarming.

Cafu became the first player to play in three consecutive World Cup finals; in the other two Brazil had failed to score, winning on penalties in 1994 and losing 3-0 to France in 1998.

Over The (Blue) Moon

The Manchester City Dream Team

ALTHOUGH OFTEN IN THE SHADOW of their neighbours, this team would give the current Manchester United side a run for its money.

Few teams in the history of the game can boast a stronger goalkeeping duo; Frank Swift was the finest keeper of his generation and relegates Joe Corrigan to the familiar role of understudy, a position he filled so often for England, covering for Shilton and Clemence in the 1970s.

In defence, Book and Doyle are obvious candidates from the side that won the Championship, FA Cup and Cup Winners' Cup in the 1960s, while Dave Watson was England's finest centre-half of the 1970s. In midfield, Kinkladze and Summerbee would stretch opponents wide, leaving Bell and Revie to surge forward into the gaps. Up front, Lee justifies his place on the grounds that City, and later Derby, enjoyed their most successful spells with him leading the line. Tilson fired the bullets in City's other championship-winning side in 1937. The bench is conspicuous by its lack of defenders, so in the event of a back-four injury this team would have to revert to 3-5-2. This shouldn't pose a problem; attack has always been City's preferred form of defence.

Managers: Joe Mercer and Malcolm Allison

4-4-2

Frank Swift (30s/40s)

Tony Book (C) (60s/70s) Mike Doyle (60s/70s) Dave Watson (70s)
Willie Donachie (70s)

Georgiou Kinkladze (90s) Don Revie (50s)
Colin Bell (70s) Mike Summerbee (70s)

Francis Lee (70s) Fred Tilson (30s)

Subs: Joe Corrigan (G) (70s) Asa Hartford (M) (70s) Peter Doherty (M/F)
(30s) Rodney Marsh (W) (70s) Dennis Tueart (F) (70s)

1968: Joe Mercer presents the League Championship at Maine Road

↖ Frank Swift became a distinguished football journalist after retiring. Tragically, he died in the 1958 Munich air crash.

↖ Dennis Tueart would be encouraged to attempt as many overhead kicks as possible. His effort won the 1976 League Cup and remains one of Wembley's most eye-catching goals.

↖ Colin Bell could stake a claim for inclusion in a post-war England side. His pace over short distances earned him the nickname 'Nijinsky'.

↖ Steve Daley or Michael Robinson are not selected; despite their expensive price tags, neither justifies inclusion.

↖ Mercer and Allison formed a potent manager/coach team in the 1960s. Can Mercer forgive Allison for ruining his legacy?

Owen, Michael

FEW FOOTBALLERS ACHIEVE in a lifetime what Michael Owen had achieved by the age of 22. At 17 years and 144 days he became the youngest player ever to appear in the Liverpool first team, then followed that by becoming the youngest England player of the twentieth century. By the time he was 18 he was a world star, largely on account of his exploits at France 98 where, against Argentina in the second round, he scored one of the greatest World Cup goals of all time.

Having spent two years learning to live with vulnerable hamstrings, Owen re-emerged late in the 2000/01 season to lead the Liverpool line as they won a unique treble of cups. His performance in the FA Cup final, when he scored both goals in Liverpool's 2-1 defeat of Arsenal, was probably his best, but it was his consistency over this period that most impressed.

Owen's principal asset is his blistering pace, but to dismiss him as merely a speed-merchant would be to take him lightly. He is able to use either foot, has a good first touch, good balance, and takes a high percentage of his chances. He scored his 100th Premiership goal in April 2003, a remarkable achievement for a 22 year-old.

VITAL STATISTICS

Place of Birth: Chester, England
Date of Birth: 14 December 1979
Died: n/a   Caps: 47
Goals (International): 20
Clubs: Liverpool
Appearances: Club (League): 187
Goals: Club (League): 92
Trophies: FAC 2001; LC 2001, 2003; EUFAC 2001

Munich, 2001. Owen celebrates one-third of his hat-rick in England's famous 5-1 triumph.

LEGEND RATING

Achievement	7
Skill	9
Teamwork	8
Passion	8
Personality	8
Overall Legend Rating	**40**

- Like Liverpool icons Kenny Dalglish and Alan Hansen before him, Owen is a class golfer.
- Owen scored his 100th goal for Liverpool in 2002, still aged only 22.

- He was voted PFA Young Player of the Year in 1998 and European Footballer of the Year in 2001.
- He was also BBC Sports Personality of the Year in 1998, and came third in the same poll in 2001.

- A fit Owen is key to England's international fortunes. Without him too many of the chances created by the likes of David Beckham and Steven Gerrard go begging.

Own Goal

SOME OWN GOALS are just down to plain bad luck. A defence can hardly legislate for a cruel deflection or unavoidable ricochet. Gary Mabbutt could hardly be blamed for the goal that won the FA Cup for Coventry in 1987, as his outstretched leg diverted a cross over Ray Clemence.

Other instances are simply inexplicable. Des Walker's combination of a cushioned defensive header and a clearance placed the ball neatly in the top corner to give Spurs the trophy they had handed to Coventry four years earlier. You'll never beat Des Walker? On this occasion he did it all by himself.

Spare a thought for Sunderland, whose wretched form and luck in 2003 were never better illustrated than in their home match against Charlton. Three down in half an hour was dire enough. The fact that two own goals from Michael Proctor and two wicked deflection were the cause summed up their season.

The best, however, are those moments that, had they occurred at the other end, would be lauded as pieces of sublime skill achieved only after months of work on the training ground.

Gary Mabbutt's Knee.

Title of a Coventry City fanzine, named after the cause of their only piece of silverware

Life isn't always rosy for the Manc Machine.

↩ The start of season 1999/2000 brought a rash of own goals in the Premier League. Frank Sinclair became Leicester's top scorer in reverse with two in successive games, both in the last minute.

↩ Occasionally, goalkeepers have obliged the opposition by throwing the ball into the net. Gary Sprake can take a bow for this: his video of gaffes would run to several hours.

↩ Pat Kruse got Cambridge United off to a flyer in 1977, scoring after only eight seconds. Unfortunately he was playing for Torquay, thus making history with the quickest-ever own goal.

↩ Chelsea's championship-winning season of 1954/55 was helped with a bizarre own goal at Leicester. It entered the records as 'Froggatt and Milburn, shared own goal', a unique achievement.

Paisley, Bob

Liverpool

BOB PAISLEY MADE HIS DEBUT as a professional footballer for Liverpool in 1939, and retired as the most successful manager in the club's history in 1983 after 54 years service. Although never a glittering international star, as a player Paisley was good enough to win a championship medal with Liverpool in 1947. When his playing career came to an end he joined the Anfield back-room staff, becoming a redoubtable deputy to the legendary Bill Shankly. When Shanks quit, Paisley took over as manager reluctantly, believing he was no more than a stop-gap for a bigger name. How wrong he was. Building on Shankly's legacy, Paisley remained at the helm for nine seasons, during which time Liverpool dominated both domestic and European soccer, winning six league titles, three European Cups and three league Cups – a haul of silverware that made this shy, quietly-spoken old man in a cardigan the most successful manager in the history of the English game.

VITAL STATISTICS

Place of Birth: Hetton-le-Hole, England
Date of Birth: 23 January 1919
Died: 12 February 1996
Caps: 0
Goals (International): 0
Clubs: As Player: Bishop Auckland, Liverpool;
As Manager: Liverpool
Trophies: LT (1947) 1976, 1977, 1979, 1980, 1982, 1983; LC 1981, 1982, 1983; EC 1977, 1978, 1981; UEFAC 1976

LEGEND RATING

Achievement	10
Tactical Awareness	9
Motivation	9
Transfer Dealing and Team Selection	9
Personality	6
Overall Legend Rating	**43**

- Paisley was the first Liverpool manager to lift the European Cup.
- He never won the FA Cup, either as a player or manager.
- Between January 1978–81, Liverpool were unbeaten at Anfield for a staggering 85 games (63 in the league).
- In 1978/79 Liverpool coasted to the title using only 15 players, two of whom played four games between them.
- He was voted Manager of the Year six times.

Parc des Princes

Paris, France

SITUATED ON THE EDGE of the capital's Bois de Boulogne, the Parc des Princes was established as the centre of French sport for over a century. It became the home of national teams for football, rugby and has been used as the final staging post of the Tour de France.

Originally the base for the now-defunct Racing Club of Paris, it underwent complete reconstruction in the early 1970s following the formation of Paris Saint-Germain. Its modern seating and good vantage points bore more than favourable comparison with the ageing concrete bowls in London and Italy, despite the lower profile of the beautiful game in France.

PSG were the first truly competitive side to be formed in Paris for 20 years. With the demise of Stade Français, French sport needed a stadium to suit. The housing of national rugby union team in the same venue guaranteed financial backing and all major French rugby and football finals were held there until the Stade de France was built for the 1998 World Cup.

VITAL STATISTICS

Location:	Paris, France
Local Club:	Paris Saint-Germain
Date Built:	1887 (rebuilt 1932 and 1972)
Current Capacity:	48,500
Max. Capacity:	49,700

- In 1997, PSG fans voted to stay at the stadium rather than relocate to the Stade de France.
- A £15 m modernisation programme ensured the Parc des Princes became a key venue when France hosted the 1998 World Cup.
- The proudest French football moment at Parc des Princes? The 1984 European Championship final, as Michel Platini lifted the trophy for the host nation.
- The Parc des Princes is a fine example of what can be achieved when football and rugby authorities join forces: can't imagine the Twickenham and FA top brasses collaborating so easily.
- The stadium hosted one of the best games of France 98, Brazil eventually prevailing in the semi-final against Holland.

Passarella, Daniel

Argentina

IN A NATION BETTER KNOWN for hatchet-men defenders, Daniel Passarella broke the mould. The first Argentine to lift the World Cup was a cultured sweeper who, by and large, eschewed the brutal and often violent tactics deployed by some of his team-mates.

After nine years in the Argentine national league with Sarmiento and then River Plate, Passarella was eventually lured to Serie A where he enjoyed seven distinguished seasons (with Fiorentina and Internazionale) before returning for a second spell with River Plate.

A move from player to manager in 1989 brought further success. Four domestic titles in the 1990s saw him promoted to national

team boss, and he led Argentina to the quarter-finals at France 98 before retiring. For such a fine player, his tally of domestic honours was modest, but it was a different story at international level. In 1978 Passarella famously skippered Argentina to victory in the World Cup, his promptings from the back providing the ammunition with which Mario Kempes was to shoot down Holland in the final.

VITAL STATISTICS

Place of Birth: Buenos Aires, Argentina

Date of Birth: 25 May 1953

Died: n/a   Caps: 71 (Argentina)

Goals (International): 21

Clubs: River Plate, Fiorentina, Inter Milan

Appearances: Club (League: for River Plate): 298

Goals: Club (League: for River Plate): 99

Trophies: WorC 1978

LEGEND RATING

Achievement	8
Skill	7
Teamwork	8
Passion	9
Personality	6
Overall Legend Rating	**38**

- Passarella had an incredible goal-scoring record for a defender (143 goals in 486 appearances).
- Passarella was not averse to bouts of nastiness. In the 1978 Final he 'caught' Johan Neeskens in the face with an elbow.
- The memory of Passarella receiving the World Cup was tarnished by the image of General Jorge Videla, murderer of children, smiling at his country's triumph.
- Passarella's style of play bore an uncanny resemblance to Stuart Pearce, right down to the thunderous shooting imparted by vast muscular thighs.
- Passarella was an unpopular manager of Argentina before the 1998 World Cup Finals, due to his reluctance to pick Batistuta.

Pearce, Stuart

THERE CAN BE FEW better examples of a player making the most of modest natural ability than Stuart Pearce; what he lacked in pace he made up for in sheer will and an almost clairvoyant ability to read the game, and what he missed in skill he overcame with brute strength. Those thunder thighs meant Pearce rarely lost a tackle, and his crossing and powerhouse shooting made him a potent weapon in attack, especially from set-pieces.

Pearce spent time in non-league soccer before signing for Coventry, from where, having been spotted by Brian Clough, who was quick to recognise his leadership qualities, he moved on to

Nottingham Forest, making 522 appearances in over 10 years at the City Ground. As it appeared his career was ending, Pearce had a flirtation with the manager's job at Forest but, quickly realising a struggling Premiership club was no place for a beginner, he stood down and elected to further his playing career at Newcastle. Spells at West Ham and Manchester City followed. His passion and naked aggression made 'Psycho' first choice for England for a decade, and they have struggled to find an adequate replacement since. Football fans love a trier, and no one gave more for his country than Stuart Pearce.

VITAL STATISTICS

Place of Birth: London, England

Date of Birth: 24 April 1962

Died: n/a Caps: 78 (England) Goals (International): 5

Clubs: Coventry, Nottingham Forest, Newcastle United, West Ham, Manchester City

Appearances: Club (League): 570

Goals: Club (League): 72

Trophies: LC 1989, 1990

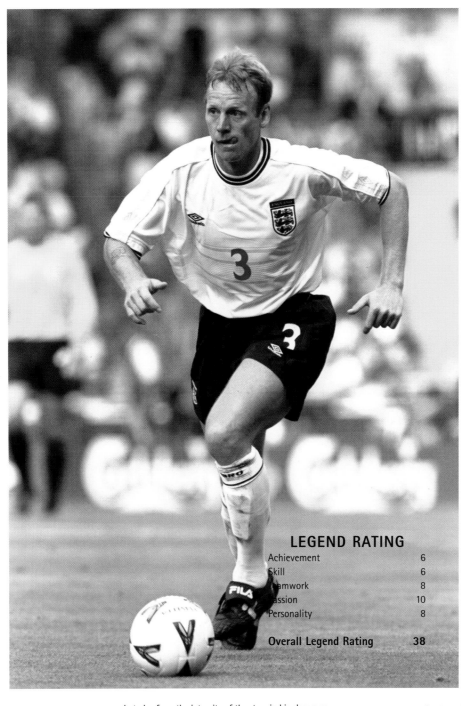

LEGEND RATING

Achievement	6
Skill	6
Teamwork	8
Passion	10
Personality	8
Overall Legend Rating	**38**

◄⌐ Pearce was distraught to have missed a crucial penalty in the shoot-out at the 1990 World Cup. His fierce exultation when he made amends at Euro 96 became an iconic image.

◄⌐ The 'Psycho' nickname comes not just from his raw playing style,

but also from the intensity of the stare in his clear eyes.

◄⌐ Pearce was awarded an MBE in 1999.

◄⌐ In 1999 Pearce was involved in a horrific accident in which his car was crushed by a lorry: the lorry came off worst.

◄⌐ Pearce's fondness for crunching punk rock has caused much mirth amongst press and team-mates. He claims that the more conventional music favoured by his colleagues gives him a headache.

Pelé

EDSON ARANTES DI NASCIMENTO is the greatest footballer of all time. No arguments.

Born in Tes Coracoes, a small provincial town in the Brazilian state of Minas Gerais, Pelé (as he is better known) began his career at Santos, forcing his way into the first team by the age of 16, and made his debut for Brazil a year later in 1958 when, at 17, he collected his first World Cup winner's medal in Sweden. Pelé went on to play in three more World Cup tournaments; he struggled with injuries in 1962, and again in 1966, but in 1970, playing in a deeper role, he was the architect of some of the finest football the game

has ever known. Surrounded by players who were in tune with his alert mind and quick feet, Brazil produced unforgettable, almost perfect football.

Pelé played all his domestic football in his beloved white shirt for Santos, a career that spanned nearly 20 years. He retired in 1974, but was persuaded to return to the game a year later when, like Franz Beckenbauer, Bobby Moore and many other of his old adversaries, he signed a $4.5 m contract to play in the newly-formed NASL with New York Cosmos. Pelé has remained in football as an ambassador for the game, and has served a spell as Brazil's Minister for Sport.

VITAL STATISTICS

Place of Birth: Tres Coracoes, Brazil

Date of Birth: 21 October 1940

Died: n/a **Caps:** 91 (Brazil) **Goals (International):** 77

Clubs: Bauru, Santos, New York Cosmos

Appearances: (All Senior matches): 1363

Goals: Club (All Senior matches): 1283

Trophies: WorC 1958,1970; BLT: 1956, 1958, 1960, 1961, 1962, 1964, 1966, 1967, 1968; WCC: 1962, 1963

LEGEND RATING

Achievement	10
Skill	10
Teamwork	10
Passion	10
Personality	9
Overall Legend Rating	**49**

◀ᴵᵛ Only Ferenc Puskas of Hungary has bettered Pelé's tally of 77 international goals.

◀ᴵᵛ When Pelé retired from Brazilian soccer, Santos also 'retired' his No. 10 shirt.

◀ᴵᵛ Pelé scored a hat-trick in the 1958 World Cup semi-final, then two more in the final, including a mesmerising, acrobatic volley.

◀ᴵᵛ Pelé's record as the only man to have played in three World Cup winning squads is unlikely to be matched.

◀ᴵᵛ Pelé scored in excess of 1,200 first-class goals in his career.

Penalty Shoot-Outs

Despair and Derring-Do

THEY MAY BE A TERRIBLE WAY to lose a game, but they make for great theatre. Penalty shoot-outs made their debut in 1970, a device introduced to settle the mind-numbing tedium of something called the Watney Cup. Since then of course, they have gone on to settle some of the world's most important matches.

For England fans, memories of high-profile failures are fresh. At Italia 90, the team were just a few kicks away from the World Cup final, but with the scores locked at 3-3, Stuart Pearce and Chris Waddle missed to send Bobby Robson's team home. Lightning struck for a second time at Euro 96 with Germany again proving to be England's nemesis from 12 yards. Gareth Southgate was the culprit this time. Then in France 98 it was Argentina's turn to expose England's vulnerability from the spot, David Batty making it a hat-trick of shoot-out failures with a feeble effort in St Etienne.

The prospect of penalties has even entered some teams' pre-match thinking. In the 1986 European Cup final, Steaua Bucharest, figuring they had little chance of beating Barcelona in open play, shamelessly played for 0-0 in the hope of pinching victory in the lottery of a penalty shoot-out. Incredibly it worked. Barcelona missed all their penalties and Steaua were crowned champions of Europe.

'Maybe they were kicking the s**t out of O'Leary for missing it.'

Roddy Doyle misinterprets the reaction of David's team-mates after he scores the winning penalty against Romania during Italia 90, in *The Van*

Pearce misses for England at Italia 90 and scores in Euro 96.

◁ Pearce, Waddle and Southgate turned their failure to financial advantage, starring in a TV advertising campaign for PizzaHut.

◁ Controversially, penalties replaced second replays in the FA Cup in 1991. Exeter beat Colchester 4-2 in the first shoot-out.

◁ In 1994 Italy's Roberto Baggio blazed over the bar to hand Brazil victory in the 1994 World Cup Final. The other errant Italian was the great Franco Baresi.

◁ David Batty volunteered to take a penalty against Argentina in France 98, even though he had never taken one in a game before.

◁ 1997. Marlow beat Littlehampton 11-10 on penalties in the FA Cup first qualifying round. The first 21 spot-kicks were scored.

Peters, Martin

THE THIRD OF THE 'HOLY TRINITY' of West Ham players in the 1966 World Cup winning side, alongside Bobby Moore and Geoff Hurst, Peters had forced his way into the England reckoning the previous season, making his debut only weeks before the tournament began. An extremely versatile player – appearing in virtually every position for West Ham – he was a good tackler and passed the ball well with either foot, but his real gift was his ability to steal into the penalty area and score vital goals, a knack that earned him the nickname 'The Ghost'. His overall scoring record was better than nearly one in three games, an exceptional return for a midfield player. Unlike Moore and Hurst, Peters left West Ham while still in his prime, and won further trophies with Tottenham. Like many of his England contemporaries, he wasn't a success as a manager. It would have been interesting to see Peters in the modern game – his style would have suited the Premiership.

VITAL STATISTICS

Place of Birth: London, England
Date of Birth: 8 November 1943
Died: n/a   Caps: 67
Goals (International): 20
Clubs: West Ham, Tottenham, Norwich City, Sheffield United
Appearances: Club (All Matches): 882
Goals: Club (All Matches): 220
Trophies: WorC 1966; CWC 1965; LC 1971, 1973; EUFAC 1972

LEGEND RATING

Achievement	8
Skill	8
Teamwork	8
Passion	7
Personality	6
Overall Legend Rating	**37**

◁ Peters scored 'the other goal' in the 1966 World Cup final, and one of England's goals in the 3-2 defeat by Germany in the 1970 World Cup quarter-final.

◁ Peters teamed up with his England colleague Geoff Hurst after their playing careers were over – selling car insurance.

◁ The £200,000 Bill Nicholson paid West Ham for Peters was a British record.

◁ Peters even appeared in goal for West Ham, deputising as a substitute in only his third appearance for the club.

◁ As Spurs captain in 1975, Peters led a deputation to try and persuade Bill Nicholson to rescind his resignation.

Pinch Me...

ALL THOSE YEARS of angst and frustration at England's inability to beat Germany were washed away in one glorious evening. Only a year before, England had given an abject performance at home to the same opponents, losing to a soft Dietmar Hamann free-kick. There were five changes to the team from the previous October; Adams, Keown, Le Saux, Andy Cole, and Gareth Southgate all giving way to younger legs. England played with the exuberance of youth and, even after going a goal down in the early stages, remained determined to set the agenda. Gerrard crunched his Liverpool team-mate Hamann to remind him he wasn't going to dictate *this* game.

The Germans were inept (they weren't very good in 2000, but Keegan was scared to have a go at them). Poor at the back, unimaginative in midfield and ponderous up front, they carried no threat. On this occasion England did what a good team should do and destroyed vastly inferior opponents. A team with four world-class players beat a team with (maybe) one.

OK, that's enough critical analysis. WASN'T IT GREAT!?

SCORERS: Germany: Jancker
England: Owen (3) Gerrard, Heskey
EVENT: World Cup qualifier, Munich, 1 September 2001

GERMANY (Man: Rudi Voller)		ENGLAND (Man: Sven-Goran Eriksson)	
1 Kahn	8 Ballack	1 Seaman	8 Scholes
2 Worns	9 Jancker	2 Neville, G	9 Heskey
3 Linke	10 Neuville	3 Cole	10 Owen
4 Nowotny	11 Deisler	4 Gerrard	11 Barmby
5 Boehme		5 Campbell	
6 Hamann		6 Ferdinand	
7 Rehmer		7 Beckham	

That scoreboard still brings tears to the eyes.

- German goalkeeper Oliver Kahn, one of the greats of the last decade, flapped about like a baboon in a strait jacket.
- The Germans were missing key players like Scholl and Jeremies. Tough.
- Canadian-born Owen Hargreaves, substitute for Gerrard, was playing on his home ground. He had impressed for Bayern in the European Cup final against Valencia.
- Eriksson exploited the space behind the German wing-backs to great effect, Beckham and Gerrard dropping balls in for the excellent Gary Neville and Ashley Cole to pick up.
- Ferdinand was at fault for the German goal, but was near flawless after that.

Pires, Robert

Arsenal, France

DESPITE THEIR PERIODS of success and the consistent emergence of Double winning teams, only the current Arsenal squad has shaken off the club's reputation for producing dour, efficient sides. 'Boring Arsenal' was always the last resort of the envious. The jibes have been rammed down critics' throats in the last two years. At the heart of this flair renaissance is Robert Pires.

Contrary to popular opinion; fast, exciting wing play is not an innovation at Highbury. It is simply that the likes of George Armstrong and Brian Marwood can not hold a candle to the Frenchman, whose arrival for £6 m in July 2000 from Marseille as

a direct replacement for Marc Overmars relegated even the talented Dutchman to the role of yesterday's man.

Pires could hardly have failed to catch the eye. As a member of the French squad that held World and European championships simultaneously, he proved too valuable a prize to remain in the backwater of the French league. The only unanswered question was whether he could shine in top-class European domestic competition. The answer, as Arsenal fans will testify, has been an emphatic yes.

VITAL STATISTICS

Place of Birth: Reims, France
Date of Birth: 29 October 1973
Died: n/a   Caps: 56 (France)
Goals (International): 11
Clubs: Metz, Marseille, Arsenal
Appearances: Club (All Matches): 374
Goals: Club (All Matches): 86
Trophies: LT 2002; FAC 2002; 1998 WorC; EuroC 2000

LEGEND RATING

Achievement	9
Skill	9
Passion & Commitment	7
Inspiration	7
Personality	7
Overall Legend Rating	**39**

- 2000. Sets up the golden goal for David Trezeguet that wins Euro 2000 for France.
- 2001/02. Wins the Football Writers' Player of the Year award
- March 2002. Damages cruciate ligaments in an FA Cup 6th Rd. tie v Newcastle. Pires is sidelined for six months but makes full recovery.
- 2000/01. Scores away to Lazio to clinch Arsenal's place in the Champions League's second phase.
- 2001. Scores winner in FA Cup semi-final v Spurs.

Platini, Michel

Juventus, France

THE FINEST EUROPEAN MIDFIELDER of the past 30 years, Michel Platini combined sublime skill with a goals-coring record that would put many international forwards to shame. Touch, vision and great accuracy with either foot made him a divine playmaker, but he added the virtue of a constant flow of goals, both from set-pieces and open play. After 10 years in the French league, he turned down a move to Arsenal in 1982 claiming, perhaps justifiably, that English clubs played too many games. The Gunners' loss was Juventus' gain, as trophies followed for the Italian giants. Platini's high point came in the 1984 European Championships when, teaming up with Jean

Tigana and Alain Giresse in midfield, he skippered France to a famous victory on home soil. Platini's astonishing return of nine goals in five games, including two hat-tricks, made him the tournament's top scorer. His business interests brought about a shock retirement in 1987, but he was tempted by the French national manager's job three years later. An uneasy tenure, Platini resigned after France's premature exit from Euro 92 but became president of the France 98 World Cup committee and continues to enjoy a high profile as a special advisor to FIFA.

VITAL STATISTICS

Place of Birth: Joeuf, France
Date of Birth: 21 June 1955
Died: n/a   Caps: 72 (France)   Goals (International): 41
Clubs: AS Joeuf, Nancy, St Etienne, Juventus,
Appearances: Club (All Matches): 576
Goals: Club (All Matches): 307
Trophies: EuroC 1984; FLT 1981; SA 1984, 1986; CWC 1984; EC 1985

Mexico, 1986. Platini scores against Brazil in the World Cup quarter-final.

LEGEND RATING

Achievement	9
Skill	10
Teamwork	9
Passion	9
Personality	8
Overall Legend Rating	**45**

- Platini's penalty won the European Cup at Heysel in 1985, but the evening's earlier tragedy overshadowed everything.
- Platini remains a strong critic of English club football, particularly its reliance on foreign players.
- His three World Cups included two as French captain, both of which brought semi-final defeats in 1982 and 1986.
- He scored the winner a minute before the end of a ding-dong-do against Portugal in the semi-final of Euro 84.
- Platini is the only player to have been voted European Player of the Year in three consecutive years – 1983, 1984 and 1985. Even the great Johann Cruyff had a year off!

Play-Offs

DERIDED BY MANY at their inception in 1987, the play-offs have become an integral part of the season, adding tension to matches that previously would have been meaningless. Initially the play-offs involved the top division side immediately above automatic relegation, and the three sides immediately beneath automatic promotion in the division below. This system was discarded after two years, and since 1989 the play-offs have involved only sides jostling for promotion, with relegation being automatic. The system still has its critics (Swindon Town's promotion in 1993, when they finished 12 points behind Portsmouth in Division One, is often cited as an example of the iniquities of the system). The first beneficiaries were Charlton, Swindon and Aldershot. Charlton edged out Leeds 2-1 in a replay after the two-legged final finished level, thus preserving their status in Division One. There have been one or two classic confrontations since. In 1995 Bolton reversed a two goal deficit to overcome Reading 4-3, while Sunderland and Charlton battled out a memorable 4-4 draw in 1998, the Addicks eventually winning 7-6 on penalties to retain their place in the Premiership.

'Not only have I had to give up chess because I don't have time anymore, but I'm also smoking myself to death. If we go through and win the play-offs at Wembley, I'll be smoking more than my old boss Menotti.'

Ossie Ardiles, then manager of Swindon, 1990

Bolton complete a remarkable turnaround against Reading in 1995.

◁ Sunderland had a ball in 1990. They scraped into the play-offs in sixth place in the Second Division, beat their great rivals Newcastle and lost 1-0 to Swindon at Wembley. The gods were shining on the Wearsiders though; Swindon were demoted for financial irregularities, and Sunderland got their promotion.

◁ In 1999, Manchester City were 2-0 down to Gillingham with a minute to go. They drew level and won on penalties. Not untypical of City's ups and downs in recent years.

◁ Ipswich lost to Sheffield United on away goals in 1997, Charlton in 1998 and Bolton after a 4-3 ding-dong-do at Portman Road in 1999. Revenge was sweet in 2000 as they battled past Bolton (5-3 this time) and beat Barnsley in the final.

Pride and Passion

NOTHING RAISES SUPPORTERS' passions more than a match against local rivals. Some of the game's most atmospheric occasions are derby days, whether in Liverpool, Manchester, North London, Glasgow or Milan. Although an Old Firm derby is no place for the faint-hearted, these games aren't necessarily the ones where feelings run highest. Provincial areas can spurn rivalries as heated as any found in big cities.

Local rivalry is often at its most intense at clubs where success is evasive. Absurd as it seems, supporters can often get more pleasure from seeing a rival fail than watching their own team win. This usually stems from envy – witness the 'Stand Up If You Hate Man U' factor in recent seasons. Sometimes one local team lords it over another, leading to resentment, and occasionally mutual dislike between twin towns intrudes on football. These intense rivalries are not always geographical; Chelsea and Leeds are still carrying around baggage from the 1970 FA Cup final, and Tottenham and Southampton have been doing their best to nurture ill feeling over the last few years

'I sometimes think you love Norwich more than you love me,' moans the wife.

'Aye,' husband replies, 'And I sometimes think I love Ipswich more than I love you.'

Wolves and West Brom get neighbourly.

◀️ West Bromwich Albion and Wolves have a bitter enmity. Both top sides in the 1950s, they have only flirted with the big time since, and it clearly rankles.

◀️ Stoke City were top flight for years, but their fall from grace coincided with John Rudge's successful stewardship of local rivals, Port Vale, and the battle for Potteries pre-eminence was resumed.

◀️ Cardiff and Swansea share a mutual loathing that may even transcend their dislike of the English. Some recent encounters have been blood-curdling affairs.

◀️ Suggestions that Hearts and Hibs merge to form one Edinburgh club saw the men behind the scheme bombarded with hate mail and death threats.

Puskas, Ferenc

SHORT AND BARREL-CHESTED, slightly overweight, one-footed and useless in the air, nonetheless Ferenc Puskas is rightly regarded as one of the best attacking players in history. His pace and blistering left foot shot took Puskas straight into the Hungarian side after the war, still aged only 18. His success with Hungarian army side Honved led Real Madrid to lure him to Spain, where he teamed up with Alfredo Di Stefano in arguably the greatest attacking pairing, well, er, ever. The duo led Real to unprecedented domestic and European success. 'The Galloping Major' won the award for Spain's top goal scorer four times, and when he didn't win it Di Stefano did.

Internationally Puskas played in another remarkable team, the great Hungarian side that went unbeaten for four years between 1950 and 1954, before losing out in the World Cup final to Germany. Critics and crowd could only watch and admire as Puskas, Czibor, Hidegkuti and Kocsis thrashed England 6-3 at Wembley – the first-ever home defeat for England. The side broke up in 1956 after the revolution in Hungary, and Puskas was later to make four appearances for his adopted country, Spain.

VITAL STATISTICS

Place of Birth: Budapest, Hungary

Date of Birth: 2 April 1927

Died: n/a **Caps:** 84 (for Hungary); 4 (for Spain)

Goals (International): 83 (for Hungary)

Clubs: Kispest, Honved, Real Madrid

Appearances: Club: All Matches: 1300 **Goals:** All Matches: 1176

Trophies: PLA 1961,1962, 1963, 1964, 1965; HLT 1950, 1952, 1954, 1955; EC 1960

LEGEND RATING

Achievement	8
Skill	10
Teamwork	9
Passion	9
Personality	8
Overall Legend Rating	**44**

◂)) Injured for the quarter-final and semi-final, Puskas insisted on playing in the 1954 World Cup Final, even though only half-fit. Typically he scored, but Germany recovered from 2-0 down to win 3-2.

◂)) Scored four times in Real's legendary 7-3 annihilation of Eintracht Frankfurt in the 1960 European Cup final.

◂)) Puskas' 83 goals for Hungary is a world record (and in only 84 matches).

◂)) In 1993 Puskas made an emotional return to a more liberal Hungary as caretaker-manager of the national side.

◂)) Even at 35 Puskas managed a hat-trick in the European Cup final against Benfica in 1962. Sadly for him, Real lost 5-3.

WITH A CAREER spanning five decades, Roy Race's evergreen qualities put even Roger Milla and Peter Shilton to shame. Signing for his local club Melchester Rovers, he carried the dreams of every British schoolboy with a career that brought a string of league titles and European Cups. Unlike Bobby Moore, he never had the distinction of lifting the World Cup, but it was one of the few honours that eluded him. A blonde, dashing centre-forward he wore the red and yellow of Melchester for nearly 40 years, first as player, then as player-manager. In 1993 Roy cheated death in a helicopter crash that forced the amputation of his left foot. He left Melchester for a short spell as boss of Italian legends AC Monza, but his heart was never in it. Surviving by the skin of his teeth, he suffered a crushing blow with the closure of *Roy Of The Rovers Monthly* in 1994, but rallied briefly with *Roy Race: The Playing Years* (1995). A comeback in *Match Of The Day* magazine ended when it ceased publication in 2001. Oh, and did we mention he was a cartoon character?

VITAL STATISTICS

Place of Birth: Melchester, England
Date of Birth: Unknown, Roy is timeless
Died: n/a **Caps & Goals (International):** Unknown, but Roy has played for England for over 25 years
Clubs: Melchester Rovers (player-manager from 1974); As player/manager: Walford Rovers
Appearances & Goals: Club (League): Lost count over 35 years
Trophies: Too many to list – he is very successful

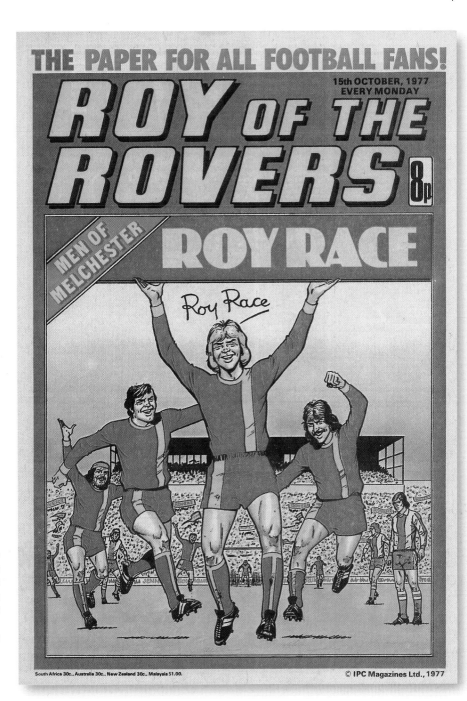

LEGEND RATING

Achievement	9
Skill	10
Teamwork	10
Passion	10
Personality	10
Overall Legend Rating	**49**

◄))) **1954.** He appeared on the front cover of boy's magazine *Tiger*, but it was a year before he made his debut, scoring twice in a 3-3 draw.
◄))) **1959/60.** Roy is endorsed by Bobby Charlton, who lent his name to the writing of the Race saga.

◄))) **1974/75.** Appointed player-manager of Melchester Rovers. After a chequered career he resigned live on TV 18 years later, only to be reinstated the same season.
◄))) **1981/82.** Survives a shooting. Five years later Race survives a

terrorist bomb attack that kills eight team-mates.
◄))) **1994/95.** In an increasingly desperate plot twist, Roy's wife Penny is killed in a car crash as the Races become the most tragic family since the Kennedys.

Racism   Don't Pretend It's Gone Away

ONE OF SOCIETY'S LARGEST BARNACLES has been attached to the game for decades. It was 1884 when Arthur Wharton turned out for Darlington to become Britain's first black footballer. One can only wonder what reception awaited him.

In the 1970s the rise of the National Front brought chanting inside grounds and the selling of racist literature at the gates. Clubs were not only ignorant of the problem but contributed to it, perpetuating the stereotype that black players lacked bottle or commitment. One popular theory also suggested they couldn't play in cold weather.

The situation today is much improved. Black players have successfully integrated all over Europe, although the problem has not disappeared. Attitudes have improved in Britain but worrying hotbeds remain in Italy, Iberia and the Balkans. Today's challenge for the British game lies in increasing the number of black people operating in football across the board. Black executives, referees, coaches, managers and board members are still an exception (the only current black member of England's set-up is Hope Powell, coach of the national women's team). Asian players and fans need to be similarly welcomed. Verdict? Much improved, but must try harder.

'When I came into the assembly hall in South Africa it was full of blackies and it was getting f*****g dark when they were all sitting together.'

UEFA boss Lennart Johansson.
(If you find this amusing, please take the book back to the shop, we don't want your money.)

◁》 Chairman of the PFA, Brendon Batson, is a rare example of a black player in a senior administrative position within football.
◁》 Less than one per cent of season-ticket holders in England are black or Asian. Football remains the preserve of the white spectator, despite the number of black players.
◁》 In the 1980s, anti-racist groups infiltrated some clubs. The efforts of Leeds United fans pioneered a belated Football League campaign 'Let's Kick Racism Out Of Football'.
◁》 Prejudice extending into religious bigotry, Rangers' policy of signing only Protestants proved ignorance is not only skin deep.
◁》 In 1995, followers of the racist group Combat 18 caused the abandonment of England's friendly in Dublin.

Rahn, Helmut

Rot-Weiss-Essen, West Germany

THE WEST GERMAN SIDE that won the World Cup for the first time contained two great players; their captain and playmaker, Fritz Walter, and the winger, Helmut Rahn.

A natural athlete and sprinter, Rahn was a relative unknown before the 1954 World Cup Finals. His first impact came against Yugoslavia, when he seemed to beat the entire team before ramming the ball home, but his speed and directness were also a major factor in the final as West Germany, with two goals from Rahn, came from behind to beat favourites Hungary 3-2.

Four years later Rahn went to Sweden, having stirred up German club football with his unfashionable team Rot-Weiss-Essen. He was a star of the German side again, showing great skill for such a big, imposing man, but after getting his team into the semi-finals with a brilliant solo goal against Yugoslavia, he was finally subdued by Sweden in the semis. A man for the big occasion, Rahn scored 21 goals in 40 games for Germany, a fantastic strike rate for a winger.

VITAL STATISTICS

Place of Birth: Germany

Date of Birth: 16 August 1928

Died: n/a   **Caps:** 40 (West Germany)

Goals (International): 21 (West Germany)

Clubs: Rot-Weiss-Essen, MSV Duisburg

Trophies: WorC 1954; WGLT 1955

LEGEND RATING

Achievement	8
Skill	8
Teamwork	7
Passion	7
Personality	8
Overall Legend Rating	**38**

- Unstoppable in full flight, he is known as 'The Train' in Germany.
- In the 1954 final, with Germany 2-1 down, Rahn scored with a sharp volley. Then, six minutes from the end, he ran through the Hungarian defence to strike the winner.
- Rahn's club, Rot-Weiss-Essen won the German cup in 1953 and the league in 1955 (the only time in their history).
- Rot-Weiss-Essen didn't make much impact in the inaugural European Cup, going out to Hibernian in the first round.
- Before the 1958 tournament Rahn had been out of the German side. He was drinking heavily and overweight. Coach Herberger worked some magic, and a fit and motivated Rahn arrived at the Finals.

Rams Rampant

The Derby County Dream Team

LEANING HEAVILY on Derby's championship-winning teams of the 1970s, this is a combative and solid line-up. Shilton was probably past his best when he played at Derby, but he was still a formidable keeper and earns his place in the face of mediocre competition. The excellent Mart Poom keeps Colin Boulton off the bench – Poom kept the Rams in the top flight in 2001.

The back four features three of Brian Clough's team; Todd and McFarland were a complementary pair who served England as well as Derby, while Tom Cooper was England captain in the 1930s, spending eight years at Derby before moving to Liverpool.

The destructive Rioch, with his dead-ball expertise, and the workaholic Gemmill anchor the midfield, with Ted McMinn and Alan Hinton providing width on the right and left respectively.

The legendary Steve Bloomer, England's first superstar footballer, leads the line, with another legend, Raich Carter, alongside.

Managers: Brian Clough and Peter Taylor
4-4-2

Peter Shilton (80s)

Tom Cooper (20s/30s) Roy McFarland (70s) Colin Todd (70s)
David Nish (70s)

Ted McMinn (80s) Bruce Rioch (70s) Archie Gemmill (C) (70s)
Alan Hinton (60s/70s)

Steve Bloomer (00s) Raich Carter (30s/40s)

Subs: Mart Poom (G) (90s) Mark Wright (D) (80s) Peter Doherty (M) (30s) Kevin Hector (F) (60s/70s) Jack Stamps (F) (30s/40s)

The early 1970s squad – easily Derby's best.

◄ Carter, Doherty and Stamps all played in the 4-1 FA Cup final win over Charlton in 1946.

◄ Rioch scored an impressive 15 goals in the 1975 championship-winning team, mostly left-foot rockets from free-kicks or penalties. Gemmill failed to score a league goal in 41 games that season.

◄ Striker Kevin Hector sits on the bench ahead of more talented but less committed souls like Charlie George and Ravanelli.

◄ Alan Hinton was one of the first players to usher in the modern affectation for white boots. With a touch more aggression he could have been an international standard player.

Ramsey, Alf

'ENGLAND WILL WIN the World Cup in 1966'. In 1963, this was a rare boast from a reserved and modest manager named Alf Ramsey. And yet, amazingly, it came true. The sight of Ramsey still seated impassively on the bench as the final whistle blew to signal England's victory over West Germany was in stark contrast to the outpourings of joy around him, but inside you can be sure his heart was stirring. Thirty minutes before he had roused an England team, shattered by Germany's injury-time equaliser to force the game into extra time, with the words: 'You've won it once, now you've got to win it again.'

Ramsey's motivational skills had been proven even before 1966. Four years earlier, in charge of what was a modest array of talent at Ipswich, he brought the First Division title to Portman Road for the first and only time in their history. His style was pragmatic rather than entertaining, and was a reflection of a playing style that brought him 32 England caps and a league title with Spurs. Knighted in 1967, he seemed untouchable, but England's capitulation to Germany and their failure to qualify for the 1974 finals cost him his job. A brief managerial flurry at Birmingham notwithstanding, it was the end for Ramsey.

VITAL STATISTICS

Place of Birth: Dagenham, Essex
Date of Birth: 22 January 1920
Died: 28 April 1999
Caps: 32 (England)
Goals (International): 3
Clubs: As Player: Southampton, Tottenham; As Manager: Ipswich Town, England national side, Birmingham (caretaker)
Trophies: WorC 1966; LT 1962

LEGEND RATING

Achievement	9
Tactical Awareness	9
Motivation	9
Transfer Dealing and Team Selection	8
Personality	6
Overall Legend Rating	**41**

- Won the Second and First Division titles in successive seasons as player and manager.
- Furiously dubbed Argentina 'animals' following the 1966 World Cup quarter-final.
- Ramsey's innovative 4-4-2 formation led England to be dubbed the 'wingless wonders'.
- Ramsey was the FA's second choice for the England job; Burnley's Jimmy Adamson turned it down.
- Ramsey's first England game was a disaster. England lost 3-0 to France and were eliminated from the European Nations Cup.

Rangers

LIKE THEIR OLD-FIRM NEIGHBOURS, Rangers' have a large pool of successful candidates to pick from. Yet, while it's tempting to select a team based on medals won, the quality control needs to be more stringent.

For all the tabloid revelations and weight problems, in his prime Andy Goram was probably Scotland's finest goalkeeper. George Young represents the 'Iron Curtain' defence in the immediate post-war era, and the twin legends of Greig and Gough are impossible to ignore in central defence. Sandy Jardine is not on his natural flank, but is a far classier option than the left-back alternatives. The midfield is not short of trickery: Baxter and Gascoigne's on-field skills were every bit as extravagant as their bar bills. The other half of midfield is tinged with sadness. Who knows the heights Ian Durrant would have scaled had one rogue tackle not put paid to his career, while memories of Davie Cooper's wing play are always tempered with the tragedy of his sudden and shocking death at 39. In attack, Brian Laudrup, Rangers' most gifted forward of all time, is paired with their most prolific goalscorer.

Manager: Graeme Souness

4-4-2

Andy Goram (90s)

George Young (40s/50s) Richard Gough (80s/90s)
John Greig (C) (60s/70s) Sandy Jardine (60s/70s)

Paul Gascoigne (90s) Jim Baxter (60s)
Ian Durrant (80s) Davie Cooper (70s/80s)

Brian Laudrup (90s) Ally McCoist (80s/90s)

Subs: Peter McCloy (G) (70s/80s) Terry Butcher (D) (80s) Ian Ferguson (M) (80s/90s) Jorg Albertz (M) (90s) Derek Johnstone (F) (70s/80s)

Paul Gascoigne (left) and Ally McCoist celebrate another trophy.

- Rangers' 49 league titles are a Scottish record.
- Graeme Souness led Rangers out of their longest barren spell, laying the foundations in the late 1980s for a side that equalled Celtic's record of nine successive titles.

- On the bench, Derek Johnstone is preferred to one-time team-mate Colin Stein. Johnstone's two spells with the club over more than a decade earned him hero status.
- Terry Butcher was the pick of Rangers' English signings of the late 1980s. Other notables included Trevor Steven, Ray Wilkins and Chris Woods.
- John Greig was voted Rangers' greatest player of the twentieth century in an end-of-millennium poll.

'LORD NELSON! Lord Beaverbrook! Sir Winston Churchill! Sir Anthony Eden! Clement Attlee! Henry Cooper! Lady Diana! (lapses into frenzied Norwegian, roughly translated as 'we have beaten them all!') Maggie Thatcher, can you hear me? Maggie Thatcher! Your boys took a hell of a beating! Your boys took a hell of a beating!'

The scene: Oslo, 9 September 1981. A hapless England looked to have blown their World Cup qualifying hopes for the third successive tournament by losing 2-1 to a Norwegian team considered to be cannon fodder. News enough in itself, but the match passed into footballing folklore thanks to this joyful rant at the final whistle

from the Norwegian radio commentator, Bjorge Lillelien, who, in a few breathless seconds, outdid even the most frenzied Brazilian broadcaster with his random grasp of British celebrity. England would love to consign this banana skin to a permanently sealed archive, but thanks to our hero it will be mentioned in perpetuity whenever the teams meet. Henry Cooper has never been in such exalted company.

SCORERS: **Norway:** Albertsen, Thoresen
England: Robson
EVENT: World Cup qualifier, Oslo,
9 September 1981

NORWAY (Man: Tor Roste Fossen)		ENGLAND (Man: Ron Greenwood)	
1	Antonsen	1	Clemence
2	Bernsten	2	Neal
3	Aas	3	Mills
	(Pedersen)	4	Osman
4	Hareide	5	Thompson
5	Grondalen	6	Robson
6	Giske	7	Keegan
7	Albertsen	8	Francis
8	Thorensen	9	Mariner
9	Okland		(Withe)
10	Jacobsen	10	Hoddle
11	Lund		(P. Barnes)
	(Dokken)	11	McDermott

Lord Nelson holds the telescope to his blind eye – could have been FA chairman.

❧ Lucky England still qualified for Spain 82 thanks largely to Romania's home defeat by Switzerland.

❧ England had been vilified months earlier by also losing to Switzerland.

❧ The team in Oslo contained four all-conquering Liverpool players, plus Kevin Keegan and Bryan Robson.

❧ The rant may have inflicted lasting damage, as the commentator died prematurely a few years later.

❧ Although Lord Nelson had only a single eye and one arm, he may have performed better than many of England's players that night.

Rattin, Antonio

Argentina

UNFORTUNATELY FOR one of Argentina's most durable players, Antonio Rattin is best known for a single match in the 1966 World Cup Finals. An obdurate Argentine team were taking no prisoners against England in the quarter-final, with Rattin a persistent culprit. Eventually the referee's patience snapped and Rattin was ordered off. Initially he refused to go and it looked at one stage as though his team-mates may leave with him in protest, but he eventually departed and his team were not required to play again following England's 1-0 victory. At the final whistle, Alf Ramsey refused to allow his players to swap shirts with the opposition, and later described the Argentines as 'animals'. There can be little doubt he had Rattin in mind when his words were chosen.

The tough-tackling centre-half honed his skills in 14 seasons with Boca Juniors, where his height and strength allowed him to intimidate opponents. In the cynical Argentine league his bullying style was considered a prudent and legitimate survival technique, but at Wembley it brought him nothing but ignominy.

VITAL STATISTICS

Place of Birth: Tigre, Argentina
Date of Birth: 16 May 1937
Died: n/a   Caps: 34 (Argentina)
Goals (International): 1
Clubs: Boca Juniors
Appearances: Club (League): 353
Goals: Club (League): 26
Trophies: ALT 1962, 1964, 1965, 1969, 1970

Wembley, 1966. Rattin initially declines the referee's invitation to leave the field.

LEGEND RATING

Achievement	6
Skill	6
Teamwork	8
Passion	9
Personality	7
Overall Legend Rating	**36**

◁ As a teenager Rattin rejected overtures from several clubs in favour of his beloved Boca Juniors.

◁ He appeared in two World Cup Finals tournaments, 1962 and 1966.

◁ Became the first player to be sent off in Wembley's 43-year history.

◁ A knowledgeable all-rounder, Rattin directed gymnastics and fencing teams after his playing career ended.

◁ 1980. Appointed technical director of football at Boca Juniors.

Real Madrid

The Dream Team

THE GREATEST CLUB SIDE of the twentieth century has boasted some of the finest players in the history of football. Most of those included here date back to a more agreeable era when, to be permitted the honour of wearing the white shirt, meant you played for as long as was humanly possible (not two or three years until your agent fixed you up with a tidy signing-on fee in Milan, Rome or Turin).

Hence we've opted for durable, long-serving Spanish players, not the likes of Figo and Zidane. The overseas players featured are those who served their time, many of them risking the wrath of their native authorities by choosing club over country. The first great Real

side from the 1930s is represented by the great goalkeeper, Zamora, and the full-back, Quincoces, while several others have been plucked from the team that dominated European football in the late 1950s. The rest are stalwarts of the 1970s and 1980s, when Real were less of a force in Europe, but remained powerful domestically, winning La Liga several times with a team peppered with Spanish internationals.

Manager: Miguel Munoz

4-3-3

Ricardo Zamora (30s)

Quincoces Lopez (30s) Jose Santamaria (60s)
Jose Camacho (C) 70s/80s) Manolo Sanchis (90s)

Michel (80s) Alfredo Di Stefano (50s/60s) Paco Gento (50s/60s)

Emilio Butragueno (80s) Ferenc Puskas (60s) Pirri (60s/70s)

Subs: Miguel Angel (G) (80s) Uli Stielike (D/M) (80s)
Amancio Amaro (F) (60s) Raul (F) (90s/00s)
Raymond Kopa (M) (50s)

Steve McManaman holds yet another European Cup for Real.

↩ Jorge Valdano, Martin Vazquez, Hector Redondo, Luis Del Sol, Hector Rial, Carlos Santillana, Roberto Carlos, Hugo Sanchez ... all great internationals, but none of them make the bench.

↩ The much-capped Jose Camacho, a mainstay of Real and Spain throughout the 1980s, has had spells as manager of the club, including one of 22 days in 1998.

↩ Pirri made 414 *La Liga* appearances for Real over 16 years, winning a European Cup aged 21 in 1966, and ten league titles.

↩ Of the modern generation, Manolo Sanchis is the most decorated, having won two European Cups, two UEFA Cups and eight Spanish league titles.

Red Devils

LOVE 'EM OR LOATHE 'EM, you can't deny that Manchester United have enjoyed the services of some fabulous footballers. Many international teams would struggle to assemble a squad like this.

In goal, the choice of Schmeichel brooks no argument, while the defence is built around the post-war era, with Irish international Carey ably supported by fellow Busby Babes Edwards and Byrne, and Martin Buchan, United's one truly class player from the team that struggled through the 1970s.

The midfield pays homage to the strength of the current team. Only an unlucky Paul Scholes misses out, but Beckham, Keane and

Giggs all stand up to scrutiny. Add the power and shooting of Bobby Charlton, and you're in dreamland. Bryan Robson, upon whom England were almost exclusively dependent for inspiration during the 1980s, has to settle for a place on the bench. (Imagine a midfield with Paddy Crerand, Robson, Paul Scholes and Billy Meredith. They're the reserves).

The forwards would be guaranteed to provide entertainment. Both volatile and intolerant of those less gifted, Best and Cantona would frustrate and fascinate in equal measure. And if it didn't work, Denis Law would enjoy playing alongside either of them.

Director of Football: Sir Matt Busby
Manager: Sir Alex Ferguson

4-4-2

Peter Schmeichel (90s)

Johnny Carey (40s/50s) Duncan Edwards (50s)
Martin Buchan (C) (70s) Roger Byrne (50s)

David Beckham (90s) Bobby Charlton (60s) Roy Keane (90s)
Ryan Giggs (90s)

Eric Cantona (90s) George Best (60s/70s)

Subs: Alex Stepney (G) (60s/70s) Bill Foulkes (D) (60s)
Bryan Robson (M) (80s/90s) Denis Law (F) (60s/70s)
Ruud Van Nistelrooy (F) (00s)

Players' cars were more modest affairs in the Seventies.

◄» How do you choose between Matt Busby and Alex Ferguson, both knights of the realm? We couldn't.

◄» After the incomparable Charlton, Bill Foulkes' 682 appearances make him United's most loyal servant.

◄» Johnny Carey was an early example of the attacking full-back, a solid defender with good ball skills. He later became a successful manager of Blackburn Rovers.

◄» In the 1978 World Cup, Scotland manager Ally McLeod played

Martin Buchan at full-back. Only when he returned him to the centre did their performances begin to pick up.

◄» Van Nistelrooy merits inclusion even after two seasons. Now we know why Fergie was prepared to wait to sign him.

Red Machine

The Soviet States Dream Team

FROM 1960 to the dissolution of the Soviet Union, the USSR had a vast array of talent, especially in the 1980s when the Dynamo Kiev team were one of the most talented sides in Europe. Their downfall in big tournaments might have had something to do with their lack of a collective identity; playing for an entity is not the same as playing for your country – which might explain why Ukraine and Russia are every bit as strong as the old USSR.

This team's defence is as cultured as they come. Shesternev was a huge man, but comfortable on the ball, and Demianenko was an excellent footballer, either at full-back or in the middle. Onopka,

experienced and mobile, completes the trio. Mostovoi and Mikhailichenko fill the central midfield positions. Both have the ability to create and finish and, supported on the flanks by wingers Rats and Chislenko, are guaranteed plenty of crosses to meet their late runs into the box. The three forwards, all Ukrainian, are outstanding: two European Footballers of the Year, plus Shevchenko, one of the best strikers currently playing.

If all else fails they can always count on Yashin, the best goalkeeper of all time. His understudy, Dasaev, is unlucky, because he too was one of the greats.

Manager: Valery Lobanovski

3-4-3

Lev Yashin (50s/60s)

Viktor Onopko (90s) Albert Shesternev (C) (60s)
Anatoli Demianenko (80s)

Igor Chislenko (60s) Alexander Mostovoi (90s)
Vassily Rats (80s) Alexei Mikhailichenko (80s/90s)

Igor Belanov (80s) Andrei Shevchenko (90s) Oleg Blokhin (70s/80s)

Subs: Renat Dasaev (G) (80s) Aleksandr Chivadze (D) (70s/80s)
Aleksandr Zavarov (M) (80s) Valentin Ivanov (M/F) (50s/60s)
Anatolyi Byshovets (F) (70s)

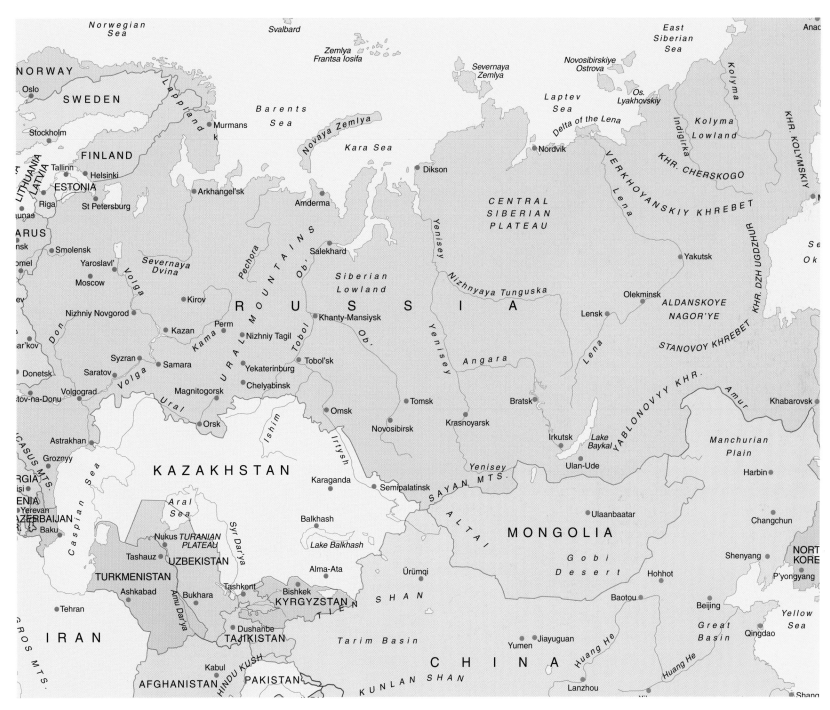

In the 1986 World Cup, coach Lobanovsky based the USSR team almost exclusively on the formidable Dynamo Kiev team he had led to victory in that year's European Cup Winners Cup. Ten of the Kiev team played some part in that World Cup campaign.

Chislenko was a quicksilver winger whose sending off, for an innocuous trip, contributed to the USSR's defeat by West Germany in the 1966 World Cup semi-final.

Shesternev was the captain of the 1966 and 1970 World Cup

teams, presiding over a defence one writer described as 'more Hammer than Sickle'.

The smaller republics from the old Soviet Union are now makeweights in the qualifying rounds of the major tournaments.

Referees

REFEREES HAVE A TOUGH JOB, and media exposure has done them no favours. They make decisions without the benefit of seven cameras and slow-motion, and yet they still get far more right than wrong.

A good referee is like a well-behaved child or dog; all the more worthy of praise when their presence goes unnoticed. But in the modern game too many referees at the top level forget that people are there to watch the football, not them. Intoxicated by the fame offered by TV exposure, they go out of their way to make decisions based on fussy interpretations of rules that they would be better served ignoring altogether. Hang your head in shame Mr David

Elleray. And Mike Riley. And Graham Poll. And Paul Durkin. And Paul 'Ballet Shoes' Alcock....

It seems nowadays that pandering to authority is more important than helping the game remain a good spectacle. Witness the treatment of Dermot Gallagher, an excellent referee, who was demoted for having the temerity to use common sense instead of wielding the FA whip.

'I wasn't sure whether the linesman was indicating the ball had crossed the goal line or whether he had spotted the same offence as me. It wasn't offside. I saw an offence, although I can't remember what it was. In fact there were about eight or nine infringements I could have blown for before the player shot.'

Having denied Chesterfield a place in the FA Cup final, Elleray compounds an abysmal decision by justifying it with a nonsensical rant

Pierluigi Collina, the best referee in the world. Would you argue with him?

◁⫶ A dreadful offside decision probably cost Leeds United the League title in 1971. In a crucial end of season clash, West Brom scored a blatantly offside winning goal. Leeds went mad, as did their fans, resulting in Elland Road being closed for a spell.

◁⫶ In a World Cup match between Brazil and Sweden, Clive Thomas awarded a corner in the dying seconds. Brazil scored from a header straight from the corner, but Thomas claimed he had already blown for full-time and disallowed the goal.

◁⫶ A better, and braver, decision by a British referee was Jack Taylor's award of a penalty to Holland in the first minute of the 1974 World Cup final. Sadly he ruined it by giving West Germany the oft-seen tit-for-tat penalty later in the game.

Renaissance for Rossi

Italy 3 Brazil 2, 1982

IF FIFA EVER DECIDE to award medals for the greatest matches in the World Cup, this one will be on the podium. The eventual winners knocked out the pre-tournament favourites in an absolute classic.

Brazil were defending a 24-game unbeaten record and needed only a draw to progress to the semi-finals while, by contrast, Italy had started the tournament in stuttering fashion, struggling in the first group stage with three draws.

The match twisted and turned throughout. Three times Italy led, only to be pegged back by Zico's brilliance in setting up Socrates and then Falcão who scored with a thunderbolt from the edge of the

area. The difference between the teams proved to be the rejuvenated Paolo Rossi. None of his goals were exceptional, but a hat-trick against the world's best team was no mean feat. Admittedly, Brazil's back line was average at best, and their goalkeeper was just plain incompetent. Italy's back four, on the other hand, were immense. Marshalled by the evergreen Zoff in goal, they withstood everything Brazil could chuck at them in the last 15 minutes to win the day and break the hearts of neutral supporters around the globe.

SCORERS: Italy: Rossi (3)
Brazil: Socrates, Falcão
EVENT: World Cup second round, Barcelona, 5 July 1982

ITALY (Man: Enzo Bearzot)		BRAZIL (Man: Tele Santana)	
1 Zoff	8 Conti	1 Waldir Peres	8 Socrates
2 Gentile	9 Rossi	2 Leandro	9 Serginho
3 Cabrini	10 Antognoni	3 Junior	10 Zico
4 Tardelli	11 Graziani	4 Cerezo	11 Eder
5 Collovati		5 Oscar	
6 Scirea		6 Luizinho	
7 Oriali		7 Falcão	

Rossi (centre, blue shirt) strikes another dagger into Brazilian hearts.

◁)) Bergomi showed impressive maturity after coming on as a first-half substitute. Most 18-year-olds would have shrunk from dealing with Zico and Eder.

◁)) For Paolo Rossi, this was the day he came in from the cold. His ban following his part in a Serie A betting scandal was only lifted a few weeks before the tournament.

◁)) 40-year-old Dino Zoff denied Brazil throughout. His save from Oscar with two minutes left won the game.

◁)) It had been a torrid time for both Italy's forwards. Antognoni had only recently recovered from a fractured skull.

◁)) Rossi's goals against Brazil were his first of the tournament. He finished as its leading scorer with six.

Revie, Don

Manchester City, Leeds United, England

WHETHER ONE REGARDS HIM as one of England's great club managers or the father of modern cynicism, Don Revie's influence on the domestic and national game is considerable. A competent, if unspectacular, player Revie was always a deep-thinking tactician, adapting his role as target man to a more deep-lying centre-forward in a copy of the tactic deployed by the Hungarian striker, Hidegkuti. But it was as a manager that he excelled, notably with Leeds United.

A struggling Second Division outfit in 1961 Revie had transformed Leeds into runaway league champions by 1969. His team, comprised of gifted and ruthlessly determined players like Jack Charlton, Billy Bremner and Johnny Giles, became feared as much for their ruthless professionalism as for their talent. The natural choice as England manager in 1974 following the sacking of Sir Alf Ramsey, Revie turned from saviour to sinner in three years. England's failure to qualify for a second successive World Cup Finals – and the discovery that he had been secretly negotiating a deal to manage the United Arab Emirates – saw him pilloried in the press. His boats burned, Revie disappeared completely from public life. Obituaries on his death in 1989 showed old wounds were not easily healed, although, to a man, his Leeds team spoke in his defence.

VITAL STATISTICS

Place of Birth: Middlesbrough, England
Date of Birth: 10 July 1927
Died: 28 May 1989   **Caps:** 6 (England)
Goals (International): 4
Clubs: As Player: Leicester City, Hull City, Manchester City, Sunderland, Leeds United. As Manager: Leeds United, England national side, United Arab Emigrates national side
Trophies: LT 1969, 1974; FAC 1972; LC 1968; UEFAC 1968, 1971

LEGEND RATING

Achievement	8
Tactical Awareness	9
Motivation	8
Transfer Dealing and Team Selection	9
Personality	4
Overall Legend Rating	**38**

◄ PFA footballer of the year in 1955.
◄ Despite Leeds' success, Revie's team should have won much more, finishing league runners-up five times and losing three Cup finals.

◄ Leeds lost only two games in the 1969 season, the fewest ever in a 42-game campaign.
◄ 1969. Leeds establish a record of 34 consecutive league games unbeaten.

◄ Bob Stokoe claimed that Revie offered him a bribe to throw a vital league game. Stokoe gained his revenge years later in 1973, as manager of the Sunderland side that upset Leeds to win the FA Cup final.

Ricky's Goal

OSVALDO ARDILES and Ricky Villa were at the end of their third successful season with Spurs, and they capped it with Wembley's most entertaining FA Cup final for a generation. For Villa, the game was a resurrection. Five days earlier, his ineffectual performance in the first match had seen him substituted in the second-half. But in the replay, he was the two-goal hero.

His winner was the final twist in a game in which the lead changed hands three times. It has become the stuff of Cup final legend. What began as a speculative dribble on the edge of the box took him past three defenders, and climaxed with him slipping the ball under the advancing Joe Corrigan. For City, who had led 2-1 shortly after the break following Kevin Reeves' penalty, it was a bitter pill. Many sides have played worse and left Wembley with the Cup.

SCORERS: **Tottenham:** Villa 2, Crooks
Manchester City: MacKenzie, Reeves (pen)
EVENT: FA Cup final replay, Wembley, 14 May 1981

TOTTENHAM (Man: Keith Burkinshaw)		MANCHESTER CITY (Man: John Bond)	
1 Aleksic	8 Archibald	1 Corrigan	8 MacKenzie
2 Hughton	9 Galvin	2 Ranson	9 Reeves
3 Miller	10 Hoddle	3 McDonald	10 Bennett
4 Roberts	11 Crooks	4 Caton	11 Hutchison
5 Perryman		5 Reid	
6 Villa		6 Gow	
7 Ardiles		7 Power	

◁ Villa's goal is the only one regularly repeated. Tough luck on City's Steve Mackenzie, who scored a waist-high volley from outside the penalty area for their first equaliser.

◁ For Manchester City, this was their last major final, making the recent successes of their Manchester neighbours all the more galling.

◁ History was on Spurs' side. This was their fifth Cup final victory out of five.

◁ The first game finished 1-1, with City's Tommy Hutchison scoring at both ends.

◁ Spurs retained the Cup the following year, becoming the first team to do so since their predecessors 20 years before.

Rijkaard, Frank

Ajax, AC Milan, Holland

THE DUTCH TEAM that won the European Championship final of 1988 – Holland's first major triumph – was built around the most talented trio of players they had produced since Cruyff, Rep and Neeskens. Their names? Ruud Gullit, Marco van Basten and Frank Rijkaard. If Gullit was their spokesman and leader and Van Basten their executioner and inspiration, then Rijkaard was their pendulum, the metronomic midfield force that made them tick. Utterly dependable, fit, strong and skilful, Rijkaard was the epitome of the modern midfield player, and it was his work that allowed the others to wreak their havoc. His copybook was blotted in the 1990 World

Cup when he was sent off for spitting at Rudi Voller as the Dutch, tournament favourites, were beaten by Germany.

When AC Milan linked Rijkaard up with his two compatriots at club level, they continued to sweep all before them. Rijkaard even managed to steal the spotlight in 1990, scoring the winning goal against Benfica in the European Cup final. A return to Ajax brought yet more domestic trophies, and a third European Cup.

Rijkaard was a surprising choice as Holland coach in 1998. He had no experience and, though his team rallied well to reach the semi-finals of Euro 2000, he resigned shortly after.

VITAL STATISTICS

Place of Birth: Amsterdam, Holland
Date of Birth: 30 September 1962
Died: n/a Caps: 73 (Holland) Goals (International): 10
Clubs: Ajax, Sporting Lisbon, Real Zaragoza, AC Milan
Appearances: Club (All Matches): 415
Goals: Club (All Matches): 74
Trophies: CWC 1987; EuroC 1988; EC 1989, 1990, 1995; SA 1992, 1993; DLT 1982, 1983, 1985, 1994, 1995

LEGEND RATING

Achievement	9
Skill	8
Teamwork	9
Passion	7
Personality	7
Overall Legend Rating	**40**

- In 1988 Rijkaard made a disastrous move to Real Zaragoza, playing only 11 games before moving to Milan.
- Seven league titles, one in each of his last four seasons (two at Milan, two at Ajax).
- The problems with racism in Dutch football have never been resolved – Gullit and Rijkaard, then later Davids, Kluivert and Seedorf have all complained about 'hidden agendas' within the squad.
- Rijkaard laid on Kluivert's goal in Ajax's 1995 European Cup success – against Milan of all teams....
- Rijkaard never played for a side that finished lower than third in the League.

Riva, Luigi

Cagliari, Italy

ONE OF ITALY'S BRIGHTEST STARS in the 1960s, Luigi Riva emerged from humble beginnings with Legnano and Cagliari to become the hero of the *Azzurri* attack with seven goals in the 1970 World Cup qualifiers. He continued this form at the Finals, hitting the winner in the semi-final with Germany and finishing as Italy's top scorer, boosting his international tally to 22 goals in 21 games.

Riva approached the 1970s Finals on a high. He had finished the previous season at the top of the Serie A scoring charts (for the third time in four years), and his goals had helped Cagliari to their first ever *scudetto*.

A few months after the Finals, however, Riva broke a leg for the second time in his career. Initially there were fears he may never play again, but he defied the doubters and made a full recovery – they did not call him 'The Rumble Of Thunder' for nothing. Indeed, he alleviated fears about his fitness to such an extent that, in 1973, Juventus made a massive bid of £1.5 m for him. At that price Cagliari were tempted to sell, but Riva refused to budge, preferring to remain loyal to his native Sardinia. A disappointing swansong at the 1974 World Cup Finals was followed by his retirement, and elevation to the Cagliari boardroom.

VITAL STATISTICS

Place of Birth: Leggiuno, Italy

Date of Birth: 7 November 1944

Died: n/a   Caps: 42 (Italy)

Goals (International): 35

Clubs: Legnano, Cagliari

Appearances: Club (All Matches): 338

Goals: Club (All Matches): 170

Trophies: EuroC 1968, SA 1970

LEGEND RATING

Achievement	7
Skill	8
Teamwork	9
Passion	8
Personality	7
Overall Legend Rating	**39**

- He made his international debut in 1965, aged 21, but it was another three years before he held down a regular place.
- Riva's thunderous shot once broke a spectator's arm during a pre-match warm-up.
- A few days later, he broke his leg and was out of action for six months.
- 35 goals in 42 internationals; one of the highest ratios of the past 40 years.
- Riva came into the team for the replayed final in the 1968 European Championship, scoring the opener in a 2-0 win.

Rivaldo, Vitor Barbosa Ferreira

Barcelona, AC Milan, Brazil

RIVALDO EMERGED with Corinthians and Palmeiras in Brazil, but failure in the 1996 Olympics led to him being pilloried in the press and prompted his departure to Spain.

The 1998 World Cup was a better tournament both for him and Brazil. Rivaldo started every game in France as playmaker from the left-hand side, running at defences and creating space for the lethal Ronaldo to exploit. His best game came in the 3-2 win over Denmark when he scored twice, and was at the heart of all his team's best attacking moments. Victory in the 1999 Copa América confirmed Rivaldo's status as a player of the highest international calibre, but even he struggled to inspire a lacklustre Brazil until they exploded in the 2002 World Cup Finals, having only narrowly qualified.

It was Rivaldo's move to Spain that seems to have been the turning point in his career. Given a free role at his first Spanish club, Deportivo La Coruna, he was a revelation and Barcelona had to pay a massive £18 m to prise him away. The money was well-spent though, as Rivaldo's dribbling and shooting skills proved to be a major factor in successive championship triumphs.

VITAL STATISTICS

Place of Birth: Recife, Brazil

Date of Birth: 19 April 1972

Died: n/a **Caps:** 69 (Brazil) **Goals (International):** 33

Clubs: Paulista, Santa Cruz, Mogi-Mirin, Corinthians, Palmeiras, Deportivo La Coruna, Barcelona, AC Milan

Appearances: Club (League): 319

Goals: Club (League): 157

Trophies: BLT 1994; PLA 1998, 1999; WorC 2002, EC 2003

LEGEND RATING

Achievement	8
Skill	9
Teamwork	8
Passion	7
Personality	7
Overall Legend Rating	**39**

◁ Rivaldo, and others, have invited huge criticism from the Brazilian press for their lack of availability for internationals. ◁ Scored in the 3-0 win over Venezuela that clinched Brazil's qualification for the 2002 World Cup Finals. Cometh the hour...

◁ Rivaldo's ratio of a goal every other game is outstanding for a midfield player. In 1998/99 he hit 24 in 37 league games for Barca.

◁ Voted European and World Player of the Year in 1999.

◁ Rivaldo has a pet dog called 'Pepsi', named in honour of his fondness for the fizzy beverage.

Rivelino, Roberto

Corinthians, Brazil

ONE OF THE ABIDING memories of the great 1970 World Cup Finals was Rivelino's shooting, especially from set-pieces. His ability to impart vicious swerve on the ball, while maintaining velocity on his shot, was a phenomenon the world had never witnessed before. He could place the ball seemingly wherever he wanted. And he didn't always bend it; sometimes he would simply instruct Jairzinho to stand in the wall, hit it straight at him, and hoped he remembered to duck.

Rivelino played for his local team, Corinthians, for 10 years without ever winning anything significant, although towards the end of his career he moved to the more fashionable Fluminense. In Brazil opponents grew wise to his free-kick expertise, but his international foes never seemed to learn their lesson. At the 1974 Finals, in a vastly inferior Brazil team, he continued to enjoy success; against Zaire he scored with a shot struck so hard the ball rebounded back out of the opponents' penalty area.

By the 1978 World Cup Rivelino was a peripheral figure, overshadowed by the emerging Zico, but with his famous left foot, missile free-kicks and magnificent gaucho moustache his mark on the game had already been made.

VITAL STATISTICS

Place of Birth: Sao Paulo, Brazil
Date of Birth: 1 January 1946
Died: n/a   Caps: 92 (Brazil)
Goals (International): 26
Clubs: Corinthians, Fluminense, El Helal
Trophies: WorC 1970

LEGEND RATING

Achievement	9
Skill	9
Teamwork	8
Passion	7
Personality	7
Overall Legend Rating	**40**

- Rivelino's end of career payola came, not in the USA like so many others, but in Saudi Arabia.
- Rivelino became a well-respected commentator on Brazilian TV on his retirement in 1981.

- Rivelino is credited with scoring the world's fastest goal, belting the ball from the kick-off over a goalkeeper who was still completing his pre-match prayers.
- Corinthians fans dubbed him 'Little King of the Park' – his

loyalty to an unsuccessful club made him something of a folk hero.
- Rivelino's 'Zapata' moustache sparked a craze amongst South American footballers. Oh dear.

Roberto Carlos da Silva

Real Madrid, Brazil

TRADITIONALLY the most exciting Brazilian footballers have been their forwards, but over the last few years one of the superstars of their game has been a brilliant attacking full-back. Thrilling runs from left-back have always been a feature of Brazilian football – Nilton Santos, Branco, Leonardo – but Roberto Carlos has taken the art of marauding to a new dimension. Whether overlapping the midfielders, or cutting in with the ball to attempt one of his outrageous, swerving strikes, Carlos commits himself wholeheartedly to attack. His ability to bend the ball makes him a real danger at set-pieces – many a goalkeeper has scoffed as Carlos has lined up a 35-yarder, only to watch open-mouthed as the ball flies into the top corner. He and Cafu were an exciting combination at the 1998 and 2002 World Cup Finals.

Carlos moved to Europe from Palmeiras in 1995, and had an unproductive year at Inter Milan before enjoying a hugely successful spell at Real Madrid where he has collected winner's medals in La Liga and the Champions League.

VITAL STATISTICS

Place of Birth: Garca, Brazil

Date of Birth: 10 April 1973

Died: n/a Caps: 95 (Brazil) Goals (International): 7

Clubs: Palmeiras, Inter Milan, Real Madrid

Appearances: Club (League): 336

Goals: Club (League): 40

Trophies: PLA 1997, 2001; EC 1998, 2000, 2002; WorC 2002

LEGEND RATING

Achievement	8
Skill	9
Teamwork	9
Passion	7
Personality	6
Overall Legend Rating	**37**

‹ᴵᴵ Cafu, his full-back partner, helped Roma win their first Italian League title for nearly 20 years in 2001.

‹ᴵᴵ At Inter, Roy Hodgson tried to move Roberto Carlos into midfield – a logical move, but not to the player's liking.

‹ᴵᴵ Capped at 18 in the 1992 Olympic tournament, he was disappointed to miss the 1994 World Cup, where Leonardo and Branco filled the 'left-back who can't defend' slot.

‹ᴵᴵ Roberto Carlos was Ronaldo's room-mate at the 1998 World Cup Finals, and witnessed the convulsions the striker suffered before the final.

‹ᴵᴵ Won two successive Copa América tournaments in 1997 and 1999.

Robson, Bobby

Ipswich Town, England, Newcastle United

EXCELLENT PLAYER. Great manager. Nice bloke. Few figures in football are treated with the universal respect accorded Bobby Robson.

Robson's 34 years as a manager, eight of them with England, followed 17 years as a successful midfield player with West Brom and Fulham, where he played alongside the legendary Johnny Haynes. After retiring as a player Robson managed Ipswich for 13 years. During that time Robson bought and sold countless players but it was the signings of the Dutchmen Arnold Muhren and Frans Thijssen, two of the first overseas players to make a significant impact in English football, for which he is probably best remembered.

As England manager he survived an indifferent start, failing to qualify for the European Championships, but his record in two World Cups was impressive. In 1986 he took England to the quarter-finals and then, four years later, led them to the semis at Italia 90. On both occasions England lost out to the eventual tournament winners. Now, after seven years abroad, he's back home in north-east England, revitalising a Newcastle club in sharp decline after careless management by Kenny Dalglish and Ruud Gullit.

VITAL STATISTICS

Place of Birth: Sacriston, England

Date of Birth: 18 February 1933

Died: n/a Caps: 20 (England) Goals (International): 4

Clubs: As Player: Fulham. West Bromwich Albion; As Manager: Vancouver Whitecaps, Fulham, Ipswich, PSV Eindhoven, Sporting Lisbon, FC Porto, Barcelona, Newcastle United

Trophies: FAC 1978; EUFAC 1981; CWC 1997; DLT 1991, 1992; PLT 1995, 1996

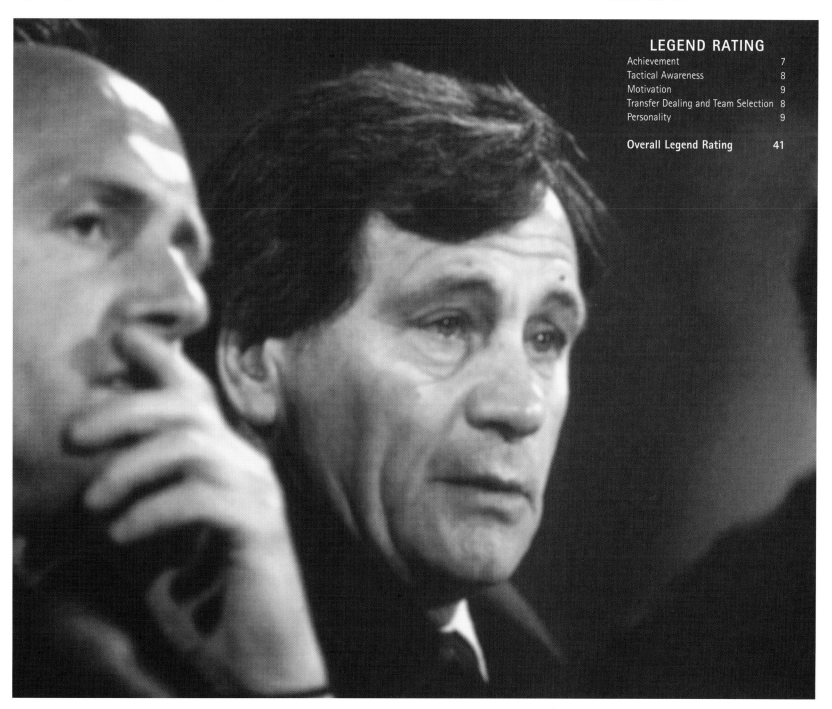

LEGEND RATING

Achievement	7
Tactical Awareness	8
Motivation	9
Transfer Dealing and Team Selection	8
Personality	9
Overall Legend Rating	**41**

◁» He caused immediate controversy as England manager by omitting Kevin Keegan from his first squad in 1982.

◁» He enjoys good relations with the media these days, but was subjected to a vicious tabloid campaign to oust him as England manager in 1988 following a 1-1 draw with Saudi Arabia.

◁» He scored twice on his England debut in a 4-0 defeat of France, 1957.

◁» He has won only one English domestic trophy as a manager, the FA Cup with Ipswich in 1978.

◁» He left Ipswich for the England job after finishing second in the First Division in successive seasons.

Robson, Bryan

West Bromwich Albion, Manchester United, England

ENGLAND'S FINEST PLAYER of the 1980s was also one of their unluckiest. Although 'Captain Marvel' brought a huge midfield presence to bear for club and country, his catalogue of injuries threatened to make him more celebrated in the *Lancet* than the back pages. Robson's first World Cup Finals in 1982 saw him come of age, but the sight of him limping prematurely out of the following two tournaments left England fans mouthing the words 'if only'.

The heartbeat of West Bromwich Albion's finest post-war side, Robson later moved to Manchester United in search of the major prizes. It worked. He won FA Cup winner's medals in 1983, 1985 and 1990 and picked up a European Cup Winners' Cup gong in 1991. It looked like a league championship was going to elude him but, in the latter stages of his Old Trafford career, United finally came good, picking up their first title in 26 years in 1993. Robson played in only five matches that season, but no one in the country begrudged him his medal. His self-motivation and determination seemed ideal qualities for management, but despite leading Middlesbrough to two Wembley finals, his record in the league was poor, and his record in the transfer market was even worse. He was replaced as Middlesbrough boss by Steve McLaren in 2001.

VITAL STATISTICS

Place of Birth: Chester Le Street, England

Date of Birth: 11 January 1957

Died: n/a   **Caps:** 90 (England)

Goals (International): 26

Clubs: West Bromwich Albion, Manchester United, Middlesbrough

Appearances: Club (League): 568

Goals: Club (League): 114

Trophies: LT 1993, 1994; FAC 1983, 1985, 1990; CWC 1991

LEGEND RATING

Achievement	7
Skill	7
Teamwork	10
Passion	9
Personality	7
Overall Legend Rating	**40**

- He captained England 65 times, second only to Bobby Moore.
- With 26 international goals he is the only non-striker in England's top ten.
- 1982. Scored after 27 seconds versus France, the quickest goal in World Cup Finals history.
- He lifted the FA Cup as captain three times (1983, 1985 and 1990).
- £1.5 m fee paid to West Brom by Man United in 1981 was a British record.

Ronaldo

IT WAS CLEAR from an early age that Ronaldo Luis Nazario de Lima had the lot. Playing in Brazilian football as a teenager he proved unstoppable, and was promptly shipped off to Europe to play for PSV Eindhoven in Holland.

The shaven-headed waif with the buck teeth isn't a complete striker by any means; he can't head the ball well and doesn't have the finishing of, say, Gerd Muller or Gary Lineker, but he has serious pace, great close control and impressive strength. In full flight he is a breathtaking sight and pretty much unstoppable, like Jimmy Greaves with a rocket up his shorts.

In Europe he has torn apart Dutch, Spanish and Italian club defences with equal relish, and had a brilliant Copa América with Brazil in 1997. He came into the 1998 World Cup billed as the world's greatest player and lived up to the hype with some fine performances, but the events surrounding his 'funny turn' prior to the final against France (and his subsequent insipid performance) meant fans came away discussing his health rather than his football. Not any more. The Golden Boot in Japan and Korea in the World Cup Finals in 2002 confirmed that the comeback kid had truly returned.

VITAL STATISTICS

Place of Birth: Rio de Janeiro, Brazil

Date of Birth: 22 September 1976

Died: n/a   **Caps:** 69 (Brazil)   **Goals (International):** 47

Clubs: Cruzeiro, PSV Eindhoven, Barcelona, Inter Milan, Real Madrid

Appearances: Club (League): 232

Goals: Club (League): 200

Trophies: WorC 2002; CWC 1997; EUFAC 1998

LEGEND RATING

Achievement	8
Skill	9
Teamwork	7
Passion	8
Personality	6
Overall Legend Rating	38

◁ Doubts first emerged over Ronaldo's fitness at PSV but Barcelona gambled £10 m on him and struck gold: 34 goals in La Liga and a winning goal in the Cup Winners' Cup final.

◁ April 2003: scores memorable hat-trick at Old Trafford as Real eliminate Manchester United from the Champions League.

◁ He was voted world Player of the Year 1996 and 1997.

◁ For Cruzeiro, aged 18, he scored 58 goals in 60 games.

◁ He was European Footballer of the Year in 1997.

Ronnie's Rocket

Hereford United 2 Newcastle United 1, 1972

THE GAME THAT still keeps Ronnie Radford in personal appearances was notable for more than just non-leaguers scalping top-division opponents. Hereford had already produced a major surprise by drawing 2-2 at St James's Park.

Due to bad weather the replay had already been postponed several times and, when it was finally given the go-ahead, the pitch resembled a treacle pudding. The state of the playing surface was undoubtedly a factor, and made Malcolm MacDonald's pre-match boast that Newcastle would win by double figures seem even more foolhardy. The general perception is that this was a typical blood-and-thunder FA Cup tie. In fact, nothing much happened for 80 minutes, and when MacDonald rose at the far post to give Newcastle the lead the anti-climax appeared complete. But Radford had other ideas. His 40-yard screamer, replayed so frequently on TV it is often mistakenly believed to have been the winner, was in fact just the prelude to Ricky George's extra-time decider and the pitch invasion, a delirious mass of snorkel parkas and bad hair-cuts, that it prompted. Just four days later, Hereford held West Ham in the fourth round, before a Geoff Hurst hat-trick in the replay made Upton Park the final stop in a memorable ride.

SCORERS: Hereford: Radford, George
Newcastle: MacDonald
EVENT: FA Cup Third Round replay, Edgar Street, 5 February 1972

HEREFORD UNITED
(Man: Colin Anderson)
1 Potter
2 Gough
3 Mallender
4 Jones
5 McLaughlin
6 Addison
7 George
8 Tyler
9 Meadows
10 Owen
11 Radford

NEWCASTLE UNITED
(Man: Joe Harvey)
1 McFaul
2 n/k
3 n/k
4 n/k
5 Moncur
6 n/k
7 n/k
8 n/k
9 Macdonald
10 Tudor
11 n/k

Ronnie Radford (No.11) attracts a few admirers.

◁)) Commentator John Motson, previously second fiddle on *Match of the Day*, became a household name after this match.

◁)) Ronnie Radford's equaliser was *Match of the Day*'s goal of the season, the only time a non-league player has won the award.

◁)) Hereford's third round in 15 years made it third time lucky.

◁)) Hereford's scorers had more illustrious namesakes; double-holders Arsenal also played twin strikers called Radford and George.

◁)) Hereford were elected to the Football League that season, largely on the strength of this game.

Rossi, Paolo

Juventus, Italy

THE HERO OF ITALY'S greatest post-war triumph was nearly on the scrapheap as a teenager. Two knee operations, the result of injuries picked up playing for Juventus' youth team, nearly strangled the career of one of Italy's most notable forwards. Offloaded by the Turin giants in 1975 after three years as a professional, he spent two seasons with Como before Vicenza offered him another chance. His reputation was made during a highly successful 1978 World Cup Finals, and prompted his £3.5 m world-record transfer to Perugia the following year. However, after only one season, Rossi found himself in serious bother after being implicated in a betting scandal that rocked Italian football, and was later banned for two years (Perugia were relegated for their part in the scam). His ban completed, Perugia got rid of him to Juventus for just £650,000, but within a year Rossi was the toast of the nation, firing Italy to the summit of World football at the 1982 World Cup Finals. Rossi was the tournament's top scorer with six, a haul that included a hat-trick against Brazil in the decisive group game, and the goal that set Italy on their way to a 3-1 win over West Germany in the final. His career came full circle in 1986, when that troublesome knee forced his early retirement at 29.

VITAL STATISTICS

Place of Birth: 23 September 1956
Date of Birth: Prato, Italy
Died: n/a   Caps: 48 (Italy)
Goals (International): 20
Clubs: Prato, Juventus, Como, Lanerossi, Vicenza, Perugia, AC Milan
Appearances: Club (League): 251
Goals: Club (League): 103
Trophies: WorC 1982; CWC 1984; EC 1985; SA 1982, 1984

LEGEND RATING

Achievement	9
Skill	8
Teamwork	8
Passion	7
Personality	6
Overall Legend Rating	**38**

World Cup Final, 1982. Rossi (no.20) receives the attentions of West Germany's Breitner.

- Rossi had played only three games since the lifting of his ban before appearing at Spain 82.
- Rossi failed to score in the first four matches of the 1982 Finals. You know the rest...
- Like Perugia, AC Milan were also kicked out of Serie A for their part in the betting scandal.
- He was World and European Footballer of the Year in 1982.

Rossoneri

The AC Milan Dream Team

WHAT A DEFENCE! Nils Liedholm was a superb all-round player, Cesare Maldini sound and intelligent, and the other three are simply fantastic: the steel and guile of Franco Baresi, speed and subtlety of Maldini, and 'The Rock', Marcel Desailly.

Further insurance against an opposition raid is also provided by the midfield, notably Rijkaard and Gullit who, for all their ball-playing gifts, never shirked their defensive responsibilities. Those two, along with Milan icon Rivera, give this team a compact and efficient midfield. The one thing it possibly lacks is width, hence the inclusion of Swedish winger, Hamrin, on the bench. There is also the option of

bringing Donadoni on for Rijkaard at half-time. (Gullit, Donadoni and Rivera – shall we play football or have a fashion shoot?)

Up front a steady supply of goals is guaranteed. Marco Van Basten, a three-time winner of the European footballer of the year award, is one of the greatest finishers of all time, and the powerful Swede, Nordahl, not far behind. Sadly, there is no room for the gifted Daniele Massaro, and only the bench for the moody genius of Dejan Savicevic. A fabulous team, but even Silvio Berlusconi might blanch at the wage bill.

Manager: Ariggo Sacchi

1-4-3-2

Fabio Cudicini (60s)

Franco Baresi (C) (70s/80s/90s)

Nils Liedholm (50s/60s) Cesare Maldini (60s) Marcel Desailly (90s)
Paolo Maldini (80s/90s)

Frank Rijkaard (80s) Ruud Gullit (80s) Gianni Rivera (60s/70s)

Marco Van Basten (80s) Gunnar Nordahl (50s/60s)

Subs: Sebastiano Rossi (G) (90s) Alessandro Costacurta (D) (90s)
Roberto Donadoni (M) (80s) Kurt Hamrin (W) (50s/60s)
Dejan Savicevic (F) (90s)

Barcelona, 1989. AC Milan after thrashing Steaua in the 1989 European Cup Final. Note lack of sweat.

◁》 Fabio Cudicini is father of Chelsea goalkeeper, Carlo Cudicini.

◁》 Cesare and Paolo Maldini are also father and son. As manager of Italy, it was Cesare who persuaded Paolo to move to centre-half in the absence of Franco Baresi.

◁》 More defensive talent sits on the bench in the shape of Alessandro Costacurta. An unlikely footballer, Costacurta collects art and owns a part share in a gourmet restaurant.

◁》 Unlucky omissions? Gunnar Gren, Milan's other great Swede,

Prati, scorer of a hat-trick in the 1969 European Cup final, and Demetrio Albertini, gifted midfielder in the 1990s.

◁》 Only half this squad are Italian, evidence of Milan's reliance on overseas stars to bring them success.

Rough Justice

West Germany 3 (5) France 3 (3), 1982

THIS MATCH HAD EVERYTHING, including one of the great injustices a World Cup audience had ever witnessed. The game was delicately poised at 1-1 when France's Patrick Battiston burst clear onto the German goal, only to be cynically brought down on the edge of the area by a head-high challenge from German goalkeeper, Schumacher. Amazingly, Dutch referee Charles Corver failed to award even a foul – rough justice for the French full-back who was stretchered off with concussion and broken teeth.

With all neutrals baying for German blood, justice appeared to have been served as France swept into a 3-1 lead in extra-time with only 17 minutes left. But, settling for their two-goal advantage, the French sat back inviting German pressure. Germany seized the initiative and two goals in five minutes, the second a brilliant overhead kick from Fischer, saw them force a penalty shoot-out. Amazingly, France threw it away a second time. Schumacher saved Didier Six's kick to prevent a 4-2 lead, and repeated the trick to keep out Bossis's effort with the scores at 4-4. Then, as the shoot-out moved into sudden-death, Hrubesch applied the final, killer blow. The tears shed by French players were shared by football lovers everywhere.

SCORERS: W. Germany: Littbarski, Rummenigge, Fischer.
France: Platini (pen.), Tresor, Giresse
EVENT: World Cup Semi-Final, 8 July 1982

WEST GERMANY (Man: Jupp Derwall)		FRANCE (Man: Michel Hidalgo)	
1 Schumacher	7 Dremmler	1 Ettori	(Battiston)
2 Kaltz	8 Breitner	2 Amoros	(Lopez)
3 K-H Förster	9 Littbarski	3 Janvion	8 Giresse
4 Stielike	10 Magath	4 Bossis	9 Platini
5 Briegel	(Hrubesch)	5 Tigana	10 Rocheteau
(Rummenigge)	11 Fischer	6 Tresor	11 Six
6 B. Förster		7 Genghini	

An anxious Platini escorts the stricken Battiston.

◄⋓ 'I'm convinced the world knows the best team lost. We only have ourselves to blame, though,' Michel Platini.

◄⋓ Substitute Patrick Battiston had only been on the pitch for five minutes.

◄⋓ 'He [Schumacher] is very sorry for what happened. It was an accident.' German coach Jupp Derwall, who even managed to keep a straight face.

◄⋓ A French newspaper poll after the game revealed Schumacher to be the least popular man in French history, edging Adolf Hitler into second place.

◄⋓ Justice finally prevailed as Italy beat Germany 3-1 in the final.

Rovers

BLACKBURN ROVERS' HEYDAY was in the nineteenth century. In an era when the FA Cup was the blue riband trophy, Rovers claimed it six times between 1884 and 1891, thanks largely to the goal-scoring exploits of their centre-forward, Jack Southworth. After a brief decline another great side emerged just before the onset of the First World War. With Bob Crompton at the team's heart, George Chapman at centre-half, and Danny Shea banging in the goals, Rovers won the title in 1912 and 1914.

Under the management of Irishman, Johnny Carey, another Rovers revival took place in the 1950s. Although Carey's team contained no megastars, it was not short on fine players: Peter Dobing, Bryan Douglas and the prolific Bill Eckersley could hold their own in any company. They reached the FA Cup final in 1960.

The end of the maximum wage meant financial challenges for a small club like Blackburn, and an exodus of their best players led inevitably to another fallow period. Only when Jack Walker began to pour millions into the kitty did Rovers again become a force, the signings of Alan Shearer and Chris Sutton giving them a strike force good enough to bring the FA Premiership title to Ewood Park in 1995.

Manager: Johnny Carey

4-4-2

Tim Flowers (90s)

Colin Hendry (90s) George Chapman (00s/10s)
Derek Fazackerley (70s/80s) Keith Newton (60s)

Damien Duff (90s) Peter Dobing (50s/60s)
Bob Crompton (C) (10s) Ronnie Clayton (50s/60s)

Alan Shearer (90s) Bill Eckersley (50s)

Subs: Jimmy Ashcroft (G) (10s) Mike England (D) (60s) Tim Sherwood (M) (90s) Jack Southworth (F) (1890s) Danny Shea (F) (10s)

"Uncle' Jack Walker indulges in a little cabaret.

◁ Centre-half George Chapman was pressed into service as a centre-forward during the 1911/12 season. He responded with eight goals in as many games as Rovers surged to the title.

◁ The loyal and willing Fazackerley deserved to play in better Blackburn sides. He stayed at the club after retiring and contributed almost as much as a coach.

◁ Despite winning the championship the 1995 team was criticised for its direct tactics: two wingers, Ripley and Wilcox, providing the bullets for the SAS (Shearer and Sutton).

◁ Only the tricky winger Damien Duff makes it from the current team, but Graeme Souness has other exciting young talents in Matt Jansen and David Dunn in his improving side.

Rummenigge, Karl-Heinz

Bayern Munich, West Germany

AS THE GREAT GERMAN SIDE of the early 1970s broke up, manager Helmut Schoen looked around in vain for stars to replace Beckenbauer, Netzer, Overath and Muller. How he must have rejoiced at the emergence of Karl-Heinz Rummenigge. Quick and mobile, with distinctive blonde hair and a typically Bavarian swagger, Rummenigge was a hard player to mark, always seeming to find a yard in which to fashion a shot at goal.

However, fortune never smiled on Rummenigge in the World Cup. He played in a poor side in 1978, and had the unique misfortune to captain two losing finalists, in 1982 and 1986. In both those tournaments Rummenigge was hampered by injuries, and Germany were a blunt edge without him. He had better luck in the European Championships though, winning the tournament in 1980 when, with the young playmaker Bernd Schuster feeding him with passes, he performed with customary vivacity. In 10 years at Bayern Munich, Rummenigge won a full set of domestic honours and two European Cup winner's medals. He tried his luck at Inter for three seasons, but they never really hit the heights, and he later played out his career in the relative obscurity of the Swiss league with Servette.

VITAL STATISTICS

Place of Birth: Lippstadt, Germany

Date of Birth: 25 September 1955

Died: n/a   Caps: 95 (Germany)

Goals (International): 45

Clubs: Bayern Munich, Inter Milan, Servette

Appearances: Club (All Matches): 424

Goals: Club (All Matches): 220

Trophies: EC 1975, 1976; EuroC 1980; BLG 1980, 1981

LEGEND RATING

Achievement	9
Skill	8
Teamwork	9
Passion	9
Personality	6
Overall Legend Rating	**41**

- The £2.5 m fee paid to Bayern Munich by Inter was a German record.
- He was European Footballer of the Year, 1980 and 1981.
- His 1982 World Cup hat-trick against Chile was a masterclass in finishing – one with each foot and a text-book header.
- Had the talented Schuster not absented himself from international football, Rummenigge's goal tally would surely have been higher. For most of his career Germany lacked both a quality playmaker and a quality target man for Rummenigge to feed off.
- The decision to play the injured Rummenigge in the 1982 World Cup final is alleged to have prompted a fierce row in the West German dressing room at half-time.

Rush, Ian

Liverpool, Wales

ONE OF THE GREAT instinctive finishers, Rush broke a stack of goal-scoring records in his time with Liverpool. Discovered at Chester as a teenager, he was bought by the Anfield club in 1979 for £300,000.

As well as great poise in front of goal, Rush's best asset was his movement. Blessed with great stamina, he constantly dragged defenders out of position and deceived them with late feints and runs – the perfect foil for the spontaneous creativity of Kenny Dalglish. A defender once claimed that keeping tabs on him was 'like marking a ribbon'.

Rush never achieved the recognition he deserved abroad. This was due in part to being Welsh, which meant he never had the opportunity to shine in a good international team, and to his unhappy season with Juventus. Bought by the Italians for £3.2 m, Rush was sold back to Liverpool for £2.8 m the following year, observing, profoundly, that the experience had been 'like being in a foreign country'. Rush should have retired at Liverpool, as lacklustre spells at Leeds and Newcastle did nothing for his reputation. Better to remember him as the highest scorer in Liverpool's history.

VITAL STATISTICS

Place of Birth: Flint, Wales
Date of Birth: 20 October 1961
Died: n/a **Caps:** 73 (Wales) **Goals (International):** 28
Clubs: Chester, Liverpool, Juventus, Liverpool, Leeds United, Newcastle
Appearances: Club (League): 584
Goals: Club (League): 253
Trophies: LT 1982, 1983, 1984, 1986, 1988, 1990; FAC 1986, 1989, 1992; LC 1981, 1982, 1983, 1994, 1995; EC 1981, 1984

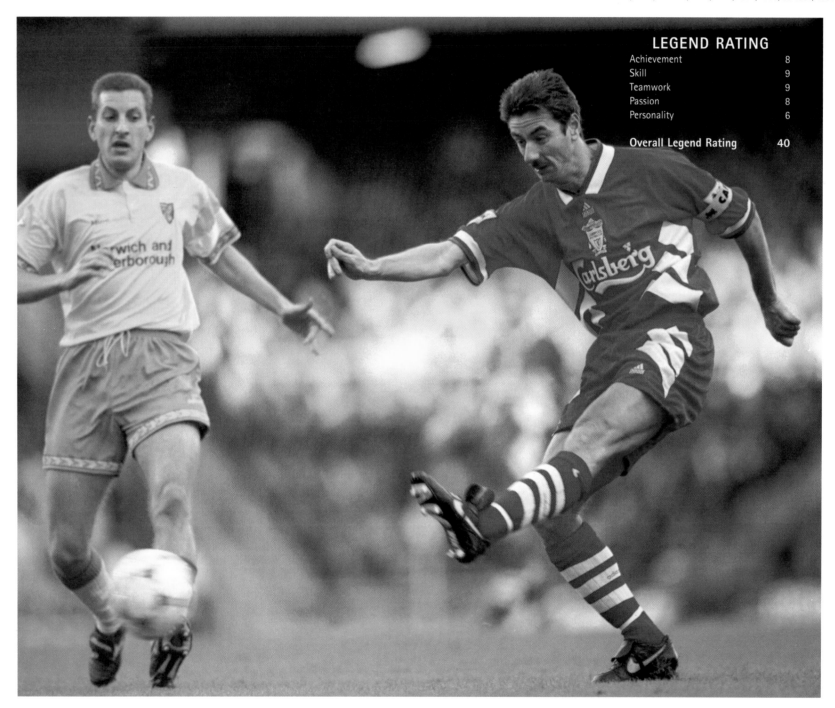

LEGEND RATING

Achievement	8
Skill	9
Teamwork	9
Passion	8
Personality	6
Overall Legend Rating	**40**

◁┃ He scored a record 44 FA Cup goals, including five in finals (also a record).

◁┃ He scored 49 League Cup goals (this is a record held jointly with Geoff Hurst).

◁┃ Rush the record breaker: 'I am proud and privileged to have beaten the record of a great player like Roger Hunt.'

◁┃ Rush had played only 33 games in the Fourth Division for Chester when Liverpool stepped in.

◁┃ He was PFA and Football Writers' Player of the Year, 1984

Saints

APART FROM a couple of Cup runs at the turn of the century, Southampton failed to establish themselves amongst the game's elite until the modern era. It was only in the 1960s, when former star Ted Bates took over as manager, that they built themselves into a force, with talented players like Gabriel, Paine and Melia.

In their most successful spell in the early 1980s, Lawrie McMenemy built Southampton's team around a number of top international players whom he managed to pick up for small fees because, in the eyes of the clubs who sold them, they were past their best. Maybe it was the sea air blowing in off the coast, but Shilton,

Ball, Keegan, Watson and Mills rolled back the years at the Dell, combining splendidly with homegrown stars like Mick Channon. Amazingly, all were previous England captains.

Southampton's sole major trophy came in 1976 when, as an unfancied Second Division team, they overturned the odds to beat Manchester United 1-0 in the FA Cup Final. Recent teams have had to concentrate more on staying in the top flight rather than winning trophies, and to that end no players have made more valuable contributions than Matt Le Tissier and Alan Shearer.

Manager: Lawrie McMenemy

3-4-1-2

Peter Shilton (80s)

Dean Richards (90s) Chris Nicholl (70s/80s) Jimmy Gabriel (60s)

Nicky Holmes (70s/80s) Terry Paine (60s/70s) Alan Ball (C) (80s) Jimmy Melia (60s)

Matthew Le Tissier (90s)

Kevin Keegan (80s) Mick Channon (70s/80s)

Subs: Paul Jones (G) (90s) Dave Watson (D) (80s) Steve Williams (M) (80s) Alan Shearer (F) (90s) Marian Pahars (F) (90s)

Southampton's home for 103 years, The Dell, usurped by St Mary's in 2001.

↝ This side would not wilt: Holmes, Paine, Ball and Keegan were industrious players who would not allow Le Tissier's wayward talents to go to waste.

↝ Paul Jones followed his old Stockport manager Dave Jones to the Dell, and has proved a great asset. We've included him despite his demotion to the bench during 2002/3.

↝ Terry Paine played a staggering 808 games for Southampton in an 18-year career, a league record later broken by Peter Shilton.

↝ Chris Nicholl won 37 of his 51 caps for Northern Ireland while with Southampton; Channon 45 of his 46 England caps.

San Siro

Milan, Italy

THE SPECTACULAR SAN SIRO was built in 1925. Remodelled to the tune of £50 m for the 1990 World Cup Finals, it superseded even the original to remain one of the world's great sporting venues.

Originally home to AC Milan, they were joined after the Second World War by their local rivals Internazionale; the two have been happily co-habiting ever since. One can only imagine parochial outrage if Manchester City were rehoused at Old Trafford or Rangers became tenants at Celtic Park.

Today the ground is known as the Giuseppe Meazza Stadium, after it was renamed before Italia 90 in honour of the legendary Inter and Italian star of the 1920s and 1930s (he later played a swansong for Milan).

As a result of the improvements, the stadium has a unique system of spectator access, ramps running around its perimeter, an additional third tier of seating extending the capacity to 82,000, and a new roof enhancing the already intimidating atmosphere. Its spiralling towers corner give the impression of a modern-day fortress. The psychological advantage to its two home teams is immense.

VITAL STATISTICS

Location:	Milan, Italy
Local Club:	AC Milan, Internazionale
Date Built:	1926
Current Capacity:	83,107
Max. Capacity:	83,107

◁ The original stadium was funded from an unlikely source. Tyre magnate Piero Pirelli provided much of the funding.
◁ The San Siro has hosted two European Cup Finals. Internazionale enjoyed home advantage in 1965 to beat Benfica. In 1970, Feyenoord overcame Celtic.
◁ One of the great World Cup shocks occurred at the San Siro. The opening match of Italia 90 saw holders Argentina succumb 1-0 to Cameroon.
◁ The San Siro was so named after a local saint,
◁ The addition of the roof has restricted the amount of sunlight reaching the pitch. In recent years millions of pounds have been spent keeping the playing surface up to standard.

Sanchez, Hugo

MEXICO'S BEST PLAYER wasn't the greatest servant to his home nation. Absent in Europe for most of his career and with a habit of crying off for all but the most important internationals, he was in frequent dudgeon with the authorities. This was a shame because an ordinary Mexican team needed his inspiration. Lively and mobile, Sanchez could shoot with either foot, and was exceptional in the air for a smallish, slim man. He is probably best remembered by European audiences for his trademark goal celebration, an acrobatic handspring he had perfected long before that sort of thing became de rigeur.

He appeared in two World Cup tournaments, although his first – as a 19-year-old prodigy in 1978 – was a disaster; the team were abject and Sanchez failed to live up to his pre-tournament billing. 1986 was much better. On home soil the Mexicans put on a decent show, reaching the quarter finals. Sanchez enjoyed a sensational career in Spain with Real Madrid where his partnership with Emilio Butragueno was the spearhead of a team that collected five consecutive Spanish titles.

VITAL STATISTICS

Place of Birth: Mexico

Date of Birth: 11 June 1958

Died: n/a   Caps: 57 (Mexico)

Goals (International): 26

Clubs: UNAM, Atletico Madrid, Real Madrid, Rayo Vallecano

Trophies: PLA 1986, 1987, 1988, 1989, 1990; EUFAC 1986

LEGEND RATING

Achievement	7
Skill	9
Teamwork	7
Passion	8
Personality	8
Overall Legend Rating	**39**

◁ The closest Sanchez got to a European Cup final was in 1989, when Real were beaten by AC Milan in the semi-final.

◁ Sanchez's famous goal celebration was inspired by his sister, an Olympic gymnast.

◁ Sanchez was top scorer in La Liga from 1985–88.

◁ Sanchez scored the opener in Real Madrid's 5-1 first-leg win in their UEFA Cup final victory over Cologne. Surprisingly, this was his only success in Europe.

◁ Butragueno, 'The Vulture' was one of Spain's finest strikers – he scored 4 goals in a 5-0 mauling of Denmark at the 1986 World Cup Finals.

Santamaria, Jose

WITH ALL THOSE FABULOUS attacking players – Ferenc Puskas, Alfredo Di Stefano and Francisco Gento – no one took much notice of Real Madrid's defence. At its heart was Jose Santamaria. A fair-haired centre-half with an intimidating physical presence, Santamaria took a no-nonsense approach to defending. If it moved he kicked it. A young star with Nacional, he was the central defensive pivot in the splendid Uruguay side that reached the semi-finals of the 1954 World Cup, brushing aside both Scotland and England along the way. Santamaria returned to the big stage in Chile in 1962, this time with Spain (he became an adopted national) but a poor side went out early and he suffered the indignity of being left out of the team. By this stage Santamaria had made the switch to Real Madrid, where he collected three European Cup winner's medals, and a place in history as a member of the best club side ever.

VITAL STATISTICS

Place of Birth: Montevideo, Uruguay
Date of Birth: 31 July 1929
Died: n/a
Caps: 35 (for Uruguay); 17 (for Spain)
Goals (International): 0
Clubs: Nacional, Real Madrid
Trophies: ULT 1950, 1952, 1955, 1956; PLA 1958, 1961, 1962, 1963, 1964, 1965; EC 1958, 1959, 1960

LEGEND RATING
Achievement 9
Skill 7
Teamwork 8
Passion 8
Personality 6

Overall Legend Rating 38

➤ Santamaria is one of four players to have represented two nations in the World Cup Finals. The others are Puskas (Hungary/Spain), Monti (Argentina/Italy) and Altafini (Italy, appeared as Mazzola for Brazil in 1958).

➤ If Di Stefano had played in the World Cup Finals he would have made it five players, and an extraordinary three from Real Madrid. FIFA rules now ensure there will be no additions to this list.

➤ Santamaria was involved in an ongoing feud with John Charles when the Welshman was at Juventus. Three matches in the 1962 European Cup were marred by a series of confrontations between the two.

Santos, Djalma & Nilton

THE SANTOS 'TWINS' of the Brazil team of the 1950s were not actually brothers at all. They were known as the twins because they operated as twin full-backs in that fabulous team. Brazil had developed their 4-2-4 formation with modern full-backs and conventional centre-halves, and Djalma and Nilton Santos were ideally suited to those defensive wide positions. Djalma, a thunderous tackler and solid marker, was the more defensive player while Nilton was more of a modern wing-back, fond of surging runs.

They both appeared in the 1954 World Cup Finals, but failed to distinguish themselves as Brazil were beaten in a violent debacle against Hungary. In 1958 Nilton was a vital part of Brazil's vibrant attacking team, scoring in the first game against Austria. By 1962 the two were veterans, but still an integral part of the Brazilian side. That was the last World Cup tournament the two played in together. But it was not the end of the story. At the age of 37 in 1966, Djalma was recalled to the team after a considerable gap. Unfortunately, he was way over the hill by this stage and was horribly exposed by the Hungarian wingers as Brazil failed to get past the group stage for the first time since the war.

VITAL STATISTICS

DJALMA SANTOS

Place of Birth:	Brazil
Date of Birth:	27 February 1929
Died: n/a	Caps: 107 (Brazil)

Goals (International): 3

Clubs: Portuguesa, Palmeiras, Atletico Curitiba

Trophies: WorC 1958, 1962

NILTON SANTOS

Place of Birth:	Brazil
Date of Birth:	16 May 1927

Died: n/a Caps: 75 (Brazil) Goals (International): 3

Clubs: Botafogo

Trophies: WorC 1958, 1962

Nilton Santos (left) models an early example of short shorts.

LEGEND RATING

Djalma:		Nilton:	
Achievement	9	Achievement	9
Skill	6	Skill	7
Teamwork	8	Teamwork	7
Passion	7	Passion	7
Personality	7	Personality	8
Overall Legend Rating	**37**	**Overall Legend Rating**	**38**

◁ Djalma, the right back, was only brought into the 1958 team for the final to counteract the flying Swedish wingers, Hamrin and Skoglund. This was tough on Di Sordi, who played the rest of the tournament – but it worked.

◁ In the 'Battle of Berne' against Hungary, Nilton was dismissed for fighting and Djalma was lectured for chasing Hungarian winger Zoltan Czibor around the pitch.

◁ Nilton Santos played his entire career for Botafogo.

◁ Nilton Santos led the deputation that persuaded coach Vicente Feola to reinstate Garrincha for the 1958 final.

◁ Djalma Santos played for the Rest of the World against England to mark the FA's centenary in 1963.

Saturday Night Fever

UNTIL THE BBC tried an experiment with its fledgling minority channel BBC2 in 1964, the only way to watch a league game was to turn up at the ground. That experiment was called *Match Of The Day*, and became a national institution and staple ingredient of Saturday-night viewing. Its first commentator, Kenneth Wolstenholme, was of the old school, a master of understatement and circumspect pronunciation. The programme was to eventually rely on Barry Davies and John Motson for its real colour, two men whose voices became synonymous with the show over a period of 30 years. In the early days only edited highlights from one or two games were transmitted

but, following the arrival of Sky to the marketplace, the format was overhauled to include highlights of all matches from the top division. Presenters have come and gone down the years, the analytical approach of Jimmy Hill giving way to the smoothness of Des Lynam. More recently Gary Lineker was promoted to the anchor role, and it is he who currently introduces the show's coverage of FA Cup and international matches. Whatever the personnel, the signature tune has remained the same, acting as a musical comfort blanket to armchair fans for nearly four decades.

'Those who participate provide the poetry. Those who commentate provide the prose – and not very good prose at that. That's why so many ex-players have taken up commentating. It's called missionary work.'

Gary Lineker addressing the Oxford Union in 1990 in a debate on the motion that 'this house believes it is better to commentate than participate'

Desmond Lynam, Match of the Day's smoothest anchorman.

◀ The first broadcast on 22 August 1964 attracted only 20,000 viewers, less than half the crowd at Anfield as Liverpool beat Arsenal 2–0. First ever *MOTD* goal is scored by Roger Hunt.

◀ 1966. Promoted to regular Saturday-night slot following success of the BBC's World Cup coverage.

◀ 1980–82. *MOTD* yo-yoed between Saturday night and Sunday afternoon as ITV muscled in on the BBC monopoly.

◀ 1983. Live deal agreed with ITV, but a strike left screens football-free. Two years later *MOTD* lost league games for seven years to ITV.

◀ 1992. Deal with Sky returned league action to *MOTD*. A nine-year run is ended on 19 May 2001.

Savo's Day

AC Milan 4 Barcelona 0, 1994

THE 1994 EUROPEAN CUP FINAL brought together two genuine heavyweights. Barcelona had won the tournament two years before, and Milan didn't fancy becoming the first team to lose consecutive finals, having lost 1-0 to Marseille in 1993. Both sides had registered 3-0 wins in their semi-final matches, Barcelona against Porto and Milan against Monaco. So both were bullish about their chances. Before the match Barcelona coach Johan Cruyff had told anyone who would listen that his team was superior, and with the gifted Hristo Stoichkov in his ranks he had a right to feel upbeat. But Milan had confidence in their wonderful defence, where Capello used

Marcel Desailly to compensate for the loss of Franco Baresi. In the end it was no contest. Barcelona were not awful, they were simply blown away by some of the most accomplished football ever played. The Italians were compact and organised, and in Dejan Savicevic they had the man for the occasion. While Stoichkov pouted ineffectually, Savicevic ran rings around Ronald Koeman and the Barcelona defence, making two first-half goals for Daniele Massaro and adding an outrageous third. Desailly scored a fourth before the hour, and the game was over.

SCORERS: Massaro 2, Savicevic, Desailly
EVENT: European Cup Final, 18 May 1994, Athens

AC MILAN		BARCELONA	
(Man: Fabio Capello)		(Man: Johann Cruyff)	
1 Rossi	9 Massaro	1 Zubizarreta	9 Sergi
2 Tassotti	10 Savicevic	2 Ferrer	10 Stoichkov
3 Maldini	11 Desailly	3 Koeman	11 Romario
4 Albertini		4 Nadal	
5 Galli		5 Berguiristan	
6 Panucci		6 Bakero	
7 Donadoni		7 Guardiola	
8 Boban		8 Amor	

Savicevic gets a hug after scoring Milan's third.

◄)) Desailly had won the European Cup with Marseille the year before, but the French club were later stripped of their title.

◄)) Milan returned to the final the following year, but Savicevic was left out. A late Patrick Kluivert goal saw Ajax rob their title.

◄)) Savicevic was a memeber of the Red Star Belgrade team that won a sterile 1991 final on penalties.

◄)) The third goal was outstanding, Savicevic lobbing Zubizarreta from close to the touchline.

◄)) Cruyff set about rebuilding his team the following season, off-loading Koeman and Zubizarreta among others.

Schiaffino, Juan

Uruguay

THE FIRST POST-WAR WORLD CUP, held in Brazil in 1950, saw the re-emergence of Uruguay as a powerful force. Built around a solid defence with an excellent goalkeeper in Maspoli, this attritional side wore down their opponents to claim the trophy. What creative spark they had came from inside-forward Schiaffino and the lively winger, Ghiggia. Fittingly these two scored the goals against Brazil that clinched the Cup.

Four years later Ghiggia had 'become' Italian, but Schiaffino remained as the main playmaker. Gaunt to the point of being emaciated, his physique concealed a rare determination and supple strength. An inventive passer and fine dribbler, Schiaffino was the orchestrator of Uruguay's finest displays at the 1954 World Cup, where the *Azzurri* proved too good for Scotland (7-0) and England (4-2), but bowed out 4-2 to Hungary in one of the classic semi-finals. That Juan Alberto Schiaffino stood tall against Hidegkuti, Czibor and the rest is testimony to his talent. His displays led AC Milan to invest in the talented Uruguayan. And it was money well spent as they won three of the next five Italian championships, and reached the 1958 European Cup final, where they went down narrowly to Real Madrid.

VITAL STATISTICS

Place of Birth: Montevideo, Uruguay

Date of Birth: 28 July 1925

Died: n/a   Caps: 22 (for Uruguay); 4 (for Italy)

Goals (International): 12

Clubs: Penarol, AC Milan, Roma

Appearances: Club (for Serie A): 188

Goals: Club (for Serie A): 50

Trophies: WorC 1950; SA 1955, 1957, 1959

Schiaffino (bottom row, second from left) with the rest of the 1950 World Cup winning squad.

LEGEND RATING

Achievement	7
Skill	9
Teamwork	8
Passion	8
Personality	6
Overall Legend Rating	**38**

🔾 Though Uruguayan, Schiaffino won four caps as a nationalised Italian.

🔾 He later managed Penarol and, briefly, the Uruguayan national team.

🔾 He scored the equaliser in the 1950 World Cup's deciding match against Brazil. He was set up by the brilliant Ghiggia, who scored the winner himself.

🔾 Schiaffino played in the 1958 European Cup final for Milan against the mighty Real Madrid, scoring in a 3-2 defeat.

🔾 AC Milan smashed the world-record transfer fee to land Schiaffino, paying a staggering £72,000.

Schmeichel, Peter

Manchester United, Denmark

OF ALL SIR ALEX FERGUSON'S signings as a manager, few were as shrewd as his capture in 1991 of goalkeeping giant Peter Schmeichel. (Knowing what they know now Brondby would surely have charged and received 30 times the £500,000 fee they asked United to cough up for the great Dane.) A giant presence between the sticks, Schmeichel's arrival provided a defensive platform that launched United on a decade of dominance. Though famous for bellowing vocal 'encouragement' to his team-mates – outbursts to match even the hair-drying performances of his manager – he was far more than just a big gob. His starfish presence shrank the goal for any onrushing forward and made him the best one-on-one keeper in the world (some would say of all time), while his last-gasp charges into the opposing penalty area started a trend and brought him a European goal. The burdens of United's year-round schedule saw him depart at the top, weeks after winning the treble, but retirement was a long way off for this enthusiastic fitness fanatic. A surprise return to the Premiership has seen him past his best at Aston Villa, but the void left by his departure at Old Trafford has never been truly filled. The sight of him at Maine Road in 2002/03 was a strange one for United fans. He finally retired in May 2003.

VITAL STATISTICS

Place of Birth: Gladsaxe, Denmark

Date of Birth: 18 November 1963

Died: n/a Caps: 122 (Denmark) Goals (International): 2

Clubs: Hidvovre IF, Brondby, Manchester United, Sporting Lisbon, Aston Villa, Manchester City

Appearances: Club (League): 587 Goals: Club (League): 9

Trophies: DLT 1987, 1988, 1990, 1991; LT 1993, 1994, 1996, 1997, 1999; FAC 1994, 1996, 1999; EC 1999; EuroC 1992

LEGEND RATING

Achievement	9
Skill	9
Teamwork	7
Passion	10
Personality	7
Overall Legend Rating	**42**

- He was a member of the Danish 1992 European Championship team. They won despite being rank outsiders.
- In season 1996/97, after a highly-publicised row at Highbury, Ian Wright accused him of racism.
- He is the only goalkeeper to have scored with two English clubs, Manchester United and Aston Villa.
- 'People say we have the best goalkeeper in the world. I wonder why we didn't bring him.' Danish team-mate Fleming Povlsen lowers Schmeichel's popularity rating at the 1992 European Championships.
- Schmeichel's penalty save from van Basten won the semi-final for Denmark. Povlsen's comments went unrecorded.

Schoen, Helmut

AFTER A MIDDLING CAREER as an inside-forward either side of the war, Helmut Schoen turned to coaching. In 1955 he teamed up with the seasoned German national coach, Sepp Herberger, and served an eight-year apprenticeship at the feet of the master. This period saw the World Cup winning side of 1954 break up, and a new squad emerge, centred around the balding centre forward Uwe Seeler and a dynamic young star by the name of Franz Beckenbauer. It also saw West Germany reaffirm their reputation for durability and resolve. In the 1966 World Cup they gave some typically powerful displays, eventually losing to England in the final and, with the phenomenal

Gerd Müller added to their squad, they showed commendable consistency in reaching the semi-finals in 1970.

The emergence of yet another great player, Gunther Netzer, saw West Germany win the European Championship in 1972; but it was the World Cup this squad really wanted. And sure enough, their time came in 1974. With two world-class full-backs in Vogts and Breitner now in their armoury, West Germany won through to the final where, against expectations, Holland were worn down in true German style, and Schoen was able to retire a happy man.

VITAL STATISTICS

Place of Birth: Dresden, Germany

Date of Birth: 15 September 1915

Died: 23 February 1996

Caps: 16 (Germany)

Goals (International): 17

Clubs: As Player: Dresden SC, Hertha berlin, Wiesbaden, Saar; As Manager: Saar, West Germany

Trophies: WorC 1974; EuroC 1972

LEGEND RATING

Achievement	10
Tactical Awareness	8
Motivation	8
Transfer Dealing and Team Selection	8
Personality	6
Overall Legend Rating	**40**

◁ The German penchant for diving forwards seemed to start under Schoen. Helmut Haller was a proficient early exponent, and Bernd Holzenbein's antics won penalties in the semi-final and final in 1974.

◁ In 1966 Schoen received some criticism for playing Beckenbauer in midfield instead of at the back. By 1970 'Der Kaiser' was *in situ* as the greatest attacking central defender of them all.

◁ Schoen accommodated the explosive Müller in 1970 by moving Seeler back into midfield, where his wiles compensated for his diminishing speed.

◁ West Germany only narrowly qualified for the 1970 tournament, a last-gasp win over Scotland seeing them home.

Scholes, Paul

Manchester United, England

DESPITE UNITED'S big money signings of recent seasons, a key reason for their success has been the ability to spot and nurture young English talent. Whilst Beckham has grabbed the lion's share of off-the-field attention, none can doubt the huge contribution of a local Salford lad.

Scholes' great asset is his versatility. A ball-winning midfielder, his willingness to roll up his sleeves has been the chief reason why aesthetes like Cantona and Beckham found room to breathe. His ability to take up and prosecute goalscoring positions has also produced a goals-to-games ratio that many Premiership strikers struggle to emulate.

Scholes has suffered in the 2000/1 and 2001/2 seasons from Ferguson's willingness to accommodate expensive imports, which marginalised him with less familiar roles. United's trophy-less 2001/2 was not a coincidence.

For England, he is one of the first names on the team-sheet. His performance against Argentina at the 2002 World Cup finals was one of the finest by any player in the tournament. But it is as the embodiment of Old Trafford's Nineties' success that he will be remembered in years to come, destined to be mentioned by United fans for years to come in the same breath as Charlton and Stiles.

VITAL STATISTICS

Place of Birth: Salford, England
Date of Birth: 16 November 1974
Died: n/a Caps: 54 (England) Goals (International): 13
Clubs: Manchester United
Appearances: Club (All Matches): 371
Goals: Club (All Matches): 101
Trophies: LT 1996, 1997, 1999, 2000, 2001, 2003; FAC 1996, 1999; EC 1999

LEGEND RATING

Achievement 8
Skill 7
Passion & Commitment 9
Inspiration 8
Personality 4

Overall Legend Rating 36

- First season 95/96 – makes immediate impact with 14 goals in 18 games.
- 1999 – scores in FA Cup Final victory over Newcastle, thus winning a second double at 24.
- Biggest disappointment – suspended for 1999 Champions League Final.
- 1999 – scores hat-trick for England in World Cup qualifier v Poland.
- Scholes made his England debut on his home ground, appearing in 1997 as a substitute v South Africa at Old Trafford. He has never started on the bench since.

Scifo, Enzo

Belgium

BELGIUM'S MOST STYLISH modern player was in fact born of Italian parents, and was the subject of interest by the Azzurri's scouts before finally settling for Belgian citizenship. A boy wonder, he debuted for Anderlecht at 17 and won full international caps while still a teenager. Belgium's gain became more apparent as Scifo went on to lead their midfield in four World Cups from 1986–98. Even with Scifo, though, the Red Devils were never more than bridesmaids, their best performance being a surprise semi-final appearance in 1986.

Scifo's obvious talents made a move inevitable and a transfer to Internazionale ended his five-year spell in Belgium. Unhappy in Milan, he later enjoyed a couple of spells in French football before a better spell in Italy with Torino brought a rare trophy, the Italian Cup. Things came full circle in 1998 with a return to his first major club, Anderlecht. Scifo as club footballer will not be remembered, but as the most talented member of a succession of good, if not exceptional, Belgian sides, he deserves his place in European football history.

VITAL STATISTICS

Place of Birth: Le Louvierre, Belgium

Date of Birth: 19 February 1966

Died: n/a   Caps: 84 (Belgium)

Goals (International): 14

Clubs: Anderlecht, Inter Milan, Bordeaux, Auxerre, Torino, Monaco

Trophies: BLT 1985, 1986, 1987; FLT 1997

LEGEND RATING

Achievement	5
Skill	9
Teamwork	8
Passion	7
Personality	6
Overall Legend Rating	**35**

- Although a teenage prodigy, Scifo only won one trophy after the age of 21.
- Best moment? Scoring one of the penalties as Belgium beat Spain to win a 1986 World Cup semi-final place.
- Scifo nearly retired at 23 after his experiences at Milan, but was persuaded to reconsider by Auxerre manager Guy Roux.
- A dead-ball specialist, Scifo scored a memorable free kick against Paraguay in the 1986 World Cup – only to realise it was indirect.
- Scifo is one of only a handful of players to have played in four World Cup Finals' tournaments.

Scottish Goalies

SCOTTISH GOALKEEPERS are not usually treated with as much respect as they deserve – an old footballing cliché. But clichés, whilst overused, are usually born out of fact. And the fact, in this instance, is that Scotland, particularly in the last 40 years, has not been well served for goalkeepers. Many times in their history they have had a team the equal of England's, but without an international-class goalkeeper, never mind truly great performers such as Banks and Shilton.

Forget the performances of Frank Haffey in 1961 and Stewart Kennedy in 1975; they were one-off bad games by two poor goalkeepers who never played again for Scotland. The real issue is selection. The sheer number of caps given to Alan Rough (53) and Jim Leighton (91) is mind-boggling. Rough, a decent shot-stopper but ordinary all-round goalkeeper kept out David Harvey, the excellent Leeds goalkeeper. Leighton, occasionally inspired but more often indecisive and nervy, won more than twice as many caps as Andy Goram. Outspoken and controversial Goram may have been, but he was a far better goalkeeper than Leighton.

'Two Andy Gorams, there's only two Andy Gorams,'

Kilmarnock fans after Goram was diagnosed with mild schizophrenia

Jim Leighton's gaps in ability were nothing compared to those in his top set.

↙ Haffey, in his second match, conceded nine goals in an avalanche at Wembley – odd, it had taken a Bobby Charlton penalty to beat him in his first game.

↙ Kennedy's performance against England in a 5-1 defeat at Wembley made him a figure of fun for years. He was a bag of nerves and was discarded afterwards.

↙ Leighton played in Alex Ferguson's excellent Aberdeen team in the 1980s. He briefly re-joined Ferguson at Manchester United, but left in acrimonious circumstances after being dropped for the Cup final replay. They are still not on speaking terms.

↙ Scotland's current custodian, Neil Sullivan is an excellent goalkeeper. He's a Londoner.

Seaman, David

DAVID SEAMAN cost Arsenal £1.3 m from QPR in 1990. Perhaps not a bargain on the same scale as Alex Ferguson's swoop for Peter Schmeichel, but not a bad bit of business. Since joining the Gunners Seaman has helped the club to a succession of trophies, including League and Cup doubles in 1998 and 2002.

A usually reliable keeper, Seaman has been harshly pilloried for a couple of high-profile errors; in the 1995 European Cup Winners' Cup final he was lobbed by Real Zaragoza's Nayim from the half-way line and, against Germany in a World Cup qualifier in 2000, he was beaten from 35 yards by a Dietmar Hamann free-kick. But those who criticise him for this conveniently forget the countless hours of impeccable service he has given both Arsenal and England. Seaman has been England's number one for most of the last 10 years, a period in which only Tim Flowers and Nigel Martyn have seriously threatened to displace him. Seaman was outstanding at Euro 96, France 98 and the 2002 World Cup Finals despite his over-publicised mistake against Brazil. His fantastic, last-minute save in the 2003 FA Cup semi-final was the perfect riposte to critics who thought he was past his best.

VITAL STATISTICS

Place of Birth: Rotherham, England
Date of Birth: 19 September 1963
Died: n/a Caps: 75 (England) Goals (International): 0
Clubs: Peterborough United, Birmingham, Queens Park Rangers, Arsenal
Appearances: Club (League): 711
Goals: Club (League): 0
Trophies: LT 1991, 1998, 2002; FAC 1993, 1998, 2002; LC 1993; CWC 1994

LEGEND RATING

Achievement	8
Skill	8
Teamwork	7
Passion	7
Personality	7
Overall Legend Rating	**37**

◄ Seaman flirted with professional cricket as a youngster; he was a powerful fast bowler in Yorkshire league cricket.

◄ Not bad in the kitchen, either, Seaman was winner of a celebrity *Ready Steady Cook* programme in 1998.

◄ Seaman's reputation as a good penalty saver didn't help England in Euro 96 or the 1998 World Cup.

◄ In a 1997 World Cup qualifier against Moldova, Seaman captained England for the first time.

◄ Seaman redeemed himself for the Hamann goal, making a fabulous save moments before England took a 2–1 lead in the return game in Munich.

Seeler, Uwe

PELÉ IS ONE OF TWO PLAYERS to have scored in four World Cup Finals tournaments. The other is Uwe Seeler, who played and scored in the same four tournaments graced by the great Brazilian. Seeler first appeared for Germany as a precocious teenager in the World Cup of 1958, but by the time the next Finals came around he was the finished article – a powerful, mobile centre forward, two-footed and decent in the air.

In the 1966 World Cup Seeler, a little slower but still a potent goalscorer, led the Germans to the final – and we all know what happened next. Despite their failure in England, Germany stuck with

Seeler for the next tournament in Mexico where, aged 34, he played in a midfield role that allowed Helmut Schoen to accommodate Gerd Müller. The satisfaction of gaining revenge over England was tempered by defeat in a great semi-final against Italy. Seeler won several trophies at club level with Hamburg, mainly a succession of regional championships prior to the formation of the joint Bundesliga in 1964. He was top scorer with 30 in the first season of the new national league, and remains Hamburg's most celebrated star. Even more popular than Kevin Keegan.

VITAL STATISTICS

Place of Birth: Hamburg, West Germany
Date of Birth: 5 November 1936
Died: n/a **Caps:** 72 (West Germany)
Goals (International): 43
Clubs: Hamburg
Appearances: Club (All Matches): 710
Goals: Club (All Matches): 551
Trophies: BLG 1960

LEGEND RATING

Achievement	9
Skill	8
Teamwork	9
Passion	7
Personality	7
Overall Legend Rating	**40**

- Seeler was only 17 when he made his debut for Germany, with relatively few Bundesliga performances behind him.
- His 21 World Cup appearances remained a record until the arrival of Lothar Matthaus.
- Seeler scored 404 goals in 476 league appearances. In total he scored over 500 goals in over 700 games.
- Inter Milan offered the vast sum of £1 m for Seeler in 1961, but still he stayed at Hamburg.
- Seeler scored a hat-trick against reigning Bundesliga champions Borussia Dortmund, as Hamburg won the 1963 German Cup final 3-0.

Shackleton, Len

ENGLAND MANAGERS have traditionally regarded talented individual players with suspicion, often ignoring them in favour of more workaday but malleable players. In recent times Glenn Hoddle and Matt Le Tissier were both victims of this peculiar mindset, while an earlier example is Len Shackleton. A plain-speaking Yorkshireman 'Shack's' blunt observations did not always go down well with managers and administrators, but plain was never an adjective to describe his play. He was the most skilful English player of the 1940s and 1950s. A small inside-forward, he cut swathes through opposing defences with instant ball control and supreme dribbling ability.

Moving to Newcastle in 1946 proved an important step in his career, as his performances at St James's Park made him a crowd favourite. But a clash with management saw him sold to neighbours Sunderland. It is at Roker Park where he will be most fondly remembered. If Shackleton was on form, so were Sunderland. His performances made a struggling First Division side a competent one, and it was probably no fluke that the fading of the great man's powers coincided with the club being relegated in 1957/58. That was to be Shackleton's final season. Sunderland have never found another like him.

VITAL STATISTICS

Place of Birth: Bradford, England

Date of Birth: 3 May 1922

Died: 28 November 2000 Caps: 5 (England)

Goals (International): 0

Clubs: Bradford Park Avenue, Newcastle, Sunderland

Appearances: Club (for Sunderland): 348

Goals: Club (League): 101

Trophies: None

LEGEND RATING

Achievement	5
Skill	9
Teamwork	7
Passion	8
Personality	9
Overall Legend Rating	**38**

- In 1935/36 Shackleton became the shortest-ever English schoolboy international, standing at a Lilliputian 4 ft 0 in.
- He scored six times on his debut for Newcastle in a 13-0 win over Newport.
- In his autobiography, Shackleton headed one chapter 'The Average Director's Knowledge of Football'. The rest of the page was left blank.
- The British transfer record was broken twice to buy Shackleton.
- Newcastle paid Huddersfield £13,000 in 1946, receiving over £20,000 from Sunderland sixteen months later.
- His five England caps are a scandalous under-use of his talent. Paul Mariner won 35.

Shankly, Bill

AFTER A PLAYING CAREER severely curtailed by the war, in which the highlight was an FA Cup winner's medal with Preston in 1938, Shankly entered football management with Carlisle, and started on his road to destiny. The apprenticeship was long and unglamorous; several years in the lower divisions with unfashionable clubs gave no indication of what was to come. Shankly seemed an odd choice for a struggling Liverpool in 1959, and their lean spell continued until 1964 when a league title finally came their way for the first time in 17 years. A further two championships, two FA Cups and a UEFA Cup followed before Shankly's retirement in 1974.

His contribution to Liverpool could never be measured in trophies alone, though. The wisecracking Scot laid the foundations of the 'boot-room' dynasty at Anfield, a think-tank of ideas and tactics that was to serve Liverpool well for 20 years. The continuity of playing style and management, and the philosophy of self-belief that characterised the club across that time were Shankly's legacy.

VITAL STATISTICS

Place of Birth: Glenbuck, Ayrshire, Scotland

Date of Birth: 2 September 1913

Died: 28 September 1981

Caps: 5 (Scotland) Goals (International): 0

Clubs: As Player: Carlisle United, Preston North End; As Manager: Carlisle United, Grimsby Town, Workington, Huddersfield Town, Liverpool

Trophies: LT 1964, 1966, 1973; FAC 1965, 1974; UEFAC 1973

LEGEND RATING

Achievement	9
Tactical Awareness	9
Motivation	10
Transfer Dealing and Team Selection	9
Personality	9
Overall Legend Rating	**46**

- Liverpool won the title in 1966 using only 14 players.
- Shankly never won the European Cup – the closest he came was a controversial defeat by Inter Milan in the 1965 semi-finals.
- An earthy humorist, Shankly's most famous observation was:

'Football is not a matter of life and death, I can assure you it is much more important than that.'

- 'The socialism I believe in is not really politics. It is a way of living. It is humanity. I believe the only way to live and be truly successful is by collective effort, with everyone working for each other, everyone helping each other, and everyone having a share of the rewards at the end of the day ... it's the way I see football and the way I see life.' Bill Shankly

Shearer, Alan

Blackburn Rovers, Newcastle United, England

NOT ESPECIALLY TALL, or particularly quick come to that, Alan Shearer is a striker who relies on strength and timing. He is also an exceptionally fine header of the ball – probably the best since Andy Gray – and possesses a thumping right foot.

Shearer emerged as a prodigy at Southampton, where he managed to shine in a mediocre side without making the breakthrough at international level. Then Jack Walker's cash, plus the promise of winning the sort of trophies that were always going to elude him at Southampton, lured him to Blackburn Rovers. At Ewood Park Shearer's scoring rate increased immediately, and his prolific partnership with

Chris Sutton propelled Blackburn to the league title in 1995. Later he struck up a similarly fruitful partnership for England with Teddy Sheringham, a double-act that climaxed with the destruction of Holland at Wembley in the group stages of Euro 96.

That same year Shearer returned to Newcastle, his boyhood team. Since then he has been hampered by a series of injuries, but when fit has continued to score goals. Now retired from international football to protect his body from further punishment, Shearer has been touted as a managerial successor to Bobby Robson at St James's Park. Watch this space....

VITAL STATISTICS

Place of Birth: Newcastle, England
Date of Birth: 13 August 1970
Died: n/a   Caps: 63 (England)
Goals (International): 30
Clubs: Southampton, Blackburn Rovers, Newcastle
Appearances: Club (League): 462
Goals: Club (League): 244
Trophies: LT 1995

LEGEND RATING

Achievement	8
Skill	8
Teamwork	9
Passion	8
Personality	7
Overall Legend Rating	**40**

- Both Shearer's domestic transfers were record fees; his £15 m move to Newcastle was a then world record.
- He scored 37 goals in Blackburn's title-winning season. The following season he got 30 again, becoming the first player to reach the target in three consecutive seasons having scored 30 plus in the previous campaign.
- He was the youngest top-division player to score a hat-trick (17 years, 140 days, for Southampton in 4-2 win over Arsenal).
- He scored in normal time and in the shoot-outs in two of England's recent high-profile matches (against Germany at Euro 96 and Argentina at France 98).
- He is the third-highest England goal scorer.

Sheringham, Teddy

Tottenham Hotspur, Manchester United, England

'OH, TEDDY, TEDDY, he went to Man United and he won f*** all!' In 1998, following Teddy Sheringham's first and unsuccessful season at Old Trafford, this became a popular chant across the country. Having been in and out of the team all year (Yorke and Cole were Fergie's preferred combination), Sheringham, with a Premiership winner's medal already in the bag, came on as a ninth-minute substitute in the 1999 FA Cup final and scored as United beat Newcastle 2-0. The following week he again made a substitute appearance and hit the equaliser in the unforgettable 2-1 triumph over Bayern Munich. From 'f*** all' to a hat-trick of medals in just 12 months.

Recognition for Sheringham came relatively late. Regarded as a journeyman at Millwall and Nottingham Forest, he blossomed at Spurs, forming a deadly combination with Jurgen Klinsmann. Accusing Spurs of lacking ambition he then left for United, but returned to his spiritual home for a swansong in 2001, immediately adding another dimension to an otherwise prosaic side. Just as he had at club level with Klinsmann, Sheringham struck up an instinctive rapport with Alan Shearer at international level. The two were an awesome pairing, inspiring England to the semi-finals of Euro 96.

VITAL STATISTICS

Place of Birth: Highams Park, England

Date of Birth: 2 April 1966

Died: n/a Caps: 45 (England) Goals (International): 11

Clubs: Millwall, Aldershot, Nottingham Forest, Tottenham, Manchester United

Appearances: Club (League): 604

Goals: Club (League): 234

Trophies: LT 1999, 2000, 2001; FAC 1999; EC 1999

1999. Sheringham tries the European Cup for size.

LEGEND RATING

Achievement	9
Skill	8
Teamwork	8
Passion	7
Personality	7
Overall Legend Rating	**39**

◁ 1999. Scored as a substitute for United in both the FA Cup final (after 90 seconds) and European Cup final.

◁ Repeated the feat in England's vital World Cup qualifier against Greece in 2001, scoring with his first touch to level at 1–1.

◁ Sheringham's finest international performance came at Euro 96 as he and Alan Shearer scored two apiece in the 4-1 destruction of Holland.

◁ Sheringham was voted both PFA and Football Writers' Player of the Year in 2001.

Shevchenko, Andrei

Dynamo Kiev, AC Milan, Ukraine

THE BRIGHTEST STAR in the current Milan team, Shevchenko has a winger's pace coupled with a centre-forward's predatory instincts. A fearsome shot in either foot, often delivered on the run, make him a complete forward. He came to prominence for Dynamo Kiev, where his performances in the shop window of the Champions League made a move inevitable.

The bigger the opposition, the better he played. Shevchenko's displays against Barcelona and Real Madrid earned him rave notices, but it was the Italians and not the Spaniards who broke the bank for him.

Although his own performances have been consistently high, Milan have not found it easy to find the right attacking partner for Shevchenko. He failed to click with either Oliver Bierhoff or George Weah. Not that it really matters. Shevchenko is a natural-born goal scorer, and would probably continue to find the net if Milan partnered him with a one-legged octogenarian.

In 2003, he struck Milan's fifth and decisive penalty to win the European Cup after a dramatic shoot-out.

VITAL STATISTICS

Place of Birth: Dvirkivshchyna, Kiev, Ukraine
Date of Birth: 29 September 1976
Died: n/a   Caps: 46 (Ukraine)
Goals (International): 19
Clubs: Dynamo Kiev, AC Milan
Appearances: Club (League): 229
Goals: Club (League): 127
Trophies: ULT 1995, 1996, 1997, 1998, 1999, EC 2003

LEGEND RATING

Achievement	7
Skill	9
Teamwork	8
Passion	8
Personality	6
Overall Legend Rating	**38**

⏵ In 1986, Shevchenko started with the Dynamo Kiev junior training scheme aged 10. Five years later, he was evacuated to avoid the radioactive fallout from Chernobyl.

⏵ His value to Milan was emphasised when club president Berlusconi awarded Shevchenko a four-year contract worth a reported £64,000 per week.

⏵ He is often compared with great Russian strikers Blokhin and Belanov. All three are great finishers, although Shevchenko is probably the most complete.

⏵ Shevchenko was rumoured to be following Milan team-mate Rebrov to Spurs in 2001, but the London club were unable to afford them both.

Shilton, Peter

Nottingham Forest, Southampton, England

PETER SHILTON CONTINUED PLAYING for so long that it seemed the only thing likely to persuade him to hang up his gloves was the arrival of his bus pass in the post. Having made his debut for Leicester in 1966, aged 17, he was still playing league football aged 47.

His best spell as a club footballer was in Brian Clough's Nottingham Forest that won the European Cup twice, but he also played in the Southampton side that contained five England captains – himself, Keegan, Watson, Mills and Channon.

For a number of years Shilton played second fiddle or alternated with Ray Clemence in the England goal; at times it seemed that everyone bar the managers could see he was the better of the two men. He later made the number one jersey his own, and though he went on to record a record number of England caps (125), one wonders what tally he may have reached if his international managers had been more decisive. Shilton played in three World Cups, conceding only one goal in the 1982 tournament as England were eliminated without losing. Once he had ironed out early gremlins in his technique, Shilton became the complete goalkeeper. A great shot-stopper, although perhaps not in the same class as Gordon Banks, dominant in the area, and fast off his line.

VITAL STATISTICS

Place of Birth: Leicester, England
Date of Birth: 18 September 1949
Died: n/a Caps: 125 (England) Goals (International): 0
Clubs: Leicester City, Stoke City, Nottingham Forest, Southampton, Derby County, Plymouth Argyle, Wimbledon, Bolton Wanderers, Coventry City, West Ham, Leyton Orient
Appearances: Club (League): 1005
Goals: Club (League): 0
Trophies: EC 1979, 1980 LT 1978; LC 1979

LEGEND RATING

Achievement	9
Skill	9
Teamwork	8
Passion	9
Personality	7
Overall Legend Rating	**42**

◁▷ Shilton played his 1,000th league game for Leyton Orient against Brighton. Fittingly, he kept a clean sheet.

◁▷ Surprisingly, he only ever played in one FA Cup final, finishing on the losing side with Leicester in 1969.

◁▷ The £325,000 Stoke paid Leicester for Shilton was a world record for a goalkeeper.

◁▷ Shilton filed for bankruptcy in the 1990s, amid reports he had accrued heavy gambling debts.

◁▷ Shilton received an MBE in 1986, and an OBE in 1991.

Shirts Off

Charity Shield, 1974

THE CHARITY SHIELD is invariably billed as the season's 'curtain raiser'. In truth it's usually nothing of the sort; if watching two ring-rusty teams pussyfoot around each other for 90 minutes is raising the curtain then it might be better to keep it drawn. But not all Charity Shield matches are dull. Take 1974 for instance. After an hour of simmering ill-feeling, the flashpoint occurred on the hour. Billy Bremner and Kevin Keegan, neither with the longest of fuses, traded blows at the edge of the penalty area. Their dismissals were inevitable, and the pair compounded their shame by petulantly throwing off their shirts en route to the tunnel. The FA was

particularly sensitive to accusations that it was failing to put its hooligan house in order. These were the dark days of the mid-1970s, and images of Spurs fans rioting in Rotterdam a few weeks earlier were still fresh in the mind. For Bremner and Keegan, Wembley 1974 was the wrong place and the wrong time. The FA felt compelled to act. The fine of £500 each was huge, the 11-week bans bigger still. Scapegoats they certainly were, but Bremner and Keegan had only themselves to blame.

> 'Players must learn that they cannot throw punches at each other.'
>
> FA Secretary Ted Croker after throwing the book

Bremner (left) and Keegan receive the inevitable.

- Niggle was usually in the air with Revie's Leeds, and wounded Merseyside pride at surrendering the title to them the previous season gave the occasion an extra dash of spice.
- Bremner and Keegan became the first British players to be sent off at Wembley. Only Argentina's Rattin had enjoyed the dubious honour before them.
- The Charity Shield was televised live for the first time that year, a fact that hardly lessened the outrage.
- Opportunistic MPs had a field day. Some called for a life ban and a civil prosecution, but they probably wanted to hang shoplifters as well.

Showboating

THE NEW YORK COSMOS sparked a major international influx of world stars into American football when they brought the game's greatest player Pelé to the States in 1975. The Brazilian star's mere presence brought unprecedented attention to the North American Soccer League and over the next few years a string of stars ended their playing careers playing for the Cosmos.

The former West German World Cup winning captain Franz Beckenbauer joined Pelé in the same line-up, as did the silky skilled former Brazilian skipper Carlos Alberto. The trio helped establish the Cosmos as a major force in the league but their main contribution was to ignite widespread interest in the game. It worked to such a degree that 77,691 fans packed the Giants stadium to watch a playoff game against Fort Lauderdale in 1977. The Cosmos went on to win the Championship three years out of four up to 1980 but eventually the bubble burst and in 1984 the NASL folded due to spiralling costs and dwindling attendances.

Key Players

Carlos Alberto (D) Franz Beckenbauer (D) Giorgin Chinaglia (F)
Johan Neeskens (M) Pelé (F)

Pelé receives deification after his final game.

◁⊳ The New York Cosmos were established in 1971. They won the North American Soccer League championship for the first time the following season.

◁⊳ NY Cosmos executive on Franz Beckenbauer: 'Tell the Kraut to get his ass up front. We don't pay a million for a guy to hang around in defense.'

◁⊳ It cost the Cosmos $4.5 m to bring Pelé out of retirement to play for them in 1975.

◁⊳ Ex-Coventry and Derby midfielder Steve Hunt played for the Cosmos in two spells in 1977 and 1982.

Simply The Best

Brazil 4 Italy 1, 1970

IT WAS THE GAME that settled the argument as to the greatest-ever team. Brazil had saved the best until last, perpetuating a philosophy that simply believed in scoring more goals than the opposition.

Their opponents were hardly makeweights. A team with Facchetti at its defensive heart and Luigi Riva a spearhead had seen off Germany in an epic semi-final – but they had the misfortune to run into a forward line with every great player at his peak.

The main surprise was that after 65 minutes, the score was still 1-1. Pelé's opener inside 20 minutes appeared to set up a procession, but the Achilles' heel that was Brazil's defence handed Boninsegna

an equaliser before half-time. Once Gerson had restored the lead with a trademark long-range strike though, normal service was resumed. The fourth goal was pure Brazil, Carlos Alberto joyously lashing home after a gorgeous build-up saw the ball rolled languidly into his path by Pelé. It remains one of the World Cup's most repeated goals – a glorious souvenir of a peerless team.

SCORERS: **Brazil:** Pelé, Gerson, Jairzinho, Carlos Alberto
  Italy: Boninsegna
EVENT: World Cup Final, Estadio Azteca, Mexico City, 21 June 1970

BRAZIL (Man: Mario Zagallo)		ITALY (Man: Feruccio Valcareggi)	
1 Felix	8 Jairzinho	1 Albertosi	8 Mazzola
2 Carlos Alberto	9 Tostao	2 Cera	9 de Sisti
3 Brito	10 Pelé	3 Burgnich	10 Boninsenga
4 Piazza	11 Rivelino	4 Bertini (Juliano)	(Rivera)
5 Everaldo		5 Rosato	11 Riva
6 Clodoaldo		6 Facchetti	
7 Gerson		7 Domenghini	

The match that won Brazil their third World Cup saw them awarded the Jules Rimet trophy outright.

Jairzinho's goal meant he scored in all six games of the tournament.

Mario Zagallo was the first man to win the World Cup as both a player and a coach.

Zagallo coached Brazil again at France 98. They failed to repeat the performance, falling ingloriously to the hosts in the final.

Pelé's opener was Brazil's 100th goal in the World Cup Finals.

Small Nation's Pride

The Uruguayan Dream Team

ADMIT IT, you're probably thinking to yourself, what are Uruguay doing here? Actually, they're here because they deserve to be.

It's easily forgotten, but Uruguay have won two World Cups (that's one more than England), and for 40 years they proved themselves to be a more powerful footballing force than Brazil.

We have gone against conventional Uruguayan tactics and picked a team packed with creative players. The wide players, Ghiggia and Borges, were both fast and direct, and Poyet's eye for goal is well-known in England. Schiaffino was Uruguay's greatest player, best remembered for his majestic performance in Uruguay's

narrow defeat to Hungary in the 1954 World Cup semi-final. Francescoli was a genius striker, good enough for Zinedine Zidane to name one of his sons after him, and Scarone, centre-forward in 1930 World Cup winning team, remains Uruguay's leading international scorer. But don't go thinking we've gone soft. There are some good old-fashioned thugs in this team as well. Nasazzi was a frightening defender, and his colleague in the 1930s, Andrade, was a hard nut too. Varela was another physical presence, as was the forceful, Santamaria.

Manager: Juan Lopez

3-4-1-2

Roque Maspoli (50s)

Jose Nasazzi (C) (30s) Obdulio Varela (50s) Jose Santamaria (50s)

Alcide Ghiggia (50s) Jose Andrade (30s)
Gus Poyet (90s) Carlos Borges (50s)

Juan Schiaffino (50s)

Hector Scarone (30s) Enzo Francescoli (80s)

Subs: Ladislao Mazurkiewicz (G) (60s) Paolo Montero (D) (90s)
Alvaro Recoba (M/F) (90s) Pedro Rocha (M/F) (60s) Omar Miguez (F) (50s)

The 1930 World Cup winning team.

↰ Ghiggia was outstanding in the 1950 World Cup, scoring the winning goal in the decisive match against Brazil.

↰ Four years later, Ghiggia was replaced by Abbadie on the right, and the explosive Carlos Borges was drafted in on the left. With

Schiaffino pulling the strings, Uruguay's wingers electrified the tournament once again.

↰ Gus Poyet has been one of the Premiership's most successful and popular imports in recent years. His goal, a volley with both feet

off the ground, at the start of the 2000/2001 season was one of the best in recent years.

Socceroos

AUSTRALIA'S ONLY World Cup Finals appearance so far came in West Germany in 1974. Their style was rugged and uncompromising, but their supreme all-round fitness took them to the finals in good spirits despite a cruel draw which pitched them against the hosts West Germany as well as East Germany and Chile. They were given little chance of progressing to the second phase, but in their opening encounter with East Germany the Socceroos more than matched their opponents until an unfortunate Col Curran own goal shortly after half-time. The East Germans added a second shortly afterwards which left the Socceroos needing a point against the tournament favourites,

West Germany, to stand any chance or progressing to the next phase. Two first-half goals underlined the Germans' title credentials and Australia had to work hard to keep the score-line to 3-0. That left a final game against Chile with Australia still looking for their first World Cup Finals goal. That looked likely for long periods until Ray Richards was sent off seven minutes from time but the Socceroos held on to a 0-0 draw to secure their first World Cup point.

'Great players don't make great teams, great people do. There is no question that we qualified in 1974 because I selected players with great character. My greatest strength was off the field.'

Rale Rasic, manager, Australia, 1974

◁ Due to an oversight by the referee, midfielder Ray Richards was allowed to play on for four minutes despite earning a second booking in the rain-soaked match against Chile. The error was finally spotted by a linesman.

◁ The Australia National Soccer League was set up following the Socceroos' 1974 World Cup appearance but with star players constantly leaving to play abroad, the league has struggled.

◁ Former England coach Terry Venables took the Socceroos to within one game of qualification for the 1998 Finals.

◁ February 2003: Australia underlined their status as a footballing nation by beating England 3–1 at Upton Park.

Socrates

SOCRATES' LAST KICK in a Brazilian shirt was missing one of the penalties in the quarter-final shoot-out defeat by France at the 1986 World Cup. It was a sad end for the tall, bearded midfielder who, much as he did four years earlier in Spain, had illuminated the tournament with his repertoire of impudent, lazy skills. No fitness fanatic – he smoked 20 cigarettes a day – Socrates appeared to stroll through games, spraying passes and shots like a merchant dispensing largesse to the less fortunate. The 1982 midfield of Socrates, Zico, Falcao and Cerezo would have won most World Cups, but the strikers were uncharacteristically lightweight for a Brazilian

side. Four years later a generally lethargic Brazilian team failed to do themselves justice, and France's penalty win was deserved. Socrates played the majority of his club football for various sides in Brazil, apart from a disastrous season at Fiorentina in 1984 where the physical demands of European club football and the alien lifestyle quickly saw him scurry home. Socrates has remained an opinionated and intelligent observer of the game, and in recent years has been a fierce critic of the officials running Brazilian football.

VITAL STATISTICS

Place of Birth:	Brazil
Date of Birth:	19 February 1954
Died: n/a	Caps: 60 (Brazil)

Goals (International): 22

Clubs: Botafogo, Corinthians, Fiorentina, Flamengo, Santos

Appearances: Club (For Corinthians): 302

Goals: Club (For Corinthians): 166

LEGEND RATING

Achievement	7
Skill	10
Teamwork	8
Passion	8
Personality	9
Overall Legend Rating	**42**

◁᷄ Socrates' goal against the USSR in 1982 was a classic, sidestepping two tackles and thrashing a missile of a shot into the top corner.

◁᷄ In the 1986 World Cup Socrates scored with a cheeky penalty, without a run-up, against Poland. When he tried a repeat in the quarter-final shoot-out, French goalkeeper Bats saved easily.

◁᷄ Known as 'The Doctor' due to his medical training, it is ironic that Socrates was a high-profile sporting smoker.

◁᷄ Socrates younger brother played for Brazil under the pseudonym Rai.

◁᷄ No boy-wonder, Socrates was 25 before he played for Brazil.

Somersaults and Salsa

The Fine Art of Goal Celebration

OLD BLACK-AND-WHITE newsreel shots of footballers scoring goals and trotting, stony-faced back to the centre circle seem to come from a different game. No kissing, no cuddling, no diving, no fist-clenching, no ripping the shirt off, no gymnastics, no mime, no tableaux vivants. How dull it all must have been.

However, the amateur dramatics of the modern goal scorer have become tedious. The obligatory cupping of the ear to mock a silenced home crowd, the plunge to the knees by the corner flag – no wonder referees were instructed to curb the worst excesses. Whole teams were charging towards the scorer, engulfing them in scrums of adulation.

Who knows where it all started? Charlie George lying flat out on the Wembley turf after firing in the winner against Liverpool? Others have refined and re-defined the art: Hugo Sanchez, Real Madrid's great Mexican, with his trademark somersault; Klinsmann plunging to the ground in self-mockery of his reputation as a diver; Roger Milla and Lee Sharpe posing around the corner flag. Entire teams got involved in complicated routines, the most bizarre being Chelsea's reproduction of a classical painting following a strike by Roberto di Matteo. Oh dear.

'I made a two-fingered gesture towards the fans to show that I had scored twice. It must have been misinterpreted.'

Paul Peschisolido

Lee Sharpe: 'Tonight Matthew, I'm going to be Elvis'.

- ◁ The most athletic? Peter Beagrie, the much-travelled winger, has treated many a ground to a somersault worthy of Sanchez.
- ◁ The worst? Has to be the awful baby-cradling pantomime introduced by Brazilian Bebeto at the 1994 World Cup.

- ◁ The silliest? Aylesbury Town, after a cup goal, waddling around on their knees doing the Aylesbury duck.
- ◁ The most irresponsible? Robbie Fowler pretending to snort cocaine off the dead-ball line.

- ◁ The most ill-judged? Not strictly after a goal, but at the end of the 1993 League Cup final, Tony Adams threw goal scorer Steve Morrow over his shoulder. Morrow broke his arm and missed the FA Cup final as a result.

Souness, Graeme

AS A PLAYER Graeme Souness was a manager's dream. Possessed of great vision, passing ability and a tremendous shot, he was also blessed with a steel and aggression that set him apart from other playmakers. The downside was his short fuse, and seeming inability to curb his violent streak.

It was Souness' form in a moderate Middlesbrough side that prompted Liverpool to shell out £325,000 for his signature – a British record that was to last only a month. He later left Anfield for a successful spell in Italy with Sampdoria before returning to Britain as player-manager of Glasgow Rangers. Souness' first season at Rangers saw them win their first Scottish title for nine years. An orgy of success at Ibrox was followed by a fraught period as Liverpool manager where, after some less-than-prudent transfer business, he was eventually forced into tending his resignation (the end came following an embarrassing FA Cup defeat by Bristol City in 1994). After a spell in Portugal as Benfica boss, Souness is now in charge at Blackburn Rovers, with whom he won promotion to the Premiership in 2001.

VITAL STATISTICS

Place of Birth: Edinburgh, Scotland
Date of Birth: 6 May 1953
Died: n/a **Caps:** 54 (Scotland) **Goals (International):** 4
Clubs: As Player: Tottenham Hotspur, Middlesbrough, Liverpool, Sampdoria, Rangers; As Manager: Rangers, Liverpool, Benfica, Blackburn Rovers
Appearances: Club: 528
Goals: Club: 78
Trophies: LT 1979–80, 1982–84; LC 1981–84, (2000); EC 1981, 1984; FAC (1992); SLT (1987, 1989–91)

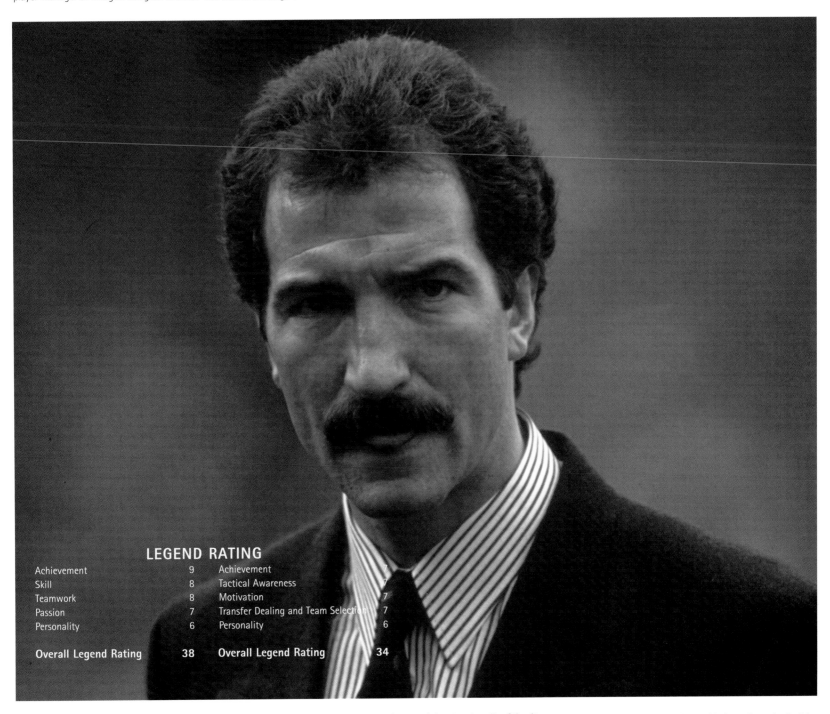

LEGEND RATING

Achievement	9	Achievement	7
Skill	8	Tactical Awareness	7
Teamwork	8	Motivation	7
Passion	7	Transfer Dealing and Team Selection	7
Personality	6	Personality	6
Overall Legend Rating	**38**	**Overall Legend Rating**	**34**

- He signed Paul Stewart from Tottenham with a view to using him as Liverpool's main striker – possibly one of the worst signings ever by a major club.
- Souness was pilloried in Liverpool for his dealings with *The Sun* newspaper, the paper that earned the eternal enmity of the city for their crass coverage of the Hillsborough disaster.
- Souness has recovered impressively from a heart by-pass operation.
- At Rangers Souness reversed a trend by importing major English stars to Scotland, notably Terry Butcher and Trevor Steven.
- Souness also signed Rangers' first Roman Catholic player, former Celtic striker Mo Johnston.

Southall, Neville

Everton, Wales

JUST WHEN YOU THOUGHT he had finally hung up his gloves, Neville Southall had a habit of popping up as stand-in keeper for yet another injury-hit club. What's more, each time he did so he seemed to have put on at least another stone, giving him the unfortunate appearance of a flying pudding. Yet, it is only recently that Southall has emerged as a figure of fun. In his heyday he was arguably the best goalkeeper in the world. His performances made Everton the only team in the 1980s to consistently challenge their rivals from across Stanley Park, and helped make the league title Merseyside's personal property. If Liverpool had enjoyed his services rather than

the erratic Grobbelaar, Anfield's domination of club football would surely have been total. Oddly, despite such a lengthy playing career, Southall was a figure who shunned the camaraderie of his team-mates; after Everton matches he preferred a long, solitary drive home to his Welsh farm to a night on the town with his colleagues. Despite his heroics for Wales, they never qualified for a major tournament. So, like his countrymen Mark Hughes and Ian Rush, he was never afforded an opportunity to validate his reputation at the top level.

VITAL STATISTICS

Place of Birth: Llandudno, Wales

Date of Birth: 16 September 1958

Died: n/a Caps: 92 (Wales) Goals (International): 0

Clubs: Bury, Everton, Port Vale, Southend, Stoke City, Torquay United, Bradford City

Appearances: Club (League): 701

Goals: Club (League): 0

Trophies: LT 1985, 1987; FAC 1984, 1995; CWC 1985

LEGEND RATING

Achievement	7
Skill	8
Teamwork	9
Passion	10
Personality	6
Overall Legend Rating	**40**

◁ᴺ 1990. Fined a week's wages after staging a one-man sit-down protest on the Goodison Park pitch at half-time.

◁ᴺ 1995. Already PFA Footballer of the Year, Southall won Everton the FA Cup with a great Wembley display against Man United.

◁ᴺ 1998. Southall won Torquay's Player of the Year award despite playing in only half their games.

◁ᴺ 2000. Southall played his last Premiership game at the age of 41, pressed into emergency service by Bradford.

◁ᴺ His 92 caps are a Welsh record.

Spend! Spend! Spend!

'AND NOW ON TO THE Pools news...' Words that have become a ritual footnote to Saturday's football results, as coupons up and down the country are shredded in frustration. Strange to think that such a national institution was once illegal. The Pools began on the right side of the law in the 1909/10 season, with the *Racing And Football Outlook* offering five guineas for the correct forecasting of six away wins.

The relationship between the Football League and the pools companies was a stormy one. In 1935, in an attempt to prevent the printing of coupons, the League refused to reveal away teams until the day before kick off. This was quickly abandoned after attendances plummeted. After the war the dominant organisation was Littlewoods, making the Liverpool-based Moores family one of the wealthiest in the country. Their prizes were also the largest; the first six-figure win in 1950/51 could have bought a village, let alone a new house. Meeting 'the man from Littlewoods' became a pipe dream for millions of people every Saturday and, for some, it remains their only connection with the game.

'I'm going to spend, spend, spend!'

Viv Nicholson became a one-woman retail boom after a six-figure Pools win; true to her word, she blew the lot

A man with a tab, Viv Nicholson, a smarmy looking Bruce Forsyth and a fat cheque.

◄ॐ 1959/60. The Football League finally triumphed after a court verdict awarded them copyright of the fixture list. Pools companies were forced to sign a deal guaranteeing the league 0.5% of their gross receipts in return for printing rights.

◄ॐ During the Second World War, the Post Office threatened to withdraw delivery of coupons as they were not essential mail, forcing pools firms to make a charitable donation.

◄ॐ 1973. The Football League doubled its pools income to £23 m in a 10-year deal. Most clubs thought they were selling themselves short.

◄ॐ With the first dividend dwarfed by National Lottery rollovers, the 1990s saw a dramatic reduction in pools companies' income.

Spot-Luck

Brazil 1 France 1, 1986 (aet) (France won 4-3 on penalties)

WOULD PLATINI'S GENIUS carry the day against a talented, but curiously defensive Brazil? The match proved to be a tight affair – technically excellent but with few clear-cut chances. Careca opened the scoring with a fine strike, but Platini, celebrating his 31st birthday, pulled the French level. The game came alive in the last 20 minutes. Two minutes after Zico's entrance as a substitute, Brazil were awarded a dubious penalty. Four years before, Zico had tucked away a penalty in similar circumstances, but history was not to repeat itself – he missed, and the game headed into extra-time.

France were denied an obvious penalty when Bellone was upended by the goalkeeper, and Socrates, of all people, spurned an easy chance a minute later. And so to penalties. Socrates attempted a repeat of his nonchalant chip earlier in the tournament, but succeeded only in effecting a back-pass to Joel Bats. Platini, with a chance to all but seal the result, then blazed high over the bar, but following a miss by Julio Cesar, his midfield colleague Luis Fernandez struck the winning penalty for France.

SCORERS: Brazil: Careca, 17
France: Platini, 41
EVENT: World Cup quarter-final, Guadalajara, 21 June 1986

BRAZIL
(Man: Tele Santana)
1 Carlos   8 Alemao
2 Josimar   9 Socrates
3 Branco   10 Careca
4 Elzo   11 Müller
5 Julio Cesar
6 Edinho
7 Junior

FRANCE
(Man: Henri Michel)
1 Bats   8 Tigana
2 Amoros   9 Stopyra
3 Tusseau   10 Platini
4 Fernandez   11 Rocheteau
5 Bossis
6 Battiston
7 Giresse

Zico (right) wriggles free from Fernandez.

◁ Penalty Shoot-out: Brazil: Socrates (missed), Alemao, Zico, Branco, Julio Cesar (missed)
France: Stopyra, Amoros, Bellone, Platini (missed), Fernandez.
◁ France lost to Germany in the semi-final (again), and their team broke up after the tournament. They would win the next Finals tournament in which they competed, in 1998.
◁ Socrates and Zico never played for Brazil again – the end of an era.
◁ Careca vied with Gary Lineker as the best striker in the tournament. Brazil might have achieved more if they had found him a decent partner.

376

DESPITE SHEFFIELD'S SIZE, it has never produced great sides with the regularity of its Northern neighbours. The city remains without a League title since 1930 (in United's case since the 19th century). This is a team high on talented individuals but low on silverware.

Springett is the best keeper by a mile. An England understudy to Gordon Banks, he would walk into the current international side. The defence is all Wednesday, picked mostly from their decent top-flight teams of the Eighties and Nineties. Walker and Swan are classy centre-halves, England left-back Ernie Blenkinsop was one of the star turns of Wednesday's most successful era.

Despite his international reputation as a man out of his depth, Palmer's holding and tackling skills can release some sublime midfield talent, particularly from Tony Currie, one of the Seventies mavericks whose ability was underused by Ramsey and Revie. Sheridan is another whose talent shone only fitfully but his ability to unlock a defence with a killer pass will serve his attackers royally.

Dooley stars up front. Johnson would be a willing workhorse and provider but the Wednesday man would fire the bullets. But for the leg amputation that ended his career prematurely, he would have been a centre-forward mentioned in the same breath as Lofthouse.

Manager: Robert Brown

4-4-2

Ron Springett (60s)

Mel Sterland (80s) Des Walker (80s)
Peter Swan (60s) Ernest Blenkinsop (20s/30s)

John Sheridan (80s) Carlton Palmer (80s)
Tony Currie (70s) Jim McAlliog (60s)

Harry Johnson (20s) Derek Dooley (50s)

Subs: Alan Kelly (90s); Joe Shaw (50s/60s); Nigel Worthington (90s); Michael Tonge (00s); Andrew Wilson (1900s/10s)

Apr 3, 1993: Alan Cork (left) and Carlton Palmer in the FA Cup semi-final.

◁ Robert Brown as manager is a largely forgotten figure. Overshadowed by Herbert Chapman, he led Wednesday to successive League titles in 1929 and 1930.

◁ Peter Swan earns his place despite being a convicted criminal.

He served an eight-year ban following a match-fixing scandal in the early Sixties.

◁ Andrew Wilson earns his place on the bench as Wednesday's record holder for both goals and appearances.

◁ Jim McAlliog's claim to fame was as scorer of Scotland's winner at Wembley in 1967, a goal which inflicted the World Champions' first defeat since winning the Jules Rimet trophy.

Stein, Jock

JOCK STEIN'S EXPLOITS as a player merit more than a passing mention in the Celtic history books, having won the League and Cup in a five-year career at Parkhead. But it was his feats as manager that ensured his legendary status. Stein broke Rangers' domination of Scottish football in the 1960s, and presided over the most successful period in Celtic's history – a record run of nine consecutive league titles, including two domestic trebles.

Football and this son of a Lanarkshire miner nearly parted company in the early days, as he drifted from Albion Rovers to Llanelli before Celtic gave him his big break. Stein's most memorable accomplishment was bringing the European Cup to Glasgow in 1967 when, against an all-star Inter team, he masterminded a stunning 2-1 victory in Lisbon. In 1978, following a near-fatal car crash and a row over his appointment to the Celtic board, he left the club to take up the job of Scotland manager, where his eight-year tenure brought two successive qualifications for the World Cup. Tragically, Stein was not around to take his team to Mexico in 1986. During Scotland's final, victorious qualifying match against Wales in Cardiff he collapsed on the touchline and died of a heart-attack.

VITAL STATISTICS

Place of Birth: Burnbank, Scotland
Date of Birth: 5 October 1923
Died: 11 September 1985 **Caps:** 0
Goals (International): 0
Clubs: As Player: Albion Rovers, Llanelli, Celtic;
As Manager: Dunfermline, Hibernian, Celtic, Leeds United
Trophies: SLT 1966, 1967, 1968, 1969, 1970, 1971, 1972, 1973, 1974, 1977; SFAC 1961, 1965, 1967, 1969, 1971, 1972, 1974, 1975, 1977; EC 1967

LEGEND RATING

Achievement	10
Tactical Awareness	9
Motivation	9
Transfer Dealing and Team Selection	7
Personality	7
Overall Legend Rating	**42**

- Only one of his 26 managerial honours was not with Celtic (the 1961 Scottish Cup with Dunfermline).
- Stein managed Leeds United in 1978 for just 44 days, the same number as Brian Clough four years earlier.
- He reached the World Cup Finals as Scotland manager in 1982, but lost out to Brazil and the USSR in a strong group.
- Bill Shankly to Stein after Celtic's European Cup final win: 'John, you're immortal.'
- Alex Ferguson took temporary charge of Scotland after Stein's death, but failed to get them through the group stage at Mexico 86.

Stiles, Nobby
Manchester United, England

OF THE MANY IMAGES from 1966, none captures the exultant English mood more than a gap-toothed Nobby Stiles jigging joyfully on the hallowed Wembley turf. Stiles had already created his national persona as a tough-tackling defensive midfielder, and developed seamlessly from an old-fashioned wing-half into the artful dislodger of Sir Alf's famous 'wingless wonders' formation.

And yet it could have been so different. After the first round match against France, during which Stiles had perpetrated a nasty, high tackle in front of the royal box, Ramsey was instructed by the FA to drop him. He refused. The decision was not well received but,

mindful of the player's value to the team, Ramsey stuck to his guns. Thus the stage was set for Stiles' greatest game, the semi-final versus Portugal and a memorable encounter with Eusebio. For all his trophies with Manchester United, including the European Cup also won at Wembley, Stiles' popularity was never higher than during that glorious, unforgettable fortnight in 1966.

VITAL STATISTICS

Place of Birth:	Manchester, England
Date of Birth:	18 May 1942
Died: n/a	Caps: 28 (England)

Goals (International): 1

Clubs: Manchester United, Middlesbrough, Preston North End

Appearances: Club (League: for Manchester United): 311

Goals: Club (League: for Manchester United): 17

Trophies: WorC 1966; LT 1965, 1967; EC 1968

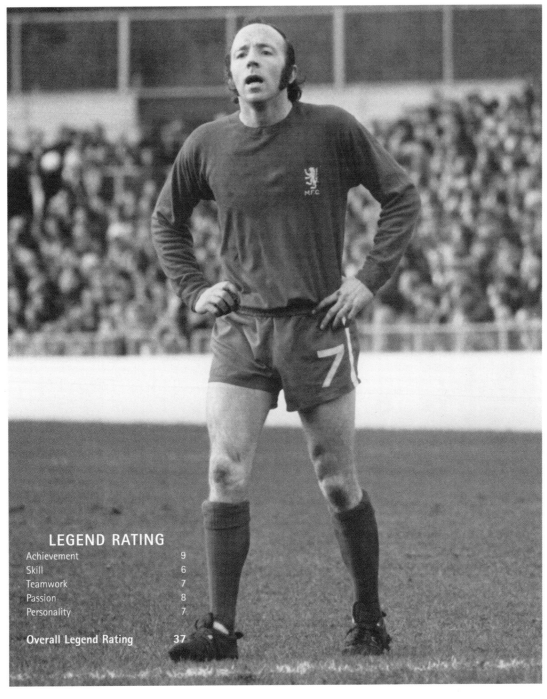

LEGEND RATING

Achievement	9
Skill	6
Teamwork	7
Passion	8
Personality	7
Overall Legend Rating	**37**

◁ Dubbed 'The Assassin' by the Argentine press before Man United's World Club Championship match versus Estudiantes in 1968. A marked man, he was headbutted and unluckily sent off for dissent.

◁ He played for and managed Preston North End. Although promoted to Division Two in 1978, they were relegated three years later.

◁ He was awarded an MBE for services to football.

◁ Stiles' 420 United and England games yielded just 19 goals.

◁ He took over at the Canadian club Vancouver Whitecaps, but management was never his forte.

Stoichkov, Hristo

Barcelona, Bulgaria

ONE OF THE GREAT CHARACTERS of the 1990s, Stoichkov was in the news as much for his fiery outbursts as his brilliant football. Exceptionally quick for a big man, he was hard to dispossess when he got going and packed a vicious left-foot shot. As a youngster he played for CSKA Sofia, where some impressive goalscoring drew the attention of scouts from the big European clubs. A move to Barcelona in 1990, as a replacement for Gary Lineker, brought him copious rewards, including four consecutive Spanish titles, and the European Cup.

Stoichkov arrived at the 1994 World Cup in the USA at the height of his powers, but the Bulgarians were not expected to go far;

except for Stoichkov, their captain Mikhailov, a world-class goalkeeper, and the balding Letchkov in midfield, their team was a collection of European journeymen. But, after surviving a tough group they saw off Mexico on penalties, came from behind to beat Germany, and were unlucky to lose to Italy in an entertaining semi-final. Stoichkov scored in every game except the first and finished as the tournament's joint-top scorer. It proved to be his finest moment. The fire later burned out and he retired in 2000.

VITAL STATISTICS

Place of Birth: Plovdiv, Bulgaria

Date of Birth: 2 August 1966

Died: n/a **Caps:** 83 (Bulgaria) **Goals (International):** 37

Clubs: CSKA Sofia, Barcelona, Parma, Kawisa Reysol, Chicago Fires

Appearances: Club (For Barcelona): 174

Goals: Club (For Barcelona): 83

Trophies: EC 1992; CWC 1997; BLT 1985, 1987, 1989, 1990; PLA 1991, 1992, 1993, 1994

LEGEND RATING

Achievement	8
Skill	10
Teamwork	6
Passion	9
Personality	8
Overall Legend Rating	41

◁ Stoichkov was given a lengthy suspension in his first season at the Nou Camp after stamping on a referee's foot.

◁ He also fell out with manager Johann Cruyff; like Lineker before him he didn't take kindly to being asked to play out wide.

◁ Stoichkov missed the 1985/86 season. He was banned for his part in a riot involving players and spectators at the 1985 Bulgarian Cup final. The league disbanded both clubs for four years.

◁ His goal against Mexico in 1994 summed up his game; running on to a through ball, he took it in his stride and lashed it over the goalkeeper. No frills, just great power and precision.

◁ He was voted European Footballer of the Year in 1994.

Strachan, Gordon

Aberdeen, Manchester United, Scotland

GORDON STRACHAN'S TENACITY while still a player has served him just as well as manager. His career in the dugout saw him rise in 1996 as the people's choice at Coventry, only to depart with his reputation tarnished a few months after the Sky Blues' relegation five years later.

Lesser men may have banked the cash and retired to the golf course. Weeks later, David Jones' misfortune at Southampton created an opening that Strachan was swift to seize. Eighteen months on, perennial strugglers Saints reach an FA Cup final in May 2003 while narrowly missing a UEFA Cup place through the league.

One need not look far for a mentor. As a ball-winning midfielder, Strachan was the pivot of Sir Alex Ferguson's Aberdeen which won domestic and European glory in the early Eighties. Reunited at Old Trafford, the League title was to elude both men but Strachan beat his manager by a season courtesy of a move to Leeds.

As captain, Strachan galvanised Leeds to the Second Division title in 1990, the League Championship following only two seasons later. Ferguson opened the floodgates the following season. For Strachan, Highfield Rd. provided an end to his playing career but the real learning curve was yet to come.

VITAL STATISTICS

Place of Birth: Scotland

Date of Birth: 9 February 1957

Died: n/a Caps: 50 (Scotland) Goals (International): 5

Clubs: As Player: Aberdeen, Manchester United, Leeds United, Coventry City; As Manager: Coventry City, Southampton

Trophies: SLT 1980, 1984; SFAC 1982, 1983, 1984; CWC 1983; FAC 1985; LT 1992

LEGEND RATING

Achievement	7	Achievement	5
Skill	7	Tactical Awareness	6
Teamwork	9	Motivation	8
Passion	8	Transfer Dealing and Team Selection	7
Personality	8	Personality	9
Overall Legend Rating	**39**	**Overall Legend Rating**	**35**

- Strachan played in the 1982 and 1986 World Cup Finals for Scotland. He scored against West Germany in the latter but, like his team-mates, never shone.
- Has won greater popularity than Ferguson due to blending Caledonian canniness with engaging humour. His post-match TV interviews are always good value.
- Strachan's transfer from Aberdeen in 1984 prompted a UEFA enquiry. Cologne claimed the player was already theirs, the Dons were forced to pay the German club £100 k despite his move to Old Trafford.
- Scottish Footballer of the Year 1980, English Footballer of the Year 1992.

Suarez, Luis

SPAIN'S FAILURE to make an impact on major tournaments remains one of the mysteries of world football. Time after time in the last 40 years Spanish sides packed with talent have turned up as fancied outsiders, only to head for the door marked 'undignified exit' within the first week. The only exception was the side that won the European Championship in 1964, when the platform provided by their goalkeeper, Iribar, and defensive colossus Jose Santamaria, allowed Luis Suarez to create mayhem.

Suarez was the prompter, a great passer and crosser, able to change the direction of play at will. Spotted by Barcelona as an 18-year-old playing for Deportivo La Coruna, he moved on to become the *generalissimo* in the great Inter side of the 1960s under controversial coach Helenio Herrera. Inter were the first proponents of the *catenaccio* sweeper system, and Suarez's speed of thought and passing allowed them to break quickly and counter-attack in numbers. He masterminded both their European Cup triumphs, including the memorable 3-1 victory over the great Real Madrid in 1964.

VITAL STATISTICS

Place of Birth: La Coruna, Spain

Date of Birth: 2 May 1935

Died: n/a   Caps: 32 (Spain)

Goals (International): 14

Clubs: Deportivo La Coruna, Barcelona, Inter Milan, Sampdoria

Appearances: Club (for Barcelona): 373

Goals: Club (for Barcelona): 153

Trophies: EuroC 1964; PLA 1959, 1960; SA 1963; EC 1964, 1965

Achievement	8
Skill	9
Teamwork	7
Passion	8
Personality	7
Overall Legend Rating	**39**

◁) Inter paid Barcelona a world record £150,000 for Suarez in 1962.

◁) Suarez was a member of the Barcelona side that beat Real in the European Cup for the first time in 1961.

◁) Suarez missed Inter's 1967 European Cup final defeat to Celtic through injury.

◁) Suarez was Spain's manager at the 1990 World Cup, where they lost in the second round against Yugoslavia.

◁) He was European Footballer of the Year in 1960.

Substitutes

BEFORE THE MID-1960s you just had to be lucky. If a player lay writhing on the ground, his manager had to pray that the mysterious powers of the magic sponge would work their recuperative spell. If that failed, there was no bench to turn to – you were down to 10 men. Eventually the authorities realised the unfairness of the situation, not least because a succession of Cup finals had been ruined by injuries. And so it was that on 21 August 1965 Keith Peacock duly trotted on to the field as the league's first substitute, pressed into action for Charlton against Bolton Wanderers. Now the tables have turned completely. Three from five substitute choices are permitted today, making old-fashioned dugouts standing-room only. In friendly internationals the habit has reached epidemic proportions, with games fragmented by the replacing of entire teams. But whether enforced or tactical, substitutes still have the power to turn a game. Just ask Alex Ferguson. With United trailing 1-0 to Bayern Munich in the closing minutes of the European Cup final in 1999 he turned to the bench, had a brief chat with his assistant, Steve McClaren, and invited Teddy Sheringham and Ole Gunnar Solskjaer to strip for action. You probably know the rest....

> 'He accepts the situation when he is on the bench ... very few players can come into the heat of a game and be so totally tuned in.'
>
> Alex Ferguson on
> Ole Gunnar Solskjaer

David Fairclough, Liverpool's Supersub.

◁)) The 1970s saw the coining of the word 'Supersub'. It was invented for Liverpool striker David Fairclough, who had a happy knack of coming on late to score vital goals.

◁)) In 1983, a league proposal to double the number of substitutes to two was rejected by clubs on grounds of expense. They were fearful of paying more appearance money and win bonuses.

◁)) Substitutes had been permitted in friendly matches since 1922. It took the Football League 43 years to cotton on.

◁)) Most effective substitute? Ole Gunnar Solskjaer. His catalogue of off-the-bench heroics include a four-goal salvo in 11 minutes against Nottingham Forest.

Sunderland's Stunner

Arsenal 3 Manchester United 2, 1979

ACTUALLY, it wasn't a great match. But for exciting climaxes, no FA Cup final had witnessed drama like it since Stanley Matthews moved into overdrive in 1953. Arsenal had established a two-goal cushion by half-time and were content to run down the clock during the second half. United scarcely looked up to the task.

But with five minutes remaining, Gordon McQueen, still loitering in the penalty area after a badly-worked set-piece, turned in a speculative cross. Even now, Arsenal looked more than capable of holding their nerve. Enter Sammy McIlroy, who dribbled through a nervous and transfixed Gunners' defence two minutes later to toe-end the ball past the advancing Jennings. It squeezed tantalisingly inside his right-hand post, like a gently caressed snooker ball falling into a side pocket. In the stands the United fans lost it big time. Unfortunately for them, so did their team. From the restart, with just seconds to go, Arsenal moved the ball to Brady on the left wing, and the Irishman hit a wicked, curling cross over a flailing Gary Bailey on to the outstretched right boot of Alan Sunderland. The goal gaped, he scored, and the Cup was won at last.

SCORERS: Arsenal: Talbot, Stapleton, Sunderland
Manchester United: McQueen, McIlroy
EVENT: FA Cup Final, Wembley, 12 May 1979

ARSENAL
(Man: Terry Neill)

MANCHESTER UNITED
(Man: Dave Sexton)

ARSENAL		MANCHESTER UNITED	
1 Jennings	8 Sunderland	1 Bailey	8 Greenhoff J
2 Rice	9 Stapleton	2 Nicholl	9 Jordan
3 Nelson	10 Price	3 Albiston	10 Macari
4 Talbot	11 Rix	4 McIlroy	11 Thomas
5 O' Leary		5 McQueen	
6 Young		6 Buchan	
7 Brady		7 Coppell	

Alan Sunderland (foreground) after scoring that late, dramatic winner.

◁» This was the second of Arsenal's hat-trick of successive Cup final appearances, and the only time they won. Ipswich and West Ham beat them in 1978 and 1980 respectively.

◁» This was Arsenal's eleventh game of the competition, having taken five matches to overcome Sheffield Wednesday in the third round.

◁» This was Pat Rice's fourth final in an amazing run.

◁» For Dave Sexton, this was the nearest he came to a major trophy as United manager. He was sacked in 1981 after four barren seasons.

◁» Several hundred United fans left the stadium when their team were 2-0 down.

384

Tale of Two Maradonas

Romania 3 Argentina 2, 1994

ARGENTINA HAD STARTED the tournament with Maradona in fine form ... until urine tests found his body to be crammed with drugs. Romania, meanwhile, had the man they called the 'Maradona of the Carpathians', Gheorghe Hagi, fit and hoping to show a world audience that he was as good as he thought he was. Romania had come through their group despite losing 4-1 to Switzerland and, allaying fears that they might adopt a cagey strategy, took the lead after just 12 minutes through a splendid Dumitrescu free-kick. A Batistuta penalty pulled Argentina level four minutes later, but Dumitrescu, collecting a subtle pass from Hagi, hit his second to make it 2-1 on 16 minutes.

Argentina pressed but Romania defended valiantly, and retained a constant threat on the break, thanks largely to Hagi whose exquisite close control and ability to launch passes from deep in his own half provided them with a reliable outlet. Supporting Dumitrescu on one such foray, he put Romania 3-1 up with a fine, rising strike from distance. Back came Argentina, a mistake by the otherwise sound Prunea letting in Balbo, but it was to prove no more than a consolation. Romania, inspired by Hagi and the commanding Belodedici, held on to clinch a famous and popular victory.

SCORERS: Romania: Dumitrescu 12, 18 Hagi 56
Argentina: Batistuta (pen) 16 Balbo 75
EVENT: World Cup Second Round, Pasadena, 3 July 1994

ROMANIA (Man: Angel Iordanescu)		ARGENTINA (Man: Alfio Basile)	
1 Prunea	7 Selymes	1 Islas	7 Simeone
2 Petrescu	8 Munteanu	2 Sensini	8 Redondo
3 Prodan	9 Hagi	3 Caceres	9 Ortega
4 Belodedici	10 Dumitrescu	4 Ruggeri	10 Balbo
5 Lupescu	11 Mihali	5 Chamot	11 Batistuta
6 Popescu		6 Basualdo	

Romanian keeper Prunea gets a deserving hug at the final whistle.

◁ If the match had gone to extra-time, Romania would have struggled. Their coach, Iordanescu, withdrew both Dumitrescu and Hagi to help protect his lead.

◁ Dumitrescu only played at centre-forward because Florin Raducioiu was suspended. His goals earned him a move to Spurs, where his performances ranged from the sublime to the downright risible.

◁ Romania lost their quarter-final with Sweden. An entertaining game ended 2-2, both goals from the returning Raducioiu.

◁ Argentina's flair players disappointed. Batistuta worked hard as usual, but the talented Ortega failed to fill the gap left by Maradona, and Redondo, terrific for Real Madrid, was anonymous.

Tartan Army

IN DAYS OF YORE, the England versus Scotland match brought the curtain down on the domestic season. For Scotland fans the visit to Wembley every two years became a pilgrimage of biblical proportions; ritual bathing in the fountains of Trafalgar Square was followed by a route march to Wembley that evoked echoes of Moses and the Promised Land. Inside the ground, England would invariably play out their 'home' game to the accompaniment of 75,000 baying Caledonians intent on witnessing a re-enactment of the Battle of Bannockburn. With the demise of the Home Internationals, the Tartan Army developed a worldwide reputation, as they cheerfully followed Scotland from one World Cup disaster to another. Their seemingly routine meetings with Brazil led to a sea of white legs twinkling a samba from beneath thousands of swirling kilts. They may have drunk the place dry, but they were generally more welcome, and always better behaved than the English.

'Anneka Rice – a challenge – get a drink in Genoa'

or

'Italy – land of no poll tax'

Tartan Army Banners during 'dry' World Cup Finals, 1990

◁▷ Wembley 1977. The Tartan Army outraged English sensibilities by dismantling the goalposts and hacking lumps from the pitch following Scotland's 2-1 win.

◁▷ In the 1970s and 1980s, London Underground opted to stage a weekend strike rather than transport the Tartan Army.

◁▷ In their World Cup single of 1978 Ally McLeod's Tartan Army famously claimed that they 'would really shake them up when we win the World Cup'. Scotland lost to Peru.

◁▷ London's last traditional visit from the Tartan Army was in 1988. The Home Internationals ended the following year, dismissed by the FA as an anachronism in a crowded season.

Taylor Report

A Legacy of Laziness

IN THE WAKE of the Hillsborough disaster, the government realised that further legislation was necessary. The aftermath of the 1971 Ibrox tragedy had brought the Safety of Sports Grounds Act, but this had failed to solve the problems of crumbling stadiums and terracing, and was anachronistic in its recommendations on crowd control. The responsibility for reform was placed in the hands of Lord Justice Taylor, a High Court judge. His first report, an interim version in August 1989, produced the Football Spectators Act and created the Football Licensing Authority (FLA), while his second in 1990 criticised many aspects of football administration and put forward

76 recommendations for improvement. The sobering conclusion of the Taylor Report was that British football could not be relied upon to put its own house in order, and that all parties – administrators, police and fans – had to share in the blame for the failings that had made British football grounds a serious threat to public safety.

A welcome side-effect of the Football Spectators Act was the scrapping of the Thatcher-inspired plans for compulsory identity cards. Perimeter fencing, a contributing factor in the Hillsborough disaster, has disappeared from British grounds but remains in Europe.

The major issues addressed in the report:
- Terrace capacities. Taylor called for a 15 per cent reduction, with restrictions on self-contained pens and the opening of perimeter gates.
- A need to drastically modernise old grounds and increase safety facilities, including the replacing of terracing with seats.
- Ticket touting should be made illegal.
- A need for responsible behaviour by players and the media.
- An urgent need for consultation between clubs, officials and fans, in particular regarding hooliganism, segregation and racist chanting.

Plough Lane, Wimbledon. Condemned, and now dismantled.

◁ March 1990. Chancellor John Major announced a 2.5 per cent reduction in the tax on football pools, releasing £100 m for ground redevelopment. The Football Trust added £40 m later in the year.

◁ Many wondered why clubs that lavished millions on transfers and wages should receive extra help from the taxpayer. Both Liverpool and Glasgow Rangers received £2 m, the maximum grant permitted to one club.

◁ Taylor's recommendations on all-seater stadiums have not been slavishly followed. All English league grounds should have converted by 1999/2000, yet Fulham were allowed to keep terraces open during their first season back in the Premiership.

Taylor, Graham

Watford, England

AFTER AN ORDINARY playing career with Grimsby Town and Lincoln, Graham Taylor moved into management at 28, his playing days ended by a serious hip injury. Moderate success led to his appointment as manager of Watford, and it was here that he made his reputation as he took the club from Division Four to the top flight in less than five years. Even more remarkably, his team even got amongst the big boys in 1983, finishing second in the First Division and losing in the FA Cup final to Everton. A strong defence and two fine wingers in Kevin Callaghan and John Barnes, later of Liverpool, enabled Watford to play a direct style with which many of their opponents simply couldn't cope. A move to more glamorous Aston Villa led to another second placed finish in 1990. An excellent club manager, particularly adept at getting the maximum return from modest players, it is unfortunate that Taylor will be eternally damned as the manager of one of England's poorest-ever national sides.

During his spell as boss in the early 1990s his selections were odd, and his long-ball tactics entirely unsuited to international football. Although his overall record is better than you might imagine, he will be remembered for his team's consistent failure to make any impact on major tournaments.

VITAL STATISTICS

Place of Birth: Worksop, England
Date of Birth: 15 September 1944
Died: n/a   Caps: 0
Goals (International): 0
Clubs: As Player: Grimsby Town, Lincoln City;
As Manager: Lincoln City, Watford, England national side, Wolverhampton Wanderers, Aston Villa
Trophies: None

October 1993. An irate Taylor is restrained by the fourth official as England lose a crucial World Cup qualifier in Rotterdam.

LEGEND RATING
Achievement 6
Tactical Awareness 7
Motivation 9
Transfer Dealing and Team Selection 8
Personality 8

Overall Legend Rating 38

After the debacle of the 1992 European Championships, Taylor's vilification in the press was unprecedented, and famously climaxed with one tabloid turning his head into a turnip on their back page.

His return to management saw Watford achieve another promotion to the top flight in 2000, but this time immediate relegation followed.

Taylor probably regrets allowing the shooting of a documentary that showed him issuing confusing, contradictory instructions to his players during England's 1994 World Cup qualifying campaign. The programme spawned a new national catchphrase: 'Do I not like that.'

388

Ten-Goal Payne

LUTON V BRISTOL ROVERS, Third Division South. True, 1936 was a time of simpler pleasures, but this wasn't a match that was likely to quicken the pulse. Except perhaps for Joe Payne who, with both of Luton's first-choice centre-forwards out injured, was pressed into service as an emergency striker. Most of the home fans had never seen Payne before, so the opposition can hardly have quaked in their boots when the team-sheets were pinned up. But he soon changed that, helping himself to a first-half hat-trick. According to the cliché, you make your own luck in football. If this is true then Payne had his own factory and was mass-producing it. Incredibly, in the second-

half he kept on scoring and Bristol Rovers were buried in the avalanche. With five minutes remaining, Payne's tenth goal of the game sealed a 12-0 win. No player had ever scored as many in a league game, and no one has come close to emulating his feat since. Joe Payne's piece of history is secure.

'How long left, ref?'

Bristol Rovers' keeper in the 89th minute realises that the game might just be up. (Yes, you're right, we made it up.)

◁ Most irritated man? Tranmere's Robert 'Bunny' Bell, who had held the league record of nine goals in a game for less than four months.

◁ Despite this blip on the radar, 1935/36 was an uneventful season for both clubs. Bristol Rovers finished eighth, while Luton were 11 points off the pace in fourth.

◁ Unsurprisingly, Payne became first choice for the Hatters the following season. He carried on where had left off, and his 55 goals in the campaign remain a club record.

◁ Oddly, Payne did not score at all in the first 20 minutes. One hopes that any premature barrackers were suitably embarrassed at the final whistle.

That Save, Pelé and Moore

Brazil 1 England 0, 1970

THE SCORELINE may not suggest a classic, but this was a match for the football purist. Pitting the defending champions against the team that would replace them at the tournament's end, this was a game notable as much for its defensive and goalkeeping qualities as it was for attacking flair. England appeared to have got out of jail in the first half as Gordon Banks made an incredible stop from Pelé's header, probably the best – and certainly the most replayed – save of all time. England could not repel the Brazilian attack for ever though, and on the hour they finally surrendered to the irrepressible Jairzinho, who fired home after good work from Tostão and Pelé.

The tone of the match was set by Bobby Moore's duel with Pelé, a real clash of the titans. This was Moore's finest game, his calm, interventionist style won the admiration of the Brazilian genius who made a point of exchanging shirts with the England captain after the two had embraced warmly at the final whistle. This mutual display of respect and affection, caught by camera lenses the world over, epitomised the dignity and style with which both players conducted themselves throughout their glittering careers.

SCORERS: Jairzinho

EVENT: World Cup Finals Group Match, Estadio Jalisco, Guadalajara, Mexico, 7 June 1970

BRAZIL (Man: Mario Zagalo)		ENGLAND (Man: Sir Alf Ramsey)	
1 Felix	7 Paulo Cesar	1 Banks	8 Ball
2 Carlos	Lima	2 Wright	9 R. Charlton
Alberto	8 Jairzinho	3 Cooper	(Bell)
3 Piazza	9 Tostão	4 Mullery	10 Hurst
4 Brito	(Roberto)	5 Labone	11 Peters
5 Everaldo	10 Pelé	6 Moore	
6 Clodoaldo	11 Rivelino	7 Lee (Astle)	

Banks makes THAT save.

◄)) Both teams qualified for the quarter-finals, Brazil with a 100 per cent record, England with wins against Czechoslovakia and Romania.

◄)) The match signalled the start of a great friendship between Moore and Pelé. The Brazilian paid a heartfelt tribute on Moore's death.

◄)) Jairzinho's goal was one of seven in the tournament; he netted in all six games and finished as the top scorer.

◄)) England nearly snatched a draw, only for Jeff Astle to miss a sitter after coming on as substitute.

◄)) This result was no disgrace for England; Brazil scored at least three goals in every other game at the Finals.

Theatre of Dreams

Old Trafford, Manchester

MANCHESTER UNITED'S MAGNIFICENT 'Theatre of Dreams' is currently the biggest club ground in England, having been modernised extensively in recent seasons. Its 68,000 seats are filled for every home game.

First opened in 1910, Old Trafford has enjoyed an eventful existence, not least during the Second World War. German bombing destroyed the main stand and extensively damaged other sections of the ground, forcing United to play home games at Maine Road for a couple of seasons. Old Trafford has long been a natural choice for important games needing a neutral venue. It staged three matches

during the 1966 World Cup and was a key host in Euro 96, providing the semi-final arena for the Czech Republic's nail-biting penalty win. In domestic football, it was chosen as the venue for the 1915 'khaki' Cup final and replays in 1911 and 1970, in addition to countless semi-final ties.

Today, fans from around the globe make daily pilgrimages to the stadium, not least to add to United's impressive coffers in the huge superstore adjacent to the ground. The modern Old Trafford is no longer just a place to watch football.

VITAL STATISTICS

Local Club:	Manchester United
Date Built:	1910
Current Capacity:	68,936
Max. Capacity:	76,962

◁)) Despite the magnificent surroundings, sections of the crowd persist in standing, leading to periodic threats of closure by the city council.

◁)) The most poignant monuments are the plaque and memorial clock commemorating the players, officials and journalists who died in the 1958 Munich air crash.

◁)) Old Trafford's record crowd of 76,962 stands for the 1939 FA Cup semi-final between Wolves and Grimsby.

◁)) The giant new North Stand is the biggest in the UK and supports the world's longest cantilevered roof.

◁)) Old Trafford's address is now Sir Matt Busby Way. A statue to its greatest manager stands outside the ground.

They Think It's All Over

'SOME PEOPLE ARE ON THE PITCH, they think it's all over ... it is now. It's four'. Thus BBC commentator Kenneth Wolstenholme brought the curtain down on the 1966 World Cup. If he could claim royalties, he would now be wealthy enough to buy the FA itself. England's sixth game of the Finals brought a unique experience; for the first time in the tournament they went a goal behind, Haller taking advantage of a Ray Wilson error. But six minutes later, rising to meet a perfectly weighted free-kick from Moore, Hurst leveled with a crisp header. In the second half England appeared to have won it through Peters with 12 minutes left, only for Weber to put celebrations on ice with

a last-gasp equaliser. After 10 minutes of extra-time came the flashpoint. Hurst's shot rebounded off the underside of the bar and, controversially (and probably wrongly), Azerbaijani linesman Tofik Bakhramov awarded a goal to England. Hurst completed his hat-trick in the dying moments but by then the Germans were already a beaten side. The country that invented the game could finally call itself world champions.

SCORERS: England: Hurst (3); Peters
West Germany: Haller, Weber
EVENT: World Cup Final, Wembley, 30 July 1966

ENGLAND (Man: Alf Ramsey)		WEST GERMANY (Man: Helmut Schoen)	
1 Banks	8 Hurst	1 Tilkowski	8 Haller
2 Cohen	9 R Charlton	2 Hottges	9 Seeler
3 Wilson	10 Hunt	3 Schnellinger	10 Overath
4 Stiles	11 Peters	4 Beckenbauer	11 Emmerich
5 J Charlton		5 Schulz	
6 Moore		6 Weber	
7 Ball		7 Held	

Hurst, far right, watches his second and England's third bounce on, sorry over, the line.

◁ Geoff Hurst remains the only scorer of a hat-trick in a World Cup final. He found the net with his head, right and left foot.

◁ Germany added to an unenviable record. In five successive World Cup Finals, the team scoring first had lost.

◁ Ramsey rallied his troops before extra-time with his most famous words: 'You've won it once, now go and win it again'. He remained impassive on the bench at the final whistle.

◁ Hurst's selection was vindication for Ramsey. Greaves was the

popular choice but Hurst replaced him for the quarter-finals and retained his place.

◁ Ramsey was knighted shortly after the victory. Both Bobby Charlton and Hurst have since received the same award.

Thijssen, Frans & Muhren, Arnold

Ipswich Town

IN 1970s BRITAIN, foreign footballers were as rare as short back and sides, so when Spurs announced the signings of the Argentine stars Osvaldo Ardiles and Ricky Villa it caused a sensation. In comparison, Frans Thijssen and Arnold Muhren slipped into Portman Road almost unnoticed. But their deft skills and vision were soon the talk of the First Division.

Cultured midfielders both, they brought the passing principles of 'Total Football' to Ipswich and, in combination with the tigerish John Wark, formed the engine of Bobby Robson's 1981 UEFA Cup winners. Muhren later moved on to Manchester United in a lucrative deal.

Although he won the FA Cup in 1983, his frequent injuries meant neither he nor United prospered (some would argue that his lengthy absence in the 1983/84 season cost United the title). His signing by Ajax in 1984 proved to be Muhren's Indian summer, and resulted in his recall for Holland. Aged 37, he was a member of the Dutch team that won the European Championships in 1988. Thijssen, meanwhile, struggled to maintain his form after leaving Ipswich, becoming an itinerant and peripheral figure.

VITAL STATISTICS

FRANS THIJSSEN
Place of Birth: Heuman, Holland
Date of Birth: 23 January 1952
Died: n/a Caps: 14 (Holland) Goals (International): 3
Clubs: FC Twente, Ipswich, Vancouver Whitecaps, Nottingham Forest
Appearances: Club (for Ipswich): 125
Goals: Club (for Ipswich): 10
Trophies: EUFAC 1981

ARNOLD MUHREN
Place of Birth: Volendam, Holland
Date of Birth: 2 June 1951
Died: n/a
Caps: 23 (Holland)
Goals: (International): 3
Clubs: Twente, Ajax, Ipswich Town, Manchester United
Appearances: Club (for Ipswich and Man Utd): 226
Goals: Club (for Ipswich and Man Utd): 34
Trophies: CWC 1971; EUFAC 1981; FAC 1983; EuroC 1988

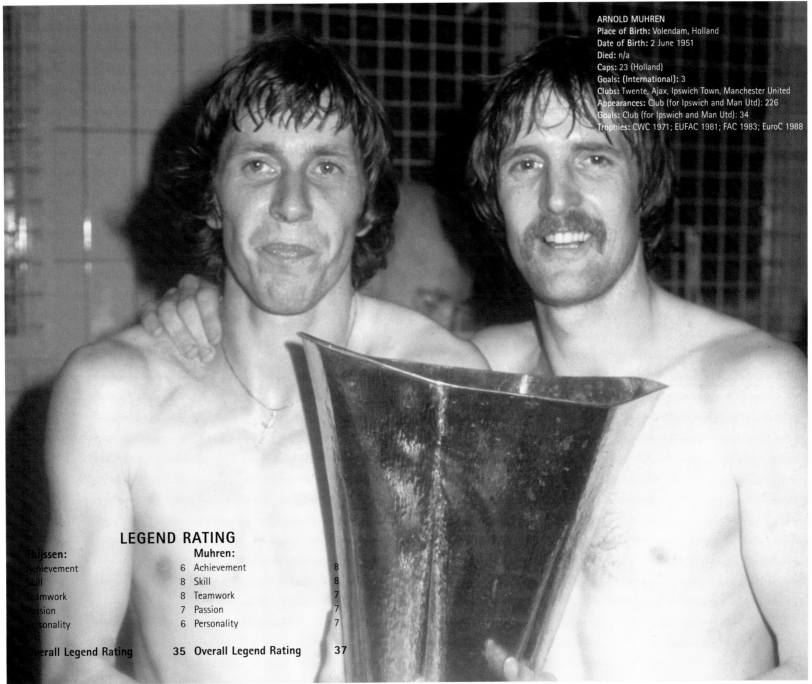

1981. Muhren (left) and Thijssen hide their modesty with the UEFA Cup.

LEGEND RATING

Thijssen:		Muhren:	
Achievement	6	Achievement	8
Skill	8	Skill	8
Teamwork	8	Teamwork	7
Passion	7	Passion	7
Personality	6	Personality	7
Overall Legend Rating	**35**	**Overall Legend Rating**	**37**

- Thijssen was PFA Footballer of the Year in 1981, while Muhren won Ipswich's Player of the Year award in his first season (1978/79).
- Both were members of the Ipswich team that won the UEFA Cup in 1981, defeating their Dutch countrymen, AZ67 Alkmaar, 5-4 in the two-legged final.
- 'The man with velvet feet.' John Motson waxes lyrical over Arnold Muhren.
- In 1988 Muhren provided the cross for the best goal ever in the European Championships – Van Basten's stunning volley in the final against Russia.

IMAGINE, IF YOU WILL, a possible post-match interview with the Bon Accord manager: 'Aye, the lads are naturally disappointed. We always knew it would be a tough game, it's difficult to come to one of the big clubs like Arbroath and get a result. Obviously, with some of our boys being a bit sketchy on the rules, like forgetting to change ends at half-time, it made it an uphill battle. But I do feel the game turned on a couple of major decisions. One was the kick-off. Had it not happened we might well have held out for a draw. Also, the referee missed a blatant handball leading up to their 29th goal, he must have been the only person in the ground who didn't see it. If television had been invented the replay would definitely have vindicated us. Still, at least we can concentrate on the league now.' One supposes the Bon Accord keeper didn't give up his day job as a piano tuner. Scotland's biggest slaughter since Culloden is a scoreline that will probably never be topped.

EVENT: Scottish FA Cup First Round, 12 September 1885

ARBROATH		BON ACCORD	
1 Milne, Jim snr	10 Crawford	1 Stevie Wonder	Langford
2 Collie	11 Buick	2 Long John Silver	7 Basil Fotherington-Thomas
3 Salmond		3 Blind Pew	8 Thora Hird
4 Rennie		4 David Blunkett	9 Adeola Akinbiyi
5 Milne, Jim jr		5 Douglas Bader	10 Don Estelle
6 Bruce		6 Bonnie	11 Toulouse Lautrec
7 Petrie			
8 Tackett			
9 Marshall			

THE HIGHLAND POST

INCREDIBLE VICTORY FOR ARBROATH

AFTER BEATING opponents Bon Accord by 36 goals to nil in the first round of the Scottish FA Cup yesterday, Arbroath's manager was said to be 'satisfied' with the way the match had gone for his team and that 'it was quite a convincing defeat'.

The Bon Accord side did not appear to find their form throughout the whole game, despite highly vocal support from their supporters, mainly family and friends of the players who all come from a small hamlet in the Grampian Mountains. Some questionable decisions were made by the referee, which worked in Arbroath's favour, giving them their 29th goal of the match.

↪ On the same day and in the same competition, Dundee Harp beat Aberdeen Rovers 35–0.

↪ Arbroath met their match in the fourth round, losing 5–3 at Hibernian.

↪ Arbroath's only other Cup exploit is a run to the semi-final in 1947.

↪ The score would have been even higher but for the absence of goal nets, which were not yet in common use.

↪ This is still a world-record victory in an official match.

Those Who Died Young

Footballers Cut off in Their Prime

DYING AS A RESULT of a playing injury is mercifully rare. The most famous example was Celtic goalkeeper John Thomson, who in September 1931 was Scotland's hottest prospect. Diving at the feet of Rangers' Sam English, he sustained serious head injuries and died hours later in hospital aged just 22. The funeral briefly united the sectarian divide, but English was mercilessly barracked by some Celtic fans in the following fixture. Deeply upset, he was never the same player and left Rangers the following season.

Rangers can point to a more recent tragedy. In March 1995 their former winger and legend Davie Cooper collapsed and died from a brain haemorrhage while coaching youngsters for a television programme. The 39-year-old Cooper was as fit as he had ever been and had no previous history of illness. There are other examples, but the deaths of this Glasgow pair are particularly poignant, putting football, sectarianism, rivalry and trophies in their rightful perspective.

'Bill Nicholson started to talk about identifying John White's body. He broke down ... he never broke down like that.'

Dave Mackay describes the effect of John White's death.

Rangers' Davie Cooper, and Laurie Cunningham. RIP.

⤴ In 1964 John White, a key member of Tottenham's double-winning side, was killed by lightning while sheltering under a tree during a round of golf.

⤴ Laurie Cunningham and David Rocastle are the most recent English internationals to die prematurely. In 1989 Cunningham met his end behind the wheel of a car in Madrid, while Rocastle succumbed to cancer in 2001.

⤴ Andres Escobar paid the ultimate penalty for scoring an own goal while playing for Colombia in the 1994 World Cup Finals. He upset a betting cartel and was murdered on his return.

⤴ In 1897, Aston's Thomas Grice was fatally stabbed by his own belt buckle after what looked an innocuous tumble.

Thrashings

Well, Des, It Was a Bit One-Sided Really

ARBROATH'S 36-0 DEFEAT of Bon Accord in 1885 is well documented as the world's biggest drubbing in a first-class game. Early fixtures were notorious for their mismatches; it would be churlish not to mention Preston's 26-0 caning of Hyde in 1887, the largest English score. In cup ties of yore, the pummelling of works' teams by well-drilled professionals was commonplace.

Despite tighter competition, mismatches still occur even at the top level (Revie's Leeds toying with Southampton in a 7-0 hammering in 1972 springs to mind). Even in the 1990s the cliché that there are 'no easy games nowadays' doesn't stand up to intense scrutiny. Manchester United versus Ipswich may have been a home banker in 1995, but 9-0 didn't result in too many claimed betting slips. But United's dominance of English football in the 1990s didn't stop them being humiliated 5-0 by Newcastle and Chelsea. Spare a thought, though, for Stanley Milton. On 6 January 1934 the Halifax goalkeeper trotted out for his debut against Stockport – and promptly let in 13 goals. Happily, he survived to be picked another day, which doesn't say much for their reserve keeper.

'We are asking the Lord to keep the score down.'

American Samoa's coach, Tunoa Lui, prays for a miracle before a World Cup qualifier against Australia in April 2001; they lost 31-0

Ryan Giggs and Andy Cole celebrate United's latest mauling.

◁ᴺ American Samoa's 31-0 defeat set a new international record. FIFA weren't able to ratify the score immediately, as the scoreboard claimed 32-0.

◁ᴺ When Newcastle's keeper and outfield stand-in were both injured during a match at Upton Park in 1986, they turned to the vertically challenged Peter Beardsley to keep goal. West Ham won 8-0.

◁ᴺ Europe's record aggregate win is held by Chelsea, who once beat Jeunesse Hautcharage 21-0. The Luxembourg part-timers fielded a player with only one arm, and it wasn't the goalkeeper.

◁ᴺ 'We were lucky to get nil.' Oft-quoted preserve of the tight-lipped and ashen-faced manager.

Tigana, Jean

JEAN TIGANA HAS PROVED as cultured, intelligent and successful a manager as he was a player. As one-third of Europe's finest-ever midfield, Tigana helped France to victory in the 1984 European Championships and was instrumental in his country's advance to the semi-finals of the 1982 and 1986 World Cups. Tigana's long legs could run all day, as could the shorter limbed Alain Giresse, allowing team-mate Michel Platini to work his genius. France would surely have won at least one of those World Cups with a world-class striker at their disposal. Tigana played all his club football in France, his spells at Bordeaux and Marseille bringing him four league titles and a European Cup final appearance in 1991. Although inexperienced in team management, Tigana nevertheless guided his first club, Monaco, to the French title in 1997. In April 2000 he took his first job outside France, as Mohamed al Fayed's millions lured him to the manager's job at Fulham. Although the Nationwide League was in theory a step down, the combination of a hugely increased transfer budget and the application of Tigana's theories on technique, passing and fitness helped bring top-flight football back to Craven Cottage for the first time in 32 years. Season 2002/3 saw Fulham's progress stutter and Tigana's departure. He will be much in demand.

VITAL STATISTICS

Place of Birth: Toulon, France

Date of Birth: 23 June 1955

Died: n/a Caps: 52 (France) Goals (International): 1

Clubs: As Player: Toulon, Lyon, Bordeaux, Marseille;

As Manager: Lyon, Monaco, Fulham

Appearances: Club (League): 411 Goals: Club (League): 26

Trophies: EuroC 1984, FLT 1984, 1985, 1987, 1990, 1991, (1997)

LEGEND RATING

Achievement	8	Achievement	7
Skill	8	Tactical Awareness	8
Teamwork	9	Motivation	8
Passion	7	Transfer Dealing and Team Selection	7
Personality	6	Personality	6
Overall Legend Rating	**38**	**Overall Legend Rating**	**36**

- As coach, Tigana lead Lyon to an impressive second place in the French league in only his second year in management.
- Scored once in 52 internationals, starting and finishing a superb passing move against Hungary in the 1986 World Cup.
- Tigana's Monaco knocked Manchester United out of the Champions League at the quarter-finals stage in 1998.
- Fulham won the First Division title in 2001 with over 100 points. But for fatigue and indifferent form towards the end of the season they might have got 100 goals as well.
- Like Arsène Wenger at Arsenal, Tigana has filled his team with French imports. He will need to balance this with British talent to progress further in the Premier League.

Todd, Colin & McFarland, Roy

Derby County, England

COLIN TODD AND ROY McFARLAND formed the best English centre-back partnership in post-war club football. McFarland had already been at Derby for four years before Colin Todd arrived from Sunderland in 1971 and, under the watchful gaze of manager Brian Clough, the two slotted together instantly. Unfancied Derby won their first title within a year, and went on to prove it was no fluke by winning a second title in 1975 and reaching the semi-final of the European Cup. The two were also effective at international level, helping cushion the blow of Bobby Moore's retirement. Like Moore, they did not possess lightning pace but both were exceptional

tacklers. Their pragmatic styles made them competent but only modest managers. Todd took Bolton to the Premier League but the task of keeping them there proved beyond him, while McFarland's only success came early, with promotion at Bradford in 1982.

VITAL STATISTICS

COLIN TODD

Place of Birth: Chester Le Street, England

Date of Birth: 12 December 1948

Died: n/a Caps: 27 (England) Goals (International): 0

Clubs: Sunderland, Derby County, Everton, Birmingham City, Oxford United, Vancouver Whitecaps

Appearances: Club: 417

Goals: Club: 7

Trophies: LT 1972, 1975

ROY MCFARLAND

Place of Birth: Liverpool, England

Date of Birth: 5 April 1948

Died: n/a Caps: 28 (England)

Goals (International): 0

Clubs: Tranmere Rovers, Derby County, Bradford City

Appearances: Club (for Derby County): 437

Goals: Club (League – for Derby County): 44

Trophies: LT 1972, 1975

LEGEND RATING

Todd:		McFarland:	
Achievement	8	Achievement	8
Skill	9	Skill	8
Teamwork	7	Teamwork	7
Passion	7	Passion	8
Personality	6	Personality	6
Overall Legend Rating	**37**	**Overall Legend Rating**	**36**

Todd (left) and McFarland advertise Bolton's current sponsors.

◄► When Brian Clough rang the local paper to break the news that he was signing McFarland, the reported reply was: 'Who the bloody hell is Roy McFarland?'

◄► Todd played under Clough twice, rejoining him at Forest in 1982.

◄► McFarland's England career was effectively ended after he snapped his Achilles tendon against Northern Ireland in 1975. He was a regular with 24 caps but only won four after the injury.

◄► Both men managed Derby and were joint-managers for a spell at

Bolton. Todd's career has been especially eventful. While assistant to former team-mate Bruce Rioch at Middlesbrough, they went into receivership. In 2002 he was sacked at Derby after just 17 games.

Tomaszewski, Jan

Poland

THE PRESS HAD LED the public to believe that England's qualification for the 1974 World Cup was a mere formality. After all, who in their right mind could imagine them failing to secure the home victory against Poland they needed to ensure their passage to Germany? Not Brian Clough that's for sure. Before the game, live to a national TV audience, he predicted a comfortable England win and dismissed Poland's goalkeeper Jan Tomaszewski as a clown.

But Clough's words proved more pathetic than prophetic as Tomaszewski, by a combination of technique, athleticism and some outrageous good fortune, helped Poland to a 1-1 draw (he was only beaten by a penalty), that saw them qualify for the Finals at England's expense. He maintained that form in two Finals appearances, during which his five clean sheets in 11 matches helped Poland build a growing international reputation. And, were it not for Polish working regulations that prevented the foreign transfer of any player under 30, Tomaszewski would almost certainly have been snapped up by one of Western Europe's big clubs. His long service for LKS Lodz finally ended with a move to Belgian side Beerschot in 1978, and he later moved to Spain where, after a spell with Hercules, he retired in 1982. Tomaszewski is now a TV commentator and newspaper journalist.

VITAL STATISTICS

Place of Birth: Poland

Date of Birth: 9 January 1948

Died: n/a Caps: 59 (Poland)

Goals (International): 0

Clubs: LKS Lodz, Beerschot, Hercules

Trophies: None

LEGEND RATING

Achievement	6
Skill	7
Teamwork	7
Passion	7
Personality	9
Overall Legend Rating	**36**

◁ᴵᴵ He was the first man to save two penalties in a World Cup. Tomaszewski saved from Sweden's Tapper, and Uli Hoeness of West Germany at the 1974 Finals.

◁ᴵᴵ The public had no right to expect a comfortable England win at Wembley. Poland had won the first match 2-0 in Chorzow.

◁ᴵᴵ Tomaszewski remains Poland's most-capped goalkeeper, although Dudek may well pass his tally of 59.

Too Much Bottle

DRINK HAS ALWAYS BEEN a strange contradiction in football. The misdemeanours of Premier League stars under the influence make for familiar tabloid revelations, yet at the same time Carling have poured millions into the FA's coffers with their sponsorship of the Premier League. At club level, the Blue Star brewery has added their familiar logo to Newcastle's black-and-white stripes in recent years. For British players, a lifestyle providing both plenty of spare time and plenty of cash has led to a thriving drinking culture. The skills of George Best and Jim Baxter can scarcely be mentioned without rueful references to the habit that so affected their lives. The great

Brazilian Garrincha was to meet with an untimely end through his own alcohol addiction, while Billy Bremner's international career was curtailed following alcohol-induced incidents in a Danish nightclub. Modern casualties have included Paul Merson, and his former Arsenal team-mate Tony Adams who published an autobiography called *Addicted* in reference to his problems with the bottle. Today's use of dieticians and the cleaner habits of most continental imports have reduced the problem but, as the US government found, prohibition is completely unenforceable.

'I saw an advert saying "Drink Canada Dry" and thought it was an instruction.'

George Best explains his decision to cross the pond

Merse calls for a swift one from anyone with a hip-flask.

◁ A wilting Denis Compton was famously revived with a half-time tot of brandy during the 1950 FA Cup final. His second-half display helped Arsenal beat Liverpool 2-0.

◁ 1971. West Ham lost 4-0 at Blackpool in the FA Cup after several players break a club curfew and go drinking the night before. Among the players dropped for the next game is England captain Bobby Moore.

◁ England's footballers are snapped in the infamous 'dentist's chair' days before the start of Euro 96. The antics are repeated on the pitch, minus chair and alcohol, following Paul Gascoigne's goal in their group match against Scotland.

Top Toffees

NINE ENGLISHMEN and two Welshmen make up this blend from Everton's four great eras. All positions are contentious save two; Southall is easily the best keeper and Dixie Dean is English football's most prolific goal machine. In defence, Newton and Wilson were two of England's best full-backs, while the combination of Watson and Ratcliffe brought Everton a brace of titles in the 1980s. In the centre of midfield Ball and Kendall edge out Colin Harvey, with Trevor Steven and Joe Mercer, who ousts Kevin Sheedy, providing balance and no little guile on the flanks. In attack, Everton enjoy an embarrassment of riches in the classic centre-forward tradition.

Tommy Lawton and Andy Gray would make most other club dream teams, but here they can only kick their heels on the bench. With Dean a natural first pick, the reaming candidates were fighting for one place. Eventually we went for Lineker, figuring his pace and opportunism would make him a better foil for Dean than the more physical Lawton. The prospect of Lineker latching on to Dean's knock-downs would make mouth-watering fare for the Goodison faithful, particularly given the current diet.

Manager: Harry Catterick

4-4-2

Neville Southall (80s/90s)

Keith Newton (60s/70s) Dave Watson (80s/90s)
Kevin Ratcliffe (C) (80s/90s) Ray Wilson (60s)

Trevor Steven (80s) Alan Ball (60s/70s)
Howard Kendall (60s/70s) Joe Mercer (30s)

Dixie Dean (30s) Gary Lineker (80s)

Subs: Gordon West (G) (60s/70s) Brian Labone (D) (60s)
Colin Harvey (M) (60s/70s) Tommy Lawton (F) (30s) Andy Gray (F) (80s)

Manager Howard Kendall beams with another League title.

◁) Everton's rich tradition of forwards is highlighted by the omissions from this squad: Joe Royle, Bob Latchford, Roy Vernon and Graeme Sharp.

◁) Harry Catterick is preferred to Howard Kendall as manager.

Although both won two titles, Kendall's second and third spells in charge presided over increasingly poor sides.

◁) Apart from Kendall, Colin Harvey also managed the side. His spell from 1987–90 was spent in Kendall's shadow, starting a

decline from which they are only recently recovering.

◁) Seven of Everton's nine championship-winning teams are represented, the exceptions being 1891 and 1915 when competition was weaker.

Top Toon

The Newcastle United Dream Team

A TRUE REFLECTION of Newcastle's colourful history, this squad pays respect to all the great Newcastle teams. Jimmy Lawrence, Colin Veitch and Peter McWilliam won three titles in the early part of the century, and Stan Seymour's wing-play helped Hughie Gallacher bring the bacon home in 1927. Mitchell and Milburn performed similar feats immediately after the war, while Frank Brennan and Bobby Cowell provided the solid defensive base for Milburn's heroic goal-scoring deeds. Craig and Moncur were ever-present as Newcastle struggled in the 1960s, but enjoyed better days when Malcolm Macdonald started tearing defences apart a decade later. Despite the skills of Beardsley,

Gascoigne and Chris Waddle another decline followed in the 1980s and then early-1990s when, only the arrival of Kevin Keegan as manager, averted a disastrous drop into the Third Division. Keegan's unique brand of attacking football won the hearts of many neutrals as they challenged the might of Man United at the top of the Premier League. Alan Shearer is the only current player in our Dream Team. The former England captain was once overlooked by Newcastle in a trial game but, since being signed for a club record £15 m by Keegan, he has wasted little time writing himself into Geordie folklore.

Manager: Kevin Keegan

4-2-4

Jimmy Lawrence (1900s)

David Craig (60s) Frank Brennan (40s/50s)
Bobby Moncur (C) (60s/70s) Colin Veitch (1900s)

Paul Gascoigne (80s) Peter Beardsley (90s)

Alan Shearer (90s) Jackie Milburn (40s/50s)
Malcolm Macdonald (70s) Bobby Mitchell (40s/50s)

Subs: Shay Given (G) (00s) Bobby Cowell (D) (40s/50s)
Peter McWilliam (M) (1900s) Stan Seymour (W) (20s)
Hughie Gallacher (F) (20s)

◁) Three Geordie omissions: Frank Hudspeth, holder of the most outfield appearances for the club (1910–29); Joe Harvey, player and manager across five decades; and Malcolm Macdonald's striking partner, John Tudor.

◁) Malcolm 'Supermac' Macdonald once scored all five goals in an England win over Cyprus. Sadly, he was never the same player after he left Newcastle for Arsenal.

◁) The squad has a distinctly Celtic flavour: six were capped by

Scotland; Given is the current Republic of Ireland goalie; and David Craig won 25 caps for Northern Ireland.

◁) Seven Geordie boys feature in the 16. The Toon Army has always reserved its loudest applause for the local talent.

Total Football

Holland, 1970s

BUILDING ON THE SUCCESS of the great Ajax club team, Michels took a squad assembled around that side to the 1974 World Cup Finals. They had scraped through qualification, a late goal against Norway eliminating Belgium, but in Germany they were a revelation, comfortably the best team of the tournament despite their loss to the hosts in the final. All the players were comfortable on the ball, while their movement and passing were exquisite. 'Total Football' at its poetic best. Van Hanegem, stately and cultured, and the vigorous Neeskens were the team's engine room in midfield. What is often forgotten is how tough the Dutch were. If the attack wasn't firing,

they were able to dig in; Krol, Rijsbergen, Haan and Neeskens were superb footballers, but they were not afraid to leave a foot in when necessary. And above all there was Cruyff. With all that talent behind him and the wiry strength of Rensenbrink next door, he was the icing on the cake, full of tricks and pace. Four years later in Argentina, without Cruyff and Van Hanegem, they were less persuasive, but still formidable opponents, and some awesome long-range shooting at altitude saw them through to a second final. Sadly, they lost again, securing their status as the greatest team never to win anything.

Manager: Rinus Michels

Key Players
Wim Suurbier (D) Ruud Krol (D) Wim Rijsbergen (D)
Arie Haan (M) Wim Jansen (M) Wim Van Hanegem (M)
Johan Neeskens (M) Johnny Rep (M/F) Johan Cruyff (F)
Rob Rensenbrink (F)

Trophies
None (beaten in 1974 and 1978 World Cup Finals)

Johan Cruyff, the best of an extremely talented bunch.

⫶ The managers who built the two great club sides were the managers for the two World Cup campaigns (Michels from Ajax, and the Austrian, Ernst Happel, from Feyenoord).
⫶ Cruyff missed the 1978 World Cup after a dispute with Happel.

⫶ Van Hanegem followed suit when Happel refused to promise the 33-year-old a starting place.
⫶ The 1978 campaign saw twins play in a World Cup final for the only time. Winger Rene van der Kerkhof had featured in the

1974 Final as a sub, and he was joined by brother Willy in 1978.
⫶ Arie Haan's winning goal against Italy in 1978, effectively propelling Holland into the final, was from a preposterous distance, easily 40 yards.

Tractor Boys

The Ipswich Dream Team

WHEN, IN 1962, just a year after winning promotion, Ipswich sneaked past Spurs to win the First Division title it was a triumph of tactical acumen over talent, and won Alf Ramsey the England's manager's job. This might sound a tad churlish, but the fact that the club were relegated two years later lends powerful support to the theory. The star of that 1962 team was undoubtedly the prolific Ray Crawford, and he leads the line in this dream team in preference to his old striking partner, Ted Phillips.

While Ramsey's champions drew professional admiration, it was the team built by Bobby Robson in the 1970s that won the hearts of neutral supporters. By introducing two Dutchmen, Arnold Muhren and Frans Thijssen, Robson brought a new dimension to the First Division. Ipswich went on to mount two serious title challenges, finishing in the runners-up spot in 1981 and 1982. The defence of Burley, Beattie (later replaced by Russell Osman), Butcher and Mills was fabulous, while John Wark and Brian Talbot added grit and graft to the Dutch skills in midfield. The modern team, despite an excellent manager in George Burley, still live in the shadow of that team; a great return to the top flight in 2000/2001 hid a lack of depth in the squad that caught up with them in 2002.

Manager: Bobby Robson

4-4-1-1

Paul Cooper (70s)

George Burley (70s) Terry Butcher (70s)
Kevin Beattie (70s) Mick Mills (C) (70s)

Jimmy Leadbetter (60s) John Wark (70s/80s) Matt Holland (90s/00s)
Arnold Muhren (70s/80s)

Kieron Dyer (90s)

Ray Crawford (60s)

Subs: Richard Wright (G) (90s) Allan Hunter (D) (80s) Colin Viljoen (M)
(80s) Clive Woods (W) (70s/80s) Ted Phillips (F) (60s)

Wembley, 1978. Ipswich pose with the FA Cup, Bobby Robson resplendent in cream ensemble.

◄ Mick Mills made 737 appearances for Ipswich. An intelligent defender with good distribution, he also won 42 caps for England.

◄ Goalkeeper Paul Cooper was an underrated player who, in another era, might have collected full England honours. He made 447 appearances for Ipswich.

◄ Kevin Beattie's career was blighted by injuries. Powerful, skilful and mobile he should have been the dominant defender of his generation. Instead, it was Butcher who became England's defensive totem.

◄ Wark was a wholehearted performer who, along with Thijssen, scored in both legs of Ipswich's 1981 UEFA Cup triumph.

Transfers

'WHAT A WASTE OF MONEY!' This familiar chant rings out many times a season, as another striker with an inflated price-tag picks out the corner flag. These days millions of pounds routinely change hands in football's equivalent of the stock market, but it was not always thus. Alf Common's transfer fee may have been what Michael Owen now earns in the pre-match warm up, but in Edwardian England it caused a sensation. Herbert Chapman raised the stakes even further when, as Arsenal boss in 1928, his £20,000 spree (including the capture of David Jack for the world's first ever five-figure transfer) led to the Gunners being dubbed 'the Bank of England club'. But the real money was in

Italy where, from around 1950 onwards, the Serie A superclubs have broken the world transfer record on an almost monthly basis; John Charles, Jimmy Greaves and Denis Law all moved to Italy for fees that were double the budget of British clubs. Yet what were once mindblowing figures are now relatively common. Looking back it is hard to believe the fuss that was made over Trevor Francis, Britain's first £1 m player. Hell, these days £1 m doesn't buy a decent reserve left-back. When Real Madrid's chairman signed the £45 m cheque for Zinedine Zidane in 2001, did the thought flicker through his mind that he was signing 45,000 Alf Commons? I doubt it.

'...as a matter of sport the Second Division would be more honourable than retention of place by purchase.'

Athletic News gets pious over Middlesbrough's signing of Alf Common, the first £1,000 transfer in 1905

Alf Common, a grand man.

◁ Middlesbrough signed Alf Common to save them from relegation. They are still trying to buy their way out of trouble nearly a century later.

◁ The 1960s Celtic and West Ham teams are rare examples of teams built purely with home-grown talent. A big cheque book is usually the pre-requisite of success.

◁ Best bargains? Eric Cantona and Peter Schmeichel were signed by the canny Alex Ferguson for a combined fee of less than £2 m.

◁ Inflation was rampant in nineties Britain. The record rose from £3.5m (Keane) to £15m (Shearer) in six years.

Trautmann's Final

Manchester City 3 Birmingham City 1, 1956

ON THE FACE OF IT, this was a routine FA Cup final. The underdogs did not defy the odds, there were no comebacks, last-minute winners or 40-yard scorchers. One goalkeeper's performance, though, was unique. Bert Trautmann was already giving a fine display for Manchester City when he dived at the feet of Birmingham forward Peter Murphy and was knocked unconscious. Only partially revived, he was involved in another jarring collision five minutes later. The newsreel footage of Trautmann massaging his neck did not reveal the whole story. It wasn't until days later, after he had completed the match and picked up a winner's medal in

City's 3-1 victory, that the full extent of his injury was diagnosed. Incredibly, x-rays revealed that he had suffered a broken neck and should not even have been standing up, let alone playing football. Had the modern system of three substitutes and a keeper on the bench been applied, Trautmann would almost certainly have been replaced immediately and his heroism thus diluted. In the event, his performance produced one of the FA Cup's most famous episodes in an otherwise unremarkable match.

SCORERS: Manchester City: Hayes, Dyson, Johnstone
Birmingham City: Kinsey
EVENT: FA Cup Final, Wembley, 5 May 1956

MANCHESTER CITY (Man: Leslie McDowall)		BIRMINGHAM CITY (Man: Arthur Turner)	
1 Trautmann	8 Hayes	1 Merrick	8 Kinsey
2 Leivers	9 Revie	2 Hall	9 Brown
3 Little	10 Dyson	3 Green	10 Murphy
4 Barnes	11 Clarke	4 Newman	11 Govan
5 Ewing		5 Smith	
6 Paul		6 Boyd	
7 Johnstone		7 Astall	

Trautmann dives in the challenge that was to break his neck.

◁⑴ Trautmann was Footballer of the Year in the same season.

◁⑴ Having been a German soldier and POW in the Second World War, his arrival at Maine Road brought protests and boycotts by City fans.

◁⑴ Trautmann made a full recovery and was back in the team six months later.

◁⑴ This match saw Trautmann overshadow Manchester City's star player, future England boss Don Revie.

◁⑴ Trautmann was a converted keeper, having preferred to play centre-half in his native Bremen.

Treble Dutch

Ajax, 1970s

RINUS MICHELS' APPOINTMENT as coach of Ajax Amsterdam started a sequence of three successive Dutch titles, followed by a European Cup final in 1969. But even more importantly it started a culture of coaching that became 'Total Football' – the successful method of play adopted by Ajax and Holland in the 1970s. They weren't quite ready in 1969, and were easily beaten by a craftier AC Milan side, but two years later they were back and made no mistake against Panathanaikos. Michels left for Barcelona that summer, but the blueprint was in place and Ajax followed up with two more European Cups and three more titles. While Cruyff was the undoubted star and

spokesman, he was not the team's only great player. A defence of Suurbier, Krol, Blankenburg and Hulshoff, with Stuy in goal didn't concede a goal in any of the European Cup finals in which they played. Haan and Rep were sound players too, both with tremendous shots from range, and Neeskens was almost the equal of the other Johan, a skilled playmaker with a steely edge.

Manager: Rinus Michels

Key Players
Wim Suurbier (D) Ruud Krol (D) Johann Neeskens (M)
Arie Haan (M) Johnny Rep (F) Johann Cruyff (F)

Trophies
DLT 1970, 1972, 1973, 1977, 1979 EC 1971, 1972, 1973
ESC 1972, 1973 WCC 1972

◁ Ajax brushed aside the double winning Arsenal team on the way to winning the 1971 European Cup, beating them both home and away.

◁ Even in the 1970s, Dutch players gave better interviews in English than English players. Krol, Haan and Cruyff were all articulate and interesting.

◁ Feyenoord were not only Ajax's main domestic threat, they were also a major rival in Europe. In 1970, under another great coach, Ernst Happel, they pipped Ajax and became the first Dutch side to win the European Cup.

◁ The Ajax side was entirely Dutch. As they faded an all-German Bayern side took over, and after them English clubs dominated.

FOOTBALL HAS PROVIDED a source of inspiration for dozens of filmmakers over the decades, yet for the most part they have been of a distinct 'B' movie standard. Perhaps the most famous football film is the improbable *Escape to Victory*, which tells the unlikely story of a group of prisoners of war – Bobby Moore, Pelé and Ossie Ardiles included – who plot their escape during a match against a German army team. *There's only one Jimmy Grimble*, is the latest attempt to depict the dreams and despairs of any football-mad youngster while *Gregory's Girl* cleverly used football to give an insight into the angst of adolescence. Television drama-makers have also turned to football on a regular basis, and seem particularly fascinated by the increasing presence of women in the game. In 1989 Cheri Lungi topped the ratings as *The Manageress* in charge of a struggling club, while the long-running BBC drama *Playing the Field*, based on the Doncaster Belles, charted the trials and tribulations of a women's team.

Later film offerings have included a decent stab at dramatising Nick Hornby's groundbreaking book *Fever Pitch*. In 2002, *Bend it Like Beckham* provided a novel take on an Asian girl trying to break into UK women's football. The greatest success story has to be Vinnie Jones, who has reinvented himself as a hard-man movie actor.

> 'The fans' favourite, a movie which understands like no other what makes football great.'
>
> A *Guardian* film critic referring to the star-studded 1981 movie, *Escape to Victory*

A scene from the risible *Escape to Victory*. Look, no dirt.

◁ Pelé flirted with the big screen twice in the 1980s. He first appeared in the POW drama *Escape to Victory* and again two years later in the little known *Young Giants*.

◁ *Beyond The Promised Land*, a Man Utd authorised fly-on-the-wall glimpse of Becks and the rest during the 1999/00 season, was only shown in Manchester cinemas.

◁ The boot was on the other foot when *Footballers' Wives* hit the small screen recently. 'They're young, they're rich, they're sexy, and they've got everything money and fame can buy,' screamed the publicity puff.

◁ *The Arsenal Stadium Mystery* is the earliest example – a 1939 black and white murder mystery set against a Highbury backdrop.

Ukraine Train

Dynamo Kiev, late 1980s

IF THE DUTCH TEAM of the 1970s were the fathers of 'Total Football', the Dynamo Kiev team of the late 1980s were their second cousins once removed. Coach Lobanowski was an intelligent and imaginative man, his sullen demeanour hiding a purity of vision about what could be achieved on a football pitch.

His Kiev team came closest to achieving that vision in the 1986 European Cup Winner's Cup final against Atletico Madrid. It may have finished 3-0, but Kiev could have won by two or three times that margin and it wouldn't have flattered them. Their technique, movement and pace were outstanding and, had they not been part

of the Soviet state, would surely have been celebrated more widely for their skills. Lobanovski was immediately installed as national coach. His team played outstandingly at the 1986 World Cup, and reached the final of the 1988 European Championships where, having beaten the Dutch in the group stage, they surprisingly froze against them on the big day. Kiev remain a potent side, particularly at home, but the loss of their main stars to Italian and Spanish clubs has reduced their effectiveness in European competition.

Manager: Valery Lobanowski

Key Players
Sergei Baltacha (D) Vladimir Bessonov (D Oleg Kuznetsov (D)
Anatoly Demianenko (D) Vassily Rats (M)
Aleksandr Zavarov (W) Sergei Aleinikov (M) Igor Belanov (F)
Oleg Blokhin (F)

Lyon, 1986. Kiev celebrate another goal in the European Cup Winners' Cup Final victory over Atletico Madrid.

◄)» Vassily Rats scored one of the great World Cup goals in 1986, beating French goalie Joel Bats with a strike from 40 yards.
◄)» Belanov scored an even better one in the 4-3 defeat by Belgium in the second round, a raking shot across goal after swerving

past his marker. The Soviets always looked the better side in the game, but Belgium somehow scored more goals.
◄)» This was a team without stars, the one exception being Oleg Blokhin ('The Ukraine Train') who was the only survivor of the

side that won the European Cup Winners' Cup in 1975.
◄)» Kuznetsov signed for Rangers in 1990, but struggled with injuries inflicted by the 'hammer throwers' (Graeme Souness) in Scottish football.

Ulster Untouchables

The Northern Ireland Dream Team

LIKE WALES, Northern Ireland are a nation who traditionally have been forced to rely upon spirit, passion and solid organisation rather than individual brilliance to get results and, with the exception of the last few years, they have proved better at this than the Welsh. Two memorably courageous squads made waves in the 1958 and 1982 World Cups, and those squads rightly provide the core of this side (11 of the 16).

Jennings is one of the all-time great keepers, and Gregg a more-than competent reserve. The back four were all tough, honest pros but would be dreadfully vulnerable to pace – the alternatives, like

Hunter and Worthington were unfortunately from the same mould. The midfield is pretty good, the craft and industry of O'Neill and McIlroy providing a complement to Blanchflower's distribution.

Dougan provides height and power while McParland, scorer of five goals in the 1958 World Cup, gets the nod for his perseverance and pugnacity. And then there is Best. Imagine the damage he might have wreaked for his country if he had been surrounded by team-mates as talented as this.

Manager: Billy Bingham

4-3-1-2

Pat Jennings (forever!)

Pat Rice (C) (70s) Terry Neill (60s)
Chris Nicholl (70s/80s) Mal Donaghy (70s/80s)

Martin O'Neill (70s) Danny Blanchflower (50s/60s) Sammy McIlroy (70s/80s)

George Best (60s)

Peter McParland (50s) Derek Dougan (60s)

Subs: Harry Gregg (G) (50s) Allan Hunter (D) (70s) Neil Lennon (M) (90s)
Norman Whiteside (M/F) (80s) Jimmy McIlroy (W) (50s)

Valencia, 1982. Gerry Armstrong scores the historic winner against Spain, Northern Ireland's most famous goal.

◀ Plenty of managerial advice for Bingham; Terry Neill, Martin O'Neill and Blanchflower all cut the mustard in their club roles.

◀ Unlucky omissions? Gerry Armstrong, scorer of Northern Ireland's goal that beat hosts Spain in 1982, and his fellow forward Billy Hamilton.

◀ Omissions? Colin Clarke and Ian Dowie. Being among the top scorers does not obscure their lack of international ability.

◀ A pre-match curfew may be difficult to enforce; not too many health food and mineral-water disciples here. Be sure to get a ticket for the party if they win.

◀ There are enough jokers included without needing the slapstick of Sammy Nelson dropping his shorts.

United Bury Their Ghosts

Manchester United 4 Benfica 1, 1968

TEN YEARS ON, this was the night that laid the ghosts of Munich to rest. At the final whistle Bobby Charlton's face, distorted with emotion, told its own story. This was a victory for the dead as well as for the living, a fitting tribute to the Busby Babes who had perished on the tarmac on that fateful night of 6 February 1958.

The pre-determined venue for the European Cup final was a huge advantage for Matt Busby's team, as half of Manchester decamped to Wembley to cheer on their heroes. They saw a cagey, goalless first half, but a rare header from Charlton appeared to have won it for United just before the hour. But Benfica pulled level through Jaime

Graca after 75 minutes, and the goal galvanised the Portuguese champions. Pressing hard, Eusebio eluded Stiles in the dying minutes, only to be denied by Stepney's parry when a winner seemed certain. This incident proved to be the turning point. In extra-time United, lifted by their supporters, were irresistible. A goal of characteristic genius from George Best set them on their way, his dribble through the entire defence unleashing raptures of relief around Wembley. Kidd and Charlton twisted the knife, and Benfica were finished.

SCORERS: United: Charlton (2), Best, Kidd
           Benfica: Graca
EVENT: European Cup final, Wembley. 29 May 1968

MAN. UTD (Man: Matt Busby)		BENFICA (Man: Otto Gloria)	
1	Stepney	1	Enrique
2	Brennan	2	Adolfo
3	Dunne	3	Humberto
4	Crerand	4	Jacinto
5	Foulkes	5	Cruz
6	Stiles	6	Jaime
7	Best		Graca
8	Kidd	7	Coluna
9	Charlton	8	Jose
10	Sadler		Augusto
11	Aston	9	Eusebio
		10	Torres
		11	Simoes

Best (no. 7) turns away after scoring United's crucial second.

◖)) Apart from Busby and Bobby Charlton, centre-half Bill Foulkes was the only other Munich survivor involved in the match.

◖)) For Denis Law, it was a bittersweet night. He watched the match from a hospital bed recovering from a knee operation.

◖)) Foulkes' words after the game were moving: '...for those of us who lost our friends ... our victory seemed the right tribute to their memory'.

◖)) The aftermath brought several more honours. Busby was

knighted, while George Best was named English and European Footballer of the Year.

◖)) The 1968 team, like the Busby Babes, was largely home-grown. Only Alex Stepney and Paddy Crerand had cost a fee.

Unsung Heroes

Never Mind the Badge Kissers

LOYALTY IS OFTEN cited as the quality most lacking in the modern game. Ronaldo's search for a bigger pot of gold at Real Madrid, thus ignoring Internazionale's patience with his rehabilitation, is the most glaring example.

For the less gifted, the options are more prosaic. Some players, whether out of devotion or expediency, have demonstrated season after season of unyielding service. Goalkeepers often figure in clubs appearance records due to their ability to eke out a longer career. Pride of place must go to Steve Ogrizovic. He remained as understudy for years at Anfield watching Ray Clemence positively ooze rude health. He not only lasted another 16 years as Coventry's No.1 but showed enough consistency to set a club record for number of appearances.

As far as clubs go, West Ham has enjoyed a greater percentage of long-servers than almost any other. Some, like Bobby Moore, enjoyed almost every decoration possible. Spare a thought for fellow defender Billy Bonds, who chalked up a Hammers' record of 663 appearances. Despite proving himself a model of consistency, his sole reward was a single England call-up. He never even got on the pitch.

> 'He is part of the furniture, like a grandad. He's a miserable old git but he has such presence'
>
> Veteran Portsmouth keeper Alan Knight receives a dubious tribute from team-mate Paul Hall.

Tony Brown of West Bromwich Albion.

◁ March 1978. Chelsea's twin stalwarts Ron Harris and Peter Bonetti each make their 700th appearance for the club on the same day.

◁ Ian Callaghan, despite eighteen years of success at Anfield, waited 12 years between England caps before being recalled by Ron Greenwood in 1978.

◁ John Trollope played 770 games for Swindon over 20 years, finally hanging up his boots in 1980 – an amazing record for an outfield player.

◁ The award for Best Uncapped Player. Step forward Tony Brown of West Brom. He holds two club records, 574 appearances and 218 goals, but never got an international sniff in 17 years.

Unsung Success

ARSENAL LADIES FC came into being in 1987 and quickly established itself as a major force in the English game. The side was formed by Arsenal's then-community liaison officer Vic Akers to improve the club's links with women, and included an amalgamation with Aylesbury Ladies. Akers, kit man for the Arsenal first team, is currently manager of the side. Since their arrival on the scene 14 years ago Arsenal Ladies have landed 16 major trophies and have twice completed the treble of National League, FA Cup and League Cup. They have also collected the league title on two other occasions, have four other FA Cups to their credit and have lifted the League

Cup on a further five occasions. Such is the strength of the club today that Arsenal Ladies now run teams down to under-10 level. It has also formed its own soccer academy for girls aged 16–19, where they can combine studies with daily training. The students will become qualified coaches, enabling them to earn a living as well as continuing to play for the club.

Manager: Vic Akers

Key Players
Emma Byrne (G) Toni-Anne Wayne (G) Jess Wright (D)
Faye White (D) Clare Wheatley (D) Yvonne Tracy (D)
Casey Stoney (D) Kirsty Pealling (D) Leanne Champ (D)
Kelley Few (D) Pauline MacDonald (D) Emma Coss (M)
Ciara Grant (M) Jayne Ludlow (M) Sian Williams (M)
Marieanne Spacey (F) Ellen Maggs (F) Emma Moore (F)
Megumi Ogawa (F) Angela Banks (F)

Trophies
LT 1993, 1995, 1997, 2001, 2002 FAC 1993, 1995, 1998, 1999, 2001 LC 1992, 1993, 1994, 1998, 1999, 2000, 2001

- Top honours on the field have won the team top sponsorship too, with the likes of Nike, Lucozade and the *Daily Star* among their supporters.
- Foreign interest is high. More than 20 internationals are already in the senior team and enquiries have been received from players in Brazil, Nigeria, Japan, Australia, New Zealand and the USA.
- Midfielder Sian Williams, the captain, is manager of the Welsh Ladies international side and is the English Universities coach.
- Twelve first-team squad players also have FA coaching certificates, which they use to help local community teams.
- First-team players Ciara Grant and Angela Banks are employed by Arsenal FC to develop and co-ordinate the club's female side.

Valderrama, Carlos

Colombia

A FLAMBOYANT PLAYER even by the standards of South American football, Carlos Valderrama scarcely needed a huge corkscrew hairstyle to attract attention. The Colombian midfielder's abilities were plain to see; he passed and moved with intelligence and vision, directing his team around the field with his artistic promptings. On the minus side his theatrical tendencies stretched patience during the 1990 World Cup Finals, where he was stretchered off in apparent agony only to return miraculously minutes later. Following 11 seasons with his native Santa Marta he made the move to Europe where, during four years with Montpellier and Valladolid of Spain, he

largely flattered to deceive and picked up just a single Spanish Cup winner's medal.

Like many great players Valderrama usually reserved his best for the big occasion, his greatest game being the pivotal performance in a sensational 5-0 demolition of Argentina still fondly remembered by Colombian supporters. Much like his national side, however, Valderrama always promised more than he actually delivered.

VITAL STATISTICS

Place of Birth: Santa Marta, Colombia
Date of Birth: 2 September 1961
Died: n/a Caps: 110 (Colombia) Goals (International): 10
Clubs: Santa Marta, Millonarios, Montpellier, Valladolid, Medellin, Atletico Junior Barranquilla, Nacional, Tampa Bay Mutiny, Miami Fusion

LEGEND RATING

Achievement	5
Skill	9
Teamwork	6
Passion	8
Personality	8
Overall Legend Rating	**36**

◁❚▷ In 1997, Valderrama became the first Colombian to be capped 100 times.
◁❚▷ He was South American Footballer of the Year in 1987 and 1993.
◁❚▷ Most critics believe Valderrama couldn't adjust to the pace of

European football. Colombia, too, were often undone by technically inferior, but quicker and stronger sides.
◁❚▷ Unlike his compatriot Andres Escobar, he wasn't shot as a result of his team's shortcomings in the 1994 World Cup Finals.

◁❚▷ The hair really was a thing to behold, deserving of the captaincy of our Hairstyles XI (see Fashion Victims, Part 1).

Van Basten, Marco

IF MARCO VAN BASTEN had not been forced out of the game prematurely, who knows what he might have achieved. He was not yet 30 when a suspect ankle gave way in the 1993 European Cup final, a game in which he probably ought not to have played. That injury meant van Basten was denied the opportunity to make amends for the one failure in his career – a miserable showing in an abject Dutch display at the 1990 World Cup Finals. Van Basten and Bergkamp? Now that would have been interesting.

Still, his admirers – and he had many – can at least console themselves with memories of his performances in Holland's 1988 European Championship success in Germany, where he scored a hat-trick against England, the winner in the semi-final against the hosts, and a sensational volley from an impossible angle in the final against Russia. At club level van Basten won the lot. Starting as a 17-year-old with Ajax, he collected medals galore in Holland before a move to AC Milan in 1987. There, with compatriots Gullit and Rijkaard, he was the spearhead of the best club side in Europe and picked up three Serie A titles and two European Cups. His strike rate against the cynical defences of the Italian league was, to quote David Coleman, quite remarkable.

VITAL STATISTICS

Place of Birth: Utrecht, Holland

Date of Birth: 31 October 1964

Died: n/a Caps: 58 (Holland) Goals (International): 24

Clubs: Ajax, AC Milan

Appearances: Club (All Matches): 280

Goals: Club (All Matches): 218

Trophies: EuroC 1988; EC 1989, 1990; CWC 1987; DLT 1982, 1983, 1985; SA 1988, 1992, 1993

LEGEND RATING

Achievement	9
Skill	9
Teamwork	8
Passion	9
Personality	7
Overall Legend Rating	**42**

◁ᴵᴵ He was voted European footballer of the year in 1988, 1989 and 1992 and World Player of the Year 1992. He was also Golden Boot winner in 1986 (37 goals in 26 games for Ajax).

◁ᴵᴵ At the 1988 European Championships he became the first player to score a hat-trick against England since the Peruvian Juan Seminario in 1959.

◁ᴵᴵ He scored two goals as Milan routed Steaua Bucharest 4–0 in the final of the 1989 European Cup.

◁ᴵᴵ In 1991 van Basten objected to being used as a lone striker for Milan. It is alleged he gave Milan President Silvio Berlusconi an ultimatum: him or the boss; Coach Arrigo Sacchi left to coach in Italy that summer.

Van Nistelrooy, Ruud

Manchester United, Holland

WHEN MANCHESTER UNITED unveiled £19 m Ruud Van Nistelrooy from PSV Eindhoven in April 2000, only for him to fail a medical, the snigger from their rivals was almost audible. When the same player ruptured cruciate ligaments a few weeks later during routine training in Holland, they could hardly contain themselves. To paraphrase the chant, they're not laughing anymore.

Since recovering from injury the Dutchman has become one of Europe's most complete and feared strikers. Strong, skilful, with acute positional sense and a deadly finish, the footballing world lies at van Nistelrooy's feet.

His impact was immediate. A goal on his debut in the 2001 Charity Shield was followed by two more on his first Premiership appearance. So began a season that was to finish with 36 goals, an incredible total in these days of squad rotation. Even though his fee was a British record, albeit a short-lived one, it already looks judicious compared to the £58 m lavished by United on Veron and Ferdinand.

Holland's failure to qualify for the 2002 World Cup Finals robbed the world stage of his talents. Euro 2004 should provide the showcase for a striker in his prime and at his peak.

VITAL STATISTICS

Place of Birth: Oss, Holland
Date of Birth: 1 July 1976
Died: n/a Caps: 24 (Holland) Goals (International): 11
Clubs: Den Bosch, SC Heerenveen, PSV Eindhoven, Manchester United
Appearances: Club (League): 264
Goals: Club (League): 163
Trophies: LT 2003

LEGEND RATING

Achievement	6
Skill	9
Passion & Commitment	8
Inspiration	8
Personality	7
Overall Legend Rating	**38**

◁)) Van Nistelrooy was leading scorer in the Dutch League for two successive seasons.

◁)) 2001/2. Voted PFA Player of the Year. Van Nistelrooy also won the Dutch equivalent whilst at PSV.

◁)) Most memorable performance – helps United turn a two-goal deficit into a 3-2 victory at Aston Villa in a 2002 FA Cup 3rd Rd. tie. The second of his two goals is a masterly controlled volley.

◁)) Biggest disappointment – knee injury not only scuppers his United transfer but robs him of the entire Euro 2000 tournament.

◁)) 2002/03 – Van Nistelrooy breaks the Premiership record by scoring in nine consecutive League games.

Venables, Terry

Tottenham Hotspur, England

UNTIL RESCUING MIDDLESBROUGH from the clutches of Division One in 2001, Terry Venables had never taken a footballing job north of Tottenham. In a managerial career that has spanned three decades his English employers have been almost exclusively in London, serving to reinforce his reputation as the cockney geezer with more than a hint of the Essex wide-boy about him – a reputation, it has to be said, he added to by resigning as England coach to defend himself in court against accusations of financial misdoings. Fans were sorry to see him leave the England post. As 'the people's choice' to succeed Graham Taylor he was a huge success, only narrowly failing to take England to the final of Euro 96. Venables has always had a reputation as a manager with imagination and foresight; from his time at Crystal Palace to his resurrection of Barcelona, his teams have played with flair and innovative tactical formations. At the Nou Camp he led Barca to their first league title for 11 years in 1985, and was unlucky not to add the European Cup to his sideboard the following year when, famously, all five of his allotted penalty-takers missed their kicks in the shoot-out against Steaua Bucharest in the final. He was a better coach than he was a player; despite being tipped for greatness at schoolboy level his career drifted after his second and final England appearance.

VITAL STATISTICS

Place of Birth:	London, England
Date of Birth:	6 January 1943
Died: n/a	Caps: 2 (England)

Goals (International): 0 Clubs: As Player: Chelsea, Tottenham Hotspur, Queens Park Rangers, Crystal Palace; As Manager: Crystal Palace, Queens Park Rangers, Barcelona, Tottenham Hotspur, Portsmouth, Australian national side, Middlesbrough, Leeds United

Trophies: PLA 1986; FAC 1991

LEGEND RATING

Achievement	6
Tactical Awareness	9
Motivation	8
Transfer Dealing and Team Selection	9
Personality	7
Overall Legend Rating	**39**

Venables was one of the few to bring out the best in Paul Gascoigne (right).

◄)) Venables has the same birthplace as Sir Alf Ramsey: Dagenham.

◄)) 1991. In partnership with Alan Sugar, Venables bought Spurs. Two years later, a bitter High Court battle ended with Sugar gaining sole control.

◄)) 1995. A judge described Venables' court evidence as 'wanton' and 'not entirely credible'.

◄)) 1997. Venables enjoyed a brief spell as Australian national coach, then bought Portsmouth for £1.

◄)) He has represented England at every level; schoolboy, youth, under–23, full international and, finally, coach.

◄)) 2002/3 proved a tough one for Venables. He started it as Leeds' potential saviour but left before its end with Leeds in trouble.

Vialli, Gianluca

Chelsea, Italy

A 20-YEAR CAREER at the summit of European football ought to have been sufficient, yet it is typical of Luca Vialli's motivation that, at an age when most of his peers were looking to Serie A for coaching jobs, he should be determined to accept the challenge to resurrect his managerial career in Division One with Watford.

By rights, his first experience of management should have put him off for life; thrust into the hot seat at Chelsea in 1998 following Ruud Gullit's sacking, he was to suffer the same fate within two years despite a top-three league finish and five trophies. The Chelsea supporters certainly did not consider him a failure; such was Vialli's popularity at Stamford Bridge his name was still being chanted around the ground over a year after his departure.

As a Chelsea player Vialli was underused and played only two minutes of the 1997 FA Cup final – strange for a player who had won every major honour in his native Italy, including a League and Cup double in a glorious season in 1994/95. His international career never produced the headlines of Paolo Rossi or Roberto Baggio, but he remains one of Italy's most popular players. Latterly, Vialli's attempts to buy Watford out of trouble backfired. He left the club after a little more than a season and is still in dispute over payments.

VITAL STATISTICS

Place of Birth: Cremona, Italy
Date of Birth: 9 June 1964
Died: n/a **Caps:** 59 (Italy) **Goals (International):** 16
Clubs: Cremonese, Sampdoria, Juventus, Chelsea
Appearances: Club (League): 467
Goals: Club (League): 156
Trophies: CWC 1990, (1998); EUFAC 1993; EC 1996; SA 1991, 1995; FAC 1997 (2000); LC (1998)

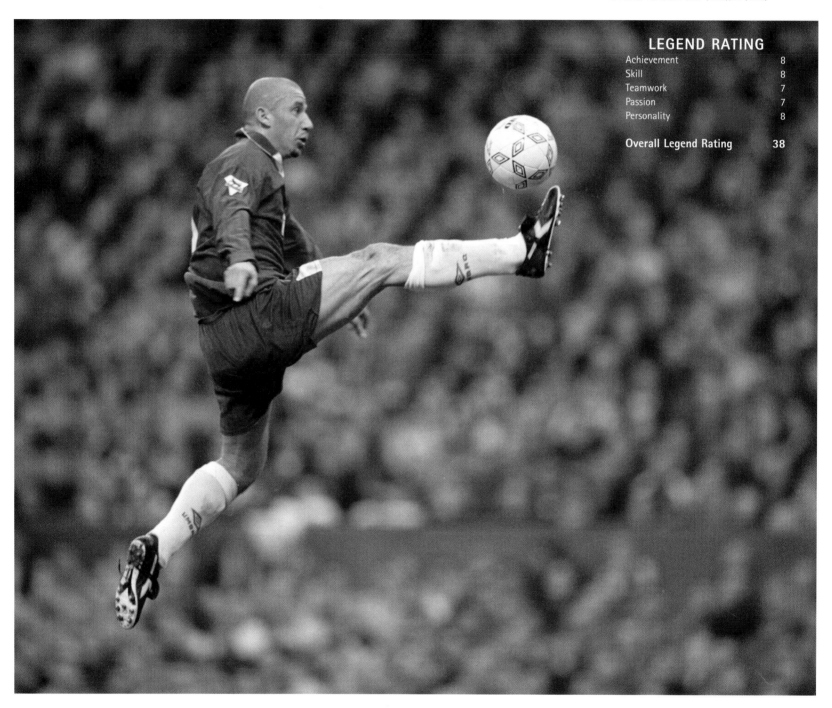

LEGEND RATING

Achievement	8
Skill	8
Teamwork	7
Passion	7
Personality	8
Overall Legend Rating	**38**

- He is one of only a handful of players to have won all three European club trophies.
- He scored both goals for Sampdoria in the 1990 European Cup Winners' Cup final.
- As Ruud Gullit's first foreign signing, Vialli's arrival started a Chelsea trend for imports.
- Discarded early from international football, Vialli won the last of his 59 caps at 28.
- 'Cheer up Luca, we love you.' Dennis Wise's T-shirt slogan, inspired by Vialli's unhappiness at Chelsea's squad rotation and his frequent omission.

Vieira, Patrick

Arsenal, France

PATRICK VIEIRA and Emmanuel Petit were the twin midfield turbines of the Arsenal side that won the league in 1998, a season the pair rounded off by collecting World Cup winner's medals with France. Two years later Vieira was again in the medals, picking up a winner's gong at Euro 2000 following France's victory over Italy – all in all a fairly tidy haul for the Senegalese-born midfielder.

Vieira first emerged at Cannes, where he captained the side in the French First Division at the age of 18. From there he wasted little time securing a move to AC Milan but, after failing to break into the side, he was rescued from his Milanese nightmare by Arsène Wenger

who paid £3.5 m to bring him to Highbury. That fee now looks like a steal. Wenger bought a player with skill and good distribution, but also immense strength.

Since arriving in England Vieira has improved with every season, and there are signs that the fuse on his temper, so often the source of his disciplinary problems, is growing longer with age. His intense rivalry with Roy Keane, another uncompromising figure with an equally quick temper, has been one of the Premiership's great sub-plots in recent years. Both had a terrible time in the 2002 World Cup Finals in Japan and Korea, for very different reasons.

VITAL STATISTICS

Place of Birth: Dakar, Senegal
Date of Birth: 23 June 1976
Died: n/a   Caps: 62 (France)
Goals (International): 4
Clubs: Cannes, AC Milan, Arsenal
Appearances: Club (League): 271
Goals: Club (League): 21
Trophies: LC 1998, 2002; FAC 1998, 2002

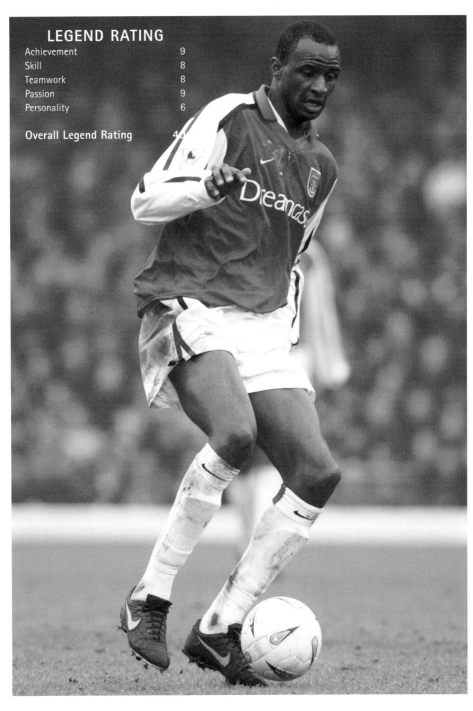

LEGEND RATING

Achievement	9
Skill	8
Teamwork	8
Passion	9
Personality	6
Overall Legend Rating	40

- After being dismissed in his first two games of the 2000/01 season, Vieira had to be persuaded not to quit English football by Arsène Wenger.
- He played only two games in Milan's first team – their loss.

- He was comfortably the best player in the 2001 FA Cup final, but still ended up on the losing side, thanks to Michael Owen.
- Vieira is exceptionally tall for a midfield player, giving his side an extra threat in the air at set-pieces.

- Vieira was not a first choice for France at the 1998 World Cup, having to wait until Euro 2000 before establishing himself as his country's leading central midfielder.

419

Villa Park

Birmingham, England

ASTON VILLA'S HISTORIC HOME is one of the oldest grounds in football. Built in 1897, Villa moved in from their former Perry Barr ground just a week after completing a League and Cup double.

The stadium originally had seating for 5,500 fans, all of whom must have watched with glee as Villa, inspired by the founding father of the Football League, George Ramsey, dominated the English game around the turn of the century.

Despite Villa's banishment from football's top table for much of the last century, Villa Park has always remained in the limelight. It hosted several matches during the 1966 World Cup and was selected as one of the venues for Euro 96. It is as an FA Cup semi-final ground that Villa Park has become a ground synonymous with domestic triumph, tension and disappointment.

In recent years the ground has undergone major redevelopment to become one of the most sophisticated in the country, with further modernisation planned. The improvements meant fans had to say farewell to the popular and massive Holte End, but the red-brick external façade still retains Villa's strong links with a bygone era.

VITAL STATISTICS

Location:	Birmingham, England
Local Club:	Aston Villa
Date Built:	1897
Current Capacity:	43,250
Max. Capacity:	76,588

The Holte End (behind far goal) is now two-tier and no less impressive with seating.

◄" Record attendance – 76,588 packed in for Villa's sixth round FA Cup tie against Derby County in 1946. The match was a 1-1 draw with Derby winning a thrilling replay 4-3.

◄" Best semi-final – Crystal Palace 4 Liverpool 3, 1990. Unfancied Eagles toppled the Champions-elect, Alan Pardrew creating his 15 minutes of fame with a dramatic winner.

◄" Best goal – 1999 semi-final replay. Ryan Giggs destroyed an international Arsenal defence with a 50-m run and finish.

◄" Best individual performance – Ted Drake's seven goals for Arsenal on 14 December 1935.

Villa, Veni, Vici

ASTON VILLA'S LONG HISTORY dictates that their dream team draws its personnel from a group of players spanning several generations. One of the dominant sides in the early years of the Football League, Villa won the championship six times before 1910, and remained in the top division for most of the next five decades, before the rot set in the 1960s. The next Villa side to make an impact won the league in 1981, and were a team largely without international stars – which might explain why only Cowans, Gray and Gidman make this all time XI (Dennis Mortimer and Peter Withe also came close).

Goalkeeper Sam Hardy was the first great England goalkeeper, and John Devey was Villa's most glamorous player in those early years. Massie, Walker and Dixon, though unfamiliar names to modern fans, were all excellent midfielders and David Platt would have enjoyed feeding off the nod downs of aerial superpowers, Hitchens and Gray. There are no representatives from the current, rather colourless team, although Ian Taylor deserves a mention for service and consistency, and Darius Vassell has the potential to develop into a genuine claret-and-blue icon.

Manager: Ron Saunders

4-4-2

Samuel Hardy (10s)

Stan Lynn (50s) Paul McGrath (90s)
Gareth Southgate (C) (90s) Charlie Aitken (70s)

John Devey (1890s) Gordon Cowans (80s)
David Platt (80s/90s) John Dixon (40s/50s)

Gerald Hitchens (50s) Andy Gray (80s)

Subs: Nigel Spink (G) (80s/90s) John Gidman (D) (80s)
Alex Massie (M) (30s) Billy Walker (M/F) (20s) Peter McParland (50s)

1982. Villa's European Cup triumph.

◁〕 Charlie Aitken made a club record 656 appearances, many of them during Villa's days in the lower divisions.

◁〕 Nigel Spink's second game for Villa was the 1982 European Cup final. He was drafted into the team just 10 minutes after kick-off, after Jimmy Rimmer ricked his neck in the warm-up.

◁〕 Gerry Hitchens ('The Blond Bomber') shocked Villa fans by leaving for Internazionale in 1961, the same summer Jimmy Greaves also departed for Milan.

◁〕 Dixon and McParland played in the 1957 FA Cup final against Man United, with McParland scoring both goals in a 2-1 win.

◁〕 Gordon Cowans, though never given a lengthy run in the England team, was the lynchpin of Villa's European Cup success.

Vogts, Hans-Hubert (Berti) Borussia Monchengladbach, West Germany

BERTI VOGTS WAS KNOWN in Germany as 'Der Terrier', an acknowledgement of his tenacity and fighting spirit. Picked up by Borussia Monchengladbach at an early age, he developed into a competitive right-back and was an automatic choice for West Germany by the time the 1970 World Cup came around. Four years later he was still around, and part of an even better team (with Franz Beckenbauer, Paul Breitner, Wolfgang Overath and Gerd Muller) that had won the 1972 European Championships at a canter. This time, at home, West Germany prevailed, largely thanks to their manager Helmut Schoen's decision to deploy Vogts as a man-to-man marker

on Johann Cruyff. After a torrid first 20 minutes Vogts got to grips with the Dutch master, and Germany came back from the shock of an early penalty to win 2-1. Four years later he was captain for a disappointing campaign in Argentina. Vogts stayed at Monchengladbach for his entire career where, during the early 1970s when only Bayern Munich could match them, he collected a stack of domestic medals, as well as the UEFA Cup. After hanging up his boots, Vogts became a manager and coached the German national team that won the European Championship in England in 1996. In early 2002 he became the first overseas coach to be placed in charge of Scotland.

VITAL STATISTICS

Place of Birth: Büttgen, Germany
Date of Birth: 30 December 1946
Died: n/a Caps: 96 (West Germany) Goals (International): 1
Clubs: VFR Buttgen, Borussia Monchengladbach
Appearances: Club (League): 419
Goals: Club (League): 32
Trophies: WorC 1974; BLG 1970, 1971, 1975, 1976, 1977; EUFAC 1975, 1979; EuroC (1996)

LEGEND RATING

Achievement	9
Skill	7
Teamwork	8
Passion	9
Personality	7
Overall Legend Rating	**40**

◁❯ Cruyff was so frustrated by the close attentions of Vogts in the 1974 World Cup final he was booked for complaining vociferously at half-time. Sad as it was to see a great player suppressed, the tactic won the game.

◁❯ Vogts was frustrated in his quest to win the European Cup, the one trophy that eluded him. Monchengladbach were beaten 3-1 by Liverpool in the 1977 final.

◁❯ In 96 internationals Vogts scored only one goal.

◁❯ His last match for West Germany was in the 1978 World Cup Finals – he scored an own goal.

◁❯ Vogts will have his work cut out with Scotland. Don Hutchison is a decent player, but Matthaus, Effenberg or Klinsmann he ain't.

Walter, Fritz

Kaiserslautern, West Germany

THE FIRST GREAT GERMAN FOOTBALLER, Fritz Walter started his career during the war, and emerged afterwards as the biggest influence on the newly formed West German national team. A goal-scoring centre-half, Walter was a typically German player: strong and physical, he was a driving influence in the middle of the field, a genuine forerunner of Franz Beckenbauer and Lothar Matthaus. Walter was 33 when he first played at a World Cup, in Switzerland in 1954. And, as if mindful that it might be his one and only chance, he performed like a man on a mission. After destroying Austria 6-1 in the semi-final, the formidable Hungarians awaited West Germany in

the final. Hungary took an early 2-0 lead but, inspired by the aggression and sheer will of Walter and the pace and finishing of Helmut Rahn, they came back to win 3-2. As it happened, 1954 was not Walter's first and last appearance at the Finals. Still going strong in 1958, he took West Germany to the semi-finals against host-nation Sweden, but picked up an injury in the game that, in addition to contributing to Germany's defeat, ended his international career.

VITAL STATISTICS

Place of Birth:	Kaiserslautern, West Germany
Date of Birth:	31 October 1920
Died: n/a	Caps: 61 (West Germany)

Goals (International): 33

Clubs: FC Kaiserslautern

Trophies: WorC 1954; BLG 1951, 1953

LEGEND RATING

Achievement	9
Skill	7
Teamwork	9
Passion	8
Personality	7
Overall Legend Rating	**40**

Walter poses with the Jules Rimet trophy after West Germany's victory in 1954.

◁)) Walter's brother, Otto, also played for the West German side in 1954 – they were the first pair of brothers to play in a final.

◁)) Kaiserslautern provided six players for the West German team in the 1954 final.

◁)) All Fritz Walter's club football was played with Kaiserslautern, his home team. They re-named their stadium in his honour in 1985.

◁)) Walter's goal-scoring rate was much higher early in his career,

but he still managed two in the thrashing of Austria. Otto also scored twice.

◁)) National coach Sepp Herberger tried to persuade Walter to come out of retirement for the 1962 World Cup Finals, aged 41!

Wandering Stars

BOLTON, ONE OF THE Football League's founder members, have had two outstanding sides, and both are well represented here. Dick Pym and Jimmy Seddon played in all three of their FA Cup wins in the 1920s, while David Jack, Ted Vizard and Joe Smith played in the first two. In the 1950s another well-drilled outfit reached two more FA Cup finals, winning in 1958. The three representatives from that team, left-back Tommy Banks, goalkeeper Eddie Hopkinson and striker Nat Lofthouse, were all England internationals.

Since then the club has been up and down, including a brief period in Division Four. In the 1970s Bolton were inspired by the flamboyant genius of Frank Worthington and the graft of Peter Reid, both of whom make the squad. So too does Paul Jones, who formed a formidable central defensive pairing with current manager Sam Allardyce, during the same era. Of the more recent stars, only Bergsson and Frandsen make the cut, with Stubbs and the lionhearted McGinlay providing cover on the bench.

Manager: Bill Ridding
4-4-2

Eddie Hopkinson (50s/60s)

Gudni Bergsson (90s) Paul Jones (70s)
Jimmy Seddon (20s) Tommy Banks (50s/60s)

Sasa Curcic (90s) David Jack (20s)
Per Frandsen (90s) Ted Vizard (20s)

Frank Worthington (70s) Nat Lofthouse (50s)

Subs: Dick Pym (G) (20s) Alan Stubbs (D) (90s) Peter Reid (M) (70s)
Joe Smith (F) (10s/20s) John McGinlay (F) (90s)

Wembley, 1958. Nat Lofthouse is chaired with the FA Cup.

◁ Although he was at the club for less than a year (1995/96), Sasa Curcic played some of the most dazzling football the Bolton crowd had ever seen.

◁ Long-serving Welsh winger Ted Vizard won 22 caps while with the Trotters. Though not a prolific goal scorer, he was the main supply line for striker Joe Smith.

◁ Gudni Bergsson joined with a reputation as a jobbing right-back, but was transformed into an excellent centre-half and crowd favourite, playing better at 36 than he had at 26.

◁ Bolton have made handsome profits by transferring Alan Stubbs, Jason McAteer, Nathan Blake, Alan Thompson, Claus Jensen and Eidur Gudjohnsen for millions in recent years.

Weah, George

AC Milan, Liberia

DISCOVERED IN 1987 by Arsène Wenger in Cameroon, where he was playing for his fifth club side, Tonerre Yaounde, Weah became the most talented and celebrated African player since Eusebio. His ceaseless charity efforts for his war-torn homeland showed a depth of personality that earned him the epithet 'light of Liberia'. His success in Europe convinced big European clubs that African players could adapt, and paved the way for a myriad of talented Africans to follow.

The North London connection continued a year later in 1988 as Weah linked up with Glenn Hoddle at Monaco. From there, in 1992,

he was transferred to Paris Saint-Germain, where he collected a league championship medal before moving on to even greater glories with AC Milan in Serie A. His pace, skill and directness frightened Italian defences, and was never better demonstrated than in the stunning length-of-the-field dribble that brought him one of the greatest goals of all time in a 4-0 win over Verona at the San Siro. Some have suggested an element of tokenism in his World and European Footballer of the Year awards, but let that not obscure the fact that he leaves an important legacy, both sporting and humanitarian.

VITAL STATISTICS

Place of Birth:	Monrovia, Liberia
Date of Birth:	1 October 1966
Died: n/a	Caps: 42 (Liberia) Goals (International): 7

Clubs: Tonerre, Yaounde, Monaco, Paris Saint-Germain, AC Milan, Chelsea, Manchester City, Marseille

Appearances: Club (League): 368

Goals: Club (League): 148

Trophies: FLT 1988, 1994; SA 1996, 1999; FAC 2000

LEGEND RATING

Achievement	7
Skill	8
Teamwork	7
Passion	8
Personality	8
Overall Legend Rating	**38**

- Two of Weah's splendidly named African clubs include Bong Range and Invincible Eleven.
- Weah is three times African Footballer of the Year (1989, 1994, 1995) and World and European Footballer of the Year in 1995.

- Playing for Liberia guaranteed that Weah would achieve nothing at international level. Had Nigeria or Cameroon had a striker of his potency, their 1990s World Cup campaigns might have been even more interesting.

- A late move to England in 2000 brought an FA Cup winner's medal with Chelsea, but he was clearly on the wane.
- His career in England ended on a sad note when he left Man City after a public disagreement with manager Joe Royle.

Wembley

ORIGINALLY NAMED The Empire Stadium, Wembley has several nicknames including 'The Old Lady' and 'The Venue of Legends'. Built in the space of 300 days at a cost of under £750,000, it was the brainchild of architects John Simpson and Maxwell Ayrton, who worked together with the engineer Sir Owen Williams.

It opened for the 1923 Cup final between Bolton and West Ham. The first myth was duly created, as over 200,000 fans stormed the gates and were cleared with the aid of PC George Storey on his famous white horse Billy. Since then, the famous twin towers have played host to 72 FA Cup and 24 League Cup finals, as well as several European club finals. It was England's venue for Euro 96, but its greatest moments were reserved for the 1966 World Cup.

In staging the Finals, England had the advantage of playing all six games at Wembley. Charlton's goal against Mexico and Rattin's dismissal for Argentina provided the prologue and first act. The dramatic finale was reserved for the final; Hurst's hat-trick, Stiles jig and Moore receiving the trophy are national mementos destined to be handed down through the generations.

VITAL STATISTICS

Location:	London, England
Local Club:	None
Date Built:	1923
Current Capacity (before closure):	80,000
Max. Capacity:	126,947

◁)) Wembley was the main venue for the 1948 Olympic Games.
◁)) Amazingly for a stadium then holding 100,000, it was built in less than a year by construction experts McAlpine. Its first intended use was for the British exhibition.

◁)) Despite its pageantry, Wembley was overdue a refit and closed in 2000. Its last game was very disappointing, as England squelched to a 1–0 defeat against Germany in a World Cup qualifier. It was also the last England game with Kevin Keegan as coach.

◁)) Wembley today is demolished. Squabbling between the government, the FA and Sport England have delayed the start of the new stadium. After much prevarication, Wembley was reinstated as the venue after fending off a Midlands lobby.

Wembley Wizards

THIS WAS A TEAM celebrated not for its domination of an era, but for one game. And if, as the chant goes, you know your history, it was the sweetest game ever for all Scotland fans. The England versus Scotland clash at Wembley in 1928 ought not to have held any terrors for the home side; in the corresponding fixture the previous season, England had triumphed 2-1 at Hampden Park. Nothing could have prepared them for what was to come. Some of Scotland's best players, like so many after them, were plying their trade in England so, in theory at least, the two teams should have known each other's games well. Indeed, many of them were club team-mates. Scotland's half-back and

captain Jimmy McMullan was the passing playmaker of Manchester City, and was to emerge as the man of the match. With targets as mobile as Alex James (Preston, later Arsenal), Alex Jackson (Huddersfield) and Hughie Gallacher (Newcastle) he was not short of players to hit. With England frozen like startled rabbits in the headlights of a juggernaut, Jackson helped himself to a hat-trick, leaving James and Gibson to notch the other two in a thumping 5-1 victory. For Scottish fans, that 1928 win was a symbolic act of defiance, a footballing equivalent of Bannockburn – which is why they still sing about it today.

**Manager: None
(team was picked by committee)**

Key Players

McMullan (M) Alex James (M) Gallacher (F) Jackson (F)

Trophies

None (but this Scottish side became famous for inflicting such a heavy defeat on the Auld Enemy on their own turf)

Man-of-the-match Jimmy McMullan is mobbed after Scotland's 5-1 demolition of England.

◄⫽ In the context of the Home Internationals, Scotland's victory was meaningless. Both teams were playing merely to avoid the ignominious wooden spoon.

◄⫽ England blamed the heavy pitch for the result, claiming it gave the smaller, nippier Scots an advantage.

◄⫽ Not only was it a thrashing, it was England's first defeat at Wembley.

◄⫽ Gallacher and James commanded huge transfer fees. Gallacher was sold to Chelsea in 1930 for £10,000, while James cost over £8,500, when Herbert Chapman took him to Arsenal in 1929.

◄⫽ England's team contained no lack of firepower; Dixie Dean scored a record 60 goals in the same season. He scarcely got a kick.

Wenger, Arsène

WHEN BRUCE RIOCH FAILED to cut the mustard at Arsenal, everyone was looking around for the big-name British manager who would take his place. It therefore came as something of a shock when they appointed a little-known coach plucked from the Japanese J-league. The initial reaction of fans was 'Arsène who?'

Wenger's managerial career began in inauspicious style. In his first season in full charge at Nancy his team were relegated, but a move to Monaco in 1987 allowed Wenger to show his worth and, with a team containing Glenn Hoddle (who was later to recommend him to Arsenal) he won the French league championship a year later.

In his time at Arsenal he has introduced a new methodology, turning them from a dour, functional outfit into an exciting and creative force. On the downside the team have been beset by disciplinary problems, and Wenger has seemed all too ready to condone some of the excesses of his players, even citing a small pitch at Highbury as an excuse for their roughhouse behaviour.

Winning the double in his second season earned Wenger huge kudos at Highbury, but he was under no small amount of pressure after a couple of lean years, and a second double in 2002 came as a huge relief.

VITAL STATISTICS

Place of Birth: Strasbourg, France

Date of Birth: 1 January 1950

Died: n/a

Caps: 0

Goals (International): 0

Clubs: As Player: Strasbourg; As Manager: Nancy, Monaco, Nagoya Grampus Eight, Arsenal

Trophies: FLT 1988; LT 1998, 2002; FAC 1998, 2002, 2003

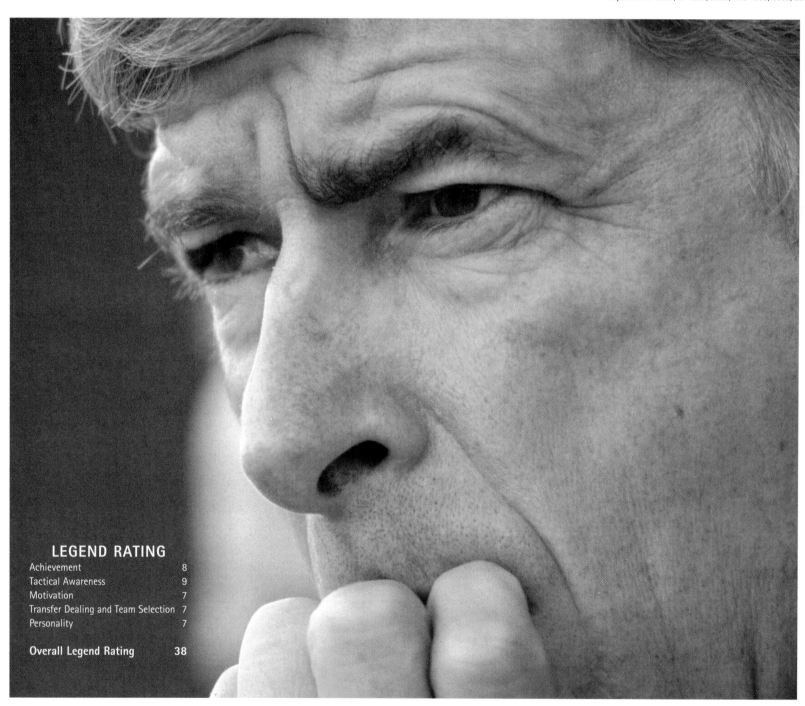

LEGEND RATING

Achievement	8
Tactical Awareness	9
Motivation	7
Transfer Dealing and Team Selection	7
Personality	7
Overall Legend Rating	**38**

- Strasbourg won the French First Division when Wenger was a player there, but he only appeared three times that season.
- Wenger took Nagoya Grampus Eight from third-bottom to runners-up in the J-League in his first season.
- He was charged with serious disrepute after an altercation with the fourth official in the opening game of the 2000/01 season. A 12-match touchline ban was later overturned.
- Has earned plaudits (rightly) for importing some exciting overseas players like Patrick Vieira, Marc Overmars, Kanu and Thierry Henry.
- Has earned criticism (also rightly) for buying and picking some very ordinary imports (Nelson Vivas and Luis Boa Morte anyone?).

White Horse Wembley

Bolton Wanderers 2 West Ham United 0, 1923

THE NEWLY COMPLETED Empire Stadium at Wembley had been chosen as the venue for the Cup final. Amazingly, it was not an all-ticket event, a fact which resulted in mayhem.

A realistic estimate is that 250,000 people turned up to a stadium built to hold 100,000. Most of them were allowed in, with a result that at the scheduled kick-off time of 3 p.m., thousands of fans covered the pitch.

The day was saved by one PC Storey. Mounted on his horse Billy, he helped push back the throng to just beyond the touchlines with such success that the game started only 44 minutes late. Legend has it (falsely) that he managed this feat single-handed when in fact, Billy's distinctive white appearance was the only one visible from a distance.

After such a delay, and with the crowd encroaching to within inches of the pitch, the game was not a classic. David Jack gave Bolton an advantage after two minutes that they seldom looked like losing. J.R. Smith's goal after 53 minutes would have grabbed the headlines in any other year. They had already been written by a single white horse.

SCORERS: Jack, JR Smith
EVENT: FA Cup Final, Wembley. 28 April, 1923

BOLTON (Man: Charles Foweraker)		WEST HAM (Man: Syd King)	
1 Pym	8 Jack	1 Hufton	8 Brown
2 Haworth	9 JR Smith	2 Henderson	9 Watson
3 Finney	10 Joe Smith	3 Young	10 Moore
4 Nuttall	11 Vizard	4 Bishop	11 Ruffell
5 Seddon		5 Kay	
6 Jennings		6 Tressdern	
7 Butler		7 Richards	

The FA was worried about the appeal of the new stadium and had advertised widely for fans to attend. They had to refund 10 per cent of the gate to spectators with pre-paid tickets who were unable to get to their seats.

PC Storey was not scheduled to be at Wembley that afternoon. He answered an emergency call in Central London to report to the ground once the crowds got out of hand.

The FA could not abandon the game: King George V was there.

Bolton's first goal was aided by West Ham defender Jack Tressdern, who was caught up in the crowd after taking a throw-in, allowing David Jack a free passage. Jack's shot knocked out a spectator pressed against the net.

White Supremacy

IT CAN'T HAVE BEEN much fun coaching Real Madrid in the 1970s or 1980s. How on earth do you satisfy the supporters of a club who have won the European Cup five times on the run, and have grown used to winning the league almost every year? The answer is you can't – which might explain why Real went 32 years before reclaiming their crown as champions of Europe.

Unlike the FA, the Spanish football authorities relished the opportunity the European competition presented, and this enthusiasm helped Real in those early tournaments. It also gave exposure to talented players from less prestigious clubs; even before playing Reims in the 1956 final, Real had decided to buy their playmaker, Raymond Kopa.

After that first flush of victories in Europe, Real found it harder going. Benfica and the two Milan teams emerged as threats to their supremacy (as Real struggled to replace Di Stefano and Puskas, these three won the next five tournaments). Although they never could replace those great players, Real did manage a swansong, winning the European Cup in 1966

Managers: Pepe Villalonga (1955–57), Luis Carniglia (1957–59) and Miguel Munoz (1960–74)

Key Players
Alonso (G) Zarraga (D) Alfredo Di Stefano (M)
Francisco Gento (W) Jose Santamaria (D) Ferenc Puskas (F)
Raymond Kopa (M) Ignacio Zoco (M) Hector Rial (F)
Amancio Amaro (F)

◄ Real knocked the young Busby Babes out of the European Cup in the 1957 semi-finals. Were it not for the air crash, they may have met again in the 1958 final, but AC Milan easily beat the makeshift United team in the semis.

◄ Miguel Munoz was a half-back in the 1956 and 1957 European Cup Final teams. Three years later he coached Real to their most famous victory over Eintracht Frankfurt. He remained as manager for 14 years. (The longest run since has been three!)

◄ Amancio Amaro won nine league titles with Real Madrid, and scored their first goal in the 1966 European Cup final against Partizan Belgrade.

Wingless Wonders

IT IS A LINE-UP that England fans can recite like a mantra. And yet it is a team almost as notable for the players it does not include as those that it does. The full-backs were good, honest professionals – but functional. Jimmy Armfield was a classier right-back than George Cohen, whilst Ray Wilson can count himself lucky that Terry Cooper did not arrive on the other flank until three years later. Bobby Moore and Gordon Banks provided the defensive class, natural choices in any England team. And though the midfield was solid, the emergence of Alan Mullery and Colin Bell for the next World Cup certainly hadn't weakened it (indeed, some would argue it was improved by

their inclusion). The forwards present a knotty problem. Geoff Hurst vindicated his late selection, his four goals in the last three games saw off Argentina in the quarter-finals and West Germany in the final, but the player he replaced, Jimmy Greaves, was an even more prolific scorer (his 44 goals in 57 games is England's most impressive modern ratio by a distance). Roger Hunt may be the lucky man here. Whatever the argument, and many feel the 1970 side was even better, no one can deny this XI their place in England's hall of fame as the nation's only World Cup winners.

Manager: Alf Ramsey

Line-Up

Gordon Banks George Cohen Ray Wilson Nobby Stiles Jack Charlton Bobby Moore Alan Ball Geoff Hurst Roger Hunt Robert Charlton Peters

Trophies

WorC 1966

Alf Ramsey and Bobby Moore flank the Jules Rimet trophy.

- ◁ This side was dubbed the 'wingless wonders' due to Alf Ramsey's reluctance to use wide players.
- ◁ From 1958 to 1970, only England broke Brazil's dominance of the World Cup.
- ◁ Cohen and Wilson were capped for a further two years. The young Alan Ball was a regular until 1975.
- ◁ The England team who defended the World Cup in 1970 was arguably a better side.
- ◁ After winning the Jules Rimet trophy, England remained undefeated for nearly a year, until Scotland beat them 3-2 at Wembley.

Winterbottom, Walter

IN THESE DAYS of professional managers surrounded by teams of assistants and advisers, it seems hard to believe that England's first manager was not even full-time. Until 1947 the national team was selected by a time-serving committee, and Winterbottom was promoted from chief coach after an embarrassing 1-0 defeat by Switzerland. His team's performance in 1950 at England's first World Cup in Brazil proved a flop, as they failed to make the final pool after suffering their most humiliating reverse – 1-0 to the United States. The tabloids were less vitriolic back then, so happily Winterbottom was spared the indignity of having his head metamorphosised into a root vegetable on the back page of the *Daily Mirror*. Throughout his tenure, the influence of the committee never fully disappeared, and it was not until Alf Ramsey took over in 1962 that the power of team selection was transferred exclusively to the manager.

Under Winterbottom, England had been carefully transformed from the team of Finney, Matthews and Lofthouse to the newer breed of Greaves and Haynes. In so doing Winterbottom started the job that was so successfully completed by Alf Ramsey in 1966.

VITAL STATISTICS

Place of Birth: Oldham, England
Date of Birth: 31 January 1913
Died: 16 February 2002
Caps: 0
Goals (International): 0
Clubs: Manchester United
Trophies: None

LEGEND RATING
Achievement 5
Tactical Awareness 8
Motivation 7
Transfer Dealing and Team Selection 8
Personality 7

Overall Legend Rating 35

- In Winterbottom's first game in 1947, England beat Portugal 10-0.
- Winterbottom led England in four World Cups; no other England manager has managed more than two.
- After England's defeat by the United States, some English news gatherers assumed the reported score was incorrect and printed the result as 10-1 to England
- Winterbottom's most successful World Cup was in 1962 when

England reached the quarter-finals, losing 3-1 to eventual winners, Brazil.
- Despite winning the World Cup four years after Winterbottom stood down, Alf Ramsey never qualified for the Finals.

Women's World Cup

New World Order

THE BRAINCHILD of former FIFA President Joao Havelange, the official Women's World Cup did not come into existence until 1991. The first tournament was staged in China and was dominated by America. They scored 20 goals in six games with striker Michelle Akers grabbing 10 on her own, including five in one game against Chinese Taipei. However, the Americans were made to fight all the way in the final by Norway, whom they eventually defeated 2-1. The second tournament was held in Sweden, and Norway gained sweet revenge by knocking the USA out at the semi-final stage. Norway then went on to lift the title courtesy of a 2-0 victory over Germany.

In the last Women's World Cup – staged in the States in 1999 – the USA returned to the top of the women's game after winning a dramatic penalty shoot-out against China after the final finished goalless. The next Women's World Cup is to be played in China in September 2003.

'In some ways it's the biggest sporting event of the last decade. It's new and exciting for the United States. It will have a very far-reaching impact, not only for the United States, but for the world.'

President Bill Clinton after the USA's Women's World Cup victory over China in 1999

Pasadena, 1999. The USA raises its second World Cup.

◄)) More than 63,000 fans watched the USA beat Norway in the first official World Cup final in 1991.

◄)) Brandi Chastain stripped off her top after scoring the decisive penalty for the US in the 1999 World Cup final. She later claimed it was 'momentary insanity'. The incident was given disproportionate and unedifying coverage.

◄)) The US trio of strikers Michelle Akers, Carin Jennings and April Heinrichs scored 20 goals in six games to reach the first title.

◄)) 90,185 fans watched the 1999 Women's World Cup final in Pasadena and millions more tuned in to it on television.

◄)) The introduction of professionalism at Fulham could herald a new era for English women's football.

Wright, Billy

Wolverhampton Wanderers, England

WHEN BILLY WRIGHT passed Bob Crompton's record number of England caps in May 1952 it was his 42nd appearance. That he went on to more than double that record is a testimony to his talent, consistency and downright resilience. Wright was unlucky to play in an era when insularity reigned in British football, so was never able to develop his game properly against the more creative European sides. In 1953 he bore the brunt of criticism after England had been led a merry dance by the Hungarians at Wembley, having taken flak after the humiliating defeat to the USA in the 1950 World Cup. Abysmal tactics and selection meant Wright never made an impact on a major tournament – that was left to his natural successor, Bobby Moore.

His experiences at club level were not dissimilar. Despite Wolves' dominance of the domestic game in the 1950s, their performances in the European Cup were disappointing – a narrow defeat to Schalke, and a hammering by Barcelona. Old-fashioned he might have been, but Wright was a player of enormous integrity, an honest pro who never gave less than his lung-busting best whether playing at half-back or, as he did later in his career, in the centre of defence. Disciplined, determined and fearless he was also the perfect captain.

VITAL STATISTICS

Place of Birth: Ironbridge, England
Date of Birth: 6 February 1924
Died: 3 September 1994   Caps: 105
Goals (International): 3
Clubs: Wolverhampton Wanderers
Appearances: Club (League): 490
Goals: Club (League): 13
Trophies: FAC 1951; LT 1954, 1958, 1959

LEGEND RATING

Achievement	8
Skill	8
Teamwork	9
Passion	10
Personality	6
Overall Legend Rating	**41**

◀ In 1959 Wright made his 100th appearance for England, fittingly against Scotland. England won 1-0.

◀ Wright missed only three games in reaching his century. Eighty-five of his 100 appearances were as captain.

◀ Wright's last match for England was against the USA; an 8–1 win was partial revenge for the embarrassment in 1950.

◀ Wright had four years as Arsenal manager in the early 1960s, but achieved nothing and was lost to the game soon after.

◀ Wright was PFA Player of the Year in 1952, and was awarded a CBE on his retirement. A monument was constructed two years after his death, and now stands outside Molineux.

Yashin, Lev

USSR

AS RUSSIA'S MOST FAMOUS and charismatic player, Lev Yashin's presence dominated Soviet football for two decades, while appearances in three World Cups brought his talents to a wider audience. Yashin made his name with Moscow Dynamo; five League titles for the club were due in no small part to his ability between the sticks.

Emerging in the European Championships in 1960, Yashin rapidly established himself as the world's top goalkeeper, a position only Gordon Banks would later challenge him for. Known as 'The Octopus' (to strikers it sometimes seemed as if he had eight arms) Yashin revolutionised the image of goalkeepers, transforming them from anonymous men in polo necks to swashbuckling match-winners. His swansong was the 1966 World Cup Finals, which found him in peak form. The tournament won him so many admirers that, later, in 1971, his testimonial was attended by Pelé, Eusebio, Bobby Charlton and Franz Beckenbauer.

Yashin's promotion to team manager of the Soviet Union was immediate upon his retirement, but with a poor squad he could never scale the heights he reached as a player.

VITAL STATISTICS

Place of Birth: Moscow, Russia
Date of Birth: 22 October 1929
Died: 20 March 1990   Caps: 78 (USSR)
Goals (International): 0
Clubs: Moscow Dynamo
Appearances: Club (League): 326
Goals: Club (League): 0
Trophies: EuroC 1960; SLT 1954, 1955, 1957, 1959, 1963

LEGEND RATING

Achievement	6
Skill	10
Teamwork	8
Passion	10
Personality	8
Overall Legend Rating	**42**

- He was, and still is, the only goalkeeper to have ever been voted European Footballer of the Year, in 1963.
- The Soviet Union won the inaugural European Championships in 1960.
- Yashin always wore a trademark black jersey.
- Yashin skippered the Soviet Union to the semi-finals of the 1966 World Cup, where they lost 2-0 to Germany.
- One of the great shot-stoppers, Yashin saved over 100 penalties.

Yorkshire Grit

HERBERT CHAPMAN'S REPUTATION is largely based around his success with Arsenal in the 1930s, but his achievements at Huddersfield in the 1920s are no less praiseworthy. Chapman took a nondescript mid-table team and turned them into a side that went on to win the FA Cup and three successive league titles. His spell at Huddersfield, whom he joined as manager in 1921, was almost a dummy run for the Arsenal job. In an era when player movement was less common than it is today, Chapman was quick to realise the benefits to be gained from buying and selling players. It became his trademark. The purchase of playmaker Clem Stephenson for £4,000 from Aston Villa was a typical Chapman buy. Considered by many to be past his best, Stephenson became a pivotal member of a new team. Lured to Highbury in 1925, Chapman's first trophy at Arsenal was the FA Cup – almost inevitably, they beat Huddersfield in the final.

Huddersfield's 1922 FA Cup victory over Preston came courtesy of a penalty kick. The authorities frowned upon the antics of Preston goalkeeper J.F. Mitchell, who hopped around and tried to distract the taker. In future it was decided that goalkeepers would have to keep still.

Manager: Herbert Chapman

Key Players
Ray Goodall (D) Tommy Wilson (D) Clem Stephenson (M)
Billy Smith (W) Alex Jackson (F)

Trophies
LT 1924, 1925, 1926 FAC 1922

JUVAT·IMPIGROS·DEUS

◄» The first of Huddersfield's trio of titles was won on goal average from Cardiff City. Had the modern system of goal difference been in use, the Welshmen would have been champions.
◄» In 1924/25 Huddersfield did not concede more than two goals in a league match. Their heaviest defeat that season was a 3-0 reversal at Bolton in the first round of the FA Cup.
◄» Huddersfield went undefeated away from home on 15 November 1924 and 14 November 1925 (18 games with 12 wins).
◄» Scottish international Alex Jackson was one of the Wembley Wizards of 1928; he also had a spell playing soccer in America, for Bethlehem Steel.

You English $&@#

Each successive World Cup is approached in an ever-increasing frenzy of media coverage. Amidst the injury bulletins and who's in/who's out speculation there is usually a juicy tale to enliven the tabloids. 2002 saw a tale to match the Bobby Moore 'shoplifting' episode and Johann Cruyff's 1978 no-show.

The Irish training facilities were crude, unworthy of a side that had exceeded expectations by even qualifying for the tournament. Roy Keane had every right to express his disappointment at this shabby treatment, and the Irish FA were deserving of scorn for their parsimony at such a high-profile event.

Mick McCarthy was in a difficult position; he probably didn't entirely disagree with Keane, but couldn't back him publicly against his employers. His already uneasy relationship with Keane was compromised, and being something of a straight-backed disciplinarian, he demanded that Keane step in line. At this point compromise was required, but that is not Keane's way. At a public team-meeting he launched a fusillade of personal abuse at McCarthy that took all sense of proportion out of the matter. McCarthy, rightly on this occasion, dug his heels in even further and Keane was sent home.

'What do you think it's been like for me?'

McCarthy upbraids pressman for inane questioning

◁)) The saga lingered on for a week as rumours of Keane's return to the Far East abounded. But rumours they proved to be; there was no prodigal return for Keane.

◁)) Keane's biographer Eamonn Dunphy, the opinionated Irish journalist, defended his charge vociferously. His credibility was shot away when he subsequently tried to vilify the Irish tactics after their splendid performance against Cameroon.

◁)) Keane has a history of verbal fireworks; previous tirades include pillorying the 'prawn sandwich brigade' in the United corporate boxes, and castigating his United colleagues for lack of desire after exit from the 2001 Champions League.

Zagallo, Mario

WHEN BRAZIL WON the 1958 World Cup in Sweden, Mario Zagallo was an ever-present on the left wing. Similarly, in Chile in 1962, Zagallo played in every game in the tournament, scoring Brazil's opening goal against Mexico. By the time Brazil won the tournament again in 1970, Zagallo had been installed as coach.

It was another 24 years before Brazil reached the final again, winning on penalties in 1994, with Zagallo as assistant coach. In 1998, when they experienced the pain of losing a final for the first time (their 1950 loss was in a decisive group match, not a final), their coach was? Yup, you've guessed it, Mario Zagallo.

As a player Zagallo was an underrated contributor to the team. His stamina and industry allowed him to be the most effective defender of the Brazilian forwards, making him a perfect foil for the strolling Didi. As a coach he was a calming influence, realising that the key to the job was getting all his great players into a relaxed and confident frame of mind before letting them loose on the opposition. In both roles he has always been full of enthusiasm and vigour.

VITAL STATISTICS

Place of Birth: Brazil

Date of Birth: 9 August 1931

Died: n/a Caps: 35 (Brazil) Goals (International): 0

Clubs: Flamengo, Botafogo

Trophies: BLT 1953, 1954, 1961, 1962; WorC 1958, 1962 (1970 as coach, 1994 as technical advisor)

LEGEND RATING

Achievement	9	Achievement	9
Skill	8	Tactical Awareness	8
Teamwork	8	Motivation	8
Passion	6	Transfer Dealing and Team Selection	7
Personality	7	Personality	8
Overall Legend Rating	**38**	**Overall Legend Rating**	**40**

➤ In 1970 Zagallo took over as coach after Brazil had already qualified. Joao Saldanho, his predecessor, was deemed too unstable after he waved a revolver at one of his critics.

➤ Zagallo has had three spells as coach of Brazilian giants Flamengo, accepting the third job offer from the club in October 2000, at the age of 68.

➤ Zagallo scored Brazil's fourth goal in the 1958 World Cup final, using his pace and forcing the ball in at the near post.

➤ Between 1958 and 1962, Zagallo lost his place to livewire Pepe.

Zico, (Artur Antunes Coimbra)

Flamengo, Brazil

AT THE 1982 WORLD CUP, inspired by Socrates, Falcão, Cerezo and Zico, Brazil played football of an attacking brilliance not seen since 1970. It was a breath of fresh air after their dour tactics in 1978, and it allowed Zico, a huge disappointment in that earlier tournament, to show his true colours. His wiry strength and fierce shooting added firepower to the intricate movements of the men in gold – which was just as well because their other main striker, Serginho, was a donkey. Brazil's second-phase games were both classics; a 3-1 win over Argentina, featuring three brilliant goals, and an undulating 3-2 defeat by a Paolo Rossi-inspired Italy. Sadly, the

1986 tournament saw Zico back to the fitful and fretful shadow of eight years earlier. Zico's club football was principally with Flamengo, for whom he once starred in a win over a top-notch Liverpool team in the World Club Championship. A £2.5 m move to Udinese proved a bit of a waste of money for the Italians. Indeed, save for that one tournament in 1982, Zico would have been in danger of being remembered as one of the world's great unfulfilled talents.

VITAL STATISTICS

Place of Birth: Rio de Janeiro, Brazil
Date of Birth: 3 March 1953
Died: n/a Caps: 71 (Brazil) Goals (International): 48
Clubs: Flamengo, Udinese, Kashima Antlers
Appearances: Club (For Flamengo): 902
Goals: Club (For Flamengo): 727
Trophies: WCC 1981

LEGEND RATING

Achievement	8
Skill	9
Teamwork	7
Passion	7
Personality	8
Overall Legend Rating	**39**

◁ Sadly, Zico's last match for Brazil saw them crash out of the 1986 World Cup in a penalty shoot-out to France. After coming on as a sub, Zico had missed a penalty during the match, but had the balls to step up and score in the shoot-out.

◁ Zico scored a stunning hat-trick against Bolivia to clinch Brazil's place in the 1982 World Cup Finals.
◁ Zico scored with a trademark free-kick on his debut for Brazil in 1975.

◁ Kashima Antlers persuaded Zico to come to Japan to help launch the J-League.
◁ Zico was later appointed Sports Minister in Brazil, and was assistant coach under Zagalo at the 1998 World Cup.

Zidane, Zinedine

Juventus, Real Madrid, France

MARSEILLES' MOST FAMOUS footballing son has seen his career soar to unimaginable heights from inauspicious beginnings at Cannes. A three-season period from 1998 brought him winners' medals in World and European finals for France, and a record £45 m transfer from Juventus to Real Madrid.

His biggest achievement? Look no further than the goals, two emphatic headers from corners, that set France on their way to that famous 3-0 win at the Stade De France in the 1998 World Cup final in Paris against Brazil. Zidane's two-footed skills and movement bemused Brazil throughout the game, just as they had bemused

defenders all through the tournament. The dose was repeated two years later at Euro 2000, where Zidane again proved himself to be without peer in the modern game. His stunning volley in the 2002 European Cup final was the icing on the cake.

A slightly stooping, balding figure, some say he lacks the charismatic looks of Gabriel Batistuta or the natural athleticism of Luis Figo, but he remains an inspiration for late developers everywhere. Zidane did not make his professional debut until 1986 and remained in relative obscurity, with Cannes and Bordeaux, before Juventus signed him 10 years later. He's certainly made up for lost time since.

VITAL STATISTICS

Place of Birth: Marseille, France
Date of Birth: 23 June 1972
Died: n/a   Caps: 82 (France)
Goals (International): 22
Clubs: Cannes, Bordeaux, Juventus, Real Madrid
Appearances: Club (League): 407
Goals: Club (League): 73
Trophies: SA 1997, 1998; WorC 1998; EuroC 2000; EC 2002

LEGEND RATING

Achievement	10
Skill	9
Teamwork	8
Passion	7
Personality	7
Overall Legend Rating	**41**

◁ Amazingly, Zidane's first goal did not arrive until five years after his debut for Cannes.

◁ Not always the hero, his five years at Juventus brought six red cards.

◁ He was voted World Footballer of the Year in 1998 and 2000 and European Footballer of the Year in 1998.

◁ £45 m is proving hard to live up to: Zidane struggled with form and injury at Real Madrid in 2002.

◁ He received the *Legion d'Honneur* from the French President.

Zoff, Dino

Juventus, Italy

IN A PLAYING CAREER that lasted 20 years, Dino Zoff performed with a consistency and casual excellence that earned him a reputation, alongsidze Banks and Yashin, as one of the best goalkeepers Europe has ever produced. Success took its time to discover Zoff. He did not make his debut for Italy until he was 26, but quickly found his feet and was soon picking up top honours. His first triumph was at the European Championships of 1968, when Italy claimed the trophy on home soil, but his most notable achievement was to captain his country to 1982 World Cup glory in Spain at the age of 40.

It was similarly late in his career that Zoff began to pick up club trinkets, but once he got a taste for victory there was no stopping him; following his move to Juventus in 1972 he collected eight major trophies, including six Serie A titles. His retirement saw him remain with Juventus, where he became team coach in 1988, winning the UEFA Cup in 1990, but in 1992 he left to fill the vacant manager's position at Lazio.

VITAL STATISTICS

Place of Birth: Mariano del Friuli, Italy

Date of Birth: 28 February 1942

Died: n/a **Caps:** 112 (Italy) **Goals (International):** 0

Clubs: Udinese, Mantova, Napoli, Juventus

Appearances: Club (For Juventus): 330

Goals: Club (Juventus): 0

Trophies: EuroC 1968; WorC 1982; SA 1973, 1975, 1977, 1978, 1981, 1982; UEFAC 1977 (1990)

LEGEND RATING

Achievement	9
Skill	9
Teamwork	8
Passion	8
Personality	7
Overall Legend Rating	**41**

◁ Zoff set an international world record in 1974 by not conceding a goal for 1,143 minutes, a sequence broken in unlikely fashion by Haiti.

◁ Zoff carried on playing just long enough to feature in the great Juventus side of the early 1980s – with Platini, Boniek, Tardelli and Rossi.

◁ His 112 Italian appearances was a national record at the time, but has since been overhauled by Paolo Maldini.

◁ Zoff preserved Italy's 3–2 lead over Brazil in the classic 1982 World Cup encounter with a formidable save from Oscar's header in the dying minutes.

Zola, Gianfranco

Chelsea, Italy

HE MAY BE SARDINIA'S most celebrated footballer since Luigi Riva but, after thrilling crowds at Stamford Bridge during the closing seasons of his career, Gianfranco Zola is now regarded as an adopted Londoner. Too small to be a target man and never a prolific goal scorer, Zola's mercurial ball skills have created countless goals for grateful team-mates and made many accomplished defenders look like hapless novices. His trademark free-kicks rely on guile and spin rather than outright power, but he still boasts a strike rate better than some penalty-takers. None was more memorable than his opener for Chelsea on their most famous European night, a 3-1 victory over Barcelona in a Champions League quarter-final in 2001. Zola repeatedly cut an international defence to ribbons that night.

Ironically, given his dead-ball prowess, it is a missed penalty for which Italian audiences will best remember him; his uncharacteristic failure against Germany in Euro 96 resulted in the *Azzuri's* elimination from the tournament. Never a Championship winner in Italy or England, and never a huge international success, Zola will nonetheless be remembered as one of the most abundantly gifted players of his generation.

VITAL STATISTICS

Place of Birth: Sardinia, Italy
Date of Birth: 5 July 1966
Died: n/a **Caps:** 35 (Italy) **Goals (International):** 8
Clubs: Nuorese, Torres, Napoli, Parma, Chelsea
Appearances: Club (League): 468
Goals: Club (League): 150
Trophies: SA 1990; UEFAC 1995; FAC 1997; CWC 1998; LC 2000

LEGEND RATING

Achievement	6
Skill	9
Teamwork	9
Passion	8
Personality	7
Overall Legend Rating	**39**

◁ﹶ 1996. Zola became a *bête noire* for England fans after scoring the only goal in a World Cup qualifier at Wembley.
◁ﹶ 1997. Named Footballer of the Year, despite joining Chelsea in mid-season.

◁ﹶ 2000. Voted Chelsea's greatest-ever player.
◁ﹶ 2001. 'There's only one Mrs Zola.' Song sung by Chelsea fans after Zola's wife was reported to have persuaded him to remain at the club for another season.

◁ﹶ 2002. Scored an audacious mid-air back-heeled volley versus Norwich in an FA Cup replay, probably his best-ever strike for Chelsea.

Zubizarreta, Andoni

Barcelona, Spain

SPAIN'S MOST CAPPED PLAYER was one of Europe's most consistent goalkeepers of the last 20 years. Unfussy and dependable, Zubizarreta was a fixture in the Spanish side much in the way Zoff and Shilton had been for England a few years earlier. He played his entire career in his homeland, where he won incalculable respect, and a few trophies to boot. His talent was spotted early by Athletic Bilbao who recognised his potential while 'Zubi' was still at his first club, Alaves. But after four seasons at Bilbao, during which time he won two La Liga titles, Barcelona whisked him off to the Nou Camp for £1.2 m.

The European Cup provided Zubizarreta with both his greatest triumph and disaster. In 1992 his clean sheet made a single goal against Sampdoria sufficient for Barca to win their first European Cup, but that was all forgotten two years later when the final of the same competition produced a 4-0 thrashing by Milan. Football's reputation for showing little sentiment to its heroes was again demonstrated after that defeat; Zubizaretta was made a scapegoat and unceremoniously offloaded to Valencia.

VITAL STATISTICS

Place of Birth: Vitoria, Spain
Date of Birth: 23 October 1961
Died: n/a Caps: 126 (Spain) Goals (International): 0
Clubs: Alaves, Athletic Bilbao, Barcelona, Valencia
Appearances: Club (League):
Goals: Club (League):
Trophies: EC 1992; PLA 1983, 1984, 1991, 1992, 1993, 1994; CWC 1989

LEGEND RATING

Achievement	7
Skill	8
Teamwork	7
Passion	8
Personality	6
Overall Legend Rating	**36**

◁ᐳ The £1.2 m paid for Zubizarreta by Barcelona in 1986 made him the world's most expensive goalkeeper.

◁ᐳ Zubizarreta won six La Liga titles, two with Bilbao and four with Barca.

◁ᐳ Sadly, his final game for Spain saw him make a howler against Nigeria at France 98.

◁ᐳ Zubizarreta is the only goalkeeper to lose a penalty shoot-out against England – in the quarter-final of Euro 96.

◁ᐳ Spain's defeat to England that day ended a 31-match unbeaten run.

Statistics

These statistics are correct up until end of the UK 2002/03 season. The following websites are a good source of the most up-to-date information on statistics, players, teams, leagues, managers and the game in general:

www.fifa.com
www.4thegame.com
www.englandfootballonline.com
www.football-league.co.uk
www.optasoccer.com
www.planetfootball.com
www.soccer-europe.com
www.soccernet.com
www.sportall.co.uk
www.sporting-heroes.net
www.stararchive.com
www.worldcupsoccer.com
www.wsoccer.com

Adams, Tony
Place of Birth: Romford, England
Date of Birth: 10 October 1966
Caps: 66 (England)
Goals (International): 5
Clubs: Arsenal
Appearances: Club (League): 504
Goals: Club (League): 32
Trophies: LT 1989, 1991, 1998, 2002; FAC 1993, 1998, 2002; LC 1987, 1993; CWC 1994

Ademir, Marques de Menezes
Place of Birth: Recife, Brazil
Date of Birth: 11 May 1926
Died: 1996
Caps: 39 (Brazil)
Goals (International): 32
Clubs: FC Recife, Vasco da Gama, Fluminense
Trophies: BLT 1945, 1946, 1947, 1949, 1950, 1952

Albert, Florian
Place of Birth: Hungary
Date of Birth: 15 September 1941
Caps: 75 (Hungary)
Goals (International): 27
Clubs: Ferencvaros
Trophies: HLT 1963, 1964, 1967, 1968

Allchurch, Ivor
Place of Birth: Swansea, Wales
Date of Birth: 16 October 1919
Died: 9 July 1997
Caps: 68 (Wales)
Goals (International): 23
Clubs: Swansea, Newcastle, Cardiff
Appearances: Clubs: 692
Goals: Club: 251
Trophies: None

Allison, Malcolm
Place of Birth: Dartford, England
Date of Birth: 5 September 1927
Caps: 0
Goals (International): 0
Clubs: As Player: West Ham; As Manager: Plymouth, Manchester City, Crystal Palace, Middlesbrough, Bristol Rovers
Trophies: LT 1968; FAC 1969; LC 1970

Anderson, Viv
Place of Birth: Nottingham, England
Date of Birth: 29 August 1956
Caps: 30 (England)
Goals (International): 2
Clubs: Nottingham Forest, Arsenal, Manchester United, Sheffield Wednesday, Barnsley
Appearances: Club: 574
Goals: Club: 31
Trophies: LT 1978; LC 1978, 1979, 1987; EC 1980

Ardiles, Ossie
Place of Birth: Cordoba, Argentina
Date of Birth: 3 August 1952
Caps: 53
Goals (International): 8
Clubs: Intstituto de Cordoba, Huracan, Tottenham Hotspur, Paris Saint Germain, Blackburn Rovers, Queen's Park Rangers
Appearances: Club (for Tottenham): 315
Goals: Club (for Tottenham): 25
Trophies: WorC 1978; FAC 1981, UEFAC 1984

Armfield, Jimmy
Place of Birth: Manchester, England
Date of Birth: 21 September 1935
Caps: 43 (England)
Goals (International): 0
Clubs: Blackpool
Appearances: Club (League): 568
Goals: Club (League): 0
Trophies: None

Atkinson, Ron
Place of Birth: Liverpool, England
Date of Birth: 19 March 1939
Caps: 0
Goals (International): 0
Clubs: As Player: Aston Villa, Oxford United; **As Manager:** Kettering Town, Cambridge United, West Bromwich, Manchester United, Atletico Madrid, Sheffield Wednesday, Aston Villa, Coventry City
Trophies: FAC 1983, 1985; LT 1991, 1994

Baggio, Roberto
Place of Birth: Caldogno, Italy
Date of Birth: 18 February 1967
Caps: 55 (Italy)
Goals (International): 27
Clubs: Fiorentina, Juventus, AC Milan, Bologna, Inter Milan, Brescia
Appearances: Club (League): 464
Goals: Club (League): 203
Trophies: EUFAC 1993; SA 1995, 1996

Ball, Alan
Place of Birth: Farnworth, Lancashire, England
Date of Birth: 12 May 1945
Caps: 72 (England)
Goals (International): 8
Clubs: Blackpool, Everton, Arsenal, Southampton, Bristol Rovers
Appearances: Club (League): 743
Goals: Club (League): 170
Trophies: WorC 1966; LT 1970

Banks, Gordon
Place of Birth: Sheffield, England
Date of Birth: 20 December 1937
Caps: 73 (England)
Goals (International): 0
Clubs: Chesterfield, Leicester City, Stoke City, Fort Lauderdale Strikers
Appearances: Club (Football League): 510
Goals: Club (Football League): 0
Trophies: WorC 1966; LC 1964, 1972

Baresi, Franco
Place of Birth: Travagliato, Italy
Date of Birth: 8 May 1960
Caps: 81 (Italy)
Goals (International): 1
Clubs: AC Milan
Appearances: Club (League): 470
Goals: Club (League): 12
Trophies: SA 1979, 1988, 1992, 1993, 1994, 1996; EC 1989, 1990, 1994; WCC 1989, 1990

Bastin, Cliff
Place of Birth: Exeter, England
Date of Birth: 14 March 1912
Died: 4 December 1991
Caps: 21 (England)
Goals (International): 12
Clubs: Exeter City, Arsenal
Appearances: Club (for Arsenal): 395
Goals: Club (for Arsenal): 178
Trophies: LT 1931, 1933, 1934, 1935, 1938; FAC 1930, 1936

Batistuta, Gabriel Omar
Place of Birth: Reconquista, Santa Fe, Argentina
Date of Birth: 2 January 1969
Caps: 75 (Argentina)
Goals (International): 55
Clubs: Newell's Old Boys, River Plate, Boca Juniors, Fiorentina, AS Roma
Appearances: Club: 411
Goals: Club: 220
Trophies: SA 2001

Baxter, Jim
Place of Birth: Hill O'Beath, Fife, Scotland
Date of Birth: 29 September 1939
Died: 14 April 2001
Caps: 34 (Scotland)
Goals (International): 3
Clubs: Rangers, Sunderland, Raith Rovers, Nottingham Forest
Appearances: Club (for Rangers): 254
Goals: Club (for Rangers): 24
Trophies: SLT 1961, 1963, 1964; SFAC 1962, 1963, 1964

Beckenbauer, Franz
Place of Birth: Munich, Germany
Date of Birth: 11 September 1945
Caps: 104 (West Germany)
Goals (International): 15
Clubs: Bayern Munich, Hamburg, New York Cosmos
Appearances: Club: 720
Goals: Club: 94
Trophies: WorC 1974 (1990), Euro C 1972; BLG 1969, 1973, 1974, 1975, (1994); EC 1974, 1975; CWC 1967

Beckham, David
Place of Birth: Leytonstone, England
Date of Birth: 2 May 1975
Caps: 59 (England)
Goals (International): 11
Clubs: Manchester United
Appearances: Club: 386
Goals: Club: 86
Trophies: LT 1996, 1997, 1999, 2000, 2001, 2003; FAC 1996, 1999; EC 1999

Bellamy, Craig
Place of Birth: Cardiff, Wales
Date of Birth: 13 July 1979
Caps: 20 (Wales)
Goals (International): 6
Clubs: Norwich City, Coventry City, Newcastle United
Appearances: Club: 196
Goals: Club: 64
Trophies: None

Bergkamp, Dennis
Place of Birth: Amsterdam, Holland
Date of Birth: 18 May 1969
Caps: 79 (Holland)
Goals (International): 36
Clubs: Ajax, Inter Milan, Arsenal
Appearances: Club (League): 472
Goals: Club (League): 189
Trophies: LT 1998, 2002; FAC 1998, 2002, 2003; DLT 1993; EUFAC 1992, 1994

Best, George
Place of Birth: Belfast, Northern Ireland
Date of Birth: 22 May 1946
Caps: 37 (Northern Ireland)
Goals (International): 9
Clubs: Manchester United, Stockport County, Cork Celtic, Los Angeles Aztecs, Fulham, Hibernian, Fort Lauderdale Strikers, San Jose Earthquakes, Golden, Bournemouth
Appearances: Club (League: for Man Utd): 361
Goals: Club (League: for Man Utd): 137
Trophies: LT 1965, 1967 EC 1968

Bettega, Roberto
Place of Birth: Torino, Italy
Date of Birth: 27 December 1950
Caps: 42 (Italy)
Goals (International): 19
Clubs: Varese, Juventus
Appearances: Club (League: for Juventus): 326
Goals: Club (League: for Juventus): 126
Trophies: EUFAC 1977; SA 1972, 1973, 1975, 1977, 1978, 1981, 1982

Bingham, Billy
Place of Birth: Belfast, Northern Ireland
Date of Birth: 5 August 1931
Caps: 56 (Northern Ireland)
Goals (International): 10
Clubs: As Player: Glentoran, Sunderland, Luton Town, Everton, Port Vale; **As Manager:** Southport, Plymouth Argyle, Linfield, Everton, Mansfield
Appearances: Club (for Luton): 87
Goals: Club (for Luton): 27
Trophies: None

Blanchflower, Danny
Place of Birth: Belfast, Northern Ireland
Date of Birth: 10 February 1926
Died: 9 December 1993
Caps: 56 (Northern Ireland)
Goals (International): 2
Clubs: Glentoran, Swindon Town, Barnsley, Aston Villa, Tottenham
Appearances: Club: 735
Goals: Club: 40
Trophies: LT 1961; FAC 1961, 1962; CWC 1963

Blokhin, Oleg
Place of Birth: Kiev, Russia
Date of Birth: 5 November 1952
Caps: 101 (USSR)
Goals (International): 39
Clubs: Dynamo Kiev, Vorwarts Styer
Appearances: Club (League): 432
Goals: Club (League): 211
Trophies: SLT 1971, 1974, 1975, 1977, 1980, 1981, 1985, 1986; CWC 1975, 1986

Bloomer, Steve
Place of Birth: Cradley Heath, England
Date of Birth: 20 January 1874
Died: 16 April 1938
Caps: 23 (England)
Goals (International): 28
Clubs: Derby County, Middlesbrough
Appearances: Club (League): 598
Goals: Club (League): 353
Trophies: None

Boniek, Zbigniew
Place of Birth: Bydgoszcz, Poland
Date of Birth: 3 March 1956
Caps: 80 (Poland)
Goals (International): 24
Clubs: Zawisza Bydgoszcz, Widzew Lodz, Juventus, Roma
Trophies: EC 1985; CWC 1984; SA 1984

Bosman, Jean-Marc
Place of Birth: Belgium
Date of Birth: 30 October 1964
Caps: 0
Goals (International): 0
Clubs: Ajax, FC Liege
Appearances: Club (League): 73
Goals: Club (League): 3
Trophies: None

Brady, Liam
Place of Birth: Dublin, Ireland
Date of Birth: 13 February 1956
Caps: 72 (Republic of Ireland)
Goals (International): 9
Clubs: Arsenal, Juventus, Inter Milan, Ascoli, West Ham
Appearances: Club (for Arsenal): 306
Goals: Club (for Arsenal): 59
Trophies: FAC 1979; SA 1981, 1982

Breitner, Paul
Place of Birth: Freilassung, Germany
Date of Birth: 5 September 1951
Caps: 48 (West Germany)
Goals (International): 10
Clubs: Bayern Munich, Real Madrid, Eintracht Braunschweig
Trophies: WorC 1974; EuroC 1972; EC 1974, PLA 1975, 1976; BLG 1972, 1973, 1974, 1980,1981

Bremner, Billy
Place of Birth: Stirling, Scotland
Date of Birth: 9 December 1942
Died: 7 December 1997
Caps: 54 (Scotland)
Goals (International): 3
Clubs: Leeds United, Hull City, Doncaster Rovers
Appearances: Club: 845
Goals: Club: 121
Trophies: LT 1969, 1974; FAC 1972; LC 1968; EUFAC 1968, 1971

Brooking, Trevor
Place of Birth: Barking, London, England
Date of Birth: 2 October 1948
Caps: 47 (England)
Goals (International): 5
Clubs: West Ham United
Appearances: Club (League): 528
Goals: Club (League): 88
Trophies: FAC 1975, 1980

Busby, Matt
Place of Birth: Bellshill, Glasgow, Scotland
Date of Birth: 26 May 1909
Died: 20 January 1994
Caps: 1 (Scotland)
Goals (International): 0
Clubs: As Player: Manchester City, Liverpool; As Manager: Manchester United
Trophies: FAC 1948, 1963; LT 1952, 1956, 1957, 1965, 1967; EC 1968

Butcher, Terry
Place of Birth: Singapore
Date of Birth: 28 December 1958
Caps: 77 (England)
Goals (International): 3
Clubs: As Player: Ipswich Town, Glasgow Rangers, Coventry, Sunderland; **As Manager:** Motherwell
Appearances: Club (League): 445
Goals: Club (League): 24
Trophies: EUFAC 1981; SLT 1987, 1989, 1990

Campbell, Sol
Place of Birth: London, England
Date of Birth: 18 September 1974
Caps: 54 (England)
Goals (International): 1
Clubs: Tottenham, Arsenal
Appearances: Club (League): 404
Goals: Club (League): 21
Trophies: LT 2002; FAC 2002

Cantona, Eric
Place of Birth: Paris, France
Date of Birth: 24 May 1966
Caps: 45 (France)
Goals (International): 19
Clubs: Martigues, Auxerre, Marseille, Bordeaux, Montpellier, Leeds United, Manchester United
Appearances: Club: 317
Goals: Club: 166
Trophies: LT 1992, 1993, 1994, 1996, 1997; FAC 1994, 1996

Carter, Raich
Place of Birth: Sunderland, England
Date of Birth: 21 December 1913
Died: 9 October 1994
Caps: 13 (England)
Goals (International): 7
Clubs: Sunderland, Derby County, Hull City
Appearances: Club (For Sunderland): 276
Goals: Club (for Sunderland): 127
Trophies: LT 1936; FAC 1937, 1946

Channon, Mick
Place of Birth: Orcheston, Wiltshire, England
Date of Birth: 28 November 1948
Caps: 46 (England)
Goals (International): 21
Clubs: Southampton, Manchester City, Norwich City
Appearances: Club (League: for Southampton): 510
Goals: Club (League: for Southampton): 185
Trophies: FAC 1976

Chapman, Herbert
Place of Birth: Kiverton Park, England
Date of Birth: 19 January 1878
Died: 6 January 1934
Caps: 0
Goals (International): 0
Clubs: As Player: Kiverton Park, Ashton North End, Stalybridge Rovers, Rochdale, Grimsby Town, Sheppey United, Worksop, Northampton Town, Sheffield United, Notts County, Tottenham Hotspur; **As Manager:** Northampton Town, Leeds City, Huddersfield Town, Arsenal
Trophies: LT 1924, 1925, 1926, 1931, 1933; FA Cup 1922, 1930

Charles, John
Place of Birth: Swansea, Wales
Date of Birth: 27 December 1931
Caps: 38 (Wales)
Goals (International): 15
Clubs: Leeds United, Juventus, Roma, Cardiff City, Hereford United
Appearances: Club (League: for Juventus): 150
Goals: Club (League: for Juventus): 93
Trophies: SA 1958, 1960, 1961

Charlton, Bobby
Place of Birth: Ashington, Northumberland, England
Date of Birth: 11 October 1937
Caps: 106 (England)
Goals (International): 49
Clubs: Manchester United, Preston North End
Appearances: Club: 798
Goals: Club (League): 257
Trophies: WorC 1966; EC 1968; LT 1957, 1965, 1967; FAC 1963

Charlton, Jack
Place of Birth: Ashington, Northumberland, England
Date of Birth: 8 May 1935
Caps: 35 (England)
Goals (International): 6
Clubs: As Player: Leeds United; **As Manager:** Middlesbrough, Sheffield Wednesday, Republic of Ireland national side.
Trophies: WorC 1966; LT1969; FAC 1972; LC 1968

Chilavert, Jose Luis
Place of Birth: Luque, Paraguay
Date of Birth: 27 July 1965
Caps: 111 (Paraguay)
Goals (International): 8
Clubs: Cerro Porteno, San Lorenzo, Velez, Sarsfield, RC Strasbourg
Appearances: Club: 521
Goals: Club: 24
Trophies: None

Clough, Brian
Place of Birth: Middlesbrough, England
Date of Birth: 21 March 1935
Caps: 2 (England)
Goals (International): 0
Clubs: As Player: Middlesbrough, Sunderland; **As Manager:** Hartlepool United, Derby County, Brighton & Hove Albion, Leeds United, Nottingham Forest
Trophies: LT 1972, 1978; EC 1979, 1980; LC 1978, 1979, 1989, 1990

Collins, Bobby
Place of Birth: Govanhill, Scotland
Date of Birth: 19 February 1931
Caps: 31 (Scotland)
Goals (International): 10
Clubs: Celtic, Everton, Leeds, Bury, Greenock Morton, Oldham Athletic
Appearances: Club (for Leeds): 168
Goals: Club (for Leeds): 25
Trophies: SLT 1954, SFAC 1954

Compton, Leslie/Dennis
Place of Birth: Woodford/Hendon, England
Date of Birth: 12 September 1912/23 May 1918
Died: 27 December 1984/ 23 April 1997
Caps: 2/12 (England)
Goals (International): 0
Clubs: Arsenal
Trophies: LT 1948; FAC 1950

Cruyff, Johann
Place of Birth: Amsterdam, Holland
Date of Birth: 25 April 1947
Caps: 48 (Holland)
Goals (International): 33
Clubs: Ajax, Barcelona, Los Angeles Aztecs, Washington Diplomats, Levants, Feyenoord
Appearances: Club: 704
Goals: Club (League): 392
Trophies: DLT 1966,1967, 1968, 1970, 1972, 1973, 1982, 1983, 1984, (1986, 1987); PLA 1974, (1991, 1992, 1993, 1994) EC 1971, 1972, (1992); CWC 1987, 1989

Cubillas, Teofilo
Place of Birth: Puente Piedra, near Lima, Peru
Date of Birth: 8 March 1949
Caps: 117 (Peru)
Goals (International): 47
Clubs: Alianza, Basel, FC Porto, Fort Lauderdale Strikers

Cullis, Stan
Place of Birth: Ellesmere Port, Cheshire, England
Date of Birth: 25 October 1916
Died: 27 February 2001
Caps: 12 (England)
Goals (International): 0
Clubs: As Player: Wolverhampton Wanders. **As Manager:** Wolverhampton Wanderers, Birmingham City
Trophies: LT 1954, 1958, 1959; FAC 1949, 1960

Dalglish, Kenny
Place of Birth: Glasgow, Scotland
Date of Birth: 4 March 1951
Caps: 102 (Scotland)
Goals (International): 30
Clubs: As Player: Celtic, Liverpool; **As Manager:** Liverpool, Blackburn, Newcastle
Appearances: Club (League): 559
Goals: Club (League): 230
Trophies: SLT 1972, 1973, 1974, 1977; SFAC 1972, 1974, 1975, 1977; EC 1978, 1981, 1984; LT 1979, 1980, 1982, 1983, 1984, (1986), (1988), (1990); LC 1981, 1982, 1983, 1984; FAC (1986), (1989)

Dean, William 'Dixie'
Place of Birth: Birkenhead, England
Date of Birth: 27 January 1907
Died: 1980
Caps: 16 (England)
Goals (International): 18
Clubs: Tranmere, Everton, Notts County
Appearances: Club (League): 438
Goals: Club (League): 379
Trophies: LT 1928, 1932; FAC 1933

Desailly, Marcel
Place of Birth: Accra, Ghana
Date of Birth: 7 September 1968
Caps: 104 (France)
Goals (International): 3
Clubs: Nantes, Marseille, AC Milan, Chelsea
Appearances: Club (League): 491
Goals: Club (League): 17
Trophies: WorC 1998; EuroC 2000; EC 1993, 1994; SA 1994, 1996; FAC 2000

Di Canio, Paolo
Place of Birth: Rome, Italy
Date of Birth: 9 July 1968
Caps: 0
Goals (International): 0
Clubs: Terrana, Lazio, Juventus, Napoli, AC Milan, Celtic, Sheffield Wednesday, West Ham
Appearances: Club (League): 327
Goals: Club (League): 94
Trophies: None

Di Stefano, Alfredo
Place of Birth: Barracas, Argentina
Date of Birth: 4 July 1926
Caps: 7 (Argentina); 31 (Spain)
Goals (International): 7 (Argentina); 23 (Spain)
Clubs: Los Cardales, River Plate, Huracan, Millonarios, Real Madrid, Espanyol
Appearances: Club (All matches for Real Madrid): 510
Goals: Club (All matches for Real Madrid): 418
Trophies: EC 1956, 1957, 1958, 1959, 1960; PLA 1954, 1955, 1957, 1958, 1959, 1961, 1963, 1964, (1971)

Docherty, Tommy
Place of Birth: Glasgow, Scotland
Date of Birth: 24 April 1929
Caps: 25 (Scotland)
Goals (International): 1
Clubs: As Player: Celtic, Preston North End, Arsenal. **As Manager:** Chelsea, Rotherham United, Queens Park Rangers, FC Porto, Hull City, Scotland national side, Manchester United, Derby County, Sydney Olympic, Preston North End, Wolverhampton Wanderers, Altrincham
Trophies: LC 1965; FAC 1977

Drake, Ted
Place of Birth: Southampton, England
Date of Birth: 16 August 1912
Died: 30 May 1995
Caps: 5 (England)
Goals (International): 6
Clubs: Southampton, Arsenal
Appearances: Club (All Matches for Arsenal): 184
Goals: Club (All Matches for Arsenal): 139
Trophies: 1935, 1938, (1955); FAC 1936

Edwards, Duncan
Place of Birth: Dudley, England
Date of Birth: 1 October 1936
Died: 21 February 1958
Caps: 18 (England)
Goals (International): 5
Clubs: Manchester United
Appearances: Club (League): 175
Goals: Club (League): 21
Trophies: LT 1956, 1957

Eriksson, Sven-Goran
Place of Birth: Torsby, Sweden
Date of Birth: 5 February 1948
Caps: 0
Goals (International): 0
Clubs: As Player: KB Karlskoga; **As Manager:** Degerfors IF, IFK Göteborg, Benfica, AS Roma, Fiorentina AC, Sampdoria, Lazio
Trophies: SA 2000; SLT 1981, 1983, 1984, 1991; UEFAC 1982; CWC 1999

Eusebio
Place of Birth: Lourenco-Marques (now Maputo), Mozambique
Date of Birth: 25 January 1942
Caps: 64 (Portugal).
Goals (International): 41
Clubs: Sporting Club of Lourenco-Marques, Benfica, Monterrey, Boston Minutemen, Toronto, Metros-Croatia, Las Vegas Quicksilver
Appearances: Club: 651
Goals: Club: 686
Trophies: PLT 1961, 1963, 1964, 1965, 1967, 1968, 1969, 1971, 1972, 1973, 1974; EC 1962

Facchetti, Giacinto
Place of Birth: Treviglio, Italy
Date of Birth: July 18 1942
Caps: 94 (Italy)
Goals (International): 3
Clubs: Inter Milan
Appearances: Club (League): 475
Goals: Club (League): 59
Trophies: SA 1963, 1965, 1966, 1971; EC 1964, 1965

Ferguson, Alex
Place of Birth: Glasgow, Scotland
Date of Birth: 31 December 1941
Caps: 0
Goals (International): 0
Clubs: As Player: Queens Park, St Johnstone, Dunfermline, Rangers, Falkirk, Ayr United; **As Manager:** East Stirling, St Mirren, Aberdeen, Scotland national side (as caretaker

Statistics

manager), Manchester United
Trophies: SLT 1980, 1984, 1985; SFAC 1982, 1983, 1984, 1986; CWC 1983, 1991; FAC 1990, 1994, 1996, 1999; LC 1992; LT 1993, 1994, 1996, 1997, 1999, 2000, 2001, 2003; EC 1999

Figo, Luis
Place of Birth: Lisbon, Portugal
Date of Birth: 4 November 1972
Caps: 92 (Portugal)
Goals (International): 28
Clubs: Sporting Lisbon, Barcelona, Real Madrid
Appearances: Club (Spanish League): 357
Goals: Club (Spanish League): 77
Trophies: PLA 1998, 1999, 2001: CWC 1997; EC 2002

Finney, Tom
Place of Birth: Preston, England
Date of Birth: 5 April 1922
Caps: 76 (England)
Goals (International): 30
Clubs: Preston North End
Appearances: Club (League): 433
Goals: Club (League): 187
Trophies: None

Fontaine, Just
Place of Birth: Marrakesh, Morocco
Date of Birth: 18 August 1933
Caps: 21 (France)
Goals (International): 30
Clubs: AC Marrakesh, USM Casablanca, Nice, Reims
Appearances: Club: 213
Goals: Club: 200
Trophies: FLT 1956, 1958, 1960, 1962

Foulke, Bill
Place of Birth: Sheffield, England
Date of Birth: 12 April 1874
Died: 1916
Caps: 1 (England)
Goals (International): 0
Clubs: Sheffield United, Chelsea, Bradford City
Appearances: Club (League): 347
Goals: Club (League): 0
Trophies: FAC 1899, 1902; LT 1898

Francescoli, Enzo
Place of Birth: Montevideo, Uruguay
Date of Birth: 12 November 1961
Caps: 122
Goals (International): 20
Clubs: Wanderers, River Plate, Matra Racing, Marseille, Cagliari, Torino
Appearances: Club (River Plate): 197
Goals: Club (River Plate): 115
Trophies: FLT 1990

Gallacher, Hughie
Place of Birth: Bellshill
Date of Birth: 2 February 1903
Died: 1957
Caps: 19 (Scotland)
Goals (International): 22
Clubs: Queen of the South, Airdrieonians, Newcastle United, Chelsea, Derby County, Notts County, Grimsby Town, Gateshead
Appearances: Club (League): 541
Goals: Club (League): 387
Trophies: LT 1927

Garrincha
Place of Birth: Pau Grande, Brazil
Date of Birth: 28 October 1933
Died: 20 January 1983
Caps: 50 (Brazil)
Goals (International): 13
Clubs: Botafogo, Santos, Corinthians, Flamengo, Bangu, Portuguesa Santista, Olaria, AJ Barranquilla, Red Star Paris
Appearances: Club (Botafogo): 581
Goals: Club (Botafogo): 232
Trophies: BLT 1964, 1965; WorC 1958, 1962

Gascoigne, Paul
Place of Birth: Gateshead, England
Date of Birth: 27 May 1967
Caps: 57 (England)
Goals (International): 10
Clubs: Newcastle United, Tottenham, Lazio, Rangers, Middlesbrough, Everton, Burnley
Appearances: Club: 378
Goals: Club: 81
Trophies: FAC 1991; SLT 1996, 1997; SFAC 1996

Gemmill, Archie
Place of Birth: Pailsey, Scotland
Date of Birth: 24 March 1947
Caps: 43 (Scotland)
Goals (International): 8
Clubs: St Mirren, Preston North End, Derby County, Nottingham Forest, Birmingham City, Wigan Athletic
Appearances: Club: 317
Goals: Club: 21
Trophies: LT 1972, 1975, 1978; EC 1979

Gentile, Claudio
Place of Birth: Libya, Tripoli
Date of Birth: 27 September 1953
Caps: 71 (Italy)
Goals (International): 1
Clubs: Arona, Varesse, Juventus, Fiorentina
Appearances: Club (League): 473
Goals: Club (League): 14
Trophies: SA 1975, 1977, 1978, 1981, 1982, 1984, 1986; UEFAC 1977; CWC 1984; WorC 1982

Gento, Francisco
Place of Birth: Guarnizo, Spain
Date of Birth: 22 October 1933
Caps: 43 (Spain)
Goals (International): 5
Clubs: Nuevo Montana, Astillero, Rayo Cantabria, Real Santander, Real Madrid
Trophies: EC 1956, 1957, 1958, 1959, 1960, 1966; PLA 1954, 1955, 1957, 1958, 1961, 1962, 1963, 1964, 1965, 1967, 1968, 1969

Giggs, Ryan
Place of Birth: Cardiff, Wales
Date of Birth: 29 November 1973
Caps: 40 (Wales)
Goals (International): 8
Clubs: Manchester United
Appearances: Club: 543
Goals: Club: 116
Trophies: LC 1992; LT 1993; 1994, 1996, 1997, 1999, 2000, 2001, 2003; FAC 1994; 1996; 1999; EC 1999

Giles, Johnny
Place of Birth: Dublin, Ireland
Date of Birth: 1940
Caps: 59 (Republic of Ireland)
Goals (International): 5
Clubs: Manchester United, Leeds United, West Bromwich Albion, Shamrock Rovers, Vancouver Whitecaps
Appearances: Club (League): 702
Goals: Club (League): 128
Trophies: LT 1969, 1974; FAC 1972,; LC 1968; EUFAC 1968, 1971

Gough, Richard
Place of Birth: Stockholm, Sweden
Date of Birth: 5 April 1962
Caps: 61 (Scotland)
Goals (International): 6
Clubs: Dundee United, Tottenham, Rangers, Kansas City Wizz, San Jose Clash, Nottingham Forest, Everton
Appearances: Club (League): 590
Goals: Club (League): 48
Trophies: SLT 1983, 1989, 1990, 1991, 1992, 1993, 1994, 1995, 1996, 1997; SFAC 1992, 1993, 1996

Graham, George
Place of Birth: Bargeddie, Fife
Date of Birth: 30 November 1944
Caps: 12 (Scotland)
Goals (International): 3
Clubs: As Player: Aston Villa, Chelsea, Arsenal, Man United, Portsmouth, Crystal Palace; As Manager: Millwall, Arsenal, Leeds United, Tottenham Hotspur
Trophies: LT 1989, 1991; FAC 1993; LC 1987, 1993, 1999; CWC 1994

Gray, Andy
Place of Birth: Glasgow, Scotland
Date of Birth: 30 November 1955
Caps: 20 (Scotland)
Goals (International): 6
Clubs: Dundee United, Aston Villa, Wolves, Everton, West Bromwich Albion, Rangers, Cheltenham Town
Appearances: Club: 593
Goals: Club: 202
Trophies: LC 1980; FAC 1984; LT 1985; CWC 1985; SLT 1989

Greaves, Jimmy
Place of Birth: London, England
Date of Birth: 20 February 1940
Caps: 57 (England)
Goals (International): 44
Clubs: Chelsea, AC Milan, Tottenham, West Ham
Appearances: Club: 528
Goals: Club: 366
Trophies: FAC 1962, 1967; CWC 1963

Greenwood, Ron
Place of Birth: Burnley, England
Date of Birth: 11 November 1921
Caps: 0
Goals (International): 0
Clubs: As Player: Bradford Park Avenue, Brentford, Chelsea, Fulham; As Manager: West Ham, England national side
Trophies: FAC 1964; CWC 1965

Greig, John
Place of Birth: Edinburgh, Scotland
Date of Birth: 11 September 1942
Caps: 44 (Scotland)
Goals (International): 3
Clubs: Rangers
Appearances: Club: 755
Goals: Club: 120
Trophies: SLT 1963, 1964, 1975, 1976, (1978); SFAC 1963, 1964, 1966, 1973, 1976, (1978), (1979), (1981); CWC 1972

Gren, Gunnar
Place of Birth: Gothenburg, Sweden
Date of Birth: 31 October 1920
Died: 10 November 1991
Caps: 57 (Sweden)
Goals (International): 33
Clubs: Garda, IFK Gothenburg, AC Milan, Fiorentina, Genoa, Orgryte, Gais, Skogens
Appearances: Club (League: Serie A): 217
Goals: Club (League: Serie A): 35
Trophies: SLT 1942; SA 1951

Gullit, Ruud
Place of Birth: Surinam
Date of Birth: 1 September 1962
Caps: 65 (Holland)
Goals (International): 16
Clubs: Harlem, Feyenoord, PSV Eindhoven, AC Milan, Sampdoria, Chelsea
Appearances: Club (League): 465
Goals: Club (League): 175
Trophies: EuroC 1998; DLT 1984, 1986, 1987; SA 1988, 1992, 1993; EC 1989, 1990; FAC (1997)

Hagi, Gheorghiu
Place of Birth: Constanta, Romania
Date of Birth: 5 February 1965
Caps: 125 (Romania)
Goals (International): 34
Clubs: Farul, Constanta, Sportul Studentesc, Steaua Bucharest, Real Madrid, Brescia, Barcelona, Galatasaray
Appearances: Club: 550
Goals: Club: 269
Trophies: RLT 1987, 1988, 1990; TLT 1997, 1998, 1999, 2000; UEFA 2000

Hansen, Alan
Place of Birth: Clackmannashire, Scotland
Date of Birth: 13 June 1955
Caps: 26 (Scotland)
Goals (International): 0
Clubs: Partick Thistle, Liverpool
Appearances: Club (Liverpool): 623
Goals: Club (Liverpool): 13
Trophies: LT 1979, 1980, 1982, 1983, 1984, 1986, 1988, 1990; FAC 1986, 1989; LC 1981, 1983, 1984; EC 1978, 1981, 1984

Happel, Ernst
Place of Birth: Vienna, Austria
Date of Birth: 29 June 1925
Died: 14 November 1992
Caps: 51 (Austria)
Goals (International): 5
Clubs: As Player: Rapid Vienna, Racing Club de Paris; As Manager: Rapid Vienna, Feyenoord, Sevilla, Club Bruges, Standard Liege, Hamburg, Innsbruck
Trophies: ALT 1946, 1948, 1951, 1952, 1954, 1957, (1960), (1989), (1990); DLT (1969); BLT (1976), (1977), (1978); BLG (1982), (1983); EC (1970), (1983)

Haynes, Johnny
Place of Birth: London, England
Date of Birth: 17 October 1934
Caps: 56 (England)
Goals (International): 18
Clubs: Fulham, Durban City
Appearances: Club (League): 594
Goals: Club (League): 145
Trophies: None

Henry, Thierry
Place of Birth: Paris, France
Date of Birth: 17 August 1977
Caps: 46 (France)
Goals (International): 18
Clubs: Monaco, Juventus, Arsenal
Appearances: Club (League): 257
Goals: Club (League): 105
Trophies: WorC 1998; EuroC 2000; LT 2002; FAC 2002, 2003

Hidegkuti, Nandor
Place of Birth: Budapest, Hungary
Date of Birth: 3 March 1922
Caps: 68 (Hungary)
Goals (International): 39
Clubs: MTK Bucharest (then known as Voros Lobogo)

Hill, Jimmy
Place of Birth: Balham, London
Date of Birth: 22 July 1928
Caps: 0
Goals (International): 0
Clubs: As Player: Brentford, Fulham; As Manager: Coventry City
Trophies: None

Hoddle, Glen
Place of Birth: Hayes, Middlesex, England
Date of Birth: 27 October 1957
Caps: 53 (England)
Goals (International): 8
Clubs: Tottenham, Monacco, Swindon Town, Chelsea
Appearances: Club (League: for Tottenham): 377
Goals: Club (League): 88
Trophies: FAC 1981, 1982; EUFAC 1984; FLT 1988

Houllier, Gerard
Place of Birth: Therouanne, France
Date of Birth: 3 September 1947
Caps: 0
Goals (International): 0
Clubs: As Player: Le Tourquet; As Manager: Le Tourquet, Neoux Les Mines, Lens, Paris Saint Germain, France national side, Liverpool
Trophies: FLT 1986; FAC 2001, LC 2001, 2003; EUFAC 2001

Hughes, Emlyn
Place of Birth: Barrow-in-Furness, England
Date of Birth: 28 August 1947
Caps: 62 (England)
Goals (International): 1
Clubs: Blackpool, Liverpool, Wolverhampton, Rotherham United, Hull City, Mansfield Town
Appearances: Club: 723
Goals: Club: 50
Trophies: LT 1973, 1976, 1977, 1979; FAC 1974; EC 1977, 1978; EUFAC 1973, 1976

Hughes, Mark
Place of Birth: Wrexham, Wales
Date of Birth: 1 November 1963
Caps: 72 (Wales)
Goals (International): 16
Clubs: Manchester United, Barcelona, Bayern Munich, Chelsea, Southampton, Everton, Blackburn
Appearances: Club (League): 646
Goals: Club (League): 164
Trophies: FAC 1985, 1990, 1994, 1996; CWC 1991; LC 1992; LT 1993, 1994

Hunt, Roger
Place of Birth: Golborne, Lancashire, England
Date of Birth: 20 July 1938
Caps: 34 (England)
Goals (International): 18
Clubs: Liverpool, Bolton Wanderers
Appearances: Club (for Liverpool): 492
Goals: Club (for Liverpool): 245
Trophies: LT 1964, 1966; FAC 1965; WorC 1966

Hurst, Geoff
Place of Birth: Ashton, England
Date of Birth: 8 December 1941
Caps: 49 (England)
Goals (International): 24
Clubs: West Ham, Stoke, West Bromwich
Appearances: Club: 518
Goals: Club: 210
Trophies: FAC 1964; CWC 1965; WorC 1966

Jack, David
Place of Birth: Bolton, England
Date of Birth: 3 April 1899
Died: 1958
Caps: 9 (England)
Goals (International): 0
Clubs: Plymouth Argyle, Bolton, Arsenal
Appearances: Club (League: for Arsenal): 181
Goals: Club (League: for Arsenal): 113
Trophies: FAC 1923, 1926, 1930; LT 1931, 1933, 1934

Jairzinho
Place of Birth: Rio de Janeiro
Date of Birth: 25 December 1944
Caps: 98 (Brazil)
Goals (International): 37
Clubs: Botafogo, Marseille, Cruzeiro, Portuguesa, Caracas
Trophies: WorC 1970

James, Alex
Place of Birth: Mossend, Scotland
Date of Birth: 14 September 1901
Died: 1953
Caps: 8 (Scotland)
Goals (International): 4
Clubs: Raith Rovers, Preston North End, Arsenal
Appearances: Club (League: for Arsenal): 231
Goals: Club (League: for Arsenal): 26
Trophies: FAC 1930, 1936; LT 1931, 1933, 1934, 1935

Jennings, Pat
Place of Birth: County Down, Northern Ireland
Date of Birth: 12 June 1945
Caps: 119 (Northern Ireland)
Goals (International): 0
Clubs: Watford, Tottenham, Arsenal
Appearances: Club (League): 757
Goals: Club (League): 0
Trophies: FAC 1967, 1979; LC 1971, 1973; EUFAC 1973

Johnstone, Jimmy
Place of Birth: Viewpark, Lanarkshire, Scotland
Date of Birth: 30 September 1944
Caps: 23 (Scotland)
Goals (International): 4
Clubs: Celtic, San Jose Earthquakes, Sheffield United, Dundee
Trophies: EC 1967

Jones, Vinnie
Place of Birth: Watford, England
Date of Birth: 5 January 1965
Caps: 9 (Wales)
Goals (International): 0
Clubs: Wimbledon, Leeds, Sheffield United, Chelsea, Queens Park Rangers
Appearances: Club (League): 393
Goals: Club (League): 33
Trophies: FAC 1988

Kanu, Nwankwo
Place of Birth: Owerri, Nigeria
Date of Birth: 1 August 1976
Caps: 35 (Nigeria)
Goals (International): 12
Clubs: Federation Works, Iwuanyanwo Nationale, Ajax, Inter Milan, Arsenal
Appearances: Club (League): 234
Goals: Club (League): 58
Trophies: DLT 1994, 1995, 1996; LT 2002; FAC 2002, 2003; EC 1995

Keane, Roy
Place of Birth: Cork, Ireland
Date of Birth: 10 August 1971
Caps: 58 (Republic of Ireland)
Goals (International): 9
Clubs: Nottingham Forest, Manchester United
Appearances: Club (League): 374
Goals: Club (League): 51
Trophies: EC 1999; LT 1994, 1996, 1997, 1999, 2000, 2001, 2003; FAC 1994, 1996, 1999

Keegan, Kevin
Place of Birth: Armthorpe, Yorkshire, England
Date of Birth: 14 February 1951
Caps: 63 (England)
Goals (International): 21
Clubs: Scunthorpe United, Liverpool, Hamburg, Southampton, Newcastle
Appearances: Club (for Liverpool): 323
Goals: Club (for Liverpool): 100
Trophies: LT 1973, 1976, 1977; FAC 1974; EUFAC 1976; EC 1977; BLG 1979

Kempes, Mario
Place of Birth: Bellville, Cordoba, Argentina
Date of Birth: 15 July 1952
Caps: 43 (Argentina)
Goals (International): 20
Clubs: Insituto de Cordoba, Rosario Central, Valencia, River Plate
Trophies: CWC 1980; WorC 1978

Kewell, Harry
Place of Birth: Sydney, Australia
Date of Birth: 22 September 1978
Caps: 14 (Australia)
Goals (International): 4
Clubs: Leeds United
Appearances: Club (League): 184
Goals: Club (League): 45
Trophies: None

Klinsmann, Jurgen
Place of Birth: Goppingen, Germany
Date of Birth: 30 July 1964
Caps: 108 (Germany)
Goals (International): 47
Clubs: Stuttgart Kickers, VfB Stuttgart, Inter Milan, Monaco, Tottenham, Bayern Munich, Sampdoria
Appearances: Club (League): 491
Goals: Club (League): 194
Trophies: SA 1989; WorC 1990; BLG 1997; EuroC 1996; EUFAC 1996

Kocsis, Sandor
Place of Birth: Budapest, Hungary
Date of Birth: 30 September 1928
Died: 22 July 1979
Caps: 68 (Hungary)
Goals (International): 75
Clubs: Fernecvaros, Honved, Young Boys Berne, Barcelona
Trophies: EUFAC 1960; HLT 1949, 1952, 1954; PLA 1959

Kopa, Raymond
Place of Birth: Noeux-les-milnes, France
Date of Birth: 13 October 1931
Caps: 45 (France)
Goals (International): 18
Clubs: Angiers, Reims, Real Madrid
Trophies: EC 1957, 1958, 1959; PLA 1957, 1958

Larsson, Henrik
Place of Birth: Helsinborg, Sweden
Date of Birth: 20 September 1971
Caps: 64 (Sweden)
Goals (International): 21
Clubs: Hogabog BK, Helsingborgs BK, Feyenoord
Appearances: Club (League: for Celtic): 183
Goals: Club (League: for Celtic): 143
Trophies: SLT 1998, 2001, 2002; SFAC 2001, 2002

Lato, Grzegorz
Place of Birth: Malbork, Poland
Date of Birth: 8 April 1950
Caps: 100 (Poland)
Goals (International): 42
Clubs: Stal Mielec, KSC Lokeren, Atlante
Trophies: PLT 1973, 1976

Laudrup, Brian
Place of Birth: Vienna, Austria
Date of Birth: 22 February 1969
Caps: 82 (Denmark)
Goals (International): 21
Clubs: Brondby, Bayer Uerdingen, Fiorentina, AC Milan, Rangers, Chelsea, Copenhagen
Appearances: Club (For Rangers): 151
Goals: Club (Rangers): 45
Trophies: SLT 1995, 1996, 1997; SFAC 1996; DLT 1987, 1988; SA 1994; EuroC 1992

Laudrup, Michael
Place of Birth: Copenhagen
Date of Birth: 15 June 1964
Caps: 104 (Denmark)
Goals (International): 37
Clubs: KB Copenhagen, Brondby, Juventus, Lazio, Barcelona, Real Madrid, Vissel Kobe, Ajax
Appearances: Club (League): 464
Goals: Club (League): 117
Trophies: EC1992, PLA 1991, 1992, 1993, 1994, 1995; SA 1986; DLT 1998

Law, Denis
Place of Birth: Aberdeen, Scotland
Date of Birth: 24 February 1940
Caps: 55 (Scotland)
Goals (International): 30
Clubs: Huddersfield Town, Manchester City, Torino, Manchester United
Appearances: Club: 566
Goals: Club: 301
Trophies: FAC 1963; LT 1965, 1967

Lawton, Tommy
Place of Birth: Bolton, England
Date of Birth: 6 October 1919
Died: 6 November 1996
Caps: 23 (England)
Goals (International): 22
Clubs: Burnley, Everton, Chelsea, Notts County, Brentford, Arsenal, Kettering Town
Appearances: Club (League): 390
Goals: Club (League): 231
Trophies: LT 1939

Le Tissier, Matthew
Place of Birth: Guernsey
Date of Birth: 14 October 1968
Caps: 10 (England)
Goals (International): 0
Clubs: Southampton
Appearances: Club (League): 443
Goals: Club (League): 163
Trophies: None

Leonidas
Place of Birth: Sao Cristovao, Brazil
Date of Birth: 11 November 1912
Caps: 25 (Brazil)
Goals (International): 25
Clubs: Havanesa, Barroso, Sul Americano, Sirio Libanes, Bomsucesso, Nacional, Vasco da Gama, Botafogo, Flamengo, Sao Paulo

Liddell, Billy
Place of Birth: Dunfermline, Scotland
Date of Birth: 10 January 1921
Died: 3 July 2001
Caps: 28 (Scotland)
Goals (International): 6
Clubs: Liverpool
Appearances: Club (League): 537
Goals: Club (League): 229
Trophies: LT 1947

Liedholm, Nils
Place of Birth: Sweden
Date of Birth: 8 October 1922
Caps: 23 (Sweden)
Goals (International): 5
Clubs: Valdemarsvik, Sleipner, IFK Norrköping, AC Milan
Appearances: Club (for AC Milan): 359
Goals: Club (for AC Milan): 81
Trophies: SLT 1947, 1948; SA 1951, 1955, 1957, 1959

Lineker, Gary
Place of Birth: Leicester
Date of Birth: 30 November 1960
Caps: 80 (England)
Goals (International): 48
Clubs: Leicester City, Everton, Barcelona, Tottenham, Nagoya Grampus
Appearances: Club: 447
Goals: Club: 236
Trophies: CWC 1989; FAC 1991

Litmanen, Jari
Place of Birth: Lahti, Finland
Date of Birth: 20 February 1971
Caps: 82 (Finland)
Goals (International): 22
Clubs: Reipas Lahti, HJK Helsinki, MyPa, Ajax, Barcelona, Liverpool
Appearances: Club (League): 346
Goals: Club (League): 147
Trophies: DLT 1991; 1994, 1995, 1998; EC 1995

Lofthouse, Nat
Place of Birth: Bolton, England
Date of Birth: 27 August 1925
Caps: 33 (England)
Goals (International): 30
Clubs: Bolton Wanderers
Appearances: Club (For Bolton): 485
Goals: Club (For Bolton): 285
Trophies: FAC 1958

Mackay, Dave
Place of Birth: Edinburgh, Scotland
Date of Birth: 14 November 1934
Caps: 22 (Scotland)
Goals (International): 4
Clubs: As Player: Heart of Midlothian, Tottenham Hotspur, Derby County, Swindon Town; As Manager: Swindon Town, Nottingham Forest, Derby County, Walsall, Birmingham City
Appearances: Club: 669
Goals: Club: 88
Trophies: SFAC 1956, 1957; SLT 1958, 1959; LT 1961 (1975); FAC 1961, 1962, 1967

Maier, Sepp
Place of Birth: Haar, Germany
Date of Birth: 28 February 1944
Caps: 95 (West Germany)
Goals (International): 0
Clubs: TSV Haar, Bayern Munich
Appearances: Club (League): 473
Goals: Club (League): 0
Trophies: CWC 1967; BLG

1969, 1972, 1973, 1974; EC 1974, 1975, 1976; EuroC 1972; WorC 1974

Maldini, Paolo
Place of Birth: Milan, Italy
Date of Birth: 26 June 1968
Caps: 126 (for Italy)
Goals (International): 7
Clubs: AC Milan
Appearances: Club: 521
Goals: Club: 25
Trophies: SA 1988, 1992, 1993, 1994, 1996, 1999; EC 1989, 1990, 1994, 2003

Mannion, Wilf
Place of Birth: Middlesbrough, England
Date of Birth: 16 May 1918
Died: 14 April 2000
Caps: 26 (England)
Goals (International): 11
Clubs: Middlesbrough, Hull City
Appearances: Club (For Middlesbrough): 368
Goals: Club (For Middlesbrough): 110
Trophies: None

Maradona, Diego
Place of Birth: Lanus, Argentina
Date of Birth: 30 October 1960
Caps: 91 (Argentina)
Goals (International): 34
Clubs: Argentinos Juniors, Boca Juniors, Barcelona, Napoli, Seville, Newell's Old Boys
Appearances: Club: 749
Goals: Club: 311
Trophies: WorC 1986; SA 1987; EUFAC 1988

Matthaus, Lothar
Place of Birth: Erlangen, Germany
Date of Birth: 21 March 1961
Caps: 144 (Germany)
Goals (International): 22
Clubs: Borussia Monchengladbach, Bayern Munich, Inter Milan, New Jersey Metrostars
Appearances: Club (League): 581
Goals: Club (League): 160
Trophies: BLG 1985, 1986, 1987, 1994, 1997; SA 1989; EUFAC 1991, 1996; WorC 1990;

Matthews, Stanley
Place of Birth: Stoke-on-Trent, England
Date of Birth: 1 February 1915
Died: 23 February 2000
Caps: 54 (England)
Goals (International): 11
Clubs: Stoke City, Blackpool
Appearances: Club (League): 698
Goals: Club (League): 71
Trophies: FAC 1953

Mazzola, Sandro
Place of Birth: Torino, Italy
Date of Birth: 8 November 1942
Caps: 70 (Italy)
Goals (International): 22
Clubs: Inter Milan
Trophies: EC 1964, 1965; SA 1963, 1965, 1966, 1971; EuroC 1968

McCoist, Ally
Place of Birth: Glasgow, Scotland
Date of Birth: 24 September 1962
Caps: 61 (Scotland)
Goals (International): 19
Clubs: St Johnstone, Sunderland, Rangers, Kilmarnock
Appearances: Club: 637
Goals: Club: 363
Trophies: SLT 1987, 1989, 1990, 1991, 1992, 1993, 1994, 1995, 1996, 1997; SFAC 1992, 1993, 1996

McFarland, Roy
Place of Birth: Liverpool, England
Date of Birth: 5 April 1948
Caps: 28 (England)
Goals (International): 0
Clubs: Tranmere Rovers, Derby County, Bradford City
Appearances: Club (for Derby County): 437
Goals: Club (League: for Derby County): 44

Trophies: LT 1972, 1975

McGrath, Paul
Place of Birth: Greenford, England
Date of Birth: 4 December 1959
Caps: 83 (Republic of Ireland)
Goals (International): 8
Clubs: Manchester United, Aston Villa, Derby County
Appearances: Club: 519
Goals: Club: 25
Trophies: FAC 1985; LC 1994, 1996

McLeish, Alex
Place of Birth: Glasgow, Scotland
Date of Birth: 21 January 1959
Caps: 77 (Scotland)
Goals (International): 1
Clubs: Aberdeen
Appearances: Club (League): 492
Goals: Club (League): 25
Trophies: SLT 1980, 1984, 1985; SFAC 1982, 1983, 1984, 1986, 1990, (2002); CWC 1983

McNeill, Billy
Place of Birth: Blantyre, Scotland
Date of Birth: 2 March 1940
Caps: 29 (Scotland)
Goals (International): 3
Clubs: Celtic
Appearances: Club (League): 486
Goals: Club (League): 22
Trophies: EC 1967; SLT 1966, 1967, 1968, 1969, 1970, 1971, 1972, 1973, 1974; SFAC 1965, 1967, 1969, 1971, 1972, 1974, 1975

Meazza, Guiseppe
Place of Birth: Milan, Italy
Date of Birth: 23 August 1910
Died: 21 August 1979
Caps: 53 (Italy)
Goals (International): 33
Clubs: Ambrosiana, AC Milan, Juventus, Varese, Atalanta, Inter Milan
Appearances: Club (League): 439
Goals: Club (League): 264
Trophies: WorC 1934, 1938; SA 1938, 1940

Mercer, Joe
Place of Birth: Ellesmere Port, Cheshire
Date of Birth: 9 August 1914
Died: 9 August 1990
Caps: 5 (England)
Goals (International): 0
Clubs: As Player: Everton, Arsenal; **As Manager:** Sheffield United, Aston Villa, Manchester City, Coventry City
Trophies: LT 1948, 1953, (1968); FAC 1950, (1969); LC (1970)

Meredith, Billy
Place of Birth: Black Park, Chirk, Wales
Date of Birth: 30 July 1875
Died: 19 April 1958
Caps: 48 (Wales)
Goals (International): 11
Clubs: Northwich Victoria, Manchester City, Manchester United
Appearances: Club (League: for Man Utd): 303
Goals: Club (League: for Man Utd): 35
Trophies: LT 1908, 1911; FAC 1904,1909

Milburn, Jackie
Place of Birth: Ashington, England
Date of Birth: 11 May 1924
Died: 9 October 1988
Caps: 13 (England)
Goals (International): 10
Clubs: Newcastle United
Appearances: Club (League): 354
Goals: Club (League): 177
Trophies: FAC 1951, 1952, 1955

Milla, Roger
Place of Birth: Yaounde, Cameroon
Date of Birth: 20 May 1952
Caps: 81 (Cameroon)
Goals (International): 42
Clubs: Leopaerd Douala, Tanerre Yaounde,

Valenciennes, Monaco, Bastia, Saint Etienne, Montpellier, Saint Pierre

Miller, Willie
Place of Birth: Glasgow, Scotland
Date of Birth: 2 May 1955
Caps: 65 (Scotland)
Goals (International): 1
Clubs: Aberdeen
Appearances: Club (League): 556
Goals: Club (League): 21
Trophies: SLT 1980 1984, 1985; SFAC 1982, 1983, 1984, 1986; CWC 1983

Monti, Luis
Place of Birth: Buenos Aires, Argentina
Date of Birth: 15 May 1901
Died: 9 September 1983
Caps: 18 (Italy) He also played for Argentina in the 1930 World Cup
Goals (International): 1 (for Italy)
Clubs: Huracan, Boca Juniors, San Lorenzo, Juventus
Appearances: Club (League: for Juventus): 225
Goals: Club (League: for Juventus): 24
Trophies: ALT 1923, 1924, 1927; SA 1932, 1933, 1934, 1935; WorC 1934

Moore, Bobby
Place of Birth: Barking, Essex, England
Date of Birth: 12 April 1941
Died: 24 February 1993
Caps: 108 (England)
Goals (International): 2
Clubs: West Ham United, Fulham, Seattle Sounders, San Antonio Thunder
Appearances: Club: 823
Goals: Club: 29
Trophies: WorC 1966; FAC 1964; CWC 1965

Mortensen, Stanley
Place of Birth: South Shields, England
Date of Birth: 26 May 1921
Died: 7 May 1991
Caps: 25 (England)
Goals (International): 23
Clubs: Blackpool, Hull City, Southport
Appearances: Club (League: for Blackpool): 316
Goals: Club (League: for Blackpool): 197
Trophies: FAC 1953

Muhren, Arnold
Place of Birth: Volendam, Holland
Date of Birth: 2 June 1951
Caps: 23 (Holland)
Goals: (International): 3
Clubs: Twente, Ajax, Ipswich Town, Manchester United
Appearances: Club (for Ipswich and Man Utd): 226
Goals: Club (for Ipswich and Man Utd): 34
Trophies: CWC 1971; EUFAC 1981; FAC 1983; EuroC 1988

Müller, Gerd
Place of Birth: Zinsen, Bavaria, Germany
Date of Birth: 3 November 1945
Caps: 62 (Germany)
Goals (International): 68
Clubs: TSV Nordlingen, Bayern Munich, Fort Lauderdale Strikers
Appearances: Club (League: for Bayern Munich): 427
Goals: Club (League: for Bayern Munich): 365
Trophies: WorC 1974; EC 1974, 1975, 1976; BLG 1969, 1972, 1973, 1974; CWC 1967

Neeskens, Johann
Place of Birth: Heemstede, Holland
Date of Birth: 15 September 1951
Caps: 49 (Holland)
Goals (International): 17
Clubs: Haarlem, Ajax, Barcelona, New York Cosmos, Groningen, Fort Lauderdale Strikers, Baar
Appearances: Club (League): 481
Goals: Club (League): 92

Trophies: DLT 1972, 1973; EC 1971, 1972, 1973; CWC 1979

Netzer, Gunter
Place of Birth: West Germany
Date of Birth: 14 September 1944
Caps: 37 (West Germany)
Goals (International): 6
Clubs: Borussia Monchengladbach, Real Madrid, Grasshopper
Appearances: Club (League: for Borussia): 230
Goals: Club (League: For Borussia): 82
Trophies: BLG 1970, 1971, (1979 as manager of Hamburg); EuroC 1972; PLA 1975, 1976

Nicholson, Bill
Place of Birth: Scarborough, England
Date of Birth: 26 January 1919
Caps: 1 (England)
Goals (International): 1
Clubs: As Player: Tottenham **As Manager:** Tottenham
Trophies: LT (1951), 1961; FAC 1961, 1962, 1967; LC 1971, 1973; CWC 1963; UEFAC 1972

Nordahl, Gunnar
Place of Birth: Hornefors, Sweden
Date of Birth: 8 October 1922
Died: 15 September 1995
Caps: 33 (Sweden)
Goals (International): 43
Clubs: Hornefors, Degerfors IF, IFK Norrköping, AC Milan, Roma, Karlstad BIK
Appearances: Club (League: in Serie A): 291
Goals: Club (League: in Serie A): 225
Trophies: SLT 1945, 1946, 1947, 1948; SA 1951, 1955

O'Leary, David
Place of Birth: Dublin, Ireland
Date of Birth: 2 May 1958
Caps: 68 (Republic of Ireland)
Goals (International): 1
Clubs: As Player: Arsenal; **As Manager:** Leeds United
Appearances: Club (League): 558
Goals: Club (League): 10
Trophies: LT 1989, 1991; FAC 1979; LC 1987

O'Neill, Martin
Place of Birth: Kilrea, County Derry, N. Ireland
Date of Birth: 1 March 1952
Caps: 64 (Northern Ireland)
Goals (International): 8
Clubs: As Player: Distillery, Nottingham Forest, Norwich City, Manchester City, Notts County. **As Manager:** Wycombe Wanderers, Norwich City, Leicester City, Celtic
Trophies: EC 1979, 1980; LT 1978; LC 1978, 1979, (1997), (2000); SLT (2001), (2002); SFAC (2001)

Owen, Michael
Place of Birth: Chester, England
Date of Birth: 14 December 1979
Caps: 47
Goals (International): 20
Clubs: Liverpool
Appearances: Club (League): 187
Goals: Club (League): 92
Trophies: FAC 2001; LC 2001, 2003; EUFAC 2001

Paisley, Bob
Place of Birth: Hetton-le-Hole, England
Date of Birth: 23 January 1919
Died: 12 February 1996
Caps: 0
Goals (International): 0
Clubs: As Player: Bishop Auckland, Liverpool; **As Manager:** Liverpool
Trophies: LT (1947), 1976, 1977, 1979, 1980, 1982, 1983; LC 1981, 1982, 1983; EC 1977, 1978, 1981; UEFAC 1976

Passarrella, David
Place of Birth: Buenos Aires, Argentina
Date of Birth: 25 May 1953

Caps: 71 (Argentina)
Goals (International): 21
Clubs: River Plate, Fiorentina Inter Milan
Appearances: Club (League: for River Plate): 298
Goals: Club (League: for River Plate): 99
Trophies: WorC 1978

Pearce, Stuart
Place of Birth: London, England
Date of Birth: 24 April 1962
Caps: 78 (England)
Goals (International): 5
Clubs: Coventry, Nottingham Forest, Newcastle United, West Ham, Manchester City
Appearances: Club (League): 570
Goals: Club (League): 72
Trophies: LC 1989, 1990

Pelé
Place of Birth: Tres Coracoes, Brazil
Date of Birth: 21 October 1940
Caps: 91 (Brazil)
Goals (International): 77
Clubs: Bauru, Santos, New York Cosmos
Appearances: Club: 1363
Goals: Club: 1283
Trophies: WorC 1958,1970; BLT: 1956, 1958, 1960, 1961, 1962, 1964, 1966, 1967, 1968; WCC: 1962, 1963

Peters, Martin
Place of Birth: London, England
Date of Birth: 8 November 1943
Caps: 67
Goals (International): 20
Clubs: West Ham, Tottenham, Norwich City, Sheffield United
Appearances: Club: 882
Goals: Club: 220
Trophies: WorC 1966; CWC 1965; LC 1971, 1973; EUFAC 1972

Pires, Robert
Place of Birth: Reims, France
Date of Birth:
Caps: 56 (France)
Goals (International): 11
Clubs: Arsenal
Appearances: Club (League): 374
Goals: Club (League): 86
Trophies: LT 2002; FAC 2003; WorC 1998; EuroC 2000

Platini, Michel
Place of Birth: Joeuf, France
Date of Birth: 21 June 1955
Caps: 72 (France)
Goals (International): 41
Clubs: AS Joeuf, Nancy, St Etienne, Juventus,
Appearances: Club: 576
Goals: Club: 307
Trophies: EuroC 1984; FLT 1981; SA 1984, 1986; CWC 1984; EC 1985

Puskas, Ferenc
Place of Birth: Budapest, Hungary
Date of Birth: 2 April 1927
Caps: 84 (for Hungary); 4 (for Spain)
Goals (International): 83 (for Hungary)
Clubs: Kispest, Honved, Real Madrid
Appearances: Club: 1300
Goals: Club: 1176
Trophies: PLA 1961,1962, 1963, 1964, 1965; HLT 1950, 1952, 1954, 1955; EC 1960

Ramsey, Alf
Place of Birth: Dagenham, Essex
Date of Birth: 22 January 1920
Died: 28 April 1999
Caps: 32 (England)
Goals (International): 3
Clubs: As Player: Southampton, Tottenham; **As Manager:** Ipswich Town, England national side, Birmingham (caretaker)
Trophies: WorC 1966; LT 1962

Rattin, Antonio
Place of Birth: Tigre, Argentina
Date of Birth: 16 May 1937
Caps: 34 (Argentina)
Goals (International): 1
Clubs: Boca Juniors

Appearances: Club : 353
Goals: Club (League): 26
Trophies: ALT 1962, 1964, 1965, 1969, 1970

Revie, Don
Place of Birth: Middlesbrough, England
Date of Birth: 10 July 1927
Died: 28 May 1989
Caps: 6 (England)
Goals (International): 4
Clubs: As Player: Leicester City, Hull City, Manchester City, Sunderland, Leeds United. **As Manager:** Leeds United, England national side, United Arab Emigrates national side
Trophies: LT 1969, 1974; FAC 1972; LC 1968; UEFAC 1968, 1971

Rijkaard, Frank
Place of Birth: Amsterdam, Holland
Date of Birth: 30 September 1962
Caps: 73 (Holland)
Goals (International): 10
Clubs: Ajax, Sporting Lisbon,Real Zaragoza, AC Milan
Appearances: Club: 415
Goals: Club: 74
Trophies: CWC 1987, EuroC 1988; EC 1989, 1990, 1995; SA 1992, 1993; DLT 1982, 1983, 1985, 1994, 1995

Riva, Luigi
Place of Birth: Leggiuno, Italy
Date of Birth: 7 November 1944
Caps: 42 (Italy)
Goals (International): 35
Clubs: Legnano, Cagliari
Appearances: Club: 338
Goals: Club: 170
Trophies: EuroC 1968, SA 1970

Rivaldo
Place of Birth: Recife, Brazil
Date of Birth: 19 April 1972
Caps: 54 (Brazil)
Goals (International): 28
Clubs: Paulista, Santa Cruz, Mogi-Mirin, Corinthians, Palmeiras, Deportivo La Coruna, Barcelona, AC Milan
Appearances: Club (League): 319
Goals: Club (League): 157
Trophies: BLT 1994; PLA 1998, 1999; WorC 2002; EC 2003

Rivelino
Place of Birth: Sao Paulo, Brazil
Date of Birth: 1 January 1946
Caps: 92 (Brazil)
Goals (International): 26
Clubs: Corinthians, Fluminense, El Helal
Trophies: WorC 1970

Rivera, Gianni
Place of Birth: Allessandria, Italy
Date of Birth: 18 August 1943
Caps: 60 (Italy)
Goals (International): 4
Clubs: Allessandria, AC Milan
Appearances: Club (League): 527
Goals: Club (League): 128
Trophies: EC 1963, 1969; CWC 1968, 1973; SA 1962, 1968, 1979; EuroC 1968

Roberto Carlos
Place of Birth: Garca, Brazil
Date of Birth: 10 April 1973
Caps: 95 (Brazil)
Goals (International): 7
Clubs: Palmeiras, Inter Milan, Real Madrid
Appearances: Club: 336
Goals: Club (League): 40
Trophies: PLA 1997, 2001; EC 1998, 2000, 2002; WorC 2002

Robson, Bobby
Place of Birth: Sacriston, England
Date of Birth: 18 February 1933
Caps: 20 (England)
Goals (International): 4
Clubs: As Player: Fulham. West Bromwich Albion; **As Manager:** Vancouver Whitecaps, Fulham, Ipswich, England national side, PSV Eindhoven, Sporting Lisbon, FC Porto, Barcelona,

Newcastle United
Appearances: Club (League): 583
Goals: 123
Trophies: FAC 1978; EUFAC 1981; CWC 1997; DLT 1991, 1992; PLT 1995, 1996

Robson, Bryan
Place of Birth: Chester Le Street, England
Date of Birth: 11 January 1957
Caps: 90 (England)
Goals (International): 26
Clubs: West Bromwich Albion, Manchester United, Middlesbrough
Appearances: Club (League): 568
Goals: Club (League): 114
Trophies: LT 1993, 1994; FAC 1983, 1985, 1990; CWC 1991

Ronaldo
Place of Birth: Rio de Janeiro, Brazil
Date of Birth: 22 September 1976
Caps: 69 (Brazil)
Goals (International): 47
Clubs: Cruzeiro, PSV Eindhoven, Barcelona, Inter Milan, Real Madrid
Appearances: Club (League): 232
Goals: Club (League): 200
Trophies: CWC 1997; EUFAC 1998; WorC 2002

Rossi, Paolo
Place of Birth: 23 September 1956
Date of Birth: Prato, Italy
Caps: 48 (Italy)
Goals (International): 20
Clubs: Prato, Juventus, Como, Lanerossi, Vicenza, Perugia, AC Milan
Appearances: Club (League): 251
Goals: Club (League): 103
Trophies: WorC 1982; CWC 1984, EC 1985; SA 1982, 1984

Rummenigge, Karl-Heinz
Place of Birth: Lippstadt, Germany
Date of Birth: 25 September 1955
Caps: 95 (West Germany)
Goals (International): 45
Clubs: Bayern Munich, Inter Milan, Servette
Appearances: Club: 424
Goals: Club: 220
Trophies: EC 1976; EuroC 1980; BLG 1980, 1981

Rush, Ian
Place of Birth: Flint, Wales
Date of Birth: 20 October 1961
Caps: 73 (Wales)
Goals (International): 28
Clubs: Chester, Liverpool, Juventus, Liverpool, Leeds United, Newcastle United
Appearances: Club (League): 584
Goals: Club (League): 253
Trophies: LT 1982, 1983, 1984, 1986, 1988, 1990; FAC 1986, 1989, 1992; LC 1981, 1982, 1983, 1994, 1995; EC 1981, 1984

Sanchez, Hugo
Place of Birth: Mexico
Date of Birth: 11 June 1958
Caps: 57 (Mexico)
Goals (International): 26
Clubs: UNAM, Atletico Madrid, Real Madrid, Rayo Vallecano
Trophies: PLA 1986, 1987, 1988, 1989, 1990; EUFAC 1986

Santamaria, Jose
Place of Birth: Montevideo, Uruguay
Date of Birth: 31 July 1929
Caps: 35 (for Uruguay); 17 (for Spain)
Goals (International): 0
Clubs: Nacional, Real Madrid
Trophies: ULT 1950, 1952, 1955, 1956; PLA 1958, 1961, 1962, 1963, 1964, 1965; EC 1958, 1959, 1960

Santos, Djalma
Place of Birth: Brazil
Date of Birth: 27 February 1929
Caps: 107 (Brazil)
Goals (International): 3
Clubs: Portuguesa, Palmeiras, Atletico Curitiba
Trophies: WorC 1958, 1962

Santos, Nilton
Place of Birth: Brazil
Date of Birth: 16 May 1927
Caps: 75 (Brazil)
Goals (International): 3
Clubs: Botafogo
Trophies: WorC 1958, 1962

Schiaffino, Juan
Place of Birth: Montevideo, Uruguay
Date of Birth: 28 July 1925
Caps: 22 (for Uruguay); 4 (for Italy)
Goals (International): 12 (for Uruguay)
Clubs: Penerol, AC Milan, Roma
Appearances: Club (in Serie A): 188
Goals: Club (in Serie A): 50
Trophies: WorC 1950; SA 1955, 1957, 1959

Schmeichel, Peter
Place of Birth: Gladsaxe, Denmark
Date of Birth: 18 November 1963
Caps: 122 (Denmark)
Goals (International): 2
Clubs: Hidvovre IF, Brondby, Manchester United, Sporting Lisbon, Aston Villa, Manchester City
Appearances: Club (League): 587
Goals: Club (League): 9
Trophies: DLT 1987, 1988, 1990, 1991; LT 1993, 1994, 1996,1997, 1999; FAC 1994, 1996, 1999; EC 1999; EuroC 1992

Schoen, Helmut
Place of Birth: Dresden, Germany
Date of Birth: 15 September 1915
Died: 23 February 1996
Caps: 16 (Germany)
Goals (International): 17
Clubs: As Player: Dresden SC, Hertha Berlin, Wiesbaden, Saar; **As Manager:** Saar, West Germany
Trophies: WorC 1974; EuroC 1972

Scholes, Paul
Place of Birth: Salford, England
Date of Birth:
Caps: 54 (England)
Goals (International): 13
Clubs: Manchester United
Appearances: Club: 371
Goals: Club: 101
Trophies: LT 1996, 1997, 1999, 2000, 2001, 2003; FAC 1996, 1999; EC 1999

Scifo, Enzo
Place of Birth: Le Louvierre, Belgium
Date of Birth: 19 February 1966
Caps: 84 (Belgium)
Goals (International): 14
Clubs: Anderlecht, Inter Milan, Bordeaux, Auxerre, Monaco
Trophies: BLT 1985, 1986; FLT 1997

Seaman, David
Place of Birth: Rotherham, England
Date of Birth: 19 September 1963
Caps: 75 (England)
Goals (International): 0
Clubs: Peterborough United, Birmingham, Queens Park Rangers, Arsenal
Appearances: Club (League): 711
Goals: Club (League): 0
Trophies: LT 1991, 1998, 2002; FAC 1993, 1998, 2002, 2003; LC 1993; CWC 1994

Seeler, Uwe
Place of Birth: Hamburg, West Germany
Date of Birth: 5 November 1936
Caps: 72 (West Germany)
Goals (International): 43
Clubs: Hamburg
Appearances: Club: 710
Goals: Club: 551
Trophies: BLG 1960

Shackleton, Len
Place of Birth: Bradford, England
Date of Birth: 3 May 1922

Statistics & Acknowledgements

Died: 28 November 2000
Caps: 5 (England)
Goals (International): 0
Clubs: Bradford Park Avenue, Newcastle, Sunderland
Appearances: Club (for Sunderland): 348
Goals: Club (League): 101
Trophies: None

Shankly, Bill
Place of Birth: Glenbuck, Ayrshire, Scotland
Date of Birth: 2 September 1913
Died: 28 September 1981
Caps: 5 (Scotland)
Goals (International): 0
Clubs: As Player: Carlisle United, Preston North End;
As Manager: Carlisle United, Grimsby Town, Workington, Huddersfield Town, Liverpool
Trophies: LT 1964, 1966, 1973; FAC 1965, 1974; UEFAC 1973

Shearer, Alan
Place of Birth: Newcastle, England
Date of Birth: 13 August 1970
Caps: 63 (England)
Goals (International): 30
Clubs: Southampton, Blackburn Rovers, Newcastle
Appearances: Club (League): 462
Goals: Club (League): 244
Trophies: LT 1995

Sheringham, Teddy
Place of Birth: Highams Park, England
Date of Birth: 2 April 1966
Caps: 45 (England)
Goals (International): 11
Clubs: Millwall, Aldershot, Nottingham Forest, Tottenham, Manchester United
Appearances: Club (League): 604
Goals: Club (League): 234
Trophies: LT 1999, 2000, 2001; FAC 1999; EC 1999

Shevchenko, Andrei
Place of Birth: Dvirkivshchyna, Kiev, Ukraine
Date of Birth: 29 September 1976
Caps: 46 (Ukraine)
Goals (International): 19
Clubs: Dynamo Kiev, AC Milan
Appearances: Club (League): 229
Goals: Club (League): 127
Trophies: ULT 1995, 1996, 1997, 1998, 1999; EC 2003

Shilton, Peter
Place of Birth: Leicester, England
Date of Birth: 18 September 1949
Caps: 125 (England)
Goals (International): 0
Clubs: Leicester City, Stoke City, Nottingham Forest, Southampton, Derby County, Plymouth Argyle, Wimbledon, Bolton Wanderers, Coventry City, West Ham, Leyton Orient
Appearances: Club (League): 1005
Goals: Club (League): 0
Trophies: EC 1979, 1980 LT 1978; LC 1979

Socrates
Place of Birth: Brazil
Date of Birth: 19 February 1954
Caps: 60 (Brazil)
Goals (International): 22
Clubs: Botafogo, Corinthians, Fiorentina, Flamengo, Santos
Appearances: Club (For Corinthians): 302
Goals: Club (For Corinthians): 166

Souness, Graham
Place of Birth: Edinburgh, Scotland
Date of Birth: 6 May 1953
Caps: 54 (Scotland)
Goals (International): 4
Clubs: As Player: Tottenham Hotspur, Middlesbrough, Liverpool, Sampdoria, Rangers;
As Manager: Rangers, Liverpool, Benfica, Blackburn Rovers
Appearances: Club: 528
Goals: Club: 78
Trophies: 1979, 1980, 1982, 1983, 1984; LC 1981, 1982, 1983, 1984, (2000); EC 1981, 1984; FAC (1992); SLT (1987), (1989), (1990), (1991)

Southall, Neville
Place of Birth: Llandudno, Wales
Date of Birth: 16 September 1958
Caps: 92 (Wales)
Goals (International): 0
Clubs: Bury, Everton, Port Vale, Southend, Stoke City, Torquay United, Bradford City
Appearances: Club (League): 701
Goals: Club (League): 0
Trophies: LT 1985, 1987; FAC 1984, 1995, CWC 1985

Stein, Jock
Place of Birth: Burnbank, Scotland

Date of Birth: 5 October 1923
Died: 11 September 1985
Caps: 0
Goals (International): 0
Clubs: As Player: Albion Rovers, Llanelli, Celtic;
As Manager: Dunfermline, Hibernian, Celtic, Leeds United
Trophies: SLT 1966–75, 1977; SFAC 1965, 1967, 1969, 1971, 1972, 1974, 1975, 1977; EC 1967

Stiles, Nobby
Place of Birth: Manchester, England
Date of Birth: 18 May 1942
Caps: 28 (England)
Goals (International): 1
Clubs: Manchester United, Middlesbrough, Preston North End
Appearances: Club (League: for Manchester United): 311
Goals: Club (League: for Manchester United): 17
Trophies: WorC 1966; LT 1965, 1967; EC 1968

Stoichkov, Hristo
Place of Birth: Plovdiv, Bulgaria
Date of Birth: 2 August 1966
Caps: 83 (Bulgaria)
Goals (International): 37
Clubs: CSKA Sofia, Barcelona, Parma, Kawisa Reysol, Chicago Fires
Appearances: Club (For Barcelona): 174
Goals: Club (For Barcelona): 83
Trophies: EC 1992; CWC 1997; BLT 1985,1987, 1989, 1990; PLA 1991, 1992, 1993, 1994

Strachan, Gordon
Place of Birth: Edinburgh, Scotland
Date of Birth: 9 February 1957
Caps: 50 (Scotland)
Goals (International): 5
Clubs: As Player: Aberdeen, Man Utd, Leeds, Coventry;
As Manager: Coventry, Southampton
Trophies: SLT 1980, 1984; SFAC 1982, 1983, 1984; CWC 1983; FAC 1985; LT 1992

Suarez, Luis
Place of Birth: La Coruna, Spain
Date of Birth: 2 May 1935
Caps: 32 (Spain)
Goals (International): 14
Clubs: Deportivo La Coruna, Barcelona, Inter Milan, Sampdoria
Appearances: Club (for Barcelona): 373
Goals: Club (for Barcelona): 153

Trophies: PLA 1959, 1960; SA 1963; EC 1964, 1965; EuroC 1964

Taylor, Graham
Place of Birth: Worksop, England
Date of Birth: 15 September 1944
Caps: 0
Goals (International): 0
Clubs: As Player: Grimsby Town, Lincoln City;
As Manager: Lincoln City, Watford, England national side, Wolverhampton Wanderers, Aston Villa
Appearances: Club (for Lincoln): 169
Goals: Club (for Lincoln): 2
Trophies: None

Thijssen, Fran
Place of Birth: Heuman, Holland
Date of Birth: 23 January 1952
Caps: 14 (Holland)
Goals (International): 3
Clubs: FC Twente, Ipswich, Vancouver Whitecaps, Nottingham Forest
Appearances: Club (for Ipswich): 125
Goals: Club (for Ipswich): 10
Trophies: EUFAC 1981

Tigana, Jean
Place of Birth: Toulon, France
Date of Birth: 23 June 1955
Caps: 52 (France)
Goals (International): 1
Clubs: As Player: Toulon, Lyon, Bordeaux, Marseille;
As Manager: Lyon, Monaco, Fulham
Trophies: EuroC 1984, FLT 1984, 1985, 1987, 1990, 1991, (1997)

Todd, Colin
Place of Birth: Chester Le Street, England
Date of Birth: 12 December 1948
Caps: 27 (England)
Goals (International): 0
Clubs: Sunderland, Derby County, Everton, Birmingham City, Oxford United, Vancouver Whitecaps
Appearances: Club: 417
Goals: Club: 7
Trophies: LT 1972, 1975

Tomaszewski, Jan
Place of Birth: Poland
Date of Birth: 9 January 1948
Caps: 59 (Poland)
Goals (International): 0

Clubs: LKS Lodz, Beerschot, Hercules
Trophies: None

Valderrama, Carlos
Place of Birth: Santa Marta, Colombia
Date of Birth: 2 September 1961
Caps: 110 (Colombia)
Goals (International): 10
Clubs: Santa Marta, Millonarios, Montpellier, Valladolid, Medellin, Atletico Junior Barranquilla, Nacional, Tampa Bay Mutiny, Miami Fusion
Trophies: None

Van Basten, Marco
Place of Birth: Utrecht, Holland
Date of Birth: 31 October 1964
Caps: 58 (Holland)
Goals (International): 24
Clubs: Ajax, AC Milan
Appearances: Club: 280
Goals: Club: 218
Trophies: EuroC 1988; EC 1989, 1990; CWC 1987; DLT 1982, 1983, 1985; SA 1988, 1992, 1993, 1994

Van Nistelrooy, Ruud
Place of Birth: Oss, Holland
Date of Birth: 1 July 1976
Caps: 24 (Holland)
Goals (International): 11
Clubs: Den Bosch, SC Heerenveen, PSV Eindhoven, Manchester United
Appearances: Club (League): 264
Goals: Club (League): 163
Trophies: LT 2003

Venables, Terry
Place of Birth: London, England
Date of Birth: 6 January 1943
Caps: 2 (England)
Goals (International): 0
Clubs: As Player: Chelsea, Tottenham Hotspur, Queens Park Rangers, Crystal Palace;
As Manager: Crystal Palace, Queens Park Rangers, Barcelona, Tottenham Hotspur, Portsmouth, Australian national side, Middlesbrough, Leeds United
Appearances: Club: 534
Goals: Club: 54
Trophies: PLA 1986; FAC 1991

Vialli, Gianluca
Place of Birth: Cremona, Italy
Date of Birth: 9 June 1964
Caps: 59 (Italy)
Goals (International): 16

Clubs: As Player: Cremonese, Sampdoria, Juventus, Chelsea;
As Manager: Chelsea, Watford
Appearances: Club (League): 467
Goals: Club (League): 156
Trophies: CWC 1990, (1998); EUFAC 1993; EC 1996; SA 1991, 1995; FAC 1997 (2000); LC (1998)

Vieira, Patrick
Place of Birth: Dakar, Senegal
Date of Birth: 23 June 1976
Caps: 62 (France)
Goals (International): 4
Clubs: Cannes, AC Milan, Arsenal
Appearances: Club (League): 271
Goals: Club (League): 21
Trophies: LC 1998, 2002; FAC 1998, 2002

Vogts, Berti
Place of Birth: Büttgen, Germany
Date of Birth: 30 December 1946
Caps: 96 (West Germany)
Goals (International): 1
Clubs: VFR Buttgen, Borussia Monchengladbach
Appearances: Club (League): 419
Goals: Club (League): 32
Trophies: WorC 1974; BLG 1970, 1971, 1975, 1976, 1977; EUFAC 1975, 1979; EuroC (1996)

Walter, Fritz
Place of Birth: Kaiserslautern, West Germany
Date of Birth: 31 October 1920
Caps: 61 (West Germany)
Goals (International): 33
Clubs: FC Kaiserslautern
Trophies: WorC 1954; BLG 1951, 1953

Weah, George
Place of Birth: Monrovia, Liberia
Date of Birth: 1 October 1966
Caps: 42 (Liberia)
Goals (International): 7
Clubs: Tonerre, Yaounde, Monaco, Paris Saint-Germain, AC Milan, Chelsea, Manchester City, Marseille
Appearances: Club (League): 368
Goals: Club (League): 148
Trophies: FLT 1988, 1994; SA 1996, 1999; FAC 2000

Wenger, Arsène
Place of Birth: Strasbourg, France
Date of Birth: 1 January 1950

Caps: 0
Goals (International): 0
Clubs: As Player: Strasbourg;
As Manager: Nancy, Monaco, Nagoya Grampus Eight, Arsenal
Trophies: FLT 1988; LT 1998, 2002; FAC 1998, 2002, 2003

Winterbottom, Walter
Place of Birth: Oldham, England
Date of Birth: 31 January 1913
Died: 16 February 2002
Caps: 0
Goals (International): 0
Clubs: Manchester United
Trophies: None

Wright, Billy
Place of Birth: Ironbridge, England
Date of Birth: 6 February 1924
Died: 3 September 1994
Caps: 105
Goals (International): 3
Clubs: Wolverhampton Wanderers
Appearances: Club (League): 490
Goals: Club (League): 13
Trophies: FAC 1951; LT 1954, 1958, 1959

Yashin, Lev
Place of Birth: Moscow, Russia
Date of Birth: 22 October 1929
Died: 20 March 1990
Caps: 78 (USSR)
Goals (International): 0
Clubs: Moscow Dynamo
Appearances: Club (League): 326
Goals: Club (League): 0
Trophies: EuroC 1960; SLT 1954, 1955, 1957, 1959, 1963

Zagallo, Mario
Place of Birth: Brazil
Date of Birth: 9 August 1931
Caps: 35 (Brazil)
Goals (International): 0
Clubs: Flamengo, Botafogo
Trophies: BLT 1953, 1954, 1961, 1962; WorC 1958, 1962, (1970), (1994)

Zico
Place of Birth: Rio de Janeiro, Brazil
Date of Birth: 3 March 1953
Caps: 71 (Brazil)
Goals (International): 48
Clubs: Flamengo, Udinese, Kashima Antlers
Appearances: Club: 902
Goals: Club: 727
Trophies: WCC 1981

Zidane, Zinedine
Place of Birth: Marseille, France
Date of Birth: 23 June 1972
Caps: 82 (France)
Goals (International): 22
Clubs: Cannes, Bordeaux, Juventus, Real Madrid
Appearances: Club (League): 407
Goals: Club (League): 73
Trophies: SA 1997, 1998; WorC 1998; EuroC 2000; EC 2002

Zoff, Dino
Place of Birth: Mariano del Friuli, Italy
Date of Birth: 28 February 1942
Caps: 112 (Italy)
Goals (International): 0
Clubs: Udinese, Mantova, Napoli, Juventus, Lazio
Appearances: Club (For Juventus): 330
Goals: Club (Juventus): 0
Trophies: SA 1973, 1975, 1977, 1978, 1981, 1982; EUFAC 1977 (1990); EuroC 1968; WorC 1982;

Zola, Gianfranco
Place of Birth: Sardinia, Italy
Date of Birth: 5 July 1966
Caps: 35 (Italy)
Goals (International): 7
Clubs: Nuorese, Torres, Napoli, Parma, Chelsea
Appearances: Club (League): 468
Goals: Club (League): 150
Trophies: SA 1990; UEFAC 1995; FAC 1997; CWC 1998; LC 2000

Zubizarreta, Andoni
Place of Birth: Vitoria, Spain
Date of Birth: 23 October 1961
Caps: 126 (Spain)
Goals (International): 0
Clubs: Alaves, Athletic Bilbao, Barcelona, Valencia
Trophies: EC 1992; PLA 1983, 1984, 1991, 1992, 1993, 1994; CWC 1989

Authors

Nick Holt (author) Nick Holt was born and raised in Bolton. Unlike its favourite son Nat Lofthouse, he spent much of his footballing career on the wing. An early penchant for alcohol and good living produced a wide player in the John Robertson mould, only without the talent. A natural abrasiveness made him ill-suited for retail; he is now a successful buying magnate. He lives in a small village with wife Emma, rendered less peaceful than it should be by his four large dogs.

Guy Lloyd (author) Guy Lloyd was raised and schooled in Slough, and to his credit managed to survive the experience. He attended university, but declined their kind offer of a fifth term. His working career has taken in the wacky world of record retailing and a number of years in various roles in publishing. Guy's awesome knowledge of obscure footballing trivia is of concern to friends and family alike. At 6 ft 3 in he has the natural physique of a goalkeeper. If only he'd had the talent.

Mark Gonnella (Contributor) Mark Gonnella is a freelance sports writer with a number of football books to his credit. A journalist since leaving school, his career has spanned local and national newspapers and broadcasting. He also works as a media consultant to a number of bluechip companies and sporting organisations. Married with two children, Mark holds an FA coaching badge, continues to play local league football and is a lifelong fan of his hometown club Reading.

Jeff Fletcher (statistics) Jeff Fletcher is a life-long Chelsea supporter and in recent years has taken up the extreme sport of following Kingstonian. He was sports administration manager for the press agencies Exchange Telegraph Company and The Press Association but now works as a freelance writer and sports media consultant. He has written books on several sports, including cricket and basketball, and now prefers to concentrate on football.

Scott Morgan (editor) Scott Morgan is a former Features Editor on *FourFourTwo* magazine, and has written on football for several publications including *Total Football* and the *Daily Telegraph*. As Events Producer he was a founding member of the team that launched the sports website Rivals.net, and now works as a freelance writer/editor.

Picture Credits

All photographs courtesy of Allsport, except:

Action Images: 17

Empics: 44, 74, 90, 157, 185, 190, 203, 234, 269, 275, 327, 352, 367, 389, 396

Foundry Arts: 25, 42, 49, 82, 122, 183, 292, 325, 394

Orion Books: 128

Popperfoto: 9, 45, 60, 71, 113, 141, 169, 179, 187, 216, 236, 246, 284, 338

Topham: 11, 12, 27, 72, 76, 87, 94, 95, 99, 110, 111, 136, 140, 147, 152, 155, 161, 172 173, 178, 181 (l), 193, 200, 212, 223, 224, 228, 230, 237, 240, 256, 261 (r), 279, 281, 291, 317, 321 (all), 324, 333, 345, 348, 349, 350, 354, 358, 368, 375, 382, 386, 398, 399, 400, 408, 410, 411

VinMag Archive: 315

Index